P9-CQQ-510

TORONTO

Biography of a City

TORONTO

Biography of a City

BY ALLAN LEVINE

Douglas & McIntyre

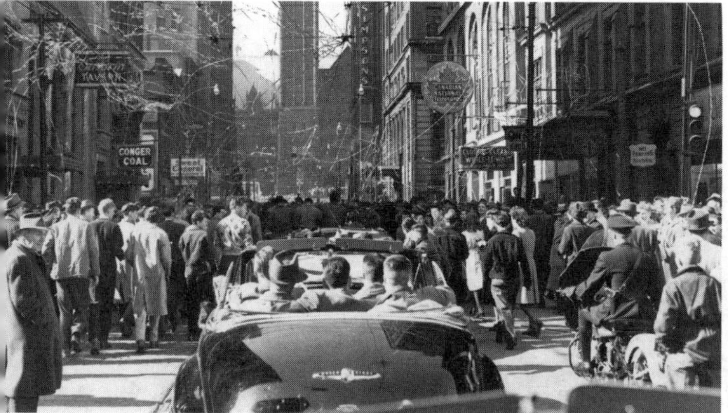

1 2 3 4 5 — 18 17 16 15 14

Douglas and McIntyre (2013) Ltd.
P.O. Box 219, Madeira Park, BC, V0N 2H0
www.douglas-mcintyre.com

Jacket illustration of Toronto skyline by paulrommer/Thinkstock
Pages ii–iii, complete view of Toronto harbour showing the eastern and western entrances *circa* 1910, courtesy Library of Congress, Geography & Map Division; page iv, Maple Leafs' Stanley Cup victory parade on Bay Street, 1948, courtesy Archives of Ontario F 223-3-2-10; page viii, detail from 1893 bird's-eye view of Toronto, looking north from harbour, courtesy Toronto Public Library.
Edited by Audrey McClellan
Jacket design by Anna Comfort O'Keeffe and Carleton Wilson
Text design by Diane Robertson
Indexed by Ellen Hawman

Canada Council for the Arts
Conseil des Arts du Canada

Printed and bound in Canada

Douglas and McIntyre (2013) Ltd. acknowledges financial support from the Government of Canada through the Canada Book Fund and the Canada Council for the Arts, and from the Province of British Columbia through the BC Arts Council and the Book Publishing Tax Credit.

Cataloguing information available from Library and Archives Canada

ISBN 978-1-77100-022-2 (cloth)
ISBN 978-1-77162-043-7 (ebook)

Grateful acknowledgment is made to the many archives, libraries and individuals that granted permission to reproduce copyrighted images and illustrations from their collections, and to the following authors and publishers for granting permission to use extended quotations from copyrighted works:

My Life as a Dame: The Personal and Political Writings of Christina McCall edited by Stephen Clarkson, copyright © 2008. Reproduced with permission from House of Anansi Press, Toronto. www.houseofanansi.com

The Perilous Trade: Publishing Canada's Writers by Roy MacSkimming. Copyright © 2003 Roy MacSkimming. Reprinted by permission of McClelland & Stewart.

The Acquisitors: The Canadian Establishment. Vol. II by Peter C. Newman. Copyright © 1981 Peter C. Newman. Reprinted by permission of Peter C. Newman.

Cabbagetown by Hugh Garner. Copyright © 1950 Hugh Garner. Reprinted by permission of McGraw-Hill Ryerson.

"The Battle to be Megamayor" by John Lorinc, *Toronto Life*, October, 1997. "Rob Ford's Powers of Persuasion" by Sarah Fulford, *Toronto Life*, October, 2010. "Editor's Letter: The Real Spadina Expressway Legacy" by Sarah Fulford, *Toronto Life*, September 2011. "What Toronto Needs Now" by Richard Florida, *Toronto Life*, November 2012. Reproduced with permission from *Toronto Life*.

"The Heather & Gerry Show" by Marci McDonald, *Toronto Life*, June 2005. "The Incredible Shrinking Mayor" by Marci McDonald, *Toronto Life*, May, 2012. Reproduced with permission from *Toronto Life* and Marci McDonald.

"No tears here for Gardens' farewell" by Christie Blatchford, *National Post*, February 13, 1999. "Protest coverage fails fairness test" by Christie Blatchford, *National Post*, June 17, 2000. "This is why people hate Toronto" by Robert Fulford, *National Post*, June 9, 2007. "Drop the witch hunt, it's decided; Time to get over Mayor Ford's small error" by Kelly McParland, *National Post*, January 26, 2013. "Letters to Editor: Voice from Ford Nation" *National Post*, May 30, 2013. Reproduced with permission from the Postmedia Network, Inc.

In memory of Professor
J.M.S. Careless (1919–2009),
who first introduced me to
the history of Toronto

ALSO BY ALLAN LEVINE

Non-Fiction

THE EXCHANGE: 100 Years of Trading Grain in Winnipeg

YOUR WORSHIP: The Lives of Eight of Canada's Most Unforgettable Mayors (editor)

SCRUM WARS: The Prime Ministers and the Media

FUGITIVES OF THE FOREST: The Heroic Story of Jewish Resistance and Survival During the Second World War

SCATTERED AMONG THE PEOPLES: The Jewish Diaspora in Ten Portraits

THE DEVIL IN BABYLON: Fear of Progress and the Birth of Modern Life

COMING OF AGE: A History of the Jewish People of Manitoba

KING: William Lyon Mackenzie King: A Life Guided By The Hand of Destiny

Fiction: Historical Mysteries

THE BLOOD LIBEL

SINS OF THE SUFFRAGETTE

THE BOLSHEVIK'S REVENGE

EVIL OF THE AGE

I am frequently asked whether I find Toronto sufficiently exciting. I find it almost too exciting. The suspense is scary. Here is the most hopeful and healthy city in North America, still unmangled, still with options.

—JANE JACOBS, 1969

I think of Toronto as a big fat rich girl.

—ROBERTSON DAVIES, *THE TABLE TALK OF SAMUEL MARCHBANKS*, 1949

TABLE OF CONTENTS

ACKNOWLEDGMENTS

THIS BOOK HAD its genesis in a conversation I had with Trena White, my former editor at Douglas & McIntyre. One day a few years ago, not long after the publication of my biography of Mackenzie King, which we worked on together, Trena and I discussed my next project, and the idea of writing a biography of Toronto came up in a conversation about biographies of other cities. I thank Trena for her initial interest, enthusiasm, and belief in me and this book. Likewise, I continue to be grateful for the support, advice, and friendship of my wise literary agent, Hilary McMahon of Westwood Creative Artists.

I also thank the new D&M team, including managing editor Anna Comfort-O'Keeffe, as well as Brianna Cerkiewicz, Carleton Wilson, Diane Robertson, and Patricia Wolfe. Anna paired me with Audrey McClellan, a talented and skillful editor, who has been a pleasure to work with. Her diligence and keen eye have immensely improved the manuscript.

A number of individuals have offered me advice, answered my questions, made recommendations, suggested research angles, put me in touch with key people, and offered expert opinion on a variety of Toronto-related topics. I am most appreciative to Peter C. Newman, my friend and writing colleague of thirty years, Jonathan Kay, Kelly McParland, Rosemary Sexton, Royson James, Richard Gerrard, and Chris Gainor.

I thank the following for taking the time to read different sections of the manuscript and for their able assistance and expertise: Dr. John Steckley of Humber College; Dr. Ronald Stagg of Ryerson University; Dr. John Zucchi of McGill University (my old friend from graduate student days at the U of T); Dr. Jay Young, co-editor and public outreach coordinator of ActiveHistory.ca; Bill Gladstone, writer, genealogist, and publisher, whose website billgladstone.ca is a treasure trove of history about the Jewish community of Toronto; journalist John Lorinc, who answered my never-ending queries in a timely manner; and journalist and Toronto expert Mike Filey, who reviewed the entire manuscript.

Among the many Torontonians I interviewed for this book, I am especially thankful to former mayors David Crombie, Art Eggleton, David Miller, June Rowlands, and

John Sewell for their insightful comments on civic politics, as well as to former Ontario premiers Bill Davis and Mike Harris, and to Paul Godfrey, former chairman of Metro Toronto (among the other Toronto institutions he has been associated with during his career). Thanks as well to David Mirvish, John Sewell, and David Crombie for providing me with photographs as well as my well-connected cousin Leanne Wright (another former Winnipegger now in Toronto), vice-president of Communications for ZoomerMedia, for putting me in touch with an assortment of Torontonians.

My family, Angie and our two children, Alexander and Mia (along, of course, with Maggie, our beagle), were as supportive as they have always been. Angie and Alexander lived with the daily ups and downs involved in such a complex writing project and kept me moving forward. And Mia, who has now become part of the ever-expanding community of former Winnipeggers living in Toronto, happily accompanied me on my various journeys around the city. For this and much, much more, I am most grateful to them.

This book is dedicated to the late Professor J.M.S. Careless, who it was my great fortune to work with many years ago as a graduate student at the University of Toronto. (He was "Maurice" to his friends and family, but never to his respectful students.) He first piqued my interest in urban history and the history of Toronto in his lively history of Ontario seminar, and he later served as my advisor on my PhD thesis. His own survey of the city's early years, *Toronto to 1918: An Illustrated History*, published in 1984 as part of the History of Canadian Cities series, was a valuable resource for this book. He was a brilliant and diligent scholar and a genuinely sincere individual who made those stimulating and hectic years at the U of T all the more enjoyable.

It goes without saying that all omissions, misinterpretations, and errors of fact and judgment are solely my own.

ALLAN LEVINE
Winnipeg, March 2014

Introduction

YONGE AND BLOOR

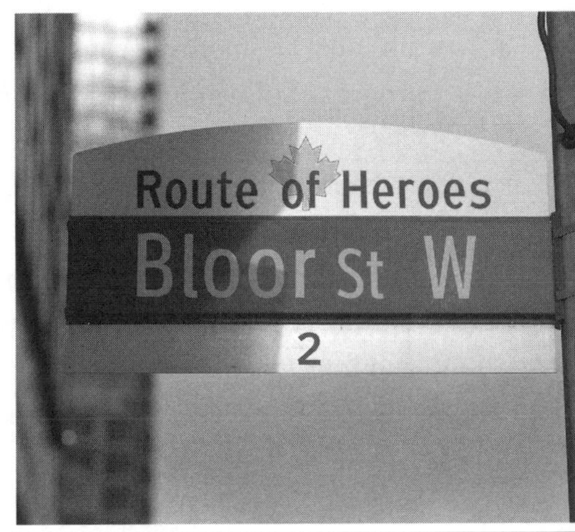

If you're born in a city like London or Paris you know you were born to one of the oldest cultures in the world. If you're born in a city like New York, you know you were born to be one of the kings of the world. If you're born in Toronto—that's destiny.

—MOSES ZNAIMER, 1995

Named after innkeeper and brewer Joseph Bloor (1789–1852), Bloor Street has been one of the city's major east-west arteries for 150 years, though at one time it was nothing more than a dirt road. Today, on Bloor Street from Avenue Road to Yonge Street can be found the most expensive shopping area in the country. *Felix Lam photo*

THE ANSWER IS NO. The opening of this biography of Toronto—an account of the people and major events which over nearly four centuries have played a pivotal role in transforming a backwater village beside Lake Ontario into Canada's largest and most important city—will decidedly not begin with me peering down at the vast metropolis from a perch high atop the CN Tower's observation deck. There will be no romantic descriptions of the Don and Humber Rivers and the Scarborough Bluffs; no astute or cute observations about ravines and raccoons; no insight (for the moment, at any rate) into how skyscrapers like the TD Centre and First Canadian Place have influenced downtown development.

Instead, I am participating in a truly aggravating Toronto experience. It is two-thirty in the afternoon on a hot and muggy June day, and I'm in a rental car going nowhere at the corner of Queen Street and Spadina Avenue. A news update on the radio reports that yet another piece of concrete has fallen from the aging Gardiner Expressway—"the Gardiner" in Toronto lingo—and construction crews are on the scene. Hence, the cars backed up on Spadina and the adjacent streets.

As any Torontonian will tell you, there are too damn many cars on the road each day as thousands of stressed drivers make their way to their jobs in the downtown area from the suburbs or, in a relatively new twist, make their way from their downtown condos to their suburban places of employment. According to the Toronto Board of Trade's 2012 survey, the average daily return commute time in Toronto was sixty-six minutes, an improvement from the eighty minutes in 2010, but still worse than Los Angeles, Chicago, and Berlin. Under any circumstance, Toronto drivers are spending close to a month each year in their vehicles. And in one of the few cases of unwanted attention for Toronto from the United States, the U.S. Department of Transportation has deemed Highway 401, the Macdonald-Cartier Freeway, aka "the 401," "officially the busiest stretch of freeway anywhere in North America." The reason: despite jammed subway cars each morning and evening, 70 percent of Torontonians are still driving to and from work because public transportation remains inadequate.

To the English poet Rupert Brooke, who visited a much smaller Toronto on his North American journey in 1913, the city was the "soul" of Canada. "The only depressing thing," he prophetically added in his travelogue *Letters From America*, "is that it will always be what it is, only larger."

He was right, of course. Today, Toronto is a victim of its own success. With an estimated population of 5.5 million, the freeways and roads of the Greater Toronto Area or GTA cannot handle the traffic. (The GTA comprises the city of Toronto with a population of 2.79 million—itself an amalgamation in 1998 of Metropolitan Toronto that included the city of Toronto, East York, Etobicoke, North York, Scarborough, and York—and the four regional municipalities of Durham, Halton, Peel, and York.) Owing to a multitude of factors, including poor planning, excessive political bickering, and inadequate government funding, the public transportation system has not expanded fast enough. The consequence is that Toronto has the reputation of being one of the most congested cities in the western world; in Canada, only Vancouver and Montreal are ranked slightly worse. Any deviation from the norm, such as a burnt-out traffic light, road construction, or too much snow makes a bad situation much worse.

WHEN I WAS A GRADUATE STUDENT at the University of Toronto in the late seventies, getting around the city was much easier. I rarely ventured north of Eglinton Avenue, less than five kilometres from the corner of Yonge and Bloor Streets—except, occasionally, to dine slightly farther north at United Dairy on Bathurst and Lawrence and get a full dose of Jewish Toronto. Everything I wanted or needed was only a few subway stops away. I lived in the city for about five years during the dynamic David Crombie–John Sewell years at city hall when, as will be told, a clash of visions erupted over Toronto's future. Would it become another American metropolis, a city in which everyone lived in the suburbs, and the downtown after six o'clock in the evening was the realm of cops and muggers? Or would it be inspired by such creative thinkers as Jane Jacobs, with people working and living in the downtown area? As a twenty-two-year-old,

I was only minimally aware of this fierce and passionate battle. Nor, in my youthful ignorance, was I cognizant of the fact that one of my neighbours, a few doors down from the house I shared with a friend from Winnipeg on Albany Street, was none other than the urban prophet herself, Jane Jacobs, imparting wisdom from her front porch.

As a diehard Toronto Maple Leafs fan, however—I was eleven years old when I watched the Leafs win their last Stanley Cup in 1967—there was nothing as memorable as that glorious day in 1979 when the entire team came into Delaney's, the bar and restaurant on Church and The Esplanade where I was working part-time as a bartender. To this day I can recite what such stars as Darryl Sittler, Lanny McDonald, and Börje Salming ordered; what the bill came to; and how much the team generously tipped me—$75, a fair amount of money for a struggling grad student.

Toronto did resonate with me then as a city with a touch of London's style and flavour and a vitality that was hard to find anywhere else in the country. Since then, in the many times I have returned, nothing has altered my initial impression that Toronto has a singular importance in Canada and a particular distinctiveness worth exploring—which is the main objective of this biography.

One day while doing research I just wandered, starting from the Brickworks at the bottom of Broadview, Toronto's Jurassic Park, where the bricks that built the city were churned out. From there it was an urban panorama: the mob scene at the Yonge and Bloor subway station at eight in the morning; watching the pretty people (most yakking on their cell phones) in Yorkville; having a bite at one of the stands at the St. Lawrence Market; traversing the underground city of commerce around Bay and King; looking around Regent Park and Cabbagetown; taking a stroll down Spadina, with the requisite dim-sum stop; into Kensington Market and then west into the Annex, revisiting some of my old haunts (Saturday afternoon drinking beer at the Brunswick) and beyond into Koreatown. That evening, near the corner of Clinton Street and Barton Avenue, I came face to face with the nastiest critter to walk the mean streets of Toronto, a raccoon, one of thousands that, owing mainly to the city's celebrated ravines, inhabit what has been proclaimed the "raccoon capital of the world" (according to the CBC documentary *Raccoon Nation*)—and I ran away from it as fast as I could. This and other travels throughout the city confirmed what one of my U of T professors, the late Robert Harney, founder of the Multicultural History Society of Ontario, said in a 1986 *Maclean's* magazine interview: that Toronto embodied "all that is potentially rich in neighbourhood terms—multiracial harmony, commitment to quality, private initiative and integration of employment and residential life."

This book is not an encyclopedic account of the city's history or an academic survey; many excellent ones are available, including the story of Toronto up to 1918 by another of my former U of T professors and thesis advisor, the late J.M.S. Careless. It is not a travel book or an architectural treatise, nor does it offer a description and analysis of every Toronto street, neighbourhood, building, organization, association, club, sports team, restaurant, theatre, or person who has lived in the city. Many of these significant institutions, groups, cultural activities, and people do indeed form part of the mainly chronological narrative that follows. Yet this is a popular-style "biography" aimed at general readers, and like any biography it offers a selective, sometimes arbitrary, chronicle of Toronto's collective character in all of its different forms and contexts. The city has not lacked local-history enthusiasts, and there are several terrific websites (*Torontoist* is my favourite) that offer rich and offbeat tales. These as well as the fairly impressive list of books and articles about Toronto found in the bibliography have been invaluable sources of information.

It is hardly surprising that Toronto, home to some of Canada's best writers, has also been featured in many novels and short stories. Michael Ondaatje's *In the Skin of the Lion*, Timothy Findley's *Headhunter*, Anne Michaels' *Fugitive Pieces*, and a handful of novels by Margaret Atwood immediately come to mind, but as Amy Lavender Harris relates in her creative study *Imagining Toronto* (2010), the city has appeared in countless guises and moments in dozens of works of fiction and poetry going back more than seventy years. In different ways, with affection as well as criticism, each of these authors, prominent and otherwise, have utilized the city's streets, characters, and collective personality as a backdrop to explore the human condition.

Great cities can offer hope and redemption as well as despair and defeat. They are unpredictable, wondrous, and devastating, often all at the same moment, "living, breathing organisms"—to paraphrase Peter Ackroyd, the author of a 2000 biography of London, England—whose laws and growth cannot be controlled. That is what has made cities such as Toronto so vital and enticing, but also disappointing and, on occasion, dangerous.

THE STORY OF TORONTO is really the story of Canada. Like it or not, the adage "as goes Toronto, so goes Canada" is all too true. The city fixes the pulse of the rest of the country and has done so for a long time. Its economic fortunes are disconnected from the boom-and-bust cycles that have characterized the history of western Canadian urban centres. Toronto is Canada's only emerging city-state in a world dominated by such city-states as London, New York, Hong Kong, and Paris. A few months after Mike Harris and the Progressive Conservatives were elected in the June 1995 provincial election, he travelled to Asia on a trade mission. Revelling in his new status, he introduced himself to one dignitary as the "Premier of Ontario." The man stared at him with a puzzled look. "Is that near Toronto?" he asked.

That question made sense. The GTA has about 17 percent of Canada's population and produces at least 20 percent of the country's total economic output. It is the financial capital, and the Toronto Stock Exchange at Bay and King, the largest in Canada, sets the pace of the business world far beyond the 401.

As the hub of the media, culture, and entertainment industries, Toronto is home to all three national television networks; headquarters for *Maclean's*, the country's only true national newsmagazine; and the centre of the Canadian publishing industry, as shaky as that has become. Among its four daily newspapers, it boasts two, the *Globe and Mail* and the *National Post*, which are distributed across the country (though the *Post* misses a few major cities). Thus, despite best efforts to the contrary, the Canadian news, whether in print or on radio, television, or the Internet, has a decidedly Toronto-centric spin. "What Toronto chose to publish or broadcast was what the rest of the country read, heard and saw," wrote journalist and author Peter C. Newman in 1995. Stories on the CBC from Toronto tend to be regarded as "national," while those from Atlantic Canada or the Prairies are relegated to "regional" status.

Part of the issue, explains CBC news anchor Peter Mansbridge, is that, due to economic constraints, most of the people he works with each day producing *The National* live in Toronto. "Consciously or subconsciously," he says, "the staff is impacted by Toronto values, whether it is riding the subway or streetcar and listening to the buzz that's going on. Their kids go to Toronto schools and they are impacted by civic issues. All of that stuff weighs on them and it does influence *The National* and reflects a Toronto thinking." One of Mansbridge's solutions to avoid that inevitable Toronto centricity is to take *The National* on the road once a month, but he also argues, "You cannot ignore the fact that what happens in Toronto, from the weather to business, does impact on the rest of the country."

John Macfarlane, a veteran editor who has at various times in his career been at the helm of *Maclean's*, *Saturday Night*, and *Toronto Life*, answers the accusation of a Toronto-centric media slightly differently. From his office at the *Walrus* magazine he says, "It was just that the most important things that were happening in the country were then happening in Toronto. At *Maclean's*, we were desperate to find stories elsewhere in the country, but there weren't always as many of them as there were in Toronto."

Toronto's fairly remarkable demographic change over the centuries has also mirrored Canada's transformation from a British and Scottish outpost to an urban, cosmopolitan, and multicultural nation. It is a given that immigration has had a powerful and profound impact on the country, especially in the latter part of the twentieth century. No city has been as altered by the arrival of newcomers and their attendant diversity as Toronto. By 2006, approximately half of the city's population had been born outside Canada, and within its boundaries could be found people of two hundred different ethnic origins. This gradual multicultural metamorphosis was not without a gut-wrenching introspection about the acceptable meaning of being "Canadian."

In 1921, 85 percent of Torontonians were of British ancestry; by 1951, that figure had dropped only to 69 percent. The city was still very much the WASP capital of Canada, "a nest of Methodists and Orangemen, of Puritans and Pharisees, who had not yet learned that Queen Victoria was dead," as one of Francis Pollock's characters cleverly puts it in his 1936 novel *Jupiter Eight.*

Skip ahead sixty years and Toronto was feted by the United Nations and other commentators as "the most multicultural city in the world." That turned out to be an "urban legend," as convincingly shown by geographer Michael Doucet, yet Toronto is certainly one of the most multicultural cities in the world. "There is a school of thought that if you want to see what it means to be Canadian, all you have to do is walk up and down Bloor Street in Toronto," wrote the Nigerian-born journalist and author Ken Wiwa in 2003. "There are, depending who you talk to, anything from 80 to 135 languages spoken on the street. It has a United Nations of cultures, a collection of fugitive pieces, historical ironies and exotic hybrids. Eritrean, Italian and Ethiopian restaurants stand side by side, there is an Indo-Japanese sari shop and the oldest mosque in Canada is in a converted Anglican church in a Ukrainian neighbourhood. Bloor Street is a long billboard to tolerance, a panoramic route to the mythology of a Canada for all."

Still, for much of its history Toronto was an unwelcoming environment for anyone who did not fit the prescribed British mould. Ethnic neighbourhoods like "Little Italy" around College Street West, or Chinatown with its hub at Spadina and Dundas, were at first hardly celebrated; rather, they were a cause for concern, even shame. In a world of British Imperialism, Social Darwinism, and eugenics, Toronto was a city of "Antis": anti-Catholic, anti-Semitic, anti-Asian. In that, too, it was a microcosm of Canada.

Even with the prejudice and discrimination, the immigrants kept coming in search of better opportunities. What was so special about the Toronto "pull factor"? Geography, a reasonable climate (no small thing in a country like Canada), the availability of natural resources, and access to technology have all contributed to the city's rise. So, too, has the history of North America. During the American Revolution, sheer necessity brought thousands of Loyalists to the British-controlled area, and they possessed the vision and drive to lay the foundation of the city's agricultural hinterland and urban development. Politics and Toronto's status as the capital of Upper Canada, Canada West (from 1840 to 1867), and Ontario after Confederation gave it the sense of importance and clout it has always seemed to have.

From its earliest days to the present—from the Family Compact of the 1820s and 1830s through to pork baron Joseph Flavelle, banker Edmund Walker, and department store magnate John Craig Eaton in the early 1900s, business tycoon E.P. Taylor in the 1950s, and grocery store mogul Galen Weston, newspaper billionaire Ken Thomson and his son David, mining executive Seymour Schulich, Donald Walker of Magna

International, and savvy entrepreneur Gerald Schwartz in later years—the city's financial and business community has led the way. These last four are also among the most prominent members of an ever-expanding exclusive club. According to WealthInsight of London, Toronto is home to five billionaires, 1,184 multi-millionaires (those with $30 million U.S. or more in net assets), and 118,000 millionaires (28 percent of the Canadian total).

No matter the era, these men, mainly until the eighties, have often run the city as their personal fiefdom. (And they are men, even still. Of the fifty most influential people in the city in 2012, selected by *Toronto Life* magazine, only twelve were women.) Frequently arrogant and self-centred, they have, nonetheless, provided the leadership and financial resources that have advanced Toronto's infrastructure, everything from its roads and hospitals to its museums, art galleries, concert halls, and universities. This, in turn, has nurtured the city's cultural life. "For cities to have sustained success, they must compete for the grand prize: intellectual capital and talent," argued Michael Bloomberg, mayor of New York City until 2012. "I have long believed that talent attracts capital far more than capital attracts talent. The most creative individuals want to live in places that protect personal freedoms, prize diversity and offer an abundance of cultural opportunities."

Building a vibrant city is thus no easy feat, nor has it been inexpensive, but it is possible. Toronto's evolution did not take place overnight. For what seemed like an eternity, the city had to endure Montreal's superior urban position as the most important city in the country. Besting Montreal (including in professional hockey, and that has not happened since 1967) was, for a time, Toronto's chief preoccupation. Moving from the number two spot to number one was a complicated process that began in the early twenties, but was not complete until well after the Second World War—despite Torontonian bragging to the contrary during the thirties.

Likewise, shaking its staid image as a stoic bastion of Victorian morality, "Toronto the Good," a moniker given to it by William Howland, the well-intentioned social reform mayor of the late 1880s, took a long time. "Christ, I hate to leave Paris for Toronto the City of Churches," Ernest Hemingway, then a reporter for the *Toronto Daily Star*, protested to a friend in a 1923 letter. Five decades later, Margaret Atwood could still caustically comment on virtuous Toronto in her 1988 novel *Cat's Eye*. "Once it was fashionable to say how dull it was," her protagonist says. "First prize a week in Toronto, second prize two weeks in Toronto, Toronto the Good, Toronto the Blue, where you couldn't get wine on Sundays."

With success and greatness come envy, satirical sneering, and outright hostility. Hating Toronto has seemingly become a national pastime. "Clearly, if Confederation is to survive another 100 years," wrote humorist Eric Nicol in 1966, "Canada must find a national esprit de corps. Cohesion cannot depend indefinitely on hating Toronto." Forget about westerners who deride the city as "the centre of the known universe"; some of the most cutting comments about Toronto have emanated from its own disillusioned citizens.

The first shot was fired by CBC Toronto radio broadcaster Lister Sinclair in his witty skit from 1947 "We All Hate Toronto"—"We all hate Toronto! It's the only thing everybody's got in common"—and has continued to the present in the same vein with the 2007 documentary film *Let's All Hate Toronto* by filmmakers Albert Nerenberg and Rob Spence. In the film, they host "Toronto Appreciation Days" across the country and, not surprisingly, receive the expected hissing and derision. The mockingly outrageous "The Toronto Song," by the Edmonton musical comedy group Three Dead Trolls in a Baggie, begins,

I hate the Skydome and the CN tower too,
I hate Nathan Phillips square and the Ontario Zoo,
The rent's too high, the air's unclean,
The beaches are dirty and the people are mean...
The water is polluted and their mayor's a dork,
They dress real bad and they think they're New York,
In Toronto, Ontario-o-o.

A harsher and more serious critique was penned by *Toronto Life* magazine columnist Bert Archer in a 2005 essay entitled "Making a Toronto of the Imagination." Toronto, Archer judged, is "a city that exists in no one's imagination, neither in Toronto, nor in the rest of the world," adding, "Toronto is a place people live, not a place where things happen." More recently, business tycoon and author Conrad Black was of the same mind. "Toronto is recognized to be liveable by world standards, and relatively safe and prosperous," he wrote in his *National Post* column on October 6, 2012. "But as a great city, it lacks history, drama and flair."

Archer and Black were dead wrong in this assessment, and the fascinating characters featured in *Toronto: Biography of a City*—everyone from Étienne Brûlé, French explorer and the first European to stand near where the Humber River flows into Lake Ontario in 1615, to the bombastic Rob Ford, mayor of Toronto in 2013, who has polarized the city as few, if any, other politicians have—prove on the contrary that things, often important and critical things, do really happen in Toronto. (Or, as the Toronto-born rapper Drake remarked when he hosted *Saturday Night Live* in early January 2014: Toronto, where "the rappers are polite and the mayor smokes crack.") The history of the city, like that of any city, is not a celebration of perfection, but it is a saga worth probing, praising, and critiquing.

Chapter One

THE CARRYING PLACE

My people have survived for thousands of years on this continent and will continue to do so.

—BRYAN LAFORME, CHIEF OF THE MISSISSAUGA OF NEW CREDIT FIRST NATION, 2012

Étienne Brûlé, the young French adventurer and interpreter, may have been the first European to explore the Toronto area in early September 1615. *Library and Archives Canada, Acc. No. 1970-99*

NOT FAR FROM THE corner of Jane Street and Bloor Street West is a quiet and family-friendly green space on the rolling land alongside the Humber River. It is called Étienne Brûlé Park and is named for the young French adventurer and interpreter who may have been the first European to explore the Toronto area in early September 1615.

The French referred to the Humber as Rivière Taronto or the Toronto River. The name was likely derived from the Mohawk term *tkaronto*, which probably meant "where there are trees standing in the water" and which was connected to the stakes the First Nations put into the water to catch fish. For a time, the French called Lake Simcoe, 80 kilometres north, Lac de Taronto. The name was then used to describe the whole region down to Lake Ontario and eventually, more specifically, the area where the Humber meets the lake—present-day Toronto.

Étienne Brûlé was no more than sixteen years old when he arrived in Quebec in 1608 as an indentured servant or *engagé*, who had little say in his own fate. He was among the colonists accompanying Samuel de Champlain on the founder of New France's first voyage to the New World. Daring and spirited, Brûlé gladly complied with Champlain's request that he spend time with the local aboriginal tribes to learn their language and customs. For more than two years, from about 1610 to 1612, Brûlé lived with the Montagnais and then with the Algonquin (or Algonkin) under the leadership of Chief Iroquet, an ally of the Huron. In exchange, Champlain took in a young Huron named Savignon.

After many months had passed, Champlain saw Brûlé again. He commented that his "French boy" now "dressed like an Indian." Brûlé had mastered the local aboriginal language and gained an important insight into aboriginal culture and daily routines. A devout Catholic, however, he definitely was not. "It is clear that Brulé was a bad man and guilty of every vice and crime," wrote Father Du Creux in his history of New France, written in Latin and published in Paris in 1664. That critical assessment was partly based on a report left by Champlain. "Brûlé was unfortunately guilty of reprehensible actions that have sullied his memory," Champlain recorded. "In espousing the customs of the Indians, he had also adopted their morals... This man was recognized as being very vicious in character, and much addicted to women." Then a rugged man in his early twenties, Brûlé might indeed have been the womanizer Champlain claimed he was. Or, like other young Frenchmen who transformed themselves into *coureurs de bois* (runners of the woods), Brûlé may simply have been attracted to the freedom of the North American aboriginal way of life.

Questionable morals or not, Brûlé remained valuable to Champlain in his efforts to maintain his alliance with the Huron against their bitter enemies, the Iroquois or Five Nations Confederacy: the Mohawk, Oneida, Onondaga, Cayuga, and Seneca nations (the confederacy expanded to six nations with the addition of the Tuscarora in 1722). In time, the Iroquois tribes aligned themselves with the British and against the French in the war the two European powers waged over North America.

In September 1615, Champlain sent Brûlé on an expedition with a dozen Huron warriors to secure the military support of the Susquehannahs in an area that is now western New York state and northern Pennsylvania. To get there, Brûlé and his group probably navigated the Humber River, which included a forty-five-kilometre portage between Lake Simoce and Lake Ontario known as the Toronto Carrying Place or Toronto Passage. This ancient trail or portage, which Aboriginals had likely used for thousands of years, may well have taken Brûlé along the banks of the Humber through Brûlé Park and along present-day Riverside Drive straight under the Gardiner Expressway to the mouth of the Humber at Lake Ontario. Then and later, the Carrying Place had a certain mystique. As historian Percy Robinson wrote in his early account of Toronto during the French regime, it "possessed a permanence very different from casual paths through the forest. It was as old as human life in America."

Was Brûlé the first European to see the present-day site of Toronto? The best answer might be perhaps. Some historians now believe that Brûlé and his party took a more westerly route to Lake Erie and then crossed the Niagara River on their way south to avoid running into the Iroquois. Still, with Brûlé Park named after him, his legacy—however dubious—as the first non-aboriginal to gaze across the Humber remains intact.

The problem is that Brûlé left no written record of his experience traversing the Carrying Place. The English fur trader Alexander Henry did. He made the trip in 1764 and was accompanied by (unfriendly) Ojibwa warriors on their way to a British–Indian peace conference at Old Fort Niagara, near Youngstown, New York, during the time of Ottawa chief Pontiac's fight against the British. In his memoir *Travels and Adventures in Canada and the Indian Territories, Between the Years 1760 and 1776*, published in 1809, Henry recalled the harrowing journey: "The day was very hot, and the woods and marshes abounded with mosquitoes; but, the Indians walked at a quick pace, and I could by no means see myself left behind. The whole country was a thick forest, through which our only road was a foot-path, or such as, in America, is exclusively termed an Indian path. Next morning, at ten o'clock, we reached the shore of Lake Ontario."

As it turned out, Brûlé's mission was futile. Though he did enlist the support of the Susquehannahs, the warriors arrived too late to assist Champlain and the Huron, who had already suffered a defeat at the hands of the Iroquois. Brûlé continued his explorations to Chesapeake Bay, though on his return trip he was captured by the Senecas. They tortured him, a sign of respect from the Iroquois' point of view. He managed to win his release by convincing them that a thunderstorm was a symbol of a higher power watching over him; or perhaps the Senecas hoped that he would help them make peace with the French. Either way, in the years that followed, as he journeyed to other parts of the continent, he gained a well-deserved reputation as a skilled interpreter.

In 1628, on one of several voyages Brûlé made between France and Canada, the ship he was travelling on was apprehended by the English Kirke brothers, who were in a fierce competition with Champlain for control of the lucrative fur trade in the region around the St. Lawrence River. Brûlé later claimed that the Kirkes compelled him to work for them, yet he was paid handsomely for his services. Needless to say, Champlain was furious when he discovered this treachery, accusing Brûlé of abandoning his faith and selling out his people. Brûlé soon sought refuge with the Huron. But some of them turned against him, possibly because of his relations with aboriginal women or perhaps because he was perceived as a threat to their trading operations. Whatever the reason, Brûlé was killed in 1633 and reportedly eaten—an act which the Hurons involved later declared they deeply regretted.

THOUSANDS OF YEARS before Étienne Brûlé explored the area around Toronto, the Great Lakes region was home to nomadic hunters whose lives were governed by the seasons and the supply of animals. Though these hunting and gathering societies were primitive, they had developed their own traditions, culture, and spiritual beliefs that dictated the routine of daily life as well as trading, war, and death rituals. As far back as AD 500, for instance, rules over territorial rights were established, as well as the permission and gifts that had to be presented to the chief in order to venture into another tribe's land. Over the years, ancient animal bones, spear heads, and stone tools belonging to these earliest inhabitants of Toronto have been uncovered in excavations, including at the construction site of the Eaton's store at College and Yonge Streets in 1910. Around the same time, a burial site, probably dating back three thousand years, was found close to Grenadier Pond in High Park. More recently, entire Huron villages containing thousands of artifacts have been discovered in archaeological digs undertaken near York University as well as on the Alexandra site at L'Amoreaux Park in Scarborough.

By the time Jacques Cartier reached the St. Lawrence in 1535, the area around Toronto in and around Lakes Ontario and Erie and north to Georgian Bay was populated by the Huron, Petun, Neutral, and several Algonquian tribes. In all, they totalled about 65,000 people, with their Iroquois enemies located not too far away, south of the lakes, in what is today the state of New York. The arrival of the Europeans in this wilderness, with their iron pots, guns, alcohol, and disease, altered forever the aboriginal way of life. Both the Europeans and the aboriginals initially embraced the contact, with each side generally seeing more positives than negatives. Almost immediately the French allied themselves with the Huron, and in the late 1670s the English formed a similar alliance with the Iroquois, reshaping the fur trade and the art of war.

In time, however, smallpox and other diseases the Europeans inadvertently brought with them to the New World wiped out half of the aboriginal population in southern Ontario. This high death rate took its toll on the Huron, hurt the lucrative French fur trade, and allowed the Iroquois to extend their territory north beyond the Great Lakes. In 1649 the Iroquois destroyed the Huron village of Ataratiri, as well as the Jesuit missionary settlement of Sainte-Marie, near present-day Midland, Ontario. More than three hundred years later, Toronto politicians would reluctantly use the name Ataratiri—suggested by aboriginal studies specialist John Steckley of Humber College—for a massive residential redevelopment proposed for the industrial West Don Lands, at the bottom of the Don Valley just north of Gardiner Expressway. (Steckley recalls that there was some opposition to using that name, and at least one civic official believed it sounded too much like the popular video game Atari.) Alas, that project crumbled due to the extensive costs. But another soon replaced it, and a section of the area is a village once more, built for athletes participating in the 2015 Pan-Am Games held in Toronto.

By the middle of the seventeenth century, the Seneca had established a village along the Toronto Carrying Place in the vicinity of the corner of Jane Street and Baby Point Road, six blocks or so from Étienne Brûlé Park. They called it Teiaiagon. It had easy access to the Humber River and hence north to the hunting region where beaver was plentiful, but was also accessible for the French from the east and the British to the south. "The site was a natural stopping place for canoeists, as they could ford the river at this spot," notes University of Toronto anthropologist Ronald Williamson, "and it was not navigable much farther upstream, even for small canoes."

Teiaiagon does not figure largely in the historical record, though it is clearly indicated as "Toioiugon" on a globe dating from 1683 that belonged to Louis XIV. Father Louis Hennepin, a Recollect missionary and adventurer based at Fort Frontenac (near what is now Kingston, Ontario), visited the village for three weeks in late 1678, as did the great French explorer René-Robert Cavelier, Sieur de La Salle in 1680 and possibly in 1681. (Some of La Salle's men might have travelled to Teiaiagon in the mid-1670s, causing serious trouble with a keg of brandy they brought with them.)

The Europeans likely found a typical Iroquois village, protected by palisade walls, with as many as fifty longhouses and nearby agricultural fields. In those days, the Humber was abundant with salmon, another source of food. Estimates suggest Teiaiagon's population was about two thousand people. In 1701, the Seneca were either pushed out of the village or voluntarily left it to the Ojibwa, known to the French and English as the Mississauga, who were based on the north shore of Lake Ontario. The Mississauga became the "masters of the Great Lakes region" (to use historian Peter Schmalz's term) for the next six decades. But the Ojibwa wisely made peace with the Iroquois so they could take advantage of the goods supplied by both French and English and could control the trade farther north. (Another theory suggests that negotiation led to the Seneca abandoning the village and the Ojibwa replacing them as part of a larger Iroquois plan to expand their trading interests.)

Throughout this period, the French, from their main base in the region at Fort Frontenac, did whatever they could to thwart the English, who were based at Albany. The English were attracting the trade along the St. Lawrence River and in and around Lakes Ontario and Erie. Bothersome, too, were the coureurs de bois, or free traders, whose "illicit" dealings with the Indians were beyond the control of the French authorities in Montreal. In 1720, under the direction of twenty-two-year-old Captain Alexandre Dagneau, Sieur de Douville, a tiny outpost or *magasin royale* (King's Store) was erected near Baby Point beside the Humber. It was not much more than a small two-storey log building with room for only a few soldiers to live and an attic to keep the supplies, trading goods—everything from buttons and ribbons to powder and shot—and furs acquired. Nonetheless, for a few years it diverted sufficient trade away from the English at New York. Unhappy with this reduction in their profits, they countered in 1726 with the construction of a stone fort at Oswego, New York, on the southeast shore of Lake Ontario. That soon spelled the end of Douville's Toronto trading post.

As the French and British warred over North America from 1697 to 1763, with occasional periods of peace, each side persistently sought strategic and geographic military and trading advantages. In 1750, the French again built a storehouse near the mouth of the Humber River with the intention of diverting aboriginals using the Toronto Carrying Place from proceeding to the British at Fort Oswego. In charge of this operation was Pierre Robinau de Portneuf, a young French officer from Fort Frontenac. The small post was opened in the early summer and was an immediate success; by mid-July, a shipment of furs valued at 18,000 livres (with purchasing power equivalent to about $400,000 in 2011 dollars) had been forwarded to Montreal. Aboriginal demand outstripped the supply of European goods (and, it must be said, of alcohol) on hand. Not wanting to lose a profitable opportunity, and with an eye on consolidating French territory in the Ohio region, the governor general of New France, Jacques-Pierre de Taffanel de La Jonquière, ordered Sieur de Portneuf to supervise the construction of a larger fort, with more trading capacity and military potential, approximately five kilometres east at the foot of present-day Dufferin Street, where the Canadian National Exhibition (CNE) grounds are now located.

Fort Rouillé, named after the French Minister of the Marine, Antoine-Louis Rouillé, comte de Jouy—and also more colloquially called Fort Toronto or *le fort royal de Toronto*—was completed by the spring of 1751. After another successful trading season was finished, Sieur de Portneuf returned to Fort Frontenac in the fall, and Thomas Robutel de La Noue, forty-nine years old, was made commander at Toronto.

Governor La Jonquière had high hopes for the economic future of the fort, which was built of squared oak timbers and entirely enclosed. The trade with the Indians "cannot but increase in future," he reassured Minister Rouillé back in France in early October. "In fact, the tribes in the regions about Toronto who hitherto had resorted only to the English, have not been at [Oswego] at all; they have preferred to barter their furs at Toronto." Still, by the time hostilities between the French and British broke out again in North America in 1754—two years before the decisive Seven Years War erupted in Europe—Fort Rouillé remained a limited garrison with seven soldiers and a storekeeper.

The fort's end came six years later, during the critical battles of 1758–59. Fort Frontenac fell to the British in August 1758, and a year later the French fort at Niagara suffered the same fate after a nineteen-day siege led by the British commander Sir William Johnson. From Quebec City, the Marquis de Vaudreuil, the governor, had ordered that if Fort Niagara was captured, Fort Rouillé should be evacuated and burned before the British could seize it. That destruction was carried out, and the inhabitants at Toronto fled to Montreal. When the British arrived to inspect what was left at the fort, all they found were "five heaps of charred timbers and planks, with a low chimney-stack of coarse brick and a shattered flooring," as one early chronicler of Toronto's history described it. After nearly two centuries, the French had yielded control of the Great Lakes region to the British.

The end of French rule in North America came two months later with the British victory on the Plains of Abraham outside Quebec City. The subsequent capitulation of Montreal in 1760 and the cession by the French of their North American empire in the Treaty of Paris in 1763 meant that any future settlement at Toronto would be British.

The British lost little time asserting their claim to Toronto and the surrounding area. In mid-September 1760, Major-General Jeffrey Amherst, head of the British forces, dispatched his chief scout and intelligence officer, Robert Rogers, with two hundred men and fifteen whale boats to take formal control of the forts deserted and destroyed by the French. Born in Massachusetts in 1731, Rogers achieved some fame during the war against the French as the daring, and occasionally ruthless, leader of "Rogers' Rangers," a freewheeling company of British irregulars who fought the enemy, both the French and their Indian allies, guerrilla-style from a base in the forest. Rogers and his men actively participated in the attack on Quebec in September 1759 and witnessed the surrender of Montreal a year later.

Rogers and his flotilla reached Toronto on September 30, 1760, having two days earlier encountered a group of fifty Mississauga who supplied them with salmon and freshly killed deer. He later described his first sighting in one of two books he wrote when he was back in London in 1765, a project he partly undertook to pay off his notorious gambling debts. "Round the place where formerly the French had a fort, that was called Fort Toronto, there was a tract of about 300 acres of cleared ground," he wrote. "The soil here is principally of clay. The deer are extremely plentiful in this country. Some Indians were hunting at the mouth of the river, who ran into the woods at our approach, very much frightened. They came in, however, in the morning, and testified their joy at the news of our success against the French... I think Toronto a most convenient place for a factory, and that from thence we may easily settle the north side of Lake Erie."

No sooner had Rogers secured the region than merchants who had been living south of Lake Ontario jumped to take advantage of the new commercial opportunities in the fur trade. Toronto was to be built by such business visionaries. One of these was Jacques Dupéront Baby, of noble French heritage, whose father, Raymond, was a fur trader. Raymond Baby was born in Montreal in 1731 and as a young man ventured south as part of an extended family enterprise. During the French and Indian War, the North American part of the Seven Years War from 1754 to 1763, he was working as a trader and Indian agent at Chiningué or Logstown in western Pennsylvania. At some point, Baby lost an eye, but it hardly slowed him down; he also possessed, as historian Dale Miquelon puts it, "the stubborn tenacity of the self-made man."

Baby planned to return to France when the conflict ended. He had been a loyal French patriot and initially disdained the British victory, but he soon found that he was able to successfully continue his fur-trading operations under British rule. By 1762, he and his wife had relocated to Detroit. In time he accepted the change of government and swore an oath of allegiance to King George III. Baby even assisted the British army during the uprising against it led by the great Ottawa chief Pontiac. This uprising, from 1763 to 1765, was a protest against the new political order and what was perceived as unfair British treatment of aboriginals.

Competition in the fur trade was intense as merchants from Albany and New York also eyed the old French territory. The business potential enticed Baby to expand his operations in and around Toronto as soon as the British granted him a pass or licence to do so. His past friendly relations with the aboriginals in the Great Lakes area proved beneficial as well. Baby remained in Detroit even after the American Revolution, and he died there in 1789. By then his eldest son, Jacques or James, born in 1763, had joined his father in the business, which continued to thrive in the fur trade as well as in the acquisition and development of land rich with timber. It was James Baby who eventually settled in Toronto, becoming an Upper Canada politician, judge, wealthy landholder, and key member of the ruling elite, the so-called Family Compact, in addition to giving his family name to the west Toronto neighbourhood of Baby Point.

Two more wily French fur traders who anticipated Toronto's future prospects were Jean-Bonaventure Rousseau, dit Saint Jean, and his son Jean-Baptiste (who later anglicized his name to Rousseaux St. John). In 1770, the elder Rousseau, then forty-three, was in Montreal working as a trader and as an interpreter with the Indian Department. That year, after he took the oath of allegiance to the Crown, he obtained a licence to trade with the Indians living along the Humber in the vicinity of Toronto. He set out with one canoe, six men, and cargo, which included "eighty gallons of rum and brandy, sixteen gallons of wine," gunpowder, shot, and balls. That was not quite what the British had in mind when they granted him the licence. General Thomas Gage, the commander of British forces in North America, and one of the few British or French officials who opposed widespread trading of alcohol with aboriginals, denounced Rousseau for "debauching" the Indians by selling it to them.

Jean-Bonaventure Rousseau died in 1774, and his sixteen-year-old son carried on the trade around Lake Ontario. Jean-Baptiste had learned to speak several aboriginal languages and was also employed by the British as an interpreter during the American Revolutionary War. He likely knew Joseph Brant or Thayendanegea, the Mohawk leader who sided with the British during the conflict. In 1787, Rousseaux married Margaret Clyne (his second marriage; his first marriage had broken up a year earlier), who was under Brant's care. Brant thought highly of Rousseaux, and the couple named one of their six children after him.

Rousseaux engaged in trading around the Bay of Quinte, west of Kingston, but maintained his business interests around Toronto. Though he built a corn mill close to present-day Brantford, he and his family finally moved to the Toronto area in 1792, where he established a trading post at the foot of the Toronto Carrying Place, near where the Seneca village of Teiaiagon once stood. Though he eventually relocated his business west to Ancaster, Rousseaux was among the first Europeans to settle permanently in Toronto. In his role as an interpreter, Rousseaux assisted the British in their 1785 negotiations with the Mississauga for the purchase of land around Lake Simcoe. This paved the way for the much larger Toronto Purchase of 1787—arguably the most significant land deal in the city's history.

For strategic military and trading purposes, and to prepare for the settlement demands of the Loyalists, who were migrating north after the humiliating loss to the Americans after seven years of war, the British needed to acquire the land around Lake Ontario, including that in the vicinity of the Toronto Carrying Place. They could have merely declared the land their property, but that would have gone against legal precedent and custom. Since 1763, the British had accepted the principle of Indian land rights in the area around the Great Lakes and were committed to negotiating with the Mississauga before any surveying commenced. Moreover, Guy Carleton—who in 1786 became Lord Dorchester, the newly appointed governor-in-chief of Quebec—well understood that, in the aftermath of Pontiac's Rebellion, maintaining positive relations with the First Nations population was essential.

On September 23, 1787, Dorchester arranged for Sir John Johnson of the Indian Department and deputy surveyor-general John Collins to meet at the Bay of Quinte with three Mississauga chiefs, Wabukanyne (or Wabakinine, who was later killed in Toronto by a Queen's Ranger in 1796), Neace, and Pakquan. With apparently little discussion, the chiefs agreed to sell to the British for a payment of £1,700 (roughly $175,000 in current dollars) plus 149 barrels of goods—containing everything from axes, guns, and brass kettles to fishhooks, mirrors, and laced hats—a tract of land "on the north side of Lake Ontario," which encompassed more than a thousand square kilometres in the area of present-day Toronto. The deal had holes in it, however. The official documents were incomplete, and there was no actual description of the land that had been purchased.

Once land surveyors got to work a year later, the Mississauga objected to the British claim. Ultimately, the Purchase of 1787 was declared invalid, and a new agreement was negotiated in August 1805, witnessed by Jean-Baptiste Rousseaux. Yet again the British failed to explain the legal process to the aboriginals, and the deal of 1805 incorporated more land than had been included in 1787—including the Toronto Islands, which were not surrendered in the original treaty. For this extra land, the British paid an additional 10 shillings, or about the equivalent of $60 today. More than two centuries would pass before the Canadian federal government agreed to settle this land claim in 2010 (after a decade of legal wrangling and negotiation) for $145 million.

Lord Dorchester's initial vision for Toronto's future has often been overlooked. True, within a few years of the original Toronto Purchase, his enthusiasm for making the city Upper Canada's new capital waned. But he had played a historically significant role in the city's development, certainly as important as Lieutenant Governor John Graves Simcoe, who has reaped most of the credit.

Chapter Two

BRITISH MUDDY YORK

Toronto was born of the water...[But] Toronto has treated its watery heritage recklessly over the years and many times appeared to turn its back on the shores of the bay. Railway tracks and expressways, land fill and buildings, storage elevators and parking lots have blocked the view here.

—WILLIAM KILBOURN, 1984

John Graves Simcoe, the first lieutenant governor of Upper Canada from 1791 to 1796, was the visionary who conceived Toronto, which he renamed York, as a viable settlement with an unlimited future. *Library and Archives Canada, Acc. No. 1991-30-3*

WHEN HE FIRST LAID eyes on Toronto Harbour in early May 1793, Lieutenant-Colonel John Graves Simcoe is supposed to have turned to the surveyors accompanying him and grandly declared: "Here let there be a city." It was not quite like Moses ordering Pharaoh to "Let my people go," but in the annals of Toronto it conveys the same biblical repercussions.

There is no forgetting Simcoe, the first lieutenant governor of Upper Canada. He is remembered in Ontario with a county, town, streets in Toronto and Niagara Falls, schools, and a regal statue near the Ontario Legislature in Queen's Park. Plus, in Toronto, the holiday Monday of the August long weekend is known as Simcoe Day to commemorate his vocal stand against slavery. (Simcoe named Lake Simcoe after his father, John.) Considering that he was only in his post in Upper Canada for three years, the accolades, with the exception of the last one, seem slightly exaggerated. Still, Simcoe was a visionary. And visionaries whose prophecies come true are frequently immortalized—whether or not they played an active role in transforming the dream into a reality.

John Graves Simcoe was an ambitious, proud, and innovative military man with an intellectual bent; he also appreciated history and poetry, like any want-to-be aristocrat. He was born in 1752 in Cotterstock, England, 140 kilometres north of London. His father John, a naval officer, brought troops to General James Wolfe during the war for Quebec and died from pneumonia prior to the British victory at the Plains of Abraham in September 1759. Some years earlier, he had composed for his sons John Graves and Percy a guide to an ordered and disciplined life entitled "Rules for Your Conduct," a list of nineteen tenets that they should follow. It included the patriotic, religious, moral, and military principles that guided John Graves Simcoe's future behaviour and actions as a commander and political official.

Simcoe was educated at several of Britain's finer private schools and at Oxford University before opting for a career in the army. He made a name for himself as a competent and creative officer during the Revolutionary War in America, most notably as the commander of the Loyalist corps, the Queen's Rangers, which he reorganized and expanded. He was a fair but tough leader and tolerated no disobedience or transgressions. For Simcoe, war was never an excuse for crime or immorality. Plundering and abusing civilians were forbidden, and he sentenced two of his men to death for raping an American woman. This assault was an aberration among the Rangers, though it is true that some of Simcoe's troops (along with their aboriginal allies) seized black slaves with the intention of selling them in Montreal and on the Niagara peninsula. Another British commander, Sir Guy Carleton (Lord Dorchester), heard of these events, so readily believed many unfounded stories about the Loyalist soldiers' inappropriate actions, tainting his opinion of the corps as well as their leader.

In a skirmish with the enemy in 1778, Simcoe was injured—wounds that contributed to his increasingly poor health as he got older—and a year later he was captured. He endured six harsh months as a prisoner before a deal was negotiated for his release. A serious illness forced him to return to England days before the humiliating British surrender to American forces at Yorktown in mid-October 1781. He recuperated at the estate of Admiral Samuel Graves, his godfather, where he fell in love with twenty-year-old Elizabeth Posthuma Gwillim.

Her father, Lieutenant-Colonel Thomas Gwillim, had died in Germany in 1762, while her mother, also named Elizabeth, was pregnant. She died giving birth to her baby daughter. Young Elizabeth was raised by her mother's sister Margaret, who soon married Admiral Samuel Graves, a man of means. Both of Elizabeth's parents had left her a substantial amount of money and land, and she grew up surrounded by servants and immersed in literature and the fine arts. She was attractive, outgoing, and a Renaissance woman, who appreciated the arts and high culture. She was, in short, the perfect bride for a determined man like Simcoe, who coveted prestige and status. The two were married in 1782, and they proceeded to have a large family. Despite being wealthier than him—owing to her money the newlyweds were able to acquire Wolford, an impressive estate in the county of Devon—she deferred to his authority as was the custom of the times; in the diary she kept after they moved to Upper Canada, she almost always wrote of him as either the "Colonel" or the "Governor."

In 1789, Simcoe was elected to the British House of Commons, but life as an MP proved too sedate. Events in the remaining British colonies in North America were about to provide him with a much more adventurous opportunity. Near the end of the Revolutionary War and after the signing of the Treaty of Paris, in which Britain was compelled to recognize American independence, nearly ten thousand Loyalist refugees, some with their slaves, arrived in Quebec—many more went to Nova Scotia and the new colony of New Brunswick as well as British islands in the Caribbean—happy to accept the British offer of free land and a chance to start their lives over again. They were a mixture of Brits, Scots, Germans, Dutch, and free blacks making up a diverse group of Anglicans, Presbyterians, Lutherans, and Catholics. All that was required to obtain the land was an oath of allegiance to the Crown.

The influx of so many non-French-speaking newcomers necessitated yet another geographical realignment of Quebec. In 1791, the British Parliament passed the Constitutional Act, which authorized the division of Quebec into Upper and Lower Canada (technically accomplished through an order-in-council on August 24, 1791), with provision for an elected legislative assembly. Power, however, remained firmly in the hands of Guy Carleton, now Lord Dorchester and governor-in-chief of Upper and Lower Canada, who was based in Quebec City. Circumstances forced him to return to Britain in August 1791, and he did not get back to Canada until September 1793. Lieutenant governors were appointed in both colonies to manage the administration—with advice and assistance from appointed executive and legislative councils—but both were to be subservient to Dorchester.

For the top position in Upper Canada, Dorchester recommended Sir John Johnson, the superintendent-general and inspector-general of Indian Affairs in British North America, who had distinguished himself as an able commander in the war against the Americans. A strong supporter of the Crown, Johnson had worked closely with Loyalists who settled on the Upper St. Lawrence and the Bay of Quinte, and he had supported their demands for a separate and English colony. He was a natural choice to be Upper Canada's first lieutenant governor. Instead, angering both Dorchester and Johnson, British officials in London, guided by the judgment of Lord Grenville, the secretary of state, selected John Graves Simcoe, who eagerly accepted the new assignment despite his unhappiness at having to answer to Dorchester. The governor-in-chief's two-year absence from Canada did permit Simcoe a certain degree of autonomy. But the two men, who clearly did not like each other—despite the fact that they never actually met in person—soon clashed repeatedly over policy, military expenditures, and an overall vision for transforming Upper Canada, and Toronto in particular, into more than a wilderness outpost. In this instance, Simcoe's idealism won out—or, at least, that is how it is perceived today—over Dorchester's pragmatism.

Several interrelated ideas shaped Simcoe's thoughts about Upper Canada as he prepared for his new task. He was convinced that the American Revolution had been perpetrated by a rebel minority and that a majority in the former thirteen colonies were still loyal to the British Crown. Like most Tories of his generation, Simcoe stood for law and order and a society in which the wealthy and educated elite controlled the world. He disdained American-style (and French) republicanism with its premise of democracy, a dangerous form of mob government if there ever was one. Simcoe was certain that most Americans would welcome British rule again, provided they were shown the proper and civilized model, which he aimed to build in Upper Canada. The new colony, he assured his friend, the naturalist Sir Joseph Banks, was "destined by nature, sooner or later to govern the interior world [of North America]." Achieving that noble objective meant for Simcoe that Upper Canada must become "a bastion of imperial power" in which British liberty, justice, and Anglicanism would prevail. This is the Simcoe vision that partly moulded Toronto's character for more than a century. It was given more credence in the nineteenth century by an influx of British immigrants and by conservative Presbyterian Scots who dominated the city's business interests. Still, until such time as the Americans renounced their rebellion, Simcoe maintained that they posed a serious threat to British sovereignty in North America. That fear, too, directed early Toronto's development.

THE SIMCOES, with their two youngest children, Francis and Sophia, in tow, arrived in Quebec City in early 1792. When summer came, the family made its way up the St. Lawrence River to Kingston and then to the designated Upper Canadian capital of Niagara. Simcoe, who detested "uncivilized" aboriginal names, rechristened the settlement Newark (today it is Niagara-on-the-Lake). There, Elizabeth indulged her passions for painting and sketching, and drew the great falls as well as other scenic locales. In January, she gave birth to her seventh and last child, Katherine, who died fifteen months later of unknown causes. She was buried at the garrison. (The name "Fort York" was not used for the garrison until the 1870s, according to Carl Benn, a historian of the fort, and it became "Old Fort York," a museum, in the 1930s.)

Unhappy with the choice of Newark as the seat of government—one contemporary observer referred to it as "a poor, wretched straggling village"—Simcoe favoured the site of present-day London, Ontario, on the River La Tranche, soon to be called the

Thames. In his opinion, its interior location offered a safer locale for civilian government, though building a road to reach it proved difficult. Simcoe's vision angered the many Loyalist pioneers in and around Kingston, who had expected that its geographic location, linking it to the trade in Montreal in one direction and Newark in the other, made it a natural choice. Moreover, Kingston was the preference of Lord Dorchester, which might explain why Simcoe rejected it, though he also judged it to be too close to American territory. The collective anger in Kingston and Niagara intensified when, by default, Toronto won the capital sweepstakes. Many officials who had built residences in Kingston or Newark stubbornly refused to relocate until they were forced to do so. And that most popular of Canadian pastimes—resenting Toronto—was born.

Simcoe first visited the Toronto site in May 1793 on a trip through his new "kingdom." Given his overarching concern about an American attack, he was immediately impressed with the harbour as the most strategic spot from which to defend the colony. He told Major-General Alured Clarke, his counterpart in Lower Canada, who was filling in for the departed Lord Dorchester, "I found it to be without comparison the most proper situation for an arsenal in every extent of that word that can be met with in this Province." He soon decided to move, if temporarily, his main headquarters from Newark to Toronto and to build up its fortifications and civilization.

On July 29, 1793, Simcoe returned with Elizabeth and the children by boat. "We embarked on board the 'Mississauga,' the band playing in the ship," Elizabeth recorded in her diary. "It was dark, so I went to bed and slept until eight o'clock the next morning, when I found myself in the harbour of Toronto. We had gone under an easy sail all night, for as no person on board had ever been at Toronto, Mr. Bouchette was afraid to enter the harbour till daylight, when St. John Rosseau, an Indian trader who lives near, came in a boat to pilot us."

An isolated wilderness, cut off from the rest of the world by lake and lack of roads, is what the Simcoes found in Toronto. Decades later, Joseph Bouchette, only nineteen years old at the time, who had surveyed the area prior to Simcoe's first visit, also remembered the tranquility. "I still distinctly recollect the untamed aspect which the country exhibited when first I entered the beautiful basin... Dense and trackless forests lined the margin of the lake and reflected their inverted images in its glassy surface. The wandering savage had constructed his ephemeral habitation beneath their luxuriant foliage—the group then consisting of two families of Mississauga—and the bay and neighboring marshes were the hitherto uninvaded haunts of immense coveys of wild fowl. Indeed, they were so abundant as in some measure to annoy us during the night."

The family's first home was a "canvas house," as it was dubbed, a large tent that Simcoe had brought with him to Upper Canada, and which had once belonged to Captain James Cook, the celebrated British explorer. It was set up near the foot of what was to become Bathurst Street, close to the soon-to-be constructed garrison near the Fort York site. Despite her outwardly timid nature, the glass of life was always half-full for Elizabeth Simcoe. As she reasoned, "did People but consider their happiness, the first point of their Creed would be not consider things as serious which are of no consequence." In good spirit she tolerated the rain and wind in the spring, humid heat and mosquitoes in the summer, frigid temperatures and snow in the winter, and lack of nearly every convenience imaginable, even for the eighteenth century, with nary a complaint. To remind her of her beloved Wolford estate, she had her "Nankeen" ware, blue and white porcelain china, and hung fine tapestry on the tent's canvas walls.

Peter Russell, a former British officer who served under Simcoe in Upper Canada as receiver and auditor general, was far less impressed. "The Governor and Mrs. Simcoe received me very graciously," he wrote to his sister Elizabeth Russell. "But you can have no conception of the Misery in which they live... in one room they lie and see company... and in the other are the Nurse and Children squalling... an open Bower covers us at dinner... and a tent with a small Table and three Chairs serves us for a Council Room." In 1794, a brutal winter uncharacteristically dragged into March, and even the indefatigable Mrs. Simcoe admitted in her diary that one evening it was so cold inside the family's tent that she could barely hold her cards for her regular game of whist.

In the spring of 1794, the Simcoes found a serene picnic spot on a high wooded ridge overlooking the Don River near the eastern end of Cabbagetown. There they built a summer retreat they called "Castle Frank," named after their son Francis, who was to perish at the siege of Badajoz in Spain during the war against France in 1812. With its four pine columns in the front, Elizabeth imagined the house as a Greek temple, but in reality it was a roughly constructed log cabin, which the lieutenant governor and his wife used to host social occasions.

After the Simcoes left Upper Canada, the property was managed by other local government administrators. It was burned in a fire in 1829, likely started by careless fishermen, and a portion of the property became the southern part of St. James Cemetery. Many years later, long after the Simcoes' land had been sold, Sir Edward Kemp, a Toronto MP and the minister of militia and defence during the First World War, erected a palatial mansion he also called Castle Frank, which was close to the site of the original house. This mansion was demolished in 1962. Today, in Toronto, the name "Castle Frank" adorns two schools, two streets, and a subway stop on Bloor Street East.

Paintings of John Simcoe show Toronto's founder as a regal military hero and country squire. And while he was an excellent administrator and town planner as well as adventurer, the list of ailments he suffered was long. He routinely and variously endured gout, neuralgia, and brutal migraine headaches. On one occasion, Hannah Jarvis, the wife of provincial secretary William Jarvis, noted of the lieutenant governor that "his eyes and skin are as yellow as saffron and he is peevish beyond description."

Health concerns aside, Simcoe could be a pretentious bore. "His favourite topics are his projects and war, which seem to be the objects of his leading passions," complained the pro-monarchist politician François-Alexandre-Frédéric de La Rochefoucauld, who had fled the French Revolution for the United States and visited with the Simcoes in the spring of 1795. "He is acquainted with the military history of all countries; no hillock catches his eye without exciting in his mind the idea of a fort, which might be constructed on the spot." Kingston businessman and über-Loyalist Richard Cartwright (grandfather of the Liberal politician Sir Richard Cartwright), who loathed Simcoe's Toronto-centred focus, found the lieutenant governor's need to replicate in Upper Canada all things British highly annoying. "He thinks every existing regulation in England would be proper here," griped Cartwright. This included imposing harsh discipline on the men of his Queen's Rangers, whom he had brought to Toronto to clear the bush and begin the construction of much-needed roads to connect the settlement with the outside world. Minor transgressions of military decorum were frequently punished with a flogging.

In another move that angered Cartwright, Simcoe, as he had done at Niagara, quickly ditched the aboriginal "Toronto" and declared the soon-to-be town's new name "York," in honour of King George III's second son Prince Frederick, Duke of York and Albany, who as the commander of British forces in Flanders had—according to the official version, at least—saved Holland from a French invasion. There was some unhappiness with the name change, and many original residents continued to fight for and use "Toronto." Nonetheless, Simcoe had his way and "York"—or, rather, "Little York" and "muddy York," as it came to be known to differentiate it from the other more distinguished Yorks—remained in use until "Toronto" was finally adopted again when the city was incorporated in 1834.

In time, Simcoe reluctantly abandoned his plans for a capital at London and dedicated himself to establishing York as the seat of Upper Canada's government. Soon Lord Dorchester supported the idea, though York maintained its "temporary capital" status until late 1796, at the end of the Dorchester and Simcoe era. Years earlier, in 1788, Dorchester had assigned engineer Captain Gother Mann the task of laying out the townsite, with the harbour as its focus. Mann came up with what might be expected from a military engineer: "a gridiron settlement" reminiscent of Roman architecture. The government and military buildings were focussed around a central square, with residences located nearby.

Simcoe opted to reinvent the wheel and in 1793 had his own surveyor, Alexander Aitkin, complete another plan. He devised a slightly more "practical" gridiron blueprint for a smaller town of about ten square blocks—"bounded by George, Berkeley, Adelaide, and Front streets, with the areas from Parliament to the Don [River] and from Peter to the Humber [River] set aside for government and military purposes." Both surveyors lacked imagination, according to Toronto architect Eric Arthur. In his view, they "ignored completely the very features that give character and beauty to Toronto—the hill and the wooded ravines," and they left the city with the dull, yet easy to navigate, gridiron layout. In the decades that followed, Toronto spread northward, almost completely oblivious to its unique river valleys and ravines. "A more imaginative city," suggests journalist and long-time resident Robert Fulford, "would have used local topography as an organizing principle, building the districts around the valleys and waterways; that would have led naturally to a more intelligent use of Lake Ontario, the eventual destination of all the waterways."

Simcoe was of a different mindset, and his vision for York as the guardian of Upper Canada took shape slowly. Lord Dorchester, still on leave in England, absolutely refused to provide him with the additional soldiers he requested or the necessary funding to build up the garrison. Nonetheless, he did what he could. Barely adequate barracks and a stockade were built near Garrison Creek, the beginnings of what would become Fort York. (In those days, Lake Ontario's shoreline was much closer to the garrison, but over the decades it was significantly altered by landfills, extending farther into the lake.) In an early example of Canadian patronage, Simcoe distributed hundred-acre parcels of land north of Lot Street—renamed Queen Street in about 1843 to honour Queen Victoria—to his loyal officials, possibly, the rumour went, to compensate them for the burden of transferring to York. Many of the recipients of this largesse developed their land into profitable farms, which they later sold for inflated prices as the city gradually expanded north.

Government buildings were erected near Parliament and Front (then called Palace) Streets. Two main roads, which have defined the city, were also laid out: a mainly east-west artery, Dundas Street, named after Sir Henry Dundas, the home secretary; and the north-south route of Yonge Street, honouring Simcoe's mentor Sir George Yonge, Britain's secretary of state for war. Thanks to the diligent efforts first of the Queen's Rangers and later of conscripted German settlers—under the supervision of the talented, albeit financially struggling, land developer, artist, and architect William Berczy—Yonge Street was hacked out of the forest. In reality, it was nothing but a treacherous muddy wagon path, yet it soon enough provided York's inhabitants, including merchants and traders, with a route north to the Holland River. By 1794, its southern end reached approximately to what is today Yorkville Avenue, north of Bloor Street.

Another path was dug out, for a time called "Road to Yonge Street" that extended Yonge to Lot Street and then down to the water, though due to private property it was not quite the straight line it is currently. Farther north, farms were cleared, mills were built, and Berczy's hard-pressed and frequently hungry settlers tried to make a go of it at his Markham Township, part of a large grant made to him by Simcoe.

Yet a third key outlet linking York eastward to the mouth of the Trent River and the Bay of Quinte was constructed between 1799 and 1800 by Asa Danforth, an American salt producer (though today's Danforth Avenue is not the route he carved out) and land speculator of dubious success. Danforth, whose name is now immortalized east of the Don River in the street known as "The Danforth," eventually completed the job after facing difficulties with money and supplies. Embroiled in a feud with the Upper Canada government over unpaid fees and land claims, he returned to New York, where he spent the rest of his days trying to sell salt and battling with creditors.

The American attack Simcoe feared never did materialize during his stint in Upper Canada. Plans for a university and elite preparatory schools—for only the truly educated could rule the lesser classes, in his view—and a full endowment for the Church of England also did not pan out. Law courts, however, were established, and he had more success ensuring the gradual abolition of slavery in Upper Canada, forty years before abolition became law in the British empire. The Simcoe-inspired legislation was not perfect. Given the shortage of labour in York and elsewhere, Loyalists who had brought slaves with them had no desire to lose or free them. So a compromise was agreed to: any slaves residing in the colony in 1793 would remain so for the duration of their lives, but no new slaves would be allowed. And children born to slaves would be freed when they reached their twenty-fifth birthday.

Simcoe had set Upper Canada and Toronto on their way. He entrenched top-down government in the colony, and encouraged York's superiority, with its haughty customs and attitudes, and the distinctive British and Anglican character it would retain for decades. Poor health forced him to return with his family to England in July 1796. This temporary leave became permanent, and he officially resigned as lieutenant governor a year and half later. Hence, it was left to his successors to complete the task of transforming York from a "military camp" (as Edith Firth aptly described it), with a sprinkling of log houses and cottages and a tiny population of only about 240 people, to a more vibrant, though admittedly still primitive, nineteenth-century town.

WITH HIS LONG, STRAGGLY WHITE HAIR, beady eyes, long thin nose, and military demeanour, Peter Russell might well have been a minor character in a Charles Dickens novel, perhaps the domineering operator of a London workhouse. Born in Ireland in 1733, Russell attended St. John's College at the University of Cambridge for a few years before opting to join the British army. During the Seven Years War, he fought in North America and Gibraltar, rising to the rank of lieutenant by 1758. Two years later he was back in North America, though he functioned mainly as a military administrator.

For a time, the ups and downs of the gaming tables dictated Russell's life. One week he would lose £1,000 only to cover his losses the following week with a winning streak. In the mid-1760s he had such a run of good fortune that he was able to acquire a Virginia tobacco plantation, which he then proceeded to gamble away. After selling his estate to settle his debts, he returned to England and wound up as a humiliated debtor in notorious Fleet Prison. When he was released, he returned again to North America to take part in the American Revolutionary War. His administrative talents proved invaluable. He served as a secretary to Sir Henry Clinton, the commander of the British forces, and had a propitious encounter with John Graves Simcoe. As the war was ending, he went back to England with bleak career prospects. In 1791, mainly due to Simcoe's influence, he was appointed the first receiver and auditor general for Upper Canada, a post he reluctantly accepted.

Russell got along well with Simcoe and played a significant role devising the structure and institutions of Upper Canada's government. By the time Simcoe left York, Russell had been appointed administrator of the colony, the most senior bureaucratic position. He expected that he would eventually succeed Simoce as lieutenant governor. That did not transpire—the second lieutenant governor of Upper Canada was Peter Hunter, a career army officer and formerly the (temporary) superintendent of British Honduras—yet it was Russell, with input from Hunter, who was responsible for managing York's affairs in Simcoe's absence and giving the settlement a sense of order, society, and life as he narrowly defined it.

During Russell's tenure, York's first jail—nothing more than a log cabin—was built on the south side of King Street at the corner of Leader Lane, and land was set aside for a church, hospital, school, and market, each duly erected. The Cathedral Church of St. James, the city's most notable Anglican sanctuary, had its genesis at the corner of King and Church Streets as a modest wooden structure opened in 1807. A public market for farmers—which over the course of two centuries and many renovations morphed into the St. Lawrence Market—opened in 1803 on a plot of land bounded by Market, Jarvis, and King Street and Front Street East. Russell expanded the town's boundaries west to Peter Street and north to Lot Street. He also curbed land speculation. By 1808, when Russell died, York's population had risen to nearly five hundred people. This was partly through immigration from the United States, Britain, and Ireland and partly due to what Elizabeth Russell noted was the "prolific" nature of York's women, who married young and quickly thereafter had lots of children.

Accompanying this population increase was the gradual development of a middle class that provided York's residents with a wide range of required services—everything from bakers and blacksmiths to druggists and hairdressers. A few enterprising citizens like William Cooper, who arrived in the town in the early 1790s, seemed to have done it all. At different times he was a tavern keeper, schoolteacher, preacher, butcher, wharf operator, miller, and auctioneer.

There is no denying, however, that Peter Russell was a cautious plodder, who ensured that he and his friends and associates, members of York's rising frontier upper class, were adequately rewarded with government stipends, offices, and land. The members of the executive council, Russell among them, were rewarded with grants of six thousand acres as compensation for the move to York. Russell and his half-sister, Elizabeth, lived in one of the nicest houses in the town, located near King and Palace Streets. Designed by William Berczy in 1797 to replace a house on the same property that Russell had purchased the year before, but which had been destroyed in a fire, the "Russell Abbey" (as it came to be known some years later due to a loose connection with the popular romantic novel *The Children of the Abbey*) was, according to contemporary accounts, an "elegant and pretentious" Georgian-style frame house with large windows that looked out onto the bay. An ornamental fence surrounded it.

Russell was an early York booster. "You would be pleased to see this place now that it is really beautiful [and] makes a very different appearance from what it did when we were here about this time six years ago," he reported in September 1798 to William Osgoode, Upper Canada's first chief justice. "I have a very comfortable house near the Bay, from whence I see everything in the harbour and entering it."

Where Russell differed from Simcoe was in his support of slavery and his use of black slaves, a consequence of his experience on his Virginia plantation. At best, Russell and his sister barely tolerated their six slaves and one free black servant named Pompadore (who was married to Russell's slave Peggy) and generally regarded them as dishonest and "very indolent and dirty." The other major slaveholder in York was Russell's colleague William Jarvis, the provincial secretary, who owned six.

Russell was a fair, yet no-nonsense master. He hired a schoolmaster for one of the slave children in his care, provided Peggy with a small weekly allowance, and assisted her when she got in occasional trouble with legal authorities. At the same time, when Peggy and Pompadore's teenage son Jupiter violated one of Russell's rules, he was punished and "trussed up in a storehouse" on public display like a dead chicken. Such harsh discipline was commonplace in York and across British North America, where blacks, slave or free, received only marginally better treatment from their owners and the legal system than they did in the American south.

In a February 1806 ad in the *Upper Canada Gazette*—the colony's first newspaper, which moved its presses from Niagara to York in 1798—Russell advertised Peggy and Jupiter for sale as, respectively, "a tolerable Cook and washerwoman [who] perfectly understands making Soap and Candles" and "a house servant." The asking price for Peggy was $150 and for Jupiter $200, payable over a three-year term. One reason for the sale was that Elizabeth Russell could no longer stand to be around Peggy, who continued to leave without permission. Elizabeth had banned her from the house. It is not known whether anyone in Upper Canada purchased mother or son. Similar advertisements about slaves and servants were routine in the *Gazette*. "A Slave for Sale. To be sold—A healthy strong negro woman, about thirty years of age; understands cooking, laundry and taking care of poultry. N.B.—She can dress ladies' hair," said one. Or "Wanted to purchase, a negro girl from seven to twelve years of age, of good disposition."

A majority of York's most prominent citizens did not own slaves, but in the insular hierarchical society that evolved, they certainly lamented the lack of decent servants. "For God's sake," William Jarvis wrote to his father-in-law in England, who was about to visit him and his wife in Upper Canada, "try and bring out a servant or two with you, the whole country cannot produce one fit to put in 'Hell's Kitchen.'" John White, the first attorney general of the colony and a close confidant of Peter Russell, complained to a friend in late 1798 that the labour shortage had forced him to cut his own firewood and dig up his potatoes, however "incompatible with my station and education" those menial tasks were. Civic duty meant that if the good citizens of York were called upon, and they usually were, they were required to either spend so many days a year working on the town's roads or pay a labourer to do the chore for them.

RANK, PRIVILEGES, GOVERNMENT POSITIONS and patronage, fine homes, and good manners meant everything in early nineteenth-century York. These would-be aristocrats continued to powder their hair long after the practice had gone out of fashion in England. The men enjoyed fox and deer hunting and salmon fishing during the spawning season, when the salmon in the Humber were so abundant that you could catch them by hand. With their wives, they played whist, enjoyed sleigh rides in the winter, picnicked on the Island (a peninsula connected to the mainland until the 1850s), read novels aloud to each other, and attended music and theatre productions and extravagant dinner parties and balls. To mark the occasion of King George III's sixtieth birthday on June 4, 1798, Peter Russell hosted a celebration for fifty-two of the town's luminaries at the King Street Inn (and general store) operated by Abner Miles. The cost was £68, more than half of which was for wine, brandy, and port.

That was typical of York social gatherings for the rich or poor: drinking spirits at balls and local taverns was the favourite pastime. The soldiers at the garrison, who tended to keep to themselves, preferred the rum at Mrs. McLean's popular Crown and Anchor tavern, located off King Street close to St. James's Church. Public drunkenness, especially on Sundays, was so bad in the summer of 1802 that the magistrates in charge of law and order in York had to have their constables (the city's first woefully underpaid policemen) visit several "Keepers of Public Entertainment" to sternly warn them about the "indecency and impropriety of allowing people to drink intoxicating liquors and be guilty of disorderly behaviour during the hours of Divine Service, and generally on the Sabbath days." It was enough to make the Methodist minister Nathan Bangs claim that York's early settlers were "as thoughtless and wicked as the Canaanites of old."

He was not entirely wrong. York attracted its fair share of discharged soldiers and drifters "with no stake in the community and little pride in its development," as the town's expert historian Edith Firth pointed out. York's good name was at stake, so deviant acts were not tolerated and, as in medieval England, the punishment for murder, theft, vandalism, prostitution, vagrancy, and other wrongdoing was swift and harsh. In November 1798, for instance, Joseph McCarthy and William Hawkins were found guilty of "grand larceny"—they stole from Elisha Beaman, a tavern keeper, an iron tea kettle, an axe, a tea canister, a hat, a keg with a few pints of brandy left in it, and a few other items. For their crime, McCarthy was branded on his hand and Hawkins was whipped; both sentences were carried out at the York marketplace so all could witness it. The market's pillory awaited anyone found guilty of being a nuisance or, in the case of one woman in April 1804, for running what must have been one of York's first brothels—a "disorderly house for the reception of loose, vicious and lewd persons."

Hangings for more serious crimes were less frequent during York's first decades. The first man hanged was John Sullivan, an Irish tailor, who was found guilty of passing a forged note for three shillings and three pence (less than one dollar) at a tavern where he had been drinking heavily. For this grave offence, Chief Justice John Elmsley sentenced him to death, an indication of how significant the judges regarded York's economic well-being. At his public execution, the inexperienced hangman bungled his assignment and poor Sullivan slipped out of the noose. The second time the hangman got it right.

In contrast, four years earlier, Charles McCuen (or possibly McEwan), a Queen's Ranger stationed at the York garrison, killed the aboriginal chief Wabakinine by hitting him on the head with a rock during an altercation over McCuen's attempt to sexually assault Wabakinine's sister. Both men had been drinking. McCuen later claimed that he had paid the woman a dollar and some rum and was therefore entitled to do what he wished. McCuen was arrested and charged, but the case was dismissed due to insufficient evidence. And in truth, it's unlikely any York jury, tainted as they were by inherent white prejudice against aboriginals, would have convicted a soldier of murdering an Indian.

Russell and those who followed him were not magicians. None of their society-building achievements should hide the fact that York remained a frontier settlement, where stray pigs, horses, and chickens often roamed freely. Some contemporary observers were not convinced that York had much of a future; its many deficiencies far outweighed any of its positives. "York never was intended by nature for a metropolis; and that nothing but the caprice and obstinacy of General Simcoe raised it to that Dignity," the educator and clerical leader Rev. John Stuart pointed out in an 1801 letter to Bishop George Mountain in Montreal. "The Harbour is not commodious, as the wind that carries a vessel out of it, is a head wind when it enters the Lake. The Town is a Hot Bed, where every Thing is forced, unnaturally by English money. I know of no Trade now existing, or to be expected at any future Period, to support or enrich it. The Lands contiguous, to the Distance of some miles, are ingrossed by what we call *the Servants of Government*, so that a Pound of Butter must travel at least four or five miles before it reaches the market."

Getting in and out of York was indeed a tough chore. As late as 1807, Alexander Wood complained about the tremendous difficulties in using Yonge Street in the spring or after a bad rain in the summer. (A popular joke of the time told of a man strolling down King Street who saw a hat on a muddy road. When he picked it up, he found it on the head of its owner, who had sunk deep in the mud. "Help me," the man shouted, "and my horse is beside me.") A toll gate was put up near Yorkville and Yonge Streets in 1820, and a few more went up after that farther north. But the paltry collection did not cover the expense of altering the street's excessive mud with crushed stone, and the government eventually had to take charge of the pricey project. Mary (Gapper) O'Brien lived during the 1820s and 1830s on farms between Thornhill and Richmond Hill. She recalled that a usual trip to York, twenty-four kilometres away, took about two and a half hours if the roads were decent. In 1816, a stagecoach trip between York and Niagara, a distance of 134 kilometres, took about three days. Shipping goods across the lake on sailing vessels was easier, though until steamers were used, starting in 1817, water travel was slow.

Most buildings were constructed of wood, and fires were a constant problem. By 1800, York magistrates had ordered that every householder in town have two fire buckets (usually made of leather) handy, as well as a ladder that could reach the roof. It was, therefore, a big event in late 1802 when Lieutenant Governor Peter Hunter presented York with its first horse-drawn fire engine.

Sanitation was poor, even for the nineteenth century. Outbreaks of ague (or malaria) were frequent, and garbage was usually strewn here and there. In an 1802 ordinance, butchers were required to properly bury the remains of their slaughtered animals "so that it may cease to be (what it now is) a public nuisance." When it rained, the streets were "seas of mud," giving more impetus to the town's "muddy York" nickname. Worse, during the winter, dead animals piled up on the ice, and the residue from carcasses seeped into the water that was used for drinking. As late as the 1830s, Francis Collins, an Irish Catholic immigrant and the editor of the *Canadian Freeman*, pointed out that there was "not a drop of good well-water about the Market-square and the people are obliged to use the Bay water however rotten." Such a serious deficiency exacerbated the cholera epidemic of 1832, which took Collins's life.

As might be expected in such a small, social-climbing environment, gossip, no matter how trivial, was rampant. And in a town where duelling was still foolishly used by gentlemen to settle their differences, gossip could have dangerous and lasting consequences. Neither John White, the thirty-nine-year-old attorney general, nor John Small, the fifty-three-year-old clerk of the executive council, was especially happy on New Year's Eve in December 1799. White, one of the chief founders of the Law Society of Upper Canada two years earlier, had a prestigious government position, yet he was hopelessly in debt. His £300 annual salary, a not insignificant amount, plus other legal fees he received for private work (permitted in those days), was never enough. Consequently, he and his wife, Marianne, the parents of three children, lived beyond their means (as many of their neighbours did), and it strained their marriage. White had a mistress, Susanna Page, and they had two daughters. In 1799, he also likely had a brief affair with Elizabeth Small, the wife of John Small, which ended badly.

John Small had his own troubles. Though Simcoe had thought highly of him, his successor, Peter Hunter, was far less impressed with Small's lack of diligence and efficiency. Both Small and White were thus under pressure, aggravated, and looking for a fight.

At some point in late 1799 during a meeting of the legislative assembly, the spurned Mrs. Small was rude to Mrs. White, who informed her husband of this slight. Angered, John White denounced the Smalls, implied that their marriage was not legal, and, to add insult to injury, impugned Elizabeth's character in a letter to David Smith, the surveyor general. Smith, in turn, informed Chief Justice John Elmsley of the accusations. When word of this exchange became public and got back to Elizabeth Small, she demanded that her husband confront John White. Small did so and challenged White to a duel. They agreed to meet on a nearby field on January 3, 1800.

That evening, White wrote to Peter Russell, "Being obliged to meet Mr. Small tomorrow the Event of which no man can tell...let me implore your present protection to my family." He was right to be apprehensive. The next morning, each accompanied by a friend, the two men faced off and Small won the duel. He shot White through the ribs and he died in agony—"under the most excruciating torture," according to Russell. As in nearly all cases of duelling in York, Small was arrested and charged with murder, but acquitted by a jury whose members respected the code of honour.

The victory did little for the Smalls. Mrs. Small's reputation never recovered, and she was blamed for years for causing White's death. In 1808, merely the hint that Mrs. Small would be attending a gathering hosted by Lieutenant Governor Francis Gore and his wife, Annabella, was enough for hostile tongues to wag in York. Later, the Smalls' son,

John Edward, acted as second for his friend John Ridout in another of York's famous duels, which pitted the eighteen-year-old Ridout, son of Surveyor General Thomas Ridout, against twenty-four-year-old Samuel Jarvis, son of government official William Jarvis. The Ridout and Jarvis families had never liked each other, and in the summer of 1817 it boiled into a fight between John and Samuel that was settled on a field north of the town. Ridout shot first but missed; Jarvis did not and killed Ridout. Jarvis was charged with manslaughter and acquitted.

YORK PROSPERED IN ITS EARLIEST DAYS and continued moving forward mainly due to the confluence of personal ambition and a devoted sense of community among many of its leading officials, merchants, and professionals. Motivated as they were by self-interest and a traditional outlook tied strongly to the mother country, some of them did not easily, if at all, tolerate criticism or opposition to their rule—a reality that would in time provoke a violent challenge to their elite control. They and their sons would soon be castigated by the rabble-rousing journalist William Lyon Mackenzie, who labelled them the "Family Compact" for their cozy, conservative, and authoritarian version of nineteenth-century democracy. They were, however, never the homogeneous group that Mackenzie portrayed. Some were more open-minded, others less so. Whatever their particular business acumen, accomplishments, or politics, each in his own unique way contributed to Toronto's growth as a city. Among the who's who in the first few decades of the eighteenth century were William Allan, Quetton de St. George, and Dr. William Baldwin.

Allan ventured to Canada as a young man from Scotland, worked as a business clerk in Montreal, and then moved first to Newark and later to York. There he established himself as a highly successful agent and merchant before becoming the premier financier of his day and one of the key founders of the Bank of Upper Canada in 1821. Allan, who was identified as the "leading businessman of the Compact," was also active in local affairs as a justice of the peace, customs officer, postmaster, and judge. In his role as Major Allan, he led the 3rd York Militia during the War of 1812 and had some trying times dealing with the American enemy. His magnificent estate, Moss Park, which he built for his family in 1828 on the west side of Sherbourne Street between Queen and Shuter Streets, was testament to his wealth and influence (the current Moss Park neighbourhood took its name from the estate). By the time he died in 1853, Allan was one of Toronto's oldest residents, though the death of nine of his and his wife Leah's eleven children before the age of twenty (many from tuberculosis) cast a shadow over his life.

More colourful was Laurent Quetton de St. George (also known as Quetton de St. Georges), a French royalist, who escaped to England after a brief military career fighting revolutionaries. From there he wound up in Upper Canada in 1798 as part of a group of exiles led by Joseph-Geneviève, Comte de Puisaye, who had been awarded a large land grant far north up Yonge Street in Oak Ridges, north of Richmond Hill, about forty-five kilometres from York and difficult to reach. At the age of twenty-seven, St. George, who cut a dashing figure, had no desire to be a farmer for the rest of his life (nor did a majority of the forty other émigrés, who detested the winter cold and deserted the settlement only a year after they arrived). Instead, like Allan, he steadily built a career as a merchant, starting first in the fur trade before establishing from his base in York a network of general stores across the colony, with a diversified stock that served the community well. Here was Ontario's first chain store magnate. He also built the town's first brick house (and York's second brick building) in 1807, a two-storey Georgian-style mansion at the corner of King and Frederick Streets, which was both his residence and a storage facility.

St. George was undaunted when it came to protecting his commercial interests. In 1808, U.S. authorities, following the federal government's orders, refused to permit the transport of a substantial shipment of tea and other goods he had paid for. Undeterred, he and one of his clerks, with the assistance of a local smuggler, accosted a deputy sheriff in Lewiston, New York, who had seized the shipment, and brought the goods back across the Niagara River into Upper Canada.

Half of York likely owed St. George money at one time or another, and collection of these debts proved tricky. In the era before banks and uniform currency and rates were established in the 1840s, this was one drawback of a small economy based on a barter system and a hodgepodge of mainly British, American, and Nova Scotian coins and notes.

Despite his wealth and stature, St. George felt more comfortable with the soldiers of the garrison, with whom he did a profitable business, than he did with the members of York's genteel society. Moreover, his passable English-language skills marked him as a "foreigner" and therefore not quite acceptable to the latter group, who generally lived in fear of Americans and other "aliens." In the fall of 1807, his proposal to marry one of Judge William Powell's daughters was immediately rebuffed. Dr. William Baldwin (who had designed St. George's house) and his wife, Phoebe, on the other hand, found St. George charming and an amusing dinner guest. Later, after the War of 1812, during which St. George did a brisk business as an army supplier, he formed a partnership with William Baldwin's brother John and Jules-Maurice Quesnel, both of whom were already working for him. St. George returned to France in 1815, at the conclusion of the Napoleonic war and restoration of the Bourbons, and never returned, though his interests were protected and augmented by William and John Baldwin and Jules-Maurice Quesnel.

Few families played as significant a role in the history of Toronto and Ontario as the Baldwins. Dr. William Baldwin, of Irish Protestant descent, immigrated to York with his family in 1799, two years after he had completed his medical studies at the

University of Edinburgh. Baldwin, who spent his first few years in Upper Canada on a farm east of York, was miserable about his future prospects, writing to his brother in 1801 that he had been "banished from all that is engaging in life, flattering to our hopes, or grateful to our industry." Not one to surrender, he made the best of the situation and quickly relocated to the capital, where he was one of only two doctors in the town.

Using his natural intelligence and creative talents, Baldwin was York's Renaissance man. He became a lawyer in 1802 and thereafter a judge, an architect (and designer of many of York's early buildings), the founder of a private classical school for young gentlemen, and an articulate politician who, with his more famous son Robert, pushed for liberal constitutional reform. Thanks in part to his wife Phoebe's inheritance of the Russell properties (she was a cousin to Peter and Elizabeth Russell), Baldwin was a wealthy landowner. His most lasting contribution to Toronto's street names was the £1,500 estate, complete with stables and a garden, he designed and built near the Casa Loma site in 1818 on his two-hundred-acre property, which he christened "Spadina"—always pronounced "Spa-deena," unlike the current "Spa-dina"—for the aboriginal term *espadinong* or "hill."

Baldwin would have probably considered himself an honourable gentleman (impolite table manners annoyed him) and above the pettiness and backbiting of York society. On one occasion he challenged another lawyer, who had insulted his reputation, to a duel, which ended without incident when his opponent did not raise his pistol. Like many others he was the beneficiary of lucrative government patronage and maintained a slightly arrogant tone about his own abilities. He was, however, true to his political principles and supported such outspoken critics of government privileges and alleged mismanagement as Judge Robert Thorpe, an early advocate of responsible government, who was suspended from the bench in 1807 for being an agitator and all-around troublemaker.

Baldwin was no republican; his push for constitutional reform and his opposition to the Family Compact in no way detracted from his ardent faith in hierarchy and aristocratic leadership. He merely saw the world through a more nineteenth-century and decidedly narrow liberal lens, which advocated civil liberties for most people along with "limited government." Later in his life, he was elected to the Upper Canada assembly and unconditionally backed his son Robert in his quest for moderate and peaceful constitutional change.

OPPOSING MODERATES like Baldwin and, later, radicals like William Lyon Mackenzie was the indomitable Reverend John Strachan, "a stocky figure... with a straight nose, a firm cleft chin, and drooping eyes," as one chronicler described him. At the behest of Major-General Isaac Brock, commander of the garrison and the recently appointed administrator of Upper Canada, Strachan came to York with his family to take up his new position as rector of the Anglican community, as well as the chaplaincy of the garrison and of the legislative council. He arrived in June 1812, at a defining moment in North American history. On June 18, 1812, mainly in response to objectionable British trade and military policies, the United States declared war on Great Britain and, therefore, Upper Canada.

The Americans might have thought that the colony and its many former Yankee residents would welcome their invasion force, but Strachan quickly quashed such treasonous ideas with a memorable sermon he delivered before the legislative council and assembly. He condemned the United States as a "formidable tyrant" and assured his fellow Upper Canadians that they would be victorious. "You will be obliged to endure many hardships and to submit to many severe restraints," he preached. "You must therefore... acquire that fortitude which we have mentioned as one of the graces of the Christian Soldier, it will enable you not only to endure the many privations of a military life, but to perform your duties with alacrity, and to be strictly obedient to your superior officers." His words stirred the town to action.

Ironically for someone who has been remembered as one of the most influential figures in Toronto's history, Strachan initially arrived with low expectations of York, its people, and their "petty politics." He figured that the only thing that would save the Upper Canadian assembly—composed as it was of "ignorant clowns," as he dismissively described the members following the 1808 election—was that, soon enough, his own students would be running the government and the colony. And, indeed, many of the leaders of the Family Compact, most notably its recognized head, Attorney General John Beverley Robinson, were mentored by Strachan.

Education was a key avenue by which Strachan had chosen to make his mark on the world. Yet there was nothing remarkable in his background that could have predicted his ascent in Canada as the personage who most embodied Tory British Anglican power and privilege. The youngest of six children, he had been brought up a Presbyterian in Aberdeen, Scotland, in a middle-class family and had attended King's College there. His father was an overseer in a granite quarry. Seeking new beginnings, John Strachan came to Kingston in 1799, at the age of twenty-one, to tutor Richard Cartwright's children.

His situation soon improved. By 1803 he had become a Church of England clergyman—to his mind, the theological distinctions between Presbyterianism and Anglicanism were minimal—and was posted to a mission church at Cornwall. There he opened a boys' school that soon attracted the sons of the Upper Canadian elite. He was a strict but benevolent headmaster who by the sheer force of his personality commanded the utmost respect from his young charges. That explains the devotion many of them felt towards him for the rest of his life. He imbued each of them with a reverence for British institutions, narrowly defined along eighteenth-century lines in which King, God, Empire, and a government led by aristocrats ruled over society with a paternalistic hand. In politics and education, there was no separation of church and state in Strachan's rigidly held views. He was as arrogant as his enemies later alleged, though even they could not question the strength of his convictions.

Strachan further cemented his position in 1807 by marrying a beautiful and wealthy widow, Ann McGill, whose first husband, Andrew McGill, a member of the Montreal-based merchant family, had left her an annual annuity of £300. This allowed Strachan, who was never well paid as either a teacher or clergyman, to live in a style that suited his upper-class tastes. The brick mansion on Front Street, called "The Palace," that he built in 1818 for his growing family was merely one sign of his affluence. He was already a member of the executive council, a position of power he held for two decades during some of the stormiest years in Upper Canada's history. As archdeacon of York in 1827, and then following his elevation to Bishop of Toronto in 1839, he continued to wield influence over religion and education—including fighting for the establishment of King's College (the beginnings of the University of Toronto) as an Anglican institution of higher learning.

It was impossible to be neutral about Strachan; either you supported him or you did not. Even his many opponents, however, could not argue with the leadership he showed in dealing with the American enemy during the War of 1812.

The war that the Americans had declared against the British ten months earlier had dragged on longer than President James Madison anticipated. Moreover, the generally unpopular conflict had not been going the Americans' way, as the British and Canadian militias and their aboriginal allies had won several decisive battles. At the Battle of Queenston Heights, near Niagara Falls, in October 1812, for example, British regulars and Loyalist militia led by Major-General Isaac Brock had defeated U.S. troops, though Brock himself was killed in the fighting.

Madison and his officials felt the need to do something to boost morale. The garrison at Kingston would have been the logical place to attack, but General Henry Dearborn was apprehensive about taking on the British regulars stationed there. York was less protected. And as the capital of Upper Canada, it was a significant target.

Before his untimely death, General Brock had begun a much-needed renovation and fortification of the garrison. When war broke out, however, there was still much more work to do. The town's small militia of 120 men under the command of merchant Major William Allan, with assistance from government bureaucrat Captain William Chewett, were fairly defenceless against any large-scale attack. As head of the Loyal and Patriotic Society of Upper Canada, Reverend Strachan did his part raising money and providing relief to wounded soldiers brought in from other battlefields. More importantly, his tireless efforts gave the community a sense of hope.

On the morning of April 27, 1813, fourteen American ships with an estimated 1,700 (and possibly as many as 1,800) troops and about 800 sailors and marines on board appeared in York harbour. On landing, they were confronted by 300 British regulars, who were on a layover in the town under the command of Major-General Sir Roger Sheafe, about the same number of local militia, and approximately fifty aboriginals led by Major John Givins. It was not much of a contest, made worse by the confusion in the militia ranks. When the Americans entered the grounds of the garrison, the fort's powder magazine was blown up (probably accidentally), and the debris of rocks killed many of them, including the U.S. commander, General Zebulon Pike. It was a bloody mess, and Dr. William Beaumont, the U.S. military surgeon, recalled that he spent the next forty-eight hours "cutting and slashing" arms and legs from maimed American soldiers.

After more than half of York's defenders were either killed or wounded in a six-hour battle, Sheafe retreated to Kingston, leaving Allan and Chewett to negotiate the terms of surrender. Strachan, who had been away from York when the occupation took place, returned in time to help reach a fair agreement with the Americans he so disdained. Most importantly, civilians were to be protected and looting was forbidden—at least, that is what the American commanders consented to. They even posted sentries during the night to protect private property.

Nevertheless, during the four days of the occupation the residents of York were subjected to looting and plundering from both unrestrained American soldiers and unsavoury characters in the community, who sought to take advantage of the wartime situation to enhance their own pockets. Isaac Wilson, who had been stationed at the garrison, wrote a few months later to his brother that the "Americans had been praised for their good conduct." On the other hand, Penelope Beikie, the wife of John Beikie, the sheriff of York, claimed that "every house [the Americans] found deserted was completely sacked." According to Mrs. Beikie, when undisciplined U.S. soldiers tried to invade her house, she bravely stood her ground and refused to permit them to enter. Other residents, either to prevent the escalation of real trouble, or possibly out of sympathy to the American cause, let them have what they wanted. "Those who abandoned their houses," Sheriff Beikie later reported, "found nothing but the bare walls at their return."

The worst event of the occupation occurred on the second day, when someone—perhaps "freelancing sailors," as historian Alan Taylor suggests, though no one has ever discovered the culprits' identities—set fire to the government buildings on Front Street. The Americans dubiously claimed that the perpetrators had discovered a scalp "suspended near the speaker's chair," which set them off. Whatever the reason, the destruction of the Parliament Buildings was used a year later as an excuse by the British when they burned the White House and other government buildings in Washington D.C.

Before the burning in York, the Americans had taken the parliamentary mace, which had been first used in Newark in 1792 before it was brought to York. (The invaders kept the mace for the next 121 years, displaying it at the United States Naval Academy at Annapolis, Maryland. Then in 1934, in a gesture of good will, President Franklin Roosevelt returned it to Toronto, which was marking the centennial of its incorporation as a city.) Other property was also destroyed, and some books were seized from the small York public library. Still, compared to other atrocities of the war, such as the River Raisin Massacre a few months earlier at Frenchtown in the Michigan territory, or later ones committed during the U.S. Civil War, the occupation of York was pretty tame. No one was murdered and women were not raped.

Nearly three months later, on the last day of July, the Americans briefly returned to York for another round of looting. This time, there is more evidence that they were abetted by "renegade" Canadians, who provided them with information on where government stores had been hidden. As Jacob Clock, an elderly purported Loyalist from New York, who had settled in the area in 1805, put it, "The King had no right to anything in this country... the Americans owned everything here." When challenged, he added, according to one testimony, that the Americans "were not his enemies but his friends, that they supported him and he would support them." Though there was much anger directed towards Clock and other allegedly false Loyalists for their treasonous actions, most escaped retribution, jail, and the hangman's rope. Strachan again negotiated with the Americans for a peaceful resolution and even got them to return the books that had been taken from the library. No one in York ever forgot Strachan's commendable conduct and efforts on the behalf of the community.

As the war slowly moved to its inevitable stalemate conclusion in early 1815, Fort York (or, more accurately, the garrison at York) finally was completed, even though there was talk again of moving the capital to a better-defended locale. Not everything about the war was bad; merchants like Allan, Wood, and St. George had prospered supplying goods to the British. As John Beverley Robinson, who had served admirably under Brock at Queenston Heights and whose political career was about to take off, conceded some years later, apart from the "individual suffering and affliction" caused by the war, it also "introduced capital and gave spur to enterprise."

Nonetheless, a decided anti-Americanism gripped the 720 people now living in York as it did the rest of Upper Canada, a collective mindset that was to shape the political battles, economic progress, and social and cultural scene in the tumultuous decade ahead. But this much was clear: there was no going back, and the separation from the Americans was permanent.

Chapter Three

THE REBELLION

Toronto is like a fourth or fifth rate provincial town, with the pretensions of a capital city. We have here a petty oligarchy, a self-constituted aristocracy, based upon nothing real, nor even upon anything imaginary.

—ANNA B. JAMESON, 1838

Led by journalist and rabble-rouser William Lyon Mackenzie, a group of rebels march down Yonge Street in December 1837 with the objective of taking over the government. Three years earlier, Mackenzie had been the first mayor of Toronto in 1834, the year the city was incorporated. *Library and Archives Canada, Acc. No. 1972-26-706*

IN THE AFTERMATH of the War of 1812 and the conquest of York, there were rumblings that the seat of government in Upper Canada would be more secure in Kingston or another locale. At first, Lord Bathurst, the secretary of state for war and the colonies, was inclined to agree with the critics, but ultimately he decided to maintain the status quo. Bathurst did not spend a great deal of time contemplating this decision, yet it had lasting ramifications for Toronto's future development.

In the short term, as the provincial capital, York remained the focus for political life in Upper Canada, with all of the attendant pomp, patronage, and pettiness. In the view of Joseph Gould, an impressionable twenty-one-year-old farmer who visited in 1830 (and was soon avidly fighting for his democratic rights), "The people of York were all politicians... and excitement ran so high that quarrels between neighbours were of frequent occurrence." Nevertheless, this prominence enabled the town, during the 1820s and 1830s, to solidify its role as hub of commerce, education, religion, and culture. York was indeed, as the *Patriot*, a pro-British and conservative newspaper, put it in December 1832, "the centre of both news and money."

The Bank of Upper Canada, which, it will be recalled, was established through the efforts of William Allan and others, set business and credit on a firmer footing. Schools were established, as well as a general hospital—on the corner of King and John Streets—under the supervision of Dr. Christopher Widmer, its well-connected senior medical officer, who was also a director of the Bank of Upper Canada for more than two decades. (The influential and fashionable doctor, who was married twice, was said to be "an amazing favourite with the ladies." His first wife, the wealthy Emily Bignell, who died in 1833, was deeply offended by his extramarital activities; he had a stronger marriage with his second wife, the much prettier, though lower class, Hannah.) St. James Church (St. James Cathedral as of 1839), severely damaged in the war, was rebuilt over the next decade and a half at a cost of £10,000, mainly paid for by a government grant and the sale of pews.

Osgoode Hall opened in 1831 to train lawyers. And a year later Dr. John Rolph, who was involved in the rowdy political machinations of the day, started Ontario's first medical school. At the behest of Sir John Colborne, the lieutenant governor from 1828 to 1836, Upper Canada College (UCC) was established in 1829 to train the province's future leaders; in its first year of operation, eighty-nine boys attended, most of them from York's finer families. The school was initially located near Jarvis and Lombard Streets. It then moved to a more palatial building at Russell Square (King and Simcoe Streets) before relocating north of St. Clair Avenue to its current spot on Avenue Road in 1891. Although UCC had several serious financial problems over the years, it remained the school of choice for Toronto's elite, and the list of its alumni—everyone from Joseph Tyrell, who graduated in 1878 and discovered dinosaur bones in Alberta, to Timothy Eaton, class of 1852, who founded Eaton's department stores—reads like a Canadian who's who of the rich, powerful, and influential.

Most notably of all, the Parliament Buildings that the Americans had callously burned were rebuilt by 1820, only to be destroyed again by a fire in late December 1824. For the next six years the legislative assembly met where it could—at Jordan's Hotel, the General Hospital, the courthouse—until a more fitting headquarters was erected at Simcoe Square on Front Street between Simcoe and John Streets (close to where the Metro Convention Centre now stands).

By the early 1820s, the town was a bit more spread out. Most of its 1,100 citizens still lived in the Old Town, south of Queen Street between Jarvis and Parliament Streets. Yet enough residents were living in what was called the "New Town"—which extended west from Jarvis to Peter Street—that rival young toughs, the "Old Town Boys" versus the "New Town Boys," faced off against each other with stones and fists. The battle line was around George Street.

Getting to and from York required military precision, logistics, and planning. In 1829, George Playter began operating a horse-drawn stagecoach service between York and Holland's Landing up Yonge Street, approximately sixty-one kilometres away. Today that would be an hour's drive, but then it was a bumpy eight-hour adventure over muddy hills that cost six shillings and three pence. Frequently, passengers had to disembark and help push the coach and horses up steep slopes. The first stop after York was Daniel Tiers's Red Lion Inn, north of Bloor and Yonge (close to where Britnell's Book Store was once located), which boasted the "best strong beer" in the province. The drivers often had private side deals with tavern owners to stop their stagecoaches so that their passengers could quench their thirst. The drivers drank for free and then continued with the trip.

Besides drinking, the citizens of York enjoyed visits from travelling American theatre companies, lectures, and exhibitions of every type and variety—such as one in the summer of 1826 that featured a wax figure of "Duncan Bradley, the Yorkshire giant," or another in September 1831 which presented a "Grand Panoramic View of Bytown." There was also the fattest heifer in Upper Canada, showcased in June 1833, and for the sports enthusiasts, horse races. The Masons met regularly at a hall on Market Lane, while the union-minded members of the Typographical Society debated trade issues over dinner.

Those who had the money, like William Allan and John Beverley Robinson and other members of the so-called Family Compact, lived near the waterfront, today's Esplanade. Or they resided beyond the town's limits on a country estate. Lawyer D'Arcy Boulton, John Beverley Robinson's brother-in-law, had built an elegant Georgian-style brick house on a large lot west of University Avenue and Dundas Street. Completed in 1817 for £300, "The Grange" (as it was called, named after a family estate in England) became the "centre of social and political life in York" for years to come. Similarly, Captain George Taylor Denison, who served during the war and was to become one of Upper Canada's wealthiest property magnates, lived with his wife Esther (the daughter of a rich Loyalist) at "Bellevue," another Georgian-style mansion located on a large estate comprising much of what is now Kensington Market, with its hub around today's Denison Avenue.

Slightly farther away was "Rosedale," built by lawyer John Edward Small in 1821 and sold within three years to William Botsford Jarvis, who was appointed Sheriff of York in 1827 (the two men later ran against each other in the provincial election of 1834, with Small eking out a victory). It was actually Jarvis's wife, Mary, who famously called the property Rosedale due to the abundance of wild roses near the house. That name was later used for the entire ritzy neighbourhood east of Yonge Street and south of St. Clair Avenue. Besides his official duties, Sheriff Jarvis bought and sold land, and with brewer Joseph Bloor (whom Bloor Street is named after) was instrumental in establishing the village of Yorkville in 1830. Jarvis was a tough diehard Tory, who did what was necessary to stop radicals from seizing the province in 1837. But he was not without a heart; during the cholera epidemic of 1834, he released all of the imprisoned debtors from the congested jail, definitely improving their chances of survival.

Opinions about York naturally varied. "The Town of York is not like any other I have ever seen and [is] still less like any with which you are familiar—it seems all suburb," Mary O'Brien noted in February 1829. "The streets are laid out wide and parallel at right angles with each other... the shops are numerous but [do] not make much show." Some months later, on another visit, she found "the streets swarming with people and abounding in carriages. I have never before seen it so busy and gay."

More upbeat was writer George Henry, author of *The Emigrant Guide, or Canada As It Is*. In the 1835 edition of the book, he praised York and its "neat pretty villas, built on handsome construction." He also was impressed by the newly built bridge over the Don, "the numerous substantial brick dwelling houses," and the "really elegant" stores and shops along King Street.

More than a decade earlier, Frances Stewart, an Irish immigrant and pioneer in the Kawartha Lakes area (northeast of the city), was far less captivated by the town. "York looked pretty from the lake as we sailed up in a schooner [from Kingston]," she wrote in 1822 on her inaugural visit, "but on landing we found it not a pleasant place, as it is sunk down in a little amphitheatre cut out of the great bleak forest... It is not a healthy town (fever and ague are common) and it is said to be much fallen off with the last two years; a deadness hangs over everything."

Mrs. Stewart was not all that wrong. Beyond the pretty villas and well-kept gardens, the town exuded a harshness especially experienced by those who were not well off. There were no handouts for the poor and little tolerance for deviance or immorality. In 1818, a young unmarried servant girl who had hid her pregnancy from her employers, Chief Justice William Powell and his wife, Anne (as well as from the family physician, who did not detect the woman's condition until a day before she went into labour), received little compassion for her newborn or her predicament. Though punishment for crime in Britain was gradually becoming more humane in the early nineteenth century, this was not the case in York and Upper Canada. Public lashings and the death penalty were still meted out for petty theft, larceny, and arson, among other transgressions. In November 1827, William Jones was found guilty of killing cattle that he did not own and was hanged.

WHAT TRULY TRANSFORMED and shook York in the 1820s was the arrival of thousands of immigrants from England, Scotland, Ireland, and Wales. It was not the last time newcomers altered Toronto's character, gradually adding to its diversity. In the early nineteenth century, this multitude comprised the dispossessed and dislocated of the Great Migration, whose lives had been affected, mostly for the worse, by the onset of industrialization, the growth of factories, and changes in agricultural practices and land distribution. Unemployment was high and wages dropped. In 1803, for instance, a Scottish hand-loom weaver was paid twenty-five shillings a week, more than enough to comfortably get by. Fifteen years later, the same weaver received only five shillings a week, a "starvation rate." Poverty, slums, crime, and prostitution became the hallmark of such cities as London, where pickpockets ruled the streets during the day, and "unruly ruffians" were in control at night.

One way to escape this misery, if you could afford it or had government assistance, was emigration to North America, where available land awaited anyone who was prepared to work hard. The six-week, or longer, ocean crossing was a dreadful experience on overcrowded ships rife with rats, disease, and unsanitary conditions. A well-known joke at the time was that you could always tell an emigrant ship by its (putrid) smell. However, if you survived the ordeal, a new life awaited you. "I really do bless God every day I rise, that He was ever pleased, in the course of His providence, to send me and my family to this place," one former weaver turned Canadian farmer put it.

The population of York jumped from 1,240 in 1820 to 9,252 by 1834. True, the majority of immigrants were British, which made York (soon to be renamed Toronto) decidedly British for the foreseeable future. Yet there were Presbyterian Scots, Irish Roman Catholics, and Protestant Orangemen, who all brought their distinctive religious, cultural, and political baggage with them to have an impact on their new homeland. They were proud, principled, passionate, and somewhat tainted by the economic and social turmoil that had engulfed their lives. Moreover, they were not afraid to challenge the cozy status quo of the York elite.

Quite soon, for example, and certainly after the arrival in Upper Canada in 1829 of Ogle Robert Gowan, the chief founder of the Grand Orange Lodge of British North America, the celebration of the Glorious Twelfth—to mark the victory of William of Orange and his Protestant supporters over the Catholic King James II at the Battle of the Boyne in July 1690—became a regular event in Toronto. Then and later the Orangemen were not shy about publicly showing their support for the British Empire or their enmity towards Catholics. Orange lodge members dominated Toronto civic politics for decades. At the same time, not all immigrants were financially well off, and before too long York's first slums became part of its permanent (and enduring) landscape—"in little old log houses in its heart and in squatters' huts on the Don."

IF ANY ONE IMMIGRANT of the Great Migration era left an indelible mark on the history of Toronto and Canada it was, for good or bad, William Lyon Mackenzie. Short and stocky, Mackenzie, soon to be renowned for his fiery personality, arrived in Upper Canada in 1820 at the age of twenty-five, ready to make something of himself. As a teenager, he had contracted a bad fever and as a result had lost his hair. Thereafter, to hide his baldness he wore a loose-fitting red wig, which, as one of his many biographers wrote, "in a moment of jubilation he used to toss at a friend or hurl to the floor."

Mackenzie had grown up in Dundee, Scotland, north of Edinburgh. He had had a rough childhood; his father, Daniel, died when Mackenzie was only an infant, and he and his mother, Elizabeth, struggled financially. The lack of money was a burden Mackenzie was to endure for the rest of his life. He had no desire to work as a labourer, and as a young man demonstrated a natural affinity for education, writing, and books. Following a few unsuccessful attempts to find a vocation—as well as fathering an illegitimate son, James—Mackenzie, accompanied by his friend John Leslie, set out for the New World.

Once in York he found work with a book and drug company and began writing for a newspaper, the *Observer*, in which he immediately displayed his budding journalistic talents and his sharp wit. Newspapers, filled with accounts of events in the old country, commercial transactions, community comings and goings, and, above all, local politics, slanted and as nasty as the mood of the publisher or editor, were truly a lifeline to the rest of the world. Upper Canadians were loyal subscribers, though papers appeared and disappeared with bewildering frequency. Mackenzie was to experience this downside of the print business as well.

Within two years his mother joined him, along with the wife she had selected for him, Isabel Baxter. Mackenzie obeyed his mother's wishes. He and Isabel were married in 1822, and slightly more than nine months later she gave birth to their first child. Their fourteenth and youngest, a daughter, Isabel Grace, was born in 1843 while the family was in exile in New York, some years after Mackenzie's abortive attempt to lead an uprising against the Upper Canadian government. Isabel Grace was the mother of Mackenzie's namesake, William Lyon Mackenzie King, the long-serving Liberal prime minister. The legacy of his grandfather, as he uniquely interpreted it, loomed large in King's life.

For a brief time, Mackenzie became a partner in a store in nearby Dundas before moving to Queenston to try another business venture. He found his niche when he started the weekly *Colonial Advocate* in May 1824, the mouthpiece that was to propel him to fame... or infamy, depending on your perspective. By November, he and his family had moved back to York, where, using his newspaper, he embarked on the great crusade of his life as a champion of the people. As he later recalled this pivotal moment, "I had long seen the country in the hands of a few shrewd, crafty covetous men under whose management one of the most lovely and desirable sections of America remained a comparative desert."

With the exception, perhaps, of Louis Riel, William Lyon Mackenzie might well be the most polarizing and misunderstood figure in Canadian history. He was a loner who detested party politics, was passionate about his convictions, and consequently often acted impulsively, as he did in 1837. Idealistic and slightly naïve, he believed that it was possible to have a government that did not show "favouritism and prodigality." Still, there was much to admire about him. Progressive for his day, he supported the vote for women and wrote with heart about the brutality of slavery, which he vehemently opposed. He was equally suspicious of banks and the seemingly limitless power of the Anglican Church in Upper Canada, with its tight grip on the lands of the clergy reserves—tracts of land designated in the Constitutional Act for the "Protestant clergy."

Because his cause was considered just, he was frequently remembered later as a hero of democracy, whose radicalism made possible the achievement of responsible government. (In a May 1912 speech at the United Empire Club of Toronto, the colourful military historian and Toronto police magistrate George T. Denison III denounced Mackenzie as "a cantankerous and quarrelsome little cad." A week later, the *Toronto Daily Star* rebuked him, reminding Denison that Mackenzie took on "the enemies of freedom.") That was certainly the view of his first biographer (and son-in-law), Charles Lindsey, who asserted in his 1862 treatise on Mackenzie's life that "much of the liberty Canada has enjoyed since 1840 and more of the wonderful progress she has made, are due to the changes which the [1837] insurrection was the chief agent in producing." Not only does this interpretation discount the development of British economic and political policies that truly enabled the evolution of Canadian constitutional history and democracy; it also suggests Mackenzie was an Upper Canadian version of George Washington or Samuel Adams, which he most certainly was not. As historians Frederick Armstrong and Ronald J. Stagg put it, "As a legend, Mackenzie has a role and importance that Mackenzie the man could never achieve."

From the first edition of the *Colonial Advocate* in 1824, Mackenzie moved steadily from newspaper critic to politician to agitator to radical, who in the end was prepared to use violence to effect change. By the mid-1830s, inspired by a similar constitutional conflict being waged in Lower Canada by Louis-Joseph Papineau (which also led to a violent confrontation), Mackenzie was increasingly frustrated and unable to tolerate what he perceived as nasty conservative forces working against him and the "people." And he was not all wrong: many of his grievances against the powers that be, the group he bitterly lambasted as the "Family Compact," were indeed legitimate.

The first time influential power broker John Beverley Robinson—who served as the attorney general of Upper Canada before becoming chief justice in 1829, and who was also the Compact's chief spokesman—took note of Mackenzie's writing, he castigated him as "a conceited red-haired fellow with an apron." His opinion only got worse after that.

Robinson and his many associates and friends, some related through marriage—G. D'Arcy Boulton, James Macaulay, William Allan, Christopher Hagerman, and

Rev. John Strachan, among others—dominated the all-controlling appointed positions on the Upper Canadian executive and legislative councils and had the ear of the three governors who served during the 1820s and 1830s. Though different in skill, character, and style, this trio, Sir Peregrine Maitland (1818–1828), Sir John Colborne (1829–1836), and Sir Francis Bond Head (1836–1838), generally sided with the Tory forces in York and Upper Canada and rejected any political reforms that hinted at American-style democracy.

The lieutenant governors, especially Bond Head, who arrived with the least political experience as the situation was escalating, held the members of the Family Compact in high esteem for their wealth, industry, and seemingly sage advice. Mackenzie, on the other hand, was scathing in his criticism. By 1833 he had concluded, "It is not... to be denied that the government of Upper Canada is a despotism; a government legally existing independent of the will of the governed." This "family connexion [*sic*]," as he labelled the perpetrators, secretly controlled and used public money for its own nefarious purposes. The Compact ruled Upper Canada, he added, "according to its own good pleasure, and [there was] no efficient check from this country to guard the people against its acts of tyranny and oppression."

The various enterprises, building projects, and institutions that Mackenzie found so distasteful and bordering on corrupt—the Bank of Upper Canada, Welland Canal, and land development schemes, to list just three—the members of the Compact regarded as absolutely essential for the future well-being of the province. As the leading citizens of York, these entrepreneurs, lawyers, and officials built up the town's schools, roads, and hospitals and supported its burgeoning social life, but always on their own terms and in the manner of the frontier aristocracy they were. The Compact was probably not as unified a group as Mackenzie and others charged. But anyone within its orbit likely saw nothing wrong with dominating the government and controlling patronage and the appointment of key judges and other functionaries. Like their godfather, John Strachan, the members of the Compact believed in the God-given right of the local elite to rule for the betterment of all. Theirs was a noble calling: to protect the interests of the British Empire and the Anglican Church against encroaching Americanism, both political and religious. Methodism, which was spreading in Upper Canada, for example, was treated as an American import and considered dangerous.

However, the Compact leaders, "petty, ruthless and selfish" (as historian Gerald Craig depicts them), made mistakes. They tried to restrict the political and land rights of long-time residents who had migrated from the United States. They sought to control King's College and education in Upper Canada in a manner that fit Anglican precepts. And they monopolized the clergy reserves, angering Presbyterians and Methodists with their arrogance. Worst of all, they failed to see that their blatant manipulation of patronage and power was bound to generate a determined reform movement that took up the cry of responsible government. The Tories rebuked anyone who challenged them as "radicals," making little distinction between Mackenzie, a vocal and discontented reformer adopting a radical position, and true moderate reformers like Dr. William Baldwin and his son Robert, a lawyer, who was first elected to the legislative assembly in 1828, when he was twenty-four years old. (The Reform movement of the 1820s and 1830s, as it is often referred to, was not an organized political party; its leaders, including Mackenzie and the Baldwins, often diverged dramatically in their views, but all called themselves "Reformers" in opposition to the Tories.)

Principled and sensitive, Robert Baldwin became the celebrated champion of responsible government and a much more significant opponent to the Family Compact than William Lyon Mackenzie ever was. His great love was his younger first cousin Augusta Elizabeth "Eliza" Sullivan, whom he married in 1827, despite the family's attempts to keep them apart. Eliza suffered ill health for much of their marriage, and her situation became worse after she gave birth by Caesarean to a son, Robert Jr., in 1834. She died less than two years later from an infection, leaving Baldwin a broken man. "I am left to pursue the remainder of my pilgrimage alone," he declared, "and in the waste that lies before me I can expect to find joy only in the reflected happiness of our darling children, and in looking forward, in humble hope, to that blessed hour which by God's permission shall forever reunite me to my Eliza." A month after Baldwin died in December 1858, a physician, acting on instructions Baldwin had left, made an incision in Baldwin's torso to match the one Eliza received when she gave birth to their son.

As happens today, the louder and more strident voice is often the one that receives the greatest attention. In this regard it was no contest between Robert Baldwin and Mackenzie. And the campaign for responsible government was never as black and white an issue as we like to think it was. During the late 1820s and early 1830s, support, and election victories in York ridings and elsewhere, seesawed between the Tories and Reformers on several occasions.

THE ROAD TO THE UPPER CANADA REBELLION of 1837 might be said to have started on the evening of June 8, 1826. At the time, Mackenzie was struggling financially to make a go of the *Colonial Advocate*, and his departure from York and journalism was imminent. The members of the Compact were elated. "The Game is up—The Patriot McKenzie has 'fled his country, for his Country's good'—in other and more homely words he has 'cleared out,' in debt and in disgrace," journalist Robert Stanton happily reported to John Macaulay during the first week of June. Then fate intervened.

The Compact's younger generation had had enough of Mackenzie. His insulting references to John Beverley Robinson and Rev. John Strachan—in an article of May 18,

1826, Mackenzie had referred to Strachan as "a diminutive, paltry, insignificant Scotch turn coat parish schoolmaster"—had struck a raw nerve, and the young men decided to take matters into their own hands. Led by the hot-headed thirty-four-year-old lawyer Samuel Jarvis, about fifteen Tories—the group also included nineteen-year-old Henry Sherwood, a future mayor of Toronto from 1842 to 1844—broke into Mackenzie's office around seven o'clock in the evening, when it was still light outside, and destroyed his printing equipment by throwing his type into the bay. Everyone knew who had committed the offence, and, in fact, William Allan and Stephen Heward, John Beverley Robinson's brother-in-law (Heward's son Charles participated in the vandalism, as possibly did his son Henry), had witnessed the incident and done nothing to stop it. Mackenzie sued eight of the men in court, and the jury awarded him damages of £625, enough to settle with his creditors and put him back in business. The attack elevated his status as a "martyr for Upper Canadian liberty," and he enjoyed pointing out how the Family Compact had saved his livelihood.

Mackenzie's political career began with his election to the legislative assembly in the 1828 election as a representative of York County, an area north of Queen Street. Thereafter, he was on the more radical side of the Reform movement, frequently attacking the Tories in language so virulent that he was expelled on four separate occasions, only to return in another election to continue his fight. Few politicians could rouse and anger a crowd like Mackenzie. He was assaulted by hooligans in Hamilton and had garbage thrown at him at a public meeting in York. His supporters, conversely, feted him at the Red Lion Inn.

The political turmoil was temporarily halted by the outbreak of a cholera epidemic in York in April 1832. The disease, which had spread from India to Europe after 1817, was brought to Upper and Lower Canada by immigrants on a ship from Limerick, Ireland. Twenty of the 178 passengers had perished at sea. Many of the newcomers, as well as hundreds more who contracted the disease, made their way to York during a year in which Upper Canada welcomed approximately 41,500 immigrants, the greatest number to date.

As more and more cases broke out, Lieutenant Governor Colborne's first instinct was to declare May 16 a day of "Public Fasting, Humiliation and Prayer... for beseeching God to turn from our people that great calamity with which parts of our Dominion are at this time afflicted." Mackenzie, too, was at his poetic best when he informed the readers of the *Colonial Advocate* a month later that York had been afflicted with "the pestilence which has continued to ravage with unexampled fierceness in almost every land from India to the British Isles and has spread under every climate from the burning sands of Arabia to the snows of Russia."

Medical understanding about cholera was primitive, and it was believed that the disease was spread through "foul air" or "miasmas," rather than through contaminated drinking water. Local physicians recommended garbage be properly collected and burned and that privies be treated with lime. A ten o'clock curfew was also imposed on inns and taverns each evening to prevent excessive drinking and late-night carousing. Householders were ordered to sweep and clean the footpaths in front of their homes. By the end of June, York's first Board of Health had been created under the guidance of Dr. William Baldwin and the other dozen doctors in York. The best remedy the board could come up with, however, given its limited resources, was to issue an edict promoting cleanliness, avoiding the damp night air, and keeping warm with flannel and woollen stockings and warm coffee in the morning.

In truth, they were fighting a losing battle since, as Thomas A. Reed, an early chronicler of York, pointed out, "there were neither sidewalks, drains nor sewers [and] no water supply except from wells." (It was the "universal practice," he adds, to allow garbage "to accumulate on the vacant lots.") Needless to say, the disease rapidly spread beyond York during the summer of 1832. Victims could have sought treatment at the York General Hospital, but it was soon common knowledge that once you entered the hospital you did not come out. One oft-told story, which was later proved to be untrue, was that a female patient had still been alive when she was declared dead by the hospital staff and put inside a coffin. Only the intervention of her husband saved her.

By the time the disease had run its course at the end of September, 273 people had died in York. The health crisis confirmed what Tories and Reformers had been bickering about for more than a decade: what passed for the town's municipal administration—essentially a few magistrates with little money and no taxing authority—was far from adequate to properly serve York's expanding population. Finally, after more heated deliberations, on March 6, 1834, the town of York was incorporated as the city of Toronto, with its boundaries now extended in all directions—from Parliament Street in the east to Bathurst Street in the west and from Lake Ontario in the south to past Queen Street in the north. That geographic area was initially divided into five wards: St. Andrew's, St. David's, St. George's, St. Lawrence, and St. Patrick's. Moreover, the city also had jurisdiction over the area as far east as the Don, west to Dufferin, north to Bloor Street, and south to the peninsula (soon to be Toronto Island). Officials had opted to revert to the aboriginal name to rid the town of its unwanted status as "Little York," which did not match the weighty aspirations of its burghers.

The mayor of the city was to be chosen by the ten aldermen elected in five wards, who along with ten common councilmen formed Toronto's first city council with the responsibility to supervise everything from police and firefighters to taverns, Sabbath observance, and billiard tables. Though William Lyon Mackenzie had initially favoured incorporation, in typical fashion he did not support the plan that was passed in 1834, arguing that it forced "upon 9,000 people in Canada a closed rotten borough government of the most odious character." His opinion presumably changed again on March 27, when he was elected an alderman (of the twenty seats on the first city council, twelve were taken by Reformers and eight by Tories). Then, in a contest between him and Dr. John Rolph, a physician, lawyer, and popular Reformer, the other aldermen chose Mackenzie to be Toronto's first mayor, likely as compensation for the Tory abuse that he had been subjected to. It was certainly not the last time a colourful and troublesome personality served as the city's chief official.

Conservatives who had predicted God's wrath would rain down on the city if Mackenzie became the mayor braced for the worst. Though he designed the city's first coat of arms, with the motto "Industry, Intelligence, Integrity," which was to endure until the 1998 amalgamation of the metropolitan area, the job did not suit his temperament or larger political ambitions. Toronto in 1834 needed a mayor who could tackle the city's debt problem, fix its muddy streets, and skilfully manage a council intent on arguing more than actually accomplishing anything substantial. Mackenzie's inclination was to act in the same dictatorial fashion he had accused the Tories of.

During one heated council session, he became embroiled in a dispute and then a shouting match with George Gurnett, a Tory councilman and newspaper proprietor who was known for his temper—a few years earlier he had been involved in the tarring and feathering of a Reform opponent—about the appointment of the new city clerk. When Gurnett refused to resume his seat after Mackenzie ordered him to do so, Mackenzie had him arrested by the High Bailiff for "violating the dignity of the Council." (Gurnett later served two terms as mayor of Toronto, in 1837–38 and 1848–50.) The *Patriot* lambasted Mackenzie as a "tyrant" and "demagogue." He blatantly used the patronage at his disposal for a variety of civic posts to get rid of his conservative opponents and reward his Reform friends.

As mayor, Mackenzie was the chief magistrate at the city quarter sessions, where he was the arbiter of public morality. As was the custom of the day, he tended to show mercy to his friends and supporters—a Reform councilman's brother who was found guilty of assault and battery was fined only five shillings—and was tougher on his Tory enemies. In one notable case involving an Irish Catholic woman named Ellen Halfpenny, accused of drunken and disorderly conduct, he sentenced her—after she threw one of her shoes at him—to the stocks, which had not been used for some time, and ordered her to clean the prison. By all accounts, Miss Halfpenny was the last person to suffer the humiliation of the stocks in Toronto.

Mackenzie had to deal with a second and more deadly outbreak of cholera in the summer of 1834, during which five hundred people died. Among the victims was the outspoken thirty-five-year-old Irish Roman Catholic journalist Francis Collins, editor of the Reform *Canadian Freeman*. He was one of Mackenzie's chief rivals, who detested the Family Compact just as much as Mackenzie. Collins had become ill after visiting sick Irish immigrants in the hospital. His wife, brother, and sister-in-law died as well. Mackenzie himself contracted the disease but recovered. Nonetheless, many of Toronto's citizens were not impressed by his perceived lack of leadership during the epidemic, in contrast to the actions of Lieutenant Governor Colborne, who was overwhelmingly praised for raising funds and improving hospital facilities.

Mackenzie quickly tired of the mundane bureaucracy inherent in civic administration and focused his attention on the more exciting and, in his view, critical issues of provincial politics. He prepared himself for the next election of the legislative assembly in September 1834 and was once again successful. Having given up his interest in the newspaper business by this time, he maintained his dual provincial and civic status (allowed in those days) for a few months. By January 1835, with a new civic campaign underway, he initially resigned his position as mayor and declared he would not run as an alderman again. Then, just as quickly, he changed his mind and re-entered the race. It did not matter: in the city's second civic election, Toronto voters opted for fifteen Tories and only five Reformers; Mackenzie received a mere sixty-nine votes. He now threw himself full-time into the task of overhauling the unacceptable status quo of Upper Canadian politics in which the despotic Family Compact, as he saw it, thwarted the true wishes of the people.

FOR ABOUT THREE YEARS, including during his term as mayor, Mackenzie had tried taking a diplomatic route by directly appealing to officials in England for redress for the perceived abuse of the Family Compact. On each occasion he was stifled, which pushed him to a more radical position. In the process he lost the support of the influential Methodist leader (soon to be an educational pioneer) Egerton Ryerson, the editor of the *Christian Guardian*. Mackenzie and Ryerson had agreed that the Anglican Church's monopoly of the clergy reserves had to end. Yet Ryerson remained a moderate throughout his life and refused to countenance any talk of American-style radicalism or violence. In 1833, the two men publicly feuded in the press, with most Methodists siding with Ryerson.

From Mackenzie's perspective, the situation worsened with the appointment of Sir Francis Bond Head as lieutenant governor in 1836. A retired military engineer and author of travel books, Bond Head was decidedly unprepared for the unpleasant world of Upper Canadian politics. His hard-nosed approach and partisan embrace of the Tories—despite orders from British authorities to work amicably with the assembly—soon alienated moderates and radicals. Mackenzie, whom he later described in his memoir as a "low bred vulgar man," was an early and lasting enemy. Never discreet, Bond Head took an active role in the election campaign of 1836, speaking out against the Reformers and brazenly portraying the contest as "a moral war... between those who were for British institutions, against those who were for soiling the empire by the introduction of democracy." Mackenzie, who had toured Lower Canada, connecting with French-Canadian radical reformers, had already come to the conclusion that the intolerable government in Upper Canada had to be changed. The "people" were not as certain, and Mackenzie was shocked to the point of weeping when he did not win a seat in the assembly in July 1836.

The tipping point came in early March 1837. Lord John Russell, the colonial secretary, not only rejected the ninety-two resolutions Quebec leader Louis-Joseph Papineau had submitted in 1834, calling for true democracy, but in a show of arrogance Russell also had the British Parliament pass his own set of resolutions, which further curtailed the power of the Canadian assemblies. This ultimately incited Papineau and his Patriotes into armed rebellions. The first fighting broke out on November 23 at St. Denis, and the violence continued for another year before the rebels were defeated.

Meanwhile, throughout the summer of 1837, as a severe depression made daily life even more miserable and slowed civic projects on roads and sewers, Mackenzie travelled far and wide from Toronto, organizing "committees of vigilance," with the intent of taking action against the government. How far he was prepared to go remained unclear. By the fall, successive physical attacks on him and his followers by rowdy Orangemen, plus the unwavering support of Bond Head and the British authorities for the appointed executive council, convinced him that overthrowing the government was the only option. In his new start-up newspaper, the *Constitution*, he published his pro-American draft plans for the State of Upper Canada. Still, his objectives were hazy and his organization somewhat haphazard.

He convened meetings and rebel rallies throughout November, most at locales beyond the city limits, to rouse his followers—farmers, tradesmen, labourers, and a handful of professionals—who now numbered in the hundreds. In a more decisive move, Mackenzie recruited Colonel Anthony Van Egmond to train and command his rebel army. The colonel had fought against Napoleon at the Battle of Waterloo and detested the Compact. When violence broke out in Lower Canada, Sir Francis Bond Head, not believing rumours about a possible Upper Canada rebellion, imprudently dispatched most of his British troops to Quebec to assist in the fight against Papineau and his men. Mackenzie sat in a wagon near the corner of King and Simcoe Streets, watching in near disbelief as the militia marched away, declaring to anyone within earshot that "I'll make it hot for you before you return." Such a brazen assertion angered a group of Upper Canada College boys standing beside him, who threw pebbles at him. He laughed off the attack.

This was a fortuitous moment Mackenzie could not ignore. His plan was to march on Toronto and take over the city. He expected many of its citizens to rise up, join his cause, and overpower the Tories. Then a provisional government, possibly headed by Dr. John Rolph, would be established. This was wishful thinking at best.

During the first week of December, Mackenzie and his men attempted to gauge the preparedness of authorities in Toronto, even as their plans for how and when to proceed with an armed uprising were in disarray. Mackenzie had set Thursday, December 7, as the day for the assault. Rolph, believing that the government in Toronto was readying itself for battle, wanted the attack to begin a few days earlier. On Sunday, December 3, without consulting Mackenzie, Rolph implored Samuel Lount, a well-liked blacksmith and settler from the Holland's Landing area, who had won a seat in the assembly in 1834, to gather all available men at Montgomery's Tavern, a popular stopping place for travellers that was just a few blocks north of Eglinton and Yonge Streets. (As it turned out, that same week the owner of the tavern, John Montgomery, had rented his inn to John Linfoot, a local Tory, who was forced to serve food and drink to the rebels.)

By the time the men—probably about five hundred in all—reached the tavern, they were cold, hungry, and tired. The next night, Mackenzie, accompanied by Captain Anthony Anderson and two other men, travelled on horseback down Yonge Street to scout the situation further. Just north of the Tollgate (Davenport Road), the group encountered Alderman John Powell, a future Toronto mayor, and his friend Archibald McDonald (or MacDonnell). The rebels immediately captured the two. According to Mackenzie, he asked Powell if he had a pistol but did not frisk him—that would have been too ungentlemanly. Powell later insisted that Mackenzie had not inquired if he was armed. In any event, Mackenzie told Anderson and another man to take Powell and McDonald to Montgomery's Tavern, and Mackenzie and the third man continued on their way toward Toronto.

Powell, who did have a concealed pistol, managed to remove it from inside his coat. There was some confusion, and Powell shot Anderson in the back. He then fled in the direction of Toronto. Within a short time he came across Mackenzie and his scout. As the groups crossed paths, Powell aimed his weapon at Mackenzie, but the pistol misfired. Powell kept riding and soon warned officials in Toronto that a rebel attack was imminent. Powell's heroics, at least considered so by the Loyalists, propelled him to the mayor's office a few months later. He served in that position for two terms, until 1840.

About the same time, news that a small group of Loyalists from Richmond Hill—led by local tavern owner William Crew—had been apprehended by the rebels prompted retired Lieutenant-Colonel Robert Moodie, a former British army officer, to investigate what had transpired. He was determined to stop the rebels from murdering the governor and citizens of York "in their beds." Moodie was accompanied by two Loyalist men, David Bridgeford, another former solider, who had served during the War of 1812, and Captain Hugh Stewart. The colonel's wife, Frances, tried to convince her husband to remain home, but he felt it was his duty to intervene.

It took almost two hours for Moodie, Bridgeford, and Stewart to reach Montgomery's Tavern to ascertain the fate of Crew and his men. As the trio tried to pass the tavern, a group of armed rebels led by Samuel Lount ordered them to halt.

"Who are you that dare to stop me upon the Queen's highway," Moodie shouted.

"You will find that out by and by," was the reply.

Bridgeford made it through the blockade and eventually joined up with John Powell, who was on his way to Toronto. Moodie, however, swung around and fired his pistol in the air in a futile attempt to scare the rebel guards. Instead, a volley of shots was returned (possibly on Lount's order), hitting Moodie in his left side. He collapsed on top of Stewart's horse. "I'm shot. I'm a dead man," he whispered. Stewart helped prop him up in his saddle. The two men were taken prisoner by the rebels. Stewart was roughed up and Moodie was placed on the floor inside the tavern. When Stewart was allowed to attend to him, he found the colonel "bleeding and writhing in agony." Within an hour he was dead, one of the rebellion's first casualties. Stewart was allowed to remove the body.

Perhaps because Mackenzie was nearly killed in his altercation with Powell, he became increasingly unpredictable, even unstable, over the next few days. He also might have been drinking heavily. He spent much of December 5 attempting to inflict punishment on the families or properties of local Tories. Robert Horne, an official with the Bank of Upper Canada, who had refused to serve Mackenzie, was his first target. He went to Horne's home near Yonge and Bloor and set it on fire. Mrs. Horne and her children, whom he threatened, escaped the blaze by running through the snow. Next he moved on to Rosedale, the home of Sheriff William Jarvis, but before he could burn that property, Samuel Lount and David Gibson, a radical reformer, prevented him from doing so.

That evening, Mackenzie, who was wearing several buttoned-up overcoats as a bulletproof vest, led a larger group of men from Montgomery's Tavern towards the city. When they reached present-day College Street, they were met by a small armed band of Loyalists led by one of Mackenzie's nemeses, Sheriff Jarvis. Shots were fired and the rebels scattered in every direction. Dejected, some of them returned to their farms, but Mackenzie was not done yet. The next day he robbed the mail coach to figure out what was happening in Toronto, and a fresh batch of men arrived at Montgomery's Tavern. It was, however, too late.

Early in the morning of December 7, Anthony Van Egmond arrived at Montgomery's convinced that the uprising would fail and should be called off. A retreat, he suggested, would be the wisest course of action. Mackenzie, who had hardly slept, grew impatient with such talk. He pointed his gun at Van Egmond's head, insisting that the rebellion was to proceed as planned.

Sir Francis Bond Head sent a veritable army of more than a thousand Loyalist soldiers with two cannons towards the tavern. They were led by James FitzGibbon, a veteran of the War of 1812, and Col. Allan McNabb, a member of the legislature. Just south of Eglinton and Montgomery's Tavern, the Loyalists encountered a rebel force of about four hundred men. A brief battle ensued and the rebels were easily defeated. On instructions from the lieutenant governor, Montgomery's Tavern was burned, as was David Gibson's nearby home. Montgomery, who was merely guilty by association, was arrested for high treason but escaped to the United States. He came back to Toronto six years later, after he was granted a pardon, and rebuilt his tavern.

A £1,000 price was put on Mackenzie's head (his grandson, Mackenzie King, proudly displayed the wanted poster at Laurier House, his home in Ottawa), and his wife and children were kept under twenty-four-hour surveillance by the militia men at his modest house on York Street. Mackenzie eventually escaped to the United States, where he tried unsuccessfully to mount another attack. His family joined him there. He ended up in New York, spent about a year in jail for violating American neutrality, and remained in the United States as an exile for the next twelve years.

Back in Toronto, hundreds of his supporters were arrested; so many, in fact, that the overflow had to be housed at the market and Parliament Buildings. Among those apprehended were Samuel Lount and Peter Matthews. A farmer and soldier of Loyalist stock, Matthews had, on Mackenzie's orders, led sixty men to destroy the bridge over the Don River as part of a diversion on December 7. That ploy had failed, too.

Less than six months later, in an atmosphere hostile to the Reform movement, associated as it was with the radicals, a slew of trials took place in Toronto and in other locales. Twelve rebels were tried for high treason, and half were found guilty—among them, Samuel Lount, forty-six, and Peter Matthews, fifty-one, who had both pleaded guilty. In sentencing the two to death, Chief Justice John Beverley Robinson admonished them for their moral failings and their refusal to appreciate the sublime way of life offered to them in Upper Canada. "I hope you have endeavoured to retrace in your minds the causes of your dreadful fall," Robinson scolded them. "There is no doubt the chief cause has been your wilful forgetfulness of your duty to your Creator, and of the purposes for which life was bestowed upon you."

Petitions asking the government for clemency were circulated in Toronto, and rallies were held in support of the two men. Mrs. Lount even begged the new lieutenant governor, Sir George Arthur, to have mercy on her husband. But Upper Canadian officials could not be dissuaded; for the sake of the future province, an example had to be made of Lount and Matthews. On April 12, 1838, on the grounds of the city's second jail—near the corner of Toronto and King Streets—thousands of people gathered beside the gallows and beyond. There was no school that day so students could watch the spectacle for themselves. Loyal Orangemen with their muskets encircled the area.

As the historical plaque on the site today notes, both men stood brave. As he was led from the prison, Lount turned and declared to the other prisoners, "Be of good courage boys, I am not ashamed of anything I've done, I trust in God, and I'm going to die like a man." Matthews "struggled hard," according to one eyewitness. Lount "died instantly."

LIEUTENANT GOVERNOR ARTHUR decided that no further hangings were required. He had made his point in executing Lount and Matthews. Despite calls from the Tories for the continuance of harsh punishment, especially since they feared that an American invasion by escaped Upper Canadian rebels and their U.S. supporters was imminent, law and order was restored in Toronto and across the province. The rebel William Lyon Mackenzie was in exile in the United States, and the worst of the remaining prisoners were sent to distant penal colonies, while others were eventually set free as a sign that British justice was not entirely without compassion or good sense. Nevertheless, change was coming to the old order and the city, and there was little the members of the Family Compact could do about it.

In 1838, the British sent John George Lambton, Earl of Durham, to investigate the causes of the rebellions. In his report "On the Affairs of British North America," released a year later, Lord Durham—or "Radical" Jack, as he was nicknamed for his fairly liberal views, at least by British standards of the day—famously found in Lower Canada "two nations warring in the bosom of a single state." His solution was to unite Upper and Lower Canada and thereby gradually absorb French Canadians into a British- and English-dominated state. He also urged Britain to grant the new assembly responsible government on domestic policy so that the executive would be "responsible" to the elected representatives of the people—but that recommendation, among several others, was ignored by British authorities for the time being.

However, they did follow Durham's suggestion for Lower Canada, and by the Act of Union of 1841, Upper and Lower Canada were united as the Province of Canada. Upper Canada now became "Canada West" and Lower Canada, "Canada East." Yet because the population of French-dominated Canada East was greater than that of Canada West (approximately 650,000 to 455,000 in 1841), the British were compelled to institute equal representation for each former province in the elected assembly, rather than the representation by population they would have preferred. It was a decision based on the false premise that it was possible to rid Canada of a French Canadian people sixty-seven years after the Quebec Act of 1774 ensured French Catholic survival. In any event, the Union Act's political ramifications loomed large in the decades ahead as Canada West's population eventually eclipsed that of Canada East.

Chapter Four

A CITY OF ORANGE AND GREEN

He hated the neighbourhood, and especially the backyard squalor that was typical of the streets. He also hated the noise of the hordes of children, and the dirt and stupidity of most of its inhabitants. More than anything else he hated his address...He particularly hated having to live in Cabbagetown.

—HUGH GARNER, 1950

George Brown, the editor and publisher of the Toronto *Globe* and, next to John A. Macdonald, arguably the most important politician in pre-Confederation Canada. He also made Tory Toronto the headquarters for the new country's Clear Grit-Reform (Liberal) party. *Hunter & Co. / Library and Archives Canada / C-009553*

BY THE TIME CHARLES Dickens and his entourage arrived in Toronto on May 4, 1842, for a two-day stop, the celebrated British author had been on tour in the United States for more than three and a half months. Only thirty years old, he had already penned such bestselling novels as *Oliver Twist* and *Nicholas Nickleby* (both initially were published as monthly serials). Dickens, whose ego was as big as most of his books, delighted in the attention that engulfed him everywhere he travelled. "There never was a king or Emperor upon the Earth, so cheered, and followed by crowds, and entertained at splendid balls and dinners and waited upon by public bodies of all kinds," he wrote to his friend and solicitor Thomas Mitten. "If I go out in a carriage, the crowd surrounds it and escorts me home; if I go to the theatre, the whole house (crowded to the roof) rises as one man, and the timbers ring again."

Apart from desiring to enhance his literary reputation and connect with his army of readers, Dickens also spoke out passionately in New York and elsewhere in support of international copyright standards and proper financial compensation to authors like him from publishers and newspapers who brazenly pirated his work. Such reasonable demands—at least from our more modern perspective—fell on deaf ears among politicians in Washington D.C. and, less surprisingly, among book publishers and editors, who generally printed what they wished, yet hypocritically accused Dickens of being greedy for trying to protect his writings. This backlash troubled him, though he later got his revenge in his critique of the United States in *American Notes*, his memoir of the tour, as well as in his novel *Martin Chuzzlewit*, in which he mocked the American national character.

Following a thrilling visit to Niagara Falls, Dickens and his wife, Catherine, received a royal welcome in Toronto. "Every attention that individuals could offer was paid them there," noted the *Toronto Patriot* at the conclusion of the visit. During their brief stay, Charles and Catherine resided at the American House, a popular establishment on the corner of Front and Yonge Streets (where rooms could be rented reasonably for two dollars a day). Dickens gave a reading—in truth, more of a performance given his talents as an actor—to an enthusiastic sold-out audience at the Theatre Royal on King Street and was feted at an intimate reception for a select group given in his honour by Chief Justice John Beverley Robinson at his grand home.

One of the invitees that evening was twenty-three-year-old Larratt Smith, a young lawyer who was articling with William Henry Draper, the premier of the Province of Canada. Smith led a typical middle-class life for an up-and-coming member of the establishment in mid-nineteenth century Toronto. As his family homestead was north of the city in Richmond Hill, he boarded for a brief time at the Greenland Fishery, a large wooden tavern near Front and John Streets. Within a year, however, he was renting a cottage on Garrison Common, which he shared with two friends. (The cottage was owned by one of his Richmond Hill neighbours, Thomas Kinnear, a farmer who in 1843 was murdered along with his beautiful housekeeper/lover Nancy Montgomery by a jealous Irish manservant.) When he wasn't spending long hours in court or taking the stagecoach to St. Catharines or Niagara for business, Smith's social life was spent in the company of his young gentleman and lady friends playing chess and whist, singing in the St. James Cathedral choir (conducted by Mrs. Draper), enjoying sleigh rides in the winter, and attending theatre, dances, and dinner parties. His connection with the Drapers was a boon and provided him with an otherwise unattainable entree to government balls and such events as the Robinson reception for Charles Dickens. Still, like every other Torontonian, he also had to deal with his share of fleas, flooded lodgings and streets, and torrential rainstorms.

Smith does not record in his diary if he actually spoke with Dickens, but it must have been a highlight of the social season for him. As for the admired author himself, he was impressed by Toronto, which he described in *American Notes* as a town that was "full of life and motion, bustle, business, and improvement." He pointed out that "the streets are well paved, and lighted with gas," a recent illuminating technology introduced to the city and its approximately sixteen thousand citizens at the end of 1841 by the City of Toronto Gas Light and Water Company (gas was too pricey for most homeowners, who depended on candles and coal oil to light their residences for many years). The multitude of shops on King Street pleased him and his wife, too, and as they paraded up and down "doing King," a favourite pastime of well-to-do Torontonians, he compared the well-stocked display of goods in store windows to what could be found "in thriving county towns in England." He was equally complimentary about the private residences, St. James Cathedral, Upper Canada College, and the public offices he saw.

At the same time, he was troubled by what he discovered of the intense political divisions in Toronto and the manner in which ardent conservative forces boldly pursued their objectives, trampling anyone in their path. As a chronicler of the evils of capitalism in nineteenth-century London and a champion of the downtrodden, Dickens was taken aback by the conversation of members of the old Family Compact at Chief Justice Robinson's reception. They related to him in glorious detail the story of how Mackenzie's 1837 rebellion was crushed. The tale had an impact on him, but likely not the one his hosts intended. A week later he wrote to John Forster, his soon-to-be biographer, that the "wild and rabid Toryism of Toronto is, I speak seriously, appalling."

That critical assessment was based, too, on what he had learned about the violence and death which had occurred during and following the election in mid-March 1841—the first election in Toronto after the union of Upper and Lower Canada into the Province of Canada—Dickens heard about the post-election riot, an all-too-typical Toronto clash between Reformers, whose candidates had been victorious, and rowdy and militant Orangemen, who had supported the two losing Tories, Mayor George Munro (a member of the Orange Order) and Henry Sherwood, who would succeed Munro as mayor in 1842. The day after the election, a group of Reformers led by the two winning candidates—Isaac Buchanan, a Scottish importer, and John Henry Dunn, a veteran Upper Canadian government official—unwisely decided to celebrate their triumph at the polls by marching down Church Street.

Waiting for them at the Coleraine Tavern near King Street was a pack of angry and half-drunk Orangemen who had been brought in from Scarborough by the Coleraine's owner, George Allen, encouraged by Henry Sherwood's brother, Samuel. The tavern was used as a meeting place for several local Orange lodges, and both Allen and Samuel Sherwood were loyal Orangemen, who typically enough served as Toronto's chief constable—Allen from 1847 to 1852 and Sherwood from 1852 to 1858. Early on the day of the march, Mayor Munro had been informed that a piper in a kilt, who was to participate in the parade, had been beaten by thugs and his bagpipes destroyed. Munro was implored to dispatch more constables to supervise the parade, but he refused. "You may go to the Devil," was his response.

Sure enough, there was trouble as soon as the parade began. Near St. James Cathedral, a group of Orangemen threw stones and muck at the Reformers and their horses. The men fought back and continued the parade. A block further, they were hit by another round of rocks and bottles, which were hurled at them from inside Coleraine Tavern. As the Reformers turned towards the tavern to confront their attackers, someone inside the tavern fired a pistol at the coach carrying Buchanan and Dunn. Neither of the politicians was injured, but in the ensuing melee, one of the Reformers was killed and several were wounded. With the police refusing to intervene, the militia soon arrived to take charge of the situation.

It had been the same story throughout the election campaign. There were reported incidents of unarmed Reformers being beaten and bloodied by Orange bullies. Later, witnesses testified that the few constables who had watched some of these unwarranted attacks stood idly by, doing nothing to assist the victims.

The police apathy towards the Reformers was hardly surprising. The dozen or so constables then on the job (including a handful who had been appointed as special constables supposedly to keep order during the election) had been recruited from among the Orange Order and were thus answerable to their Tory and Orange masters, who firmly controlled the civic corporation. Upholding law and order was secondary to protecting the trinity of Orangeism—Crown, Protestantism, and Empire—and would continue to be so until employment as a police constable was no longer treated as a patronage appointment. Transforming the Toronto police force from an Orange fraternity into a professional and non-partisan organization modelled on the Metropolitan police force in London, however, took nearly another two decades and a lot more political wrangling.

Charles Dickens was not aware of the various complexities of Toronto's sectarian strife and heated civic politics, yet it was clear that during his short visit he did gain some insight into what ailed the city. "It is a matter of deep regret that political differences should have run high in this place, and led to most discreditable and disgraceful results," he added in the section on Toronto in *American Notes*. "It is not long since guns were discharged from a window in this town at the successful candidates in an election, and... one man was killed on the same occasion; and from the very window whence he received his death, the very flag which shielded his murderer (not only in the commission of his crime, but from its consequences), was displayed again on the occasion of the public ceremony performed by the Governor General, to which I have just adverted. Of all the colours in the rainbow, there is but one which could be so employed: I need not say that flag was orange."

That was substantially what William Coffin, the former commissioner of police of Lower Canada, and his fellow riot commissioner, Nicholas Fullam, who investigated the causes of the 1841 violence, concluded. They did not mince their words about

Mayor Munro's "dereliction of duty" or the more significant issue: the Orange Order's all-encompassing and "evil influence" on the inner workings of the city corporation. As a political entity, the order held a powerful sway over what went on at city hall. "The existence of Orangeism in this province is a great and growing evil," the commissioners asserted, "which should be discountenanced, denounced, and repressed by the exercise of every authority and influence at the disposal of the Government."

IN THE YEARS AFTER THE REBELLION, there had been a subtle shift of power among the Tories. Old Compact stalwarts like Chief Justice John Beverley Robinson and Bishop John Strachan (as of 1839) had not vanished from the political scene, yet they had been superseded, at least in local matters, by the more rugged middle-class members of the Orange Order. In part, this was a result of the union of the Canadas and what was initially perceived as Toronto's devastating loss of its coveted status as a provincial capital. In 1841 the capital of the United Province of Canada was moved, first to Kingston and then to Montreal, before events compelled it to alternate every five years between Toronto and Quebec City from 1849 to 1866. This left civic politics, operating from the new Italianate city hall on Front and Jarvis Streets (now part of the Market Gallery inside the South St. Lawrence Market), open to a new generation of mainly Irish Protestant businessmen. In the hallways and cigar-smoke-filled meeting rooms, "ward bosses, officials, lawyers, MPs and contractors congregated daily to talk politics or swing deals."

Former members of the Compact, and moderate conservatives like William Henry Draper, along with influential Reform politicians such as Robert Baldwin and Francis Hincks, the publisher of the *Examiner*, focused more of their attention, resources, and influence on the great issue of the day: the achievement of responsible government. For much of the forties, that constitutional quest kept them away from Toronto for long periods of time and, as might be expected, their interest in local affairs fluctuated.

The membership of the Orange Order continued to grow in the 1830s and 1840s, bolstered by the arrival of Irish Protestant immigrants and a growing fear of Catholicism, a paranoia which became even more ominous in the wake of the Irish famine and the substantial increase in Irish Catholic immigration to British North America. By the early 1860s, there were twenty active Orange lodges in Toronto with a membership of approximately 1,200 men, which represented roughly 15 percent of the adult male non-Catholic population of the city.

Tightly knit, like-minded, intimidating, and with absolutely no tolerance for their perceived enemies, they formed a powerful "political machine" reminiscent of New York City's Tammany Hall, the powerful nineteenth-century Democratic municipal administration. Few provincial or civic elections during this era were not influenced in some way by the Order. In the seven provincial general elections held between 1841 and 1863, for instance, Orange-backed candidates won five times. At city hall, their control was even more pervasive: of the fourteen men who served as mayor of Toronto from 1840 to 1866, only lawyer Adam Wilson, a Baldwin Reformer, was able to break the Orange-Tory grip on the position in the first direct popular mayoral election. For much of this period, Orangemen also dominated city council; in 1844, for instance, six of the ten aldermen were well-known Orangemen.

That was merely the most visible aspect of the Order's civic hegemony. Its loyal members were appointed to the city's dozen or so key administrative jobs, including chief constable and city inspector (the latter was the man who licensed taverns, horse-drawn taxis, and the carters who hauled goods in their wagons). In the 1840s, as today, there was money to be made in operating a tavern. Not only was it the most popular and profitable business in the city—in 1841, there were at least 140 drinking establishments, or roughly one tavern for every hundred citizens, in addition to innumerable beer shops and unlicensed bars—but city officials deliberately doled out tavern licences to themselves, their friends, and political supporters. Absolutely no attempt was made to disguise this blatant abuse of power. In 1841, for example, tavern licences were granted to City Inspector William Davis, Deputy Inspector of Licences James Bell, and Constable Thomas Earls.

Davis was not quite as corrupt as New York City's infamous William "Boss" Tweed, but for a time he controlled the patronage of the civic corporation's appointments with an iron fist, always ensuring that his friends and lodge brothers were looked after. And when a tavern owner or carter did not heed Davis's orders to support his choice of candidates in a city election, punishment was meted out: licences were not renewed and businesses were targets of police harassment. For good reason he was denounced in the *Globe*, the new Reform newspaper operated by George Brown, for bullying Toronto's citizens and unfairly influencing local elections. The newspaper cheered loudly when, soon after he took office in 1845, Mayor William Henry Boulton, a diehard, third-generation member of the Family Compact and Orangemen, nonetheless fired Davis for spreading nasty rumours about him. (This was retaliation for Boulton's decision to fire one of Davis's friends, a police constable, for being drunk on the job.)

The mayor's independent action did not sit well with many of the aldermen or, for that matter, with other Orangemen, but at least they did not physically attack him. Orange Order members could be rough and crude. In September 1841, when Larratt Smith visited the Race Ground—the track was then located on the Grange, the property of William Henry Boulton, who was also a member of the Upper Canada Turf Club—he was accosted by "pugnacious" Orangemen, as he put it, and forced to say "To Hell with the Pope," though he had not said or done anything offensive to warrant such thuggish treatment.

That was fairly mild treatment. The Order was at the centre of about twenty-nine riots in Toronto between 1839 and 1864, nearly all involving political disputes of one kind or another or violent clashes with Irish Catholics. Like the shooting and fighting that followed the 1841 election, if there was any reason to take to the streets for acts of hooliganism in defence of Protestant religious or political principles, the city's Orangemen were never reticent to do so.

In early November 1843, Robert Baldwin, then the attorney general for Canada West, piloted two pieces of legislation through the assembly (then sitting in Kingston) that took direct aim at the Orange Order: the Party Processions Act, which was supposed to halt rowdy election campaigning and Orange parades (it was only partially successful and was repealed in 1851); and the more significant Secret Societies Act, which would have outlawed all secret societies except the Masons. Yet the only other so-called secret society in Canada was, in fact, the Orange Order, so there was no disguising the aim of the legislation. Governor General Charles Metcalfe initially supported both acts—though Tories in the assembly, either Orangemen themselves or dependent on Orange votes, vehemently did not—but he had second thoughts about enacting the Secret Societies Act and asked the Colonial Office back in London for instructions. The British government ultimately killed it.

Predictably, when news of the legislation reached the streets of Toronto, a mob of Orangemen decided to show their extreme displeasure by congregating in front of Baldwin's house and burning effigies of him and his fellow Reformer Francis Hincks from makeshift gallows. Watching from a safe distance, Baldwin's nine-year old daughter Eliza later reported to her father that while the effigy of Hincks blazed bright and hot, "they could not get you to burn at all."

The Orange mob was back at Baldwin's house in 1849 to burn him and Hincks again after the assembly, sitting now in Montreal, passed the Rebellion Losses Bill. This controversial legislation, put forward by the ministry of Baldwin and Louis Lafontaine, his counterpart in Canada East, awarded compensation to individuals whose property was destroyed in the Lower Canada Rebellion of 1837, including some of the former rebels. The governor general, Lord Elgin, adhering to London's orders, assented to the bill, a symbolic act signifying that responsible government now existed in the Province of Canada. Angry Tories in Montreal pelted Elgin's carriage with eggs and rocks and caused a riot in the city for two days—an event which necessitated moving the seat of government to Toronto—and outraged Orangemen in Toronto were less than pleased by this kowtowing to the Reformers.

The government's decision to grant a full amnesty to the old rebel William Lyon Mackenzie (conditional pardons already had been granted to other rebels) triggered a similar hostile reaction. When Mackenzie visited Toronto from his exile in New York, before moving back permanently with his family in 1850, a large Orange-led mob surrounded the house of his brother- and sister-in-law, John and Helen McIntosh, on Yonge Street just north of Queen Street, where he was staying, and threatened to destroy it and tar him. Mackenzie wisely stayed inside, so the mob settled for breaking every window and smashing the doors with rocks. The four police constables watching this scene blocked the entrance, but were otherwise helpless to stop the violence, even if they had wanted to.

In the decade and a half before Confederation, there were rowdy and violent clashes between Orangemen and the newly established Irish Catholic immigrants, many of whom, like the members of the nationalist Hibernian Benevolent Society, were unwilling to be pushed around. Indeed, it was a bloody fight between Catholics and Protestants on St. Patrick's Day in 1858, in which an Irish Catholic marcher in the parade, Matthew Sheedy, was fatally stabbed, that prompted thirty-two-year-old Michael Murphy, owner of a tavern on the Esplanade, to establish the society and accept the role of its first president. The night before, at the St. Patrick's Society Dinner held at the National Hotel, a fight also broke out between Catholics and Orangemen. One of those accosted was D'Arcy McGee, an Irish Catholic member of the provincial assembly and future Father of Confederation.

In the earliest days of the Hibernian Benevolent Society, members functioned as a street-watch group, guarding Catholic neighbourhoods against Orange encroachment and attacks. The widely accepted view in the Catholic community in the 1850s was that the Orange lodge's hold on the Toronto police was firm, evidenced by the way in which the case against Matthew Sheedy's four attackers fell apart, largely because of police indifference. All those charged in the murder were acquitted.

It was not only Catholics who fought with Orangemen. In the summer of 1855, an American circus was visiting Toronto. After a performance on the evening of July 12, the day of the Orange parade commemorating the Battle of the Boyne, several of the circus clowns showed up inebriated at Mary Ann Armstrong's brothel on King Street West. Among the clientele at the "house of ill-fame" that night were several members of a local volunteer fire brigade, Orangemen celebrating the Twelfth. Some nasty words were exchanged, and within moments the clowns and the firemen started brawling. By all accounts, the clowns beat their opponents badly. The police sought to arrest one of the clowns the next day, but he had vanished. That was not sufficient for the firemen or their Orange friends. This was the background to the infamous Toronto Circus Riot.

Three days later, a mob of Orangemen intent on exacting retribution and justice marched to the circus grounds and attempted, without success, to bring down the circus tent. Another donnybrook broke out. The members of the fire brigade soon arrived and, using the hooks on their truck, pulled the tent to the ground. While at least twelve police constables stood by watching, the mob went on a rampage, burning the circus wagons and fighting with the performers. Eventually Mayor George W. Allan (the son of Upper Canadian scion William Allan) was forced to call for the militia to restore order and protect the circus workers.

Asked later to identify the perpetrators—many, presumably, their fellow Orange lodge brothers—none of the constables were able to do so. By any standard, this was an unacceptable and even absurd situation, rightly denounced in the *Globe*, whose editor argued that the city's police and fire departments had to be restructured, professionalized, and removed from political and Orange control. Establishment of a fire department that was less of a social club, with a paid staff, and a police force free of patronage—and with a chief "free of the contamination of local politics," as the *Globe* put it—was gradually accomplished over the next decade.

Sensible Tories and Reformers on city council, who accepted the need for change, worked through the provincial assembly to create the Toronto Board of Police Commissioners in late 1858. This put police matters into the hands of the mayor, recorder, and police magistrate, who proceeded to set regulations and rules of conduct and hire new constables. The new system did not completely remove the council's influence, since it still financed the police force, but it was a start.

In one of their first significant acts, the commissioners appointed William S. Prince, who had a British military background, as the new chief constable. Prince also had a well-deserved reputation for being hard-nosed and slightly arrogant, especially in his dealing with perceived city council interference, yet fair. Not only did he introduce discipline (firing several men for being drunk on the job) and adequate training for his officers, but he was also the first head of the force since 1837 who was not an Orangeman. Almost immediately, he ensured a proper police presence at both Catholic and Orange parades. Still, loosening the Orange Order's tight grip on the force was easier said than done, and as late as the 1920s, according to Toronto police historian Nicholas Rogers, "the Orange presence on the force was considerable, constituting roughly one-third of the new recruits."

Beyond issues involving the police and fire department, the Orange Order remained highly visible, no matter what the occasion. There was tremendous excitement and anticipation in Toronto during the first week of September 1860 before the arrival in the city of Albert Edward, the eighteen-year-old Prince of Wales—the future King Edward VII—who was on a tour of Canada and the United States at the behest of his mother, Queen Victoria. This was the first time an heir to the British throne had visited North America, and his every move was covered in great detail by the local press. One highlight of his visit was the official opening of Queen's Park (named in honour of Queen Victoria), which was then north of the downtown. (Within twenty-three years it was the site of the Ontario Legislature.)

For several months prior, city council had spared little expense to spruce up Toronto, and had built an amphitheatre by the waterfront for the opening celebrations. As in other cities, a parade had been planned, along with the requisite arches decorated with flags, flowers, and royal regalia.

With immense pride in the empire, Orange Order lodges had collectively erected a large arch adorned with the society's banners and insignia at the crossing of King and Church Streets, which the Prince was to pass under on his way to the Sunday service at St. James Cathedral. Accompanying the Prince was the Duke of Newcastle, secretary of state for the colonies and a Catholic. Naturally, he objected to the Order's attempt to politicize the visit, particularly since the British government of Lord Palmerston, of which the duke was a member, was in the process of passing the Party Emblems Act to halt partisan displays and demonstrations (the Orange Order was the target), which had recently contributed to deadly riots in Ulster. After problems in Kingston—where Orange intransigence led the duke to cancel the Prince's visits there—he had been assured by Toronto mayor Adam Wilson, a Reformer, that there would be no problems with the Order and there definitely would be no Orange arches under which the Prince would have to pass. Wilson had brokered a deal with the local lodges: they agreed to remove their banners and colours from the arch, provided they could hold a parade wearing their yellow and orange uniforms before the Prince's arrival. They also agreed to change into civilian clothes when they attended the welcoming ceremonies.

Early in the evening of September 7, the Prince and his party arrived by steamer and were treated to a grand reception of speeches and singing at the amphitheatre, with twenty thousand citizens of Toronto in attendance. "Thrilling, soul-stirring, heart-heaving" was how the *Globe* enthusiastically described the event. The Duke of Newcastle concurred, later reporting to Lord Palmerston that "the most magnificent spectacle I have ever seen welcomed the Prince. As an artistic effect it cannot easily be excelled, but as a popular demonstration I have never witnessed its equal."

However, when the Prince left the waterfront for a procession down King Street, his coach passed under the supposedly stripped Orange arch, which to the duke's great displeasure still displayed a transparency of William of Orange. So incensed and insulted was the duke that he refused to present the Prince the next day for a planned levee until Mayor Wilson officially apologized for this egregious transgression. For the Sunday morning journey to St. James Cathedral, the suspicious duke ordered the driver of the coach ferrying him and the Prince to take a different route and thereby avoid the arch altogether. This angered the crowd of Orangemen waiting outside the church to greet the Prince. As the service was proceeding, they strung banners and flags across the arch and shouted that they would "cut the trace and drag the Prince through the arch" after he exited the cathedral. There could have been serious trouble when the

Prince and the duke left the church through a side door to avoid the mob, but the police controlled the situation.

IN THE TWO DECADES THAT PASSED between the visits of Charles Dickens and the Prince of Wales, Toronto grew from a small town of 14,250 people to an industrial city of 45,000, and more than 50,000 by the time of Confederation in 1867. Consider that in 1850 the entire civic bureaucracy amounted to eight people, and the Toronto Fire Brigade had only seven companies. The city did not have a proper water supply, and though there were at least nine newspapers, a town crier still wandered the streets yelling "descriptions of lost children and animals."

All of this changed significantly during the next ten to twenty years with the railway boom that made the city the focus of an industrial heartland, a position it has never relinquished. Additionally, thousands of immigrants continued to arrive from Liverpool, Dublin, and Cork, seeking a refuge from the industrial revolution and the Irish famine, and fugitive slaves came from the American south in search of freedom and a new life. The revolution in transportation, and its attendant impact on banking, business, and factories, as well as the influx of newcomers, the vast majority of whom were poor, profoundly reshaped Toronto's environment for good and bad. At first it was the positive aspects of this urbanization and growth that attracted the most attention.

"It seems like magic!" the *Globe* bubbled early in 1853 in response to the tremendous increase in the city's trade. "We question whether there is a town in the world which has advanced more rapidly than Toronto." Charles Mackay, a Scottish poet and journalist who travelled throughout the United States and Canada in the late 1850s and wrote a book about his journey, was similarly impressed with Toronto. "There is a Yankee look about the whole place which it is impossible to mistake, a pushing, thriving, business-like, smart appearance in the people and in the streets; in the stores, in the banks; and in the churches," he wrote.

The city did have resilience. Late on the night of April 7, 1849, a tremendous fire, probably started accidentally by an overturned lantern or discarded cigar, began in a stable near the corner of King and Jarvis Streets. By the time it had run its course, made worse by a harsh wind, less-than-adequate volunteer fire brigades using poor equipment, and a deficient water supply, the blaze had destroyed most of the buildings in the Market Block area—about fifteen acres bounded by King East, Church, Adelaide East, and Jarvis Streets. This included Toronto's first city hall at the southwest corner of King and Jarvis Streets, and St. James Cathedral, which had to be rebuilt using imported stone, an intricate construction project that took almost four years. The fire's only casualty was Richard Watson, a printer at the *Upper Canada Gazette*, who tried in vain to rescue the newspaper's type.

By the end of the year, many of the burned buildings had been re-erected. And new ones like St. Lawrence Hall, completed in 1851, were soon the focus of a plethora of political, social, and cultural events—performances by the Swedish opera star Jenny Lind, lectures about the calamities of slavery, Orange Order rallies, and rousing partisan speeches by conservative and reform politicians like John A. Macdonald and George Brown. Of note, too, during this bustling decade was the new General Hospital on Gerrard Street East, then still a short distance from the centre of the city; the medieval castle-like University College, a secular institution, around which the University of Toronto gradually took shape, eventually connecting to the various religious-based colleges in the vicinity (the one holdout was Bishop John Strachan's Anglican Trinity College, which did not join the University of Toronto—Strachan had castigated it as a "godless institution"—until 1904 and did not relocate from its Queen Street West home to the St. George Campus until 1925); and two prestigious hotels, Rossin House (later Prince George) at King and York Streets (built and owned by Marcus and Samuel Rossin, German Jewish immigrants) and the even more regal Queen's Hotel on Front and York Streets. Until it was demolished in 1927 and the Royal York was erected on the site, the Queen's Hotel was the epitome of modernity, with the finest bathrooms money could buy and gardens adorned with statues and fountains. Later, Prime Minister Sir John A. Macdonald was noted for holding court in its Red Parlour, and during the U.S. Civil War, Confederate agents based their clandestine operations at the hotel.

Behind much of this development and expansion was the coming of railways. Canals and water transportation had served the city's economic needs, but never fully. Access to points in every direction was limited by season and weather, a problem that a railway could solve. In 1850, when the St. Lawrence and Atlantic Railway was being built, which within three years connected Montreal to an ice-free port in Maine, the ire of Toronto boosters was awakened. "Let us in the West... sink our local and personal differences," a *Globe* editorial declared, "and push through a western railroad, cheap or dear. Let us have the road!"

The newspaper got its wish. In mid-October 1851, the announcement and official sod turning for the Ontario, Simcoe and Huron Railway—the "Northern" as it was referred to (and officially renamed in 1858)—was celebrated with a parade and an elegant ball at St. Lawrence Hall, with Lord and Lady Elgin in attendance. In time, the Northern—its wooden depot located not far from the eastern entrance of the current Union Station—along with several other railroads and their branches, linked the city with Collingwood to the north, essentially following the old Toronto Carrying Place route; Hamilton, London, and Windsor to the west; Montreal in the east; and Sarnia (and the United States by a ferry) in the southwest via the Grand Trunk Railway (GTR), the most ambitious and expensive of the pre-Confederation railroad schemes.

The fact that the GTR was based in Montreal rankled Torontonians no end. Most everyone, however, cheered the fact that it now was possible to travel between the two cities in only fourteen hours—the train moved at a top speed of about thirty miles per hour—rather than having to endure a stagecoach ride that lasted several days. The busy railroad traffic necessitated the construction of a GTR platform in 1858 in a landfill near Front and York Streets, the first version of Union Station. Indeed, as Toronto railway historian Derek Boles notes, the railroads' demands for more and more space near the harbour for their network of tracks and terminals was eventually solved by the "acquisition of new land that was created by filling in Lake Ontario."

Railways were expensive to construct, requiring public support and investors who were not averse to risk. They also offered potentially gigantic profits. Nonetheless, raising funds was not always easy. Such an ambitious venture required a particular impetuous mindset and was hence attractive to a select group of daring Toronto businessmen and politicians. Frederick Capreol, the entrepreneur who had initially promoted the Northern railway project, for example, was an impulsive English-born real estate agent and auctioneer. He had cleverly proposed a "Grand Canadian Railroad Lottery." Participants were offered a chance to win land and stock worth two million dollars. Capreol tried to convince Toronto city council to purchase £100,000 in tickets by means of debentures. Civic politicians, conscious of the righteous mood that has always characterized Toronto, wisely held a referendum on the issue. And voters, who, not surprisingly, found this scheme too much of a gamble, rejected it. The city did quietly invest £50,000 in the project, permitting it to move forward, but Capreol fell out of favour with the company's board of directors, who fired him from his position as manager a few days before the official sod-turning ceremony.

Caught up in this, too, were Mayor John George Bowes, who served from 1851 to 1853, and Francis Hincks, who in the early 1850s was the premier and inspector general of finance of the Province of Canada. Their exuberance to finance the Northern railway ensnared them in an insider stock manipulation that netted them close to a £10,000 profit. It was all quite innocent, though the "£10,000 job," as it was dubbed by their political rivals, ultimately cost them both their positions.

The Toronto press expressed legitimate concerns about the power of the railway companies and their incestuous relationship with Canadian politicians. Still, it was impossible to argue with the domino effect the railways had on the city's industry and attitude. They also increased export trade with Britain during the Crimean War, and with the United States thanks to the Reciprocity Treaty of 1854, which stimulated the grain and lumber businesses. It was no coincidence that the Toronto Stock Exchange, primarily used by grain dealers in this era, as well as the Board of Trade, the city's first true business lobby group, were established in the early fifties (a smaller version of the Board of Trade had been operating since about 1844, but without a charter).

Even with a downturn in the economy in 1857 and 1858, industrial progress marched on and a Victorian city took shape. By 1861, the Toronto Street Railway Company's horse-drawn wagons transported the city's residents—about two thousand passengers a day in its first year of operation—up Yonge Street, all the way to Yorkville Town Hall, at six miles an hour for a five-cent fare. The ride on the tracks in the company's wagon-cars, which had room initially for sixteen people and later twenty-four, was usually bumpy, and chilly in the winter despite the straw on the floor. Yet the inauguration of the service was hailed at the time as one of the great moments in the annals of the city.

Typical of the new breed of businessman of the railway age was William Gooderham, a miller and distiller who had come to the Toronto area in the early 1830s. Together with his brother-in-law James Worts (who committed suicide in 1834 after his wife, Elizabeth, died in childbirth) and then with Worts's eldest son, James Gooderham Worts, William Gooderham continually expanded his stone distillery, located on the lakeshore close to the mouth of the Don River (on Mill Street, east of Parliament), until it was one of the largest enterprises in Toronto and Canada West. For a time the distillery was powered by a massive windmill—in its day the city's most unique landmark—until it was replaced by steam engines. Gooderham and Worts's marquee brands, "Toddy" and "Old Rye," were popular across the country as well as in England. Gooderham's commercial interests, naturally enough, extended into railways and banking, two enterprises he depended on for the success of his distillery and mills. He was a major investor and director in several railway companies, including the Toronto and Nipissing, as well as being president of the Bank of Toronto, an executive position he held from 1864 until his death in 1881.

A business tycoon with a social conscience, Gooderham, a Moses-like figure with a full white beard in his elder years, was instrumental in the construction of the Little Trinity Anglican Church on King Street East, where members did not have to pay for their pews as they did at St. James Cathedral. In later years, he also financed the building of small, affordable cottages on Trinity and Sackville Streets for many of his workers and the city's growing working class, which was another consequence of the railway era. His son George, who took over the family firm, broadened its financial interests and profits further and continued the philanthropy from a grand red brick mansion he erected in 1889 on the northeast corner of Bloor and St. George Streets (now the York Club).

IN THE BACKGROUND of this industrial development was the equally dramatic reshaping of Toronto by Irish Catholic immigrants. Starting in 1847—"Black '47," the year much of Ireland starved—and for the next five years or so, the arrival of the unwanted Famine Irish, impoverished, diseased, and seemingly backward, increased the city's population and significantly altered the urban landscape.

Tragic victims of the potato blight that destroyed Ireland's main food supply, and at the mercy of a harsh political and economic mentality that offered them little or no aid, the lucky ones had sufficient money to purchase a steamship ticket and escape the "frightful charnel house" (as one contemporary Irish journalist described it) that Ireland had become. Of the million who did emigrate, about 100,000 landed at Grosse Isle off Montreal, the entrance to British North America. These were the fortunate souls who survived the horrendous six-week journey aboard the infamous "coffin ships" with little food to eat or clean water to drink, crammed into fetid quarters that bred typhus, dysentery, and lice. In the summer of 1847, the *Times* of London rightly depicted the ships as akin to "the worst horrors of [the] slave-trade." Ten ships left ports in Cork and Liverpool bound for Montreal with a total of 4,427 passengers. By the time they had reached Grosse Isle, 804 had died at sea and another 847 were ill, most of whom latter perished while quarantined.

Thousands made their way to Toronto in 1847, causing a public health crisis as bad as any the city had dealt with during the cholera epidemics. Immigrant fever sheds were constructed on the northwest corner of King and John Streets, but by the end of the year 1,100 had died from typhus and were buried in plots beside St. Paul's Church as well as in St. James Cemetery. One of the early victims was the Right Reverend Michael Power, the city's first Roman Catholic bishop (he had been appointed in 1841), who contracted the disease while comforting the sick newcomers and died in October less than three weeks before his forty-third birthday. An asylum had to be opened for widows and orphans left destitute. Over the next nine months, 627 women and children, nearly all Irish Catholic, found refuge there.

Anglican bishop John Strachan was not exaggerating when he wrote at the end of the year that "this town has during the whole season resembled a lazar house." Or put more ominously by Egerton Ryerson, chief superintendent of education, "the physical disease and death" associated with the Irish famine immigrants "may be the precursor of the worst pestilence of social insubordination and disorder."

The impact of the Irish Catholic migration on Toronto's collective psyche was demographic, emotional, and, for some residents, worrisome. By 1851, one in four Torontonians (7,940) was Catholic, and nearly all of these were Irish. Ten years later, the city's population had increased to 44,821, and 12,135 or 27 percent of that total was Irish Catholic, the highest number they reached. Irish Protestants still outnumbered the Catholics, but the rise of a distinct Irish Catholic presence frightened many of Toronto's narrow-minded citizens. "No Irish Need Apply" signs were a common sight in the city's shops and factories throughout the nineteenth century. At best, many were "last hired and first fired," as historian Murray Nicholson notes. Irish Catholic immigrants "will find out through bitter experience," declared the Toronto-based newspaper *The Irish Canadian* in September 1869, "[that] their prospects are damped, their chances are curtailed, and the openings of employment lessened, because of their religion." In the years ahead, other immigrant groups to Toronto and Canada would also experience such intolerance in an age when assimilation to the white Anglo-Saxon Protestant ideal, rather than multicultural acceptance, defined the country's expectations of newcomers.

The prejudice and discrimination against Irish Catholics were based on a number of related factors: irrational fears about the power of the pope to usurp Protestantism across the world; highly exaggerated notions that all Irish Catholics were supporters of Fenianism, the early IRA-style anti-British radical militant movement based in the United States (tavern owner Michael Murphy of the Hibernian Benevolent Society embraced the movement, but he did not support the violent attacks on British North America in 1866); and the linking of Irish poverty with widely held stereotypes of Irish Catholic social ills and immorality.

Fanning the flames of this hatred was, among others, George Brown, the editor and publisher of the *Globe* and, next to John A. Macdonald, arguably the most important politician from Canada West. From the day the Scottish-born Brown arrived in Toronto via New York City at the age of twenty-four in 1843, he made himself known. A large man, Brown was over six feet tall and powerfully built. His most distinguishing feature was his long, bushy, mutton chop whiskers. He had learned liberal-minded politics, religious principals—he was an ardent supporter of the Free Church of Scotland—and, most significantly, the newspaper business from his father, Peter. Brown was hard and dogmatic but also an energetic and passionate man with strong convictions about free speech, civil liberties, and the separation of church and state. (Brown was a staunch advocate of "voluntaryism," which, as his biographer notes, affirmed that "churches should rest solely on the conscience and contributions of their members, while the state in turn should know no church connection and grant support to none.") He fell in with Robert Baldwin's Reform movement and soon rallied around him left-leaning Reformers in Toronto and western farmers he dubbed "Clear Grits" (this faction only wanted men of true grit). He was eventually elected to the Province of Canada assembly in 1851, the beginning of a journey that would culminate with his role as a leading Father of Confederation and a founder of the Liberal Party.

Brown's most enduring legacy was the *Globe*, the newspaper he established in Toronto in 1844. Initially working with his father and then with his younger brother, Gordon, the Browns made the *Globe* the organ of liberalism and, within a short time, the most widely read paper in the city and the country. It was later said that before many Liberal politicians would speak on an issue, they would ask, "What will the *Globe* say?" It was sold in every train station, hotel, and bookstore in Ontario. "There were probably many thousand voters in Ontario," the veteran Liberal politician Richard Cartwright wryly observed, "who hardly read anything except their *Globe* and their Bible." The *Globe* was Brown personified. And if he trained his acerbic pen on you, as he did with his

Tory rival John A. Macdonald, he could be vicious.

He had a particular resentment for the Catholic Church and what he perceived to be its evil machinations. In Brown's view, the pope was nothing less than a "great foreign tyrant," whose indoctrinated followers were never to be trusted. "Rome has but one aim, to make the secular serve the ecclesiastical," he wrote in an editorial of August 1857. "Rome means tyranny, and has for its mission the subversion of the civil and religious liberty of the masses." The *Toronto Mirror*, a Catholic reform weekly owned by Charles Donlevy, rightly accused Brown of waging "a kind of guerilla warfare" against the city's Irish Catholics. "His anti-Popish tendencies," suggested the *Mirror*, "preyed upon his brain like feverish disease."

His intolerance was partly a consequence of the firm religious doctrine he held so tightly (especially voluntaryism), but was also simply the reaction of a blind bigot. For such a brilliant man and devoted liberal, Brown could at times be narrow-minded. He was aghast at the successful efforts of his Conservative opponents to expand government funding for Catholic schools in Canada West in the late 1850s and early 1860s, mainly thanks to the strength of French Catholic votes from Canada East in the union assembly. That he believed Irish Catholic immigrants would burden and overwhelm Toronto's destiny was hardly surprising. In his public pronouncements he did not sound much different than the anti-Catholic, anti-immigrant nativist American extremists of the mid-nineteenth-century Know-Nothing movement.

Almost as soon as the famine victims arrived in 1847, the *Globe* declared that they would be "unaccustomed to the habits and occupations of Canadians," and that they would "sink down into the sloth to which they had been accustomed at home." Thereafter, lurid headlines screamed about "Irish Catholics the Curse of the Land," and "The Irish Papist a Rebel and a Judas." In a February 1856 editorial, Brown expressed deep concern over further Irish Catholic immigration, warning that Canada West was to be "colonized by papists," which he compared to "as great a curse... as were the locusts to the land of Egypt."

Most telling of Brown's attitude was his complete reversal of opinion about the Orange Order. For many years the *Globe* had regularly portrayed Orangemen as "thugs"; however, by the mid-1850s they had become "patriots." Remarkably, now, as an editorial of July 2, 1857, put it, the Order's "fundamental principles, fairly carried out, are all conducive to the growth of constitutional liberty and the best interests of religion." Brown's change of heart was no doubt due to the anti-Catholic view he shared so strongly with the Order, but it was equally an opportunistic desire to win Orange support for his budding political career—a ploy that worked in the election of 1858, when he won an assembly seat in a Toronto riding with a lot of help from the Orange lodges.

DESPITE BROWN'S BELIEF to the contrary, not every Irish Catholic immigrant fit the classic stereotype of the poor, drunken Irishman one step ahead of the police. Arriving in Toronto when the city's industrial economy was taking off, many eventually found work as unskilled or semi-skilled labourers in factories or for the budding railway enterprises so integral to Toronto's growth. Some, like John McGee, the owner of the large Phoenix Foundry; Patrick Hughes, who ran a successful dry goods store; and Frank Smith, a wholesaler, who literally rose from rags to riches and later became the president of the Toronto Street Railway Company and director of half a dozen major corporations, were more the exception than the rule. Most Irish businessmen were small-time shop or tavern owners best classified as "working-class entrepreneurs," or independent contractors who toiled for low wages (from about ten to less than five dollars a week) as carters, drivers, hackmen, or piecework garment tailors and seamstresses. In the case of the carters and hackmen, they received their licences at the discretion of city officials, and most of those, as noted, were loyal members of the Orange Order.

Generally excluded from positions of power, the Irish Catholics thus created their own neighbourhoods along with their own fraternal societies, religious institutions, and social culture, a unique blend of the old country with the New World. There was no Irish ghetto in Toronto, yet it existed in the hearts and minds of the Irish nonetheless, often perpetuated by the community's newspapers. "Surrounded by a hostile majority lashed into frenzied anger by the incendiary appeals of the Protestant press," the *Irish Canadian*, one of several newspapers that defended Irish Catholics, pointed out, "we have neither sympathy nor assistance to expect outside of our own body." That was probably an exaggeration of the Irish Catholic dilemma in Toronto in pre-Confederation Canada, but only a slight one. A feeling of isolation may have been only a state of mind, but it was one based in reality.

Irish Catholics lived mainly in small (and often substandard) rented houses and cottages in several downtown areas. The most popular was close to St. Paul's Church, south of Queen and east of Parliament Streets, in a community already settled by Ulster Irish Protestants and known as "Corktown" (after County Cork). Little Trinity Anglican Church was also nearby for Irish Protestant workers. Similarly, Irish Catholics and Protestants lived next to each other, along with their British working-class neighbours, in a tract of land north of Queen Street East and south of Winchester Street that soon became immortalized as Cabbagetown—which "offered jobs, soot and smells together," as historian J.M.S. Careless portrayed it—yet another by-product of railroads and factories. West from there was Macaulay Town, located north of Queen and west of Yonge Streets, and named after the family of businessman and politician John Simcoe Macaulay, who had first owned this large piece of land. As of 1853, this area was incorporated into the newly christened St. John's Ward, the most well-known impoverished immigrant quarter in the city for the next century. Irish Catholics resided, as well, in the vicinity of King and Bathurst Streets, and later farther west on Dufferin Street in a neighbourhood that ran from College to Bloor Streets.

Critics of the community especially targeted the dilapidated slums east of Yonge near King. On Dummer, Centre, Pine, and Stanley Streets, the truly horrendous Irish poverty proved an eyesore for any reporter brave enough to venture to this squalid and crime-ridden neighbourhood. Every stereotype about the depravity "idle and wretched" (two favourite adjectives in the press to describe them) Irish Catholics could inflict on a city was there for all to witness. "Irish beggars are to be met everywhere, and they are as ignorant and vicious as they are poor," the *Globe* asserted in February 1858. "They are lazy, improvident and unthankful; they fill our poor houses and our prisons, and are as brutish in their superstitions as Hindus."

A few years later, a *Globe* journalist was shocked to find in one decrepit shanty, with filth everywhere, "no less than sixteen human beings, men and women, lying indiscriminately." Another lengthier report bemoaned the "muck and filth" of the overflowing sewers on Stanley Street, homes with stagnant water in their basements "rotting the floors and breeding disease," backyards with putrid garbage breeding the "plague," and "miserable hovels which in themselves are better fitted for pig-styes and cow-pens than residences for human beings." The newspaper accounts did not necessarily single out Irish Catholics for condemnation, but the implication was clear nevertheless: these immigrants were responsible for making Toronto "one of the dirtiest cities in Canada."

Protestant sensibilities were also appalled by the petty crime, prostitution, and excessive drunkenness that were in part an unfortunate consequence of life in the slums. Alcohol and beer were plentiful and inexpensive in Toronto—a glass of ale or lager was three cents and whiskey five cents a glass in the 1870s—and a lot safer than drinking water. (Also available and popular was poteen, a banned intoxicating distilled Irish homebrew, often upwards of 180-proof.) Moreover, the neighbourhood tavern served as a popular social and entertainment spot for Irish men after a long day on the job. Women, too, imbibed in (often illegal) grog shops or in the privacy of their own homes. No Irish Catholic wedding or wake was held that did not include celebratory toasts and good cheer. That this fondness for drink sometimes turned nasty, leading to street fights and domestic violence, should not be surprising—nor should an increase of the membership in local temperance societies.

The Toronto press, high, mighty, and defenders of morality—the *Globe*, in particular, was a staunch guardian of the city's (and province's) Sabbath laws that prohibited drinking, gaming, sports, public meetings, and even outdoor bathing on Sundays—thrived on tales of small-time crime, alcohol abuse, and mayhem at local brothels. "There's no halfway house in this matter," a *Globe* editorial on the integrity of the Sabbath declared in July 1850. "Either we must recognize God's law in its full extent, or set it aside."

Newspapers recorded the salacious detail in daily and weekly police court reports, which merely reinforced negative images of Irish Catholics and their plight. "James Hoolahan and James Felton were charged with fighting and causing a disturbance," the *Globe* noted in its "Police Intelligence" column on November 21, 1856. Likewise, Matthew Evans, a carter, was charged with "stealing a pair of gloves." A few days later, Ellen Ferral was discovered in the cellar of the home of James Cleland on the corner of Nelson and Duchess Streets. One of Cleland's servants found her holding a bucket of apples, corned beef, and a dress worth three dollars. She claimed that Cleland had given the food and clothing to her but was remanded nevertheless.

At the end of May 1860, Sarah Wilson was charged with "keeping a notorious house of ill fame" on Richmond Street between Yonge and Bay. Caught up in the dragnet were her employees, Rosa Breen, Anne Breen, Anna Marie Farrell, Anne McNab, Margaret O'Keefe, and a few customers, James Payne, James Russell, and John McNab. According to the arresting officer, Sergeant Major Ferris, several of the women were found "huddled together in a most filthy condition." After a quick hearing, the entire group was sentenced to one month of hard labour.

More typical was this *Globe* report in December 1865 of an Irish family row. "Yesterday Patrick O'Brien was brought before Yorkville authorities charged with assaulting and beating his half-sister Elizabeth Graham," the paper noted. "The assault was committed in the tavern of Michael O'Hara, on account of some old grudge which existed between them. The assault consisted in O'Brien beating her with a small club on the head and pushing her out doors." He was fined a few dollars and sent on his way.

Such lurid accounts of "Irish-Catholic couples lying on their babies in a drunken stupor, of inebriated Irish labourers beating their children or kicking their pregnant wives in the belly, and of stabbings, fights and late-night brawling parties further confirmed anti-Catholic prejudices," suggests historian Brian Clarke. Of the nearly five thousand men and women whose names are found in the Toronto police register for 1857, for example, more than half were arrested because of problems connected to liquor, and most of those were likely Irish Catholics. That deplorable situation, no doubt bolstered by the deep-seated police prejudice directed at Irish Catholics, prompted James Beaty, publisher of the *Leader*, to create a new subsection in the newspaper's police court section entitled "The Drunkards." Based on arrest and city jail reports from 1858 to 1868, approximately 50 percent, and frequently more, of the total number of individuals arrested in Toronto each year—larceny, assault, and drunk and disorderly conduct were the most frequent crimes—were Irish Catholics, though they represented only 20 to 25 percent of the city's population.

More serious was a riot on Stanley Street in the hot summer of 1857, a consequence of the bad feelings that had been brewing between members of the Orange Order and Irish Catholics. The battle began following the Orange celebrations on July 12. Police constable Devlin, sporting an Orange rosette, was walking on Stanley Street with his wife when he was attacked by a gang of Irish Catholics and beaten bloody. Another constable soon arrived to arrest one of the perpetrators, but his friends refused to permit that. Stones were thrown and fighting broke out with the police until more officers arrived to rescue their colleagues and restore order. Similar often bloody confrontations between Irish Protestants and Catholics, especially on July 12 and St. Patrick's Day, when parades were held, were regular occurrences in Toronto for the next thirty years.

In 1864, the sad realities of Irish Catholic urban life—including an unusually high mortality rate for children under the age of ten—led Bishop John Joseph Lynch (who became Toronto's first archbishop in 1870) to write a pamphlet entitled "The Evils of Wholesale and Improvident Emigration from Ireland," in which he urged Catholic officials in Ireland to discourage further immigration to North America. That plea, however, fell on deaf ears.

LIVING SIDE BY SIDE with Irish Catholics in the shacks and cottages of Macaulay Town, and tolerated to about the same degree by Toronto's upstanding citizens, was another smaller group of newcomers, black refugees from the United States. From the 1830s to the 1860s, before the American Civil War was waged, the city's "coloured" residents, as they were then referred to—"darky" and "nigger" were also common and fairly acceptable euphemisms to describe them in nineteenth- and early twentieth-century Canada—had escaped the brutality of slavery and found freedom in British North America. Many had used the courageous assistance offered to them by the Underground Railroad, the clandestine network of safe houses and secret transportation routes facilitated by white and black abolitionists, including Harriet Tubman, who was herself an escaped slave from Maryland. Operating from bases in Pennsylvania and St. Catharines, where she lived from 1851 to 1857, Tubman daringly travelled back and forth to the southern states nineteen times, somehow avoiding detection or capture, rescuing as many as three hundred slaves. In 1850, when the U.S. Congress enacted the oppressive Fugitive Slave Act, which extended the legal rights of slave owners and made it easier for them to reclaim their escaped slaves, Canada became an even more attractive place of refuge.

Though it attracted a fair bit of attention in the local papers, Toronto's fugitive slave population was never that large; by 1858 the city's black community numbered fewer than two thousand people when Toronto's population was about fifty thousand.

Nevertheless, individual stories of bravery and resourcefulness in the face of bigotry and injustice remain compelling. Two of the first fugitives to settle in Toronto were Thornton and Lucie Blackburn. In 1985, the ruins and artifacts from their home on Eastern Avenue, where they had lived for more than five decades, were discovered by chance in an archeological dig at the old Sackville Public School playground.

Both had been born into slavery. Fearing that Lucie (or Ruthie, as she was then known) was about to be sold, she and Thornton—he was nineteen and she was twenty-six—escaped from their captivity in Louisville, Kentucky, in the summer of 1831. With forged papers, they posed as free blacks and somehow made it all the way north to Detroit. There they lived for two years, until a visiting clerk from Louisville recognized Thornton and informed his and Lucie's owner of their whereabouts. They were subsequently arrested by Detroit police (under the Fugitive Slave Law of 1793) and ordered to be returned in chains to their lives of misery and servitude. Aided by a small band of black and white sympathizers, they pulled off a brazen escape: another woman took Lucie's place in jail, and Thornton was freed during a staged riot, in which he pointed a gun at a Detroit sheriff, as he was about to be transported. Fleeing, they soon landed in Sandwich in Canada West, near Windsor, on the other side of the Detroit River. But their legal troubles were not over yet. The mayor of Detroit tried to have Thornton and Lucie extradited under the recently passed Fugitive Offenders Act of 1833, an arrangement between the United States and Upper Canada to deal with perpetrators of murder, larceny, and other serious crimes. The American argument was that the Blackburns had been involved in planning the riot and that Thornton had tried to kill the sheriff.

The British Parliament had abolished slavery throughout the empire in 1833, a decision wholeheartedly supported by the enlightened members of the Family Compact. Ultimately, Chief Justice John Beverley Robinson; the Rev. John Strachan, who was then a member of the executive council; as well as Governor Sir John Colborne, took the position that the evidence of any crime committed by Thornton during the riot was insufficient compared with the idea of returning two people to bondage. Some years later, Robinson took a different view of a runaway slave named John Anderson, who was guilty of killing Seneca Digges, a white farmer in Missouri who was trying to prevent his escape. In that case, Robinson did order that Anderson be extradited, but two months later this decision was overturned on appeal to the Court of Common Pleas in Toronto over a difference of opinion about the legality of the original arrest warrant.

After living in Amherstburg, south of Windsor, for a year, the Blackburns moved to Toronto, where Thornton reunited with his brother Alfred, who was also a fugitive and whom he had not seen since 1826. All three became members of the First Baptist Church, ministered by the charismatic black pastor Washington Christian, a former slave. "Elder" Christian, as he was known by his devoted followers in Toronto's black community—they often lined up two hours ahead of time to hear him speak—had started preaching in private homes and outside by the water in 1827, and then in 1834 in a schoolhouse on Richmond Street. Within seven years a small church was built for the all-black congregation at the corner of Queen and Victoria Streets, where they remained until 1905. (That year the church moved to a new building at the northeast corner of University and Edwards Streets, and it moved again in 1955 to its present location at Huron and D'Arcy Streets.)

Thornton's first job in Toronto was as a waiter in the dining room at Osgoode Hall, where he served judges and lawyers during twelve- to fourteen-hour days, six days a week. He was paid £1 per month and survived on tips. Lucie likely worked as a washerwoman, a common occupation for a black woman in Toronto in the nineteenth century. Thornton, ever ambitious, came up with a better idea to improve his lot in life.

Familiar with horse-drawn hackney cabs he had seen in U.S. cities, he noted their absence on the muddy streets of Toronto. He scraped enough money together and had a prototype built by Paul Bishop, a former Montrealer. Soon, Thornton's four-seat cab, named "The City" and with red and cream design (similar to the red with white trim colour scheme used by the Toronto Transit Commission) was a common sight. Thornton's monopoly on the nascent Toronto taxi business lasted only a brief time. So popular and profitable was his venture that other black workers abandoned their low-paying jobs, much to the annoyance of their white employers, and began driving their own cabs. There was sufficient traffic, ferrying visitors and gentlemen and ladies to all points, that the tiny staff of city bureaucrats was compelled to issue cab licences and establish regulations—merely the beginning of such government management of the industry. By the 1840s, drivers were not permitted "to leave their vehicles, needlessly or wantonly flourish their whips, or use any abusive, obscene, or impertinent language."

Thornton and Lucie prospered. In 1848 they finally were able to purchase for £60 the modest house on Eastern Avenue, and they had enough surplus cash to buy investment properties on Agnes and Elizabeth Streets in St. John's Ward, which they rented to newly arrived fugitive slaves. They both lived fairly comfortable lives; when Thornton died in 1890 at the age of seventy-eight, his estate was worth $18,000. Two years later, Lucie sold their house to the Toronto Board of Education. She died in 1895 when she was ninety years old and was buried beside Thornton at the Necropolis cemetery.

The Blackburns were by no means the only success story in the city's black community. While most, like Thornton and Lucie, were unskilled labourers or competent blacksmiths, carpenters, and tradesmen, a handful rose into the professional and business ranks in those early years. Alfred Lafferty was born in 1839. His father, William, a carter and grocery store owner who could not read or write, had come to Upper Canada in 1830 from the United States (he may have been a slave). William and his wife, Sarah, valued education and sent Alfred first to Rev. William King's school for the children of former slaves in the black settlement of Buxton near Chatham, and later to Upper Canada College, which had already accepted other black children. Alfred then attended University College at the University of Toronto, became a scholar in mathematics, and was awarded his BA in 1863 and his MA four years later. He initially embarked on a career as a teacher and principal; married a white woman, Isabella Campbell—despite the prejudice of the day, his biographer, Hilary Dawson, says that there is no evidence that Alfred and Isabella endured any problems as an interracial couple; and eventually rose to prominence as the first black lawyer in Chatham.

One of Alfred's close friends and classmates at Reverend King's school was Anderson Ruffin Abbott. His father, Wilson, was a free Negro who lived in the southern states. He had attempted to run a grocery store in Mobile, Alabama, but was literally run out of the city. He arrived in Toronto in about 1835 with his wife, Ellen, to start a new life. Wilson briefly sold tobacco before he began buying and selling property. In a matter of years, his real estate holdings expanded to more than forty homes, mostly in Toronto, but also in Hamilton and Owen Sound. By the early 1870s, he was one of the wealthiest black men in Toronto, if not the richest, and a generous leader of the community.

Anderson was one of Wilson and Ellen Abbott's nine children. He studied in Ohio and then at the Toronto School of Medicine, where he graduated in 1857. He apprenticed for four years under Dr. Alexander Augusta Thomas, an American black physician who had come to Canada West to complete his medical training because he had not been allowed to do so in the United States. In 1861, Anderson R. Abbott received his licence from the Medical Board of Upper Canada, becoming the first Canadian-born black doctor in the country. Both Thomas and Abbott served the Union Army during the U.S. Civil War.

Rich or poor, life in Toronto's self-contained black community revolved around home and church. A big annual event was Emancipation Day, August 1, marking the day in 1834 that slavery was abolished throughout the British empire, a year after the British Parliament passed the Slavery Abolition Act. This public display was all the more significant in the 1840s and 1850s, when there were stories in the press of American slave catchers on the hunt for fugitives in Toronto. The holiday was celebrated in Toronto into the 1920s with parades and banquets, and later with the "Big Picnic," held across Lake Ontario at Port Dalhousie, when thousands of African Canadians from Toronto and elsewhere gathered for the festive occasion. Emancipation is still a holiday in the Caribbean and was reborn in Toronto in 1967 with Caribana, a grand street carnival inaugurated by the city's West Indian community to commemorate Canada's centennial.

Perhaps because they had experienced such harsh treatment and injustice in their former lives as slaves, and even as freemen, in the United States, the leaders of Toronto's black community refused to endure blatant prejudice and discrimination without at least a fight. In particular, they objected with public petitions and protests to demeaning and insulting blackface or Jim Crow-style caricatures by visiting minstrel shows and circuses. They also spearheaded the North America Convention of Colored Freemen at St. Lawrence Hall. One of Toronto's five delegates at the convention was Thornton Blackburn, who along with the other fifty or so delegates voted to officially recognize the British government as "the most favourable in the civilized world to the people of colour."

Toronto civic officials heeded complaints from the community about acts of prejudice and occasionally attempted to rectify them. But for the most part, depictions of "darkies" in plays and musicals remained popular, and stereotypical attitudes about African Canadians persisted for decades. As is usual, racism only increased as more fugitives arrived in the city. Lord Elgin, who had served as governor of Jamaica before his appointment as the governor general of the Province of Canada in 1847, worried that Canada would be "flooded with blackies who are rushing across the frontier to escape from the bloodhounds whom the Fugitive slave bill has let loose on their track." Samuel Thompson, the editor of the moderately conservative *Daily Colonist*, felt the same way. "We fear that they are coming rather too fast for the good of the Province," wrote Thompson in an editorial at the end of April 1855. "People may talk about the horrors of slavery as much as they choose; but fugitive slaves are by no means a desirable class of immigrants for Canada, especially when they come in large numbers."

Abolitionists and black journalists called such attitudes, appropriately, "Colorphobia," and they defined the treatment of black Canadians in every aspect of life in Toronto—from white demands for segregated schools (admittedly, more of a problem in cities and towns outside Toronto) to the "polite," and not so polite, racism blacks encountered in their daily dealings with whites when, for example, they sat down in a restaurant or attempted to rent or buy a house in a neighbourhood outside of Macaulay Town. Likewise, it manifested itself in the less-than-fair justice meted out to blacks brought before police magistrate George Taylor Denison III, a wealthy supporter of the British empire and one-time city councillor and militia commander, who was notoriously pro-South during the American Civil War and entertained both Confederate general Robert E. Lee and Jefferson Davis, the president of the Confederacy, when they later visited Toronto.

The noble crusade against slavery, however, tugged at the hearts of many good Christian white men like George Brown. The *Globe* publisher and editor may not have wanted to hire a black printer, but he found slavery a stain on civilization that had to be blotted away. (Brown courted black votes when he was running as a Reformer in the 1850s, and he was shocked and appalled when he was presented with a petition from 150 white supporters who promised him their vote if he agreed to press for a law excluding blacks from public schools and to advocate a head tax on those wanting to come to Canada.) The *Globe* regularly published editorials denouncing the evils of slavery and the Fugitive Slave Act, and argued that in the name of "the laws of humanity," Canada must accept every fugitive slave who made it across the border. Brown and the members of his family were instrumental in establishing the Anti-Slavery Society of Canada in 1851. Headed by Rev. Dr. Michael Willis, a Presbyterian minister and professor of theology at Knox College, the society helped four hundred fugitives settle in the city during the next six years and raised more than $2,000 for them.

One of the society's major events was a lecture series in the spring of 1851, organized in conjunction with representatives of the black community, which brought Samuel J. May, a white American abolitionist; George Thompson, a British parliamentarian and anti-slavery advocate; and Frederick Douglass, the former slave and abolitionist, to Toronto. St. Lawrence Hall was packed on the evening of April 2, when Thompson, well known as an orator, delivered a passionate lecture entitled "The Evils of Slavery."

The following year, Brown reprinted excerpts from *Uncle Tom's Cabin*, the sensational and heart-wrenching anti-slavery novel by Harriet Beecher Stowe. Partly inspired by the experiences of Josiah Henson, a fugitive slave who made it to Upper Canada in 1830 and published his memoirs in 1849 (and who played a key role in the establishment of Dawn, a black settlement near Dresden, in 1842), the novel was dramatized in a celebrated play at Toronto's Lyceum Theatre to enthusiastic sold-out white audiences, who never would have understood the hypocrisy of their actions. Clearly, it was one thing to sympathize with the plight of Tom and Eliza, and quite another to socialize with the blacks they encountered on the streets of Toronto.

THE RINGING OF THE BELLS of St. James Cathedral at midnight on June 30, 1867, signified that the Dominion of Canada was now a reality, and despite the inequities of their lives, the city's black population joined with most of the other fifty thousand citizens of Toronto—the majority of whom were British Anglicans, Irish Protestants, and Scottish Presbyterians, with a couple of hundred Jews, Quakers, and assorted others—to celebrate the glory and promise offered by Confederation on July 1, 1867. There was much excitement and great "rejoicing" all that day and evening, hot and humid like many summer days in Toronto. Conyngham Crawford Taylor, an early Toronto memoirist and travel writer, later described, "What with bonfires, fireworks and illuminations, excursions, military displays and musical and other entertainments, the citizens and the thousands who crowded the streets did not want for amusement." For the poor, there was a meal of roast ox for all who desired it.

Confederation might have been worked out at animated conferences in Charlottetown and Quebec City over a three-year period, but it was very much a Toronto-driven scheme. Canada's first prime minister, the colourful and charismatic John A. Macdonald, was the face of the new Dominion, and rightly so; and it was his French-Canadian counterpart, George-Étienne Cartier, who delivered Quebec. Yet it could be argued that without the magnanimity and vision of George Brown, who embraced Confederation and his two Tory rivals—and the hostility between Brown and Macdonald, a decade in the making, was especially deep and bitter—the whole plan may well have collapsed, a fact that even Lord Monck, the governor general, conceded to Brown some months later.

During the preceding two decades, Brown, ironically, had made Conservative Toronto the headquarters for the new country's Grit-Reform (Liberal) party. At the historic Reform Convention held at St. Lawrence Hall in November 1859, Brown convinced the delegates that the answer to the intractable political divisions in the province of Canada was a new federal structure, in which contentious issues like separate schools could be dealt with more effectively at the local level. Achieving this restructuring did not happen overnight, but in 1864, with the assembly facing yet another deadlock, Brown wisely offered to join Macdonald and Cartier in a "Great Coalition," provided they agreed to support a federal union of Canada East and Canada West, or a broader confederation with the colonies in the Maritimes. Expansion to the northwest, which Brown endorsed, was also a future possibility. Macdonald and Cartier welcomed Brown's initiative, and Confederation eventually became a reality.

On June 30, 1867, Brown had stayed up most of the night composing a nine-thousand-word article about the story and meaning of Confederation that took up the entire front page of the *Globe* on July 1. "We hail the birthday of a new nationality," he wrote. "A United British America, with its four millions of people, takes its place this day among the nations of the world."

From a purely Toronto perspective, Confederation returned to the city its status as a capital, now of the new province of Ontario, with the attendant power that went with that designation. As it looked toward the millennium and experienced the full measure of the Industrial Revolution, Toronto's leadership in the Dominion and its concerns about assuming excessive responsibility for British North American debt were about to be put to the test.

Chapter Five

HOGTOWN THE GOOD

"Down to the docks" led deeper and deeper into city life, into the essential Toronto of pickup and delivery and redistribution of wealth...

—HUGH HOOD, 1975

Transporting Torontonians around the city efficiently always has been an issue embroiled in controversy since the Toronto Street Railway Company was launched with horse-drawn trams in 1861. *Library and Archives Canada / PA-171131*

WILLIAM DAVIES was a man on a mission. He wanted to produce high-quality bacon and sell it far and wide. Born in England and raised as a Baptist, Davies came to Toronto in 1854 at the age of twenty-three with his wife Emma and the first of their twelve children. Having gained experience in the grocery and meat business before he left England, he soon opened up a small operation in Toronto, the William Davies Company. Success brought expansion, and by 1860 he was exporting large quantities of bacon to England. As demand outstripped supply, he expanded again. Within a decade he was raising his own hogs, as opposed to purchasing them already butchered, and had opened an impressive packing plant on Front Street East and Overend Avenue, close to the mouth of the Don River.

The secret to his success, as business historian Michael Bliss has noted, was "constant attention to quality, reinvestment of profits, and determined innovation." His hogs were lighter and leaner, and his Wiltshire Sides bacon tastier. His profits reached approximately $30,000 annually by the 1880s.

Health problems eventually stymied Davies. He went deaf and his two eldest sons, James and William, became ill with tuberculosis. In 1892, Davies sought out a partner, Joseph Flavelle, a devout Methodist and astute businessman, who had already established himself as a provisions merchant. With Flavelle at the helm, the William Davies

Company became the largest pork-packing enterprise in the British Empire and hence earned Toronto the epithet "Hogtown." Flavelle himself was one of Toronto's and Canada's wealthiest men, a generous philanthropist involved with the University of Toronto and the Toronto General Hospital, and associated with the Bank of Commerce, National Trust Company, and Simpson's department stores.

Davies—who, despite his ailments, lived until March 1921, two months shy of his ninetieth birthday—as well as Flavelle, a millionaire with a conscience, were products of the late Victorian era. For them and other members of the ruling elite, industrialization, urbanization, and technological innovations—steam power, electricity, and the telegraph among them—were exhilarating as well as distressing. Change and imperfections abounded. A personal response to this perceived upheaval was to lead a virtuous life that stressed diligence, piety, and, in the case of Flavelle and other prominent Toronto Methodists such as Timothy Eaton and Hart Massey, sobriety. These men valued their families and believed it was essential to give back to society, enhancing community institutions such as hospitals and universities and sharing their wealth with the less fortunate. But their philanthropy and sense of morality were also derived from their wealth and class, which in turn fostered a superiority that bordered on arrogance. It was such a world view that produced the notion of "Toronto the Good" and the quest for moral perfection.

In truth, they were fighting an uphill battle. Industrialization and the demand for factory workers transformed the city in a variety of ways. Toronto's population more than tripled, from 56,000 in 1871 to 208,000 by 1901. Part of that growth was due to geographic expansion, which extended the city proper west to High Park and the Humber, north into the bushland beyond Yorkville Village (which was finally forced to surrender its independence in 1883 to secure an adequate water supply), and east of the Don. Queen Street, for instance, reached the Beaches by 1891, and in the vicinity of Danforth and Broadview, the real estate developer and dreamy self-promoter Ernest A. Macdonald—an alderman who also served as mayor of Toronto in 1900—continually advanced the interests of his small community of Chester, which ultimately became part of Toronto in 1909. Also captured within that geographic span was the area west of Spadina Avenue immortalized as "the Annex," since it was literally annexed by the city in 1887; Seaton Village, west of Bathurst, which became part of Toronto a year later; and the town of Parkdale, soon to be a fashionable residential neighbourhood, which followed a year after that.

Farther west still was High Park, given to the city by architect, surveyor, and civil engineer John Howard, who had acquired the vast estate in 1837. (In return, Howard and his wife, Jemima, received an annual pension of $1,200.) Howard was born in England in 1803, where he had been known as John Corby. He changed his name to Howard when he came to Upper Canada in 1832 with his wife, Jemima. Corby was the last name of the man his mother had married after he was born, and Howard claimed that he was actually a descendant of Thomas Howard, the fourth Duke of Norfolk, although that was likely wishful thinking. At the time Howard transferred the property to the city in 1873, the deed stipulated that the park remain "for the free use, benefit and enjoyment of the citizens of Toronto." Through further acquisitions, the city expanded the park twice, first in 1875 and again in 1930. Still, it took a while to transform the park into the inviting green space it is today and to make it accessible. Until proper boat and train service started in the 1880s, it was not an easy place to visit. Once that problem was solved, thousands of Torontonians trekked to the park each Sunday, especially in the summer.

One shocking and tragic episode occurred in July 1882. At that time, Howard (who died in 1890) was serving as a forest ranger, tasked with the duty of enhancing the site. To ward off hunters—wildlife was then plentiful—and trespassers, he hired as his assistant John Albert, a former American police constable with a tough law-and-order attitude. One evening in late July 1882, Albert came across a few teenage boys rafting on Grenadier Pond in an area where visitors were not permitted. Inexplicably, he shot a round over their heads and then apprehended one of the boys, Andrew Young. He pointed his pistol at Young's face and the gun accidentally went off, killing him. Even for the late-nineteenth-century version of law and order this was an overreaction that led to a needless tragedy. Two months later, Albert was found guilty of murder and sentenced to hang, but the death sentence was commuted by the federal government to life imprisonment.

NO MATTER HOW LARGE THE CITY GREW, there were a few constants. Toronto still remained a city divided by religion and even more by class. It was also solidly "WASP"—the operative word being "White." In 1882, when the postal service appointed Albert Jackson, a former African-American slave, as a mailman, the other mailmen protested and Jackson was soon demoted to being a hall porter. Only a protest by the black community, and the intervention of Prime Minister Sir John A. Macdonald, got Jackson back his job.

The vast majority of Toronto's citizens, no matter their station or place of origin—and by 1891, 65 percent were native born, mainly Ontarian—had roots in Great Britain or Ireland. The city was a bastion of Britishness and Protestantism, with each denomination having a plethora of churches for their flocks. "If the sons and daughters of Toronto are not as moral and godly as they can be made," one local journalist commented, "the failing is not by any means due to the lack of churches, nor of divines to teach them to shun the path of the wicked, and cling to that which is 'lawful and right, and save their souls alive.'"

On an average Sunday, people attended church twice, and many regarded the Lord's Day as sacred. The so-called blue laws, which restricted almost every activity except praying, were firmly enforced. William T. Crosweller, a British visitor in the 1890s, was less than impressed. "Altogether, Sunday in Toronto is as melancholy and suicidal a sort of day as Puritan principles can make it," he wrote in his book about his North American travels. "The Toronto Sabbath is still as gloomy and forbidding as the English institution in its palmy days."

Irish Catholics remained the proverbial outsiders, and the violence of earlier years erupted from time to time. By far the worst riot in the city's history of clashing Catholics and Protestants occurred in October 1875 during a pilgrimage parade to mark Pope Pius IX's declaration of a sacred Jubilee. This was the last and largest of a dozen such pilgrimages to various Catholic churches that had taken place in Toronto through the summer and early fall of 1875. Apart from insults and a few stones being directed at the participants by Orange onlookers, most of these religious marches had proceeded without serious trouble. Mayor Francis "Old Square-toes" Medcalf, though a lifelong Orangeman and a former Canada West grandmaster, had ensured that the Catholic pilgrims were properly protected by the police. However, an altercation had ensued during a parade on September 26, when the stone throwing got out of hand (shots were also fired), so the city was on high alert when another parade was planned for the following Sunday, October 3.

Toronto press opinion was mixed; most newspapers condemned the rioters, but blamed the Catholics, nonetheless, for public religious displays that deliberately provoked large segments of the city's population. Orange groups like the Young Britons were of the same mind, insisting that the pilgrimages violated the "tranquility" of the Sunday Sabbath and were "calculated to enflame the public mind." (Established in Toronto in the late 1860s, the Young Britons attracted men in their late teens and early twenties who enjoyed tavern life and possessed a sense of militant Protestant entitlement over what went on in their city.) At a well-attended Orange rally held at St. Lawrence Hall on October 1, one passionate speaker proclaimed that if yet another Catholic parade went ahead on Sunday, "the streets of Toronto would be flooded with innocent blood." Mayor Medcalf again defended the legal rights of the marchers, but played to the exuberant crowd with his declaration that the law ought to be changed forbidding such processions.

Sure enough, on the day of the pilgrimage, despite the presence of a large contingent of police (the force was still overwhelmingly Protestant) and soldiers, a bloody riot ensued. The trouble started soon after the close to two thousand men, women, and children who were taking part departed from their first stop at St. Michael's Cathedral on Church Street, north of Shuter Street. The defiant young men of the Hibernian Benevolent

Society and the even more nationalistic Young Irishmen were among them. Needless to say, their hatred for the Young Britons was intense. Nearly eight thousand people congregated nearby, and many of them were angry young Orangemen.

In a matter of minutes, stones were thrown and shots fired. The police and militia men did what they could, but the crowd of Protestants and Catholics was far too big for them to control. The battle raged from Church and Yonge Streets all the way over to St. Mary's Church on Adelaide Street West and Bathurst Street and then back to St. Paul's Church at Queen and Parliament Streets. All down Queen Street, fierce fighting took place between mainly anti-Catholic mobs and the police, who were trying to halt the assault. Catholic churches and taverns were attacked, resulting in massive property damage and retaliation from those inside these buildings. Even the intervention of the cavalry did not stop the battle, which continued well into the evening. Remarkably, no one died in the melee.

In the aftermath, public officials and the press, regardless of their political affiliation, condemned the riot and the bigotry as a day of "disgrace" in Toronto. Despite its past history of anti-Catholicism, the *Globe*, too, denounced the attack on the parade as "contrary to the most cherished principles of Protestantism." Surprisingly, considering the number of people involved, only twenty-nine men were arrested. Of those, only fifteen—ten Protestants and five Catholics, all of whom could be described as working class except Fallis Johnson, a prominent Protestant merchant and property owner—were indicted, most for "riot and assault." Only nine, all Protestants, were found guilty (with strong legal representation and political help, Johnson was acquitted), though each received only minor jail sentences of two or three months. For a long time, accusations were hurled back and forth between the rival communities about what had happened on October 3, 1875. The animosity between Catholics and Protestants persisted in the city, designating it, at least for a brief time, "the Belfast of Canada."

Three years later, a visit by the Irish Fenian leader O'Donovan Rossa from his home in New York City caused another outcry. (Rossa was later implicated as a leader in the 1880s "Fenian dynamite campaign," which saw bombings in several English cities including London and Manchester.) When Rossa arrived in Toronto in mid-March 1878, he was taken to a packed St. Patrick Hall, connected to St. Lawrence Hall at the market, to deliver his speech. Outside, four thousand unhappy and angry Orangemen gathered into the early evening. Before too long the booing and singing of Orange songs turned ugly; stones flew and the glass windows shattered. It took until two in the morning before the police could quiet the mob.

There were other Protestant–Catholic clashes during the next decade. Yet the actions of the police became more professional and neutral, and Torontonians, no matter their particular religious affiliation, refused to put up with riots and rowdies in their streets. The Orange Order purposely curtailed any further violence and made every effort to rein in the passions of the Young Britons. Though religious intolerance did not vanish from Toronto—animosity towards Catholics remained a staple of a few Toronto newspapers, and the establishment of the anti-Catholic Protestant Protective Association, a political lobby group with a membership of three thousand in Toronto in 1893, fanned the flames of religious prejudice—Protestants and Catholics learned to coexist in relative peace in neighbourhoods and factories.

IF TORONTONIANS WERE NOT PRAYING to the Almighty or fighting about religious differences, they were engaged, in one way or another, in the world spawned by the industrial revolution. Down by the waterfront and close to the railway yards, clouds of dark smoke from nearby factories hovered over the city, a sure sign that Toronto had entered the age of progress. In 1871, the city had 497 manufacturing enterprises; twenty years later there were 2,109. Magazine editor and city booster G. Mercer Adam, for one, was impressed. "The industrial and social evolution of Toronto, especially within the last two decades," he wrote in 1891, "is so remarkable as to be almost without a parallel in the history of the communities of the New World." That was an exaggeration to be sure; members of the Toronto business community were constantly peering over their shoulders to see how they matched up against Montreal. And losing the contract to build the Canadian Pacific Railway to the Montreal group led by Sir Hugh Allan rankled for a long time. Still, these men supported the proliferation of wholesalers and retailers. Iron foundries like the Toronto Locomotive Works and Toronto Rolling Mills, owned by David L. Macpherson (who had headed Toronto's bid for the CPR) and Casimir Gzowski, employed three hundred men. Within the city's industrial core there were shoe and tobacco operations, and wholesalers that distributed everything from stoves to pianos. Backing these various enterprises was an extensive banking network, the real beginnings of the city's ascent as a financial behemoth.

William McMaster's career showed a typical progression. A clerk in Ireland, he rose to become the most successful wholesale dry goods merchant in Toronto and from there to be, in 1866, one of the founders of the Bank of Commerce, among his numerous other business interests. He was installed as the bank's president a year later, a position he held for nearly two decades. A wealthy man, much of his nearly million-dollar estate was donated to the university that bears his name, which was relocated from Toronto to Hamilton in 1930. The original site of McMaster University on Bloor Street West became the home of the Royal Conservatory of Music in 1962.

Among McMaster's contemporaries was George Cox, an insurance executive, bank executive, ardent Liberal Party supporter, and newspaper owner. Cox had a stake in both the *Globe* (after George Brown's death) and the *Toronto Daily Star*, which had been established as the *Evening Star* in 1892 before it was bought out in 1899 by Cox and other Liberals. There was also James Austin, who made a fortune selling groceries, purchased the Spadina property from the Baldwins in 1866, and was instrumental in the founding of the Dominion Bank in 1871; and his partner Edmund B. Osler, a major shareholder in the Dominion and a pioneer of the stock business, who played a key role in building up the Toronto Stock Exchange. Osler's commercial interests in banking, railways, and land extended across the country.

Two merchants of a different breed during this era, no less significant to Toronto's development, were Timothy Eaton and Robert Simpson. Before Eaton and Simpson transformed the retail business, shopping meant "doing King." The highlights on King Street within a few blocks east and west of Yonge Street included Thomas Thompson's emporium, The Mammoth, and Robert Walker and Sons' Golden Lion (there was a large statue of a stone lion on the roof of the three-storey Italianate building, as well as a slightly smaller gilded one above the entrance), which was by all accounts "the finest retail clothing house in the Dominion." Eaton and Simpson permanently shifted the focus of Toronto shoppers north to Queen and Yonge Streets at a time when the downtown was gradually shifting westward along King towards Yonge and Bay.

One of Timothy Eaton's employees once described him as "diligent in business, fervent in spirit, serving the Lord. He never smoked, played cards, danced or drank, and would not have those who drank about him if he could help it." That was an apt depiction, though "diligent in business" does not quite capture the sheer force of Eaton's drive and personality. "We are made [to] work," he told his brother James in April 1870, "and as long as the Lord gives me a continuation of health and energy, I am determined to work and work with a will." Guided by the motto "honesty, quality and service," Eaton started each workday by dissecting the previous day's sales. He had learned the intricacies of retailing as a young man in Northern Ireland, where he was born in 1834, and steadily built his business empire step by step almost from the moment he arrived in Upper Canada in 1854.

He and his brother James opened a small general store in Kirkton, north of London, Ontario, and then relocated the business to nearby St. Marys, before he decided to end the partnership and venture out on his own in Toronto in 1869. By then he had converted to Methodism and married Margaret Beattie from Woodstock. They already had one daughter, Kathleen, the first of their large brood of eight children.

Initially Eaton ran a wholesale business on Front Street West before finding his niche and legacy in a dry goods operation he purchased from fellow Methodists at 178 Yonge Street, south of Queen Street. Here, in an area of the city regarded as somewhat dingy compared to King Street, he was to define the term "department store" and make his mark as one of the giants of the Canadian retail industry.

Several factors contributed to his success. He was one of the first merchants to truly grasp consumer behaviour. Eaton innately understood the concept of a bargain and the value of advertising. By 1900, Eaton's ran a full-page ad every day in the *Toronto Daily Star*, the newspaper he had helped financially launch as a Liberal Party organ a year earlier (the paper was renamed the *Toronto Star* in 1971).

He targeted middle- and lower-middle-class buyers by offering them fair prices, but on a cash basis only. Buying on credit, which was the current practice at almost every other store, was not permitted. As his biographer, Joy Santink, points out, despite the long-held myth, Eaton was not the first merchant to implement such a policy. "Many North American urban merchants," Santink writes, "had found that selling for cash allowed them to offer cheaper prices and thereby increase their volume of sales."

Still, few customers left Eaton's feeling cheated, and the long-term loyalty he built among his growing clientele nicely enhanced his balance sheet. Annual sales increased from $25,416 in 1870 to $154,000 by 1880 and $244,000 by 1895. That trend continued upward in the early years of the twentieth century when he opened his own wholesale depot; built a brand new and modern department store—complete with a hydraulic elevator—north of Queen Street (with several more property expansions); and, most famously, started dispatching his mail-order catalogue far and wide. Eaton became a wealthy man, living in an opulent mansion he built at the corner of Lowther Avenue and Spadina Road, which was certainly a boon for the Annex neighbourhood. His numerous philanthropic endeavours included supporting the building of Western Methodist Church close to his house (later Trinity United Church, which after a merger in 1980 became part of Trinity-St. Paul's United Church).

Like a majority of merchants and business owners of this period, Eaton had a paternalistic attitude to his employees—from four employees in 1869, the company grew to a remarkable seven thousand by 1907—though he was slightly more enlightened than most. At a huge New Year's Eve celebration he hosted on the second floor of the store in 1898, he proclaimed his wish that in the future the word "employee" might be replaced by "fellow-associate." It was a pipe dream to be sure, but he was regarded as a good and decent boss by the men and women who worked for him.

Most retail stores in Toronto were open from 8 AM to 9 or 10 PM, six days a week. Eaton sensibly reduced the lengthy workweek from eighty-five hours to a more tolerable eighty, with a closing time of six o'clock on Saturdays and even earlier during the summer months. He also offered opportunity for advancement. Twenty-five-year-old Harry McGee went from sweeping floors for six dollars a week in 1883 to managing the carpet department a year later for eight dollars a week plus commission. Single female clerks—married women were never hired—were almost always paid less than men (by approximately three to four dollars a week), as was the practice elsewhere.

Eaton's chief competitor was Robert Simpson, who was born in Scotland the same year as Eaton. His story is similar as well. He came to Canada in 1855 at the age of twenty and worked as a clerk in a general store in Newmarket. By 1867 he had his own impressive store there. A fire nearly drove him out of business in 1870, but he regrouped and opened a new dry goods store in Toronto on Yonge Street near Queen in 1872. While Simpson may have had a drinking problem and was not as skilful an accountant as Eaton—at the time of the fire in Newmarket in 1870 he was publicly accused of "a most culpable carelessness in the conduct of his business" for not having sufficient insurance to cover his vast stock—he continued to expand his operation, though not quite to the extent Eaton did. However, he was just as innovative: Simpson had "coloured dodgers" or flyers distributed across the city publicizing his store and goods. He was crippled by another fire in 1895 and had no choice but to rebuild his six-storey department store on the southwest corner of Yonge and Queen Streets. This time he erected a fireproof steel frame structure, the first in Canada, complete with a restaurant and thirty-five departments staffed by five hundred employees to serve his enthusiastic customers. Never in great health, Simpson died in December 1897, and the company was eventually taken over for $135,000 by a trio of competent businessmen, Harris Fudger, Joseph Flavelle, and Alfred E. Ames. Like Eaton's, Simpson's had great success with the mail-order business and soon began opening stores across the country.

Another businessman who came to Toronto from an outlying community was Hart Massey. He had taken over his father's foundry in Newcastle, Ontario, expanded it to produce agricultural implements, and saw it flourish after the federal government put in place a protective tariff that excluded American competitors from the market (the Toronto Board of Trade had endorsed this tariff). Massey soon operated the city's largest factory on a sizable tract of King Street West with seven hundred employees. The Massey harvester was marketed throughout Canada and the elder Massey and his sons established a dynasty—especially after their merger with the rival Harris Company in 1891—whose commercial and philanthropic interests persist to the present day.

Vincent Massey, who in 1952 became Canada's first Canadian-born governor general, recalled his grandfather as a "tall gaunt frock-coated figure, his features softened by a white beard, driving to church in an over-full landau behind a pair of well-chosen coach-horses with an old coloured coachman in antique garb on the box, while on the back seat he sat in supreme enjoyment with his adored grandchildren tumbling about his knees, a patriarchal figure of the old school." As a loving grandson, Vincent was being too kind, a fact that he privately conceded to his own sons. Hart Massey, Vincent also remembered, had been "bred in a narrow faith."

Another devout Methodist capitalist, Massey was indeed a generous philanthropist, yet he also had a large ego that required stroking and was intolerant of criticism.

Like a shepherd tending his flock, he watched over and mentored his workers, recognized those who had given him long service, and even provided employees with a library. So entrenched was this paternalistic attitude that when confronted with a challenge to his authority, as when an employee supported a union, Massey lashed out. In the old days, an employer like Massey would have had the last word, but this was changing.

HART MASSEY, TIMOTHY EATON, ROBERT SIMPSON, and other leading lights of late-nineteenth-century capitalism in Toronto understood that with the right amount of financial support and entrepreneurial acumen, there was a great deal of money to be made. But they also knew that the accumulation of profit required skilled and unskilled labour—and the cheaper the better. Canadian business owners were eventually forced to face the fact that their workers expected decent wages, tolerable working conditions, shorter and fairer hours, recognition for unions, and more out of life than they were willing to offer. Whether they realized it or not, a bitter class struggle was looming.

At every step, labour was challenged by an elite which maintained that unions were evil, collective bargaining destructive, and it was their God-given right to make as much money as they could. From the perspective of business owners, labour's demands for radical change were unacceptable and they used any means at their disposal—lockouts, police intervention, non-unionized workers ("scabs" or "rats" to the unionized), and even violence if required.

George Brown of the *Globe*, a model of Victorian liberalism, was less inclined to resort to brutality, yet he was just as adamant that he had the right to run his newspaper as he saw fit. In assessing the actions of Edward Gurney, a stove manufacturer who became embroiled in a clash with the Moulders Union in 1870 and 1871 and brought in replacement workers from Buffalo, the *Globe* pointed out that "everyone must have perfect liberty to dispose of his labour in the way he deems best, without interruption, intimidation, or insult."

A year later, Brown himself was faced with disgruntled printers, who asserted that they wanted to replace their ten-hour working day with one that was nine hours, with a wage raise of a few cents an hour. When the skilled night compositors had first approached him, Brown had acquiesced. Yet he drew the line when the less-skilled printers demanded similar contracts. His Scottish temper was roused. He dismissed out of hand the Typographical Union members who worked for him and castigated them as "being too lazy to earn their bread." All Brown's fellow newspaper owners sided with him in the Master Printers' Association he initiated except James Beaty, the outspoken publisher of the *Leader* and then a Conservative MP.

Beaty was a loyal supporter of John A. Macdonald, despite the Tory chieftain's unhappiness with the quality and direction of the newspaper, and he was no fan of Brown, which meant he was more than happy to have an opportunity to publicly oppose the *Globe* publisher. Throughout the labour dispute, Beaty, who had a soft spot for the workers, supported their position. (A year earlier, he had taken a much harsher position with shoe workers, who were making what he regarded as unreasonable wage and union demands of Toronto shoe factory owners.)

The printers went out on strike on March 25, 1872, and for a brief time their protest was the talk of the city. Unable to shut down the *Globe* or any other affected newspaper, the strikers countered with their own paper, the *Ontario Workman*, to condemn the capitalist tyranny confronting them. A pro-strike rally was held at St. Lawrence Hall on April 3, and Beaty was the keynote speaker. "What has produced the capital?" he asked the enthusiastic audience. "Why the labouring class! It is the labour put on raw material which gives all the value."

Brown continued to marshal his forces and was supported by the owners and managers of other Toronto papers, who were determined to quash the nine-hour movement. As a final resort, Brown used the justice system to bring down the strikers, since at the time it was an indictable offence to collectively conspire to impede the flow of daily business; in other words, unions were technically illegal. On April 16, more than a dozen strike leaders—among them printer Edward "Ned" Clarke, later the editor of the influential *Orange Sentinel* and a future mayor of Toronto, who as a politician milked his status as a working-class martyr—were arrested "on grounds of conspiring to keep other workmen from their employment."

Though initial legal proceedings were started against the strikers, they were soon rescued by an unlikely saviour: Prime Minister Macdonald. Never one to miss a chance to score political points, Macdonald, urged on by labour advocates in Ottawa and elsewhere, pushed through the Trade Unions Act in Parliament, giving Canadian workers the same rights as workers in England and making unions legal. While Macdonald was hailed as "a working man" at a festive gathering in mid-July at the Toronto Music Hall and benefited from working-class support in the October 1872 federal election, behind the scenes he was doing his best to assure Toronto capitalists he was still one with them.

For years, Macdonald had been trying to establish a conservative newspaper in Toronto that could challenge the mighty *Globe*—the detested "Grit Organ" to the Tories. Beaty's *Leader*, Macdonald decided, was not up to the task. Nor was John Ross Robertson's "attention-grabbing" but, from a partisan perspective, highly undependable *Daily Telegraph*, which since 1866 had been wooing Toronto newspaper readers with catchy news stories, like a sensational interview with Louis Riel in 1870. Riel had imprisoned

Robertson when he arrived at Red River, gave him the interview he wanted, and then banished him from the settlement. Robertson went on to build up the *Telegraph* as an influential Tory Orange newspaper. He was an avid chronicler of the city, a tireless promoter of amateur hockey, and a generous philanthropist who gave millions to the Hospital for Sick Children after his only daughter died from scarlet fever in 1882. He also had a reputation for being inflexible; his grandson, John Gilbee Robertson, later commented, "I never liked that son of a bitch."

In early 1872, Macdonald brought together a group of wealthy Toronto investors to establish the *Mail*. Among those who heeded Macdonald's call for funds were Frank Smith, a prominent Ontario Catholic businessman whom Macdonald had recently appointed to the Senate; John Sandfield Macdonald, the first premier of Ontario; and David L. Macpherson, who had headed the Toronto team that vied for the lucrative contract to build the Canadian Pacific Railway. John A. himself contributed $10,000 to the enterprise, a fair amount for someone who continually struggled with his personal finances.

For the newspaper's first editor, Macdonald recruited Thomas Patteson, a thirty-six-year-old government bureaucrat, lawyer, and journalist. If the venture did not pan out, Patteson was promised a federal government appointment. It was Patteson who urged John A. to adopt a policy of economic protection to counter the Liberals' free trade platform. Soon after, protective tariffs became a key plank in Macdonald's National Policy.

The arrival of the *Mail* temporarily forced Robertson and the *Telegraph* out of business. He was back four years later with the more enduring and decidedly independent *Evening Telegram*. Robertson could get under the skin of the politicians he criticized in his paper. One afternoon in June 1891, Ewart Farquhar, a contractor and city alderman, waited outside the *Telegram*'s offices. When Robertson finally came out, Farquhar beat him with a whip. The two men fought briefly until a third man, unknown to both of them, pelted them with eggs. Later, Robertson found Farquhar, threw him to the ground, and got his revenge. "As he lay there," Robertson recounted, "I read one of my editorials to him."

The first edition of the *Mail* was published on the morning of March 30, 1872, in the midst of the printers' strike, with a declaration that suggested it was not the party organ it was certainly designed to be. "With honest endeavour to do justice to the claims of new ideas and to the irresistible force of progress, the *Mail* will steer clear of partisanship," Patteson had penned. "Not local purposes, not local prejudices ought to guide, but the general good." In truth, such respectful niceties meant little. "The first number is a good one—for a first number," Macdonald told Patteson. "You must assume an appearance of dignity at the outset. The sooner, however, that you put on the war paint and commence to scalp the better." About the printers' strike, he added this: "You must take great care not to offend the employers of labour in this nine hours movement. When the present excitement is over you must look to them and to the employed for support. At the same time there is, of course, no necessity for your running your head against the navvies in the way that the *Globe* is doing."

Patteson lasted at the *Mail* until 1877, when financial problems forced him out and the newspaper was taken over by John Riordan, a St. Catharines paper manufacturer who was owed $26,000. According to Patteson, Macdonald "actually wept" when he lost control of the *Mail*. Nonetheless, for the next decade the paper was fairly supportive of John A. and the Tories, until, under the direction of editor Christopher Bunting, an Ulsterman, it became virulently anti-Catholic, alienating many of the Conservative Party's Irish and French supporters. Even the *Globe*, an ardent critic of Catholicism, was fairer to Ontario Catholics than the *Mail*. During the 1886 federal election, Macdonald had no choice but to cut all party ties with the *Mail*. The newspaper then declared itself to be independent and, interestingly, its circulation started to climb.

By this time the *Globe* was under the control of a syndicate led by Robert Jaffray and George Cox. They had acquired the newspaper from the Brown family after George Brown's death. On March 25, 1880, Brown had been working at his *Globe* office when he was interrupted by an angry and intoxicated former employee, George Bennett, who had been fired when he showed up for work drunk. Bennett demanded Brown sign a document indicating he had worked for the newspaper for the past five years. Brown was busy and told Bennett to obtain the signature he required from the foreman he had reported to. Unhappy with that suggestion, Bennett became indignant and a heated argument ensued. Suddenly, Bennett took a revolver from his pocket. Brown tried to grab the gun, but in the struggle the weapon fired, hitting Brown in the leg. Brown was examined by a doctor who assured him that he had only sustained a "flesh wound," but the leg soon became gangrenous and on May 9 the Father of Confederation, who as publisher and editor of the *Globe* had put Toronto on the map as much as anyone, died at the age of 61. George Bennett was convicted of murder and hanged, going to the gallows denying that he had intended to kill Brown.

IN THE 1880S, the new key player in the Toronto labour scene confronting Hart Massey and other business owners was the Knights of Labor, an American- based trade union association, which at its peak in 1886 had successfully organized fifty-three locals in Toronto representing about five thousand workers. The Knights supported the Toronto Trades Council and helped promote the Trades and Labour Council convention that was held in the city, to great fanfare, in 1883. The Knights were not radical; their leaders favoured negotiation and arbitration, not violent strikes. Led by Daniel O'Donoghue, who began working as a printer in Ottawa as a teenager in the late 1850s and in time was one of the country's most notable labour leaders, the Knights refused to be pushed around. The group was supported, too, by the writings of journalist Phillips Thompson, who was associated with several Toronto newspapers and was a leading authority on labour issues in the city and country.

Matters came to a head at the Massey factory in February 1886 over reduced wages. Massey would not meet with a Knights delegation and then fired without cause five of his workers, whom he identified as leaders of the local. The Knights were outraged and O'Donoghue castigated Massey as a "brute... devoid of soul." Support for the strikers swept through the city. Initially Massey's plant was guarded by the police, but after a delegation of workers met with the new mayor, William Howland—who was sympathetic to the labour movement, which had helped get him elected that year—the police were removed. Faced with the possibility of other workers joining the strike, Massey capitulated five days later. With what was surely great reluctance, he reinstated the men he had fired and accepted the Knights of Labor local in his factory. Massey had no more problems with his workers, and O'Donoghue and other labour leaders now understood that collective action could indeed yield the results they wanted.

To an extent, that was also evident during the much more bitter confrontation at the Toronto Street Railway Company (TSR) a month later. In 1881, Frank Smith (who was appointed to Prime Minister Macdonald's cabinet as a minister without portfolio a year later) gained control of the TSR from Alexander Easton. At that point there were ten years remaining on the thirty-year-monopoly contract Easton had signed with the city in 1861. Under the terms of the agreement, Easton, and now Smith, was to maintain the area in and around the tracks, pay the city an annual per car licence fee of five dollars, and not run streetcars on Sunday (this last became the most contentious issue of the 1890s).

An astute entrepreneur, Smith turned the TSR into a "goldmine" and "bonanza," as Toronto's chief satirist J.W. Bengough depicted so cuttingly in his popular weekly journal *Grip*. Smith cut corners, did not maintain the paving around the tracks, used old horse-drawn cars, and compelled his workers to toil fourteen-hour days, six days a week, for less than nine dollars a week (a paltry ten cents an hour). In 1890 the TSR showed a profit of $165,500, which did not include hundreds of thousands of dollars Smith received in bonuses and dividends. This was indeed a handsome—some said obscene—return for his initial $7,500 investment in the company.

TSR workers soon tired of Smith's bullying, though he later insisted he was a "friend of the labouring man." Urged on by the Knights of Labor, the street railway workers walked off the job on March 10, having organized themselves into a Knights local. This action was precipitated by Smith's decision to fire any worker who was identified as joining the local union—a contravention of a binding agreement Smith had forced his men to sign some months earlier. When Smith attempted to use non-union drivers and conductors to keep the streetcars running, the company's operations were disrupted by blockades.

Within a few days, the crowds challenging the non-union drivers grew larger—an estimated seven thousand by the third day of the walkout—and more ornery. Mud, stones, and bricks were routinely hurled in their direction. Smith countered with a threat to sue the city for failing to keep the streets clear and demanded city hall provide police protection, a move immediately denounced by Mayor William Howland. "You have by your act," Howland publicly declared, "produced this trouble." Nevertheless, as the strikers and their numerous supporters—average Torontonians who were dependent on the streetcars and resented Frank Smith's tyrannical behaviour—became more violent, the police had to step in to break up fights, and arrests were made.

The strikers had the strong backing of the *Evening News*, the *Mail*'s lowbrow yet sensational penny offspring (its critics called the paper a "sewer journal"). It had been established in 1881 and was soon operated and owned by the debonair and all-around rabble-rouser Edmund E. Sheppard. Distinguished by his plug hat, cloak, and high leather boots, he had, by one account, a "raffish charm" and a "fondness for chewing tobacco." Within a year, Sheppard was to be a key part of the team that launched the quintessentially Canadian magazine *Saturday Night* to provide "social intelligence" to Toronto's finer citizens.

With more trouble brewing and the mayor now determined to restore the peace, a contingent of aldermen convinced Smith to meet with representatives from the Knights of Labor. Smith uncharacteristically acquiesced and consented to permit the men to return to their jobs. Normal streetcar service resumed a few days later. The Knights mistakenly believed that Smith had had a change of heart about unions. But he had not. Only two months later, Smith's autocratic intransigence led to a second strike starting on May 8, 1886.

This time, Smith was ready with non-unionized workers to keep the cars operating, and the city directed the police to halt all street protests. The Knights' leaders, who never countenanced violence, opted for a boycott of the TSR and started running their own co-operative, the Free Bus Company, as an alternative. The *News* thought this was a wonderful tactic and would have the desired effect on Smith. "Never bother appealing to a capitalist's brain," the paper's city hall reporter noted, "when you can reach his pocket."

This strategy had limited success, however, and there were again violent clashes in the streets as workers took out their frustrations on the strikebreakers who kept the TSR's cars running. In the end, differences of opinion between the Knights' leadership and the workers, arguments about the inadequate strike pay, and problems with the Free Bus Company led to labour's capitulation. Smith had his way and unions were kept out of the TSR as long as he was in charge.

The workers might have lost this round, and Toronto was still a city dominated by a powerful business elite. Yet, as events were to show, the labour movement would not be halted, nor would its demands for equitable treatment be silenced.

AT THE HEART OF THE CLASH with labour was not only a power struggle in the factory about who was in charge of wages and unions, but also a profound difference of opinion on the future life of the city. There was no agreement among Torontonians, rich, poor, or in the middle, on how the universe should unfold, though many did share a common vision of morality and entitlement. This started with the truly wealthy, the elite circle around the lieutenant governor, the so-called four hundred, who fancied themselves on a par with the more famous Four Hundred of New York City socialite Mrs. Caroline Astor.

The chief objective of Toronto's upper crust was to get a star listing in the city's Society Blue Book or have their photograph and stories of their balls and soirées included in *Saturday Night*'s high society columns. With their private horse carriages and magnificent mansions on Jarvis and St. George Streets, Admiral Road, and farther east in Rosedale, they continued to live in a past in which few had questioned their station or privileges. They created a closed, refined, and definitely smug world of high culture, theatre, music, literature, and restricted clubs, but nevertheless relished everything modernity had to offer. They gave their children magnificent and expensive weddings and travelled in private railway cars.

In the summers, the more adventurous of the well-to-do played golf and cricket at Toronto clubs, or more likely were off to Hanlan's Point on the Toronto Islands, to the hotel and playground the champion oarsman and original sports celebrity Edward "Ned" Hanlan had erected in 1880. (Hanlan was the most famous Torontonian of his day; when he visited Australia in 1884, a town in New South Wales changed its name to Toronto, a change that remains to the present. Hanlan sold the hotel and the Island lease he had obtained from the city to financier Edmund B. Osler for $50,000 in 1892.) At Hanlan's Point the various classes mingled, with some enjoying the amusement park and others partaking in the shooting galleries, the musical presentations, or even the illicit drinking, gambling, and possibly dog fights that occurred there.

Each September starting in 1879 the mingling continued at the city's fascinating Industrial Exhibition, which in 1904 was renamed the Canadian National Exhibition or CNE. Under the guidance of its chief founder and cheerleader, businessman and civic politician John Withrow, there were creative and wondrous displays on just about anything and everything that titillated one's mind: art, business, agricultural products, food, furniture, animals, ornithology, and inventions like sewing machines and electricity, which was the big attraction in 1882.

At other times, theatre, in particular, occupied the time and interest of the wealthy. This was despite the generally uncouth atmosphere of many halls—filled as they were with "foul air and tobacco smoke," with "boot-blacks" "street arabs," and "boisterous youths" scattered in the audience—and the vaudevillian and scandalous nature of many of the productions. Regardless, as they do today, the rich supported the slew of Toronto theatres—the Grand Opera House, the City Theatre, and the Royal Theatre, among others, And, foreshadowing the hoopla surrounding the Toronto International Film Festival, they relished the "theatre party," an evening out with special friends in a private box or the best seats in the house. *Saturday Night*'s society columnist vividly described a typical theatre outing in 1890: "Row upon row of gleaming shoulders and well-starched bosoms, great unpunctuality, together with much chatter, and an attention to attractions on the right and left more constant than that given to the stage and its occupants—all these things stamp the fashionable theatre party as it is known in Toronto."

Whatever the activity, this much can be said: the rich gloried in "their" Toronto, no doubt agreeing with the *Mail*'s pretentious declaration in 1884, at the time of the city's fiftieth birthday celebrations, that it was "not too much to expect that ere another fifty years roll by her [Toronto's] fame will be worldwide and her influence felt beyond the seas."

Consider, as one representative of this moneyed class, William Mulock, a well-connected, gentle yet gruff, brusque, Cuban cigar-smoking and whiskey-drinking lawyer and politician. As Wilfrid Laurier once put it, Mulock was "the best hearted and worst-mannered man he knew." Born in 1843 in the village of Bond Head, north of Toronto, Mulock lost his father, Thomas, a physician, whose family had roots in Northern Ireland, when he was only four years old. Though his early life was difficult, his mother, Mary, was the daughter of John Cawthra, a successful merchant (and the son of Joseph Cawthra, an Upper Canadian pioneering merchant), which immediately linked Mulock to Toronto high society. His uncle William Cawthra was the richest man in the city, whose wealth a writer in the *Monetary Times* in 1871 cuttingly noted was "mainly the result of compound interest." William Cawthra and his wife, Sarah, aptly called "the Astors of Upper Canada," held court at their mansion at King and Bay Streets (torn down by the Bank of Nova Scotia in 1948 and now the site of its head office).

William Mulock was educated at University College at the University of Toronto, the start of his lifelong association with the institution. By the late 1860s he was a lawyer in the office of Senator John Ross (son-in-law of Robert Baldwin), and in 1870 he married Sarah Crowther, the daughter of the upstanding lawyer James Crowther. They had six children; their youngest son, Cawthra, president of National Iron Works, was the leader of a group of wealthy Toronto businessmen who financed the construction of the lavish

Royal Alexandra Theatre (the first theatre in the world to have makeshift air conditioning via ice in tanks beneath the floors) on King Street West which opened in 1907.

William Mulock was elected to the University of Toronto Senate and served as vice-chancellor from 1881 to 1900. He spearheaded the delicate and complex task of expanding the university through a federation with such denominational colleges as St. Michael's, Wycliffe, Knox, and Victoria. The last holdout was Bishop Strachan's Trinity College, which did not affiliate with the university until 1904. He also oversaw the development of new faculties of medicine, law, dentistry, music, and pharmacy; supported the "Toronto for Torontonians" policy by hiring University of Toronto graduates as professors; and, taking a fairly enlightened position for a gentleman of his era, supported the entrance of women despite intense opposition. (When Emily Stowe, the first practising female physician in Canada attempted to enrol for science courses at University College in 1869, she was turned down. Angry, she told university president John McCaul that "these university doors will open some day to women." According to Stowe, McCaul replied "with some vehemence": "Never in my day Madam!")

Together with Chancellor Daniel Wilson and former Liberal Party leader Edward Blake, Mulock helped to rebuild University College after a devastating fire in February 1890. And when students went on strike in 1895—the result of a clash over the university's heavy-handed firing of a popular professor and its censoring of the *Varsity*, the student newspaper—he worked behind the scenes to bring about a resolution.

Mulock's political career began with his election as a federal Liberal MP in 1882. Following Laurier's victory in 1896, he was appointed to the cabinet as postmaster general and was responsible for inaugurating the department of labour, though he was guided in these efforts by William Lyon Mackenzie King, whom Mulock appointed a deputy minister in 1900 (Mulock was a close friend of King's father, lawyer John King). In his later years, Mulock, who lived to be 101 years old, served as chief justice of the Exchequer Division of the Supreme Court of Ontario, and from 1923 to 1936 as chief justice of Ontario.

At his grand home on 518 Jarvis Street, Mulock and his wife liked to entertain. By far the highlight of the 1899 social season was the Mulocks' daughter Ethel's marriage to Arthur Kirkpatrick, son of George Kirkpatrick, lieutenant governor of Ontario from 1892 to 1896. The *Globe*'s social column referred to the extravagant nuptials as the "Wedding of the Year," with lots of white satin ribbon, ivy-covered windows in the St. James Cathedral for the ceremony, and "spreading palms" and "luxuriant ferns." The who's who of Toronto attended. Among the guests were the Coxes, Denisons, Cawthras, Gooderhams, Jarvises, Willisons, Siftons, and even such upper class "wannabes" as John and Isabel King (daughter of William Lyon Mackenzie), and their children, Bella, Willie, Max, and Jennie, who was a bridesmaid. John King was a decent man and a legal scholar, but he could never make enough money to satisfy his wife's desire to be a full-fledged and well-off member of the city's elite.

Ever serious, twenty-four-year-old "Willie" Mackenzie King felt sad during the ceremony. "Arthur and Ethel are young," he confided in his diary later that evening. "This can give them no true view of life—acting, acting, acting, that is what it all is... I could not but feel, that to a degree, they were children, playing the most sacred part, in a great drama of life."

King would have certainly noticed the presence of one other guest, the eminent professor and gentleman Goldwin Smith, who was accompanied by his wife, Harriet. Like others, King often sought out the worldly opinions of the erudite Smith, revered as the "Sage of the Grange." Before coming to Canada in 1871, Smith had taught modern history at Oxford and later at Cornell University in Ithaca, New York. In 1875, in a propitious move, he married Harriet Elizabeth Mann, the widow of William Henry Boulton, who had inherited the family's property, the Grange. Now Smith made the mansion west of University Avenue his own and its drawing room his court, where he wrote and pontificated on the various issues of the day—democracy, imperialism, Canada–U.S. relations, women's suffrage, trade unions, Darwinism, urbanization, immigration, and Jews.

Among other literary and journalistic endeavours, Smith backed the *Evening Telegram* for John Ross Robertson and published intermittently his own review of current affairs, the *Bystander*. He had little faith in democracy and took a keen interest in civic affairs, engaging himself in debates about park land, public libraries (he opposed loaning books for free), and streetcars on Sunday. Above all, he was governed by one overarching conviction: his ardent belief in the superiority of the white Anglo-Saxon race. Any obstacle or threat to the white race's God-given right to dominate the Earth was to be dealt with and expunged. Consequently, Jewish enterprise—he loathed the fact that a select number of Jews in Western Europe owned newspapers—and immigration to North America were troublesome, even to be feared.

In Smith's view, Jewish determination to maintain a separate religious identity and not embrace the "civilized" Christian world was part of the problem. The two "greatest calamities" to have "befallen mankind," he argued, were "the transportation of the negro and the dispersion of the Jews." Regularly, in his editorial articles, which were frequently reprinted in Canadian newspapers, he promoted the classic negative stereotypes of Jews as deceitful and conspiratorial. "A Jew is not an Englishman or Frenchman holding particular tenets," he opined in a May 1878 magazine feature. "He is a Jew, with a special deity for his own race. The rest of mankind are to him not merely people holding a different creed, but aliens in blood." Historian Gerald Tulchinsky rightly designated Goldwin Smith "Canada's best known Jew-hater." (In 1946, when Prime

Minister Mackenzie King was dealing with the defection of the Soviet cipher clerk Igor Gouzenko and determined that several of the spies recruited by the Soviet embassy in Ottawa were Jewish, he recalled what his old mentor Goldwin Smith had said to him once about Jews: "they were poison in the veins of a community." For much of his life, King's anti-Semitism was more subtle, but occasionally he expressed similar attitudes.)

No member of Toronto's high society (nor much of the rest of the city, for that matter) would have been troubled by such racist sentiments. Anti-Semitism was too entrenched in nineteenth-century Canada—and continued to be so until well after the Second World War—for anyone to challenge or question Smith's opinions about Jews. He touched a rawer nerve with his 1891 book *Canada and the Canadian Question*, in which he argued that the country's destiny lay in joining the United States. But that hardly diminished his status as the city's resident intellectual pooh-bah. Moreover, whatever their particular political views on the country's future relationship with the United States, nearly all of the "four hundred," as well as the burgeoning middle class at their heels, shared Smith's fears that Toronto was on the verge of a moral collapse.

YOU HAD TO SEE Madame Henault in person to appreciate the full effect of her con. Her outfit was right out of *Arabian Nights*. She sported "Turkish trousers, silk gown embroidered with cabbalistic characters, red-leather boots turned up at the toes, jewelled tiara, and fistfuls of diamond rings." For a few weeks at the end of August and early September 1882, she actually drove up Yonge Street in a horse-drawn golden chariot to an amphitheatre on the west side of James Street. There she performed her healing magic behind a "protective shield"—pulling teeth, apparently without causing her patients any real pain, and treating the blind, deaf, and crippled. Young Hattie Newman of Yorkville, who had used crutches because of a bad knee, could walk again. So could Eliza Phillips, twelve years old, who five days after seeing Madame Henault walked without crutches or pain in her damaged hip.

No one was certain where she had come from. One story claimed she was a Gypsy from Italy who had been hounded out of Glasgow. She claimed she was the daughter of a famous Italian doctor. It made no difference: the miracles she performed, and the relief she provided for a lot of toothaches, brought more and more Torontonians to see Madame Henault for themselves. Ned Hanlan and Mrs. Harriet Gooderham were among her admirers.

How she pulled off these stunts, if she actually did, is anyone's guess. Her secret was a so-called Chinese elixir of life, which she sold to the enthusiastic crowds that gathered each day. (It was later discovered that many of the people in the audience were "plants," who purchased the concoction to stimulate sales and then had their money refunded.) The *Globe* caustically called her "The Wonderful Woman." She might truly be an "expert dentist," the newspaper concluded, "but probably that is all." In the *Globe*'s view, she was a "travelling quack," "a Bohemian," and "a fraud." About two weeks after her triumphant arrival she suddenly disappeared, never to be seen in Toronto again.

Charlatan or not, Madame Henault typified the excitement of living in the big city. People might go to the theatre and the CNE or they might attend the show put on by someone like Madame Henault, and spend their hard-earned money on her elixir. Journalists noted it was often the poorest who were giving Madame their money, and they could least afford it given the financial and social pressures they continually faced. Beyond the mansions on Jarvis and St. George Streets, cities like Toronto had their dark side. Crime, corruption, prostitution seemed to lurk around every corner, and all this depravity, it was said, was fuelled by poverty. Inadequate water facilities and poor sewage systems continued to hamper Toronto and were certainly partly responsible for the worst neighbourhoods in the city.

On Christmas Eve in 1868, a bitterly cold night, a *Globe* reporter stumbled across a thinly clad young girl selling newspapers on the street. She told the reporter that she could not go home until all the papers were sold. He kindly bought the remaining newspapers and escorted the girl to a poor part of the city. There he watched as she was roughly treated by two drunk and brutish parents, who claimed she was short a few pennies.

Civic leaders, physicians, journalists, and the new breed of social reformers who wanted to solve these persistent social problems blamed them not just on "slum conditions"—a catch-all term for squalor, vice, and degeneration—but also those who dwelled in them. In short, Toronto's poor, like the poor in every Canadian and American city, were largely to blame for their predicament. Eugenicists of the era, ever popular, took this one step further, arguing that poverty, and hence criminal behaviour and immorality, was a biologically inherited trait.

"Underneath the seemingly moral surface of our national life," declared a Canadian Salvation Army journal in 1887, "there is a terrible undercurrent of unclean vice with all its concomitant evils of ruined lives, desolated hearth-stones, prostituted bodies, decimated conditions, and early dishonoured graves." According to Reverend S.W. Dean of Toronto's Missionary Society, the slum was "the lurking place of disease and impaired health, the hiding place of crime, the haunt of immorality." Quoting from the Bible, he then added for good measure that "men love darkness rather than light because their deeds are evil."

To save these people from themselves, several lasting social service organizations were established, like the Young Women's Christian Association (YWCA), set up in Toronto in 1873, with its declared purpose the "temporal, moral and religious welfare of young women who are dependent upon their own exertions for support." The Methodist

Fred Victor Mission opened at the corner of Queen and Jarvis Streets in 1894, owing mainly to a generous donation by Hart Massey to honour the memory of his twenty-three-year-old son Frederick Victor, who had died in 1890 from a complication in his lungs. Its prime mover was John Miles Wilkinson, an "audacious" local Methodist minister, who had high hopes for this "People's Tabernacle," that in time became a hostel for down-and-out men.

There was, too, the Haven, a shelter created in 1878 by evangelical Protestants led by lawyer Samuel Blake and Elizabeth Harvie, who was the daughter of a Methodist minister; the wife of real estate developer, civic politician, and teetotaller John Harvie; and a pioneering Toronto social reformer. The Haven's goal was to aid homeless women, unwed mothers, prostitutes, and those afflicted by the bottle. By the 1890s, when young Mackenzie King—then a University of Toronto student who aimed to find meaning in his life through an "ideal of service" and "moral obligation" he had learned in his political economy classes—decided to volunteer his time to save prostitutes as his idol, the British prime minister William Gladstone, had done in London, the Haven was looking after nearly eight hundred women.

Despite the best of intentions, King had his work cut out for him and he had many false starts: the women just did not want to be saved. He had better luck with a young streetwalker named Edna, who was probably about eighteen years old. Accompanied by a university friend, David Duncan, King met Edna and another girl named Jennie on King Street and accompanied them back to their room. They talked until two o'clock in the morning, and over the course of several more encounters, he and Duncan heard the "sad stories" about Edna's and Jennie's troubled lives. It broke his heart. There were more prayers, and scripture and poetry readings, and within a week Edna consented to relocate to the Haven (Jennie would not). Edna told King that God had sent him to her in answer to her mother's prayers. Naturally, he was elated by his achievement of "bringing this tossed little ship [Edna] into a quiet harbour." During the next few months, King visited Edna at the shelter many times. Eventually his relationship with her ended, and he gave no indication whether she returned to the street—was "overcome with temptation," in King's words. He later turned his attention to other girls like Maud "Maggie" Taylor, who assured him of "God changing her heart." He was able to reunite her with her family.

THE FACT WAS THAT TEMPTATION, pleasure, and sin beckoned Torontonians. That was certainly the conclusion of the young investigative journalist Christopher St. George Clark (C.S. Clark to his readers), whose sensational 1898 exposé *Of Toronto the Good* was the spiciest reading Torontonians could get their hands on. It also proved that despite the best efforts of moral crusader and businessman William Howland, elected mayor in

1886 to wipe away the evil of drink and debauchery, and the establishment of a police morality department under the guidance of no-nonsense Inspector David Archibald, elements of Sodom and Gomorrah remained in Toronto at the turn of the century.

"Houses of ill fame in Toronto? Certainly not," Clark sarcastically wrote. "The whole city is an immense house of ill-fame, the roof of which is the blue canopy of heaven during the summer months." By Clark's estimation, there was not a street in the entire business section on which he had not been solicited by a prostitute. (Clark himself favoured regulation of the "social evil" rather than suppression, which he argued would never happen.) This may have been an exaggeration. Then again, some years earlier a reporter for the *Empire* claimed that during a short stroll on King Street, he was greeted in a span of ten minutes by six women in search of customers.

If you wanted trouble—as is so colourfully depicted in Maureen Jennings's *Murdoch Mysteries* series set in Victorian Toronto—it was easy to find. In the 1870s and 1880s, York Street around Adelaide was one area that attracted a lot of attention from rowdies and the police. According to Detective Alf Cuddy, who started as a police constable when he was only nineteen years old in 1882, York was the toughest street in the city (in August 1883, he was nearly killed in a shootout with a hood named Mickey Morgan at the corner of York and Pearl Streets). At McQuarry's Saloon there was always a loud, boisterous, and heavy-drinking crowd that featured "lewd jokes," "pert little damsels," and "villainous looking fancy men," as a writer for the *Mail* described it in 1879. Down the street, Bob Berry's dance hall was usually prefaced by the adjective "notorious." At midnight, York Street was said to come "alive with . . . wretchedness," filled with pickpockets, thieves, swindlers, and loose women. Illegal whiskey joints operated by unsavoury gangsters competed with an assortment of brothels, which served as a particular enticement for rural Ontario boys visiting the big city. For the truly adventurous, there was even an assortment of opium dens run by newly arrived Chinese immigrants, as one reporter from the recently established *Empire* newspaper learned on a visit to Sam Lee's on Parliament Street in June 1892.

The "high-class" brothel Clark stopped in at during his book research was located at 248 Front Street West, the present site of the CBC building. There were no red lights and the blinds were closed. Clark determined that this particular whorehouse was "patronized by wealthy men, young and old, from every part of the city and country." Inside, he discovered "elegant and tasteful" furniture and a pleasant "proprietress." The young women who worked there, he observed, "are carefully chosen for their beauty and charms, and are frequently persons of education and refinement. They are required to observe the utmost decorum in the parlors of the house, until you are fairly well acquainted with them, and then their language is not so polite. Their toilettes are usually extremely aesthetic and voluptuous, and display their charms to the best advantage . . . Some have been led astray, some adopt this life to avoid poverty, some have entered from motives of pure licentiousness and at the same time gratify a taste for an easy life."

A *Globe* feature from December 1887, entitled "Palaces of Sin," offered a more realistic assessment. The reporter accompanied Inspector Archibald and his team of officers from the morality department on a midnight raid of illegal groggeries and brothels. It was an eye-opening experience, though Archibald later insisted that the situation had improved. Their first stop was a dingy saloon on the lower part of Jarvis Street, where they found a collection of rogues and drunks who quickly dispersed. Next was a brothel run by Alice Miller. The only customer was a young man who hid behind the prostitute he was with. He told the police he was from Parkdale and was married, and cried, "I'm ashamed of myself." The police let him go as well. This was followed by a visit to a busier brothel on Richmond Street, the "elegantly furnished house" of madam Belle Howard. Here was a "gay scene," the reporter noted. "A young man with the bloom of youth on his cheek presided at the piano, while around the apartment on scarlet cushioned chairs sat a half-dozen youths from country towns, while Belle Howard's painted women occupied seats between. They were in the height of revelry but the appearance of Inspector Archibald quickly changed the scene." The police dutifully recorded the men's names, and the inspector gave them a lecture about sinning before he told them "to get out."

Wickedness, at least by Victorian standards, came in many varieties. In 1861 the American actress Adah Isaacs Menken, the original sex goddess who went through five husbands, starred at a Toronto theatre in a production of the scandalous play *Mazeppa*, which attracted sold-out audiences in the United States and select cities in eastern Canada (due to the high demand, the concept of advance ticket sales was established). The definite highlight of the play, based on a Ukrainian folk tale and a Lord Byron poem, was when Menken, wearing only tights and appearing to be naked, rode a horse across the stage. "Her posture," her biographers Michael and Barbara Foster point out, "strapped on the bare back of the steed, legs apart, was more suggestive than any actress had previously dared." Far and wide, she was now celebrated as "The Naked Lady" (Mark Twain, who saw her perform in San Francisco in 1863, called her "The Great Bare"). A few years later, Torontonians similarly revelled in a New York ballet "extravaganza," *The Black Crook*, featuring "scantily clad female forms" in flesh-coloured tights.

Somewhat more crude and lewd were the sexually charged twenty-five-cent burlesque shows with comedy and dancing, like Lydia Thompson, "The First Lady of Burlesque," and her "British Blondes" in shapely tights, who entertained in the city in 1868. The hosting theatres were occasionally raided by the Toronto police. More refined gentlemen had to be satisfied with racy photographs on display at the Industrial Exhibition in 1894. And even then the defenders of Toronto the Good were distraught. One letter to the *Empire* about the exhibit expressed outrage at the number of young men leering at the photos. "Picture after picture of scantily dressed women was presented to our gaze," the writer stated with disgust, "it was only necessary to notice the whispered conversations of the youngsters and to overhear an occasional word to realize the evil effect it was having on their youthful minds."

Just as worrisome were young single women venturing into the streets in small groups or alone. As early as 1871, police chief William Prince expressed grave concern in his annual report that "many young women, and mere girls resort to [saloons and dancing halls] unaccompanied by guardians or any one to protect them." The consequence of such behaviour, he added, "must be detrimental to their educational and moral training, as well as to their health."

Despite any assertions to the contrary, not every woman walking the streets of Toronto, in a group or alone, was looking for trouble or sex. Yet at a time when urbanization was altering the labour market faster than long-held mores were changing (a young gentleman, after all, still had to seek permission from a father to wed his daughter), there was bound to be turbulence. Few societal issues terrified the traditionalists more than the changing role of women. In later years, questions about a woman's "proper sphere" would lead, in Toronto and across the country, to the right to vote, but initially it was about middle- and lower-class women supporting themselves and their families. More and more women, many of whom had migrated to the city from rural areas, were finding employment as factory workers, domestics, and seamstresses, and others, who had valiantly fought their way into the University of Toronto, were receiving a college education and graduating as teachers, nurses, and even doctors. Jobs as clerks and stenographers at Eaton's and Simpson's and other businesses were also available.

The fact that women were merely responding to the demand for their labour was beside the point. A young woman "'adrift' in the industrial city," wrote historian Carolyn Strange, "was accompanied by fears about the disruption of family cohesion, the decline of rural life, and the growing militancy of the urban working class." And the worst of it was that single women alone in Toronto were either the helpless prey of men or, in some cases, the predators of single (and powerless married) men. In either situation, the critics claimed, the result was the sin of sex before marriage, which frequently had dangerous consequences. They were not entirely wrong.

In the first week of July 1888, the body of a young woman was found floating in Toronto Bay. A subsequent investigation determined that the dead woman was Jennie Irving (she also went by the last name Brown), who had come to Toronto from Walkerton. For a time she had worked as a seamstress for a Mrs. Glassey in a house on Mission Avenue, where she also boarded. The job did not work out, though Mrs. Glassey allowed Jennie to stay in the house—until she was caught having sex with Mrs. Glassey's sister's husband.

Mrs. Glassey's sister forced Jennie to sign a document testifying to the affair, which Jennie later felt had disgraced her. She "threw herself in the Bay," committing suicide. At first there was great sympathy for her plight. Then the police discovered among her possessions love letters to and from other men, and questions were immediately raised about Jennie's morality.

That same year, in what the *News* dubbed "The Sad Case," an eighteen-year-old woman, Elizabeth Bray, who worked at the large Crompton Corset Company on York Street, had an affair with a Mr. Gamble, a married piano-factory worker. She became pregnant and explained this to her aunt, who was responsible for her, by claiming that she had been raped in an attack in High Park. Meanwhile, Gamble tried to arrange for Elizabeth to have an abortion, which was then illegal in Canada. He was unable to do so. Desperate, he conducted the abortion himself and botched it, and Elizabeth died from puerperal peritonitis. Gamble was charged and convicted of murder, though due to the circumstances he escaped the hangman.

Cases of young women being coerced into prostitution were not uncommon, then or later. This was a tragic occurrence that received a lot of press, especially after the July 1885 publication in the *Pall Mall Gazette* of British investigative journalist W.T. Stead's explosive series of articles "The Maiden Tribute of Modern Babylon," with its lurid account of sexual abuse in London, including the "purchase" of a thirteen-year-old chimney sweep named Eliza Armstrong.

About the same time, Torontonians were shocked, yet also mesmerized, by the heart-rending story of sixteen-year-old Eva Kenney. Eva, who was from a farm outside Toronto, had initially found a job in Brampton working at a coat factory managed by George Tate. Unbeknownst to Joseph Kenney, Eva's father, Tate had taken advantage of Eva and seduced her. Eva was too scared and ashamed to tell her family what had transpired, so she went along with Tate when he offered to find her "a nice situation" in Toronto. They had only been in the city for a few days when Tate took Eva to see a Mrs. Ellison, the madam of a brothel on Adelaide Street West. Eva soon ran away, but Tate found her and forced her to work at another brothel on Gould Street. Joseph Kenney learned of his daughter's plight, went to the police, and pressed charges against Tate, who was arrested. At the trial, the case turned into a "she said, he said" dilemma, and with help from a few prominent friends, Timothy Eaton among them, Tate was portrayed as a decent individual. In January 1886 he was acquitted of all charges.

The simple fact was that women were rarely believed, particularly by male juries. A woman by herself on the streets of Toronto after dark, it was commonly assumed, was asking for trouble—even if she was raped as Elizabeth Griffiths was in 1887. Seeking refuge for the night, and without money, Griffiths accepted the aid of a man who took her to a house on Adelaide, where he sexually assaulted her. Like Tate and many others, he was found not guilty at his trial. When the assault was on a prostitute or madam—as it was in July 1880 when Jane Harding, who ran a brothel on Adelaide Street West, was attacked by three men and raped by one of them—defence lawyers had an easy time discrediting the women's stories and testimonies. Twenty years later, Lucy Brooking, the superintendent of the Haven, reported countless other examples of women being accosted, manipulated, and taken advantage of by unsavoury men—and there was little the law did to protect them.

From 1880 to 1930, as Strange adds, "not a single Toronto domestic who laid a complaint of indecent assault or rape against her master saw him punished." If there was a transformative moment, it occurred in the spring of 1915. The sensational trial and subsequent acquittal of Carrie Davies, an eighteen-year-old maid, for murder was viewed as a step forward in advancing the rights of domestic servants and the working class throughout the city. In a moment of desperation, she had killed her employer, the philandering Charles Albert "Bert" Massey (a grandson of business giant Hart Massey), who had accosted her the night before. Her testimony was that she "lost all control" when she saw Massey returning to his home on Walmer Road and was petrified that he would rape her. Her plea of self-defence convinced the all-male jury, which found her not guilty. When the verdict was announced, both Justice William Mulock and the jury were moved to tears.

THE EXCESSIVE DRINKING and carousing; risqué burlesque shows; booming brothel trade; assignation houses, where young men, married or not, could rent rooms for illicit purposes; illegal abortionists; and flagrant violations of the Lord's Day left many of Toronto's citizens reeling. Enter William Holmes Howland.

The son of William P. Howland, a Father of Confederation, William H. was passionate about life and the causes he embraced. By the time he was twenty-seven years old in 1871, he had become fairly wealthy owing to his family's grain business. That year he was appointed president of the Queen City Fire Insurance Company, "the youngest insurance company president in Canada." Before his involvement in municipal politics, he was well known as an evangelical Christian, social reformer, philanthropist, Sunday school teacher, economic protectionist, Canadian nationalist, political independent, and founder in 1884 of the Toronto Mission Union, an organization that helped the poor. At the time of his death in December 1893, the *Globe* described him as "one of those large-hearted men who have a genial smile, a cheery word and a hearty handshake for all. He was the most approachable and kindly sympathetic of men." The great Satan that Howland sought to vanquish was alcohol, which he, like all "drys," saw as the cause of so much misery and depravity.

In late 1885, Howland decided to challenge the incumbent mayor, Alexander Manning, who had also served a term as mayor in the early 1870s. Manning was a Conservative and a rich contractor and land developer, everything Howland the Reformer was not. A downturn in the economy in the early 1880s had hurt Howland financially, though he managed to survive and recover. In some quarters, his "relative poverty," compared to Manning's wealth, was seen as a virtue according to Howland's biographer, historian Desmond Morton.

Throughout the brief campaign, Howland presented himself as the common man's law-and-order candidate, who could take on the "whiskey men" and would bring Toronto out of the immoral muck it found itself in. "Let us keep the city with the character of an honourable city, a God-fearing city, and I would rather see it thus than the greatest and richest city in the continent," he declared enthusiastically at one rally. It was a populist appeal that found support among the clergy, the nascent organized labour movement, and two thousand widows and spinsters who owned sufficient property, which permitted them to vote for the first time.

Howland promised that he would rid the city of sin and clean up city hall, where aldermen tied to the Conservative Party, who had ruled for the past few years, used blatant patronage, favouritism, and possibly graft to reward their friends and themselves. It was an effective strategy. On election day in early January 1886, Howland trounced Manning in Toronto's dozen wards by more than 1,700 votes. The following year he won a second term over David Blain, a former federal Liberal MP and a Manning supporter, by nearly 2,200 votes.

Guided by the motto "Except the Lord Keep the City, the Watchman Waketh but in Vain," which he kept in a large frame on his desk, Howland was true to his word—or at least he tried his best to be. He supported the expropriation of property (the first slum clearances in Toronto) and construction of a much-needed new city hall and courthouse on Bay Street, and though kickbacks were stopped, the building costs escalated from an unrealistic estimate of $200,000 to a final cost of $2.5 million. The new Romanesque building designed by Edward J. Lennox was opened with a great celebration in September 1899.

Howland also wanted to improve public health by replacing a poor sewage system—exacerbated by open privies in many areas of the city and vast amounts of horse manure dumped daily on the streets—yet Toronto's frugal ratepayers, whose vote of support was necessary for the $1.4-million improvement project, rejected a plan most felt was too expensive. He sought to expose a swindle hatched by coal merchants and city clerks to cheat the city out of thousands of dollars, but not enough evidence could be found to convict the city clerk and engineer who were implicated in the conspiracy. He could claim a partial victory in reducing the number of liquor licences granted by city hall, though his temperance crusade was ultimately stalled by the citizens of Toronto who did not share his aversion to drink. And, as noted earlier, he took the side of workingmen in their clashes with such capitalists as Hart Massey and Frank Smith in the battle at the Toronto Street Railway.

Howland had more apparent success working with police inspector David Archibald, formerly with the Royal Irish Constabulary, and the morality department in the metamorphosis of the city into "Toronto the Good." With the dedication of an Old Testament prophet, Archibald went after drunks, whores, and licentiousness wherever he found or imagined it. This included clamping down on young boys playing ball in the park, swimmers who bathed half-naked in the bay, and unlicensed nut carts on the streets, around which young men and women congregated at night and socialized.

Most Torontonians tolerated this excessive puritanical witch hunt, probably because they understood that its overall effectiveness would be limited, as C.S. Clark proved in his survey of Toronto sin in 1898. Asked in December 1887, at the hearings of the Royal Commission on Labor and Capital, about his efforts to stamp out prostitution, Howland blamed the problem on human nature and societal ills. "The difficulty with prostitutes is rooted in laziness, due largely to improper education," he argued. "A good woman would prefer death to prostitution, but there are young girls who have no good training and [are] not under supervision, and who can barely make a living, do the best they can."

In November 1887, Howland decided not to run for a third term. He planned for Alderman Elias Rogers, an evangelical Quaker and coal merchant, to succeed him and carry on the struggle against sin. However, the revelation that the good Mr. Rogers was party to a coal-price-fixing ring, or at any rate knew of its existence, was enough to propel to victory the debonair Conservative and Orange candidate Edward "Ned" Clarke, a fiery orator (and the former printer who had battled George Brown and the *Globe* in 1872). His status as a labour champion gave Clarke the working-class vote; upper- and middle-class citizens may have voted for him because they did not like being told how to live their lives. "The citizens of Toronto did not vote against Mr. Rogers," suggested a *Mail* columnist, "but against the attempt of [a] few cliques of well-meaning but fussily-feeble bodies to dictate to the city in a matter with which most of us took the liberty to think they had no immediate concern. Temperance associations and Leagues of Purity are very good things in their place, but their place is not everywhere and if they think it ought to be, and insist upon forcing themselves on the public... they must not be at all surprised at often receiving the severe setting down they had this week."

Yet Clarke, whose most distinctive feature was a droopy moustache, was hardly a libertarian or an advocate of sin. In fact, he was more like Howland than the *Mail* and other newspapers would have conceded. He was an active congregant of the Reformed

Episcopal Church, he understood the threat to decency posed by liquor, and, most importantly, he permitted Inspector Archibald to continue to "prowl the streets, hunting down harlots, arresting drunks, shutting down unlicensed grog shops and terrorizing vagrant boys." He also brought some professionalism to the workings of city hall, hiring more staff; by E.E. Sheppard's account, in 1888 city hall employed exactly one typist and one stenographer. Happy with his sound and generally fiscally astute administration (at least until the drop in land prices in 1890), Toronto voters returned Clarke, "the People's Ned," as mayor for three terms.

DURING THE CLARKE YEARS, as well as for the mayors who followed him—business executive and staunch temperance advocate Robert J. Fleming (1892–93 and 1896–97) and Warring Kennedy, a dry goods merchant (1894–95)—the main preoccupation at city hall was the Toronto Street Railway Company. Despite Frank Smith's best efforts to stave off the expiration of his lucrative thirty-year contract, city officials had no intention of continuing their business dealings with him any longer than they had to. His contentious actions during the 1886 strikes, and his incessant arguing with the city over maintaining the TSR's tracks, made him likely the most unpopular person in Toronto in 1891.

For a brief time there was a campaign to turn the TSR into a publicly owned corporation; that innovative and socialistic idea appealed to Phillips Thompson and his labourite friends, as well as Ernest Macdonald, the so-called Baron of Chester, who was mad at Smith for not extending streetcar service east over the Don Valley to Danforth Road. However desirable a publicly owned system would have been, it was economically unfeasible, since the main objective of city hall was to transform the TSR from a horse-drawn service to one run on electricity. And electrification was expensive, too expensive for civic government.

First things first, though. Never a poor businessman, Frank Smith demanded $5.5 million for the TSR and all its assets. The city's lawyers, with advice from an American consultant, Henry Everett, the secretary of the East Cleveland Railway Company and a recognized expert on electric street railways, countered with an offer of $1 million. Arbitrators decided on $1.45 million, and Senator Smith pocketed $500,000, while his chief partner, George Kiely, received $400,000. With Smith taken care of, a bidding war ensued for one of the greatest prizes in Toronto's history: a thirty-year TSR monopoly.

Of the three main offers, the one that was most financially attractive, with promises of nearly half a million dollars up front and electrification within one year, came from a syndicate fronted by George Kiely. Its key member was William Mackenzie, the western Canadian railway tycoon, who with his partner Donald Mann soon embarked on the development of the Canadian Northern Railway. Not taking any chances, the

Kiely–Mackenzie group mounted an impressive, if slightly sleazy, public relations campaign to win the bid. To manage it, they brought in a slick operator named Baruch "Barney" Mahler, a Jewish financier from Cleveland with some experience in the urban transportation business.

"Oiled and smoothed," as W.F. "Billy" Maclean's tabloid-style *World* depicted him, Mahler was given about $40,000 to lobby, entertain, and likely pay off city aldermen to support the Kiely–Mackenzie bid. (An 1894 investigation by Judge Joseph E. McDougall into city hall corruption suggested that Mahler had indeed made a few payoffs to several aldermen for their support, and several were also the recipients of interest-free loans that were never repaid.) Mayor Clarke cuttingly referred to Mahler as "the Clean Skater from Cleveland... owing to the light and airy manner in which [he] could glide in and out of the street railway business without leaving any tracks." The money was well spent. By the end of August 1891, Kiely, Mackenzie, and their partners had acquired the TSR for $1.45 million, with a down payment of $475,000 and an assurance that the city would have an electric trolley system within a year. Under the new ownership, the TSR was renamed the Toronto Railway Company (TRC).

The lone voice of protest against the new agreement and the corruption that led to it came from a resentful Phillips Thompson in the *Labor Advocate*. "The stolidity, stupidity and prejudice of the people of Toronto... have proved too much for the efforts of the few who cared enough about the public interest and the rights of labour to make a stand for the principle of civic operation," he wrote a few weeks after the deal had been finalized. "When in addition to this slavish indifference to the citizens, the influence of boodle is thrown into the scale the fight became a hopeless one."

Mackenzie was true to his word; by the middle of August 1892, the horses were off the roads and all of Toronto was wowed by the new electric streetcars. "Oh bliss! we went for our first ride in the new electric cars down Church St.—it really was the most exciting," the young amateur playwright and thoroughly modern Marion Chadwick recorded in her diary on August 31, 1892. Yet progress had a steep price. Many of the TRC motormen had not been trained properly on the operation of the speedier trolleys. In the middle of the afternoon on September 2, 1892, this had tragic consequences when sixty-one-year-old Hannah Heron, on a visit to the downtown from her home in Scarborough, was hit by a trolley as she tried to reach a boarding platform. She died a few hours later. The motorman driving the trolley in question, it was later determined, did not know how to work the brake.

Accidents like this aside, Mackenzie's biggest headache during these first years of the contract was gaining the right to keep the streetcars running on Sunday so he did not forgo a seventh day of profit. It took six years, three civic referendums (in 1892, 1893, and 1897), and a lot of money before the TRC finally had its way. Though 1890s Toronto was as puritanical a city as there was in North America—one visitor from Chicago praised it as "a bulwark against evil"—the factions for and against Sunday streetcars did not divide entirely on religious grounds. Those who combated the extra day of service, like Timothy Eaton and Hart Massey, naturally had the Lord on their side. In a nasty display of xenophobia, some of them even denigrated their opponents as unwanted aliens plotting an attack on Christian Canadian life. "The character of the home life of a nation depended largely upon the character of the Sabbath day," declared journalist and prohibitionist Frank Spence to great applause at an anti-Sunday streetcar rally in 1893. "They did not want a New York or European Sunday. Let those who advocated it go to Europe. Anyone who came to Canada should be made to respect Canadian laws and institutions."

In fact, the yes side consisted of a variety of Torontonians of all classes and religious affiliations—from Goldwin Smith, George Gooderham, Robert Simpson, Roman Catholic and Anglican bishops, and the most vocal proponent, Billy Maclean, who though he had opposed the Mackenzie group's acquisition of the TSR, now used the pages of the *World* to mock the saints and priests who wanted to tell him what he could and could not do on a Sunday. Besides the issues of freedom of choice and progress involved, the upper-class supporters also contended, in as paternalistic a way as might be expected, that Sunday streetcars would benefit Toronto's lowly workers, since it would permit them to escape the unhealthy, fetid confines of their miserable homes and neighbourhoods rather than spend a Sunday drinking and gambling.

In the end it probably cost Mackenzie and his associates more than $50,000 in advertising and other expenses over six years to win, just barely, the third municipal referendum held in May 1897 (the vote was 16,273 to 16,051 in favour of Sunday streetcar service). At long last, on May 23, 1897, streetcars ran in Toronto on a Sunday. The TRC magnanimously distributed that day's receipts of $1,327 to the city's hospitals. Ironically, as historians Christopher Armstrong and H.V. Nelles point out, for a brief time Hart Massey, an anti, had some revenge. As the major shareholder in the Canada Cycle and Motor Company (CCM), he took advantage of the bicycle craze that engulfed the city. (By late 1897 there were bicycle racks on Toronto streetcars.) It seems Torontonians decided they preferred bikes to streetcars, a development that marked the beginning of the war of the streets between cyclists, public transportation, and cars that persists to the present. Sunday, on the other hand, remained as dull and boring as ever in Toronto well into the twentieth century.

No one should feel too badly for William Mackenzie, however. The TRC raked in millions of dollars during the next three decades. An especially astute move was the company's investment in 1912 in Scarboro Beach Park. The Coney Island-like amusement park located south of Queen Street East on Scarboro Beach Boulevard was opened in 1907 by Harry and Mabel Dorsey, who sank $600,000 into its development. The park featured such popular attractions as a roller coaster, "Shoot the Chutes" flume ride, "Bump the Bumps" slide, and a tunnel of love. After the TRC acquired it, streetcar service was established to the beach—before that the easiest way to get to the park was on a steamer that picked people up at the foot of Yonge Street—and the number of visitors increased exponentially.

Mackenzie and his wife, Margaret, enjoyed all that Victorian Toronto had to offer. In June 1897 they bought, for approximately $100,000, "Benvenuto," a magnificent six-year-old mansion at the top of Avenue Road hill, south of St. Clair. From this base, he oversaw his vast global business empire.

PRESERVING THE LORD'S DAY was only one of many issues that occupied and divided Torontonians as the twentieth century dawned. Like other major cities in North America, Toronto was a "cradle of progress," where theatres, libraries, newspapers, and bookstores fostered culture and modernity. In 1900, cities were also technological wonders, with electricity, streetcars, and telephones appearing everywhere.

Yet technology was often changing people's lives faster than they could adapt, and it fuelled their anxieties about the future. Toronto may not have been a "jungle," as Chicago was in novelist Upton Sinclair's sensational 1906 exposé, where corruption and exploitation of workers was the norm. But some of the same urban elements—poverty, factory toil, and crime—were evident. Toronto the Good was under siege, even if its upstanding citizens did not fully grasp everything, good and bad, that the future promised. By 1900, this much was clear: industrialization had uprooted millions of people, in Europe and elsewhere, who were in search of work and opportunities. Their mass migration brought them across the ocean to North America, and many found their way to Toronto, whether they were welcome or not.

Chapter Six

THE WARD

In a part of the city that is ever
shrouded in sooty smoke,

And amid huge, hard buildings,
hides a gloomy house of

Broken grey rough-cast, like a
sickly sin in a callous soul.

—LAWREN HARRIS, 1922

In the late nineteenth and early twentieth centuries, many European immigrants lived in "the Ward," an impoverished neighbourhood located within Toronto's downtown core. The area also had important cultural and religious connections—synagogues, schools, churches, food shops—that made the struggles of day-to-day life a bit easier. *City of Toronto Archives, Fonds 1244, Item 8029*

IN 1913, on the other side of the world from Toronto in the town of Lagow, Poland, about two hundred kilometres south of Warsaw, eleven-year-old Joseph Baruch Salsberg—"Yossele" to his friends—packed his few belongings and joined his mother, Sarah-Gittel, and his two sisters for the long journey to Canada. His father, Abraham, a baker, had left his family three years earlier for North America, eventually settling in Toronto. Like almost all Jews, the Salsbergs resided in the Pale of Settlement, the Russian-controlled geographic area that defined Jewish life in Eastern Europe from the time of Catherine the Great in the mid-eighteenth century to the Russian Revolution in 1917. Joseph was studying the Talmud and was a star pupil. The local rabbi had assured Abraham and Sarah-Gittel that their son would prosper in the New World.

In the *shtetlach*, or small villages, of the Pale, Jews worked at a variety of trades, barely rising above poverty levels, but finding some comfort and relief in religion and the annual cycle of Jewish rituals and holidays. Official government repression—from a multitude of taxes to the brutal "cantonist" decree, which under the reign of Czar Nicholas I (1825–55) forcibly conscripted young Jewish boys into the Russian army for thirty years—was always present, though somehow the Jews tolerated it. Then Czar Alexander II was assassinated in March 1881. Jews were wrongly blamed for the assassination—only one young Jewish woman, Gesia Gelfman, was arrested and may have been involved in the plot—which unleashed pent-up anti-Semitism that led to pogroms or riots in the countryside, targeting Jews. The Czarist regime did not support the violence, but government officials, nevertheless, punished Jews with the "May Laws," despotic regulations that further choked Jewish life. Emigration to "America," *di goldeneh medina*, the Golden Land, was a popular way to escape the misery. And so between 1880 and 1914 more than two million Russian Jews journeyed across the Atlantic to North America. The vast majority wound up on New York City's Lower East Side and in other large American cities. About 100,000 made their way to Canada; of those, approximately 30,000 settled in Toronto, increasing the city's Jewish population from 500 in 1881 to 35,000 by 1921. Only Montreal had more Jewish immigrants.

By the time Sarah and the children arrived, Abraham Salsberg had become a peddler, a common, though not popular, occupation for many East European Jews who wanted to work for themselves and accumulate some capital. And, in fact, the Salsbergs were able to move into the home that Abraham had purchased at 73 Cecil Street, west of the city's immigrant quarter called "the Ward." Located close to Union Station (at the foot of today's University Avenue) and Toronto's core in the north and central sections of St. John's Ward, the Ward was a rectangle bounded by Queen Street in the south, University Avenue in the west, College Street in the north, and Yonge Street in the east.

Though hardly well off, the Salsbergs settled into a thriving Yiddish world of kosher shops, synagogues, and garment factories closer to Spadina Avenue, which Jewish owners and workers soon dominated. Joe Salsberg attended Lansdowne Public School, near Spadina and College (to this day, two-thirds of the student population do not speak English as their first language). He was a natural leader: in 1914, at the age of twelve, he led his first collective action, a protest by Jewish children who were compelled to sing Christmas carols each December. The local school board grudgingly allowed the Jewish students to opt out of this activity. Salsberg dropped out of school a few years later to help his family. Like so many Jewish immigrants who toiled in the city's burgeoning garment industry, he found work at a leather goods factory for three dollars a week, though he continued his Talmudic studies.

As the world of the Jewish diaspora changed, especially after the failed 1905 Russian Revolution, the Jewish immigrants coming to Toronto and North America were imbued with the spirit of the Bund, *Der Algemeyner Yidisher Arbeter Bund in Lite, Poyln un Rusland*, the Jewish workers' political and labour movement established in Russia in 1897. Their distinct cultural baggage, which had a tremendous impact on Toronto's Jewish community, comprised socialist and Marxist principles, a love for Yiddish language and culture, and a secular rather than religious emphasis on Judaism. They were the first and only generation of a true Jewish "proletariat" in Canada and were prepared to stand up for themselves in the factory, whether their boss was Jewish or not. Some were dedicated radicals; others embraced the socialist principles of their leaders only because it gave them a chance to improve their miserable lives. The successful Russian Revolution of 1917 merely reinforced this vision for a new world order based on equality.

These intellectual currents and historic developments had an impact on Toronto's Jewish working class, including on the career path of young Joe Salsberg. Much to the chagrin of his parents, who wanted him to become a rabbi, by the time he was fifteen he had abandoned Orthodox Judaism for left-wing Labour Zionism—which conceived of a socialist future for Jews in a homeland in Palestine. This was the beginning of a lifelong journey that saw him go from being a member of a Jewish labour youth club to union organizer, Communist Party member, Toronto alderman, and Labour-Progressive member of the Ontario Legislature from 1943 to 1955.

ALREADY PROSPERING and living in the Ward for many years by the time Joe Salsberg arrived was Francesco Glionna. Born in the town of Laurenzana, Italy, two hundred kilometres southeast of Naples, Glionna was part of the first wave of Italian immigrants to make their way to North America. By 1874, following brief stops in Paris and New York, he wound up in Toronto.

The "push" factors that affected Glionna's decision to migrate, as well as the decisions of millions of Italians between 1860 and 1914, included what must have seemed like the Plagues of Egypt: high taxes, unemployment, subsistence wages, terrible farm land, few resources, and, in some locales, pests and disease. For the Italians of this era it was all summed up in one word: *miseria*. They wanted out or, at any rate, a temporary reprieve. Thus they embarked on a sojourn in search of capital and opportunity. As the economic situation grew worse, the migration numbers escalated. In 1906 and then again in 1913, close to a million Italians left each year; from 1896 to 1915, about 16 million departed in total, although about a third of them later returned.

Italian migration was characterized by a chain. Several families from one village or town departed; they were soon joined by some of their relatives and friends, and a few more after that. Within a decade, in some cases, more than half the town had been transplanted to the same neighbourhoods, on the same streets, in one of many "Little Italies" that sprang up in New York, Chicago, and Toronto, among numerous other cities. Laurenzana, for instance, lost 40 percent of its population (4,300 people) between 1881 and 1908. The Old World local connections were powerful; of 246 immigrant Italian marriages in Toronto between 1908 and 1935, for instance, the probability of a man and woman from the same town, and certainly from the same province, marrying each other was high. Facilitating this mass movement of people were shipping companies and *padroni*, or labour agents, who recruited the workers to dig Toronto's roads and lay the track for the street railway. Some of them also owned and operated the boarding houses in Ward where the men resided.

Though hardly appreciated at first by Anglo-Toronto, the Italian immigrants arrived bearing trades and skills that in time enhanced the city's character and ethnic flavour. In the 1830s, for example, an Italian immigrant named Francesco Rossi opened the first ice cream shop in Toronto near Bay and King Streets. From Val Rendena came knife-grinders; from Termini Imerse, fruit merchants—who by 1925 operated 25 percent of all fruit stores in Toronto; bricklayers and barbers from Pisticci; construction workers from Codroipo; and from Laurenzana came street musicians like Francesco Glionna, as competent a musician as he was a carpenter.

Once in Toronto in the 1870s, Francesco and his family rented a house on Chestnut Street in the Ward. A wily businessman, he soon owned his home and nearly a dozen more. More impressively, in 1885 he opened the Glionna Hotel on Chestnut and Edward Streets, which immediately became a popular immigrant saloon and an office for his labour agency. The corner of Chestnut and Edwards itself, says the community's historian John Zucchi, "remained the centre of the city's laurenzanese community until the First World War." Acting as a pardrone, Glionna found fellow Italians to work on the Welland Canal, among other construction projects. By the turn of the century, Francesco was the patriarch of the city's "most influential" Italian family and a key member of the Umberto Primo Benevolent Society, which looked out for and helped the ever-increasing number of Italian newcomers. His son Donato was a key Liberal party organizer, and his grandsons George and Joseph were, respectively, the first Italian doctor and lawyer in Toronto during the twenties.

JOSEPH SALSBERG AND FRANCESCO GLIONNA were only two of the thousands of European and Asian immigrants who changed the face of Toronto in the late nineteenth and early twentieth centuries. The city's population, 208,000 in 1901, jumped to 380,000 in 1911 and then to 522,000 by 1921, only 100,000 less than Montreal. Among the 380,000 in 1911 were 3,000 Italians, 18,000 Jews, 9,800 Germans, 1,000 Chinese, and an assortment of Poles, Macedonians, and Ukrainians. Clifford Sifton, the minister of the interior in charge of immigration in Wilfrid Laurier's government from 1897 to 1905, had purposely opened Canada's doors for "stalwart peasants in sheepskin coats" to farm the prairies, but in doing so he also allowed many immigrants to populate the country's major cities.

Still, Toronto's population remained more than 85 percent white Anglo-Saxon, either British or Canadian born, and overwhelmingly Protestant. The vast majority of the

100,000 or so British immigrants who settled in Toronto between 1900 and 1914 found a niche in their new Canadian homeland. It is true that some ended up in the northwest area of the city, living as paupers in what became derisively known as "Shacktown" and at the mercy of charity. (Alice Randle, who wrote about Shacktown for *Saturday Night* in January 1914, was slightly more positive. The small cabins, she wrote, had "curtained windows [that] showed a thrifty woman's care... Each cottage seemed to have a personality all its own.") Many did suffer in silence, since they believed that there was "no sympathy for them here," as a *Globe* article in January 1908 explained. The newspaper, along with the Saint George's Society, found them "food, fuel and clothing." But most British immigrants found jobs in factories and stores, lived in working-class neighbourhoods around Gerrard or on Danforth east of the Don River, and imbued Toronto with both trade unionism and a deep affection for and pride in the mighty British empire.

Whether they wanted to or not, the non-Anglo minority attracted a lot of attention. This was the result of an ingrained xenophobia that was characteristic of Canadian society for much of the twentieth century; as sportsman and writer Frederick Barlow Cumberland stated in a 1904 speech to the Empire Club, expressing a widely shared sentiment, "We are the trustees for the British race. We hold this land in allegiance." It was also because these strange newcomers—who spoke languages other than English or French and dressed differently and ate exotic foods—resided in the squalor of the Ward, "a veritable ghetto," as the *Mail and Empire* dubbed the quarter in 1911. The neighbourhood had cheap and rundown housing and was close to the factories where many of the immigrants worked. There were also important cultural and religious connections—synagogues, schools, churches, food shops—that made the struggles of day-to-day life a bit easier.

Yet in an era when the eugenics movement, with its theories about the alleged link between biology and morality, was popular, the arrival of so many strangers was frightening and threatening. University of Toronto biology professor Ramsay Wright deemed the slums of the Ward "a cancer of the modern civic organism." Indeed, there was no denying the abject poverty, outdoor privies, and derelict atmosphere that made the Ward a blot on Toronto. "Here is the festering sore of our city life," inveighed Rev. H.S. Magee in a profile of the Ward published in the *Christian Guardian* in 1911. "The lanes, alleyways and backyards are strewn with refuse, houses behind houses, and in the yards between unsightly piles of ramshackle out-houses that are supposed to provide sanitary conveniences." After a long day touring the Ward's sweatshops in 1897 and witnessing first-hand the exploitation, abusive child labour, and grinding poverty, twenty-two-year-old William Lyon Mackenzie King, on assignment for the *Mail and Empire*, was appalled. "What a story of Hell," he wrote in his diary. "My mind all ablaze."

Politicians, church leaders, reformers, physicians, academics, and journalists raised the alarm about these undesirable and clearly primitive, uncivilized, dirty, immoral, and degenerate foreigners. The newcomers might supply some needed cheap and unskilled labour, but they could never be assimilated—or so ran the argument. "Foreign trash," "heathens," "vermin," "indolent social parasites," and "foreign scum" were just a few of the "colourful" ways the newcomers were contemptuously depicted in speeches, government documents, and newspaper and magazine articles. "Many of our non-Anglosaxon [*sic*] population are amongst the best of the people from their native lands," noted a 1915 report from the Canadian Methodist Department of Temperance and Moral Reform. "It is lamentable that such large numbers have come to Canada during the last decade bringing a laxity of morals, an ignorance, a superstition and an absence of high ideals of personal character or of national life... [They] may constitute a danger to themselves and a menace to our national life." Speaking in the House of Commons in early 1914, E.N. Lewis, a Member of Parliament from Ontario, was more succinct. "We do not want a nation of organ-grinders and banana sellers in this country," he declared.

In a November 1909 feature on the Ward in *Canadian Magazine*, journalist Augustus Bridle took some solace in the news that plans were underway to move Toronto General Hospital from its Cabbagetown site on Gerrard and Sumach to the corner of College and University Avenue, near the northern border of the Ward (the new hospital was opened in June 1913, thanks in part to the fundraising efforts of business tycoon Joseph Flavelle). As Bridle pointed out, "the Ward had a reputation for dirt and disease and diligent microbes. The Hospital was the enemy of all." It was also not a coincidence that the legendary psychiatrist Dr. Charles K. Clarke ran his clinic from the new hospital with the intent of amassing data and case studies on the connections between "feeble-mindedness, illicit sexuality, and venereal disease."

Leading the charge to keep Toronto pure from infection by foreigners, prostitutes, and liquor abuse was the evangelical Presbyterian Reverend John Shearer, likely the most puritanical moral reformer Canada has ever produced. "We may not want to copy the Puritans in every particular, but, in their respect for righteousness, law, order, religion, and the Lord's Day, we could stand a good deal more Puritanism than we are getting," he argued in a 1906 article. Six years earlier, he had become the first general secretary of the Dominion's Lord's Day Alliance and lobbied zealously for the federal Lord's Day Act, which enforced Sunday as a day of rest and which was passed in 1906. As head of the Presbyterian Department of Temperance and Moral Reform (later the Board of Social Service and Evangelism) he battled the twin evils of prostitution and liquor. With little evidence, he blamed Chinese and Japanese immigrants for operating most of the brothels and other "dens of vice" in Toronto. "We do not have to go six blocks away from Massey Hall, Toronto," he proclaimed in a 1911 address to the pre-assembly congress of the Presbyterian Church of Canada, "to find a whole city-full... of people that are at any rate non-Anglo-Saxon, a large portion of them non-Christian, and a goodly portion of them, whether non-Anglo-Saxon or Anglo-Saxon, pagan in life."

About the only reform-minded Torontonian who did not panic about the Ward, it seemed, was Mary Joplin Clarke, who worked at the Central Neighbourhood House. "The danger that lurks in these crowded streets is not always clearly formulated in the minds of those who fear it... but at any rate the fear remains, and probably it could best be analyzed as Fear of the Unknown," she pointed out in a 1915 report. But, she insisted, "for those of us who know the Ward and its inhabitants it is the safest and friendliest place on earth."

In this fight, reformers used the public school as the agent of assimilation. Teachers in schools in and around the Ward encouraged their foreign students to learn English by any means possible and, more significantly, imparted to their young charges the correct moral values. This meant teaching them respect for law and order and having them embrace "thrift, punctuality, and hygiene." As one Toronto public school teacher put it, Canadians are "tidy, neat and sincere—foreigners are not."

A more sympathetic strategy in the noble goal of "Canadianization" was employed by Frances Esther How, otherwise known by children in the Ward as "Aunt Hessie." An Irish immigrant herself, How became a teacher and in the 1880s established a school in the Ward for "delinquent and homeless boys" after being asked to do so by Mayor William Howland. Operating after 1892 from classrooms in a building on Elizabeth Street, her progressive approach to education made "men out of street Arabs," as a December 1906 *Saturday Night* magazine article noted. "If the children of the Ward are dirty, it is not the fault of Elizabeth Street school. A big bath has been installed there, and the little tots as well as the bigger chaps are given a chance to take a dip." On her retirement in 1912, a new school building was erected and called the Hester How School.

Another key figure was Dr. Charles Hastings, the city's chief medical officer from 1910 to 1929. By the time he accepted the position, Hastings, fifty-two, had had a long and distinguished career as a physician and obstetrician. He was set to cut back on his work when his youngest daughter died from typhoid fever after drinking contaminated milk. Indeed, for children and infants in the early decades of the twentieth century, no matter what their class, Toronto was a perilous place to live. Between 1900 and 1911, the city had infant mortality rates higher than London, England, and far higher than nearby Rochester, NY (in 1908, for example, Toronto's infant mortality rate was 153 per 1,000, while in Rochester it was 86). Besides improper milk pasteurization—it took Hastings until 1915 to make Toronto the first city in Canada to enact compulsory pasteurization of milk—the main cause of typhus and other related diseases remained the dreadful water supply. For years, untreated sewage was dumped into the harbour close to where the city obtained its water supply. Only when the city put a stop to this, again at Hastings's behest, did typhoid rates significantly decline. Hastings also finally rid Toronto of outdoor privies by 1918.

During the first years in his new position, Hastings targeted the Ward's slum housing, which he deemed a "menace to public health, affording hotbeds for germination and dissemination of disease, vice and crime." But he subscribed, as well, to the popular notion that the crux of the social problems in the Ward was linked to the foreign invasion. "Thousands [of immigrants] are being imported annually of Russians, Finns, Italians, Hungarians, Belgians, Scandinavians, etc," he wrote in a 1907 journal article. "The lives and environments of a large number of these have, no doubt, been such as is well calculated to breed degenerates. Who would think of comparing for a moment, in the interests of our country, mentally, morally, physically or commercially, a thousand of these foreigners with a thousand of Canadian birth?"

Hastings and others who so fervently held these "White Canada Forever" convictions were ultimately proven wrong. The immigrants of the Ward established their own ethnic enclaves, complete with dynamic infrastructure and enduring institutions—schools, shops, synagogues, churches, ethnic-language newspapers, social clubs, and benefit societies—and in the process provided the labour that built and paved Toronto's streets, sweated in its garment-manufacturing industry, did the dirty work at the Keele Street stockyards, and gradually made the city more cosmopolitan. It certainly was not an easy transition. Many white middle-class Torontonians were not fond of Jewish rag peddlers (by one estimation, in 1913 Toronto was said to have one thousand peddlers, the majority of whom were Jewish), Italian fruit salesmen and street musicians, and Chinese launderers.

But as the immigrants worked hard, and as their children were educated, learned English, and moved up in the world, the Jews and Italians who most prominently inhabited the Ward were able to relocate into better neighbourhoods while still retaining their powerful ethnic identities, a meshing of the Old World and the New. By the First World War, and certainly by the early twenties, for instance, "Little Italy," around College and Grace Streets, west of Bathurst, was thriving and developed what Robert Harney called a "commerce of migration," with *padroni* offices, saloons, insurance and real estate agencies, dry goods shops, and restaurants. Much of the social and religious life of the community was focused on St. Agnes Church on Dundas and Grace, which had been transferred from the Irish to the Italians, just as Our Lady of Mt. Carmel Catholic Church, near College and Spadina, had been in 1908. (In 1969 the Chinese community assumed control of Our Lady of Mt. Carmel.) Italian immigrants, many of them from Friuli, a region in northeastern Italy near Venice, for example, dominated the building trades and brick-making.

UNTIL ABOUT 1920, the largest ethnic group of immigrants in the Ward were East European Jews. "Twenty-five years ago there were no Jews [in the Ward] at all," explained John McAree in a *Maclean's* feature article in May 1912. "Now there is nothing but Jews." His depiction of the Jewish neighbourhoods in the Ward was a classic combination of Anglo-Canadian condescension, disdain, and wonder. "The streets swarm with old Jews and young, flashily dressed young Jews in the latest Queen Street styles, and patriarchal old Jews in gabardine and skull cap. Strange noises and smells rise on the air and blend with a Babel of tongues. You might imagine you were strolling through a bazaar in Damascus. You feel that if you had a stronger stomach you would linger a while, while inviting adventures. When you get home, you probably wonder what the medical health officer is about that he permits it. Fifteen thousand of the 20,000 Jews are herded together in these few blocks, dozens of them living, and happily living in a house, that an Englishman and a Scotchman would find far too small for them both." Though a majority of the Jews in the Ward were poor, one exception was Jacob Singer, a Jewish immigrant from Austria who came to Toronto in 1905. Working as a watchmaker, he amassed nearly a hundred houses, many of them in the Ward, and when he died in 1912 left an estate valued, after accounting for liabilities, of $347,000.

The Jewish immigrants also faced a regular barrage of anti-Semitism, a common feature of Canadian society into the 1950s and 1960s. In Toronto and across the country, Jews could not find jobs as teachers, sales clerks, or hospital interns, and appointments of Jewish doctors at teaching hospitals in Toronto did not occur until after the Second World War. (In 1898, in what was probably a Canadian first, a young Jewish woman, Etta Birkenthal, the daughter of a Reform rabbi in Hamilton, and the first Jewish high school teacher in Ontario, was appointed assistant principal of the Palmerston Avenue Public School.) At the University of Toronto it was 1930 before a Jew, Jacob Finkelman, was hired as lecturer in the faculty of law. There were no quotas on admitting Jews into the university, as there were at other Canadian universities, but into the thirties the university administration, according to its historian Martin Friedland, "kept a running tally of the number of Jews at the University."

Gentile mothers invoked the figure of the Jewish peddler, the *Canadian Jewish Times* noted in 1913, as a "bogeyman" to hush their children. Regarded as unwanted outsiders, Jews confronted restrictions at social clubs and summer resorts—although this was more a problem for the earlier generation of well-off English and German Jews who had first settled in the city during the 1840s and 1850s—and in the Ward were routinely the victims of street violence. Jewish schoolchildren were frequently bullied and attacked, as were Jewish peddlers, who were dragged from their wagons by gangs of ruffians or had garbage and stones hurled at them. In 1905, the peddlers organized themselves into the Toronto Hebrew Pedler's Protective Association, though the group was not very effective at stopping the harassment.

Hardly a day went by, it seemed, when there was not a news story in the Toronto papers about Jewish troubles. In October 1910, the *Star* reported on a case in which a seventeen-year-old "Hebrew" girl, Annie Gibble, and her mother were assaulted with stones on Victoria Street. In September 1914, the *Globe* published an account of a Jewish family, living near the corner of Adelaide and Widmer Streets, that had been terrorized by a gang of teenage thugs until the police rescued them. In 1919, yet another gang of hoodlums attacked a "Jewish huckster" behind the back of 15 Edward Street, where he resided. The peddler tried to defend himself but was eventually beaten back by a volley of bricks. The mob let the peddler's horse loose and set his wagon of rags on fire. Before the police could arrive, the mob then turned on the rest of the Ward. Jewish storekeepers shut down their shops. The police and military eventually apprehended the mob leaders, two veterans, and the riot was stopped.

Such harsh treatment reinforced the desire of Jews to live safely and slightly isolated in self-contained neighbourhoods beside other Jews. Already, the longer-established Toronto Jews—many of whom practised a more secular Reform Judaism than the Orthodox faith adhered to by the East Europeans—had built a second and more elaborate Holy Blossom Temple (the first, erected in 1876, was on the corner of Richmond and Yonge Streets) on Bond Street, east of Yonge, where the congregation remained until it relocated in the late 1930s to its current home on Bathurst near Eglinton. Its members might have thought of themselves as being more Canadian, yet, in fact, they often faced the same anti-Semitism as the poor and working-class Jews of the Ward—an anti-Semitism that reinforced the Jewish will to prosper, succeed, and create a variety of institutions that addressed the many political, class, and religious affiliations of the budding community.

By 1914 there were close to two dozen different synagogues and mutual aid societies, or *landsmanshafn*, representing what seemed like every city, town, and *shtetl* in the Pale of Settlement. There was the "Kiever" Synagogue, started in 1912 by immigrants from Kiev, which ran out of a rented house in the Ward for more than a decade until sufficient money was raised for a real sanctuary on Bellevue Avenue near Kensington Market. Jews from Minsk established the Beth Israel Anshei Minsk congregation, or the "Minsker," also in 1912, which was the first synagogue in the Kensington Market area—and remains there to this day, the lone synagogue still in operation from that era, though in another building across the street from its original location.

A private clinic, set up by Dr. S.J. Kaufman, a young Jewish doctor from Cleveland who had married a girl from Toronto and moved to the city in 1907, provided much-needed medical care for the Ward's Jewish residents. As Dorothy Goldstick Dworkin, a nurse who worked with Kaufman, recalled many years later, the Jews who sought help at the clinic "could not speak English and could not make themselves understood at the outpatient clinics of the local hospitals; they could not afford the $1 fee of the private physicians (by 1912 there were five Jewish physicians in the city with offices close to the Ward) and Dr. Kaufman charged only fifty cents in his clinic." When Kaufman and his family returned to Cleveland a few years later, Ida Seigel, a prominent Jewish activist, organized a group that took over the clinic. It became the Jewish Dispensary, evolved in 1923—following a decade-long fundraising effort—into the Hebrew Maternity and Convalescent Hospital in a building on Yorkville, and eventually became the Mount Sinai Hospital.

Great philosophical debates took place in Yiddish in the heart of the Ward. At a store at the corner of Louisa and Elizabeth Streets, run by Shimon Colofsky and by Samuel and Joseph Rosenfeld, who doubled as carpenters, a salon was convened for "formal discussions, readings from Yiddish classics, and talks on Zionism." At another store on Elizabeth Street, owned by Chanan and Boris Dworkin, radical labourites clashed with anarchists and anti-Zionists. And over at Yitzhak Herman's ice-cream store on Agnes (now Dundas) Street, Labour Zionists held court.

In the years after the First World War, as Jews made their way out of the Ward to a slightly better neighbourhood closer to Spadina and centred on the animated Kensington Market (where there were hundreds of Jewish shops within a one-and-a-half-kilometre radius), the Labour Lyceum, the headquarters of the city's Jewish garment unions, was the favourite spot for cultural and leisure activities. Here you could attend poetry recitals by the Yiddish poet Shimon Nepom, a streetcar conductor, and Yudica (Yehudit Zik), the "poet of Spadina's sweatshops," who arrived in Toronto in the late twenties at the age of thirty-three, after years of hardship in Europe, and found work as a seamstress. "Thinly fragile is dawn's early air," one of Yudica's poems began. "Spadina street of stores and factories. Lies under a web of gray; And dreams the dream of workers' fortunes."

May Day was also a special occasion, starting with a long parade down Spadina that culminated with a boisterous rally in the park at Christie Pits. That evening there would be more festivities at the packed Labour Lyceum. Community newspaper editor Ben Lappin recalled a variety of passionate Yiddish speeches "calling for an end to the exploitation of man by man, extolling the dignity of *halutziut* (pioneer movement) in Palestine, decrying the cynicism of the Communists, and pledging the might of labour in the struggle against the dark forces of fascism."

More entertaining still were the lively performances at the Lyric, the Yiddish theatre on Agnes near Terauley (at the old Agnes Street Methodist Church), and in later years at the more accommodating Standard Theatre on the corner of Spadina and Dundas.

At both theatres the hardships of Jewish life were presented in poignant dramas (Jacob Gordin's *Jewish King Lear* was a fan favourite) and hilarious comedies that reflected on the immigrants' lives and brought back fond memories of the old country.

Another source of entertainment and pride for Toronto Jews was watching boxer Sammy Luftspring, who had been born in 1916 and grew up in the Ward. (His parents made money selling home-brewed rye whiskey for twenty-five cents a shot.) He learned to box as a teenager at the Hebrew Association of Young Men's and Young Women's Clubs (later the Young Men's Hebrew Association or YMHA), then operating out of the basement of the Brunswick Avenue Talmud Torah. Like other Jewish athletes, Luftspring refused to participate in the 1936 Berlin Olympics as a protest against the Nazis' anti-Jewish policies. After he turned professional, he became famous for displaying a prominent Star of David on his shorts and was the Canadian welterweight champion from 1938 to 1940. "For us Jews," Luftspring later recalled, "the world of College and Spadina never stopped buzzing."

Before or after a Yiddish theatre performance or boxing match, there were fresh bagels to munch on at Aaron and Sarah Ladovsky's eatery United Bakers—the store, which opened in the Ward in 1912 (and celebrated its centennial in 2012), followed the Jewish migration to Spadina with a new venue near Dundas in 1920, where it remained for the next forty-six years until it moved north up Bathurst—or ice cream at Harry and Jenny Shopsowitz's tiny parlour on Spadina (some decades later their sons Sam and Izzy transformed the business with world-class corned beef and hotdogs). All these events and happenings were covered in great detail in the Toronto Jewish community's Yiddish newspaper, *Der Yidisher Zhurnal*, established in 1913 and edited for many years by Avraham Rhinewine, who shared his readers' support of unions and socialism.

Naturally, not everyone was thrilled with this development or appreciated the distinctions between Reform and Orthodox, liberals, socialists, and Zionists. To the rest of Toronto, they were all "Hebrews," and there were too many of them. The *Globe* was less than impressed with what its editors declared to be "a Jewish invasion of the public schools," and the *Telegram* expressed concern about the opening of the new and impressive Beth Jacob synagogue in 1922 on Henry Street. Under the headline "Another New Synagogue," the newspaper claimed that "the rate of increase compared with that of the Hebrews, does not put the Gentiles in a winning place. The Jews are not creeping in. They are coming by leaps and bounds, establishing churches and schools... all over the city." Two years later the same issue was addressed, but even more virulently. "An influx of Jews puts a worm next to the kernel of every fair city where they get a hold," an editorial stated. "These people have no national tradition... They are not the material out of which to shape a people holding a national spirit... Not on the frontiers among the pioneers of the plough and axe are they found, but in the cities where their low standards of life cheapen all about them."

Presbyterian and Anglican missions determined the best way to rid the city of Jews, and in the process save their souls, was to convert them to Christianity. "The foreign quarter," an editorial in *Methodist Missionary Outlook* in 1910 declared, "is bound to become a menace to our civilization unless it learns to assimilate the moral and religious ideals and standards of citizenship which go to make a Christian nation."

By this time, the first Presbyterian mission had been working among the Jews for about two years in the Ward on Terauley Street, led by Reverend Sabeti Benjamin Rohold, a converted Jew who had been born in Jerusalem. The mission offered newcomers medical, educational, and social services; it also had access to all of the students at the Elizabeth Street school for various proselytizing activities. Its main aim of conversion met with limited success, despite Rohold's claims to the contrary. In 1912, Rohold stated that he had been "privileged to listen to the testimony of hundreds of Jews confessing faith in Christ and witnessed the baptism of forty-two adults and children." Other reports, however, estimate the number of converts in a three-year span was from six to twenty. The other missions had similar low rates of success.

To be fair, such behaviour and attitudes were not universal, and some members of the city's elite adopted a more enlightened approach. In 1906, several aldermen, as well as Mayor Emerson Coatsworth, attended an early Zionist convention in Toronto. The mayor told the audience that he and other members of council "found the Jew as good a citizen as can be desired." Similarly in 1913, when Nahum Sokolow, a Zionist leader, visited Toronto, he was accorded the royal treatment by Mayor Horatio Hocken, who gave him a personal tour of the city and even hosted a kosher lunch for him at the Queen's Hotel.

BEYOND EDUCATION, intellectual pursuits, and entertainment, life was really about making a living. And for a majority of Jews in Toronto during the first part of the twentieth century that meant working as garment workers. By 1931, more than 5,200 Jews—or about one in three—were employed in some way or other in the needle trades. Their Old World skills were easily transplanted to North America. "At a machine," John McAree suggested, "two Jews are worth, at the lowest calculation, three Gentiles. One manufacturer told me the other day that one Jew is worth four Gentiles." Their labour was not only plentiful; it was also cheap. Many workers were women, underpaid and exploited by Jewish and non-Jewish factory owners alike. One of the more notable garment industry success stories was that of David Dunkelman, a Polish Jewish immigrant who founded Tip Top Tailors in 1910 at a small store on Yonge Street—he had a contest to name the business and a journalist came up with "Tip Top Tailors" and won the $25 prize. Selling tailor-made suits initially for a total price of fourteen dollars proved to be a brilliant marketing strategy. By 1931, Tip Top Tailors was the second-largest garment company in the city and employed seven hundred workers.

Toronto may not have had the infamous sweatshops of New York's Lower East Side, and there were only a handful of tenements in the Ward, yet Jews and other immigrants were systematically abused nonetheless, whether they exclusively did piecework out of their homes, were employed in a factory, or did both. So-called speed-ups, in which floor managers demanded faster work, were exhausting. Rules prohibited workers from speaking to each other, using the washroom when they wanted, and leaving the factory floor. Female employees frequently suffered sexual harassment.

A union organizer who investigated the dire situation in August 1908 discovered this typical scene in the Ward. There was a room in the basement, "about fifteen feet square," in which a family of six or seven persons were "engaged at 11 o'clock at night working on 'ready-made' garments, while in the same rooms, used for sleeping, cooking and eating, as well as working, a young girl was lying in bed sick." For these twelve- to fourteen-hour days, the Jewish workers generally were paid less than five dollars a week, hardly enough to get by on. Such severe realities naturally led to demands by workers for higher wages, better working conditions, and union protection. The owners mightily resisted, and bitter labour confrontations ensued. Jews were on both sides of these battles, and in the Ward and Kensington Market neighbourhoods, Jewish workers who did not support unions or, worse, acted as strikebreakers, were ostracized by their friends and families.

In Toronto, the most active of the so-called Jewish unions were the International Ladies' Garment Workers' Union (ILGWU) and the Toronto Cloakmakers' Union. It took until 1909 for an ILGWU local to be organized and another two years to obtain affiliation with the national union based in New York City. The local Cloakmakers' Union was established during the same period by Abraham Kirzner and Yudel Cohen after they received encouragement from Jewish tailors who visited Toronto from Rochester, NY. Any union organizing had to be done in secret, however, lest the owners find out what was afoot. Joe Salsberg told historian Ruth Frager in a 1984 interview that he recalled an incident when "one of the activists in the shop was promptly fired when the man's union book fell out of his pocket and the boss found it."

The first real test for the Jewish unions came in 1912, when they took on one of the city's most powerful and popular companies, Eaton's. By this time, Eaton's department store had its own massive clothing factory complex, which eventually employed as many as six thousand workers, a majority of them Jewish. John Craig Eaton, who had inherited the family firm following the death of his father, Timothy, in 1907 and was caustically referred to by the garment workers as the "King of Canada," ran a non-union shop and was proud to do so.

Unhappy with long days and low wages, union organizers began marshalling support. In February 1912, matters came to a head after management ordered sixty-five tailors to sew in coat linings, a task that required extra time but for which they were to receive no additional pay, and that had up to then been done by female seamstresses or finishers. The men refused. "*Mir vellen nisht aroycenemen dem bissle fun broyt fun di mayler fun undzere shvester,*" they declared in Yiddish. "We will not take the morsel of bread from the mouths of our sisters." Unwilling to tolerate such a challenge to their authority, Eaton's managers had the police escort the tailors out of the factory and locked them out. Within days, 1,200 workers were on a sympathy strike. John Craig Eaton and his managers stood firm, claiming that unions had no legal right to interfere in the affairs of his company. Eaton also declared that he would shut down the factory before he succumbed to union demands.

The Jewish community rallied to support the strikers with food and charity, and the ILGWU doled out meagre strike pay. Jewish women tried to raise money for the strikers on the streets, until city officials ordered them to stop. A huge pro-labour rally was held at Massey Hall on March 20, with three thousand vocal Yiddish and English unionists in the audience. Later that day, thousands joined in a parade of solidarity through the streets of downtown past the Eaton's factory and on to the Labour Lyceum. Cries for a boycott of Eaton's department store were heard, but little came of that.

A main problem for the strikers was that non-Jewish workers were less inclined to become involved, since the strike was perceived to be, in the words of the Toronto labour newspaper the *Lance*, "only a strike of Jews." Moreover, within the Jewish community itself the strike did not garner much support from middle-class merchants and businessmen, who definitely did not welcome the negative attention. Many of them were members of the Holy Blossom Temple (including Sigmund Lubelsky, a senior Eaton's manager), and that synagogue's leader, Rabbi Solomon Jacobs, already had cautioned that "Jews must not rebel" if they hoped to fit into Canadian society. To prove his point, Rabbi Jacobs, along with a former synagogue president, the influential Magistrate Jacob Cohen ("Jakey" to his friends, and the first Jewish magistrate in Toronto), attempted to mediate a settlement. But Eaton's management still refused to negotiate with the strikers and was, in fact, running ads in England and Wales for strikebreakers.

By mid-April, with strike pay dwindling, the union more or less surrendered. A handful of the tailors were rehired by the company, though the majority were forced to find employment elsewhere. The Eaton's Strike of 1912 was only the beginning of more than two decades of labour strife in the city. While the unions gradually won rights and recognition, many of the strikes were marked by violence, police abuse, and bitterness. Eaton's, in particular, did not moderate its anti-union position and stopped hiring Jewish workers after 1912.

A sign of the Jewish community's growth in both numbers and political clout was the election of Louis Singer to city council in the election of January 1914, Toronto's second Jewish alderman (Newman Leopold Steiner, German businessman and artisan, had been elected in St. James' Ward in 1867). Singer, who had immigrated to Toronto from Austria when he was only three years old in 1888, grew up in the Ward and graduated high school from Jarvis Street Collegiate. He eventually put himself through law school and established his own law office. He represented Ward 4, which encompassed St. John's Ward and the Spadina Jewish neighbourhood, for the next three years. Of note, too, was the election to city council in 1924 of thirty-one-year-old Nathan Phillips. Born in Brockville, Ontario, Phillips lived in Cornwall for many years until after he became a lawyer in 1914 in Toronto. His victory as one of Ward 4's three aldermen marked the start of his notable three and a half decades in civic politics, which culminated with his election as mayor in 1955—the first Jewish mayor in the city's history.

A FAR SMALLER IMMIGRANT COMMUNITY than Jews and Italians, but more ominous from the perspective of the city's leaders were the "un-assimilable" Chinese. "Let them swarm in once and the yellow stain on the country will be one that cannot be rubbed out," warned *Saturday Night* in September 1906. The *Globe* was slightly more enlightened, arguing in a October 1907 editorial that the "average Oriental is dangerous and injuriously inferior to the average Canadian." Adding that its main concern was not immorality but Canada's political future, the newspaper claimed, "Democracy is imperilled by the introduction of alien races devoid of the very capacity for democratic government."

Due to a discriminatory fifty-dollar head tax imposed by the federal government in 1885, which was increased to five hundred dollars in 1903, few Chinese immigrants could afford to enter Canada. Many of the approximately one thousand who resided in Toronto by 1911 had moved east from British Columbia after the Canadian Pacific Railway was completed in the mid-1880s. Nevertheless, their presence triggered decades of fear and apprehension that a "Yellow Peril" was engulfing the city.

Sam Ching operated the first Chinese laundry in Toronto on Adelaide Street East in 1878, and the makings of a Chinatown developed after 1901 in the Ward, around Dundas and Elizabeth Streets, not too far from its current centre at Dundas and Spadina. The city's first Chinese restaurant was likely the Sing Wing Restaurant on Queen Street West, which opened for business in 1901. Tea shops and grocery stores soon followed, but the budding community had to establish its own financial institutions because no bank in Toronto would give a loan to a Chinese immigrant, no matter how successful.

The prejudice was indeed palpable and constant. In a December 1896 story, "Danger in John's Shanty," the *Star* accused Chinese laundrymen of stealing business from white laundry operators with low prices. It also suggested, with no evidence, that Chinese laundries were spreading disease. (The article was highlighted by such sensational subheadings as "The Evil the Chinese Do" and "A Grave Danger.") The following year the *Star* claimed that Chinese laundry owners were not "worthy" of public patronage since they "contribute nothing to the city's welfare in the way of supporting public enterprise, have inferior plants, employ no Canadian help," and sent much of the money they earned back "to their native country." It was further asserted that "Canadian laundries wash and dampen their clothes with pure water, while the Chinamen dampen their clothes with water thrown from their mouths, doubtless often giving clothes a contagion which is ironed into them for the benefit of the Canadian patron." A decade later the Rosedale Ratepayers Association, Toronto's first neighbourhood organization, declared it essential that Chinese laundries be kept out of their area.

Feeding the hysteria was the widely held belief that Chinese men used opium to exploit and sexually assault white women. The Methodist Church officially deemed Chinese restaurants "dangerous places" for Canadian women, and in a series on the "Yellow Peril" in the fall of 1911, the Toronto bi-weekly tabloid *Jack Canuck* (edited by James and Louisa Rogers) issued a dire warning. "The bland smiling Oriental and his quaint pidgin English does not appear very formidable to the young woman who enters his store for the weekly wash," the paper cautioned. "She does not notice the evil lurking in the almond eyes as she accepts the silk handkerchief or other trifling Oriental knick knack." In later stories, its editors wrote of "the demoralizing of [Toronto's] young womanhood by the yellow sojourners in this city."

Arrest statistics and court records did not support such outlandish and racist claims about Chinese corruption. In one case in 1913, Horace Wing, a Chinese merchant, was arrested and charged with "procuring a white woman for immoral purposes" after he answered a young Minnie Wyatt's newspaper advertisement seeking employment as a stenographer. Her parents gave Wing's letter offering her a job to the police. On scant evidence, Wing was convicted and his appeal upheld by the Ontario Supreme Court, which declared that "interracial relationships not be condoned." Wing, however, was given a suspended sentence. Such cases, no matter how frivolous, led the Ontario provincial government of Conservative premier James Whitney to amend the Factory, Shop and Office Building Act in the spring of 1914, prohibiting Chinese businesses from employing white women. For a long time, about the only other ethnic group to patronize Chinese restaurants was the Jews—at least those who did not feel guilty about breaking kosher dietary rules—a cultural culinary taste that has prevailed for Jews in Toronto and throughout North America.

IN THE YEARS BEFORE and after the First World War, the city beyond the Ward continued to expand north above St. Clair Avenue towards Eglinton, east past Danforth and Riverdale Avenues, and west to Jane Street. The eastern extension of Bloor Street was made possible by the construction of the Prince Edward Viaduct (also called the

Don or Bloor Viaduct), a massive $2.4-million project finally approved by Toronto ratepayers in 1913. Supervised by thirty-four-year-old Roland C. Harris, the city's newly appointed Commissioner of Public Works, and built by a small army of immigrant workers, the bridge, which wisely included a second level for the future subway, linked Bloor Street with Danforth when it was completed five years later. (Harris and the building of the viaduct figure prominently in Michael Ondaatje's 1987 novel *In the Skin of a Lion.*) Meanwhile, the prime shopping area had shifted away from King Street to Yonge, with fashionable stores now right up to Bloor Street. And the best promotional gimmick was Eaton's Santa Claus Parade, first held in 1905 and thereafter a Toronto Christmas tradition.

A year earlier, on the night of April 19, 1904, the city's downtown core had been devastated by yet another raging fire—likely started by faulty electric wiring—which destroyed an estimated $10 million of property up and down Front Street and north on Yonge. Amazingly no one died, and the brave employees of the *Evening Telegram* saved their building by dousing whatever they could with water from a perch on the roof. Publisher John Ross Robertson thanked them with generous bonuses.

The *Telegram* and its chief competitors, the *Star* and the *World*, each as unique as their colourful proprietors—the *Telegram*'s Robertson, the *World*'s Billy Maclean, and the *Star*'s Joe Atkinson—filled their pages with bold headlines, local news, human interest stories, advertising, and brief and to-the-point independent editorials (though despite Atkinson's resolve, the *Star* tended to support the Liberals). The *Globe, Mail and Empire*, and *News* also fought overt partisanship, but were more sombre in their approach and style.

Within this urban kingdom, there was lots of money to be made by an unfettered and privileged business elite, which envisioned Toronto as theirs for the taking. And take it they did. New York had the Waldorf Astoria and London, the Ritz. If Toronto was to become a "world-class city," as its business leaders wished, then it too needed its own five-star "palace hotel." In late 1900, a syndicate—which included Robert Jaffray, the owner of the *Globe*; iron foundry magnate Edward Gurney (the principal investor); and distillery giant George Gooderham—began building a new first-class eight-storey hotel close to King and Yonge Streets. At a cost of about $1 million, the lavish King Edward Hotel, designed by architects Henry Ives Cobb of Chicago and Toronto's E.J. Lennox, opened to great fanfare in the spring of 1903.

The *Star* proclaimed the "King Eddy," as it was soon affectionately called, "a monument to the enterprise of Torontonians." At the Royal Canadian Yacht Club Ball on May 22, six hundred select guests dined at the hotel's inaugural social event alongside the governor general and his wife, Lord and Lady Minto, and danced to the music of D'Allesandro's twenty-piece orchestra. A week later the Mintos attended a second gala, the "Citizens' Banquet," for two hundred of the "most prominent ladies and gentlemen of the city." No banquet, the *Globe* gushed, "had so splendid a setting." It was the first banquet, the paper also noted, "where ladies and gentlemen will sit down at the tables together." Thereafter, the King Edward was noted for catering to unescorted women as well as indulging businessmen with Havana cigars and fine Scotch whisky at the oak-panelled Bar and Gentlemen's Café.

An entrepreneur missing from the guest list at the Citizens' Banquet was Senator George Cox, who was away in Montreal attending a directors' meeting for the Dominion Iron and Steel Company, one of the many enterprises he was associated with. Cox, who moved from Peterborough to Toronto in 1888, had overlapping interests in the Bank of Commerce, National Trust, Dominion Securities, and the Canada Life Assurance Company that often put him in a conflict of interest, as a federal Royal Commission later determined. He also (as noted in Chapter Five) had invested in the *Globe* in the early 1880s and was part of the group that bought the *Toronto Evening Star* in 1899 for the benefit of the Liberal Party. In 1896, he had been appointed to the Senate by Wilfrid Laurier for this service to the Liberals.

Cox was a dour man and sported a Methodist or Amish-style full beard, but no moustache. Devout, he and his family were members of the Sherbourne Street Methodist Church, the so-called Millionaires' Church, along with other wealthy luminaries who drove the city's development, like Alfred E. Ames (Cox's son-in-law), sheet-metal manufacturer and federal Conservative politician Albert Kemp, and Joseph Flavelle of the William Davies Company and, as of 1902, the publisher of the (money-losing) independent conservative *News*.

Flavelle, who lived by the Protestant values of "thrift, sobriety and hard work," was a devoted family man and churchgoer, but he was not shy about displaying his wealth. In 1901, the Flavelles built a magnificent mansion adjacent to Queen's Park they called "Holwood"; behind his back, his friends and rivals referred to the Beaux Arts home as "Porker's Palace," a reference to the pork processing that was the source of his wealth. The University of Toronto had leased the land to Flavelle as a reward for his generous financial support of the university and his role as a member of the board of governors. (Holwood eventually became the university's faculty of law.) A staunch believer, as his biographer Michael Bliss notes, that he had an obligation to use his money and talents in the service of his fellow man, Flavelle was more than happy to chair a provincial Royal Commission set up by the Whitney government in 1906 to restructure the university's ailing administration.

The university and its unimaginative president, James Loudon, had no end of critics. In the spring of 1904, the *Globe* ran a series of articles on the university, concluding that its faculty were characterized by "deadwood" and "fossilism." *Saturday Night* was more direct and cutting. "With few exceptions [the faculty] are regarded as mediocrities, a bunch of cheap men whose manners, methods, and appearance would hardly pass the inspection of a High School board in a country village," a May 1904 diatribe in the magazine declared. "You would find more dignified and better groomed men, with better carriage and deportment and more intellectual faces among the same number of policemen or firemen than you would among the professors and fellows and tutors who run the educational mill up in the [Queen's] Park." That may have been an exaggeration, but the university administration definitely needed an overhaul. Working with Flavelle on the commission were six other distinguished and prominent men of religion, education, and business—including Edmund Walker, president of the Canadian Bank of Commerce and an avid supporter of the arts and the university, who later served as chairman of the U of T's board of governors from 1910 to 1923; and eighty-two-year-old Goldwin Smith. To accommodate Smith, the commission convened in his elegant dining room at the Grange.

Once the final report was submitted—a messenger boy had secretly given a draft of the report to the *World*, which annoyed the university and government by publishing its contents ahead of the official announcement—the Whitney government followed through on its recommendations by separating the university from direct government control. From that point onward, a board of governors was to manage the university's finances, and a senate was to oversee its academic affairs, thereby eliminating charges of nepotism and bias that shadowed many faculty appointments. Loudon was forced out as president and Robert Falconer, a Halifax educational administrator, was appointed to the position, which he held with distinction for the next twenty-five years.

One of the early highlights of the Falconer years, following a recommendation of the 1906 commission—and significant fundraising by Walker and business tycoon E.B. Osler—was the opening of the west wing of the Royal Ontario Museum (ROM) in the spring of 1914, a three-storey "Byzantine-style" building that was entered off Bloor Street. The museum was a creature of the provincial government, which formally established it by an act of the legislature, and was affiliated with the university until 1968. Right from the start, the ROM "had about it the air of a temple," as its historian Lovat Dickson has described it. On display in the museum was more than a decade's worth of collections, which had up to then been kept at various colleges, including Egyptian, Chinese, and West Asian artifacts that enhanced the ROM's international reputation.

Edmund Walker and Goldwin Smith were also involved in establishing the Art Gallery of Toronto in 1919 as a permanent home for the Art Museum of Toronto, which had been founded almost two decades earlier (the Art Gallery of Toronto was renamed Art Gallery of Ontario in 1966). Neither Smith, who died in 1910, nor his wife, Harriet, who had died a year earlier, lived to see the opening of the gallery. In 1900,

Walker had convinced them to bequeath their magnificent estate, the Grange (which actually belonged to Harriet), to the City of Toronto so that it could be transformed into an art gallery. A major expansion was completed by 1918, with three new galleries, and two years after that the Art Gallery of Toronto presented the first exhibition of paintings by Group of Seven artists A.Y. Jackson and J.E.H. MacDonald. Though Jackson, MacDonald, and the other members of the celebrated group later portrayed themselves as "underdog artists fighting for their radical vision against a narrow, conservative society," Robert Fulford points out that, in truth, the "Toronto establishment blessed the group at its birth."

One of those establishment art patrons was the bombastic businessman Henry Pellatt, who donated medieval arms and armour to the ROM. Pellatt did not just want to support a museum, however; he wanted to live in one—or in a castle, at any rate. Pellatt was born in Kingston in 1859 and educated at Upper Canada College. As a young man, he learned the ups and downs of high finance from his father, Henry Sr., a partner in a stock brokerage firm with E.B. Osler. In the 1870s, the company was one of the movers at the Toronto Stock Exchange, still a small operation in those days, with trading almost exclusively in bank securities and a membership of fewer than fifty brokers.

Pellatt never looked back. During the 1890s he invested in coal and silver mines and South American utilities and reaped a fortune; by 1911 he was probably worth close to $20 million and had interests and directorships in two dozen companies. A fair chunk of his fortune was also derived from his astute investment in the Toronto Electric Light Company, which for a time had a monopoly providing electricity to the city's streets and residents. In 1903, Pellatt joined with William Mackenzie and Frederic Nicholls, a vice-president of Canadian General Electric, to develop an even greater potential source of revenue: hydroelectric power at Niagara Falls. The scheme might have worked, except that other Toronto businessmen, including most notably the "brusque and overbearing" cigar-box manufacturer Adam Beck, as well as civic-conscious and commonsense politicians like Premier James Whitney, determined that electric power was too precious to be left in the hands of opportunistic profiteers. Pellatt left the fight to the enterprising Mackenzie, who was still running the Toronto Railway Company, but it was a losing battle against the public ownership campaign led by Beck, who was elected to the Ontario Legislature in 1902. The Hydro-Electric Power Commission, today's Ontario Hydro, was established in 1906, and by 1922 the assets of Mackenzie's reorganized Electrical Development Company had been bought out.

Pellatt had yet other adventures. He had enlisted in the Queen's Own Rifles of Canada when he was seventeen and was besotted with the military thereafter. He rose to the rank of colonel and later, upon his retirement in 1939, to major-general. It was an expensive hobby: in 1910, to celebrate the regiment's fiftieth anniversary, he financed a trip for the entire six hundred-member regiment and its horses to England. "Pretentious" does not quite describe Pellatt, who was honoured with a knighthood in 1905 as reward for his work with the Queen's Own Rifles.

Naturally, as "Sir Henry," he and his family had to have the requisite mansion. Not any mansion, mind you. Pellatt owned a prime piece of Toronto property on the hill above Davenport. In 1911, he hired architect E.J. Lennox, who had designed the King Edward Hotel and city hall, to let his imagination embrace the luxury and style favoured by European aristocracy. Lennox did just that and came up with the royal (and somewhat absurd) Casa Loma, a $3.5-million project with ninety-eight rooms, elevator, central vacuum, and separate stables and servants quarters. Three bowling alleys were also in the plans. In the spring of 1914, after three years of construction by three hundred workers, Sir Henry and his wife, Lady Mary, took up residence, though Casa Loma was never actually finished.

Pellatt was spending too much money. He took a big financial hit when one of his business interests, the Home Bank, failed in 1923, and he was forced to sell off many of his assets to cover his liabilities as a director of the bank. Matters only got worse after that. The city bumped his taxes on Casa Loma from $600 in 1913 to $12,000, an amount he claimed he could not afford. There was no heat in Casa Loma during the cold winter of 1923–24, and the roof leaked. Somewhat humiliated and owing millions, Pellatt held an auction that June in which he parted with everything from high-priced paintings to bathroom fixtures—though he only recouped a small portion of what the items were worth. (An expensive mahogany writing table with five drawers and a brass rail sold for only $58; the matching chair for $18.) He and Mary soon left Toronto for his summer farmhouse in King City.

For a while it appeared that a group of American investors was going to transform Casa Loma into a hotel, and it did open in the late twenties as a popular nightclub where patrons dined and danced to the "swinging" melodies of Glen Gray and his Casa Loma Orchestra. In 1933 the city finally took over the castle, which was then in rough shape, in lieu of more than $25,000 in back taxes owing. The Kiwanis Club saved and slowly restored it, turning it into the unique tourist attraction it is to this day. Sir Henry would not have been surprised.

PELLATT WAS AN EXTREME EXAMPLE of Tory Toronto's dedication to King and Country, which reached a fever pitch during the First World War. When Canada found itself at war in early August 1914 as part of the British Empire, the vast majority of Torontonians heartily agreed with Liberal leader Sir Wilfrid Laurier's response of "Ready, Aye, Ready." Few events prompted such a spontaneous outburst of patriotism, with street parades and Union Jacks hung from every flagpole and building. A committee led by Chief Justice William Mulock, publisher Joe Atkinson, and financier Edward Wood quickly obtained pledges from fellow businessmen for $700,000 towards the war effort. Young men did not walk but ran to the armouries to enlist. Before the war was over on November 11, 1918, hundreds of Toronto women would also be involved in the fight as nurses, fundraisers, and factory workers at munitions and airplane plants. And seventy thousand men, the most from any Canadian city, would be part of the country's expeditionary force. Of those, approximately ten thousand, or one in seven, died, and many thousands more came home wounded and missing arms and legs.

On its wall of honour, Eaton's department store proudly displayed the photographs of all 2,200 of its employees who volunteered; the company even continued paying married men their full wages and single men half wages, a gesture that cost the company at least $2 million over the next four years. At the University of Toronto, 250 male students immediately signed up in August 1914. By mid-November, one of them, R.E. Mackenzie Richards, had died in a battle near Ypres, Belgium. Nonetheless, the pressure to enlist never let up. Future Canadian prime minister Lester Pearson, only seventeen years old and a student in the fall of 1914, joined as a medical orderly with the university's hospital unit and a year later was overseas with the Canadian Army Medical Corps. He was committed to the cause as much as anyone else, but also later conceded that he did not want "a white feather [a symbol of cowardice] pinned on" his lapel. The U of T campus soon became the training area for the British Flying Corps, and the men slept in tents set up on the grounds of Victoria College. By the war's end, six thousand students and faculty members were involved in the conflict in one way or another, and six hundred of them perished. Among the many wounded were two notable future professors, historian Frank Underhill and political economist Harold Innis, who was likely saved when part of the shrapnel that injured him hit a notebook in his pocket. Another university graduate who did not survive was Dr. John McCrae, the author of the war's most enduring poem, "In Flanders Fields." He died in Europe in January 1918 of pneumonia.

The ugly side of the war's patriotism was a predictable virulent anti-German hostility. Three German professors lost their jobs at the University of Toronto, though university president Robert Falconer treated them fairly, despite cries from most members of the board of governors to fire them without pay. "I cannot see why we should be paying Germans salaries here when thousands of young men of Britain are being killed by Germans at the front," E.B. Osler said in a response to Falconer's decision to keep the trio on full salary until the end of the academic year. Courses in the German language were offered throughout the war, but it lost its status as a key subject area then and for many years after.

The city's chief war booster was the animated Tommy Church, the populist mayor from 1915 to 1921. Church, who first served on city council, had the right credentials. He was an Orangeman, though not a zealous one, and an avid fan of boxing and the Argonauts football club. Church took the war, and Toronto's involvement, personally and made a point of being at Union Station, wearing his dapper suits and trademark straw fedora, to welcome soldiers back to the city. He also visited many of the wounded at their homes.

One of the few people to question Church's integrity was the soon-to-be celebrated author Ernest Hemingway, who worked as a reporter for the *Star* from 1920 to 1924. There was no middle ground for Hemingway, especially when it came to the war. In 1915 the mayor was forty-five years old, single, and partially deaf. Nevertheless, from Hemingway's obdurate viewpoint, Church was a "slacker" for not fighting at the front. "From the standpoint of an interested observer," Hemingway wondered in the first piece he wrote for the newspaper, "why should an unmarried man of Mayor Church's age, no matter how well exempted, who took no active part in the war, be so popular with returned men?" The *Star*'s editors felt the story was too disrespectful and never ran it. A librarian saved it from the trash and filed it away for posterity in the newspaper's library.

The war put added stress on the city's ethnic communities, particularly those from Germany or Austria-Hungary. Toronto Jews held a pro-war rally at Massey Hall in the spring of 1915 that received positive coverage in the press, also drawing attention, as the *Globe* noted, "to the half-million Jews who are fighting against Prussianism in Europe." As the war dragged on into 1917, returned soldiers lashed out at anyone they felt was unpatriotic. When a rumour spread that a wounded veteran had been snubbed by an employee of Austrian descent at a downtown restaurant, other soldiers attacked and destroyed the eatery. In a knee-jerk reaction, Mayor Church demanded that the chief of police compel other restaurants to tell authorities how many "enemy aliens" they employed.

Prime Minister Robert Borden's decision in June 1917 to introduce conscription for overseas service exacerbated tensions in Toronto further. Needless to say, the city was overwhelmingly supportive of the draft and of Borden's Union government (which included Borden's Conservative MPs but also a number of Liberals and independents who supported conscription). At a large public gathering at Queen's Park on June 2, with Tommy Church presiding, the ten-thousand-strong crowd cheered as speaker after speaker expressed support for conscription and urged the government to "take immediate steps to put down sedition in Canada." Rousing applause was heard after one of the officials on the dais suggested that the government "put a revolver to the head of a fit man who refused to go." A day later, at least three hundred veterans descended on the Labour Temple to break up an anti-conscription meeting of "socialists." In the "bedlam" that ensued, as the *Star* reported, the hall was thrown into disarray and many "foreigners" in attendance—a Finnish band was on hand to play the socialist song "The Red Flag"—were hurt before the police showed up to rescue them.

The highlight of the pro-conscription–Union government campaign was the Win-the-War Convention that packed the Arena Gardens on Mutual Street in August 1917. A crowd of more than six thousand cheered the thousands of war veterans present and listened attentively for three hours to a variety of speeches. "Shall we have conscription?" the audience was asked. "Ye-es!" was the cry. When one speaker referred to Quebeckers as French, there was protest against Quebec's anti-conscription stand. "Don't call them French," someone shouted. "They're not French. They're traitors." Hugh Guthrie, a Liberal MP (who later joined Borden's Union government), tried to explain Laurier's position against conscription, but the boisterous crowd would not permit him to do so. In the contentious federal election held in December 1917, Toronto's six ridings were all won by Union-Conservative candidates, most by wide margins.

During the war's final year, the flag continued to be waved at any person or group perceived to place individual or collective interests ahead of the country and its courageous soldiers. In the summer of 1918, members of the Civic Employees Union, whose wages had significantly declined, were prepared to accept a 20 percent increase. They saw this amount as only partially making up for what they had lost but accepted it as necessary because of the war. What triggered an angry response was the city's refusal to give them a retroactive increase from the beginning of the year—and they warned city council they were prepared to strike if their demand was not addressed. Mayor Church took a diplomatic approach, asking for calm, while the city controller (and future mayor) Sam McBride, known for his temper (as an alderman, McBride had famously grabbed another alderman by the neck and banged his head against the wall because he objected to some of his comments) and pro-British attitudes, chastised the workers, describing their threats as "a mean, concerted attempt of the men to take advantage of the war conditions." After several days of negotiations failed to solve the problem of the back pay, which officials claimed the city could not afford, the city employees walked off their jobs on July 5. Other unions began to talk about a general strike. The suave Tommy Church, who was not unsympathetic to the workers' demands, resolved the situation and blocked a general strike by convincing both the employees and city council to accept arbitration. Little did the mayor know that the tension in Toronto was about to become a whole lot worse as the hot summer of 1918 continued.

Many of the returned soldiers, who had experienced the horrors of the European battlefields and watched helplessly as their friends and family members died, were full of rage and hatred for all things foreign. They had fought to defend the British Empire and their Canadian homeland, and now Toronto, in their distorted perspective at any rate, was turning into a city of aliens. A small spark was all that was required to set them off. Bizarrely, their resentment was aimed at the city's then small Greek community of about three thousand—an action which ignored the fact that Greece, neutral until 1917, had then joined the fight alongside Britain and France against the Central Powers. Still, as historian Thomas Gallant points out, many Greek immigrants refused to fill out their military registration cards and were regarded as "slackers" by the veterans.

The trouble began on a Thursday night, August 1, at a Greek diner, the White City Café, on Yonge Street south of College Street. Private Claude Cludernay, who was later charged with public drunkenness and fined, became involved in an argument and fight with a Greek waiter, which left him with a bad gash on his head. News of the altercation quickly spread through Toronto's military brethren, and the following evening hundreds of soldiers laid siege to the White City Café, breaking its windows and smashing its furniture—the staff at the restaurant fled before the destruction started—before proceeding to other Greek establishments, joined by an ever-growing mob, to wreak more havoc. The soldiers waved the Union Jack and the American flag as they marched through the downtown. The police, assisted by a large contingent of reinforcements from the military police, were unable to control the situation or quell the violence that lasted until two-thirty in the morning. Two police constables were injured, one by a soldier who beat him with his crutch. Fifteen soldiers were arrested and the rioting caused as much as $45,000 worth of damage—and this was only the beginning. The following night there was another round of rioting, this time aimed at freeing the incarcerated veterans from custody, and yet more violent clashes, arrests, and injuries for both soldiers and the police.

An official inquiry later blamed the police for incompetently handling the disturbance and for being overly aggressive with many of the soldiers. One restaurateur claimed that he saw constables helping themselves to boxes of cigars during the Friday night attacks. The charges against many of the soldiers who had been arrested were eventually dropped, though some received jail sentences of three months to a year. The fanatical xenophobia that gripped Toronto, and much of the rest of the country, did not truly subside for a long time, and there were loud calls to rid the city of "aliens" for the duration of August. (Decades later, mobs of Torontonians targeted Greek citizens again over an August weekend, but this time it was to enjoy the souvlaki, pita, and other delectable delights of the "Taste of the Danforth" celebration.)

SEPTEMBER 1918 brought a different and far more deadly problem. At the end of the month, hundreds of Torontonians came down with a bad flu: high temperatures, headaches, chills, and back pains. The worst cases were reported at the Royal Air Force base. On September 29, a young girl with the last name of Robertson who attended Jesse Ketchum School on Davenport Road was the first person in the city to die of the ailment.

Unlike the response to the SARS (severe acute respiratory syndrome) outbreak in Toronto eighty-five years later, which saw medical authorities springing into action, the reaction in 1918 was muted because Dr. Charles Hastings, the city's medical officer, did not want to cause panic. Despite a growing number of sick people, Hastings took a wait-and-see approach, believing it was merely "ordinary grippe." He advised the citizens of Toronto to remain calm and "to walk more." While he did quarantine the students at Jesse Ketchum School, he absolutely refused to close all Toronto public schools or "places of amusement." Other physicians were more apprehensive, and rightly so.

The epidemic was, in fact, the Spanish Flu, so named because cases in Spain first brought attention to the disease. Hastings's diagnosis proved wrong during the next week as thousands of students and teachers became ill. Soon much of the city was under a cloud of sickness, and Hastings and other medical officials instituted more severe measures to stop the flu's spread. All public places, including schools, dance halls, theatres, sports events, and churches, were shut down. By order of the Public Health Act, sneezing and coughing in public areas was forbidden. A makeshift hospital was set up at the Hotel Mossop (now the Hotel Victoria) on Yonge Street, south of King Street.

Across the globe, the flu was responsible for the deaths of twenty million people in one year. Close to two million Canadians contracted the disease; fifty thousand of them died. By the time the worst of the crisis was over in Toronto in November, probably 260,000 people, or more than half the city's population, had become ill, and 1,300 had died.

Hastings waited until November 11, the day the First World War ended, to reopen the city's schools. As soon as news of the armistice had reached Toronto in the middle of the night, there was non-stop partying in the streets, from Rosedale to the Ward. Mayor Church read the official declaration at noon on the steps of city hall, and a steam whistle pierced the air as ticker tape was strewn onto Bay Street from the windows of offices above. The past four years had left Toronto scathed, and the loss of ten thousand young men was not easily forgotten. But the city, now somewhat less British than many of its citizens cared to admit, had survived.

Chapter Seven

TORONTO THE DULL

It must be good to die in Toronto. The transition between life and death would be continuous, painless and scarcely noticeable in this silent town. I dreaded the Sundays and prayed to God that if He chose for me to die in Toronto He would let it be on a Saturday afternoon, to save me from one more Toronto Sunday.

—LEOPOLD INFELD, 1941

The first contestants in the Miss Toronto pageant in 1926 held at Sunnyside Beach and Amusement Park. For the city's boosters, Sunnyside reflected the optimism of the era and of Toronto's potential for greatness. *City of Toronto Archives, Fonds 1244, Item 1028M*

EVEN AT THE AGE of twenty, Ernest Hemingway possessed the brash, bold, and rugged confidence, along with the arrogance and nastiness, which was soon to make him one of the most celebrated writers of the twentieth century. Born in 1899 in Oak Park, Illinois, west of Chicago, he worked briefly as a cub reporter for the *Kansas City Star* after graduating from high school. A passionate and compulsive adventure seeker, he found his way to the First World War in Europe and drove an ambulance for the Red Cross in Italy until he was seriously wounded. He returned home in 1918, ailing, but with an inspiring tale that was eventually fictionalized in his bestselling 1929 novel *A Farewell to Arms*.

As he was figuring out the course of his life, he wound up in Toronto on a bitterly cold day in January 1920. He was there ostensibly to provide companionship for troubled Ralph Connable Jr., the nineteen-year-old son of Harriet and Ralph Connable Sr., friends of Hemingway's mother. As the manager of the F.W. Woolworth department stores in Canada, Ralph Sr. had some connections at the *Toronto Daily Star*. As part of the agreement to lure Hemingway to Toronto so that he could babysit "young Ralph," Connable promised that he would introduce Hemingway to the *Star*'s editors. Initially, at least, it was a good fit: Hemingway's penchant for superb storytelling, if sometimes slightly embellished, matched the *Star*'s larger-than-life style and mass appeal.

In the intensely competitive world of Toronto newspapers and magazines of this era, the *Star*, located in a nondescript building on King Street West and under the firm guidance of "Holy" Joe Atkinson and his gruff son-in-law Harry Hindmarsh, became the most widely read newspaper in the city, with a daily circulation of nearly 135,000 in 1924. The *Star Weekly* magazine was even more popular. For years, every morning when John Ross Robertson of the *Telegram* encountered Atkinson on Bay Street, he would ask the *Star*'s publisher, "Making any money?" Atkinson's reply was invariably, "Not yet." But one day that changed and Atkinson's answer was "At last, I'm making money." Robertson never bothered him about it again.

Whether it was raising money for destitute children; campaigning for a cleaner water supply; uncovering corruption in the awarding of government contracts; or portraying Dr. Frederick Banting, one of the discovers of insulin at the laboratory of the University of Toronto in 1922, as the greatest hero of all time, there was not a cause, social crusade, disaster, or human interest story that did not receive "razzle-dazzle" treatment in the *Star*—the proverbial "paper for the people." The *Star* in those days, recalled author Morley Callaghan, who worked as a young reporter in the early twenties and became a close friend to Hemingway, was as "aggressive and raffish a newspaper as you could find in any North American city." *Star* reporters, he added "moved on great disasters in far places like shock troops poured into a breach by an excited general."

At the rate of half-a-cent a word, Hemingway churned out an array of tightly woven stories for the *Star Weekly* on everything from medicine to communism to boxing, one of his favourite subjects, and sports. Despite developing a keen appetite for local hockey and Chinese food restaurants, he later dismissed Toronto, the "city of churches," as too damn dull. In particular, he found the prohibition of alcohol—a wartime measure that lasted for about a decade—repressive and most uncivilized. Not that it was difficult to obtain a bottle of whiskey; the Ontario Temperance Act did not ban the production of booze (which, as Hemingway noted in a June 1920 article, was how so much Ontario liquor was "pouring" into the United States during its prohibition experiment) or make it illegal for physicians to prescribe it for "medicinal" purposes—and prescribe it they did. "It is necessary to go to a drug store and lean up against the counter and make a gurgling sigh like apoplexy," observed Stephen Leacock in 1919. "One often sees these apoplexy cases lined up four deep." One doctor signed two thousand medicinal liquor prescriptions in a month.

For Hemingway, that was beside the point. Toronto, where the law forbade the use of city park toboggan slides on Sunday, and the police actually padlocked playground swings on that day, was too small for his big tastes and larger ego. Though he envisioned his future as a novelist rather than a features writer, he wisely continued freelancing for the *Star Weekly* after he briefly returned to Chicago, and he became the newspaper's first European correspondent when he moved to Paris in 1921 with the first of his four wives, Hadley Richardson.

Then, freelancers had even less control over their work than they do today. Hemingway's appointment in Europe was part of a well-orchestrated and sanctioned scheme by the paper's managing editor, John Bone, to resell Hemingway's articles under Bone's byline to American and British publications. If Hemingway ever discovered what Bone was up to, he ignored it. For the next year and a half he traipsed around Europe, covering a range of events for the *Star*. This included attending his first bullfight in Spain, another fascination that made its way into the pages of his 1926 novel *The Sun Also Rises*.

When Hadley became pregnant in early 1923, she and Hemingway decided it was wise to return to Toronto so she could give birth in a North American hospital. The *Star* agreed to give Hemingway a position as a full-time reporter at a salary of $125 a week. (According to William Burrill, Hemingway's biographer, he also secretly wrote pieces for the *Globe* and the *Mail and Empire*.) The couple settled into a quaint apartment on Bathurst Street, north of St. Clair Avenue, now called "The Hemingway," and in mid-October, Hadley gave birth to a healthy son, John (also known as Jack, who became the father of actress Mariel Hemingway).

By then, however, Hemingway had had enough of Harry Hindmarsh, the *Star*'s assistant managing editor. Hindmarsh, enamoured of his own authority, decided to take Hemingway down a notch by subjecting him to what was caustically known in the *Star* newsroom as the "Hindmarsh Treatment." He drove a reporter day and night until the man broke—and thoroughly enjoyed doing so. Morley Callaghan, who also toiled for him, described Hindmarsh as "a hard-driving, good, ruthless newspaperman," but he was also childish and inexplicably moody. Each day he expected a chirpy "good morning" from the staff and relished the fact that, due to nepotism, his was the only safe job at the newspaper. That Hindmarsh and Hemingway clashed was hardly surprising. Hindmarsh felt that Hemingway was a prima donna who was not working diligently enough, while Hemingway detested Hindmarsh for being so critical and miserable.

Hemingway had been on assignment in New York City when Hadley gave birth. As soon as he arrived back in Toronto by train, he naturally headed straight to the hospital. The next day, Hindmarsh reamed him out for not reporting in and for not filing the story he was supposed to have written on a speech by former British prime minister David Lloyd George. That was the last straw. Though Hemingway wrote more articles for the *Star Weekly*, he and Hadley decided they would return to Paris, where Hemingway would find fame and glory. He formally submitted his resignation to the

Star in December. Legend has it that he also wrote an anti-Hindmarsh diatribe, which he posted on the staff bulletin board. Hindmarsh, proud as ever, never mentioned it, and no reporter ever mentioned it to him.

ERNEST HEMINGWAY was by no means the only person to claim that Toronto was stuffy and boring. Anarchist Emma Goldman, on a lecture tour in December 1927, came to the same conclusion and also deemed Toronto "deadly dull." Asked by a *Star* reporter to elaborate, she replied, "Because it's church-ridden. Toronto people are smug and don't think for themselves." Maybe so, but had either Hemingway or Goldman probed further, they might have found the city slightly more enticing. Subterfuge and misconduct occurred here as much as in any big city.

In early December 1919, Ambrose Small, the fifty-six-year-old owner of the Grand Opera House on Adelaide Street West and of theatres in Hamilton and London, Ontario, had just sold his entertainment business for $1.7 million, with a million dollars paid up front. Small was a seedy character; he cheated on his wife, Theresa, regularly with a harem of lowly mistresses and was involved in illegal gambling. Scrooge-like, he even griped about his wife's donations to charitable causes. The day after Small deposited his million-dollar cheque, he left his office to buy a newspaper and was never seen again.

Theresa Small waited two weeks to inform the police that her husband was missing. If that was not suspicious enough, the abrupt departure of Small's secretary, John Doughty, supposedly for a new job in Montreal, put the Toronto police on alert. As soon as the news of Small's disappearance was reported, Doughty vanished. The police quickly discovered that on the day Ambrose had gone missing, so had $150,000 in bonds from his office vault. The police finally apprehended Doughty nearly a year later, hiding out under an assumed name in Oregon City, Oregon. He was brought back to Toronto and, after questioning, revealed where he had hidden the stolen bonds. Yet try as they might, the police could not link Doughty to any crime involving Small's disappearance. He was convicted of larceny and received a sentence of six months.

No matter how hard they looked or how creative the investigation—and the police even enlisted the help of Sir Arthur Conan Doyle, the author of the Sherlock Holmes novels—they could find no sign of Ambrose Small. Allegations that Theresa Small, the sole recipient of Small's approximately $2-million estate, had hired someone to kill her husband were raised in 1936 (and later), after Mrs. Small's death. But the charges could not be substantiated in court or by further research. The affairs of Small's estate were not settled until 1954, and the case file was closed by the Toronto police six years later. The mystery of what happened to Ambrose Small remains.

Less tragic, but more salacious, was the story of a wild party at the Ontario Legislature in late 1921, complete with booze (a violation of the province's temperance act, which was then in force) and several attractive "scantily clad" ladies from the secretarial pool. What made these allegations extra sordid was the apparent participation of several members of the government of Ernest C. Drury. A co-founder of the United Farmers of Ontario (UFO), Drury had been catapulted into the premier's office following the UFO's remarkable victory in the October 1919 provincial election that unseated the Conservatives and William Hearst.

The shindig in question had been held in the private Queen's Park apartment of Treasurer Peter Smith, though neither Smith nor any other cabinet minister was present. When Drury learned about the gathering, he was livid. He lectured everyone involved and set up a nightly patrol of the legislature to ensure no such "terrible event" ever took place again.

The sordid story of the party did not stay secret for long; it was too juicy a tale for Conservative Party newspapers to ignore, especially when it involved a government whose motto was "moral uplift." The *Telegram* was the most prurient, with one headline pronouncing, "Wine-Women-And-Song Orgy in the Legislature." There was never an official inquiry, yet the gossip lingered and the story was a contributing factor to the Drury government's defeat in the election of 1923, which saw the Conservatives under Howard Ferguson regain office.

There was good, clean fun and excitement to be had in the city as well. And no more so than at the Sunnyside Beach and Amusement Park at the southern end of High Park, off Roncesvalles Avenue. For sheer enjoyment, Sunnyside quickly surpassed Scarboro Beach Park almost from the day it was opened at the end of June in 1922. The press was ecstatic. Sunnyside, the *Globe* enthusiastically declared, ushered "Toronto to the Threshold of Her Newer Era." Added the *Telegram*, "Sunnyside Inspires Visions of Greatness-To-Be of Toronto."

Sunnyside was often referred to as the "poor man's Riviera." It had everything from shooting galleries, dancing, a wild roller-coaster ride (the Sunnyside Flyer), a world-class merry-go-round, and the "continent's best bathing pavilion" (which cost $300,000). Special events on its wide wooden boardwalk included the Easter Parade and the Miss Toronto pageant, which started in 1926 and was modelled after the more famous Miss America contests held in Atlantic City. The first winner of the pageant was Miss Jean Ford Tolmie, a tall, striking brunette who lived with her parents near Ossington Avenue and College Street.

More risqué was the "Water Nymph Carnival," a swimsuit contest sponsored by the *Telegram* to "encourage young girls in the art of swimming." This was especially daring in an era that regarded men and women dancing too closely—if at all—as sinful and the hemline of a woman's dress which was more than six inches off the ground as scandalous. During a heat wave in 1936, when the temperature reached forty-one degrees Celsius, thirty men were arrested at Sunnyside for indecently displaying their bare chests.

In short, Sunnyside was a place where memories were made—where boyfriends asked their sweethearts to marry them on a ride in the Tunnel of Love, and where parents took their children on special occasions. Alas, the amusement park was eventually a victim of the very progress that had led to its establishment. In 1955 it was closed and torn down to make room for the Gardiner Expressway.

DESPITE ALL OF THE FUN at Sunnyside, there was more than a hint of truth to the charge that Toronto was dull. Montreal was still the financial centre of the country (and would remain so until the early sixties), though Toronto was steadily making gains. By 1920 the city was home to the corporate headquarters of five of the seven big banks in Canada, as well as eight of the thirteen leading insurance companies. Most impressive was the erection of skyscrapers around King Street between Yonge and Bay, a sure sign that, like New York City and Chicago, Toronto was caught up in the age of progress. The opulent Bank of Commerce Building at 25 King Street West, started in 1928 and completed two years later (now Commerce Court North), was the tallest building in the British Empire until about 1962. While proud of this corporate affluence, the *Star*, among others, sounded a typical note of Canadian caution, expressing grave concern about the formation of overpowering wind tunnels that would literally blow Torontonians away. And who knew what other dangers lurked in the heavens?

Puritanical Sunday laws were as firm as ever, and sin was stamped out at every opportunity, as the men who tried to swim at Sunnyside Beach without their shirts on discovered. Also in 1936, the police forced several script changes in the play *Reunion in Vienna*, performed at the Royal Alexandra Theatre. The words "bathroom" and "damn" were cut, and a kissing scene was reduced from eight seconds to three.

Toronto put the Lord first in every way. In 1927, Ernest Sterry, the editor of the *Christian Enquirer*, an atheist journal with a small following, was arrested by the city's morality inspector for writing allegedly critical comments about Jesus and describing incidents from the Old and New Testaments "in an irreverent and facetious manner." This was one of the few times section 296 of the Criminal Code, which covers blasphemous libel, was used by the authorities (it was also used in Quebec in 1935 against Reverend Victor Rahard, head of an Anglican church in Montreal, who put up posters insulting to the pope and Catholics). Before sentencing Sterry to sixty days at a jail farm, Judge Emerson Coatsworth (former mayor of the city in 1906–7), reflecting the majority values of the day, lectured, "[There is] probably nothing more sacred to us than our religion... We regard taking God's name in vain as a sin... Our conception of God is so much a part of every life that it is an integral part of our national life." Most Torontonians (the editors of the *Star* were an exception) hailed the verdict and sentence as just.

Worse was the evil of drink. It required no less than three referendums to repeal the problematic Ontario Temperance Act, plus a pledge to do so by Conservative premier

Howard Ferguson at the start of the election campaign of December 1926 (his chief opponent was the Ontario Liberal Party leader William Sinclair, a rabid prohibitionist). Only after Ferguson won another mandate was an enduring provincial government monopoly, today's Liquor Control Board of Ontario or LCBO, established.

There were limits, however, to how much Ontarians were allowed to enjoy themselves. Ferguson's intention, as he so righteously declared, was "to promote temperance sobriety, personal liberty and, above all, to restore respect for the law." For the next thirty-five years, obtaining a drink was made a bit easier—but only a bit. Before you could guzzle a beer or down a shot, there were myriad forms to fill out. Not only did you need a government-sanctioned permit to drink, but the state also had the right to monitor your drinking habits. There were no stand-up bars in Toronto, or anywhere in Ontario, until the 1960s.

Civic politics during the twenties also remained dull, as might be expected. A notable exception was the election of 1920, the first municipal election in which all women aged twenty-one or older could vote, which saw social reform advocate Constance Hamilton elected in Ward 3. She was not only the first female "alderman" on city council, but also the first woman in Ontario to hold public office (beating federal MP Agnes Macphail by nearly two years). Hamilton, one of the founders of Toronto's Bach Society, dedicated herself to helping the city's underprivileged.

Tommy Church jumped to federal politics in 1921, and the four men who succeeded him as mayor of Toronto during the twenties—C. Alfred Maguire, William Hiltz, "Honest Tom" Foster, and Sam McBride—all came from the usual collection of businessmen and property owners who had served on city council and who lacked any real vision when they assumed the mayoralty. Hiltz's claim to fame was forcing civic workers to use time clocks, while Foster took great pride in spending as little money as possible. McBride, who had been born in the Ward in 1866 and achieved success in the lumber industry, suggested reimbursing citizens who were robbed, rather than hiring more police officers.

McBride, at least, was pro-development and supported expansion of streetcar service, construction of the Coliseum at the Canadian National Exhibition grounds, and improvements to the waterfront area. His gruff, no-nonsense style and excessive British patriotism had its good and bad sides. He stamped out municipal corruption. But he also (à la a later mayor, Rob Ford, who became embroiled in a bitter feud with the *Toronto Star*) banned reporters from the *Telegram* from his office because he objected to their coverage of him. And he encouraged the police to be as tough as possible on left-wing rabble-rousers.

One fight McBride lost was to the soft-spoken controller Donald MacGregor, a music teacher. In May 1925, McBride had publicly questioned MacGregor's credentials as a music instructor and had referred to MacGregor as a "rat" for allegedly asking the newspapers to print a private letter McBride had sent him. One day MacGregor waited for McBride outside the council chamber, called him a "dirty yellow dog," and attacked him. McBride got the worst of it as MacGregor pounded him, inflicting damage with his large Masonic ring.

BY FAR THE MOST IMPORTANT DEVELOPMENT of the twenties, one that dictated the city's growth thereafter, was the celebrated end of the Toronto Railway Company's thirty-year monopoly in 1921. For as long as anyone could remember, the privately operated TRC had been accurately perceived as an impediment to the expansion and improvement of Toronto's civic transportation network. Its chief owner, William Mackenzie—who had been occupied for nearly a decade supervising the construction of the Canadian Northern Railway, his most ambitious, though, in the end, financially unsustainable, project—was still as "arrogant" and "imperious" as John Willison of the *News* had described him back in 1906. After the federal government was compelled to take over the money-losing Northern (which became part of Canadian National Railways) in 1917, the TRC was further neglected. There were never enough streetcars running, so Torontonians were forced to wait and then wait some more. When a car did arrive, it was inevitably overcrowded. The TRC had refused to extend its service to the new northern and western suburbs, so the city was forced to establish the Toronto Civic Railways and take over existing feeder lines.

Finally, on January 1, 1920, voters approved the creation of the publicly owned Toronto Transportation Commission (TTC), which took control of all the city's streetcar lines. (In 1954, the TTC was renamed the Toronto Transit Commision.) During the next few years, Toronto city council spent $50 million enhancing the street railway service. Fares were increased from four cents to seven cents. (The debt from this expansion was eventually retired by 1945.) By 1929, 200 million people were using the TTC cars annually; only New York City's civic transportation system was more in demand. As early as 1909 there had been talk of constructing a north-south subway along Yonge Street and Avenue Road that would reach St. Clair Avenue, but it took decades before the engineering reports and discussion at council became a reality. Such a proposal, which envisioned the removal of the streetcar tracks on those streets, would be expensive and the underground digging challenging, but it was also far-sighted and meant the seeds of Toronto's subway system were slowly germinating.

As significant as the TTC was to Toronto's future as a metropolis, it was the advent of the automobile age in the twenties that truly altered the geographic landscape and daily life. Thanks to the creative genius of Henry Ford and others, owning a car was no longer a luxury but a necessity. Between 1908, when Ford's Model T hit the market, and 1927, sales in Canada exceeded a million. In 1916 there were 10,000 cars on the streets of Toronto; by 1930 that number had escalated to 104,600 cars and 14,200 trucks, inaugurating the city's traffic woes that continue to the present day. The *Star Weekly* imagined special "speed highways" to ease the congestion; that perceptive solution would have to wait many years. For the time being, streets were widened and underpasses were built to avoid nuisance railway crossings. The York Street underpass, which gave easier access to the waterfront, was not finished until 1931, after many years of construction and negotiations with the railways to raise the tracks.

With no lanes, traffic lights, or stop signs, driving a car in Toronto, or elsewhere in the country, could be downright dangerous. Drivers merely honked at each other to permit a turn. It took until the summer of 1925 before Toronto's first traffic lights were installed, naturally enough, at the corner of Yonge and Bloor, and the provincial government soon introduced compulsory drivers' licences—and not a moment too soon. In 1918 in Toronto, twenty-eight people died in traffic accidents; ten years later that number exceeded two hundred. And in another sign of the times, more than eleven hundred cars were stolen in 1918 and that number kept on rising, no matter what the police did (Toronto detectives did not have their own vehicle until 1916).

Cars had an impact on women's fashion and social activities—teenagers quickly discovered all sorts of deeds were possible in the back seat of a Ford or Buick—dramatically improved public health by getting thousands of horses (and the daily deluge of manure) off the streets, and, most significantly, linked isolated rural communities with the cities. Owning a house in the suburbs was now appealing, and in Toronto's case that meant the growth of more middle-class communities in North York, East York, and Etobicoke. In 1911, approximately 33,000 people resided beyond the city's boundaries. By 1921, after the city annexed North Toronto and Moore Park, that number increased to 89,550; ten years after that it was 187,141. Blue-collar workers who lived in these growing neighbourhoods tended to work nearby—the Ford Motor plant opened in 1923 in East York—since it was more difficult to own and maintain an automobile on a blue-collar salary.

Slightly beyond the city limits, another suburb was in the making. Toronto's ever-rising downtown skyline, along with the recurrent fog from the lake, made locating the city's major airport by the waterfront problematic. The island airport was developed in the late thirties. But it was in the village of Malton, about twenty-eight kilometres away, that the federal government and the city decided in 1935 to construct an airport for use by the new Trans-Canada Airlines. Over the next forty years the city of Mississauga would grow up around it (and in 1984 the airport was renamed Lester B. Pearson International Airport, after the Liberal prime minister).

LIFE SEEMED GOOD in the city in 1929. Business appeared to be booming. The Toronto Stock Exchange was buzzing. No one seemed to notice that thousands of people were borrowing money to buy stocks they could not afford, with only 10 percent down. There were profits to be made—but on paper only. No matter.

On Front Street, directly across from nearly functional Union Station, the luxurious Royal York Hotel, owned by the CPR, opened for business on June 11 to great fanfare and was billed as the "largest hotel in the British Empire." "Apartment Houses" were all the rage in Toronto, and builders could not erect them fast enough, including the $1.25-million Claridge Apartments a few streets south of St. Clair off Avenue Road. Farther south on Avenue near Bloor Street, construction was also underway on the Queen's Park Plaza Hotel, a lavish hotel and residential complex. The project ran into design problems and was then hit hard by the stock market crash. Another six years would pass before the hotel was taken over by new owners and finally opened as the iconic Park Plaza.

Torontonians were occupied by all varieties of entertainment and sport. The "talkies," moving pictures with sound, wowed crowds in 1927 at Massey Hall. There was horse racing at the old Woodbine track in the Beaches area. At Varsity Stadium, you could cheer on such football teams as the University of Toronto Varsity Blues, the Toronto Balmy Beach Beachers, and the Toronto Argonauts as they competed for the coveted Grey Cup. The Argos, established in 1873 as part of the Argonaut Rowing Club—which chose its double blue colours as a nod to Oxford and Cambridge Universities—won the cup three times between 1921 and 1937. And the city boasted two Maple Leaf teams: the baseball version—playing in their new $300,000 home stadium at the foot of Bathurst Street—which won the International League pennant in 1926; and their hockey counterparts, the former Toronto St. Patricks, renamed the Toronto Maple Leafs in 1927, which under the sway of First World War veteran and gravel man Conn Smythe would lay the foundation for a brilliant hockey dynasty and, arguably, the city's most enduring and defining attraction.

Above all, there was radio, an innovation that generated more excitement than even automobiles and airplanes. While radio technology developed simultaneously in the United States and Canada, American broadcasters were slightly quicker in bringing this revolutionary invention into the homes of regular citizens. In 1922, two years after radio debuted in Pittsburgh, and a year after the broadcasting of the sensational heavyweight boxing championship between Jack Dempsey and Georges Carpentier, the *Toronto Star* launched the city's first radio station, CFCA, though in order to listen to it you needed a crystal radio set.

Some months earlier, the *Star*'s publisher, Joe Atkinson, had been overwhelmed when more than one thousand people waited in line for two hours for admission to the Masonic Temple at Davenport and Yonge Streets so they could hear a concert played by musicians back in a studio. The crowd was mesmerized by the sounds from the black box sitting at the front of the hall. "Men strained forward in their seats with their hands cupped to their ears... Women were rigid as if carved from stone," the *Toronto Star*, which had sponsored the event, reported the next day. Atkinson was hooked and envisioned the radio, in the earliest instance of media convergence, as a means to promote his newspaper.

In fact, the radio reached new and ever-expanding audiences, enhancing the influence of preachers and politicians, and tripling sales of Pepsodent toothpaste, Lucky Strike cigarettes, and Kellogg's breakfast cereal. Within three years approximately 100,000 Canadians, many of whom lived in Toronto, owned a radio; by 1930 this number had increased to half a million and had made the radio the "central piece of furniture in the living room." Like millions of listeners in the United States, most Canadians regularly tuned in to such popular shows as *The Happiness Boys*, *The Chase and Sanborn Hour*, *Moran and Mack* (also known as *Two Black Crows*) and especially *Amos 'n' Andy*, about two black country bumpkins trying to find their way in the big city. Played by two white actors, Freeman Gosden and Charles Correll, Amos and Andy were always trying to get themselves out of some impossible situation—or "sitchiation," as they would have put it. ("Ain't dat sumpin" was another favourite catchphrase.) White audiences adored *Amos 'n' Andy*'s urban adventures, while black listeners were more circumspect about the standard stereotyped characters.

In Toronto, the radio brought fame and fortune to many, though two individuals stand out: Ted Rogers and Foster Hewitt. As a young boy, Edward "Ted" Rogers was an avid crystal radio enthusiast. When he was twenty-one in 1921, he succeeded in transmitting a radio signal from Newmarket, Ontario, to Ardrossan, Scotland—a Canadian first that received front-page coverage in the *Star*. But that was merely the beginning of his ingenuity. Three years later, after much dedicated experimentation, he had devised a battery-less radio that could be operated by plugging it into an electric socket as opposed to using large, cumbersome, and noisy batteries.

Building on that success, Rogers, well-groomed and self-assured, established his own radio station, CFRB, in 1927 (the "RB" stood for "Rogers Batteryless"). Likely no radio station in North America broadcast as clear and crisp a signal as CFRB. Next he entered into a partnership to manufacture Rogers-Majestic electric radios.

In February 1930, Rogers married his long-time girlfriend, Velma Taylor, a nurse. They quickly became high-profile members of the Toronto social scene. Velma gave birth to their son, Edward "Ted" Jr., in May 1933. Only six years later, Edward Sr. suddenly died from an internal abdominal hemorrhage following surgery on May 6, 1939, slightly more than a month before his thirty-ninth birthday. In the decades that followed, Edward Sr.'s lucrative companies were largely mismanaged by his brother Elsworth, and it took young Ted many years to reacquire, rebuild, and greatly expand the business his father had worked so diligently to create and grow it into one of Canada's greatest media empires.

While Edward Rogers Sr. was experimenting with his battery-less radio, twenty-one-year-old Foster Hewitt, a cub reporter with the *Toronto Daily Star* who had been awed by the broadcast of the Dempsey–Carpentier fight, began writing a newspaper column about the radio. His father, W.A. Hewitt, was the *Star*'s esteemed and well-connected sports editor. On March 22, 1923, the paper dispatched young Hewitt to broadcast a local senior league hockey game at the Mutual Street Arena. Though he had already read news and sports reports on the air, Hewitt was reluctant to accept this assignment but, complying with his editor's wishes, he sat on a small stool and used a telephone to relay the play-by-play back to the station. The game went into three extra periods of overtime, and, as journalist Knowlton Nash tells it, "listeners heard for the first time the flat, nasal tones of an excited Foster Hewitt shouting what was to become one of Canada's most memorable phrases, 'He shoots! He scores!'" Within a few years, Hewitt entered into an astute and profitable arrangement with Conn Smythe to become the voice of the Toronto Maple Leafs and a staple of Canadian hockey broadcasts, first on radio and later on television.

MORE SYMPTOMATIC OF the economic and political problems about to be inflicted on Toronto and the rest of the country in 1929 was the anti-communist and anti-immigration hysteria of the period. Leading the charge were Mayor Sam McBride and Chief of Police Dennis Draper, an autocrat with a thick black moustache. The fifty-seven-year-old chief, a retired army officer with no police training, was all business. "Toronto is going to like him," the *Star* declared following his appointment in the spring of 1928. Not everyone did. Draper's priorities were threefold: keeping order, keeping Canada British, and maintaining morality as he defined it. John Gray, a University of Toronto student who later became a book publisher, recalled that Draper assigned constables "with stop-watches in the wings of the Royal Alexandra Theatre, timing the kisses in the... production of *The Guardsman*, [who were] ready to bring down the curtain if they lasted more than 20 seconds."

With the full support of McBride and the other two members of the police commission, Draper issued an edict that banned public meetings about communism in any language other than English—since the police insisted on knowing what was being said—and eventually prohibited street-corner gatherings of any kind. In early 1929 there was a Communist Party rally at the Standard Theatre on Spadina, and Draper ordered his men to be present to ensure attendees adhered to his foreign languages order. Soon after the event began, Max Shur, a garment-trade union organizer, was invited to the stage and said a few words in Yiddish before he was unceremoniously dragged off by the police. In the audience, Philip Halpern, the editor of the Yiddish weekly *Kampf*, was so incensed that he stood on his chair and made an emotional speech in Yiddish. He was promptly arrested for disorderly conduct, but in reality his only crime was that he had spoken a language other than English. Chief Draper later claimed that while the constable "who had arrested Halpern did not understand Yiddish he was sure that British institutions were being attacked."

According to legal experts, the chief's edict banning foreign languages was not enforceable, and the Crown wisely dropped the charges against Halpern. Debate about the edict persisted with the *Toronto Daily Star* on one side, guided by Joe Atkinson's liberal sensibilities, and its chief competitors on the other. "The Police are right," a *Globe* editorial declared, dismissing the complaints as "silly twaddle from pens that weep with Anglo-Saxon sympathy." The *Telegram* labelled the *Star* "the Big Brother of the Little Reds."

The bitter conflict between the authorities and local communists continued for the next few months, with the police threatening to cancel the licences of halls or theatres that permitted communist gatherings. Refusing to be intimidated, the communists organized a meeting at the bandstand at Queen's Park on the evening of August 13, but without the requisite permission from Chief Draper. Trouble was imminent. In fact, the police had roughly dispersed another Communist Party gathering in the park only two weeks earlier. On this night, about sixty people showed up to hear John MacDonald, the Secretary of the Communist Party—men, women, and children who, as John Gray remembered, "looked ordinary and harmless, not remotely dangerous to the city or the country as a whole." That, however, did not stop the police—"Draper's Dragoons," as *Saturday Night* later caustically referred to them—from descending on the small crowd as if they were assaulting an enemy bunker on a First World War battlefield. Gray and his friends had wandered over to the park to watch the spectacle and were sickened by what they witnessed. "On horseback and on motorcycles with sidecars [the police] burst from the cover of bushes round the buildings and rode straight at the group," he later recalled. "They had been only partially screened so that their eruption wasn't a complete surprise, but the size and force of it was overpowering and shocking." In the subsequent melee, participants were beaten with batons and kicked as they lay on the ground. "Get back to Russia," constables screamed as they attacked them. Two people were seriously injured and six were arrested. Many more were battered and bruised. Diana Bisgould of the Young Communist League had her blouse "ripped to pieces," and Meyer Klig, a Jewish fur worker, had his ear nearly ripped from his head by a "sadistic policeman."

Eighty years later, during the G20 Summit in 2010, the harsh treatment Toronto police meted out to protestors and bystanders was scrutinized and generally condemned, but their wanton actions in 1929 received few criticisms from politicians, the press, or the public. In fact, the response was quite the opposite. "Police Rout Communists in Queen's Park," the *Globe*'s front-page story reported. "The battle for the 'freedom of the streets' was fought and won last night by the Toronto Police Force." A *Globe* editorial two days later, entitled "Deport the Reds," was sharper still. In the newspaper's view, there was no difference between the crowd at Queen's Park and the "nucleus of professional [Bolshevik] revolutionaries working day by day for the destruction of civilization." The only solution was for the federal government to send them back where they came from. "They are not only a nuisance to Canadians, but a menace to Canada."

The other Toronto papers made similar arguments, with the lone exception of the *Star*, which saw the events of August 13 as we might today: as an unacceptable abuse of police power. "The story of what happened in the park," the *Star*'s editorial observed, "under the shadow of the parliament buildings, when the police with horses, motor cars, batons, boots and fists attacked the Communist leaders particularly and bystanders at random reads like a story of the Czar's Cossacks or of the methods of the Soviet police of Moscow against a crowd of bourgeoisie. It reads like nothing this country knows anything about... The whole thing is an exhibition of Colossal Stupidity for which we think there has been no precedent in Toronto's history."

Not surprisingly, the *Star*'s call for Chief Draper's dismissal and the disbanding of the current board of police commissioners came to nothing. If anything, the police repression of, and disdain for, the left became much worse during the next decade. As Mayor McBride declared two years later, "Our stopping of Communist meetings shows that we are truly British." Few Torontonians would have disagreed with that sentiment.

FOR WEEKS IN THE FALL OF 1929, savvy Toronto stockbrokers like C.W. Stollery and Jack Meggeson sensed the worst. Years later they would reflect that their dire predictions hardly captured the panic they and the other brokers at the Toronto Stock Exchange (TSE) were about to endure. While the market had hit new highs in early September, the buying and selling was more erratic after that. On October 4, a wave of selling cost Toronto investors $200 million on paper. Many business observers thought that the bottom had been reached and share prices were certain to bounce back. They were wrong. Thursday, October 24 was another bad day of intense selling in Toronto and New York. And still it was not over, despite assurances from U.S. and Canadian bankers to the contrary.

The crash Stollery and Meggeson had feared occurred early the following week on "Black Tuesday," October 29, 1929. At the TSE, stocks tumbled "at the rate of one million dollars a minute." There was chaos inside the exchange as stocks were sold for fire-sale prices. Outside on Bay Street, thousands of people watched in horror as their paper fortunes vanished and they were faced with meeting margin calls they could not possibly cover. Brokers did not jump from windows. Yet less than five months later, thirty-year-old Lottie Nugent, the head bookkeeper at the Monarch Brass Company, who owed $4,421.27 on her stock account—funds that she did not have and could not borrow—committed suicide by turning on the gas stove at her flat on Huron Street. She left a typewritten letter explaining her financial condition to her brokers.

It took a while for the full impact of what had transpired on October 29 to take hold. By May 1932, as an example, $1,000 invested at the TSE in May 1929 was worth only $164. Such a steep decline would have been impossible to comprehend even after the insanity of 1929.

The day after the crash, the market did rebound, and everyone seemed to breathe a sigh of relief. "Stock Lists Holding Giving Traders Hope of Regaining Losses," read the front page of the *Star*. "Utter Collapse in Stock Market Narrowly Averted," the *Globe* noted. It was also election day in Ontario, which resulted in another impressive victory and a third majority government for Premier Howard Ferguson and the Conservatives, who won all fifteen seats in Tory Toronto. Certainly Ferguson was not overly concerned by the rumblings at the TSE, and neither was Prime Minister Mackenzie King. Asked by the press to comment, King stated with confidence that "while no doubt a number of people have suffered owing to the sharp decline in stocks, the soundness of Canadian securities generally is not affected. Business was never better, nor faith in Canada's future more justified."

Less than a year later, King and the Liberals, who were criticized for not dealing effectively, if at all, with the rising unemployment in the country, were defeated by R.B. Bennett and the Conservatives. One of Bennett's first actions was to send Howard Ferguson to London as the new Canadian High Commissioner. George Henry became the new Ontario Conservative leader and premier, but he faced the new young and wily leader of the provincial Liberals, Mitch Hepburn, an opportunistic politician ready to use the Depression to his own advantage. He was to turn Ontario politics, and the legacy of Tory Toronto, upside down.

BY THE END OF 1929, the number of unemployed in Toronto had reached 8,500, and during the next five years that total kept growing. In late 1934, the year the city celebrated its centennial, 25 percent of Torontonians, or approximately 160,000 people, were on relief (across Canada the number of people on relief rose to an unprecedented two million). Hugh Garner depicted the humiliating experience in his 1950 novel *Cabbagetown*: "Look at some of these people carryin' club-bags and paper to wrap their stuff up in. They don't fool nobody. I seen a man last week walk back two car stops along Dundas before he got in a street car goin' the other way, just so's people wouldn't know he'd been here. He had his rations in a suitcase too... It wasn't only in Cabbagetown and the West End slums that were represented in the relief lines now. It seemed that the depression, as it was beginning to be called, was, like a war or revolution, a leveller of the population."

Only the truly wealthy did not worry about poverty during the thirties. Asking prices for homes dropped significantly, yet even at the absurdly low price of $150, few people could afford to buy. Taking in a boarder or two became a common way to keep your house, since more and more people could not afford to pay rent of twenty-five to thirty dollars a month for an average home. In violation of local bylaws, some landlords in the Annex subdivided their single-family houses and rented rooms to as many tenants as they could cram in. And in Cabbagetown, a group of hard-pressed residents banded together to defy bailiffs sent to evict people from their homes. The police often had to intercede in these angry confrontations.

In August 1934, Ontario lieutenant governor Herbert Bruce led a committee on housing which determined that the number of slums in Toronto had increased beyond 1,500 houses; Bruce reported to Prime Minister Bennett, "[These dwellings] are unhealthy... [and] are lacking in the elementary amenities that should be present in Canadian cities." He pointed to hard-hit neighbourhoods from the Don River to Dovercourt, and south of College and Carlton Streets, "which are especially bad and which may be termed blighted areas."

Cabbagetown, too, remained overcrowded. Half the houses in the 1930s, recalled lawyer George Rust-D'Eye, a local resident and the neighbourhood's historian, "had no central heating, depending entirely on stoves, one out of ten still had only outside toilets, and about one-quarter of them had no bathtub. Many small streets, such as Bright Street, had a row of privies sitting just outside the back doors of the houses." Worse was the "hobo jungle" of tents and huts, erected in and around the Don Valley Brickworks (on the west side of the valley), where more than a hundred homeless men found temporary refuge in 1930 and 1931 before the authorities shipped them up north to camps or local shelters.

At the luncheon celebration for the city's hundredth birthday, Bruce called for the development of a plan "that would recognize the inalienable right of every man and woman and child to a decent and dignified and healthful environment." It was a noble thought but was not followed up during the thirties, particularly in a city where a Social Darwinist mentality still persisted, as it did elsewhere in North America. Simply put, from the perspective of some of Toronto's finer citizens and leaders, the city's slums, which had been present for decades, were an unfortunate part of the so-called natural order—as unpalatable an eyesore as they were. "Improper living conditions in Toronto," city planning commissioner Tracy leMay claimed in January 1934, "are very largely caused by the tenants rather than the houses."

Slum housing and long lines at soup kitchens were merely the most visible signs of the Depression. Construction jobs dried up, and if you could find work, the odds were you toiled long and hard for paltry wages, usually less than the twelve to fifteen dollars a week a family of five received on relief. The owner of a restaurant on Spadina Avenue reportedly paid his employees $6.25 a week and expected them to work close to a hundred hours. A Red Indian service station paid $5.55 for a 64-hour workweek. In time, people advertised their services for one dollar a day—the *Star* began a "Give a man a job" promotion to find odd jobs for people—and masses of the unemployed congregated in Queen's Park as well as at Trinity Park in the west end. The police became overly anxious. Several nasty clashes broke out at Trinity Park during the summer of 1933, when the police attempted to clear the unemployed ("demonstrators" to the *Telegram*) from the area.

Survival was a family affair. Businessman and boxing promoter Irving Ungerman, who was eleven years old in 1934, recalls that his father, Isaac, a Polish-Jewish immigrant, worked as a peddler of scrap metal and chickens, and Irving and his six siblings all contributed however they could. Irving eventually got a job as a delivery boy for a drugstore and worked six days a week for $2.50, giving nearly all of it to his mother. Similarly, restaurateur Lou Bregman's father, Max, and two partners, Alex Newman and Max Robinovitch, taking advantage of Max's experience as a baker, opened the Russian Bagel Bakery (later changing the name to Canadian Bagel Bakery because in 1939 the federal government would not permit them to use the word "Russian") on Kensington Avenue in 1936. All three families lived above the store in a small apartment with one bathroom, and their eleven children helped out running the business. In time, the Bregmans became Toronto's most famous sellers of bagels.

In the city's garment industry, weekly wages fell 30 to 50 percent. On average, pieceworkers at Eaton's factory were paid $3.60 for a dozen voile dresses; after 1933, the fee the company paid was only $1.75, and work fluctuated throughout the year. On top of that, garment manufacturers like Eaton's expected their employees to work faster than humanely possible. As one young woman later told a Royal Commission on price spreads (established to look into the difference between wages paid and prices charged, most notably in the chain stores and food industry), "You had to work so hard [and] you were driven so fast that... you were a nervous wreck. The girls cried. I was hysterical myself. It almost drove me insane." The hours were so long and demanding that some workers never left the plant but slept overnight at their stations. Any complaining or talk of unions was met with the harshest of consequences.

In the summer of 1934, Eaton's introduced a new and more complicated dress pattern, yet refused to compensate its workers for the added work. Upset by what they perceived to be an unfair demand, a group of thirty-eight women, members of the ILGWU, requested that they be allowed to consult with their union representatives. Eaton's managers consented, but told the women that they had to return by 5:30 PM, which they were unable to do. The next day Eaton's locked them out, and the women declared themselves to be on strike. The company used strikebreakers and private detectives to intimidate and hassle the workers on the picket line, and the strike ultimately failed. However, the women's plight did receive national attention when several of them testified before the price spreads commission, exposing Eaton's harsh treatment of its workers and sweatshop conditions. The company vigorously defended itself, insisting that it did not "hound" its workers.

Divisive, as well, was a 1934 strike by workers, predominantly Jewish, against the Superior Cloak Company. Established by Abraham Posluns in 1916, Superior was run in the 1930s by his sons, Sam and Louis, pillars of the Toronto Jewish community (Louis's sons Irving, Jack, and Wilfred, along with Jimmy Kay, later established the clothing giant Dylex). So hostile were the Poslunses towards the ILGWU and its members that it locked out two hundred workers, hired strikebreakers, and then temporarily moved the company's plant to Guelph. During the sojourn in Guelph, visiting strikers from Toronto confronted their replacements, which over the course of several days led to violent clashes with the local police, who were assisted by reinforcements from the Kitchener police force as well as firemen. During one altercation, Sam Posluns shot a gun close enough to a striker that he was later charged with discharging a revolver with intent to injure. The strike lasted through the summer until the Poslunses eventually agreed to mediation to end the dispute.

THE GREATER THE DESPERATION of the times, the more people looked for political saviours to rescue them. The Depression was tailor-made for the brash and erratic Liberal leader Mitch Hepburn, only thirty-seven years old, who beat the all-powerful Tories in the provincial election held in mid-June 1934. Hepburn's Liberals won six of Toronto's now thirteen seats, with the Conservatives hanging on to the rest.

Hepburn was a populist and understood the common man more than most political leaders of his day. "People believe he is honest; know he is fearless; and regard him as efficient in administration," Prime Minister Mackenzie King, who famously feuded with the Ontario premier, wrote begrudgingly after Hepburn had won a second majority government on October 6, 1937. "His manners, evidently, as well, catches the man on the street. It is the 'fellow' that counts and he is one of them in language and spirit." Hepburn was indeed King's polar opposite. He was impetuous, inconsistent, impulsive, vindictive, reckless, and worst of all, from King's puritanical perspective, a sinner. Hepburn had a well-deserved and notorious reputation for being a drinker and a womanizer. There was one story about Hepburn being caught with three young girls in his suite at the King Edward Hotel and another about the premier bedding one woman in a Kingston hotel one night and another in Ottawa the next night. King had no doubt that Hepburn would "eventually destroy himself."

In the spring of 1937, Hepburn, the alleged man of the people, took a ruthless stance against United Auto Workers (UAW) strikers at the General Motors plant in Oshawa.

Apart from better working conditions and wages, the main issue of the strike was recognition of the UAW and its connection to the Committee for Industrial Organizations (CIO), a new militant American union federation actively organizing in the United States. Hepburn was determined to halt the CIO's entry into the Ontario labour movement. Yet his tactics were ruthless, treating the workers as if they were about to instigate another Bolshevik revolution. He was furious that Norman Rogers, the federal minister of labour, offered to mediate the dispute, wrongly considering it an attempt to embarrass him. He became madder still when Mackenzie King refused to put the Mounties at his disposal. Instead, he created his own police force—referred to derisively as "Hepburn's Hussars" and "Sons of Mitches"—to harass the strikers. Watching from a safe distance, King believed that Hepburn had become a fascist. (He was not the only one to hold this view.) After sixteen days, GM capitulated and the UAW was quietly recognized as the workers' union. Hepburn's tough stand, however, won him praise from many Ontarians who were not enamoured with radicals or unions, and he was re-elected for a second term in the provincial election held later that year.

Adherence to political and economic ideologies is rarely carved in stone. On occasion, personality can trump dogma as it did, if briefly, in 1935 when James "Jimmie" Simpson was elected mayor of Toronto. Trained as a printer and then employed by the *Star* for several years as its city hall reporter, Simpson, in his early sixties, was one of Toronto's most well-known labour men and a key member of the Toronto and District Trades and Labour Council. He was an inaugural member of the Ontario Co-operative Commonwealth Federation or CCF—the socialist party established nationally in 1932—and served for several years on the city's Board of Control.

As a politician, Simpson was immensely likeable and a genuinely decent fellow, though he did harbour anti-Catholic feelings, which ultimately cost him support. He was no communist, but that did not stop one of his political opponents from declaring on the radio that "the bells of Moscow will ring when Simpson is elected mayor." Despite similar concerns expressed by the press, with the exception of his former employer, the *Toronto Star*, Simpson triumphed over Alderman Harry Hunt in 1935. Ironically, staid British Tory Toronto made history as the first major city in North America to elect a socialist as mayor. Almost immediately, Simpson wanted to create more hostels for unemployed men, an idea denounced by Hepburn, who suggested the mayor was "doing everything in his power to assist men who refuse to work." His preoccupation with labour issues and his anti-Catholicism contributed to his defeat in 1936, when Sam McBride challenged him and won another term. Simpson, not in the best of health, died in September 1938 in a car accident. "To him and to his courageous progressiveness," the *Star* wrote in its editorial eulogy, "Toronto owes much."

THE ADAGE THAT RACISM and economics have an inverse relationship certainly rang true in Toronto: as the Depression worsened, racist and anti-Semitic incidents increased. The city's Jewish community, still the largest ethnic group apart from the English, Irish, and Scottish, continued to grow, reaching 46,751 in 1931 and 49,000 by the end of the decade. Symbolic of the assimilation of the upper echelon of the community was the Holy Blossom Synagogue congregation's embrace of the American Reform movement, including mixed seating, English services, and the optional wearing of prayer shawls and *kippot* or skull caps. (When the young new rabbi Maurice Eisendrath did not wear a *kippah* on Rosh Hashanah in 1929, he later recalled, "a thousand gasps, gathering into bursts of whispers, spread through the congregation.") Even at the more traditional Goel Tzedec Synagogue, English was more frequently used and women began to participate in services. The community's institutions, though financially hurt by the Depression, managed to sustain themselves through donations and through leadership from individuals like Otto Roger, a British-born Jew who emigrated to Toronto to work for the Shell Oil Company, and who helped Mount Sinai Hospital modernize and expand. The Talmud Torah on Brunswick Avenue was the focus of both Jewish education and culture, but also taught its young students about the importance of Canadian citizenship.

That process of "Canadianization" was also fostered at the nearby Harbord Collegiate on Harbord Avenue, west of Bathurst Street. During the twenties and thirties, 85 percent of the student body there was Jewish, and the parents of these students, like those of other Jewish students of the era, put a high premium on education and achieving professional success. Among the throng in 1930 were two boisterous grade ten students: Frank Shuster, who had moved with his family back to Toronto (where he was born in 1916) from Niagara Falls; and Louis Wiengarten, aka Johnny Wayne, whose father was a successful clothing manufacturer. It was in history teacher Charles Girdler's after-school Oola Boola Club that Frank and Lou—soon to be immortalized as the celebrated comedy duo Wayne and Shuster—first experimented with the amusing sketches that were to propel them to international fame.

Other notable Harbord Collegiate graduates included Sam "The Record Man" Sniderman; Sam Shopsowitz of Shopsy's deli; clothing retailer Harry Rosen; pollster Martin Goldfarb (his immigrant mother called the school "Harbord Collision"); Louis Rasminsky, the class valedictorian in 1925 and the first Jewish governor of the Bank of Canada; journalist Morley Safer of the CBS television news show *60 Minutes*; and Philip Givens, who was mayor of Toronto from 1963 to 1966. Harbord had "one other claim to fame," remembered lawyer and backroom politico Eddie Goodman, who was friends with Frank and Johnny. "The best crap games of any school in the city," he recalled, "went on in the lane just outside the schoolyard."

In and around Harbord Collegiate and east to Spadina Avenue, Jews had influence. Joseph Singer was elected to city council for Ward 4 (where Jews represented about 25 to 30 percent of the population) in the early twenties and then served on the Board of Control. More telling was the election of Liberal Sam Factor in the federal election of 1930 in the riding of Toronto West Centre, which incorporated the Spadina neighbourhood. Factor, who had emigrated from Russia to Canada when he was ten years old, defeated the former popular mayor Tommy Church, who ran for the Conservatives—the party that won a majority government under R.B. Bennett—to become Ontario's first Jewish MP. Factor was also the only Liberal elected in Toronto in 1930. On election night, a large crowd gathered to watch the results outside the *Toronto Star* building. "As Tommy's defeat emerged like a stranger at the feast," the *Star* reported the following day, "there ran gusts and shivers of surprised and possibly indignant comment that faithful Tommy had been given the 'works' by his party." Factor went on to serve as an MP for the next fifteen years, winning in the new riding of Spadina in the 1935 and 1940 elections. Mackenzie King considered appointing him to the cabinet in July 1940, until that idea met with resistance from his less tolerant Quebec colleagues.

It was the virulent anti-Semitism in Quebec during the thirties, where Adrian Arcand's Fascist party boasted a membership of eighty thousand at the height of its popularity, that Sam Factor also encountered in Ottawa. Along with two other Jewish MPs, Abraham Heaps of the CCF and Liberal Samuel Jacobs of Montreal, Factor continually lobbied King to permit German Jewish refugees into Canada after Adolf Hitler came to power in Germany in 1933. As is well documented, King, whose Christian conscience was moved by the plight of the German Jews, yielded to intense opposition from Quebec and other Liberals across the country and adhered to a heartless "none is too many" policy.

Toronto was hardly immune from such prejudice and discrimination, which during the tough times of the thirties became more volatile. It was as if the increased tension caused by the Depression left no room for tolerance. During the twenties and thirties, there were areas of the city where Jews were not able to rent or buy houses. "Is it restricted?" was a common question in any such property transaction, as Ben Kayfetz of the Canadian Jewish Congress later recalled. Signs proclaiming "No Jews and No Dogs," or the slightly more polite but just as pointed "Gentiles Only" or "Patronage exclusively Gentile," sprang up at the Lambton Park dance hall, summer resorts in the Muskoka region (including Toronto alderman Robert Siberry's new posh Bangor Lodge, opened in 1932), and golf clubs, including St. Andrews. Mayor William Stewart decided not to attend the official opening of Bangor Lodge, though he refused to explain why. When he was urged to express his opposition to Siberry's actions, he remarked to a reporter from the *Star* that "this is not the time to raise controversial issues." A year later, however, Stewart did speak against a proposal that would have barred Jews from Centre Island, quashing it. (On more than one occasion, Italian teenagers, who were mistaken for being Jewish, were also denied entry to "Gentile Only" public swimming pools. No amount of pleading with the officials at the door made a difference.)

When the St. Andrews Golf Club was established in 1925 (it no longer exists) on property in North York, several Jews had been investors. That did not stop the board of the club from erecting a sign that said "This course is restricted to Gentiles only. Please do not question this policy." As a result, the following year some of the wealthier members of the Jewish community opened their own club, the Oakdale Golf Club, on Jane Street and Sheppard Avenue West, which still has a large Jewish clientele to this day.

Jews were also often perceived to be Bolsheviks and a danger to Canadian society. (In fact, more Finns and Ukrainians were members of the Communist Party of Canada, and its leaders were largely British-born or of British heritage.) Several Toronto newspapers complained that there were too many Jews in the city, and in September 1924 the *Telegram* proposed a "Jewish poll tax" to discourage further Jewish immigration to Canada. If Jews were victims of anti-Semitism in Germany or elsewhere, a *Globe* editorial opined, it was their own fault for not assimilating—an absurd criticism and quite the opposite of the reality of German-Jewish life at the time. Besides, the *Globe* added, they were "admittedly the brains of the Communist movement in Germany as in Russia."

In the Beaches area off Queen Street East, a small Jewish enclave had developed, and in 1919 its residents had opened the quaint Beth Jacob Synagogue (or the Beach Hebrew Institute) on Kenilworth Avenue. They generally got along well with the larger Anglo population in the neighbourhood. During the summer months, however, many Toronto Jews from the Spadina area hopped the streetcar to spend a pleasant afternoon picnicking by the lake, a situation the Anglos did not appreciate. "Do you think it would be possible to place a few picnic tables under the trees in Kew Beach Park... and also to place a sign upon the trees—The area for Gentiles only," one unnamed resident asked the Parks Department in a letter of June 1933. "At the present time it is quite impossible to get a table in the Park, at all on Sunday: for the Jewish people seem to get every table in the Park and even if there were room for others to sit at the same table, one would hardly like to share the same table with them as our ways are so entirely different."

In 1933, these unwanted and "obnoxious" visitors became the target of the pro-Nazi Beach Swastika Club, whose members were young Anglo-Canadian men and boys. As the harassment increased, altercations between Jewish youth and the local toughs were inevitable. In August, when members of the Swastika Club held a dance and put up large swastikas on the side of their headquarters, they were confronted by fifty Jewish boys. The police—who were known to be unfriendly to Jews in general, if not outright anti-Semitic, and who had been reluctant to intervene in the ongoing dispute up to this point—arrived in time to ensure that no serious fighting broke out. Soon after, Mayor Stewart, who on July 12 had stood proudly alongside Chief Draper during the annual Orange parade, denounced the Swastika Club as "un-British" and "Un-Canadian." Nonetheless, further confrontations ensued; in one case, Jews enjoying a picnic at the beach were attacked by young men wearing swastikas on their shirts. More trouble was definitely on the horizon.

The simmering animosity finally exploded on the evening of August 16, 1933, at the baseball diamond in Christie Pits (officially Willowvale Park) on Christie Street, south of Bloor Street. Two nights earlier, during a softball game played between a team from St. Peter's Church and the Harbord Playground, a predominantly Jewish team, two spectators displayed a large swastika. Once the game was over, the two spectators were joined by several of their friends—members of the neighbourhood Willowvale Swastika Club—and ran onto the field shouting "Heil Hitler" at the Jewish players. No fighting broke out, but sometime late that night the troublemakers painted a large (and misspelled) "Hail Hitler" on the side of the Willowvale Park clubhouse. This set the scene for the riot on August 16.

St. Peter's Church and Harbord Playground were again playing baseball, with a crowd of about ten thousand in the stands, more than a thousand of whom were Jewish. During the second inning, members of the local Pit Gang, all from Anglo working-class families who resided near the park, started chanting "Heil Hitler." A group of Jews charged at their antagonists, armed with lead pipes and batons, and a brief fight erupted. The game continued with a small police presence on the scene to prevent further trouble. Once the game ended, however, a few Pit Gang members unfurled a white blanket with a black swastika sewn on it. That brazen act triggered a bloody six-hour riot, as more gangs of Gentiles and Jews, including workers from the Spadina garment factories, along with Ukrainian and Italian teenage boys who joined them as allies, descended on the Pits with baseball bats, broom handles, and lead pipes. The battle carried over into the street, and the few policemen present were unable to immediately do much to stop it. Nearby Jewish shops were vandalized. No one was killed in the melee, though many youths on both sides of the fight sustained serious injuries. There were two arrests, though only one of the two was charged. He had been apprehended as he was about to strike a person on the ground with a club and was sentenced to two months in jail or a fifty-dollar fine.

The Christie Pits riot naturally received a great deal of newspaper coverage and attention from Toronto politicians. The mayor immediately banned further displays of the swastika. Predictably, the *Telegram* placed the blame on "Jewish toughs" and "Communists"—an accusation echoed by the *Mail and Empire* and *Globe*—while the *Star* was more circumspect, describing the riot as an isolated incident and certainly not representative of a wave of anti-Semitism engulfing Toronto—a fair assessment.

The Jewish community's newspaper, *Der Yiddisher Zhurnal*, compared the battle to a Russian pogrom, an exaggeration to be sure.

Stories about the riot were told for years afterward, with many more people claiming to have been at the Pits on that fateful evening than were likely actually there. In the Jewish community, the battle has been steeped in mythology as a proud moment when Jews refused to be pushed around, as Cyril Levitt and William Shaffir showed in their detailed account *The Riot at Christie Pits* (1987). Most recently, on the eightieth anniversary of the confrontation in August 2013, Joe Black, who was seven years old in 1933, shared his recollections in press interviews, and the United Jewish Appeal Federation of Greater Toronto hosted a baseball game to commemorate the occasion.

The members of the Pit Gang or the Beach Swastika Club were hardly sophisticated in their intense dislike for the city's Jews, classic outsiders who they had been taught to detest. The events of August 16 were a primitive outburst of xenophobia exacerbated by the rise of the Nazis in Germany, but they were also the result of ingrained prejudice and discrimination, which was deeply held in early twentieth-century Toronto, as it was right across Canada.

JEWS WERE NOT the only targets of this abuse. Until well after the Second World War, most blacks were not permitted to stay at Toronto hotels. Jobs were hard to come by, even when there was a "Help Wanted" sign displayed in the window of a shop. "No, we have no job for coloured people," Harry Gairey Sr., a Jamaican immigrant, was told by one store owner when he inquired about employment as a young man in the twenties. Eaton's and Bell Telephone were then out of the question as well. He eventually found work for one dollar a day as a dishwasher and later as a railway porter, though he fought prejudice and discrimination whenever he confronted it. In 1943, he and his wife, Elma, put $500 down and purchased a $5,000 house on Barton Avenue, where they raised a family. They were, he recalled, "the first coloured people I know of to buy a house."

One day in late November 1945, Gairey's fifteen-year-old son, Harry Jr., and his friend Donny Jubas, who was Jewish, decided to try something new and go skating at Icelandia, a fashionable indoor arena on Yonge Street, north of Davisville Avenue. Jubas was told by the seller in the ticket booth that while he was welcome, Gairey was not. "We don't sell tickets to Negroes," Jubas was informed. "We don't let them in here. So do you want only one ticket?" The two friends departed. Yet that was not the end of it. Once Gairey Sr. learned what had happened, he complained to his local alderman, Joe Salsberg, and was invited to speak to city council about the incident. He took a logical approach to the problem by pointing out to Mayor Robert Saunders and the aldermen that if Canada ever went to war again, his son and other young black men were certain to be drafted. "If, so," he concluded, "I would like my son to have everything that a Canadian citizen is entitled to."

The story caught the attention of the *Star*'s city hall reporter, and the paper interviewed Harry Jr. That publicity triggered a brief protest in front of Icelandia by a group of University of Toronto students holding signs declaring "Color Prejudice Must Go" and "Racial discrimination should not be tolerated." Two years later, city aldermen approved an ordinance "requiring non-discrimination policies [with respect to race, creed, colour and religion] in all recreation and amusement establishments licensed by the police commission." Widespread and deeply ingrained prejudice remained firm, however.

Professional hockey was out of the question as well for black Canadians. Herb Carnegie, who died in March 2012 at the age of ninety-two, was born in Jamaica in 1919 and emigrated to Toronto as a child. He took an instant liking to hockey and developed into a brilliant player. In 1938 he played for the Toronto Young Rangers, a Junior A team. He was the only black or "coloured" player on the team and had to endure the usual racist taunts from unruly spectators. One day the Maple Leafs' boss, Conn Smythe, watched a Rangers' practice and was impressed with the young centreman. According to Carnegie, Smythe told Ed Wildey, the Rangers' owner and coach, that he would have signed Carnegie on the spot if he was white and offered $10,000 to anyone who could turn him white.

This story has been used to tarnish Smythe's reputation. It is true that Smythe was taught at a young age "to distrust Catholics," as his latest biographer Kelly McParland writes, and was not overly fond of Jews either; by one account, he would not hire young Jewish boys to sell programs or refreshments at Leaf games, and he may have traded the talented defenceman Alex "Mine Boy" Levinsky to the New York Rangers in 1934 because he was Jewish. (Levinsky's nickname was derived from his immigrant father's proud declaration as he watched his son play hockey, "That's mine boy!") But the Leafs' owner, though gruff, was probably no more racist than anyone else of his generation.

Carnegie later played for semi-professional teams in Quebec and eventually got a tryout with the New York Rangers in 1948, but he was only offered a deal to play with the team's minor-league outfit. Dissatisfied with the offer (including the money the Rangers were prepared to pay him), he refused and spent the rest of his playing days in Quebec. The first black player in the NHL was instead Willie O'Ree, from New Brunswick, who played with the Boston Bruins during the 1957–58 season.

One of the most devastating incidents of racism in Depression-era Toronto involved a Chinese man and a white woman who did not follow the mores of the time. In 1939, Velma Demerson, a white eighteen-year-old, was charged under Ontario's Female Refuges Act as being "incorrigible" because she was pregnant and living with Harry Yip, a Chinese waiter. Instituted in 1897, the "draconian" act allowed the province "to regulate the sexual and moral behaviour" of women between the ages of sixteen and thirty-five—especially women who were seemingly "out of sexual control." In

Demerson's case, her father had reported her to the police. She was sentenced to one year at Belmont House, the city's house of refuge for wayward girls on Belmont Street in Yorkville (today it is the site of a home for elderly residents). Soon after she arrived there, Belmont House was reconfigured and she was forced to spend the duration of her term in a windowless cell at the more decrepit Andrew Mercer Reformatory for Females, surrounded by thieves, prostitutes, vagrants, and an assortment of rough women. As she recalls in her autobiography, she suffered many indignities including intrusive, painful, and humiliating vaginal surgeries conducted as part of a eugenics experiment.

Three months after she gave birth to her son, Harry Jr., the infant was taken from her by provincial authorities and became a ward of the state. For a time he was raised by a friend of Harry Sr. Velma married Harry after she was released from the reformatory, although the marriage did not last. Her relationship with her son was not good either, and he ultimately died in a drowning accident in 1966, when he was twenty-six. In 2002, after bringing public attention to what had happened to her as a young girl, the Ontario government offered Velma an apology and an undisclosed settlement for the abysmal treatment she was subjected to.

THE CITY CONTINUED TO GROW, even during the hard years of the Depression. Thanks to generous grants from the Rockefeller and Carnegie Foundations, the University of Toronto was able to establish its School of Nursing in 1933 and expand its fine arts and Chinese studies programs. More impressive was the provincial government–sponsored expansion of the Royal Ontario Museum in 1932–33 into the now iconic structure on Queen's Park near Bloor Street. This was a make-work project, so "no machinery was permitted, only pickaxes, shovels, and horse-drawn wagon, and only Ontario building products could be used." Inside, four large totem poles, which had been acquired and shipped from British Columbia, were installed. Throughout the year-long construction, passersby marvelled at the beauty and elegance of the new building. And soon after it reopened in early 1933, an ever-increasing number of visitors regularly lined up to examine the enlarged and exceptional exhibits of Egyptian, Roman, and Holy Land artifacts.

A year earlier another enduring Toronto landmark on the corner of Carlton and Church Streets had received even more public interest. Maple Leaf Gardens, which opened to tremendous fanfare in November 1931, was largely the creation and dream of Conn Smythe. The legendary hockey aficionado was only thirty-two years old in 1927 when he astutely acquired an interest in the Toronto St. Patricks, the city's professional team in the then struggling National Hockey League (NHL).

Smythe was an avid sportsman with an interest in hockey as well as horse racing. He had survived three brutal years fighting on the battlefields of the First World War and then came home to marry his high school sweetheart, Irene. By 1927, he and Irene had three children—two sons, Stafford and Hugh, and a daughter, Miriam. Another daughter, Patricia, was born in 1935, though she died of an allergic reaction when she was nine, which devastated Smythe and his wife.

Besides running a profitable gravel and sand business, Smythe had developed into a successful hockey manager and coach for teams at the University of Toronto (the university's blue and white colours stuck with him). In 1926 he was hired to be the manager and coach of the NHL's New York Rangers. Before the season even began, however, a disagreement with the team's owner, Col. John Hammond, over which players to sign led to his dismissal and his contract was bought out. Smythe was angry at the way he had been treated, yet it proved to be a propitious moment in his life, as he returned to Toronto and bought his stake in the St. Pats.

He was a plain-speaking man with a hard exterior. He disdained alcohol, which had contributed to the death of his mother, Polly, at the age of thirty-eight when he was only eleven, and forbade his players to drink or carouse with women while travelling. He did not care much for tobacco, either, and forbade his players to smoke in the dressing room and certainly not on the bench (though they did anyway). Above all, he approached hockey as if he were still a soldier—in fact, he served again during the Second World War and was seriously wounded in 1944—and expected his players to show a tough resolve. Hence, his famous dictum "If you can't beat 'em in the alley, you can't beat 'em on the ice." Smythe was never bullied by anyone, and he expected his players and anyone else in his employ to adhere to his high standards—without question or comment. One of Smythe's only sinful activities was gambling and an oft-told tale has it that he won the $10,000 he used to acquire a share in the St. Pats by wagering on a few hockey games.

As difficult as it is to believe, hockey was not the most popular sport in Toronto in the mid-twenties; baseball and rugby or football garnered more attention. The NHL, which had been established in 1917, was not yet the dominant league in hockey, and the Stanley Cup was still challenged by an assortment of semi-professional and amateur teams. The deal that saw Smythe and a group of wealthy investors purchase the St. Pats, and the new owners renaming them the Toronto Maple Leafs, "wasn't big news," as Kelly McParland writes, and received only scant attention on the sports pages of Toronto newspapers. Any comment about the Leafs was more likely to involve the team's new president, the First World War flying ace Lt.-Col. Billy Barker.

Smythe's primary objective was to transform the Leafs into a winning and profitable hockey team and organization. The first goal was easier than the second. Emphasizing teamwork, discipline, fitness training, structured practices, and ruggedness on the ice, he brought together the right combination of coaches and players. "I'm not interested in hockey players who don't play to win," he once explained to sports journalist Trent

Frayne. "You can take penalties, but you gotta play to win." Almost overnight, the Leafs became Stanley Cup contenders, and the city's sports fans took notice. With assistance from the diligent and bright Frank Selke, a former player turned coach, Smythe drafted and signed a team of future Hall of Famers. Of note in the annals of the Leafs were Clarence "Hap" Day, who later became one of the team's most successful coaches; Francis "King" Clancy; Reginald "Red" Horner; right winger Irvine "Ace" Bailey, who was nearly killed in a game in December 1933 after he was hit from behind by Boston Bruins' defenceman Eddie Shore; and the "Kid Line" of Joe Primeau, Charlie "The Big Bomber" Conacher, and Harvey "Busher" Jackson. Primeau was twenty-three, Conacher nineteen, and Jackson eighteen when they started playing together in 1929. In goal by the start of the 1935 season was Walter "Turk" Broda. Smythe and Broda famously argued about Broda's up-and-down weight in what became known in the Toronto papers as the "Battle of the Bulge."

The strategy worked. Between 1927 and 1939, when the number of teams in the league varied from ten to seven, the Leafs contended for the Stanley Cup seven times and won it once, in 1932, under coach Dick Irvin. Thousands of fans started showing up to watch the team practise, and the city's passion for the Leafs began in earnest.

To achieve profitability, however, Smythe desperately required a new arena. The Leafs played in the old arena on Mutual Street, which was too small and cold, had uncomfortable wooden benches, and could only seat 7,150 paying customers. In comparison, Madison Square Gardens in New York City, the home of the Rangers, had room for at least fifteen thousand spectators. Worse still, the Leafs were hardly a priority at the arena. They were allocated only two Saturday night games a month and restricted practice time.

Smythe realized that if the team was to truly prosper, the Leafs needed their own home, a new state-of-the-art arena that he and the team owned and operated. Only then could the Leafs play games when they needed to and attract more fans. It would also allow Smythe and his board to keep all of the money from ticket and concession sales (the owners of the Mutual Arena received approximately 30 to 35 percent of the gate receipts). Thus was born the audacious scheme to build Maple Leaf Gardens at Carlton and Church Streets (on property acquired from the T. Eaton Company) during the worst economic depression in history.

The plan began to take shape in June 1929. Smythe did not want to operate in just any old hockey arena. He envisioned a classy establishment with comfortable seating for twelve thousand and a place where businessmen attired in suits would attend games accompanied by their dolled-up wives. First, he needed to raise about one million dollars—in 1930. With ingenuity, promotion, support in the newspapers, increased ticket sales even during the Depression, a lot of hard work, and a bit of luck, Smythe and his associates pulled the deal together. He and Selke convinced an assortment of investors—among the group were the Sun Life Insurance Company, Canadian National Railway, Bank of Commerce, Bank of Nova Scotia, and Eaton's and Simpson's department stores—to invest in the Leafs and the new Maple Leaf Gardens. Selke even convinced unemployed construction workers to work for less than union rates with some taking partial payment in shares in the new Gardens that would eventually be worth more than the few dollars they were owed. Smythe negotiated an agreement with Foster Hewitt, who set up his own one-man media enterprise and was soon richer than Smythe as the master of the Leafs' radio broadcasts. Foster's father, the *Star*'s sports editor W.A. Hewitt, was hired to manage non-sporting entertainment events.

Despite cost overruns and other setbacks, the Gardens rose on Carlton Street and was officially opened on schedule on November 12, 1931, to a tremendous reception. It was as if the Taj Mahal had been erected in downtown Toronto. The Gardens had it all: padded seats, ranging in price from one to three dollars; squeaky clean washrooms; pretty usherettes in adorable blue uniforms; and Foster Hewitt broadcasting high up in the gondola, accessible only via a narrow and dangerous catwalk where only the most courageous (or foolish) dared go—and that did not include Smythe, Selke, or Hewitt Sr.. Most significantly, the opening of the Gardens—the *Globe* dubbed it "the Great New Arena"—made Torontonians feel they had "blossomed forth into major league ranks to the fullest extent," as the paper's sportswriter Bert Perry put it.

With an improved product on the ice—during the 1931 Stanley Cup final against the New York Rangers there were eighty thousand requests for tickets—the Gardens lived up to Smythe's high expectations, making him not only wealthy but also the most notable sports figure in the city. Owing to the team's success, plus the radio promotion of Foster Hewitt, the Leafs became the most celebrated hockey team in Canada, swelling the chest of every Toronto sports fan and booster. During the worst years of the Depression, the Gardens, presenting everything from hockey to religious revivals to pro wrestling, rather remarkably posted profits in the $40,000-plus range, before reaching $87,000 in 1938.

CONN SMYTHE WAS ONE TYPE of Toronto celebrity to emerge during the thirties; the young business tycoon C. George McCullagh was another (in the forties the two men become business associates and political comrades). Thirty-one years old in 1936, McCullagh was the Conrad Black of his day, or "Canada's Wonder Boy," as one big American magazine anointed him; a man "who could be prime minister of Canada at will." He looked, as a *Saturday Night* article described him, like the "Arrow-collar advertisement in the flesh: dark, crisp hair, of medium size but broad-shouldered with an athletic build. Readily, he smiles or jokes, glibly he damns or consigns to hell what does not meet with his approval. But underneath this congenial exterior is an analytical mind—one that misses nothing, one that sizes up constantly and one that acts without hesitation." McCullagh certainly did act, and he turned the Toronto newspaper industry on its head by purchasing both the *Globe* and the *Mail and Empire*, merging them in the *Globe and Mail*.

Born in 1905 into a working-class family in London, Ontario, McCullagh was a go-getter at an early age. His whirlwind life and career mirrored the plot of a Horatio Alger saga. He started as a newsboy selling the early-morning *Globe* on street corners in London. Next, in 1921, at sixteen, he worked in the *Globe*'s circulation department, regularly outselling every other employee. For a brief period he worked as a financial reporter, which enabled him to make important connections with the Toronto business community. Legend has it that after being forced to leave the *Globe* in 1928 for violating the newspaper's no-smoking policy, he promised to return some day as the paper's owner.

Until then, he charmed and cajoled Bay Street as a broker, making lots of money in mining and oil investments in addition to finding an ally in mining executive and millionaire William Wright. "In the Canadian scene there are two sure-fire ways of becoming a success," wrote Pierre Berton in a 1949 profile of McCullagh. "One way is to find a gold mine. The other way is to find a man who has found a gold mine. Bill Wright found the gold mine. George McCullagh found Bill Wright." McCullagh helped Wright sort out his muddled business affairs and shared his interest in horse racing, and Wright provided McCullagh with the financial clout he required to become a press baron.

The *Globe* was first on his list. In 1936 the *Globe*'s publisher was William Jaffray, who had assumed control of the newspaper following the death of his father, Robert, in 1914. The younger Jaffray was a smart man, but eccentric, and he let his puritanical beliefs cloud his judgment and impact the *Globe*'s bottom line. A moral crusader, he was opposed to divorce, gambling, and all other forms of enjoyable vice. For this reason, he foolishly turned his back on thousands of dollars in advertising for tobacco, liquor, and women's undergarments. He insisted the *Globe* published a regular religious editorial, one of the few newspapers in North America to do so, and denounced anyone who smacked of atheism; this included author Sinclair Lewis.

Jaffray also deliberately steered the paper away from its historic partisan support of the Liberal Party—a contentious act that annoyed and angered the party's leader, Prime Minister Mackenzie King. (King maintained, with some justification, that the Liberals' terrible showing in Ontario in the 1925 federal election, in which the party won only twelve seats, was mainly the result of Jaffray's insistence that the *Globe* turn against King and the Liberals.) For years, Jaffray absolutely refused to permit the *Globe* to print horse-racing odds or news and he berated King to pass legislation banning the publication of horse-racing results. Desperate to win Jaffray's favour, King and the Liberals pushed through an amendment to the Criminal Code outlawing horse-racing statistics, but it was rejected by the Senate on three different occasions. Naturally, Jaffray blamed King for the failure each time.

With Wright supplying the capital, McCullagh bought the *Globe* from Jaffray for $1.3 million in October 1936, and within days the paper had a brand new look, including cigarette advertising and the results of the races at Pimlico and Woodbine. Not finished yet, McCullagh then decided to buy out the *Globe*'s chief morning competitor, the Conservative-leaning *Mail and Empire*, a more lively newspaper owned by the wealthy and reclusive Montreal financier Izaak Walton Killam (when he died in 1955, Killam was said to be the richest man in Canada).

When Killam got word that McCullagh was interested in the *Mail and Empire*, he arranged for the two of them to meet for breakfast at the Royal York to discuss it. The asking price was nearly double the cost of the *Globe*, $2.5 million, yet McCullagh, again with Wright's backing, came up with the funds. When Mackenzie King heard the news, he was thrilled and told McCullagh that he "hoped and prayed" the *Globe* "might again become the exponent of Liberal principles." Privately, however, McCullagh made the prime minister nervous, and King feared the merger of the *Globe* and the *Mail and Empire* might result in a "big interest, Fascist organ." That was not quite what transpired, though Toronto's newest paper did in the end turn on King and the federal Liberals.

The first edition of the *Globe and Mail* (the *Empire*, which had started as a Tory organ in the 1890s, was dropped and largely forgotten) appeared on November 23, 1936. Many, though not all, *Mail and Empire* reporters kept their jobs with the amalgamated paper, but the *Globe and Mail* in its early years reflected McCullagh's inimitable personality. "I have no politics," he claimed. "I am a Canadian." From the start, he declared the *Globe and Mail* would be supportive of the government in power, whether Liberal or Conservative, but he added that the paper reserved "the fullest liberty to criticize any actions of any government which we do not consider to be in the public interest."

What drove McCullagh was his quest for power and influence, which led him for a time into the ever-expanding orbit of the unpredictable Ontario premier, Mitch Hepburn, who by 1937 had declared himself to be a Liberal, but not "a Mackenzie King Liberal." The two men shared a fondness for carousing and drinking, though McCullagh eventually abstained from liquor entirely and tried, with little success, to convince Hepburn to do so as well. Hepburn was instrumental in McCullagh's being appointed a governor of the University of Toronto, the youngest person to hold that position, while McCullagh privately helped Hepburn make some money in gold mine investments (Hepburn lost it all by the time of his death in 1953). Still, McCullagh fiercely guarded his newspaper's independence, and his support for Hepburn was not unconditional. A diehard capitalist, McCullagh ensured the *Globe and Mail* backed Hepburn in his bitter clash with the United Auto Workers during the strike in Oshawa in 1937. Yet he was critical of the premier's Hydro policy and unhappy about Hepburn's "unholy alliance" with Quebec premier Maurice Duplessis. Independently, he promoted a coalition with the opposition provincial Conservatives and even pressured Hepburn to fire several members of his cabinet.

By 1938, McCullagh was following his own path. In a series of political sermons broadcast by private radio stations, he attacked patronage, political corruption, high taxes, communists, and fascists, following them up with his short-lived "Leadership League," an organization intended, as McCullagh explained, "to arouse the public to a new consciousness of Canada's major problems." The League became an expensive sounding board for McCullagh's pet peeves and ultimately cost the *Globe and Mail* more than $100,000. Within a few years, McCullagh's severe disenchantment with Mackenzie King's wartime policies led to a permanent and irreconcilable break with the Liberals—first at the federal level and then at the provincial—and the *Globe and Mail* became one of the Conservative Party's most ardent defenders.

In the forties, McCullagh's home away from home was a reserved table at Winston's on King Street West, close to York Street, in a building owned by the *Globe and Mail* (the newspaper's new home, the modern William H. Wright Building, was just down the block). Winston's, named in honour of Winston Churchill, was the fanciest dining establishment in Toronto for years, the headquarters of the city's nascent WASP establishment, and owned, ironically, by two Hungarian immigrants, Oscar and Cornelia Berceller. They had acquired the small diner, then a hangout for reporters, in 1940 for $10,000 and soon completely transformed it. McCullagh was the Bercellers' most enthusiastic patron and ensured that they received the proper accolades in his newspaper. An October 1946 review extolled the high quality of "the light-hearted little restaurant... [which] has blossomed into a beautiful, grown-up 'glamour job' that would make New York look several times." For years, Winston's was the favourite place to be seen by celebrities and theatregoers alike. (Later, in the mid-sixties, after the Bercellers sold the restaurant, it was rejuvenated by John Arena of the Rosedale Golf Club and again became the headquarters of the Toronto business establishment of that era.)

Celebrities dining at Winston's often presented the Bercellers with autographed pictures that were prominently displayed. One night in the spring of 1945, local artist Harold Shaw was at the restaurant and sketched Cornelia with a fountain pen. Oscar and Cornelia were so impressed with the drawing that they convinced Shaw to do a charcoal sketch of Hollywood actress Elissa Landi, who was then visiting Toronto. The drawing was hung on the wall, attracting much attention. Soon Shaw's charcoal sketches of other actors and actresses, including Joan Crawford, Lucille Ball, Betty Hutton, Danny Kaye, John Gielgud, Laurence Olivier, and Ralph Richardson, were the talk of the restaurant. (Shaw's sketch of U.S. president John F. Kennedy was treasured by his wife, Jacqueline.)

The Bercellers prided themselves on offering their select clientele excellent service and fine food—among Winston's specialties were veal fillet Pompadour, roast duckling flamed in Grand Marnier and brandy sauce, and filet mignon à la Winston's—and doing so in an establishment that promoted exclusivity. They presented about 1,500 of their regulars with keys, which did not open the restaurant's doors, but did give them immediate access and special treatment. The keys, which suggested Winston's was a private club (though it technically was not), were also a way to keep out unwanted prostitutes from nearby hotels, who in the restaurant's early days liked to stop by to prowl for potential clients.

In December 1949, actress Sarah Churchill was in Toronto, performing in a play at the Royal Alexandra Theatre, and one evening was to be the guest of honour at the restaurant named after her illustrious father. Winston's expected its patrons to dress in formal attire, but Sarah Churchill arrived at the front door wearing slacks and was refused entry. Churchill explained to the befuddled maître d', who did not recognize her, that she was the special guest he was waiting for. It was left to Oscar Berceller to clear up the misunderstanding. That was his style, and visiting celebrities and dignitaries knew there was nothing Oscar and Cornelia would not do for them (that included bringing in smoked eel from New York for Danny Kaye and spending $400 to charcoal-broil a steak for Jimmy Durante). During the forties and fifties, they bestowed on Toronto's social scene elegance and "sophistication," so that at Winston's, at any rate, the Great Depression was but a faint memory—for the rich and famous at least.

Chapter Eight

SUBWAYS, SUBURBIA, AND PAESANI

Toronto is the greatest unifying influence in this country today. Without Toronto, let me tell you, this country would dissolve into the red ruin of domestic turmoil and civil war tomorrow! Or this afternoon even! Toronto is the one thing that holds the place together.

—LISTER SINCLAIR, "WE ALL HATE TORONTO," 1948

Mayor Allan A. Lamport (left) and Metro Chairman Frederick G. Gardiner (right) at the official opening of the Yonge Street subway on March 30, 1954. City of Toronto Archives, Fonds 1257, Series 1057, Item 8962

ON THE EVENING OF September 3, 1939, the day Britain and France declared war on Nazi Germany, and a week before Canada officially did so too, Toronto had its first taste of the bloody confrontation that was to dominate the next five and a half years. Late that night the SS *Athenia*, which had left Glasgow for Montreal, with a stop at Liverpool on September 2, was hit by a torpedo fired by a German submarine about four hundred kilometres northwest of Ireland. The anxious German commander believed he had been stalking a ship carrying troops. Instead, the *Athenia* had 1,102 civilian passengers on board, at least fifty of them from Toronto and Hamilton. In all, ninety-three passengers and nineteen crew members died in the attack and subsequent rescue.

Among those killed was ten-year-old Margaret Hayworth from Hamilton, who was travelling with her mother, Georgina, and younger sister, Jacqueline. During the rescue operations that followed the blast, Margaret was taken to safety, but she soon died from a bad head injury. By all accounts, she was the first Canadian killed in the Second World

War. Once the surviving members of the family were back home, she was given a state funeral, attended by Ontario lieutenant governor Albert Matthews and Premier Mitch Hepburn, accompanied by his entire cabinet. The story of Margaret's death was covered widely in the press and united Torontonians in a common cause against the enemy.

The city had clearly changed since the last war. Its population had increased by more than 200,000 in the city proper, with growth of the surrounding suburban area of Metro Toronto about to take off. Greater diversity, however, would have to wait until after the war ended. The city's economy and industrial production expanded. Massey-Harris and Research Enterprises were mobilized for war work, while the National Steel Car plant at Malton was reorganized on federal government orders as the Crown corporation Victory Aircraft. (The latter was sold to the British aircraft group Hawker Siddeley in 1945 and became its subsidiary, A.V. Roe Canada). And the town of Ajax (named after the British war ship HMS *Ajax*), today a community in the eastern part of the GTA, was literally created as home for the thousands of employees who filled millions of shells at the Defence Industries Limited plant.

Toronto's collective response to the outbreak of war was more or less the same as it had been in 1914: when Britain is at war, Canada is at war. At Queen's Park, the odd duo of Liberal premier Mitch Hepburn (who in September 1939 acted as if a Nazi invasion of Ontario was likely) and the stiff, though debonair, Conservative opposition leader George Drew—who liked to be called Colonel Drew, since he was an honorary colonel in the Royal Canadian Artillery—was backed firmly by the *Globe and Mail* and *Telegram*. The two leaders and the newspapers' editors soon hammered away at what they regarded as Prime Minister Mackenzie King's inadequate wartime policies—mainly his refusal to institute overseas conscription.

In October 1942, the ever erratic Hepburn resigned and was replaced by Gordon Conant, who in turn was replaced as premier by Harry Nixon following an Ontario Liberal Party leadership convention in May 1943. In the provincial election held three months later, Nixon and the Liberals, still reeling from the turmoil linked to Hepburn, lost to the newly revamped Progressive-Conservatives led by Drew, who formed a minority government. In a surprise turn, and a sign that Canadian expectations of government were in flux, the CCF won thirty-four seats, including four of the thirteen Toronto ridings as well as the four York ridings, and became the official opposition. (The downtown riding of St. Andrew elected Communist Joe Salsberg of the Labor-Progressives.) Less than two years later, Drew rebounded and regained a sizable majority. The Liberals also recovered and were back in opposition, though with only a few seats more than the CCF.

Drew's impressive victory in the June 1945 provincial election marked the beginning of a forty-year PC dynasty in Tory Ontario. The Liberals and the CCF (which morphed into the New Democratic Party in 1961) battled for second spot for the next four decades. Still, Toronto voters were not as consistently Tory as is believed: in the 1948 contest, for example, the CCF captured eleven of the seventeen Toronto and York ridings. In any event, throughout the war years, no one could question Drew's commitment, his support for conscription, or his disdain for Mackenzie King's alleged "coddling" of Quebec.

Provincial efforts during the conflict were wholeheartedly supported at city hall by mayors Ralph Day, a funeral director who was a veteran of the Battle of Vimy Ridge in 1917 (and later chairman of the TTC), and dental surgeon Dr. Frederick Conboy, a devoted Orangeman with an interest in social reform. To ensure that there were no questions about civic patriotism, all council meetings during the war years started with a hearty rendition of "God Save the King" and the Lord's Prayer. Toronto voters rejected the CCF at city hall for much of the forties and fifties and stuck with tried-and-true Tory civic leaders like Robert Saunders, Hiram McCallum, and Leslie Saunders.

Canada's historic link to Britain was no trifling matter, as the outspoken University of Toronto history professor Frank Underhill discovered. At a conference in the summer of 1940, he suggested that Canada's connection with the United States was about to become stronger no matter what transpired in Europe. Pressured by such notable graduates as former prime minister Arthur Meighen, the university board voted to fire Underhill, though Canon Henry Cody, the aging president who made the final decision, eventually decided not to carry out the firing.

In the first month of the war, four thousand young men enlisted in Toronto. Many more would join them, as crowds gathered daily around the University Avenue Armouries. Some of the enlistees, who did not see action until D-Day in June 1944, would never return. Fewer Torontonians died in the Second World War than the First, but more than three thousand did perish fighting the Nazis. In this group were 557 students and 500 graduates from the University of Toronto, whose names are listed on the memorial under the university's Soldiers' Tower. Likewise, starting in 1942, the name of each fallen Toronto-area soldier was recorded on index cards that were later used to create the Golden Book of Remembrance now displayed at the Hall of Memory at Toronto City Hall.

Among those at the front of the line was the owner of the Toronto Maple Leafs, forty-five-year-old Conn Smythe, who was determined to serve his country as he had during the First World War. He also encouraged his staff at the Gardens and his players to enlist, though few volunteered for overseas service. Smythe was another vocal critic of Mackenzie King's military policies and pushed himself on the army, whose officials were not keen to accept Smythe's offer of leadership. Never one to give up, he established his own battery that was part of the 7th Toronto Regiment, Royal Canadian Artillery. He was promoted to major and saw action with his unit in France in June 1944, when he was seriously wounded.

During his recovery back in Toronto, he launched another harshly worded missive against King, denouncing the lack of Canadian reinforcements in Europe and advocating conscription. This diatribe was published with great flourish by the *Globe and Mail* on September 19, 1944, on the orders of George McCullagh, who was now aligned with Ontario Conservative leader George Drew (McCullagh was later made vice-president of the Maple Leaf Gardens board). For a brief time, Smythe's comments were the talk of the city, yet they were fairly insignificant in the larger context of the Conscription Crisis of 1944 that nearly tore apart King's cabinet.

Though Smythe had relinquished his day-to-day running of the Leafs during the war, he was present and in uniform at the Gardens in mid-April 1942 to witness the Leafs' unprecedented Stanley Cup victory after falling behind three games in the best-of-seven series against the Detroit Red Wings. And he was soon back in charge of the team as the majority shareholder and president of Maple Leaf Gardens. He oversaw five more Stanley Cup victories between 1945 and 1951, with such players as centreman Ted "Teeder" Kennedy, the team's captain, and Walter "Babe" Pratt, a rugged and talented defenceman. The Gardens was a tremendous money-maker for Smythe—the company reported a healthy profit of $190,000 in 1947—and Leaf tickets became such a sought-after commodity that the Leafs played in a sold-out arena for decades.

TORONTO JEWS were naturally encouraged to enlist as well. That was sometimes easier said than done. Ben Dunkelman, the son of Tip Top Tailors founder David Dunkelman, was a strapping young man. Because of his father's business success, he grew up in a mansion located on a ninety-acre estate called Sunnybrook Farm, then on the outskirts of the city (today on the grounds of the Sunnybrook Health Sciences Centre off of Bayview, north of Eglinton Avenue). He and his brother, Joe, attended Upper Canada College, the only Jewish students in the school at the time. Probably because of their size, the Dunkelman brothers did not experience any overt anti-Semitism.

In the fall of 1939, Ben tried to enlist in the Royal Canadian Navy but was told that he was "overqualified" to be an ordinary seaman and that "their quotas were full" for officer training. As Dunkelman subsequently discovered, the navy would never have accepted Jewish officers. (In another example of discrimination trumping patriotism, Private Stanley Grizzle, a black Canadian who had been born in Toronto, tried to book a room for himself and his bride at the Royal York in 1942, but was informed that the hotel "couldn't accommodate coloured people." According to Grizzle, it was "a rare day" when he wasn't called "nigger" on the streets of Toronto during this period.)

Dunkelman next tried the army and was able to enlist in the 1st Battalion of the Queen's Own Rifles. The Canadian army was more liberal; he was able to take an officer's course and became a lieutenant, and eventually was given command of a mortar platoon, which he courageously led during the D-Day invasion. After the war, Dunkelman, a committed Zionist, travelled to Israel, where he distinguished himself and was one of the few North Americans to be given command responsibilities.

By early 1943, approximately ten thousand Canadian Jews had enlisted, but that did not stop Leslie Saunders, a Toronto alderman (and mayor of the city in 1954–55) from publicly declaring "that the Jews of this country are not doing their duty in this war." Saunders was a loyal member of the Orange Order who later was anointed a deputy grand master, but he was stuck in the past. For him, as for many others, Toronto was "a Protestant City," plain and simple, as he proclaimed on many occasions. It is difficult to argue with the assessment of Jean "True" Davidson, the colourful mayor of East York, who later said Saunders was "bigoted, pigheaded, and in his attitude toward women, a throwback to the Stone Age."

In the face of Saunders's accusation, the Canadian Jewish Congress was compelled to defend Jewish men and women who were doing their part for the war effort. So, too, did Controllers Robert Saunders (no relation to Leslie Saunders) and Fred Hamilton, as well as the editors of the *Globe and Mail*, who questioned the alderman's claim, especially in light of the disconcerting news of mass killings of Jews in Europe. "Toronto's City Council ought to be able to adopt a resolution condemning the terrible slaughter and torture of Jews in Nazi-occupied countries without an alderman injecting a sour note into the discussions," stated an editorial of March 24, 1943. "The extent to which Jewish men have enlisted in Canada's active forces has the same bearing on the atrocities that the enlistment of other citizens has, although Alderman Saunders seemed to think there is a distinction... These figures [of the Canadian Jewish Congress] indicate there is no reason to single out the Jews as failing to hold up their end. If they are to be criticized as not doing enough, it should be along with others who are Jews, as citizens, not as followers of a particular creed." It was fitting that Leslie Saunders, who became mayor in 1954, lost the position in 1955 to Nathan Phillips, the first Jewish mayor in the city's history.

The war was everywhere. Dr. Peter Bryce, a Methodist clergyman, recalled the "vast crowds" of young soldiers at Union Station on their way to Europe in October 1943. "In the throngs of men and women representing every branch of the armed services, with their mothers and fathers, their wives and sweethearts... When the time comes for the movement of trains on one of the main lines, it seems as if a wave of emotion surges through the rotunda." For historian and alderman William Kilbourn, who was a teenager in 1939, the war "meant city hall with its tall red thermometer keeping track of the latest war-bond drive... Toronto businessmen on the train to Ottawa to run the wartime Prices and Trade Board, and some of them, such as E.P. Taylor, torpedoed in the chilly North Atlantic during production trips to England [in December 1940]. There were victory gardens and blackouts and ARP wardens... The Inglis plant producing

Bren guns, and de Havilland... turned out 1,000 Mosquito fighter bombers. Rationing meant one bottle of liquor a month, books of stamps for sugar and most other staples; a stay of execution for Toronto's horse-drawn fleets of milk and bread wagons; and the disappearance of appliances and new tires from the stores."

After Norway was invaded by the Nazis in the spring of 1940, Toronto Island Airport became the training headquarters for the exiled Royal Norwegian Air Force (RNAF). A military camp at the foot of Bathurst Street, adjacent to the airport, was soon dubbed "Little Norway" and became the home for more than 2,500 RNAF pilots and their families. One among many was mechanic Viggo Ullmann, his wife, Janna, and their two-year-old daughter, Liv, who was destined to become an international movie actress. She spent four years in Toronto until her father was injured after being struck accidentally by an active airplane propeller. The family relocated to New York, where it was discovered Viggo had a brain tumour. He died there in 1944.

The training operation was supposed to be secret, but that did not last long. At a ceremony held at the airport on November 1, 1940, Toronto mayor Ralph Day presented two Norwegian flags to two RNAF commanders. In 1943, the RNAF moved its operation to a larger area in Muskoka, though the airmen often visited the barracks in the city. Moreover, Toronto residents quickly invited the airmen to family dinners, and many, like navigator and gunner Conradi Hansen, wound up marrying city girls—Hansen married Barbara File—and returned to Ontario once the war had ended. Little Norway Park, at the southwest corner of Bathurst Street and Queen's Quay West, was established in 1986 to commemorate the wartime link between Norwegians and Torontonians. In November 1987, King Olav V officially dedicated the park, which displays as its symbol of friendship a memorial granite rock that was shipped to Toronto from Norway in 1971 with an engraving thanking Toronto and Canada for its "help and hospitality."

VE day on May 8, 1945, was declared a civic holiday in Toronto, as it was throughout Canada, with parades down Yonge Street. Unlike the victory celebration in Halifax that turned into a riot, however, Toronto officials kept everything orderly and trouble-free. About the only real inconvenience was the daily one-hour blackout in the war's aftermath to conserve electricity. Few would have suspected that the next decade and a half would transform Toronto in almost every respect from the British Protestant city, which Leslie Saunders and others wanted so desperately to preserve, into the cosmopolitan metropolis it was destined to become.

RADICAL CHANGE did not happen overnight, of course. In 1947, when journalist Pierre Berton, then working for the *Vancouver Sun*, was offered, and accepted, a job writing for *Maclean's* magazine by its esteemed editor, Arthur Irwin, his B.C. friends thought he and his wife, Janet, were leaving paradise for Outer Mongolia. Toronto, he recalled, "was regarded with fear and loathing by every Vancouverite—including me. Those who accepted a job in Toronto were thought of either as traitors, and reviled, or as victims, and pitied."

Whatever misgivings the Bertons had about moving east, they knew that this was a career advancement that Pierre could not ignore. In the late forties, Toronto was not quite the media hub it was destined to become, yet in that time before television, *Maclean's* was, by a long shot, the number one magazine in the country. Guided artfully by the shy but firm Irwin and assistant editor Scott Young, and featuring such writers as Ralph Allen (whom Irwin had lured away from the *Globe and Mail*) and John Clare, and with Blair Fraser covering politics in Ottawa, *Maclean's*, then a monthly, was a must-read for millions of Canadians.

Nevertheless, Berton was already familiar with Lister Sinclair's sarcastic CBC radio skit "We All Hate Toronto," which skewered the city for its alleged pretentiousness, and his first impressions on arriving were not especially positive. The city was too hot and humid during the summer—the formality of the era dictated that businessmen or journalists never left the house for work without wearing a long-sleeved shirt, tie, jacket, and fedora, no matter what the temperature—the streetcars too crowded, the restaurants almost non-existent (although, according to Berton, the seafood at George's on Yonge Street was not bad), liquor was still far too difficult to acquire, and on Sundays Toronto remained a holy ghost town. Yet Berton, whose fame as a journalist, writer, and television personality grew, was bound to Toronto for the rest of his life. He and his family lived north of the city in the village of Kleinburg (part of the city of Vaughan), where he became one of its most celebrated residents.

A year after Berton arrived, Budd Sugarman, who became a loyal Yorkville neighbourhood supporter, opened his decorating business in an old house on Cumberland Street. At the time, he recalled in a 2002 interview, he would ask people, "Where is the cultural centre of Toronto?" He was told, "There isn't any."

A classic example of Toronto's puritanism occurred in 1952 when University of Toronto president Sidney Smith and his officials were deeply disturbed by a prank perpetrated by the staff of the *Varsity*, the student newspaper. They replaced the world "English" with the word "sex" in a story about Smith's annual report, in which he commented on the poor English-language skills of students entering the university. Publication of the term's last issue of the *Varsity* was suspended, and in response the editors and senior staff resigned. The controversy raged for about a week, and the only punishment for members of the staff involved in the hoax was that they were not permitted to edit or write for the final issue, published later in the month.

Women at the university were expected to graduate from arts, nursing, or occupational and physical therapy. They were not banned from such professional faculties as medicine, dentistry, and law, but they were not exactly welcomed either. The real world beyond the confines of academia was colder and less inviting still. Toronto's business and legal establishments, for example, remained solidly male in the forties and for the next two decades.

After graduating with a liberal arts degree in 1941, Mabel Van Camp, who grew up in a small town northeast of Toronto, studied education with the intention of earning enough money to one day become a lawyer. Following a year and a half working as a teacher, she inquired about enrolling in law school at Osgoode Hall. The dean, John D. Falconbridge, suggested as politely as he could, as she later recalled, "that law was no profession for a lady." He urged her not to try. She ignored him, excelled, and was called to the bar in 1947. Then it took her six months to find a job at a Bay Street law firm. Out of desperation, Gerard Beaudoin, who had lost some of his staff, hired her to work on family law cases from his largely Roman Catholic clientele—a sticky problem for him since he was Catholic and forbidden by the church to be involved in divorce. By 1962, following Beaudoin's departure, she and another lawyer took over the firm. In November 1971 she received a telephone call from Prime Minister Pierre Trudeau, who asked if she would accept an appointment to the Supreme Court of Ontario, which she immediately did. She served as Madam Justice until her retirement in 1995.

So the times were changing, but slowly. In 1947, thanks to Premier Drew's idea of progress, Toronto became the first Canadian city to permit cocktail lounges. The government had proposed its plan in the spring of 1946 and, predictably, the various righteous defenders of Toronto the Good denounced the proposal as a sinful capitulation to the evil liquor interests. When evangelist (and later journalist and broadcaster) Charles Templeton asked sixteen thousand exuberant teenagers at his massive Youth for Christ rally, held at Maple Leaf Gardens, if they wanted Drew's cocktail lounges, they replied with a resounding "No!"

The backlash against cocktail lounges hit Drew personally in the 1948 provincial election; he lost his own seat in the Toronto High Park riding by 1,035 votes to the CCF candidate, William "Temperance Bill" Temple, whom Drew had referred to as a "Communist" throughout the campaign. Predictably, he attributed his defeat to a Communist conspiracy to vanquish Ontario. Within a few months, Drew resigned as premier and won the federal PC party leadership. The irony was that the regulations governing cocktail lounges were so rigid that there were only a handful open and serving customers in 1948; according to Pierre Berton, the favourite haunt was the Silver Rail on Yonge Street, which on a Saturday night was "jammed with tipplers guzzling gin fizzes, pink ladies, Manhattans, and brandy Alexanders—anything sweet and potent to unpracticed tastes."

Acceptance was gradual, and the battle continued to rage between those who enjoyed drinking and carousing, and those who regarded it as the work of the Devil. Leslie Frost, who followed Drew as leader of the Ontario PC Party and premier of Ontario (Thomas Kennedy served as the interim premier for a year following Drew's departure), had grown up in a prohibition household and believed it was his life's calling to ensure that Ontarians remained a "moral and sober people." In 1950, he was dismayed after he learned from officials at Carman Memorial United Church that there were in the neighbourhood "three night spots selling liquor until 2 a.m., two hotels dispensing it until midnight, a retail wine store, and a government liquor store."

A few years later, Rev. Frederick Brailey, head of the Committee on Evangelism and Social Service for the Toronto Conference of the United Church, wrote to the premier to complain about "the vicious evil" of the provincial liquor system. "Some proprietors of cocktail bars have encouraged the most vulgar type of entertainment," he pointed out with exasperation. "Some of the jokes, songs and actions have been a thousand times worse than anything I heard in the trenches in World War I."

Worse, the seemingly endless availability of liquor in Toronto—the fault, it was suggested, of the LCBO granting too many licences—was blamed for the increase in the number, or at least the higher visibility, of prostitutes in and around bars near Jarvis and Dundas Streets. Much to Frost's displeasure, the *Telegram* sensationalized the issue in several articles in the fall of 1953. Judge Walter Robb, chairman of the LCBO, reported to Frost one disturbing tale of an encounter between a liquor inspector and a young woman named Kay. She mistook him for a client and suggested that he meet her later at an unnamed hotel. Playing along, the inspector asked what he should do if he could not find her. "Just ask the doorman or any of the waiters where Kay is," she happily instructed him. Robb investigated the hotel in question and threatened to revoke its liquor licence.

Allowing sporting events on Sundays was the next step, and a steadfast campaign was waged successfully by the indomitable Allan Lamport, one of the most influential civic politicians of the post-Second World War period. From his first election to city council in 1937, "Lampy," as he was affectionately known by friends and foes alike, was involved in one way or another with Toronto life for more than thirty years—as an alderman, controller, Liberal MPP, mayor from 1952 to 1954 and chairman of the TTC from 1955 to 1959. In the early seventies, the sports facility on King Street West, built on the site of the Mercer Reformatory for Women, was named the Allan A. Lamport Stadium. A regatta course on Toronto Island was also named in his honour.

Built "like a fire hydrant," as one commentator observed, "solid and close to the ground," he was "the man with the turmoil touch" and was famous (or infamous, depending on your viewpoint) for his contorted malapropisms, or "Lamportisms," for which he was dubbed Metro Toronto's Sam Goldwyn. "I deny the allegations and I defy the alligators," Lamport declared. Or "I wouldn't take that job for a million bucks. I have too many mouths to feed." Better still was his comment about infighting at city hall: "If anyone's gonna stab me in the back, I wanna be there." Making a point about pollution in Lake Ontario, he said, much to the glee of every reporter present, "the only thing you'll catch swimming in Lake Ontario is a dead fish." While he was mayor, he claimed that "being Mayor of Toronto is like being a Prime Minister—without a cabinet or a majority."

He also became embroiled in an expense scandal. After Lamport left office to head the TTC, it was revealed to great fanfare in the Toronto press that he had arranged to privately use suite 1735 at the Royal York Hotel to entertain visiting dignitaries, including C.D. Howe, the powerful federal Liberal cabinet minister. Lamport charged the city for the food and booze he served; over a two-year period that tab came to about $48,000, the equivalent of approximately $400,000 today. At a brief inquiry convened in late 1954, Lamport insisted that all the expenses on entertainment had been approved by the Board of Control and city council—except the members of both bodies claimed they did not know of the suite's existence.

Lamport had a lot of allies on city council, and following a vote at the end of December 1954, the probe into his expenses was halted. Thirty years later, Lamport, then eighty-seven, was still unapologetic. He maintained that lobbying for the city at the Royal York was beneficial for Toronto. "A lot of people suddenly thought that they found a scandal because I had a suite in the Royal York," he said in an August 1987 interview, "but many of them had been in it."

As a civic politician, Lamport fought for subway expansion and subsidized housing, and in the sixties he took on the hippies in Yorkville, who he argued were destroying the neighbourhood. Near the end of his career, he traded barbs with media guru Marshall McLuhan of the University of Toronto at a public works committee meeting over the proposed widening of St. Joseph Street. It was, recalled William Kilbourn, who witnessed this spectacle, "a marvellous non-meeting of minds."

In 1946, as an alderman and then controller, he fully supported George Drew's decision on cocktail lounges, which convinced him, a boxer and football player, to tackle the thorny issue of permitting sports on the Lord's Day. Oddly, it was harder to sell Lamport's "Sensible Sunday" proposition to Torontonians than it was to gain support for making booze more easily available—three plebiscites were required before the proposal was finally (and barely) approved in January 1950. In that last vote, a citizen coalition, supported by a $25,000 fund and backed by the likes of Cardinal McGuigan, did all it could to persuade Toronto residents to reject the change, but to no avail. Of the 170,000 people who voted on January 2, 1950, 88,108 or 51.8 percent, voted in favour of commercialized Sunday sports. Lamport, who scraped by in his own election to the Board of Control, was thrilled. "The people of Toronto," he declared, "have voted themselves out of a strait-jacket and they won't regret it." However, the referendum only allowed football, baseball, hockey, soccer, and other team sports to be played on Sunday. Theatre performances, movie screenings, and horse racing were still not allowed and would not be for another decade.

In spite of the 1950 referendum win, it took nine years, until September 13, 1959, for the Toronto Argonauts to play a home game on a Sunday at Exhibition Stadium (the Ottawa Rough Riders and Hamilton Tiger-Cats had played a Sunday game during the 1958 season, but at a stadium in Philadelphia). There was not a word in the press about it. For that matter, every Grey Cup until 1969—including the renowned Mud Bowl, played in the muck and swamp-like field at Varsity Stadium in November 1950, which the Argos won over the Winnipeg Blue Bombers—was scheduled on a Saturday, probably because the revamped Canadian Football League did not want to offend churchgoers. The only exception was the 1962 Fog Bowl at Exhibition Stadium, which had to be halted on the Saturday because of the thick fog off Lake Ontario. The game was finished the next day.

Much to the chagrin of many traditional city aldermen, in a referendum held in conjunction with the December 1960 civic election, Torontonians voted overwhelmingly—81,821 to 45,399—to permit such entertainment on the Lord's Day. Starting on May 28, 1961, following the passage of provincial legislation, movies were running in Toronto seven days a week. The most popular event that day, though, was an eye-popping performance at the Lux Theatre on College Street by the well-endowed and always crowd-pleasing burlesque dancer Miss Cupcake Cassidy. Miss Cassidy, who earned a salary of $1,250 a week (a fee much higher than an average stripper was paid), dismissed all the fuss. "The people who are opposed to Sunday burlesque are family folk who like to settle down at home on Sunday," she said. "They aren't interested in entertainment but just want to watch television." Two months later, the Lux got into trouble with the police over an "immoral performance" by another dancer, Evelyn West, who had, as *Torontoist* writer Kevin Plummer tells the story, "reclined on a couch, spoken to the audience, and made gestures the morality detectives considered 'obscene.'"

THE DAILY SHENANIGANS at city hall received an extraordinary amount of attention from Toronto's three main dailies, the *Star* and *Telegram*, both late-afternoon papers, and, to a lesser extent, the *Globe and Mail*, which published in the morning. No politician, disaster, crime, or scandal was too trivial for the city's army of roving reporters to cover, especially during the blood feud between the *Star* and *Tely*. (According to local legend, reporters from both newspapers tried to outdo each other in the drinking and debauchery at the Toronto Press Club as well.) That celebrated clash, which produced some wild and sensational journalism, much of which was half true at best, was triggered in November 1948 when George McCullagh shook the Toronto newspaper world yet again by purchasing the *Telegram* from the estate of John Ross Robertson for $3.6 million.

The *Tely* had floundered for many years, and McCullagh relished the challenge of rebuilding its circulation. He and his key staff members—city editor J. Douglas MacFarlane, who innately understood that the Orange Order, a staple of the *Telegram* for decades, was far less important than a local fire or the notorious bank robbers the Boyd Gang; and his advertising director, young John Bassett, the *Telegram*'s future owner and media mogul—transformed the *Telegram* into a much more vibrant newspaper. Within about a year of MacFarlane's arrival from the *Globe and Mail*, the *Telegram*'s daily circulation had risen from just under 200,000 to approximately 275,000 (compared to the *Star*'s 400,000).

But that was only part of McCullagh's motivation. What really drove the forty-three-year-old entrepreneur was the opportunity to take on the *Star*. He considered that paper a Communist organ run by an anti-British owner, Joe Atkinson (who had died in May 1948), and his son-in-law Harry Hindmarsh (who, McCullagh told *Time* magazine in an interview, "is so ugly that if he ever bit himself, he'd get hydrophobia"). When asked about his intentions, McCullagh was as straightforward as usual. "I'm going to knock that fucking rag right off its pedestal," he declared. In fact, it was the *Star* that survived the battle—a bitter fight that McCullagh, a manic depressive, did not live to see. He committed suicide by drowning in his Thornhill swimming pool in August 1952. (In 1966, McCullagh's widow, Phyllis, married his former political ally George Drew after Drew's first wife, Fiorenza, had died a year earlier.)

The *Star–Telegram* feud did provide Torontonians with some entertaining moments. During the 1949 federal election, both newspapers were guilty not only of the industry-standard partisan editorials—the *Telegram* supported George Drew and the Conservatives; the *Star*, Prime Minister Louis St. Laurent and the Liberals—but also of blatantly slanting the news. Headlines were so distorted it was impossible to believe either paper. "Ready to Aid Any Plan to Build Decent Homes St. Laurent Declares," the *Star* noted about the prime minister's speech at Stratford, Ontario, on housing; the *Telegram*'s version of the same event was "St. Laurent Fatigued Cuts Handshakes Hurries from Meet." (In a fascinating *Maclean's* article, "How Toronto's Evening Papers Slanted the Election News," in August 1949, Sidney Katz dissected the coverage and determined that the Liberals received 1,734 inches of news columns in the *Star* and only 290 inches in the *Telegram*, while the Conservatives received 355 inches in the *Star* and 1,402 inches in the *Telegram*.)

The most outrageous journalism of the campaign was the *Star*'s allegation of a "sinister alliance" between Drew, Quebec premier Maurice Duplessis, and the mayor of Montreal, Camillien Houde, who was running federally as an independent. Two days before the vote, the *Star* ran a huge bold-faced banner on the front page:

> KEEP CANADA BRITISH
> DESTROY DREW'S HOUDE
> GOD SAVE THE KING
> (the last line was altered in later editions to: VOTE ST. LAURENT)

The story, which was accompanied by a grotesque photograph of Houde (that mostly displayed his enormous gut), absurdly claimed that if Drew won, Canada would also be run by Houde, who had been interned during the war for his opposition to the National Resources Mobilization Act (which registered men and women for possible military training and duty) that he suspected would lead to conscription.

In turn, the *Telegram* attempted to prove that the *Star* had avoided paying the 8 percent sales tax on newsprint used for its weekly magazine. "Liberals Paying Off *Star*," a *Telegram* headline proclaimed. It is difficult to gauge the extent to which the newspapers influenced the vote. When the election was called, the Conservatives held fourteen of Toronto and York's combined fifteen federal ridings; the Liberals held one. On June 27, the Conservatives lost eight seats as Toronto area citizens opted for eight Liberals, six Conservatives, and one CCF member in York South. Naturally, the *Star* declared that "the Tory grip on Toronto and district was smashed."

The two newspapers tangled again in early September 1954 over sixteen-year-old Marilyn Bell's attempt to swim across frigid Lake Ontario. It was an act of human endurance that held the attention of most Torontonians, at least for a little while. The stunt had been dreamed up by officials at the CNE, who had initially arranged for the champion American swimmer Florence Chadwick, thirty-four, to swim the lake. She was offered $2,500 when she accepted the proposition and promised another $7,500 if she was successful. In the meantime, two other swimmers, twenty-eight-year-old Winnie Roach-Leuszler from St. Thomas, Ontario, who had been the first Canadian to swim the English Channel in 1951, and Toronto's young and adorable Marilyn Bell, "freckle-faced and 119 pounds," challenged Chadwick. The CNE remained adamant that the cash prize was only offered to Chadwick, and the *Telegram* supported that decision. Within a few days, the *Star*, seizing a golden moment, declared that it would pay for Winnie's and Marilyn's expenses and guide boats. Then it became a guessing game. All three women gathered in Youngstown, New York, waiting for the lake to calm so they could attempt the fifty-two-kilometre swim to the shore in front of the

CNE, where each day as many as fifty thousand exuberant spectators gathered in great anticipation of the conclusion of the competition.

Finally, late in the evening of September 8, the three women started swimming in the very choppy water, but only Marilyn, a month shy of her seventeenth birthday, was able to tolerate the rough conditions. Both Chadwick and Roach-Leuszler were forced to quit. All through the dark night and into the next day Marilyn swam, cheered on by her coach, Gus Ryder, who was supervising her from a guide boat. The worst moment, she later wrote in a *Star* front-page exclusive, was at dawn. "At 6 a.m. after my stomach had ached for an hour and I began to have a hard time getting my breath I was in real pain and didn't care whether I went on with the swim or not," she remembered, "but Gus and the others urged me on and for them I kept going." At six minutes past eight o'clock that evening, after twenty-one hours, much of it battling waves as high as five feet, she touched the cement barrier in front of the CNE, to the delight of the estimated 300,000 people who had gathered to greet her. She became the toast of Toronto and was showered with about $60,000 worth of gifts.

Doug MacFarlane, now the *Telegram*'s managing editor, annoyed by the *Star*'s coverage of Marilyn, decided to "blanket the story," as he later put it. He dispatched nearly every reporter he had at his disposal to write about Bell and the contest. This included obtaining Marilyn's signature from an old high school yearbook and printing it in the paper along with a version of the event, leaving the false impression that she had written the story. "I liked my story better in the *Tely* than I did in the *Star*," Marilyn conceded to MacFarlane many years later. MacFarlane also instructed reporter Dorothy Howarth to disguise herself as a nurse in a surreptitious attempt to interview Marilyn as she was resting in an ambulance on shore. But the ploy failed after a *Star* reporter recognized Howarth and exposed her.

A month later the two newspapers were at it again, this time trying to surpass each other's coverage of one of the worst and most unlikely natural disasters to ever hit Toronto: Hurricane Hazel. The odds of a brutal tropical storm reaching the city with wind gusts over 150 kilometres per hour were low. It had never happened before (and would not again). When the harsh rain came thundering down on October 14, the newspapers and the rest of Toronto began to take notice. Yet the next morning the Dominion Public Weather Office issued a mild storm advisory: there was no cause for undue alarm; the remnant of Hurricane Hazel expected to touch down in southern Ontario would be moderate at best.

On October 15, most everyone in Toronto carried on as usual, even with the bad downpour. Just after eleven o'clock that night, however, the situation became much graver. Hazel, which had travelled over a thousand kilometres from the Caribbean up through the east coast of the United States, started sweeping through the city with overpowering winds and torrential rain, later described as a "wall of water." Before the storm ended more than twelve hours later, the Don and Humber had overflowed, countless streets were flooded—Raymore Drive, built imprudently in a low area beside the Humber south of Lawrence Avenue West and east of Scarlett Road, literally vanished—houses and cars were hoisted through the air, and eighty-one people died (thirty-five of them had lived on Raymore Drive). Gerald Elliott, a telephone linesman, was rescued on a washed-out bridge near the Old Mill after clinging to willow branches for four hours. On Island Road in south Etobicoke, eighteen-year-old Marilyn Topp, who was pregnant with her first child, cowered with her husband on top of a stove. Half of their home had been destroyed. The next morning they were rescued, but the house across the road, where her parents and younger sister lived, was no longer there; all three members of her family had died. There were many similar harrowing and tragic stories. The private and public property damage in the Greater Toronto Area exceeded $25 million (at least $210 million in current dollars).

For days after, the *Star* and the *Telegram*, with reporters in helicopters and planes, attempted to outdo each other with tales of rescue and courage, a battle said to be won this time by the *Tely*. The army sent eight hundred men to assist with the cleanup—not the last time the military would be called to Toronto because of bad weather—and a hurricane relief fund was established. Provincial and civic politicians sprang into action, creating regulatory boards and emergency protocols to ensure better preparedness in the event of another similar disaster. No Torontonian who survived Hazel ever forgot the frightening experience. It also reaffirmed that building homes and neighbourhoods beside the city's distinctive ravines did not make a lot of sense.

THERE WERE STILL MORE SURPRISES for Toronto the Good. At some point in the mid-1950s, the city ceased to be a British satellite of the mother country and was dragged into the cosmopolitan age by more than half a million immigrants who had planted themselves in Metropolitan Toronto between 1945 and 1965. Whereas the foreign born accounted for 31 percent of the city and suburbs' population in 1951, ten years later that figure had increased to 42 percent. "Where is the Old Torontonian today?" Pierre Berton sarcastically asked in a 1961 profile of the city. "Occasionally a rare specimen is encountered in the panelled confines of the Toronto Club or perhaps at the Hunt Club." Whether these old-stock Torontonians liked it or not—and many of them certainly did not—the city was more Hungarian, Ukrainian, Polish, Chinese (once the discriminatory Exclusion Act was repealed in 1947), and, above all, Italian by 1960.

The Soviet invasion of Hungary in 1956 brought more than fifteen thousand Hungarians to Toronto, many of whom quickly altered the culinary taste of the Annex with a slew of Hungarian restaurants on Bloor Street between Spadina and Markham—the so-called Goulash Archipelago. (In the seventies, the Blue Cellar Room's wooden platter piled high with schnitzel and other assorted fried meat, all for less than twenty dollars, was a particular favourite.) As a young war refugee from Vienna, journalist and author Peter C. Newman remembers that his parents could not find an authentic Hungarian restaurant in Toronto before 1955. And then there was only Csarda, which first opened on King Street West.

Among the Hungarian Jews settling in Toronto during this period, albeit via a more circuitous route through Vienna, Paris, and Tangier, were members of the Reichmann family. By 1958, Paul and Ralph Reichmann (soon joined by Albert) had established a Toronto branch of their Montreal-based brother Edward's Olympia Trading, a tile-importing company, and the commercial foundation for Olympia & York, the Reichmanns' titanic property development corporation that had a huge impact on Toronto as well as on New York and London, England.

Another severe bout of *miseria*—poverty, poor land, and little opportunity in the post-war economy—particularly in southern Italy and Sicily, pushed more than two million Italians out of the country between 1946 and 1961 and brought approximately 250,000 to Canada. Tens of thousands, entire villages in some cases, migrated to Toronto, where many had relatives and friends. Prime Minister Mackenzie King might not have wanted the country's fundamental character to change as a result of immigration, but that was, in fact, what happened. Canada needed more workers to build streets and dig tunnels and sewers, and Italy supplied the manpower.

Immediately, these newcomers swelled Toronto's Italian population to 140,000, a number that kept growing by the day. The majority settled in the original Little Italy, near College Street West on Grace and Clinton Streets and Manning Avenue, but in time the overflow created a satellite Little Italy on St. Clair Avenue West near Dufferin Street. Owing to this massive infusion of Italians, the number of Catholics in Metro Toronto doubled from 188,000 in 1951 to more than 437,000 by 1961. Another result was an even more vibrant, and insular, Italian community, complete with its own schools, shops, churches, theatre, and Italian-language newspaper, the *Corriere Canadese*, founded in 1954 and sustained by Dan Iannuzzi, a Montreal-born journalist, and Arturo Scotti from Milan.

Like immigrants at the turn of the century, they devoted every waking minute to getting ahead. And that meant, too, following the path of those Italians who came before them: finding arduous and generally poorly paid employment in construction and labour, more often than not in firms operated by fellow *paesani* or countrymen. In 1951, more than 30 percent of all Italian men living in Toronto were involved in one way or another with the construction business. Inevitably, many of them found work with Tridel, the construction company started by Jack DelZotto, a stonemason who emigrated from Friuli, Italy, to Canada as a young man in 1927. After helping build the Park Plaza Hotel in the early thirties, he began erecting houses, though on a small scale. After the war, his three enterprising sons, Angleo, Elvio, and Leo, took over the family business. Soon they expanded into apartment buildings, shopping plazas, and eventually condominiums, a market which they still dominate. Despite some recent financial and tax problems, the brothers and their wives became high-profile members of Toronto's upper-class philanthropic and social scene.

Another *paesano* from Friuli who became as big as, or bigger than, the DelZottos was Marco Muzzo, who came to Toronto in the fifties. A skilled plasterer, he soon established the most successful drywall business in Canada, also employing an army of inexpensive immigrant labour. Then, with his partners Alfredo De Gasperis and Rudy Bratty, he literally developed and constructed the homes, condominiums, roads, and sewers of the northern section of the GTA and throughout southern Ontario's Golden Horseshoe. His commercial interests were diverse, vast, and multi-layered. He had links as an investor and shareholder to numerous companies—Erin Mills Development Corporation, Greenpark Homes, Springtown Homes, Consolidated HCI Holdings, and the Camrost Group, among them. When he died from cancer in December 2005 at the age of seventy-three, *Canadian Business* magazine listed him as the forty-ninth-richest person in the country, worth $871 million.

Muzzo tried to remain out of the public eye, though that was not always possible. He was "the Bull of Toro Road," as Paul Palango of the *Globe and Mail* described him in a 1989 profile. "He has the reputation of being a no-nonsense tough guy with a vocabulary to match, with the intellectual wherewithal, the physical stamina and, if necessary, the sheer brawn to get his way." In the early seventies, during the hearings of a Royal Commission on the Ontario construction industry, Muzzo the drywaller was asked, "So you were not opposed to the general practice of bribery, you were only concerned about whether it worked or not?" He replied, "That is right." Judge Harry Waisberg, who headed the inquiry, was not impressed. "It goes without saying that this attitude is quite cynical and improper and, in some circumstances, illegal," Waisberg wrote. "It should be clearly understood that those who give are at least as blameworthy as those who take." As was his style, Muzzo sloughed it off, and provincial politics welcomed him. He became a philanthropist and a generous supporter of whatever party was in power, becoming close, for example, to both Progressive Conservative premier Bill Davis and Liberal premier David Peterson.

Before DelZotto and Muzzo transformed the city, finding adequate housing during the fifties was as challenging a problem as it had ever been for immigrants. Young

Fortunato "Lucky" Rao, who was later a prominent labour leader, journeyed to Toronto in 1952. He boarded with a Jewish family on Brunswick Avenue before moving in with a cousin in a house on Clinton Street where twenty-eight men shared five rooms.

The plight of the Italian immigrants was captured in a 1961 series of *Toronto Star* columns by Pierre Berton. The articles followed the first-hand experience of Ontario Liberal MPP Andrew Thompson, who lived for a week in a house with three Italian families—"a strange world that most Torontonians are only dimly aware of," as Berton put it. Twelve people shared a tiny space and subsisted on a poor diet in a situation reminiscent of the mid-nineteenth-century profiles of Toronto's Irish poor. In a telling observation, Berton pointed out how one of the men profiled, Dominic Moscone, who had been in Toronto for a decade and worked for a concrete company for seventy-five cents an hour, still existed almost entirely in an Italian environment. "Like many families, the Moscones have no contact with English-speaking Toronto," he wrote. "They have never been to a motion picture here and they have no TV. They read no newspapers, even the Italian language ones (for only the children can read)... Their diet consists largely of macaroni and fried potatoes. The children, who only mix with Italian children at the separate school, drink wine from the age of two." As well-intentioned as Berton and Thompson were, there was a paternalistic tone to the articles. Berton concluded that the children would have no future as "productive Canadians" if their families' incomes and quality of life did not substantially improve.

Yet the truth was that until the late sixties, many Torontonians regarded "Eyetalians," as they caustically referred to them, with suspicion and disdain—which merely reinforced the newcomers' desire to remain separate and apart from the larger community. (A few astute commentators, like Peter C. Newman, himself an immigrant, and Hugh Garner, pointed out the negative consequences of the prejudice and discrimination, but the adoption of more liberal attitudes was gradual.) When immigrants rode the streetcar, they often heard such remarks as "dirty wop" or "go back to Italy" directed at them. Italians were stereotyped as pool hustlers, bootleggers, and all-around troublemakers, although a 1964 *Maclean's* feature did at least acknowledge that only a tiny minority of Italians were involved with the Mafia. (Peter C. Newman tells a story of a press conference around the time of the Cuban Missile Crisis. Soviet leader Nikita Khrushchev was showing reporters a map of the various U.S. cities that Soviet missiles could hit. At the end of the conference, a Canadian journalist asked, "Mr. Chairman, do you have any missiles aimed at Toronto?" Khrushchev became very agitated at the question. "No," he declared, "I have nothing against Italians.")

Another new arrival in the early fifties was Frank Colantonio, who came to Canada at the age of twenty-six from the town of Montorio, in southeast Italy. A year before he was born, his father had gone to New York in search of work but was killed in an accident, leaving his wife back home to raise Frank and his sister. Not wanting to spend the rest of his days as a farmer and goat herder, Frank journeyed to Toronto, where his uncle lived, and was sponsored by a farmer on the outskirts of the city. When that work finished, he found his way to the city and a job digging ditches on a watermain project supervised by an Italian contractor. As he learned to speak English, he obtained more construction work on the new Hospital for Sick Children on University Avenue, where he initially toiled long and hard for forty dollars a week (in 1950, the average Canadian weekly salary for men was $40.90).

He eventually became a carpenter and for a time was an active and vocal member of the Toronto local of the United Brotherhood of Carpenters and Joiners of America. His main task was organizing other Italian workers, who, as he remembers, "were joining the union in droves." Still, the "Canadian" members were wary. According to Colantonio, they considered the Italians "simply as a flood tide of cheap, unskilled workers who were driving down wages." It was the same story in the bricklayers union; Italian organizers recruited Italian workers, despite existing prejudices.

During this period in the mid-fifties, Colantonio returned to Italy, where he met his wife, Nella, and brought her and his mother and sister to Toronto. Frank and Nella scrimped and saved and in 1958 bought a house in a new burgeoning Italian neighbourhood in North York, somewhat far from the St. Clair West Little Italy. The couple later opened a safety shoe and equipment store in a plaza on Dufferin and Finch.

On March 17, 1960, Colantonio was shaken, as were other Italians in the city, by the Hoggs Hollow disaster. Italian workers or "sandhogs" digging a tunnel in a North York watermain project were trapped deep beneath the surface and caught in an accidental fire. Despite rescue attempts, five of the Italian men suffocated or drowned. Two of the deceased were brothers, Alessandro and Guido Mantella, twenty-three and twenty-five years old, who had been sending funds back to their family in Italy. Subsequent investigations revealed that inadequate safety precautions had been taken—the construction company management, in the words of the coroner, had been "callous" with respect to safety—and, in general, the workers were treated as "slave immigrants," as Frank Drea, the *Telegram*'s labour columnist, described them in a series of articles on the accident.

"For years they've been dying in ones and twos in Don Mills and Scarborough," wrote Drea, "falling off rickety scaffolds with no safety hats, no workboots, not even gloves... The only difference about this one at Hoggs Hollow is that five guys died in a hellhole underground." Drea's stories and the outcry over the disaster forced the Frost government to significantly revise Ontario's lax workplace health and safety laws. In March 2010, five decades later, a quilt in memory of the tragedy, created by Nova Scotia-based artist Laurie Swim, was unveiled in York Mills subway station, where it permanently hangs.

Toronto's Italian community (with the full support of such civic politicians as Frederick Gardiner) rallied to raise funds for the families of the five men, most notably at a concert held at Massey Hall. That event had been arranged, naturally enough, by the unofficial mayor of Little Italy, Giovanni Barbalinardo, aka Johnny Lombardi. Born in the Ward in 1915, Lombardi (his father Leonardo changed the family name after he arrived in Canada) and his parents moved to the College Street West neighbourhood, where young Johnny developed his musical expertise as a talented trumpet player. During the Second World War he served with the Canadian army and also entertained his fellow soldiers. Back in Toronto, he used $1,500 he received as a veteran to open a grocery store, Lombardi's Italian Foods at the corner of Dundas Street West and Manning Avenue, where he held court for decades.

In 1966, Lombardi founded Toronto's first ethnic radio station, CHIN, which became a great success and the premier broadcaster of multilingual Canadian-style multiculturalism. He also promoted concerts and sports. When Pierre Berton asked him in 1961 why so many Italians came to Toronto, he pointed to the city's "freshness" and "opportunity," adding that it had a way to go when compared with the old country. "It's a funny thing," he said. "This is nothing like an Italian city. It's not on the sea... There are no fresh fish markets and no open fruit markets. There are few coffee bars of the kind the Italians know. You can't buy liquor at any place and any time. All these things are missing. Yet, somehow, there's something here that Italians can love, even though you can't put your finger on it."

A year earlier, however, a short time after the Hoggs Hollow disaster, Lombardi became embroiled in controversy after he downplayed the grievances of striking and fairly angry Italian construction workers and blamed the labour troubles on "a small group of rabble-rousers," adding that "the poolroom, coffee-counter hangers-on have no right to speak for the Italian community." His caustic comments were denounced by the strikers, who picketed his store, and by labourites like Frank Colantonio. "I know more about the construction industry than a fellow behind a salami counter," said Colantonio. "Our people—and other immigrants—are being cheated every day of the week." Lombardi had no choice but to apologize and in time declared his support for the strikers. His death in March 2002 was given front-page coverage in the Toronto press, and dignitaries, including Prime Minister Jean Chrétien, saluted Lombardi's tremendous contributions to the Italian community and the city.

SOME MONTHS BEFORE Marilyn Bell conquered Lake Ontario and Hurricane Hazel nearly conquered Toronto, the first section of the Yonge Street subway line opened to tremendous hoopla. On March 30, 1954, "Subway Day" (which was also the last day for the Yonge streetcar line that had been in operation since 1891), Premier Leslie Frost,

Mayor Allan Lamport, TTC Chairman William McBrien, and Frederick "Big Daddy" Gardiner, the first chairman of the new Metropolitan Toronto council, accompanied by a small army of local dignitaries and schoolchildren, took the inaugural trip on the country's first subway, an exciting fourteen-minute ride from the station at Eglinton Street to the one at Union Station. The 7.4-kilometre line cost $67 million and required four and a half years of back-breaking labour to complete.

In 1945, C.D. Howe, the federal minister of reconstruction in the Liberal government, had promised to contribute 20 percent of the cost of the subway, but that fell through, leaving the province and the city to fund the project. After a few false starts, city council accepted a proposal from the TTC for a north-south route in late 1945, which was approved in a civic plebiscite in January 1946. A year later the TTC was forced to slightly alter the location of its subway yards south of Davisville Avenue to what became the Davisville Yard, following a loud protest by the Oriole Park Neighbourhood Association. This was one of the first occasions, but definitely not the last, when the local citizenry banded together to fight city hall and controversial urban development.

The first ground was broken on September 8, 1949, on Yonge between Union Station and Queen Street, and the mainly Italian immigrants doing the back-breaking work were serenaded by the pipe band of the 48th Highlanders as the trench was dug. Not surprisingly, the initial estimate of $28 million turned out to be woefully low.

It would take two more decades for the line to be extended north to Finch, until 1963 for the University Avenue section to be added, another three years after that for the first part of the Bloor–Danforth line to open, and until 1968 for the line to reach Islington station in the west and Warden in the east. By then the subway was already inadequate for Toronto's growing population and spreading geography, a problem exacerbated ever since. Still, on its first day of full operation, more than 200,000 Torontonians, approximately one-sixth of the total Metro population, paid the fifteen-cent fare (ten cents if you bought five tokens) and took a ride—most travelling to nowhere in particular. There was a fair amount of griping when token machines and transfer distributors broke down and escalators stopped working. These minor inconveniences were only the beginning of Toronto's topsy-turvy love affair with the TTC subway system.

THE YONGE SUBWAY was just one significant component of a mighty wave of urbanization that swept over Toronto after the Second World War, forever altering its landscape. Acting methodically and always with great debate, politicians, technocrats, social reformers, entrepreneurs, real estate tycoons, and planning visionaries, for better or worse, reinvented Toronto with social housing projects, superhighways, sprawling suburbs, and shopping plazas—all overseen by yet another level of government, the council of the Municipality of Metropolitan Toronto, which was created to bring order to the chaos that had engulfed the city proper and its immediate region.

The council tackled social planning in the downtown area first. Critics of Regent Park, Toronto's (and Canada's) first social housing project, would probably not have been surprised to learn that young gang members from that neighbourhood were linked to the frightening shootings on Boxing Day in 2005, when fifteen-year-old bystander Jane Creba was shot and killed, as well as the Eaton Centre food court shooting on June 2, 2012, in which rival factions of Regent Park's Sic Thugs gang were implicated. Even before the initial phase was completed in 1949, serious questions swirled around the new-style housing project, located in the area now bounded by Parliament and River Streets on the west and east, and Gerrard Street East and Queen Street East on the north and south.

The idea for Regent Park (named, ironically, after elegant Regent Park in London) was given support by the City of Toronto Planning Board's 1943 master plan for city development and improvement, which envisioned large-scale public housing developments in Toronto's core. As Lieutenant Governor Bruce's 1934 report on housing had made clear, Toronto had a downtown slum problem that could be traced back to the 1890s and earlier. Little had changed by the fifties according to an extensive investigation undertaken by journalists Max Rosenfeld and Earle Beattie, which was published in the *Telegram* over a two-week period in October 1955. They detailed the misery and crime of the city's "creeping slum empire" in the Jarvis–Sherbourne–Parliament area, akin to New York City's wretched Five Points neighbourhood in the nineteenth century. Leaving no stone unturned, their series astonished civilized Torontonians with its lurid and sordid tales of destitution, prostitution, bootlegging, corruption, "vice syndicates," and the elusive Johanna Nemeth, the "mystery woman of Panama City," allegedly the queen of slum landlords with properties worth anywhere from $700,000 to $2 million. Staying one step ahead of the authorities, Nemeth and a handful of other landlords (assisted by sleazy collectors and hirelings) regularly defied city bylaws, rarely repaired their houses, charged excessive rents, openly operated a slew of bawdy houses, and amassed sizable profits. If this was not bad enough, tenants stuck in that neighbourhood, as well as other areas in Toronto, were routinely harassed by local gangs of toughs.

One solution to alleviate this "blot on the city" (as Rosenfeld and Beattie described it) had been proposed in 1944 by the grassroots Citizens' Housing and Planning Association. Led by such University of Toronto social activists as Harold Clark, Albert Rose, and Humphrey Carver, the association urged the city to construct housing that was both affordable and slum-free. City council and a majority of Toronto residents eventually agreed, and in 1947 council approved spending an estimated $5.9 million on Regent Park North (with later additions supplemented by federal funds, the total amount increased to more than $15 million). The development, managed by the new Toronto Housing Authority, was not merely slum clearance; it was also, according to John Sewell, an urban activist who was later mayor, "social reform ... based on the idea that the old city had to be replaced, not simply modified." With adequate green space, playgrounds, and traffic-free walkways, Regent Park became the model for other Toronto housing projects like Moss Park (Regent Park South) and Alexandra Park—whether the residents already living in the area agreed with the decision or not. When it came to property rejuvenation in Toronto, the march of progress might be delayed, but never halted.

Regent Park certainly provided its residents with more up-to-date housing. At the end of March 1949, when the first residents moved in, the project received a great deal of generally positive news coverage, despite the fact that the tenants had to pay higher-than-expected average rents of $53 per month. "It's like a palace," said Joan Bluett, who moved into one of the first apartments with her husband, Alfred, and their four children. The family had been living in a four-room cottage without a bathroom and with crumbling walls, but for a rent of only $19 a month. Nonetheless, Mrs. Bluett, like other new tenants, was thrilled with the accommodations. "It takes my breath away," she told a *Star* reporter.

From a sociological perspective, Regent Park placed the emphasis on "nurture" in the nurture-nature debate. Change the social environment in a positive way, Regent Park's advocates argued, and society would be altered for the better. The Citizens' Housing and Planning Association contended that it was "the slum that makes the slum dweller, not the slum dweller the slum, and therefore with the elimination of the slum one tends to get the elimination of lower social standards."

Despite numerous studies and testimonies that showed marked improvements in the quality of life of many Regent Park residents, fixing Toronto society remained easier said than done. The housing project, for instance, did not suddenly purge juvenile delinquency among the lower class—as the Toronto police affirmed in a conversation with Albert Rose and as later academic studies more or less confirmed. Rose, who saw the glass half full, maintained, however, that Regent Park's lessons in the late fifties were "that most people can and do change" and "that rehousing brings important benefits to people." Notwithstanding the idealism and noble objectives behind Regent Park, couched as they were in civic paternalism, there is also no denying that the socio-economic problems that its planners believed they could eliminate (or, at least, significantly reduce), are problems that still plague the neighbourhood and others like it today: poverty, isolation, juvenile delinquency, and crime.

In 2014, Toronto Community Housing is spearheading a long-term revitalization of Regent Park with the goal of transforming it from a low-rent, impoverished neighbourhood to a more "mixed-income, mixed-use community." Farhia Osman, an immigrant from Somalia, who lives in Regent Park with her husband and children, has yet to be convinced that the situation will change as dramatically as revitalization proponents suggest it will. At the end of May 2012, she and her family were nearly killed when they found themselves in the middle of a gun battle and stray bullets were shot through her back door. "We don't feel safe," she said in an interview with the *Toronto Star*, echoing a sentiment no doubt shared by some, though not all, of the more than twelve thousand people who live in Regent Park.

AS THE POPULATION of Metro Toronto increased by half during the fifties—from 1.1 million in 1951 to 1.6 million by 1961—the demand for housing for all levels of income and classes increased as well. The sprawl that soon defined the GTA was also fuelled by the fact that, by the early fifties, owing an automobile had become as common as owning a toaster. (Between 1954 and 1961, the number of registered cars in Metro Toronto jumped by 58 percent.) Commuting to and from work became both desirable and routine, and with it came demands for "superhighways" to facilitate this travel. Build them efficiently enough, the planners of the time argued, and you could avoid the traffic congestion already starting to plague big American cities like Los Angeles. Torontonians would soon know better, yet in the baby-boom era, when life was good and housing in the suburbs affordable, few people foresaw the problems.

The man who started this domino effect was homegrown tycoon Edward Plunkett Taylor, most commonly referred to in the press by his initials E.P., which sarcastically were said to stand for "Excess Profits." He was "big Eddie," the "beer baron," or, a bit nastier, the "Mad Miser of Millions." Born in Ottawa in 1901, Taylor was educated at Ashbury College, an independent school located in the wealthy Ottawa neighbourhood of Rockcliffe, and then attended Montreal's McGill University, graduating as an engineer. He heeded his father's advice, however, and embarked on a career in the securities business, merely a stepping stone for his rise as one of Canada's great entrepreneurs.

In creating his Toronto-based commercial empire, Taylor collected businesses, and lots of them. His sizable stable of companies, which he and his investors—Col. Eric Phillips, Wallace McCutcheon, E.W. Bickle, and later his partner, financier J.A. "Bud" McDougald, among them—merged in 1945 into a holding company, the Argus Corporation, included such breweries as O'Keefe and Carling, Dominion grocery stores, and agricultural stalwart Massey-Ferguson. Taylor's "methods were rough capitalism at its most predatory," says business historian Michael Bliss, and that may be so, but it was difficult to argue with the results. By 1958, when the Argus Corporation moved into its aristocratic headquarters at 10 Toronto Street, arguably the most serene avenue in the city's downtown business core, Taylor's Midas touch had transformed him into a multi-millionaire with a net worth of at least $35 million, equivalent today to roughly $280 million.

Taylor was an avid and successful horse breeder (he owned Northern Dancer, who won the Kentucky Derby in 1964) at his Windfields Farm estate in North York, on land adjacent to what became the city's (and Canada's) toniest address, the Bridle Path. In the late forties, Taylor's business associate George Montegu Black Jr. laid the foundations for the neighbourhood when he constructed a magnificent mansion on Park Lane Circle (since expanded by his more famous son, former newspaper baron Conrad Black, whose rise as a financial magnate began after he gained control of the Argus Corporation from Bud McDougald's widow in 1978). Thereafter, the elder Black directed who could own a home on and around the Bridle Path and what type of dwelling it had to be, ensuring the area's elitist status.

Like any astute, fabulously wealthy empire builder, Taylor had a good eye for real estate. In 1952 he bought 2,063 acres in what became Don Mills (the first idea was to call it Yorktown or EPtown), the model for suburban development in Canada. Influenced by American planners, Taylor and his architects created a self-contained residential suburban neighbourhood complete with serviced lots (a Taylor innovation) large enough for a single-family dwelling that fit middle-class tastes, and apartment complexes for lower-income factory workers who toiled nearby, as well as pedestrian walkways, schools, churches, community centres, green space, parks, and the latest fad, shopping plazas. Taylor assured its success by imposing on contractors and owners strict building requirements and deadlines. In short, as the professional journal *Architectural Forum* put it in 1954, "the new town of Don Mills is a planner's dream coming true." Taylor's one stipulation was that no blue shingles be used because, he said, "blue fades" and is "a bad colour in the sun." As Don Mills took off in the mid-fifties, Taylor expanded his property holdings, this time with six thousand acres of land farther west of the city, which ultimately was transformed into the suburb of Erin Mills.

The most telling statistic about Don Mills, however, and the one with the biggest impact on Toronto's future development, was that a mere 5 percent of the people who lived in the suburb worked close by. Without access to the subway, the majority were partaking in what became the aggravating suburban commute. And in the fifties, Toronto's roadways were not adequate for this increased traffic.

The first solution that was supposed to improve the flow of Toronto commuters was the construction of a superhighway—another Canadian first—along the lakeshore. This was the aptly named "Frederick G. Gardiner Expressway," or "the Gardiner" to a generation of Toronto drivers, which was completed between 1958 and 1964. Currently it is an out-of-date, crumbling, and frequently traffic-jammed freeway. Yet in its day it was the pride and joy of Metropolitan Toronto and its first chairman and chief advocate Frederick "Big Daddy" Gardiner. Indeed, the story of Metro from its inception in 1953 until his retirement in 1961 is really the story of Frederick Gardiner (he acquired the "Big Daddy" nickname, borrowed from Tennessee Williams's play *Cat on a Hot Tin*

Roof, from Toronto alderman Philip Givens, and it was then picked up by the *Star* and other newspapers). Gardiner, as his biographer Timothy Colton observes, "was big in size, big in ambition, big in appetites, and big in rhetoric... [He was] part tyrant, part showman... part philistine [and] the biggest story in town."

The City of Toronto would have much preferred a complete amalgamation with the twelve other suburbs in the metropolitan area (that would have to wait until 1998), but the politicians in those other suburbs absolutely refused to merge with the city (the exception was the town of Mimico). Fearful of higher taxes, excessive expenditures on roads and services, and all sorts of other bogeymen, they guarded their respective neighbourhoods like medieval warlords. So Premier Frost, following the recommendations of Lorne Cumming, chair of the Ontario Municipal Board, compromised by creating the Municipality of Metropolitan Toronto with its council on which the mayor of Toronto and his suburban counterparts served, along with a select group of aldermen and other officials. The new council was to have power over roads, sewage and water, public transportation, and Metro parks. An independent Metro school board was also established. Separate fire services remained for each suburb, though the police were wisely amalgamated in 1956. Toronto city council, not surprisingly, hated the federation scheme, comparing it to "something worthy of Marx or Stalin," but there was not much they could do about it.

In Frost's view, Gardiner was the perfect choice for the role of Metro's first appointed chairman. He had Irish Orange roots and was a veteran of the First World War. A Bay Street lawyer, who had been initiated into local politics as deputy reeve in Forest Hill, he was also a loyal backroom financial supporter of the Conservatives. For the next eight years, Gardiner lived and breathed Metro; he was Toronto's first true CEO. "I knew I was going to have to be a bit of a ham and a hell of a good actor," he recalled in a late 1970s interview. "But what came first was having a product worth buying and a well-run organization to back it up."

Gardiner was regularly criticized by other politicians and the press for behaving like a "Caesar" and a benevolent dictator. On one occasion he was holidaying in the Caribbean and ordered that a decision about the TTC be deferred until his return. He regularly bullied other Metro councillors and was given to short and snappy one-liners—"you can try if you want to bat the breeze with a broom," he once declared—that made him the darling of political cartoonists. (In one of Duncan Macpherson's many brilliant cartoons of Gardiner that appeared in the *Star*, he was aptly portrayed as the "Maharajah of Metrostan.") "When he really wanted something, he just came and beat it out of you," remarked Nathan Phillips, who as mayor of Toronto tangled with Gardiner many times.

Politicians who tried to stand up to him almost always failed miserably. Gardiner's objectionable behaviour, according to Robert Fulford, who covered Metro for the *Globe and Mail* in the early fifties, was undoubtedly the result of his penchant for drinking during council meetings, a fact that went largely unreported in Toronto's newspapers. One of the few times Gardiner retreated was in 1958, when the development of the Gardiner Expressway would have meant the relocation of Historic Fort York to a spot half a kilometre away. "If the Americans landed here today," Gardiner commented about the fort's site amidst railway yards and a bridge, "they would never find it." Nevertheless, the outcry from Toronto history enthusiasts was so loud that Gardiner came up with another plan for the expressway route.

No one could have accused Gardiner of being a procrastinator. He made things happen and certainly lived up to his operating creed: "Let's get the 'goddamn' shovels into the ground." And that he did. Several of the more significant projects initiated under Gardiner's reign included water system improvements, major subway expansion, suburban development in North York and Scarborough, new schools, and the construction of both the Gardiner Expressway and the Don Valley Parkway, which was linked to the provincially built Highway 401. He also supported Nathan Phillips's conception for a new Toronto city hall—which he caustically referred to as "a stairway to the stars"—and recommended the square in front of the new building be named in Phillips's honour. Gardiner's one planning dream not fulfilled was the Spadina Expressway, which became a great controversy in the sixties and was ultimately killed in 1971 by the provincial government of Bill Davis (see Chapter Nine).

BACK IN 1929, Gardiner and his wife, Audrey, had built a three-storey house on Spadina Road in the Village of Forest Hill. It was here that he was first introduced to feisty local politics. Forest Hill then was a quiet, independent (as of 1923), and fashionable neighbourhood that grew to be defined as the area between St. Clair Avenue in the south and Lawrence Avenue to the north, Avenue Road on the east and Bathurst Street on the west. The smaller village remained a separate entity until it was annexed by the City of Toronto in 1967. Everything about Forest Hill—which had an estimated sixteen thousand residents by 1950—smacked of elitism, a characteristic that its affluent leaders took much pride in. They considered it an "honour" to be "the foremost residential community in Canada." Many of their children attended either Upper Canada College (UCC) for boys or Bishop Strachan School for girls. Both schools were conveniently located within Forest Hill's boundaries, where, as Conrad Black, who attended UCC in the fifties, put it, students learned in a "Waspy" and "snotty" environment that at UCC, at any rate, encouraged sadistic corporal punishment. (Black was unceremoniously expelled from UCC in 1959 for stealing and selling exam papers.) Forest Hill boasted a high-powered council, whose members, including Gardiner, firmly protected the village's perceived collective interests.

Forest Hill culture and politics were meticulously probed and dissected in the absorbing 1956 sociological study, *Crestwood Heights*, about life in a typical North American middle- to upper-class suburban neighbourhood. There was little attempt to hide Crestwood's true identity. The chief author of the five-year research project was John "Jack" R. Seeley, a University of Chicago graduate. He had been born in England in 1913 and had moved to Canada as a sixteen-year-old, possibly to distance himself from his abusive mother. He worked as a farm labourer and printer and managed to save enough money to attend university. In 1948, Seeley was head of the Forest Hill Village Project, a federal-funded research initiative to study the "mental health of the community and the impact of this on its children." He later taught at the University of Toronto and York University. For its day, the five-hundred-page book was cutting edge and received a lot of publicity and commentary, some of which was not complimentary to Forest Hill. "Children Spoiled by Rich Forest Hill Parents—Research" was one *Toronto Star* headline about the book.

Around this time, Forest Hill went through a fascinating transition. Upwardly mobile Jews began leaving the Spadina–Kensington Market neighbourhood as early as 1930, but it was only a trickle. After the Second World War, that trickle became a mass migration. One reason the Jews opted for Forest Hill was that they had been "discouraged" by land covenants from purchasing homes in affluent Lawrence Park, a post-Second World War suburban development east of Yonge, north of Eglinton, and west of Bayview.

The Jewish population of Forest Hill and the adjacent York Township, centred on and around Bathurst Street, soon exceeded 18,000 and by 1961, 42,000. In 1951, 40 percent of the population in the village was Jewish, the "highest proportion in any Canadian municipality." It took somewhat longer for synagogues and Jewish community institutions to follow. In 1954, for example, of the forty-eight synagogues in Toronto, only five were located north of St. Clair Avenue. In contrast, of the ninety or so synagogues in the GTA today, fewer than ten remain south of Dupont Avenue. In any event, contractors could not build houses fast enough, and Bathurst, which up to then had been akin to a rural road in North York, was transformed into a major artery with the attendant problems (it wasn't until a tragic accident took the life of two young girls that proper sidewalks were built).

Erna Paris's *nouveau riche* parents (as she describes them) migrated to Forest Hill from their home in the Annex, as so many other Jewish families did, when Erna was a young girl, long before she became a successful journalist and writer. Forest Hill, she recalled, was a world unto itself. "Our lives in the Forties and Fifties were insular and 'unreal'—unconnected to the WASP reality of Toronto, unconnected to the rural reality of Canada," she wrote in a 1972 memoir. "We knew almost nothing beyond the Village, the downtown department stores where we'd sometimes wander on Saturday afternoon and charge clothes to our fathers' accounts, and the bits of northern Ontario where we summered and wondered at the people who stayed there after Labor Day." The "spoiled Forest Hill snobs," as they were derisively known far and wide, found a real sense of security in the Bathurst and Eglinton ghetto, which merely reinforced Jewish exclusivity and led to even more Jews finding their way there. To Toronto Jews, Bathurst Street had become "sacred space," or in the words of one Jewish resident in 1995, "what the Nile is to Egypt: a narrow strip of life with desert on both sides."

Who could fault that self-segregation? In the forties and fifties, despite the revelations of the Holocaust, anti-Semitic discrimination and racism were alive and well in Toronto. (The city was then, as Peter C. Newman, who had graduated from Upper Canada College in 1947, remembered it, "bicultural: English and Irish, except for the bankers, who were Scottish.") In 1946, a Gallup poll showed that for a majority of Canadians, the two least-desirable immigrant groups were the Japanese, followed by the Jews. Though Canadian regulations made it difficult to immigrate to the country, with some ingenuity and help from local communities, Jewish Holocaust survivors started rebuilding their broken lives in Toronto (and other Canadian cities).

Toronto was a lot better than where they came from but was certainly no multicultural, tolerant haven. The Toronto General Hospital did not hire Jewish staff and allowed only one Jewish intern a year. And though the University of Toronto faculty of medicine did not have a quota system against Jews and other minorities, its admission committee was concerned about the number of Jewish applicants. Likewise, businesses and resorts either banned Jews outright or creatively invented ways to deny them job opportunities, as Pierre Berton discovered while he was researching his bold and eye-opening article "No Jews Need Apply," published in *Maclean's* on November 1, 1948. Much to his dismay, he learned that the magazine's parent company, Maclean Hunter, did not hire Jews either. "It's company policy," he was matter-of-factly informed.

Black musicians broke through a colour barrier of sorts in 1951 when they were hired to play at the Town Tavern, a white club on Queen Street east of Yonge. Jazz drummer Archie Alleyne, now in his early eighties, was a member of that group and recalled in a recent interview that during a break a white woman asked him to "quit playing that nigger music." A feature story in the *Star* in February 1959 about Metro's nine thousand "Negroes" concluded that though the "blatant prejudice of prewar days has disappeared, a more subtle and sometimes just as acute prejudice has taken its place." Despite provincial legislation forbidding it, as late as 1959, black Torontonians were frequently denied the right to purchase real estate because of fears "that the Negro's presence would adversely affect property values."

Between 1944 and 1951, Ontario governments chipped away at this discrimination, banning discriminatory signs and advertising, forbidding race or religion from affecting the sale of property, and eliminating discrimination in the workplace through the Fair

Employment Practices Act of 1951. Changing the law was one thing, changing attitudes quite another. When the bill abolishing discrimination in the sale of property was being debated in 1950, Judge J.A. McGibbon privately complained to his friend and fishing buddy Premier Leslie Frost, whose government had introduced the legislation, that "surely we have not arrived at the stage of life where the Government is going to take it upon itself to dictate to whom I must sell property, and whom I must have as my next door neighbour. I do not want a coon or any Jew squatting beside me, and I know way down in your heart you do not." Frost disagreed and politely told the judge that his intolerance was outdated.

The reaction to this Jewish presence was more muted in Forest Hill, but that subtlety could not entirely mask the aversion many old-stock Torontonians felt about this perceived invasion. Despite efforts by non-orthodox Jews to shed their *shtetl* or old-country Yiddish mentality and embrace "Canadian" values, they still remained outsiders in the eyes of the wealthy Protestant populace. Frederick Gardiner, for instance, regarded himself as a tolerant person, yet as a Forest Hill politician he voted against synagogue construction in the village (it would have created too much traffic, the argument went) as well as alteration to a bylaw that would have allowed a Jewish private school to teach Jewish religion. As John Seeley and his team documented in *Crestwood Heights*, Christian parents did not want their children associating with Jewish children—inherent Jewish insecurity, one Christian woman said, made Jews too "materialistic" and showy—and if they could afford to do so sent them to private schools where it was far less likely they would encounter Jews. A by-product of this was that Forest Hill Collegiate became overwhelmingly Jewish, much as many schools in Thornhill are today.

THE FROST GOVERNMENT'S human rights legislation was only the beginning. Despite negative feelings towards Jews, Italians, Chinese, and other ethnic groups living in the city and the metro area, the march of liberalism could not be halted. If there was a moment during the 1950s that truly marked a turning point in Toronto's history, when the city began to shed its British Tory skin for good, it was the municipal election of December 1954.

The contest pitted incumbent Leslie Saunders, the proud and defiant Orangeman, against Arthur Brown, the former head of the Toronto School Board; Alexander MacLeod, a Communist; and long-time civic politician Nathan Phillips, who was Jewish. Phillips, who had first served as a Toronto alderman in 1926 at the age of thirty-four, had run in the mayoralty election of December 1951 and come in a distant third behind Allan Lamport, the winner, and Hiram McCallum, who had been mayor for the previous three years. He tried again the following year, but once more was badly defeated by Lamport. Phillips felt that his losses in 1951 and 1952 were directly connected to the fact that Toronto was not prepared to elect a Jewish mayor—an undoubtedly correct assessment.

So what had changed only two years later? Saunders rightly grasped that Phillips was his most serious challenger and he decided, foolishly as it turned out, to publicly raise Phillips's background. In the previous mayoralty elections Phillips had entered, the fact that he was Jewish had been a subtle factor, hinted at but not shoved in the voters' faces so they were forced to grapple with their own prejudices. Saunders decided to be more straightforward, a strategy that rubbed a lot of Torontonians the wrong way. During the campaign, he declared himself to be "Leslie Saunders, Protestant," in a listing of civic candidates included in the journal *Protestant Action*, which Saunders published. Phillips cleverly ignored the taunt and later sold himself as "mayor of all the people."

Equally as important for Phillips was the endorsement of the *Star* (which had also backed him in 1951 and 1952) as well as the *Telegram*, now under the control of John Bassett, who hosted a fundraiser for him at the Royal York (according to Bassett's biographer Maggie Siggins, Bassett established an annual $10,000 honorarium for Phillips that he was paid for the remainder of his life). The *Globe and Mail* supported Arthur Brown, who tainted Saunders's campaign with unproven accusations that while he was a member of the Board of Control (from 1949 to 1954), Saunders had been involved with Mayor Allan Lamport in the alleged misuse of public funds to maintain suite 1735 at the Royal York for secret meetings and cocktail parties. The press picked up the story, and despite Saunders's denial, the insinuation of wrongdoing hung over him.

The night before the election, Phillips's wife Esther, or Ett, was rushed to the hospital after an accidental fall down the stairs. She had a bad concussion and brain surgery was required, though she fully recovered. Election day was exceptionally difficult for Phillips as he waited for news from the hospital. By ten o'clock that evening, the last ballots had been counted and the remarkable result was official: Toronto had elected its first Jewish and non-Christian mayor. His victory was not a sweep—he defeated Saunders by only 3,927 votes and Brown by 4,070—but that hardly mattered. Bitter about the loss, Saunders later blamed Brown for splitting the "Christian and Gentile vote." This was an absurd charge, since the majority of the 40,683 people who voted for Phillips were also Christian, and if Brown had not entered the race, there is no telling how the votes he received would have been divided between Saunders and Phillips. The truth was that Saunders missed the real point of the night.

"Every person should be proud of his ancestry," Phillips declared in his acceptance speech, "and I am proud of the blood that flows in my veins." The lead *Toronto Star* editorial also addressed the issue, underlining its significance. "[Phillips's] victory was the culmination of a fine campaign on his part and tribute to the liberal-minded people of Toronto who refused to be misled by appeals to religious prejudice," the newspaper wrote. "Mr. Phillips is proud to be a Jew, and proud also to proclaim his intention to administer Toronto's affairs without regard to religious or racial differences." (Two decades later, following Phillips's death in January 1976, the *Star* extolled "his thatch of white hair, his close-cropped moustache [and] his fine Jewish features.")

In its assessment of the election, the *Ottawa Journal* proclaimed that the city was now "Toronto the Tolerant." And a year later, after Phillips won another one-year term, the *Star* rejoiced that the "liberal-minded people of Toronto . . . demonstrated once again that race or creed is not a barrier to public office—that a Jew as well as a Gentile can be elected mayor of the city." These various backslapping judgments were exaggerations to be sure. Yet like the elections of the first non–Anglo-Saxon mayors in Edmonton and Winnipeg during this period—William Hawrelak in 1951 in Edmonton and Stephen Juba in 1956 in Winnipeg, both of Ukrainian heritage—Phillips's win was evidence that Canadian attitudes were changing and that a slight power shift was taking place in all three cities as the so-called ethnic middle class asserted itself politically.

Though Nathan Phillips was not the best of administrators—he was "a duffer, incapable of running anything," recalled Robert Fulford—he had lots of help from the civic bureaucracy. As a result, he was rewarded with four more election victories, most fairly sizable ones, over the next eight years (starting in 1956, mayors were elected to two-year terms) and was the second-longest-serving mayor in Toronto history after Art Eggleton, who was mayor from 1980 to 1991. A witty raconteur with a conservative sensibility, Phillips definitely enjoyed the perks of the job; his memoir is filled with photographs of him with a bevy of dignitaries and celebrities, everyone from Queen Elizabeth II and General Charles de Gaulle to Hollywood starlets like Jayne Mansfield, Gina Lollobrigida, and Kim Novak. He loved the attention he received and was later remembered as a "mayoral Marco Polo," spreading "the gospel of Toronto" around the world. The most often heard criticism of him was that he ignored his administrative duties in favour of the banquet circuit. Yet, beyond the camera and hoopla, he ably defended the city's interests on Metro council, despite occasionally tangling with Metro chairman Frederick Gardiner. (His suggestion that the regular Tuesday 2:00 PM Metro meetings be pushed back half an hour, to 2:30, so that his lunchtime engagements could be completed did not win much favour from Gardiner or the press.) Still, Gardiner and Phillips generally agreed on the need for the Bloor Street subway and the controversial revitalization of downtown Toronto.

Phillips wanted to modernize the city. So it was out with the old—the University Armoury, the Chorley Park estate in Rosedale, and the magnificent and pricey General Post Office on Adelaide Street, among others—and in with the new—the O'Keefe

Centre on Front Street, then a state-of-the-art concert hall, funded generously (more than $750,000) by E.P. Taylor, which opened in October 1960 with *Camelot*, starring Richard Burton, Julie Andrews, and Robert Goulet; and Mayor Phillips's pride and joy and legacy, the new Toronto City Hall on Queen and Bay Streets.

(When Richard Burton came to Toronto in 1960, he was not yet involved in the tumultuous, adulterous affair with Elizabeth Taylor that began on the set of the film *Cleopatra*. Early in 1964, however, he returned to Toronto to star in *Hamlet* at the O'Keefe Centre and was accompanied by Taylor. Staying at the King Edward Hotel, the famous couple were the object of protestors, who picketed the hotel with signs condemning their behaviour. Taylor, who had brought her two poodles with her, was forced to walk the dogs on the roof because it was too dangerous for her to take them out on the streets. Her appearance at the premiere was more exciting than the play, which the *Star*'s acerbic critic, Nathan Cohen, called "an unmitigated disaster." The *Telegram*'s review was kinder.)

By the time Phillips sat in the mayor's chair, plans for a new city hall had been drafted after years of debate. In December 1955, the first time city voters were asked to approve an expenditure of $18 million on the new building, they rejected the plan, but only by four thousand votes. A year later the expenditure was put forward on the ballot again, and this time it was approved. (The 1956 election was also significant for the victory of Alderman Jean Newman as head of the Board of Control, the first woman to serve in that capacity. In the 1960 civic election she ran for mayor, the first woman to attempt that, but came in third behind Phillips and Allan Lamport.)

The redevelopment necessitated by the new city hall also meant the end of the Ward and, with it, most of the city's small Chinatown, regarded by civic leaders as an "eyesore," even if they did frequently enjoy eating at Chinese restaurants. Properties were duly expropriated, often at bargain prices, and by 1958, five hundred people had been dislocated. The businesses that survived to the north around Elizabeth Street and Dundas Street West maintained the Chinese presence, and eventually an expanded Chinatown took shape. Keeping the community—which grew from only 2,700 in 1951 to 6,700 by 1961—going were what Chinatown historian Arlene Chan calls the "big four" restaurants: the Nanking Tavern and Restaurant that opened in 1947; Lichee Garden, a higher-profile three-hundred-seat establishment operated for many years by Harry Lem; Sai Woo, which started serving food in 1957 on Dundas Street West near Bay Street and was immediately popular with non-Chinese Torontonians; and Kwong Chow, which opened on Elizabeth Street in 1959. A 1965 attempt by city hall to expand civic property on Elizabeth Street, thereby eliminating the older part of Chinatown, was successfully halted by the Save Chinatown Committee, led by Jean Lumb, Harry

Loo, Doug Chin, and Harry Lem, after a concerted four-year battle with city hall. In view of the prejudice and discrimination that was present in the city, such a community victory would have been impossible even a decade earlier.

Had Nathan Phillips had his way initially, he would have financed new city hall with the sale of old city hall to Eaton's, which probably would have meant the building's demolition, but the head of the company, John David Eaton, turned him down. Instead, Phillips convinced Gardiner and Metro council to purchase old city hall for $4.5 million; it continued to function as one of Toronto's main courthouses (and does so to the present). As a consequence, the neo-Romanesque old city hall, now 115 years old is still standing. Eaton's did try to buy the building later, in October 1965, for $8 million as part of the proposed Eaton Centre complex, and promised to preserve the clock tower and cenotaph (war memorial erected in 1925). Despite strong objections from a grassroots heritage group, city council and Metro eventually agreed to the sale, but Eaton's, sensing a backlash and unhappy with its projected return on the investment, opted not to buy it after all. According to Rod McQueen in his history of Eaton's, John David was so annoyed about what had transpired that when he decided to cancel the project he said to his associates, "Let's walk across the street and tell [Mayor William] Dennison he can shove the Old City Hall up his ass."

Plans for the new city hall had been drafted before Phillips became mayor, but the design, which incorporated the 1917 Beaux Arts registry office, did not meet Phillips's sense of grandeur; he thought the proposal looked like the "Grand Hotel with the longest balcony in the world," and he said that Toronto must have "the finest City Hall and Civic Square in the world." He urged city council to scrap the original design for the new city hall and hold an international competition, though the first vote on the issue went against him. However, the more detailed plans presented to council were disappointing. Architectural students at the University of Toronto wrote that the proposed building looked like "a funeral home of vast dimensions" and was "a monstrous monument to backwardness." Similarly, noted architect Frank Lloyd Wright criticized it as "sterilization" and "a cliché already dated," while Walter Gropius, the originator of the Bauhaus school, dismissed it as "a very poor pseudo-modern design unworthy of the city of Toronto."

Whether the criticisms were warranted (and Toronto architectural historian Mark Osbaldeston argues they were not), the harsh comments compelled the city to hold the international competition Phillips had wanted. In 1958, an esteemed panel headed by Professor Eric Arthur of the Faculty of Architecture at the University of Toronto selected the design by Finnish architect Viljo Revell from the 520 submitted. Revell's design had not made the shortlist of eight, but Michigan architect Eero Saarinen convinced his fellow panellists to reconsider it. Sadly, Revell died of a heart attack at the age of fifty-four, ten months before the new city hall was opened. The iconic landmark was distinguished by the twin curving towers of different heights and the circular council chamber. For the most part, the design received universal praise. (The exception again was Frank Lloyd Wright, then ninety-one years old and cranky. "Every graveyard in Canada, if it could speak, would say 'amen' to the slab [of Toronto's City Hall]," he remarked. "Well, that's what this building says for Toronto. You've got a headmarker for a grave and future generations will look at it and say: 'This marks the spot where Toronto fell.'")

Construction did not start until November 1961, and it took four years to complete the project. The final cost for the building and square was $31 million, nearly double the original estimate. The large square, in particular, was underappreciated at the time but soon became, as Robert Fulford has noted, "a civic space, open to an infinity of uses... This was a break with the past, something new for Toronto, a stage where the people could act out their beliefs and understand themselves as citizens rather than consumers and workers." By the time of the grand opening celebrations in mid-September 1965, Nathan Phillips was no longer mayor—he had lost the 1962 election after the *Star* (in 1958) and the *Telegram* deserted him—yet it was his day, nevertheless. And the day after he died, at eighty-three years old on January 7, 1976, six hundred Toronto citizens patiently lined up to sign the memorial book on a desk at the entrance to city hall.

There was one more footnote to the saga of Toronto's new city hall. To complement his design, Viljo Revell advocated that the city obtain an abstract bronze sculpture from artist Henry Moore. Philip Givens, who was mayor when the new building was opened, liked the idea, believing that such a work of art would be a sign of Toronto's growing sophistication. He negotiated with Moore to produce the unique sculpture *Three-Way Piece No. 2*, which, because of its arc shape, resembling a hunter's bow, became popularly known as "The Archer." The price for the sculpture was $100,000, reasonable for a work by Moore (who reduced his initial fee of $120,000), yet the high cost immediately embroiled Givens in controversy. Several city councillors as well as many taxpayers objected to spending so much money on art. Determined, Givens raised Moore's fee through public donations. That was still not enough for some councillors, who did not want the modern art statue anywhere near city hall. In the end, a majority on council voted to accept what was a gift to the city.

The Archer was officially installed close to the main flagpole in front of city hall and unveiled at a ceremony in late October 1966. "Posterity will remember tonight," declared a defiant Givens. "The Philistines have retreated in disorder."

For a while it seemed no one in Toronto talked about anything except the sculpture. All of the fuss was not a boon for Givens, however. Many voters believed, as Givens later conceded, that he should have been more concerned with streets and sewers than modern art. The Archer might have "boldly thrust modern sculpture into the consciousness of Torontonians, and legitimized installing more and more abstract sculpture in the city," as historical geographer John Warkentin has written, but the controversy also contributed to Givens's defeat in the mayoralty election on December 5, 1966.

Chapter Nine

THE FASTEST-GROWING CITY IN NORTH AMERICA

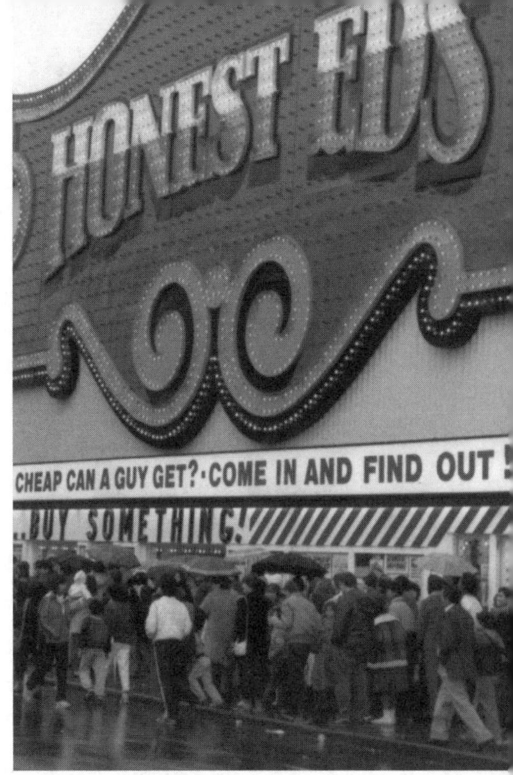

It was only below the Hill that you came into direct contact with the core of vitality that was the true essence of the city. Here you were acutely and excitingly aware of the steady heart-beat of a really great metropolis, fresh blood continuously pumped into it from the four corners of the globe.

—PHYLLIS BRETT YOUNG, *THE TORONTONIANS*, 1960

"Honest Ed" Mirvish was one of Toronto's most colourful impresarios. In 1948, he opened his block-size bargain emporium near the corner of Bloor and Bathurst Streets, where it was possible to buy everything from bottle openers and long underwear to digital cameras in later years. *Courtesy of David Mirvish*

IF YOU WERE a "somebody," the place to be on Monday evening, September 9, 1963, was the gala opening of the renovated and restored Edwardian-era Royal Alexandra Theatre on King Street West. The 700 invited guests, who had dined earlier at Winston's Grill, walked down the red carpet and gushed in awe at the Louis XVI furniture in the lobby and the wall of portraits of actors and actresses who had performed at the Royal Alex over the decades since it had first opened in 1907. At their beck and call were ushers dressed in black breeches with white stockings and black-buckled shoes.

Among the select throng were Earl Rowe, Ontario's lieutenant governor; Mayor Donald Summerville, who had unseated Nathan Phillips in the December 1962 election (and who was to die of a heart attack two months later); the kings of comedy, Johnny Wayne and Frank Shuster, who were by then full-fledged television stars on CBC-TV and *The Ed Sullivan Show* on CBS in the United States; New York actors who had flown in for the occasion, Donald Davis, Dennis King, Lou Jacobi, and June Havoc; and Lady Eaton, royalty in Toronto in those years. The play they watched that night was a forgettable and mediocre American comedy, *Never Too Late*, starring William Bendix. But it was the show's novice producer, the new owner of the theatre and the host of the celebration, who was the true star of the evening—"Honest Ed" Mirvish. "I don't really know anything about the theatre business," he said modestly. That was Ed.

There was something larger than life about Ed Mirvish on that night in September 1963—and always. Mirvish never did anything on a small scale if it could be done "big." Besides the Royal Alex, he was most famously known for Honest Ed's, his block-size bargain emporium near the corner of Bloor and Bathurst Streets, where it was possible to buy everything from bottle openers and long underwear to digital cameras in later years. Capped off by Mirvish's delightful sense of humour, astute business acumen and carny demeanour, the store shopping experience—and "experience" does not quite describe it—was complemented by 22,000 flashing lights and kitschy and in-your-face signs—"Don't Just Stand There, Buy Something!" Or "How cheap can a guy get? Come in and find out." Mirvish was much more than a merchant, however. His support of local artists in the small shops he owned in "Mirvish Village" on Markham Street, and his decision to purchase and renovate the Royal Alexandra Theatre and bring Broadway to King Street, made him a first-rate Toronto booster in the same league as Johnny Lombardi and Nathan Phillips.

Though he was born in 1914 in Colonial Beach, a resort town in Virginia, Mirvish was at heart an immigrant, like his parents David and Anna, Russian Jews who had come to the New World in search of a new life. The immigrant mentality to succeed propelled young Ed forward, even when he faced adversity. It also later connected him to his numerous Italian, Greek, Portuguese, and Jewish customers on an emotional level, as well as the many Torontonians who benefitted from his generous philanthropy; the thousands of turkeys he gave away during the Christmas season each year were only the most visible support of those in need.

His parents had named him Yehuda, but on the advice of a relative they gave him the English name Edwin so that he would be more American. His *bris* or ritual circumcision when he was seven days old was performed by Rabbi Moshe Reuben Yoelson, the father of singer Al Jolson. Mirvish was fond of pointing out that this had been his first brush with the entertainment business.

Try as he might, Ed's father, David, had a difficult time making a living. He owned a grocery store in Washington, D.C., yet could not make a go of it. Then he worked as a travelling salesman, with the same poor results. In 1923, he and Anna, with Ed, now nine years old, and two-year-old Robert, decided to try their luck in Toronto. David soon opened another small grocery store on Dundas Street West near Bathurst Street, though this, too, proved to be a faltering business. To supplement the family income, he worked after hours hawking drinks and candy on long train trips. The ordeal finally wore him out and he died in 1930 at the age of forty-two.

With his mother and brother's help, Ed, only a teenager, attempted to keep the store running and did so until 1938, when he finally surrendered. "We were broke, we were always in a state of bankruptcy," Mirvish recalled in a 1963 interview. He walked away from the store with regrets, but he also learned a valuable lesson in business. "Never give credit. My father gave credit and he died broke," he later said. He found a job with the young merchant Leon Weinstein, who owned Power Supermarkets, and gained important insight into how to operate a profitable business. His life further changed for the better in June 1940 when he married Anne Macklin, an artist from Hamilton. She gave him their only child, David, born in 1945, and introduced him to high culture—not that he always appreciated it.

Scraping together enough cash from their wedding presents, Anne's insurance policy and a bank loan, Ed and Anne opened their first store in late 1940 in a small shop they rented on Bloor Street west of Bathurst—the beginning of the Mirvish commercial empire. At the Sport Bar, as they named it, the couple sold inexpensive women's wear to working-class and immigrant women who lived in the nearby neighbourhoods. In time they were able to buy the building and expand into another store they called Anne & Eddie's. By 1948, weary of selling only dresses, Ed took over more of the adjacent shops, bought as much low-priced merchandise as he could find, and Honest Ed's was born. He urged his customers to "Name Your Own Price! No Reasonable Offer Refused!" and that they did. The cash-only store took off, and soon there were two hundred or more people lined up each morning before it opened. (Among Italian women, the store was colloquially known as "la polizia," due to the presence of uniformed security guards.) Mirvish struck gold with "loss leaders," as business journalist David Olive explained in his tribute to Mirvish in July 2007, after Ed died. "He skimped on décor, introduced self-service, and sold only those goods he was able to find at rock-bottom cost, passing the savings to his loyal shoppers."

Never one to miss an opportunity for a good joke, Mirvish hung a photograph with the sign "Honest Ed Welcomes You" at the store's entrance, except it was, by agreement, a picture of a down-and-out local, "Dirty Dick" MacDougal—thin, worn out, toothless, with a stubble beard—who did odd jobs for Mirvish. Most customers believed Dirty Dick was Honest Ed. The marketing "shtick" he was proudest of was a Marathon Sale and Dance he inaugurated in February 1958. The Toronto police tried to ruin the party, charging Mirvish for keeping the store open for seventy-two hours straight, in violation of city bylaws. With as many as eighty thousand customers coming in during that period and spending a record-setting $75,000, he gladly paid the fines and kept on running the celebratory sale. Yet another clever gimmick, recalls his son, David, "was to hire the 'wolf girl' to hitch up her dogsled in the Yukon to hunt for bargains. And he'd have the radios report where she was in crossing Canada. She would eventually stop in front of Honest Ed's and go in to find a bargain. The local papers reported that 'wolf girl arrives in Toronto to shop for bargains at Bloor and Bathurst.' In those days, they would not put the name of your store in the paper." In July 2013, David Mirvish decided to put Honest Ed's up for sale. Three months later, he sold the landmark site to Westbank Properties of Vancouver, which built the Shangri-La Hotels in Toronto and Vancouver.

Around the corner from his store, Ed bought as many houses as he could with the intention of building a large parking lot. When the local residents objected, however, he followed his wife's sage advice and transformed Markham Street and its quaint Victorian-era houses into an artists' colony. David Mirvish operated a popular gallery and bookstore in one of the homes for many years.

Anne's devotion to the theatre led Ed to buy the Royal Alexandra Theatre from the Cawthra Mulock Trust in 1963 and save the fifty-six-year-old broken-down landmark from certain destruction. This was definitely another sign of the changing times: a Jewish entrepreneur purchasing a beloved theatre from descendants of the Family Compact. Mirvish paid $215,000 in cash and then spent at least half a million dollars restoring the theatre to its former grandeur. In typical Mirvish style, the refurbished Royal Alex had a huge marquee sign with more than a thousand flashing lights.

Given the high overhead, the theatre business in Toronto and elsewhere has always been enormously risky. By bringing in touring Broadway shows, Ed Mirvish made it work and, in the process, revitalized King Street, which for decades had been essentially a warehouse district servicing the railways. "It took 90% of his effort for 5% of his profit, but he was making a profit," says David Mirvish. "He thought the theatre business isn't a business but a disease, and he was afflicted." In later years, Ed had much more success expanding his subscription list with such musicals as *Hair*, *Godspell*, *Les Miz* and *Mama Mia!*

In 1966 he bought the warehouse next door to the theatre and turned it into Ed's Warehouse, a restaurant where men had to wear jackets and ties. The furnishings were gaudy and the roast beef and mashed potatoes were fairly bland, though at a price of $3.99 as good a bargain as you would find at Honest Ed's. The unique ambience attracted the theatre crowd in search of fun (the author had first-hand experience, working briefly as a bartender at Ed's Warehouse in the late seventies), and on a busy Saturday night he could serve more than six thousand meals. According to David Mirvish, Nathan Phillips's wife, Esther, specially ordered beef rib bones, which Ed quickly added to the menu as "dinosaur ribs."

Starting in the early 1980s, he expanded with mixed results. He first bought the Old Vic Theatre in London for £550,000 and spent $4 million renovating it. The Queen was impressed enough to make him a Commander of the British Empire; he said CBE actually stood for "Creator of Bargains Everywhere." Still, no matter what he put on the stage, the Old Vic remained unprofitable and he sold it in 1998. In 1993, Mirvish Enterprises spent $22 million building the opulent Princess of Wales Theatre (and another $20 million for the land), half a block from the Royal Alex. It opened to tremendous fanfare with the successful and very expensive musical *Miss Saigon*, which played to sold-out audiences for two years.

Despite elitist grumbling, Ed Mirvish, with the able assistance of his son, David, kept theatre alive in Toronto. Indeed, the Royal Alex had 52,000 annual subscribers by 1989. "What would the theatre in this city have been like without Ed Mirvish?" *Toronto Star* critic Richard Ouzounian asked in 2007. His reply to his own question: "Don't even think about it... Had Mirvish not made the [Royal] Alex available in 1963, Toronto audiences would have missed out on hundreds of theatrical experiences over the years."

WHILE ED MIRVISH was transforming the entertainment business, Conn Smythe remained firmly in control of professional hockey in Toronto through the late fifties and early sixties. His dominating personality continued to define the Toronto Maple Leafs as well as the National Hockey League. "Behind everything he does," wrote Trent Frayne in a penetrating profile for *Maclean's* in January 1952, "is a meticulous and calculating mind and away from public view, in the confines of his richly, though conservatively, appointed office on the second floor of the Gardens, he becomes as fussily efficient as a bookkeeper." They might not have loved him, but none of his employees and few of his players would dare to have crossed him. The same went for the other NHL owners. The leadership role Smythe played, and his philanthropy on behalf of the Ontario Society for Crippled Children, was universally respected and praised.

On the ice, however, the Leafs floundered during the late fifties. This was the result of Smythe's interference with such talented coaches as King Clancy and Howie Meeker, as well as the fact the team had to face the mighty Montreal Canadiens led by Maurice "The Rocket" Richard and Jean Béliveau. There were emerging bright spots: young Frank Mahovlich, the "Big M," won the Calder Trophy for the 1957–58 season, though the Leafs finished last in the league and only won twenty-one games. In 1959 and 1960 they made it to the Stanley Cup finals under their new general manager and coach, the tough and dictatorial hockey wizard George "Punch" Imlach, yet lost both times to the gifted Canadiens. By the time Imlach was guiding the team, Conn Smythe was ailing, a consequence of his war injuries. He permitted his son, Stafford, along with Stafford's partner in the Toronto Marlboros, the irascible Harold Ballard, and a small committee, the so-called Silver Seven, to run the Leafs' on-ice affairs. (The change required Conn Smythe to unceremoniously force the devoted Hap Day to resign as general manager, soon followed by his replacement Howie Meeker, who clashed with both Smythes.) Another important member of the committee was John Bassett, the owner of the *Telegram* and the Toronto Argonauts.

Stafford, who would have preferred to remain in the gravel business, was forever burdened by living in his father's shadow. Nor did Conn Smythe relinquish his supreme control of the team very easily. Stafford's early years coincided with the formation of the NHL Players' Association, organized by Ted Lindsay, Doug Harvey, and others. Though this first attempt at creating a viable players union foundered—in part due to Conn Smyth's ardent opposition—it marked the beginning of a drawn-out and frequently nasty confrontation between the wealthy owners of the league and the poorly paid players. (Not only did most of the players have to maintain jobs outside hockey, but the owners often procrastinated when players asked to see their own contracts or obtain proper information on their pensions.) Whereas Conn Smythe made close to $100,000 a year from salary and dividends, a top player on the Leafs was lucky to make $10,000. In an era without agents, the players were literally at the mercy of the owners, who even cut them out of most of the money made on hockey cards. The real battle off the ice would not advance until 1967, when lawyer Alan Eagleson became the group's executive director.

Imlach's career in hockey had been primarily with the Quebec Senior Hockey League. "He was forty, cocky, and didn't have much hair," sports writer Scott Young recalled about his first meeting with Imlach at Maple Leaf Gardens in 1958. Within a short time, Young and every other sports journalist and fan came to appreciate Imlach's skills and overwhelming desire to succeed. And he delivered. With such homegrown stars as Tim Horton, George Armstrong, Bob Pulford, Frank Mahovlich, Dave Keon, Bobby Baun, and veteran goaltender Johnny Bower, the Leafs started winning.

At the beginning of the 1961–62 season Conn Smythe, now sixty-six years old and weary of his bitter power struggle with Stafford, challenged his son to buy him out. Stafford united with Harold Ballard and John Bassett to purchase controlling interest in the team for $2.3 million. The elder Smythe, who believed he was selling his shares exclusively to his son, did not learn of the existence of Stafford's two partners for several days (though as biographer Kelly McParland points out, Smythe was well aware of the intricacies of the deal by the time it was publicly announced and did not stop it). According to Stafford's son Tommy, Conn "was heartbroken. He felt deceived by his own son, whom he believed to be giving away two-thirds of the Smythe legacy."

The Gardens, nevertheless, prospered. Whatever his faults, Ballard knew how to make money and transformed the Gardens into "the Cashbox on Carlton Street." One of his greatest coups was astutely booking the Beatles to perform at the Gardens in early September 1964 before 35,500 screaming and deliriously happy fans. The Fab Four stayed at the King Edward Hotel on their brief visit; upon arrival, they discovered a teenage girl hiding in the linen closet. Mayor Phil Givens and his wife tried to meet the group but were turned away at the door of their room by a mysterious blonde woman, leading to the *Star*'s front-page headline "Beatles' blonde snubs mayor." Ballard did everything he could to bring in additional revenue, from adding more seats to selling more advertising and alcohol. Within three years his efforts had tripled the Gardens' profits from about $300,000 to $900,000. Conn Smythe finally resigned from the Gardens' board in the spring of 1966 after Ballard agreed to hold a boxing match between Muhammad Ali and George Chuvalo. Smythe held Ali in disdain for his declaration that he would not serve in the U.S. army if he was drafted. This incident further strained his relations with Stafford.

The 1962 season marked the beginning of Imlach's greatest success, with three consecutive Stanley Cups for the Leafs. The sixth game of the 1964 Stanley Cup final between Toronto and Detroit was especially notable. Playing in Detroit's Olympic Stadium, the Leafs' rugged defenceman Bobby Baun took a hard slapshot to his ankle and had to be carried off the ice. Baun refused to quit, so the team doctor gave him a shot of a painkiller that "froze" his ankle. The game went into overtime, and the injured Baun scored the winning goal when his shot from the point bounced off a Detroit player's stick past goaltender Terry Sawchuk. Back in Toronto, the Leafs easily won game seven. It was later revealed that Baun's ankle was broken.

Imlach was accused of being too tough on his players, pushing and berating them to perform better; or as one sports scribe put it, of having "ice water for blood and a paving stone for a heart." His practices were notoriously punishing, especially after the team lost a game. He later claimed it was all for the players' "own good," adding that he lived "by the creed that you can always be better than you are." And it was difficult to argue with the results. Still, Frank Mahovlich (who served as a Liberal-appointed senator from 1998 to 2013) would have begged to differ. Imlach, with lots of help from impatient fans, rode the "Big M" so hard that he wound up in the hospital with a severe depression and missed the first few weeks of the 1964–65 season. It happened a second time in November 1967, prompting the *Star*'s Milt Dunnell to point out in his sports column (on the front page that day) that "Mahovlich is a sensitive, easily-bruised individual." Later that season, in a blockbuster deal, Mahovlich was traded to Detroit and then in 1971 to Montreal, where he shone. Today he says he has much fonder memories of playing for the Canadiens than the Leafs.

The year before the trade he had been part of another Stanley Cup-winning team. It was Canada's centennial year and fitting that the Leafs and Canadiens battled for the

Cup. On May 2, 1967, in the sixth game of the series, Leafs' captain George Armstrong scored into an empty net, clinching the victory. The team's two "creaky old goalies," as the *Star* dubbed them, Johnny Bower and Terry Sawchuk, performed brilliantly, as did the rest of the many veterans on the team.

Few in the city or across the country would have guessed that this tremendous victory would be—as of 2014 and counting—the last time the Leafs won the Stanley Cup. Season after many a pathetic season—though there have been a few exceptions, most notably the 1978 playoffs when the Leafs made it to the semi-finals—masochistic Leaf fans have griped, but have, nonetheless, continued to financially and emotionally support the team. As one old joke has it, what do the Leafs and the *Titanic* have in common? They both look good until they hit the ice.

Trouble was on the immediate horizon after the 1967 cup win. The following year, NHL expansion to six American cities, the first of several such additions, permanently altered the hockey landscape. After two lousy seasons, Stafford Smythe and the board fired Imlach, who went on to build the new franchise in Buffalo. The year after that, Smythe and Ballard were caught stealing thousands of dollars from the Gardens' funds for their own personal use. In June 1969, at a tense board meeting, they were fired as president and vice-president. Their partner and friend John Bassett, the board chairman, had no choice but to vote against them. Significantly, they retained their shares, a mistake made by Bassett.

A few weeks later, Smythe and Ballard were charged with income tax evasion; from 1965 to 1968 they had raided the Gardens' coffers, spending money on houses, cottages, and other big items, and neither had declared the money as personal income. As their lawyers were negotiating a deal with the government tax officials, the two, as major shareholders, regained control of the Gardens' board. When that happened, Bassett sold his interest in the Gardens and Leafs for a sizable profit; in ten years he had made about $7 million on his initial $900,000 investment.

The duo's jubilation did not last long. Following an investigation by the Ontario government's attorney general's office, Smythe and Ballard were charged with defrauding Maple Leaf Gardens of a combined $477,000. The ordeal of the arrest and a possible jail term proved too much for Smythe. Through the rest of the year he drank heavily, and his health deteriorated. He died at the age of fifty on October 13, 1971, following complications from surgery for a bleeding ulcer. Much to the chagrin of Conn Smythe and his family, Harold Ballard declared to reporters, "I'll be calling the shots from now on."

Ballard dealt with the charges of tax evasion by paying the government what he owed, and he also repaid the Gardens the money he had taken. He could not talk his way out of the legal charges, however. Nearly a year later, the outspoken sixty-nine-year-old executive was convicted of fraud and theft and was eventually sentenced to two concurrent three-year sentences. That translated into one year in a minimum-security facility at Millhaven Correctional Institution near Kingston. While incarcerated, Ballard maintained control of the Gardens board via his son Bill. True to form, he later claimed that he "loved the swimming pool, golf course, sirloin steaks, pie and ice cream" at the prison.

Owing to what Tommy Smythe says was Ballard's manipulations, Ballard was able to buy all of Stafford Smythe's shares, becoming the Gardens' majority owner. For the next two decades, the Leafs' often dismal fortunes seemed to be a personification of Ballard's crusty personality. If he could antagonize his players or journalists, he did so—in a radio interview he told CBC journalist Barbara Frum to "keep quiet" and said women "are at their best" in bed. His friend Sam Shopsowitz of Shopsy's said that Ballard was merely "misunderstood."

While the hockey team, with such high-scoring stars as Daryl Sittler and Lanny McDonald, almost always made the playoffs for the duration of the seventies (including the semi-finals in 1978), Ballard consistently found ways to aggravate his players. The low point was his outrageous treatment of the Leafs' coach, the cerebral Roger Neilson, who he fired one day in March 1979 and then rehired two days later after an outcry by the players, the media, and the city. "In one of the greatest examples of baloney in the history of mankind," commented sports columnist Frank Orr, "[Ballard] tried to pass it all off as just a little hoax he'd cooked up to shake the team out of its lethargy." For his part, Neilson would not be dragged into the caper, nor did he consent to Ballard's silly idea for him to enter the arena wearing a paper bag over his head after he had been reinstated. And it was still next to impossible to get a seat at the Gardens for a regular season or playoff game, which was just the way Harold Ballard liked it.

JOHN BASSETT MAY HAVE LOST HIS INTEREST in the Leafs, but he had several other business interests to occupy him. He was debonair, stylish, and seemed to know anyone and everyone in Toronto and Ottawa, where he had grown up as the son of John Bassett Sr., the publisher of the *Montreal Gazette*. In the fifties and sixties he "dominated Toronto like a mythological Titan," wrote Peter C. Newman. Bassett rated as Newman's "favourite WASP" because "he overcame his natural WASP prejudices and was, for example, an enthusiastic booster of Israeli independence."

During the years John Diefenbaker was in power, from 1957 to 1963, Bassett, as the publisher of the Tory *Telegram*, had the prime minister's full attention—at least until 1963, when Bassett disagreed with Diefenbaker's indecision about nuclear weapons. In 1960, Diefenbaker wanted to appoint Bassett the Canadian ambassador in Washington, D.C., envisaging him as a man who could get along well with the new president, John F. Kennedy. Bassett, however, was not interested, and for good reason. He had set his sights on acquiring Toronto's first private television licence from the Board of Broadcast Governors (BBG) (later the Canadian Radio-Television and Telecommunications Commission, or CRTC).

As had been the case with radio, television's impact was initially underestimated, especially by those who had the most to lose from its ever-increasing popularity and influence, including newspapers and older politicians like Diefenbaker's predecessor, Louis St. Laurent, and his chief cabinet minister, C.D. Howe. Ironically, it was St. Laurent's government that passed the legislation allowing CBC-TV to go on the air in September 1952 as a self-governing and seemingly independent body, and then was upset when the network started reporting critically on the government's policies. It took decades, and many battles, before the CBC achieved any degree of independence from the federal government, which subsidized its operations. During the 1957 general election, the elderly St. Laurent declared that he was more "interested in seeing people than in talking to cameras." His opponent John Diefenbaker, on the other hand, used television to emphasize his vibrant energy and electric yet "folksy" personality. Diefenbaker's success at using TV to his advantage may well have been the deciding factor in the election, giving the Conservatives a slight edge and a minority government. The Tory leader had a "hot" image according to media guru Marshall McLuhan, who, following in the footsteps of his University of Toronto colleague Harold Innis, probed the true power of TV and deemed that "the medium is the message."

Newspaper editors, meanwhile, were not entirely impressed with the new invention; in 1952 the *Globe and Mail* depicted television as nothing more than a "fireside screen entertainment." A few days later, though, after the CBC was on the air, the *Globe* offered a more reflective assessment. "Undoubtedly television will have profound social effects, just as radio and the movies have had," an editorial stated. "It will tend to make the civilization in which we live more mechanical, and individuals more passive in their habits of mind. But it is here to stay, and for better or worse will affect the patterns of our lives." The editors merely had to examine the numerous advertisements on the *Globe*'s pages for Admiral and General Electric televisions to recognize that Torontonians, like Canadians everywhere, were purchasing televisions in ever-increasing numbers.

Whichever way you looked at it, television had power. One Sunday in May 1958, when Toronto's own comedy duo Johnny Wayne and Frank Shuster appeared for the first time on the American television variety program *The Ed Sullivan Show* (over the next decade they would perform a record-setting fifty-eight more times and another nine in reruns), they reached an audience of forty million viewers. On that first Sullivan appearance, they and their talented troupe performed the clever sketch "Rinse the Blood Off My Toga," a hilarious parody of Julius Caesar's murder. One of the best lines was delivered by Sylvia Lennick, as Caesar's wife, who, when questioned about the murder, tells Private

Roman Eye Flavius Maximus (played by Wayne), in her impeccable Bronx accent, "I told him, Julie, don't go." The next day, Lennick was walking down Broadway when a bus stopped, seemingly for no reason. The door opened and the bus driver shouted, "Hey, Julie, you told him: don't go. Julie, hey, you told him: don't go." Lennick was stunned. "I thought it's me, I'm in New York," she later recalled, "people listen." From that day forward, she was forever linked with those immortal words, "Julie, don't go."

Back in Toronto, CBC-TV executives, who had been having second thoughts about continuing Wayne and Shuster's weekly show, quickly offered them a new deal. When Frank reviewed the revised CBC contract, he pushed it back and said, "Double it." Johnny, a little more reticent on money matters, concurred. "He's quite right, gentlemen," he added with a glint in his eye. "We're American stars now."

Their CBC-TV specials soon attracted hundreds of thousands of viewers. In March 1963, the *Toronto Star* estimated that they were each earning about $70,000 a year, likely making them the highest-paid Canadian performers of their day. Yet their passion for comedy trumped any desire to be rich American TV stars. As their fame and celebrity spread in the United States, mainly due to their popularity on *The Ed Sullivan Show*, their agent begged them to move south permanently. "You know, there's more to life than happiness," the desperate agent pleaded with them. But no matter how much money they were offered or how sweet a deal for their own television show was dangled before them, they refused, content to work in New York on Sunday evenings, but be back for lunch in Toronto the following day. Such a position enhanced their status at the CBC.

When the opportunity arose to obtain a private television licence, Bassett, along with his partners in his company Baton Broadcasting—the Eaton family, Ted Rogers of CFRB, and Joel Aldred, a well-known radio personality and the true brains behind Bassett's proposal—made their intentions for CFTO known. With other major players of the Toronto business community also vying for the rights—among the list of bidders were Beland Honderich, the publisher of the *Star*, and such entrepreneurs as Roy Thomson, Jack Kent Cooke (later the owner of several U.S. professional sports teams), Frank McMahon, and the Sifton family—the competition was intense, though Bassett was not worried. More than once he bragged, "We've got it in the bag," implying that his close connections with the Tories on the BBG and his friendship with Diefenbaker assured him of a victory. When Bassett and his partners did indeed win the licence, charges of bias were raised. Everyone from Diefenbaker on down denied any interference, but it is difficult to believe that Bassett's close connection to the government was not a factor.

CFTO soon went on the air, to great ballyhoo, and by Bassett's design it was Toronto-centric. After Bassett linked CFTO with other private broadcasters across Canada, establishing the CTV network (a move made quickly so Bassett could broadcast four big CFL games that he had bought rights to for $750,000), CFTO became its flagship station.

At first the CTV national news was broadcast from Ottawa, yet Bassett eventually had his way and the show was moved to Toronto in 1966. Like CBC's *The National*, CTV news quickly came to reflect a Toronto view of the world: Toronto news was "national news"; Canadian stories from outside Metro, especially in the west, were perceived more as local matters. Bassett would not have wanted it any other way. "Toronto was the key market in the country," said Bassett about the decision to relocate the CTV news program from Ottawa. "Toronto is by far more dominant in the Canadian market than any single city in the United States. New York is not as dominant across America as Toronto is in Canada."

While Bassett's venture into television was on the rise, the same could not be said for his newspaper. During the sixties, the *Telegram*, though overly occupied with politics, like its majority owner, had held its own against its chief afternoon competitor, the *Star*, and both were doing better against the third-place morning *Globe and Mail*. In 1962, Monday-to-Friday circulation of the three stood at 344,486 for the *Star*; 226,857 for the *Telegram*; and 220,459 for the *Globe and Mail*.

During the decade, the *Star*, now being guided by Beland "Bee" Honderich—who had become editor-in chief in 1955 and president and publisher ten years later—was a work-in-progress. Honderich, recalled Robert Fulford, who was then writing a book column for the newspaper, "wanted a new kind of *Star* for the new Toronto slowly being born. He seems to have had in mind a combination of populism and sophistication, a paper that could be read by large masses of people but could also impress the most knowledgeable readers." To this end, Honderich hired a stable of talented writers including Pierre Berton, Charles Templeton, Mark Gayn (an expert on the Soviet Union), and drama critic Nathan Cohen, likely the most loved and hated journalist in the city. Around the *Star* newsroom, Honderich was not so affectionately referred to as "The Beast" for his obsessive micro-managing. His strategy, nevertheless, worked. By 1970, the *Star*'s daily circulation had risen to 380,000 and the *Telegram*'s to 242,000, but the *Globe and Mail* had now surpassed the *Tely* with a circulation of 264,000. Peter C. Newman, who was hired by Honderich as editor-in-chief in 1969 and tolerated Honderich's dictates for two years, was told by the indomitable publisher that the *Star* had "one and only one objective: 'To beat the *Tely*.'" On Saturdays in 1970, the *Star* under the odd-couple reign of Honderich and Newman was far and away the most popular newspaper in the city, with 489,000 papers sold. The *Telegram* was at 249,000 and the *Globe*, 264,000.

The *Telegram* had run into a number of financial problems. Its old building on Melinda Street had seen better days. The newsroom, recalled Don Obe, who joined the *Tely* in 1961, "was all just so ramshackle, totally uncoordinated, totally messy operation." Bassett decided to improve things. He borrowed $12 million to build the newspaper a brand new state-of-the art headquarters on Front Street West, but then he lost his chief financial backer after John David Eaton became ill and the Eaton's company finances were restructured. The paper had also experimented with an expensive Sunday edition in 1957, but it was poorly planned and executed—not to mention that in some parts of Toronto, selling a newspaper on the Lord's Day was still regarded as heretical. The Sunday *Telegram* lasted a brief nineteen weeks. Continuing labour troubles hampered the newspaper as well. And staff morale took a beating in 1969 when a frustrated Bassett "retired" fifty-three-year-old Douglas MacFarlane, the long-time and astute editor-in-chief.

Bassett's son John or Johnny F. was an enthusiastic supporter and tried to liven up and modernize the *Tely* with more arts and family features, among other innovations. Both father and son also pushed for expensive overseas bureaus in London, Paris, and Moscow. This European presence made the elder Bassett feel like a Fleet Street baron. Yet the expenditure seriously hurt the newspaper's bottom line, and Bassett refused to go public, relying on bank loans to keep the *Telegram* afloat. He continually declared that the newspaper was not for sale, but, in fact, he searched for possible buyers without any success (he approached Lord Thomson, as well as Charles Templeton and Pierre Berton, about taking over the paper, but they all turned him down). Under pressure to settle a contract with the Newspaper Guild, Bassett decided, following a tense meeting at John David Eaton's home, that his only option was to shut down the nearly one-hundred-year-old *Telegram*.

The newspaper's demise was a big story in the city and covered intensely by the *Tely*'s competitors. It was all a bit embarrassing for a city like Toronto. "We are told Toronto is a city like no other... a city that grows and prospers," said Art Eggleton, then an alderman. "How in this setting can the closure of the *Telegram* occur?" The Guild wanted the government to intervene, and the provincial government did offer Bassett a loan. He refused it. Bassett later said that closing the paper was "one of the most painful things in my life." Ever the wily business tycoon, however, he found that things worked out nicely for him. The *Star* bought the *Telegram*'s subscription list for $10 million and leased its presses for two years until its new building on Yonge Street was ready. The *Globe and Mail* soon purchased the *Telegram*'s property on the north side of Front Street just west of Spadina Avenue for $7 million; it remains there to this day.

As for the *Tely*'s employees: some found work at the other newspapers and many more at the *Telegram*'s enduring "cheeky" tabloid offspring, the *Toronto Sun*. The *Sun* was launched on November 1, 1971, the day after the *Telegram* ceased publication, mainly owing to the machinations of Douglas Creighton, Peter Worthington, and Donald Hunt, all formerly with the *Telegram*, plus the financial wizardry of lawyer Eddie Goodman. Toronto had never seen anything like this British-style import. It had short articles about crime and entertainment, pictures of scantily clad women, the "Sunshine girls," and a conservative slant shaped by Worthington, the paper's first editor-in-chief. Lo and behold, the *Sun* was a success in chic, upscale Toronto and it remained a city with three distinct newspapers.

THE RISE OF TELEVISION, the popularity of an academic like McLuhan—who in 1977 had a wonderful cameo in Woody Allen's Academy Award-winning film *Annie Hall*—and even the success of the *Toronto Sun* each represented in its own way that "the times they are a-changin," in the immortal words of legendary singer and songwriter Bob Dylan. In August 1967, Dylan's friend George Harrison paid an unannounced visit to the Haight-Ashbury neighbourhood in San Francisco, the unofficial hub for the Summer of Love—rock 'n' roll, folk music, drugs, sex, and good times. The Beatle was not impressed. "I went to Haight-Ashbury, expecting it to be this brilliant place," he recalled in a 1995 interview, "and it was just full of horrible, spotty, dropout kids on drugs. It certainly showed me what was really happening in the drug culture. It wasn't what I thought, of all these groovy people having spiritual awakenings and being artistic. It was like the Bowery, it was like alcoholism, it was like any addiction." His lousy experience convinced him to stop taking LSD.

Like everything critical of the magical sixties, however, Harrison's comments have been swept under the proverbial rug. This much-storied era may, truly, have been about disillusioned and idealistic baby boomers rejecting the middle-class values of their parents and embracing a freer lifestyle—a journey that involved drug experimentation, new morals and attitudes about sex, Vietnam War protests, and turning the world on to unforgettable music. But if the history of any recent era has been overhyped and overanalyzed, it has to be the story of the sixties. This is partly due to the continuing prominence of the boomers—as long as senior citizens like Paul McCartney and Mick Jagger, both now in their seventies, continue performing, the music of the sixties will remain influential—but is also because the sixties saga—the hippies, folkies, marijuana, LSD, casual sex, great causes—was too compelling a human drama for the media to ignore at the time or later.

The spectacle that played out in Toronto's Yorkville neighbourhood from 1961 to 1970 was certainly such a compelling tale, which is remembered today with nostalgia oozing a deified fondness. Some of this reverential groupthink is valid—the Yorkville scene did inspire and inaugurate the careers of a wide range of successful musicians—and some of it is a distorted recollection of one long drug-induced, drunken, and wild party. *Globe and Mail* writer Michael Valpy, who as a young reporter covered Yorkville, explained the media's fascination in a 2006 interview with the neighbourhood's latest historian, Stuart Henderson: "It had all the elements of a major media story: it had political conflict, police versus citizen conflict. It had images (real or not) of sex, of drugs, of deviant behaviors. I mean it was stuff the media would just love. And they did." In an investigation for the CBC program *Newsmagazine*, for example, Knowlton Nash and his cameraman followed a friendly young man, cigarette in hand, named Bill (the American-born speculative fiction writer William Gibson), who took them on a tour of Yorkville. Nash proclaimed Gibson to be "a real hippie."

The story of Yorkville in the decade before it became an upscale shopping mecca—"Rodeo Drive North" as record producer Bernie Finkelstein, who started his career in Yorkville, sarcastically calls it—is also a good example of Toronto's craving, even subconsciously, for national attention. Whether they were aggravated by the hippie/drug scene or not, and many civic politicians were, Torontonians had an acute awareness that what was happening in San Francisco, New York, and dozens of other locales was also taking place in a big way in their city. Yorkville, a less-than-desirable area with old Victorian houses, boutique stores, art galleries, and a small assortment of European-style coffee houses, had been attracting beatniks and folk music enthusiasts since the early sixties, but by 1967, the "hippie ghetto," as the village was dubbed by Alderman Horace Brown, had become Toronto's premier tourist attraction, akin to Amsterdam's red-light district, where visitors wandered around to gawk at the unseemly sights.

There is no disputing that Yorkville put Toronto on the map as the birthplace of Canadian pop music. In such cafes as the 71 Club, Half Beat, Purple Onion, Bernie Fiedler's Riverboat Coffeehouse, and the Village Corner ("a Hipster's Heaven," according to music journalist Nicholas Jennings), you could mellow out listening to the likes of Ian and Sylvia, Gordon Lightfoot, Neil Young—the son of Toronto journalist Scott Young, Neil made his way to Yorkville from Winnipeg, where he lived with his mother, in 1965—Joni Mitchell, Bruce Cockburn, Murray McLauchlan, and megastars Simon & Garfunkel. And groovy stuff happened. "The heavy concentration of clubs in Yorkville," music insider Colleen Riley Roberts recalled in her memoirs, "meant one simply could walk down the street and meet, at one time or another, nearly everyone in the music industry, from artists to managers to booking agents to recording company executives to promotion people. Deals were done from a sighting or a wave."

The Summer of Love, in all of its imagined glory, drew thousands of young people to Yorkville as it did to Haight-Ashbury. Some came for the music and drugs, some were searching for God, some wanted to escape the confines of their middle-class homes in the suburbs, and many just wanted to hang out, do nothing, and get laid. But in the early sixties, sex was no laughing matter in Toronto. Just four years earlier, in May 1963, Pierre Berton, who had left the *Star* and rejoined *Maclean's*, wrote a column advocating premarital sex, even for his own daughters. The magazine's young managing editor, Peter Gzowski, ran the column, not expecting it would cause any controversy. He was wrong. Berton was castigated in Toronto and across Canada as a "Godless atheist, a sexual pervert, a slug, [and] a dirty old man," as he recalled. Never one to back down, he wrote a follow-up column in which he defended himself. When advertisers threatened to pull their business from the magazine over this issue, and the Roman Catholic clergy protested mightily, executives at Maclean Hunter unceremoniously fired Berton. They did not even want him to step back into their offices. So it was hardly surprising that in 1967, Syl Apps, a former Maple Leafs star, now an MPP, decried Yorkville as a "festering sore in the middle of the city" that needed to be eradicated. This was a view undoubtedly shared by many of the city's upstanding citizens.

Yorkville had lost its innocence in early August 1961, before it was actually "Yorkville" in the Toronto and Canadian collective imagination, when the police morality squad arrested Werner Graeber, his wife, Eva, and twenty-two of their "customers" who had allegedly been drinking liquor at the Graebers' house at 71 Yorkville Avenue. The group was roughly treated, strip-searched, and incarcerated in the Don Jail. Though the case against the Graebers for illegally selling liquor, in violation of Ontario's stiff liquor laws, was subsequently dropped due to a lack of hard evidence, the highly criticized police action set a nasty precedent for how authorities were going to deal in the future with anyone caught not behaving according to prescribed standards. A few months later, the discovery of four marijuana joints in a second raid on the Graebers' place, now the 71 Club, led to further trouble. Again, the charges were dropped since the ownership of the marijuana could not be proved, but the wickedness of Yorkville had been established.

Thereafter, Yorkville moved through the hippie and folk music stage to become a neighbourhood that attracted troubled youth, motorcycle toughs, and druggies. It was no surprise that, from time to time, the situation got out of hand. On the night of April 9, 1965, a "throng" of two thousand young men and women, as the *Globe and Mail* reported, "jammed" Yorkville between Bay Street and Avenue Road. This allegedly out-of-control street party quickly brought the police, who arrested a handful of people for underage drinking and disturbing the peace.

Brian Walker, the owner of the Penny Farthing Coffee House, was not impressed by such festivities, which he said drove away his regular customers, who preferred folk and jazz music to "street riots." (Music was not the only thing going on at the Penny Farthing. Bob Segarini, a California native and member of the popular band the Wackers, landed in Toronto in the winter of 1968 and found his way to the Penny Farthing, famed for its shapely waitresses in bikini uniforms. "This is what I remember," he recalled two decades later. "I paid a dollar for a bowl of chili and a girl took me downstairs and blew me. The buck paid for the chili.")

As the drug culture intensified in Canada during 1965 and 1966, and the authorities became more vigilant about stopping it, Toronto newspapers began warning, with some exaggeration to be sure, that Yorkville was now "breeding crime." A fistfight between "hippies and greasers" at the end of May 1966, which quickly escalated into an ugly "bottle-throwing demonstration" by up to two thousand people who turned on the few policemen who tried to break it up, further contributed to Yorkville's deteriorating image. Shouts by the mob of "Kill the fuzz" were intermixed with "Kill the queers" and "Kill the greasers." A year later the *Star* published a series of articles about Yorkville which highlighted its link to marijuana abuse and underage or "teenybopper" prostitution. By November there were reports of 125 girls, "dirty, demoralized and often diseased," being arrested "for wandering at large without means of support." Many of them were on a long list of missing girls that the police were searching for.

These and similar events angered civic politicians, who felt that Yorkville was indeed the "festering sore" described by Syl Apps. In mid-August 1967, David DePoe's defence of the Yorkville scene and all it represented led to a celebrated clash with sexagenarian Allan Lamport, the crusty former Toronto mayor, who was then a member of the Board of Control. DePoe was the twenty-three-year-old bearded (it was "neatly trimmed," according to the *Globe and Mail*) son of CBC-TV journalist Norman DePoe, working in the village with the humanitarian outreach group the Company of Young Canadians. He was also a founding member of the Diggers, a small "anarchist humanitarian collective" modelled after the more famous anti-capitalist protesters of Haight-Ashbury. At a memorable meeting at city hall, initiated by Lamport (who conceded that "not all kids are bad"), DePoe and a band of more than fifty hippies "who wore flowers between their toes, in their hair and clenched between their teeth," as one news report described it, gathered to explain their grievances. But they spoke a different language. Lamport wanted to know why they refused to become "productive members of society" and why so many had not bathed in weeks. The hippies spoke about "opting out." DePoe told Lamport that most of the problems in Yorkville arose from non-residents "who come to look at us." Lamport ignored him, declaring that he would like Yorkville "to grow as a shopping centre." The hippies laughed, yet it was "Lampy's" vision that prevailed.

Three days later, another violent clash erupted between police and Yorkville protestors during a sit-in near Hazelton Avenue in an attempt to block traffic. Again the police overreacted, beating people over the head, pulling hair, and arresting fifty. Among those jailed were David DePoe and well-known journalist June Callwood, a committed and sympathetic Yorkville supporter. She later worked tirelessly to raise funds to establish a shelter for the lost and homeless youth of Yorkville, one of several philanthropic and social projects she undertook.

The August troubles were only the beginning. That summer there were further protests in front of city hall and elsewhere, which garnered the hippies, police, and besieged Toronto politicians national attention—much of it not wholly appreciated. "We failed in Yorkville," a *Globe and Mail* editorial declared on November 4, 1967. Yorkville used to be "fun" the newspaper conceded, even if it "prickled our Victorian conscience." Now it was merely a depraved neighbourhood with fifty known "carriers" of venereal disease. "This is a problem facing us," said Lamport's fellow-controller Margaret Campbell, "and we must try to solve it."

Yorkville, in a sense, solved itself. The hippies soon vanished, some returning to their middle-class families, and left on the streets were the "wounded," as Michael Valpy referred to them. In time they moved on to other areas of the city, and Yorkville was ultimately transformed into the yuppie paradise Allan Lamport and his colleagues had envisioned. On the fortieth anniversary of the Summer of Love, David DePoe, a retired elementary school teacher, bemoaned the transformation. "Yorkville today is the antithesis of what we wanted," he said in an interview with the *Star*. "It's consumerism and rich people whereas we were trying to live the simple and cheap life."

AS PASSIONATE AND CONTENTIOUS as the events that unfolded in Yorkville through the sixties were, the real fight for Toronto's soul, a battle that had begun in the fifties, was waged over its future development, both downtown and in the suburbs. In one corner were the pro-business promoters of massive skyscrapers, a freeway network, and suburban projects like the Yorkville shopping centre. And in the other were the reformers, who ardently believed that Toronto belonged to the "people" rather than to developers and automobiles.

E.P. Taylor's Don Mills had given rise to Erin Mills, where housing prices had skyrocketed to $65,000 in response to demand, and Flemingdon Park, where high-rise rental apartment complexes were the norm, bucking the trend of the Canadian dream of owning a house in the suburbs. The success of both areas reinforced a truism of the era: more and more Torontonians were living in the suburbs, and it only made sense to provide them with schools, churches, and places to shop, rather than forcing them to drive downtown. Shopping plazas with separate outdoor entrances for each store, like the ones at York Mills and Bayview or Eglinton and Bayview, came first. But the available land led to a much more ambitious project, the Yorkdale Shopping Centre, a large indoor suburban mall—another Canadian first.

Yorkdale's genesis began in 1955 with a decision by Eaton's to purchase a forty-hectare piece of farmland south of the 401. Embracing the future, the company had plans to erect a new store that would take advantage of the changing urban landscape. Three years later, in an unprecedented move, Eaton's invited its downtown rival Simpson's to join them in the venture. Eaton's thinking was that the presence of two of the largest department stores in the country was bound to attract more customers for them and the other stores in the mall, ensuring its overall success. Both retail giants would anchor the mall.

Once Simpson's was on board, more serious planning proceeded. In time, other retail stores, such as Tip Top Tailors and Birks, also signed on. Rents of approximately five dollars per square foot (compared to nearly ten dollars on Yonge Street) encouraged retailers to become part of the mall. The proposed Spadina Expressway, the anticipated main artery to the mall, which received Metro's blessing in 1959, also advanced the project. Each side used the other to its own advantage: the planners sold the mall on the strength of the expressway and Metro Chairman Frederick Gardiner used the mall to bolster support for the expressway. Metro officially approved a portion of the Spadina Expressway in 1961—a proposal that was destined to become one of the most heated controversies in the city's history (see Chapter Ten). Soon after that, construction began on the mall.

The development was handled by the Trizec Corporation, a property company operated by William Zeckendorf, a big-time American real estate developer. His partners were two British financial firms that had bailed Zeckendorf out of the mess he dug himself into during the expensive construction of Place Ville-Marie in Montreal. (Trizec, minus Zeckendorf, who was forced to surrender his interest in 1965, was involved in other major developments and acquisitions in Halifax, Winnipeg, and Calgary before reaching mega-status under Peter and Edgar Bronfman and the Reichmann brothers.)

The $40-million, 1.2-million-square-foot Yorkdale Shopping Centre, a third of a mile long, opened its doors on February 26, 1964, to great excitement. At noon that day, Miss Canada, Carol Ann Balmer, cut the ribbon before she and 350 invited guests dined on a lobster lunch. An estimated 100,000 customers then paid a visit. "In the corridors, it was like the Friday before Christmas," the *Star* exclaimed. One elderly gentleman walked into a six-foot-square plate of glass, mistaking it for a door. The *Telegram*, like a wide-eyed child visiting a carnival for the first time, enthused that "the 100 stores [actually only 61 of the stores were opened] and shops of Yorkdale are all air-conditioned, and if the cooling systems... were making ice cubes, they could produce a single stack 55 miles high every hour on the hour." The free parking in the mall's massive lot for 6,500 cars (today it has room for 7,400) was another huge incentive for Toronto shoppers used to scrambling, and paying, for parking downtown, even if it proved challenging for visitors to remember where they had left their vehicles. Until the Ala Moana Center in Honolulu, Hawaii, was expanded two years later, Toronto could boast that it had the largest shopping mall in the world.

Architects and urban commentators were critical of its design, complaining about everything from the storefronts to the shape and size of the parking lot, but that did not stop the shopping centre from becoming a commercial success. Yorkdale became the model for all other shopping centres in Canada to emulate. It was the place to go on a Saturday; or, as one publicity brochure claimed, "It's Instant Downtown—even though it's Uptown."

The most sensible expert comment was likely the one made by Alison Hymas. Writing about Yorkdale in the June 1965 issue of the *Journal of the Royal Architectural Institute of Canada*, she astutely pointed out, "The design critic must bear in mind that this is essentially real estate and not architecture; that return on financial investment is the aim of the developers and not a concern for the creation of well-ordered buildings in which buying and selling take place."

The subway reached the mall in 1978, solving transportation problems for anyone without a car. And further multi-million-dollar renovations and expansions—there are now 240 stores, more than double the number when it first opened, occupying 1.45-million square feet—were undertaken several times in the past decade, attracting popular American brand stores like Old Navy, H&M, Apple, and the Rainforest Café. On average, 400,000 people visit the mall each week. In April 2013, yet another $331-million expansion of Yorkdale was announced, with a completion date set for the fall of 2016.

PHILIP GIVENS, the mayor of Toronto from 1963 to 1966, cheered the opening of the Yorkdale Shopping Centre, as he did such other massive property developments as the Toronto-Dominion Bank's $100-million TD Centre near Bay and Wellington Streets. This latter project confirmed once and for all Bay Street's dominance over any other pretenders, like the area around Yonge and Bloor. Completed in 1967, the TD Centre was designed by the well-known German-American architect Mies van der Rohe and was the crowning achievement of the bank's imaginative CEO, Allen Lambert. He had the bank partner with the Fairview Corporation, a subsidiary of CEMP Investments owned by Montreal's Bronfman family. It was Phyllis (Bronfman) Lambert (no relation to Allen Lambert) who recommended Mies, who had designed the Bronfman's Seagram Building in New York. The erection of the fifty-six-storey black tower and subsequent additions required the demolition of older and architecturally beautiful downtown buildings, which was considered by many at the time a small price to pay to foster big-city progress. Indeed, Toronto's skyline was truly altered during the sixties, part of the boomtown mentality that made it, according to proud boosters, "the fastest-growing city in North America."

Not to be outclassed, the city's other banks followed Toronto-Dominion's lead during the early to mid-seventies. The Chinese modernist architect I.M. Pei designed the Commerce Court complex for the Canadian Imperial Bank of Commerce. The Royal Bank was next with its two-tower plaza, considered highly significant because the bank moved its main office from Montreal to Toronto. Finally, the Bank of Montreal united with the Reichmann brothers and their company, Olympia & York. After acquiring numerous properties (including the old *Toronto Star* building) and spending several years in complex negotiations with city hall, the Reichmanns built First Canadian Place, a seventy-two-storey edifice on the northwest corner of King and Bay Streets—at the time it was the tallest building in the Commonwealth—and the bank's new headquarters.

At Toronto city hall and Metro, politicians were generally receptive to these various land development schemes, no matter how unpopular or people-unfriendly they were. Some of these pro-development decisions came back to haunt Toronto aldermen in the decisive civic election of December 1972. But for the moment the *Star* could declare somewhat accurately, in early 1971, that "within ten years, downtown Toronto will be composed entirely of skyscrapers."

Two other mammoth and pivotal projects were soon unveiled. The first, the Eaton Centre, became a downtown Toronto landmark, while the second, the Metro Centre, which would have been even more sweeping in its grandeur and impact, died on the drawing table.

In the mid-sixties, Eaton's had tried to expand, but its dreams of a major redevelopment were stymied by the issues surrounding construction of the new city hall. After that, company executives took a quieter approach, working with the Fairview Corporation and holding private meetings with civic politicians and bureaucracy, and in 1971 announced their plans for a $250-million Eaton Centre, bounded by Queen, Bay, Dundas, and Yonge Streets. (Ironically, Fred Eaton did not want to call it "Eaton Centre," fearing that customers would blame the company if they received lousy treatment from other stores in the mall.) Eaton's itself was to build a new five-storey (changed later to nine storeys) retail store on Yonge and Dundas Streets, and there would be room for one hundred other stores in this downtown shopping plaza. (The development eventually prompted Simpson's to invest in a $6-million facelift to keep attracting customers.) Eaton's owned most of the land this project required, but not all of it. The company needed city hall's co-operation and its powers of expropriation. There were also many months of delicate negotiations, particularly with the congregation of the Church of the Holy Trinity, before the final deal was done. (The original plans would have had a major impact on the church's structure and view, but the plans were changed to avoid this.) There was much excitement early in February 1977 when the northern part of the centre, with its "magnificent glass-roofed galleria," was opened. "Futuristic" was one adjective used to describe it.

Everyone hoped that the Eaton Centre would revitalize this area of Yonge Street south of Dundas Street. Upstanding Torontonians of a certain age did not quite appreciate cool blues and jazz clubs like the Colonial Tavern, the Friar's Tavern, the Sapphire or the Blue Note, where you could hear Ronnie Hawkins, Jackie Shane, and

Willie Dixon. These clubs and the music they featured contributed to the birth of the "Toronto Sound," a blending of R&B with rock that catapulted David Clayton-Thomas, Domenic Troiano, Eric Mercury, and others to stardom. In the midst of the clubs was Sam Sniderman's music store, Sam the Record Man, the first store in Sniderman's retail empire, which had relocated to the east side of Yonge Street near Dundas in 1961. Not only did Sniderman's store, with its iconic neon sign of two huge LP records, have the best Boxing Day sale in the country, Sam (who died in 2012 at the age of ninety-two) made it his life's work to promote Canadian music and such successful bands as the Guess Who, Lighthouse, and Rush.

Still, Yonge had become downright seedy—the home, as a widely read and discussed *Toronto Star* series exposed with uptight disapprobation, of raunchy strip clubs, bawdy rub-and-tug massage parlours, and the number one spot in the city to seek the services of prostitutes. Less than half a block away from Eaton's on the east side of Yonge, the infamous Zanzibar, for instance, which had opened as a respectable nightclub in the fifties and then morphed into a tasteful dance club, eventually featuring topless performers, had become a crude strip club in the seventies. (Full nudity was legalized in 1975, which made these clubs even more popular.) The Zanzibar's motto was that "every bench was a waterbed," and the club assured its clientele that "the girls never stop." It took the torture and murder in 1977 of twelve-year-old shoeshine boy Emanuel Jaques, son of an impoverished Portuguese immigrant—who had been lured to a room above a Yonge Street massage parlour where three men sexually assaulted and finally killed him—for police and authorities to begin cleaning up the area.

As significant as the Eaton Centre was to remaking parts of the downtown, the Metro Centre proposal to dramatically reshape the rail yards and waterfront was more epic in its design and potential impact. Even Union Station would have been demolished, a suggestion Pierre Berton thought was "insane." The palatial railway station, he argued, was "part of our history as a transcontinental nation." Nonetheless, in the name of progress and "the largest redevelopment scheme in North American history," as it was touted, Union Station was slated to go.

In December 1968, the chief proponents, Canadian Pacific Railway and Canadian National Railway, announced that Metro Centre, a joint private and public project, would see the removal of two hundred acres of rail yards and replace it with a self-contained mini-city along the waterfront—complete with office buildings, residential units, a new railway terminal, a new building for the CBC, direct access to the subway and a tall new communications antenna, the CN Tower. Predictably, city council jumped on the bandwagon, ignoring the numerous complexities involved: the citizen protests about the destruction of Union Station, an appeal to the Ontario Municipal Board, and the Architectural Conservancy of Ontario's condemnation of the project as a "functional monstrosity." However, it was not the criticisms that sank most of the project, but a lack of money. The federal government refused to fund the new CBC headquarters (that was to not happen until the early nineties), and the TTC would not agree to pay for the subway extension. Metro Centre was finally put on hold in 1975. Union Station survived. As for the $63-million CN Tower, it was reconfigured with an observation terrace and glass floor (that will make anyone queasy) and opened in 1976. Until 2007 it was the tallest free-standing structure in the world. The tower became a popular tourist destination and the city's most notable landmark. Another decade or so would pass before new development plans for Front Street and the waterfront took hold.

IN TANDEM WITH the suburban residential and commercial development, Metro Toronto attracted a substantial amount of foreign investment during the sixties as Americans discovered untapped Canadian markets. Between 1954 and 1967, forty-eight foreign-owned plants were established, including Ford at Oakville and American Motors in Brampton.

Another was the British-controlled A.V. Roe Canada plant in Malton, which had a lucrative, publicly funded contract to construct the technologically superior, but very expensive, CF-105 or Avro Arrow jet fighter. A.V. Roe famously lost this contract when the Diefenbaker government pulled the plug on the enterprise in February 1959. More than fourteen thousand people were thrown out of work, as were thousands more employed by contractors. Ontario premier Leslie Frost, who had been aware that the cancellation was coming for about a year, learned that it had happened when a note was passed to him in the Ontario Legislature. "The decision to terminate... was completely sound," he later wrote in a personal memorandum, "but its execution was really indescribable." A.V. Roe alone took the drastic step of quickly dismissing its employees, but, much to Diefenbaker's grief, the prime minister received the brunt of the blame. The day after the official announcement, the *Star*'s entire front page displayed an assortment of stories on the issue, and a headline blared about the "Anger of Avro." The Conservative-friendly *Telegram* and the *Globe and Mail*, like Premier Frost, concluded that the "Arrow 'kill' [was] correct, but badly fumbled." However, this issue did ultimately cause an irreparable split between the *Globe*'s editor, Oakley Dalgleish, and Diefenbaker.

The perception that Diefenbaker callously threw A.V. Roe employees onto the street was compounded a few weeks later when the five completed Arrows and several uncompleted models, as well as engines and other parts, were dismantled and blowtorched. In view of the government's decision to follow the American government's advice and accept Bomarc missiles and SAGE ground-control systems to guide them, that action made sense, but the optics were bad then and later.

More than two thousand of the employees were rehired "for winding-down operations," and others found jobs with A.V. Roe's competitors. The company's plant was sold to one of these competitors in 1962 and passed through the hands of many others before it was demolished in 2005. Malton, which as of 1967 was absorbed into the Toronto township (in 1974 it was incorporated into the newly created city of Mississauga), survived the ordeal. But the myth of the Avro Arrow, and the belief that the Canadian aeronautics industry was crippled by a prime minister who lacked vision, haunted John Diefenbaker for the rest of his days and endures to the present time.

The cross-border blitz of U.S. investment dollars continued through the 1960s, and in 1970 triggered the formation of the Committee for an Independent Canada by former Liberal finance minister Walter Gordon, journalist Peter C. Newman, and University of Toronto political economist Abraham Rotstein. The trio hatched the idea for the lobby group over lunch one day in the Victoria Room at the King Edward Hotel. Their main objective was to stop U.S. corporations from allegedly taking over the Canadian economy. They were joined in their efforts by publisher Jack McClelland; Claude Ryan, then editor of the French-language newspaper *Le Devoir*; and Edmonton publisher and book aficionado Mel Hurtig, among others. Soon they boasted a membership of ten thousand and were able to influence the Trudeau government's Foreign Investment Review Agency, established in 1973.

As critical as this issue was, Toronto was by this time engulfed in the most intense battle of its history since William Lyon Mackenzie and his rebels marched down Yonge Street more than 130 years earlier—a fight to define its future growth and character.

Chapter Ten

JANE'S DISCIPLES

> Before the real city could be seen, it had to be imagined, the way rumours and tall tales were kind of a charting.
>
> —MICHAEL ONDAATJE, *IN THE SKIN OF A LION*, 1987

The proposed plan in the sixties to construct the Spadina Expressway, a major north-south freeway that would have cut through the middle of the city, led to one of the most bitter protests in Toronto's history. The members of the citizens' lobby group, the Stop Spadina, Save Our City Coordinating Committee, hailed the decision by the Ontario provincial government to kill the project in 1971. *York University Libraries, Clara Thomas Archives & Special Collections, Toronto Telegram fonds, ASC00707*

THE VARIOUS PROPOSALS to transform the downtown were referred to as "urban renewal," a catch-all term for so-called progress. What the proposals really meant, however, their many critics argued, was the expropriation of whole neighbourhoods regarded as derelict slums and their replacement with isolated Regent Park-like highrise apartments. The needs or wants of the long-time residents living in these areas were largely ignored. "If you are going to make an omelette," said Mayor Philip Givens about one urban renewal project, "you have to break eggs," implying that with sacrifice came something that was supposedly far better. From the black-and-white perspective of those in power, skyscrapers, slum clearance, and a vast expressway network linking the suburbs with the downtown was Toronto's future. Anyone who challenged this vision was out of their depth and probably a Marxist.

Yet challenge it they did. Many of the so-called agitators were in their twenties and thirties, university-educated and not afraid to question authority. Whose city was it, they wanted to know—was it the property of the developers, politicians, and automobiles, or did Toronto belong to its citizens? Their defiance was inspired by the eminent urban guru of the era, Jane Jacobs, whose 1961 book *Death and Life of Great American Cities* altered perceptions about ideal city life. A keen observer of the human condition, she rose from being a New York magazine writer in the forties with an interest in architecture to becoming a creative thinker about cities in the same way that her contemporaries Marshall McLuhan thought about the power of television, Betty Friedan wrote about women and motivated feminism, and Ralph Nader pushed the big automobile companies about safety.

Going against the accepted precepts of modern urban planning, Jacobs argued that people in cities should live in densely populated, mixed, and "lively" neighbourhoods on short blocks, surrounded by old as well as new homes and businesses. She disdained housing projects that segregated residents by income and cities built around traffic congestion. A pleasant and charming woman, Jacobs was an unrepentant critic, which drove her many detractors to distraction. Lewis Mumford, the urban historian and highly regarded expert on city life was one of them. "Like a construction gang bulldozing a site clean of all habitations, good or bad," he wrote caustically in the early sixties, "she bulldozes out of existence every desirable innovation in urban planning during the last century, and every competing idea, without even a pretense of critical evaluation."

This was an unwarranted censure of her urban philosophy. For a generation of Toronto urban reformers—John Sewell, David Crombie, and Colin Vaughan, among others—Jane Jacobs was a true visionary, not to be ignored. "It was as if somebody had torn blindfolds from my eyes," architect Eberhard Zeidler recalled, describing his reaction to reading Jacobs's first book. As fate would have it, in the midst of the contentious debate about the Spadina Expressway, she and her husband, architect Robert Jacobs, and their family moved from New York City to Toronto so that their two sons would not be drafted into the U.S. Army and sent to fight in the Vietnam War. In mid-1968, they bought a house in the Annex on Albany Avenue, where Jacobs fell in love with Toronto, made herself and her viewpoints known, and motivated her many followers.

A year later, in the civic election of December 1969, a handful of reformers Jacobs would have approved of were elected as first-time aldermen. The city hall newcomers included three future mayors: David Crombie of the Ryerson Polytechnical Institute (rebranded as Ryerson University in 2001), who ran on behalf of the non-partisan Metropolitan Civic Action Party or CIVAC; John Sewell, a twenty-nine-year-old lawyer and community activist; and accountant Art Eggleton, a confirmed Liberal. They were joined by Karl Jaffray, also a lawyer, who ran for the New Democratic Party; and historian William Kilbourn, who taught at York University, Toronto's innovative post-secondary institution, founded in 1959 with campuses eventually operating in suburban North York and north on Keele Street. A bit of a loner, Sewell found city hall "a sad, pathetic, and humorous world to enter," drowning in bureaucracy and political backbiting. His arrival, as well as that of the other reformers, stirred things up, much to the annoyance of the mayor, William Dennison, who, "un-Jacobs-like," frowned on citizen participation in civic affairs.

Several years before Sewell embarked on his political career, his ire was triggered when he became involved in an urban renewal project in the small neighbourhood of

Trefann Court. Located near Regent Park South between Parliament and River Streets, north of Queen Street East to Shuter Street, Trefann Court—a community of only 1,215 in 1966—was one of several old, blue-collar, and, arguably, rundown residential areas in the immediate vicinity that the city had targeted as early as 1956 for a drastic makeover. Still, as Edna Dixon, who lived in Trefann Court with her husband, Gus, later pointed out, the neighbourhood was definitely not a slum. "Our houses are old, but so are some of the people who live here; they have spent their lives struggling to pay for their houses."

The city's objective in Trefann Court, as in other similar projects, was to expropriate all of the residential property at the lowest cost possible and put up high-rise apartments. Civic officials, when pressed, declared that they were offering residents market value for their homes, but since the planned renewal had already depressed housing prices, the residents justifiably felt they were being cheated. (It was later determined that the city was offering residents an average of $9,800 each for their homes, when market values were more like $13,400.)

With an air of superiority, Mayor Givens and his supporters, who believed they stood for the greater good, showcased the poverty in the downtown core by touring the area in the spring of 1965, accompanied by three carloads of reporters. The group visited one street in St. James Town, north of Trefann Court, peering into private residences and tut-tutting at the visible squalor. The *Star*'s columnist Ron Haggart was scathing in his assessment of Givens's publicity stunt, denouncing him for using "the slum dwellers for his own promotion." Yet judging from the letters to the *Star*'s editor, many Torontonians supported the mayor and the city's housing authority's renewal policies.

Unwilling to back down, Trefann Court residents like the Dixons started to mobilize; it was the first time any of them had been involved in political action. They soon changed course and decided that the issue was not how much the city would pay for their homes, but, rather, the survival of their neighbourhood. Their battle would now be the concept of urban renewal itself. They rejected the expropriations and the destruction of the neighbourhood.

John Sewell became involved around this time (he was in the midst of completing his law articling, even though he had decided not to become a practising lawyer). By March 1967 he had moved into a Queen Street apartment in Trefann Court and began to organize. By then he had learned that city hall did as it wanted, no matter how logical or reasonable the residents' demands. "I was amazed and shocked," he later recalled, "when the City didn't listen to the people's arguments, when it said that no matter what the evidence, no matter what the people say about how much they are going to be hurt, the urban renewal plan was going ahead and the area was going to be wiped out."

He and his fellow community organizers were regarded by Givens, his successor William Dennison, and most aldermen as "outside agitators" who "supposedly quoted 'chapter and verse from Karl Marx.'" Civic leaders went so far as to use the police to intimidate the Trefann Court workers at city committee meetings. As the popular opposition grew louder, the city stubbornly stuck to its vision and policy.

The turning point came when the federal and provincial governments, which were contributing 75 percent of the funds for the renewal project, accepted that some type of "citizen participation" was required. Compelled now to listen to the people's wishes, the city halted the overhaul of Trefann Court in 1968 and then debated for another two years about how to proceed. In February 1970, after many meetings and hearings with Trefann Court residents, who were now supported on council by Sewell and the other reformers elected in the 1969 municipal election, the city and residents agreed on a plan to save Trefann Court. Urban renewal—which Trefann Court effectively ended, as Sewell has pointed out—was replaced by urban rehabilitation. This did not mean that slums in Toronto or elsewhere in Canada would vanish overnight, but the Trefann experience at least ensured that a fairer and more equitable system would be instated.

AS IMPORTANT AS THE FIGHT over Trefann Court was, the true *cause célèbre* of Toronto's urban grassroots movement (if you could call it that) during the sixties was the fierce battle against, and ultimate defeat of, the Spadina Expressway. The expressway's demise shocked its supporters, from retired Metro chairman Frederick Gardiner on down, and undermined the expansion-at-all-costs approach to the city's overall development.

As early as the mid-fifties, Gardiner and Metro had envisioned a major north-south traffic artery, with the requisite interchanges, connecting North York and the Lakeshore. As the plan evolved, the expressway was set to run from Wilson Avenue, north of Highway 401 (which was expanded in the early sixties from a four-lane road to a twelve-lane Los Angeles-style freeway), past the Yorkdale Shopping Centre, towards Bathurst Street, moving east after Eglinton towards St. Clair and Spadina, through the Cedarvale Ravine, through a tunnel near Casa Loma, and then possibly moving above Spadina and Bloor to its terminus near Harbord Street. An expanded Spadina Avenue would then take cars to the Lakeshore. Several other planned expressways would have linked up with Spadina, surrounding Toronto with a circular freeway system connecting the Don Valley Parkway to Highway 427 and everything in between.

It was audacious in its design and more expensive than any other transportation project in the city's history up to that point; the Spadina Expressway and subway would have cost as much as $230 million. Admittedly, if the expressway had been completed, it likely would have made getting around the GTA today much faster and easier (though Spadina detractors would still dispute that). Yet there would also have been tremendous economic and social costs. The number of cars coming into downtown Toronto each day would have substantially increased, as difficult as that is to comprehend given current traffic congestion. Demand for parking would have risen to unheard-of levels. Worse, hundreds of homeowners and their families would have been removed from their residences, dynamic and diverse neighbourhoods like the Annex would have been decimated—imagine the corner of Spadina and Bloor today with a multi-lane freeway above it—and Toronto would have been yet another city that put cars ahead of people.

At first, the expressway project started on as positive a note as Gardiner and his successor, William Allen, anticipated. Construction of the initial section between Wilson and Lawrence Avenues was approved by Metro in 1962 and underway a year later. The provincial government agreed to fund the expressway–Highway 401 interchange, providing easy access to the Yorkdale shopping mall. A revised plan also included a subway that was to be built in the middle of the expressway. By the time William Allen retired as Metro chairman in 1969—the name of the expressway was officially changed to the William R. Allen Expressway—the land and homes between Lawrence and Eglinton had been cleared. Still, Metro had exceeded its allotted budget. Additional funds would have to be borrowed, and that required the approval of the provincial Ontario Municipal Board (OMB). This should have been routine, but the involvement of the OMB ultimately proved to be the expressway's biggest stumbling block.

The opposition mobilized slowly, but it was loud. In his last year as chairman of Metro, Frederick Gardiner experienced more citizen hostility from ratepayer associations than he had in the rest of his nine-year term. The City of Toronto began to have doubts too, especially about the $80-million feeder route, the Crosstown Expressway, which had Rosedale residents up in arms. Gardiner derided their stand as a foolish example of "isolationism" that could result "in the building of a monument to stupidity." Nonetheless, at Gardiner's last meeting as chair in December 1961, Metro council ruined his farewell by voting to reconsider the Crosstown Expressway.

The battle continued through the decade. By far the most creative protest was organized by the residents of Rathnelly Avenue and the adjacent neighbourhood near Dupont Street and Davenport Road. To mark Canada's centennial on July 1, 1967, and to show their displeasure with the expressway plans, they "officially" seceded from Canada and established the independent "Republic of Rathnelly." Passports were issued, the Queen of Rathnelly was elected, and an "air farce" was created.

Metro wisely stopped any further expressway building in 1969 to reassess its plans. That October, a decisive citizens' lobby group was created, the Stop Spadina, Save Our City Coordinating Committee. Its leading proponents were mainly academics and university-educated middle-class professionals who were not afraid of publicly challenging the powers that be. Thirty-one-year-old Alan Powell, who taught urban sociology at the University of Toronto, was the group's chairman. He was ably assisted by David Nowlan, a professor of economics at York University; Alderman John Sewell; Colin Vaughan, a thirty-eight-year-old architect, who within a few years would be elected to Toronto city council and Metro council and would then cover civic politics for CITY-TV; and, of course, the resolute Jane Jacobs.

Well-connected and creative, the group did whatever it could to draw attention to its fight. "Citizens arise," Powell declared in one press release, "you have nothing to lose but your city!" A poster ominously warned "Los Angeles stinks; it has destroyed itself. The Spadina 'Express' way promises the same for Toronto." On another occasion, Stop Spadina supporters dressed in Victorian garb and drove in horse-drawn carts on downtown streets to emphasize how ancient and backwards the expressway was. Better still, Jacobs and Marshall McLuhan, a winning combination if there ever was one, surreptitiously collaborated on a short film, *The Burning Would*, which premiered in 1970. It was, according to the *Globe and Mail*'s reviewer, a "very campy" and amusing film, yet with a distinct "McLunanesque" message emphasizing the dreadful impact the expressway would inflict on the people of Toronto. Some months earlier, in a lecture at the McGill Street YWCA, Jacobs called the Spadina Expressway "the single greatest menace in this city" and predicted, with some exaggeration, that "Toronto is going to be destroyed within another 15 years."

The well-organized protest roused other voices—by January 1970 there were twenty-seven groups opposed to the project—and the province took notice. The expressway was the number one media story for two years. Urban intellectuals and activists offered their support in this battle of the corporation versus the people. On the other side, pro-expressway advocates labelled the members of the Stop Spadina group and other anti-expressway types as "hairy, snaggletoothed academics" and "romantic, Quixotic fool[s]." Archie Ginsburg, who owned a music store in North York, was blunter. "Anyone who believes Toronto doesn't need a downtown expressway from the northwest," he told the *Star*, "is a selfish idiot."

The *Globe and Mail*'s editors looked at the problem from a different perspective. "The crux of the matter is that the Spadina was conceived and begun in an age much different from what the 1970s promise to become," the paper observed in a February 1970 editorial. "Who cared about pollution in 1962? Who imagined the parking mess that is downtown Toronto today? Who was concerned about the dismemberment of urban residential neighbourhoods, which make the city civilized?" At the *Star*, publisher Beland Honderich was an enthusiastic supporter until his editorial board, led then by Peter C. Newman, convinced him in a 235-page brief that it was wrong

TOP: In 1793, Lieutenant Governor John Graves Simcoe ordered the construction of a garrison at the foot of Bathurst Street, which would later become Fort York. This is an oil painting of the garrison completed in 1907 by British-born Canadian artist Owen Staples based on a sketch done by Simcoe's talented wife, Elizabeth. *Courtesy of Toronto Public Library*

LEFT: This sketch by Canadian painter and illustrator, C.W. Jefferys, depicts the construction of Toronto's most important road, Yonge Street, which honoured John Graves Simcoe's mentor Sir George Yonge, Britain's secretary of state for war. Thanks to the diligent efforts first of the Queen's Rangers and later of conscripted German settlers—under the supervision of William Berczy—Yonge Street was literally hacked out of the forest. *Library and Archives Canada, Acc. No. 1972-26-767*

TOP: Fort York (the garrison) in 1804. In April 1813 during the War of 1812, when the Americans entered the grounds of the garrison, the fort's powder magazine was blown up and the debris of rocks killed many, including the U.S. commander, General Zebulon Pike. *Library and Archives Canada, Acc. No. 1990-336-3*

OPPOSITE PAGE, BOTTOM: Soon after he arrived in Upper Canada, John Graves Simcoe renamed Toronto "York," depicted here in 1804. Rank, privileges, government positions and patronage, fine homes, and good manners meant everything in early nineteenth-century York, where gossip was rampant. *Library and Archives Canada, Acc. No. 1970-188-2092 W.H. Coverdale Collection of Canadiana*

LEFT: In 1794, John and Elizabeth Simcoe found a serene picnic spot on a high wooded ridge overlooking the Don River. There they built a summer retreat that they called "Castle Frank," named after their son Francis, who was to perish at the siege of Badajoz in Spain during the war against France in 1812. Today it is the name of a subway station on the Bloor line. *Archives of Ontario F 47-11-1-0-228*

TOP: St. Lawrence Hall, completed in 1851, was the focus of a plethora of political, social, and cultural events—performances by the Swedish opera star Jenny Lind, lectures about the calamities of slavery, Orange Order rallies, and rousing partisan speeches by Conservative and Reform politicians like John A. Macdonald and George Brown. *Archives of Ontario F 4356-0-0-0-43*

OPPOSITE PAGE, TOP: King Street in Toronto in 1868 had the most elegant stores and shops. "Doing King," strolling up and down the street, was a favourite pastime of well-to-do Torontonians in the early to mid-nineteenth century. *Octavius Thompson / Library and Archives Canada / C-04439*

OPPOSITE PAGE, BOTTOM: King Street, looking east from Yonge Street in 1878. The highlights on King Street within a few blocks east and west of Yonge Street included Thomas Thompson's emporium, The Mammoth, and Robert Walker and Sons' Golden Lion, which was by all accounts "the finest retail clothing house in the Dominion." *Archives of Ontario F 4436-0-0-0-46*

Ready Made &
ORDER
YOUTHS

TOP: During the course of the nineteenth century, Toronto had grown from a village on Lake Ontario to an urban centre with a population exceeding 200,000 by 1893. The city now extended west to High Park and the Humber, north into the bushland beyond Yorkville Village, and east of the Don. *Courtesy of Toronto Public Library*

RIGHT: Toronto's bustling harbour area in 1901 was characterized by the boom in industry, transportation, and commerce. *Courtesy of the Library of Congress, LC-DIG-ppmsca-17944*

McCONKEY'S
TOYS

TOP LEFT: At the turn of the century, King Street still had style, but the streets beyond Toronto experienced all of the social and economic problems connected to industrialization and urbanization. *Courtesy of the Library of Congress, LC-USZ6-90*

TOP: Hanlan's Point on the Toronto Islands in 1907, the playground for Torontonians of all classes. At Hanlan's Point, tastes differed, with some citizens enjoying the amusement park and others partaking in the shooting galleries, the musical presentations, or even the illicit drinking, gambling, and possibly dog fights that occurred there. *City of Toronto Archives, Fonds 1244, Item 163*

BOTTOM: The Union Station freight yard a week after the Great Toronto Fire. On the night of April 19, 1904, the city's downtown core had been devastated by yet another raging fire, which destroyed an estimated $10 million of property up and down Front Street and north on Yonge. *Arthur F. Rust / Library and Archives Canada / PA-134533*

TOP LEFT: In the years after Timothy Eaton opened his department store on Yonge Street in 1869, Queen Street (pictured here in 1901) came into its own as a prime Toronto shopping area. *Courtesy of the Library of Congress, LC-USZ6-89*

TOP RIGHT: Yonge and Bloor in 1911, Toronto's most vibrant corner for more than a century. *Courtesy of the Library of Congress, LC-USZ62-96947*

BOTTOM: By 1910, Eaton's department store had its own massive clothing factory complex, which eventually employed as many as six thousand workers, a majority of them Jewish immigrants. *Archives of Ontario F 229-308-2-372 Used with permission of Sears Canada Inc.*

TOP: In 1913, Toronto was said to have one thousand peddlers, the majority of whom were Jewish. It was difficult work and a hard way to make a living. *City of Toronto Archives, Fonds 1244, Item 616*

LEFT: Newsboys, many of whom were the children of newcomers, were a common sight on the streets of Toronto in the early twentieth century. *Archives of Ontario Acc 6520, S 13458*

TOP: One of the more popular events of the winter season was Eaton's Santa Claus Parade, first held in 1905 and thereafter a Toronto Christmas tradition for decades. *Archives of Ontario*

BOTTOM: Toronto's chief booster during the First World War was the animated Tommy Church (left), the populist mayor of the city from 1915 to 1921. *City of Toronto Archives, Fonds 1244, Item 664*

OPPOSITE PAGE, TOP: Sunnyside Beach and Amusement Park was often referred to as the "poor man's Riviera." It had everything from shooting galleries, dancing, a wild rollercoaster ride (the Sunnyside Flyer), to a world-class merry-go-round and the "continent's best bathing pavilion." *City of Toronto Archives, Fonds 1244, Item 220A*

OPPOSITE PAGE, BOTTOM: When Canada found itself at war in early August 1914 as part of the British Empire, the vast majority of Torontonians heartily agreed with Liberal leader Sir Wilfrid Laurier's response of "Ready, aye, ready." *Canada. Dept. of National Defence / Library and Archives Canada / PA-004910*

THIS PAGE: In 1911, the bombastic businessman Sir Henry Pellatt conceived Casa Loma, a mansion with ninety-eight rooms, an elevator, a central vacuum, and separate stables and servants' quarters. The castle was too expensive to complete and manage, and the city ultimately took it over in the early thirties. *Canada. Patent and Copyright Office / Library and Archives Canada / C-022940*

OPPOSITE PAGE, TOP: The members of the Orange Order with their devotion to Crown, Protestantism, and Empire, dominated Toronto civic politics for much of the nineteenth century and well into the twentieth. The annual July 12th parade was always a popular and boisterous event. *City of Toronto Archives, Fonds 1244, Item 668*

OPPOSITE PAGE, BOTTOM: Though hardly appreciated at first by Anglo-Toronto, Italian and Jewish immigrants in the Ward and Kensington Market area arrived bearing trades and skills that in time enhanced the city's character and ethnic flavour. *John Boyd / Library and Archives Canada / PA-084812*

ONE ONE ONE
GOD FAITH EMPIRE

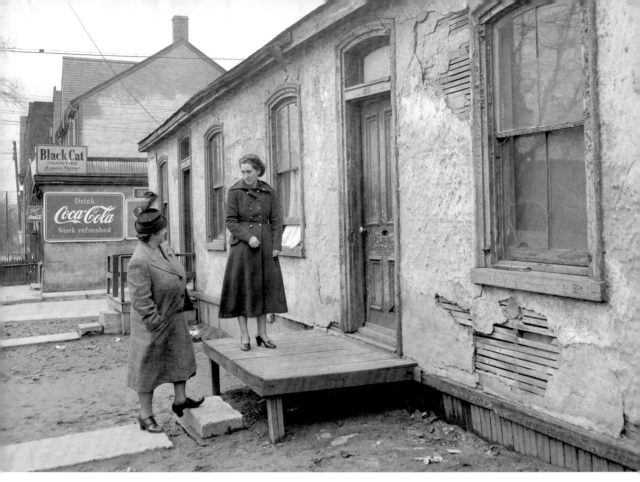

TOP: Regent Park, Toronto's (and Canada's) first social housing project in 1949. The development, managed by the new Toronto Housing Authority, was not merely slum clearance; it was also, according to John Sewell, an urban activist who was later mayor, "social reform... based on the idea that the old city had to be replaced, not simply modified." *Archives of Ontario C 3-1-0-0-540 / Gilbert A. Milne*

RIGHT: In late 1934, in the midst of the Great Depression and the year the city celebrated its centennial, 25 percent of Torontonians, or approximately 160,000 people, were on relief. *Toronto Star / Library and Archives Canada / C-029397*

TOP: In 1936, business tycoon C. George McCullagh transformed the Toronto newspaper industry by purchasing both the *Globe* and the *Mail and Empire* and merged them into the influential *Globe and Mail and Empire. Library and Archives Canada / Ronny Jaques*

LEFT: One of Toronto's great personalities was "Honest Ed" Mirvish (1914–2007), shown here with his son, David, an entrepreneur and visionary in his own right. Ed Mirvish never did anything on a small scale if it could be done "big." He was famous for his department store, Honest Ed's, and for reviving the city's theatre scene. *Courtesy of David Mirvish*

TOP: As early as 1909 there had been talk of constructing a north-south subway along Yonge Street and Avenue Road that would reach St. Clair Avenue, but it took decades before the engineering reports and discussion at council became a reality. *National Film Board of Canada. Photothèque / Library and Archives Canada / PA-111572*

RIGHT: Young swimmer Marilyn Bell with her coach, Gus Ryder, and Toronto mayor, Nathan Phillips, in September 1954, soon after Bell did the impossible and swam across Lake Ontario. It was an act of human endurance that held the attention of most Torontonians. *Archives of Ontario C 221-0-0-30*

TOP: The Lord's Day was always sacred in Toronto. It was not until Sunday, May 28, 1961, that theatre performances, movie screenings, and horse racing were permitted. One of the most popular events that day was an eye-popping performance at the Lux Theatre on College Street by the burlesque dancer, Miss Cupcake Cassidy. *City of Toronto Archives, Fonds 1257, Series 1057, Item 474*

LEFT: In October 1954, Hurricane Hazel left parts of Toronto in ruin. The private and public property damage in the Greater Toronto Area exceeded $25 million (at least $210 million in current dollars). *Courtesy of Toronto Public Library*

THIS IS ?
STOP
YOUR HOUSE IS NEXT !!
STOP SPADINA

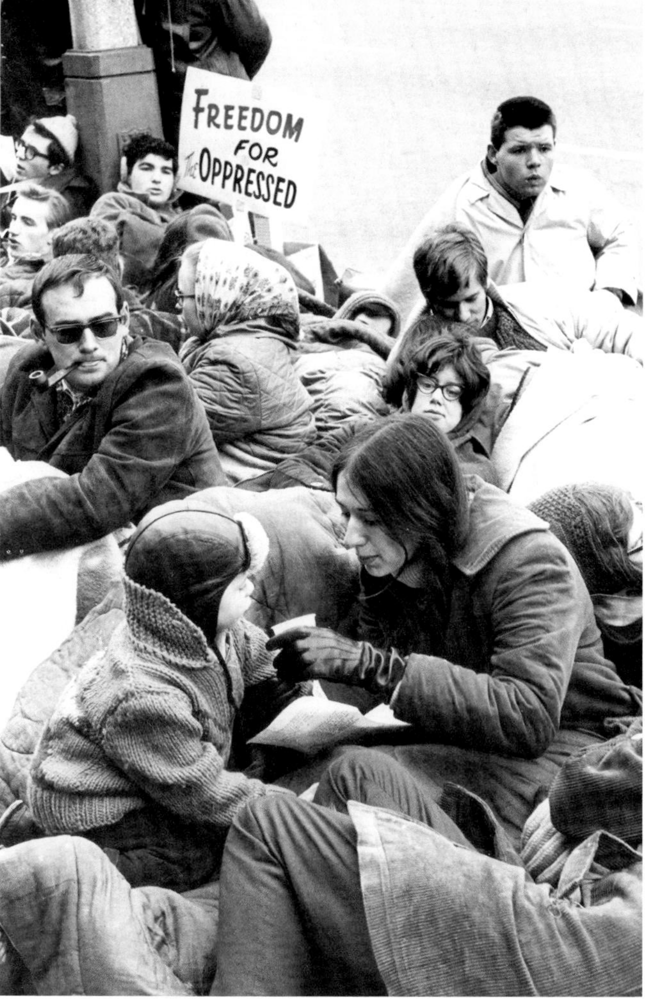

OPPOSITE PAGE, TOP: Highway 401, or the Macdonald-Cartier Freeway, runs from Windsor, Ontario, to Quebec. The section that goes through Toronto is the city's key artery, and according to some estimates, the busiest freeway in North America. *Archives of Ontario RG 14-162-5-60, #47*

OPPOSITE PAGE, BOTTOM: The cause célèbre of Toronto's urban grassroots movement during the sixties was the fierce battle against, and ultimate defeat of, the Spadina Expressway. The expressway would have linked the 401 with the city's core, but severely altered every neighbourhood in its proposed path. *York University Libraries, Clara Thomas Archives & Special Collections Toronto Telegram fonds, ASC00706*

TOP: Urban guru Jane Jacobs (1916–2006) argued that people in cities should live in densely populated, mixed and "lively" neighbourhoods on short blocks, surrounded by old as well as new homes and businesses. Her ideas and writings inspired a generation of Toronto politicians as well as civic leaders across North America. *Courtesy of the Library of Congress, LC-USZ-62-137838*

BOTTOM: Music, drugs, hippies, sex, and protests like this one held in November 1966 were part of the "scene" in Toronto's Yorkville during the sixties before it became an upscale shopping area. *Library and Archives Canada / Credit: Michael Lambeth / Michael Lambeth fonds e01962579*

TOP: Opened in 1976, the distinctive CN Tower was until 2007 the tallest free-standing structure in the world. The tower became a popular tourist destination and Toronto's most notable landmark. *Library and Archives Canada / Credit: Ted Grant / Ted Grant fonds e000940990*

BOTTOM LEFT: Lawyer and community activist John Sewell was mayor of Toronto from 1978 to 1980. While he was sometimes perceived as a controversial and radical civic politician, he never shied away from fighting for what he believed in. *Courtesy of John Sewell*

BOTTOM RIGHT: David Crombie, the mayor of Toronto from 1973 to 1978, escorted Queen Elizabeth II during the Royal Tour of 1973. Crombie was one of the most popular mayors in Toronto's history, and "the political embodiment of the city's best hopes for itself," as journalist Robert Fulford put it. *Courtesy of David Crombie*

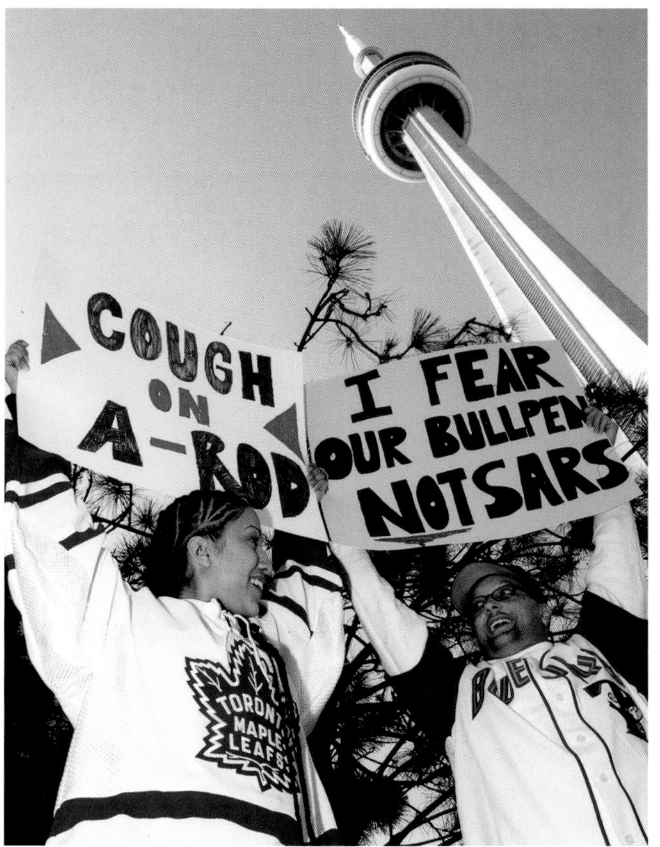

TOP: Toronto police were accused of using excessive force and tactics when the city hosted the G-20 summit of world leaders. When the police found themselves unable to control the situation or stop the black bloc, they began using tear gas, pepper spray, and rubber bullets to disperse the crowds, roughed up anyone who got in their way, and detained and arrested hundreds of people, guilty or not. *Thinkstock*

LEFT: In the spring of 2003, Toronto was one of several cities seriously affected by the deadly severe acute respiratory syndrome, or SARS, pandemic. Of the estimated eight hundred people who died worldwide from the disease, forty-four were from the GTA. *Thinkstock*

TOP: Toronto's Chinatown along Spadina Avenue, with its focal point on Dundas Street West, is a teeming collection of stores and restaurants and is emblematic of the city's multicultural character. *Thinkstock*

LEFT: In the annals of Toronto civic politics, there had never been anything quite like the manic circus surrounding Rob Ford, who became mayor of the city in 2010. His confession in November 2013, following months of denial, that he had smoked crack cocaine, led to turmoil in city council and made Toronto the subject of countless late night television jokes. *Thinkstock*

RIGHT: Toronto's Pride parade, a celebration of the city's LGBT community, has been an annual event at the end of June for more than 25 years. The festivities attract almost all of Toronto's politicians—except, most notably, Mayor Rob Ford, who has yet to participate because he spends the weekend of the parade at his cottage with his family. *Thinkstock*

TOP: Before he became a national figure as head of the federal New Democratic Party in 2003, Jack Layton served on Toronto city council for many years during which he gained a reputation as fierce defender of the underdog. When he died from cancer in August 2011 at the age of 61, there was an outpouring of emotion in Toronto and across Canada. *Thinkstock*

LEFT: For nearly a century the Toronto Maple Leafs have been the city's premier professional sports team and the most valuable National Hockey League franchise. Leaf fans are as loyal as can be, but year in, year out, the Leafs, who have not won a Stanley Cup since 1967, continually disappoint them. *Thinkstock*

BOTTOM: On April 27, 2013, Torontonians commemorated the 200th anniversary of the Battle of York during which the town was occupied by Americans during the War of 1812. For four days the residents of York were subjected to looting and plundering from both unrestrained American soldiers and unsavoury characters in the community, who sought to take advantage of the wartime situation to enhance their own pockets. *Thinkstock*

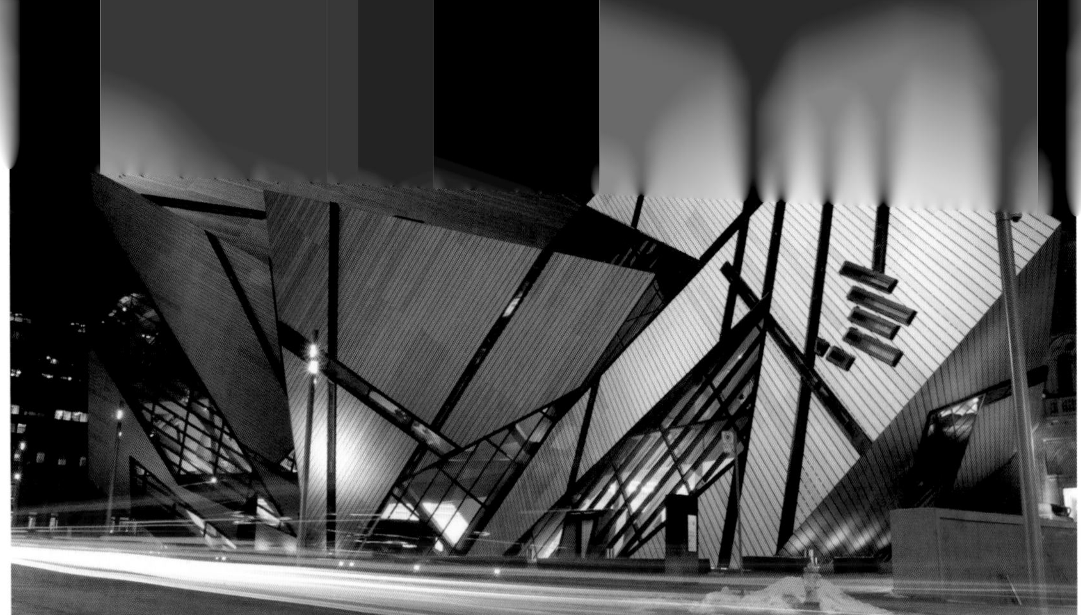

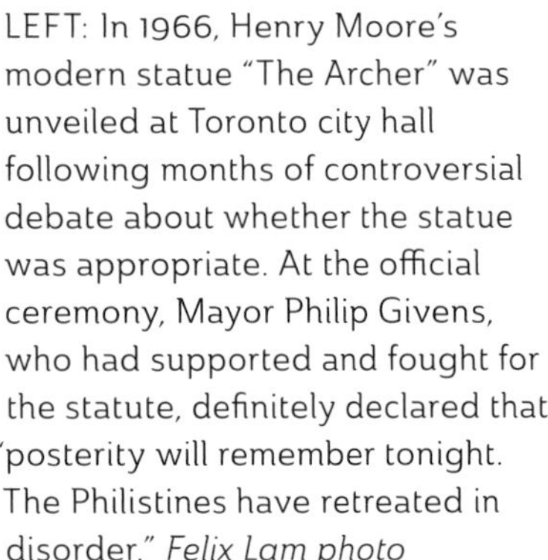

LEFT: In 1966, Henry Moore's modern statue "The Archer" was unveiled at Toronto city hall following months of controversial debate about whether the statue was appropriate. At the official ceremony, Mayor Philip Givens, who had supported and fought for the statute, definitely declared that "posterity will remember tonight. The Philistines have retreated in disorder." *Felix Lam photo*

TOP: In 2007, the opening of architect Daniel Libeskind's admittedly unique "Crystal" expansion to the Royal Ontario Museum sent the city into a tailspin. For weeks the question "Do you like the new ROM addition?" was the most common conversation starter in the GTA. *Thinkstock*

RIGHT: Toronto's waterfront long has been a source of controversy. In 2010, in a novel twist that harks back to the city's roots but with a modern design, Canada's Sugar Beach was opened at the foot of Lower Jarvis Street close to the Redpath Sugar Factory. *Stocksy*

TOP: Home to the Toronto Blue Jays and Toronto Argonauts, SkyDome (now the Rogers Centre), featuring a retractable roof, opened in 1989 with great fanfare and millions of dollars over-budget. *Thinkstock*

LEFT: Inaugurated in 1967 as a small two-day festival on Centre Island, by the late nineties Caribana attracted up to a million people and was a symbol of Toronto's celebrated cultural diversity. *Thinkstock*

AQUOS LCD Televisions
MICHAEL CERA
KAT DENNINGS
NICK & NORAH'S
INFINITE PLAYLIST
IN THEATERS THIS OCTOBER
THE PLACE YOU WANT TO BE.
FALLSVIEW CASINO
RIMMEL
Susanna Kwan & Sky Wu
OCTOBER 5 & 6
FALLSVIEW
WALL·E
visitPA
penn
STATE OF
XXII
FOREVER
milestones
GRILL + BAR
SHOPPERS
DRUG MAR
EXTREME FITNESS
FOO FIGHTERS
OASIS
amc
SUBWAY
10 DUNDAS STREET EAST
TRULY SPECTACULAR!
Dirty Dancing
MIRVISH.COM

OPPOSITE PAGE: Toronto's Dundas Square, completed in 2002 at the intersection of Yonge Street and Dundas Street East, is a focal point for celebrations, rallies, and protests. *Courtesy of Benson Kua (Flickr)*

ABOVE: Opened in 1907, the Royal Alexandra Theatre on King Street West was refurbished and restored to its grandeur by Ed Mirvish. Since then, the theatre has showcased a bevy of popular Broadway plays and musicals, attracting large audiences. *Courtesy of The City of Toronto (Flickr)*

LEFT: In late July 2013, the Toronto police killed eighteen-year-old Syrian immigrant Sammy Yatim, who was brandishing a knife on a streetcar. The shooting, which was recorded on a cellphone video and posted on the Internet, triggered protest marches and a public outcry about police brutality. *Courtesy of Joseph Morris (Flickr)*

SW2

Named in honour of Nathan Phillips, mayor of Toronto from 1955 to 1962, Nathan Phillips Square in front of new city hall is a popular Toronto spot for tourists and for skating during the winter months. *Thinkstock*

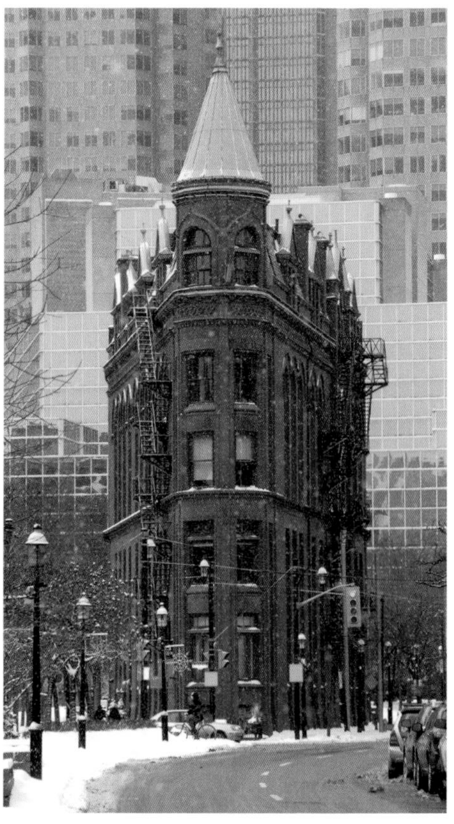

TOP: The University of Toronto dates back to King's College founded in 1827. Located in the heart of the city's downtown, it is one of Canada's premier universities. In the early twenties, the university celebrated the discovery of insulin at its campus laboratory by Frederick Banting, Charles Best, J.J.R. Macleod, and James Collip. *Thinkstock*

LEFT: Victorian-style row houses squeezed together in the neighbourhood close to the Kensington Market, off of Spadina Avenue south of College Street. The area has been home to various immigrant groups since the first decade of the twentieth century. *Thinkstock*

RIGHT: Toronto's distinctive flatiron building on Wellington Street, the Gooderham Building, was the headquarters of Gooderham and Worts distillery company for decades. *Thinkstock*

for the city. "To his credit, Honderich was swayed to accept our position," Newman remembered. "It was a first."

Metro decided to hold public hearings in the spring of 1970, which provided another opportunity for more protests and nasty name-calling. Still, Ontario premier John Robarts, who believed this project was a Metro matter, was reluctant to intercede. The beginning of the end came in early 1971, after Metro was compelled to seek permission from the OMB to borrow more funds, and more public hearings were convened. Stop Spadina joined forces with other anti-expressway factions to form the Spadina Review Corporation. They hired John J. Robinette, one of Canada's most distinguished lawyers, to represent their cause (at a cost of $50,000). Following more than two weeks of intense debate and wrangling, during which all the same pro and con arguments were heard, the three-member OMB sided with Metro and supported the completion of the expressway, though the vote was split two to one. The Spadina Review Corporation then announced it would appeal the decision to the premier and the cabinet.

John Robarts had resigned as premier of Ontario in late 1970, after nine years in office, and was succeeded by William "Bill" Davis. The new leader was first elected as an MPP in 1959, when he was only twenty-nine years old. In 1962, Robarts had appointed Davis minister of education, and in that role he skilfully ushered in an era of modernization and expansion. Guided by the advice, propaganda, and fundraising of the famous Tory "Big Blue Machine," Davis and the Progressive Conservatives easily maintained power with another majority government in the provincial election of October 1971.

Four months earlier, in one of their first major decisions, Davis and his cabinet were faced with the expressway controversy. An affable "Red Tory," Davis held strong convictions about the common good—"that all members of society are linked together through shared history, social institutions and common endeavour." He wasted little time before announcing in the legislature that he was halting the expressway project. "If we are building a transportation system to serve the automobile, the Spadina Expressway would be a good place to start," he declared. "But if we are building a transportation system to serve people, the Spadina Expressway is a good place to stop." The "march of concrete into the heart of Toronto," as the *Globe and Mail* described it, had been halted.

More than forty years later, Davis recalls that though it was a heated discussion inside and outside of cabinet, it was also an "uncomplicated" one. One person who had Davis's ear was Roy McMurtry, who was then the legal counsel for the Ontario Progressive Conservative Party. (In 1975 he was elected to the legislative assembly and entered the Davis cabinet as attorney general.) McMurtry, an old friend of Colin Vaughan, became active in the anti-expressway protest, and he advocated that position to the premier. Davis says he agreed that the consequences to the Annex, the University of Toronto, and the Spadina neighbourhood would have been terrible.

Reaction across the city was naturally mixed. Albert Campbell, who had succeeded William Allen as Metro chairman in 1969, deemed the decision a "disaster." Similarly, Toronto mayor William Dennison, one of the few on council still supporting the project, said from Italy, where he was on vacation, that he was "very disappointed and shocked" by the Davis cabinet decision.

Members of the Stop Spadina movement, on the other hand, were jubilant in victory. "It's the most fantastic day in the history of Toronto," claimed Alan Powell. "It's a tremendous victory for the rights of the people." Colin Vaughan, who said that he became involved in the fight after reading an article on urban issues by Jane Jacobs and then meeting her at a party, pointed out that a tiny group of concerned citizens had grown to a movement of 30,000 people. The citizens of Toronto learned that it was indeed possible to fight city hall and win. Dennis Lee wrote a poem to honour the triumph. "Sparrows sniffed the air, and hung," the first verse began. "Like humming-birds with bubblegum; Doing push-ups in the sun; The day we stopped Spadina." The Frederick Gardiner era truly ended that day in June 1971. Never again would a civic politician try to ignite an audience by holding out the vision of Toronto as another Los Angeles.

In the aftermath, work proceeded on the Spadina subway extension, which was opened in 1978, connecting St. George station to Wilson station. The Davis government substantially increased funding for the TTC. The next political headache became what to do with the "Spadina Ditch" between Lawrence and Eglinton, the portion of the expressway that had been under construction. After a few more years of argument, Davis approved its completion so that it was possible to reach Eglinton from north of the 401 relatively easily via the W.R. Allen Road—as it was officially renamed in 1980. Thereafter, every Toronto driver would experience the long wait to turn left from the Allen onto Eglinton.

In the decades since the expressway was killed, there have been backslapping, grey-haired, Stop Spadina reunions and museum exhibits chronicling the celebrated fight. Likewise, outside the Dupont subway station on the corner of Dupont and Spadina is a series of plaques that details the valiant struggle in all its glory. As difficult as it might be for the boomer activists to believe, some members of the younger generation, such as Sarah Fulford, editor of *Toronto Life* magazine, find the commemoration bizarre.

"Not that I'm in favour of bulldozing neighbourhoods to make room for highways," she wrote in her editor's letter of September 2011. "But it would have been nice if at some point in the last 40 years we had implemented a workable transportation plan for southern Ontario. In my view, the legacy of the Stop the Spadina Expressway movement is this: grand municipal plans are not welcome here. The population of the GTA is well over five million; we are way too big to continue congratulating ourselves for squashing big plans."

The expressway continued to impact provincial and local politics for years after its defeat. While it is true that overall support for the provincial Conservatives did decline during the next decade, Bill Davis had solidified his image in Toronto as a decidedly urban Progressive Conservative man-of-the-people. He paid attention to environmental and housing concerns, creating ministries for both in the early seventies, and, as Danielle Robinson observed, "aligned himself and his government with the priorities of urban activists." There were scandals and ups and downs, but Davis held on to power in Ontario (though from 1975 to 1981 with minority governments) until his retirement in 1985.

AT TORONTO CITY HALL, David Crombie, as genial as Bill Davis, emerged as the civic version of the premier and rode the wave of reform fervour into the mayor's office in the municipal election of 1972. Crombie was indeed the "tiny perfect mayor," as he is remembered fondly today—a charming and brilliant Red Tory who offended few, was loved by the media, worked through consensus with both radicals and conservatives, supported the local neighbourhoods and citizen initiatives, yet could not be considered anti-development. He even listed his number in the phone book and tolerated the personal calls from Torontonians who had a beef or just wanted to talk. "For years," wrote journalist and arts critic Robert Fulford, "[Crombie was] the political embodiment of the city's best hopes for itself."

Crombie had learned the skills of people management as a thirty-one-year-old administrator at Ryerson and then as the chief representative of CIVAC following his election to city council in 1969. His introduction to the theories of Jane Jacobs, he recalled, happened when he went looking for lecture material and discovered Jacobs's book. He quickly earned a reputation as a "young man in a hurry": there was not a person or issue that he shied away from. He could work through problems with William Dennison, as hard-nosed as any mayor of Toronto, as well as ease differences between the various factions in the Trefann Court community.

When Dennison announced he was not running in the 1972 election, Crombie put his name forward with a reform platform that stressed precisely what the anti-Spadina Expressway proponents had been fighting for: "neighbourhood preservation," maintaining Toronto's "sense of time and place," and "a city of civilized growth." It was idealistic, to be sure—the *Globe and Mail*, which endorsed Crombie, described his campaign team of young urban professionals as men and women "who are full of hopes, ideas, and dreams"—yet it clicked with Torontonians searching for new and vibrant leadership that fit the progressive times. No one but Crombie could have received support from both Progressive Conservatives and the opinionated Jane Jacobs.

"We knew in the late 60s that we had an interest in creating our own model out of our own understanding of who we were," Crombie reflected in a 2010 interview.

"What was really exciting is that we weren't saying let's go find out who's doing what and where—though we did some of that—and just take it off the shelf and cram it into Toronto. No, we said let's understand more about Toronto, let's understand its history, what principles guide it, what things have worked in the past, and so on."

On election day, Crombie easily defeated his two main opponents, civic politicians who had much more experience than him: Tony O'Donohue, an environmentalist; and David Rotenberg, a long-time Toronto alderman and champion of the Toronto Islands' residents, who had also served on the Metro executive. Rotenberg had been supported by the *Star*. As the new mayor, Crombie had to work with a council dominated by reformers, including John Sewell, who continually pushed Crombie in a more radical direction than he desired to go. He also had to contend with a few vocal members of the conservative and pro-development "Old Guard," though for the first time in a long time, they were in the minority.

For the next six years, Crombie was arguably the most popular mayor in Toronto's history, the epitome of the "manager of consensus." It was not by chance that American journalist Anthony Astrachan, in a profile of the city he wrote for *Harper's Magazine* in 1974, declared Toronto to be "the city that works." That was mostly Crombie's doing. Like a well-prepared lawyer, he surveyed and cajoled the aldermen so that he could fairly predict how each council vote would go. Beyond that, he innately understood, as he put it some years later, that the city was not "a canvas for someone to draw their own particular ideological or philosophical view of the world." Instead, Crombie said, city council, which reflected all of the people in the city, had to "paint the canvas" as the people saw it and not as the politicians did.

Property development naturally received his full attention. His motto, which nicely captured his approach, was "make haste slowly." He was not opposed to development, which he felt was required to achieve the ultimate goal of transforming Toronto into a "world class city," the buzzword in the seventies and later, but it had to be regulated. Nevertheless, developers were outraged when Crombie and the council passed the much maligned "45-Foot Bylaw." Intended merely as a temporary measure so the city could "catch its breath" and figure out which direction it wanted to go, the bylaw stipulated that "only new buildings under 45 feet high and less than 40,000 square feet in floor area" could be constructed until the Central Area Plan was finalized. Financiers and builders denounced it as "arbitrary," "extreme," and "immoral."

Four decades later, he says his goal was to ensure that the American urban model of people working downtown, deserting the city at six o'clock and living in the suburbs would not happen in Toronto. "We needed people, parks, residential buildings as well as offices," he says. "And, the only way was to control the height of new construction." Hospitals and other similar institutions were granted an exemption. Premier Bill

Davis, who was listening to the angry developers, was concerned and asked Crombie what he was up to. "I told him I needed two years to develop the policy," Crombie said, "and that's what we got." As agreed, the bylaw was rescinded by the Ontario Municipal Board in 1976.

One of Crombie's more notable (and enduring) accomplishments in making this Jane Jacobs-inspired vision a reality—with lots of input and argument from John Sewell and others—was the redevelopment of the St. Lawrence neighbourhood, an area bounded by Front Street East between Yonge and Parliament Streets that stretched north to Queen Street East. A fashionable part of the historic Town of York in the early nineteenth century, it had become by the early seventies a large downtrodden area of discarded warehouses and factories. It took vision and chutzpah to conceive of building a high-density, socially mixed neighbourhood beside railway yards and the Gardiner Expressway.

Under Crombie's leadership (with key advice from lawyer Michael Dennis, his young housing advisor), the city took ownership and charge of the project. Rather than creating another insulated housing development like Regent Park, St. Lawrence was turned into a livable community with row houses with front and back yards, mid-rise apartments, schools, and stores. It required two years of consultation with developers, planners, engineers, architects, citizens' groups, and others before the first housing construction was started in 1975. By the early nineties, more than three thousand housing units with 30,000 residents had been built on forty-four acres in the biggest urban development project of its kind in Canada.

In 1978, Crombie decided to jump into federal politics, soon winning a by-election as a Progressive Conservative in the riding of Rosedale in October 1978. No one could dispute that he had left city hall far better off. He modernized the mayor's office, expanded the bureaucracy to provide much-needed support for overworked aldermen, and established Cityhome, a non-profit housing company "to provide affordable rental accommodation for low and moderate income families," which was later absorbed by Toronto Community Housing.

John Sewell didn't see eye to eye with Crombie on every issue, yet today he concedes that Crombie was a superior political strategist. "He grabbed many of my ideas," says Sewell. "I was angry at that then. Now I'm happy about it. He took my ideas and made them acceptable, which I now realize was brilliant on his part." Crombie has fond memories of what he calls "a productive relationship," but with some qualification. "John was a scary guy," he says with his trademark smile. "He knew each and every issue so well and created fertile political ground. We worked well together... even though you spent a lot of time cursing the son-of-a-bitch. But you could not diminish his drive or dedication."

THAT JOHN SEWELL FOLLOWED David Crombie as mayor in the heady reform-inspired days of the 1970s was a natural progression. With his turtleneck sweaters, blue jeans, and fondness for bicycles over cars, Sewell, a youthful thirty-seven, might be remembered as Toronto's most radical mayor since William Lyon Mackenzie in 1834. Yet he did not see himself that way then or now and firmly disputes such a characterization. Instead, he considered himself a "good administrator," though he held some specific ideas about what made a great city.

For Sewell, like Crombie, this meant putting the needs of people ahead of the considerations of business, traffic, and sports stadiums. He insists that he was not anti-development; "developers always knew where I stood," he maintains. Rather, as a disciple of Jane Jacobs, he advocated affordable downtown housing, both privately developed and subsidized by the city; a more efficiently operated TTC; and commercial development—as long as it made sense. Controversy, nevertheless, trailed him throughout his two-year term, especially after he challenged the Toronto police force's treatment of the black community and when he took a progressive stand—at least for 1980—on such social issues as gay rights.

In the weeks leading up to the election on November 13, 1978, Sewell felt confident. His two main opponents were Tony O'Donohue, who had also challenged Crombie, and Alderman David Smith (who was appointed a senator in 2002). Sewell was the most left-wing of the three. O'Donohue, the more right-wing, was best known as a staunch defender of the small group of Toronto Island residents who were then in the midst of a lengthy and bitter feud with Metro, which was intent on evicting them and redeveloping Ward's and Algonquin Islands. As a populist, Sewell championed the Islanders' cause as well.

During the campaign, Sewell held Sunday afternoon walks. "The first walk had a couple of hundred people," he recalls. "The second walk more, and the last walk had five or six thousand people. That was ten days before the election. I felt like I was going to win." His reading of the electorate's mood was correct. On election day he won with more than 71,000 votes over O'Donohue in second with 62,173 and Smith, who received 45,071 votes. While later assessments suggested that Smith siphoned off key votes from O'Donohue that would have put him in first place, the *Globe and Mail* argued that Sewell's victory was no "fluke." It was, the paper suggested, "the result of a vigorously waged campaign among three well-known and well-liked candidates. Of the three, Mr. Sewell was the best-known, the best-liked and the most-disliked." Indeed, Sewell was one of the more brilliant and fascinating individuals ever to lead the city, yet by inclination and temperament he was a polarizing figure.

Sewell's chief nemesis was Paul Godfrey, another young, bright, and diligent visionary who had a decidedly different vision for Toronto. The product of hard-working Jewish parents, Godfrey grew up in the Kensington Market neighbourhood before the family migrated to North York. When Godfrey was twenty-five, his mother, Bess, who had become involved in municipal politics, convinced him to run for a seat on the North York city council—and he won. Nine years later, in 1973, when he was only thirty-four years old, he was appointed the chairman of Metro, a position he held until 1984. "I don't know how that quite happened," he says today. "I was outspoken, young and trying to raise my profile. I felt I had to be in the middle of things."

That he was. In the seventies, his most notable coup was first convincing Premier Bill Davis to contribute $8.5 million, half the amount required to upgrade Exhibition Stadium so that Toronto could attempt to acquire a major league baseball team, and then selling baseball commissioner Bowie Kuhn on the idea of expanding the league to Toronto. Working closely with Labatt Breweries; financier R. Howard Webster, the chairman of the *Globe and Mail*; and the Canadian Imperial Bank of Commerce, Godfrey was as responsible as anyone for the birth of the Toronto Blue Jays in 1977 and for the construction of SkyDome, which opened in 1989. (His four-year-old son Rob had the honour of throwing the ceremonial pitch at the Blue Jays' snowy debut on April 7, 1977.) In later years, Godfrey was directly involved with the *Toronto Sun* newspaper, the *National Post*, the Ontario Lottery and Gaming Commission (a position he was forced out of in 2013), and most recently the Postmedia Network (which acquired CanWest's newspaper chain in 2010).

He and Sewell could both claim to love Toronto and its citizens. But whereas Sewell concerned himself with TTC passes and money for daycares, Godfrey wanted to revisit the Spadina Expressway and enhance the city's sports venues. Thirty years later, in an interview with the *Star*, Sewell was still railing against Godfrey's political connections to the Progressive Conservatives, the use of taxpayers' funds to build sports stadiums, and the sins of capitalism. Godfrey, not surprisingly, dismissed his comments as wrong.

Sewell set the tone for their relationship on election night. Godfrey was working as a guest analyst on CFTO with Fraser Kelly. "As we came on air, Kelly says we are going right to Sewell headquarters and he wanted me to first congratulate Sewell for his victory," Godfrey recalls. "So I say, 'Congratulations, John, on being elected mayor. CFTO has declared you the mayor.' He says, 'Who is this?' I replied, 'It's Paul Godfrey.' His response, 'Oh, I want to get rid of you.'" Sewell repeated this objective to the press, indicating that the first item on his agenda was to try to unseat Godfrey, who in another month was up for reappointment as the chair of Metro. "I think we can do better," Sewell announced. (According to Jean Sonmor in her history of the *Toronto Sun*, in 1974 Godfrey started secretly advising the *Sun*'s editors on which city politicians the newspaper should support at election time. Ironically, more than once he chose Sewell. "I deplored his politics," he told Sonmor. "But he was an untiring worker and quite bright.")

Godfrey's reappointment as Metro chair was never in doubt, and the two men were soon arguing about the TTC, closed-door meetings on matters of public importance—which Sewell said should be open—police shootings, and treatment of blacks, gays, and other minorities in the city. Godfrey could and did wield his power as he saw fit: he and other members of Metro council, for instance, ensured Sewell did not sit on the Metro-TTC transit committee, though Godfrey later appointed Sewell to a special committee studying the future of transportation in Metro Toronto.

The protracted Toronto Islands issue was another point of conflict. Sewell supported the few hundred residents, while Godfrey, representing the view held by a majority of Metro councillors, wanted to evict them and transform the islands into a place of leisure and amusement for everyone. For decades the islands were the summer playground for Torontonians of every class. In the late thirties, the city, which owned the land, permitted a small group of individuals, who had been pitching tents on Ward's Island, to construct cottages there, and allowed another group to relocate houses from Hanlan's Point to Algonquin Island. The residents signed long-term leases with the city that led to the development of a tiny, tight-knit, year-round island community. Adequate transportation back and forth to the mainland, particularly in the winter, was always a problem; for a time the islanders were dependent on tugboats.

Questions about the residents' future were raised soon after control of the islands was transferred from the City of Toronto to Metro in 1956. For the next twenty-five years, the frazzled residents lived under the constant threat of mass eviction by a succession of Metro leaders who envisioned a redevelopment of the type that eventually did take place on Centre Island—parks, amusements, and lowbrow restaurants. Throughout this period, countless ominous declarations were made and votes taken that deemed the leases of the residents on Ward's and Algonquin Islands were to be terminated. At public meetings, the islanders were routinely labelled as "selfish, or transient or greedy," while they portrayed themselves as "historic," "colourful," and "unique." The powerful Metro parks commissioner Tommy Thompson, who served (or, rather, ruled) in that capacity from 1955 to 1981, was the residents' most ardent detractor; at one point he promoted building a par-3 golf course on Algonquin Island.

In 1969, in the age of citizen participation, the residents, aided by such reformers as Crombie, Sewell, O'Donohue, and Jane Jacobs, organized an effective lobby. One of those who rose to the forefront of the Toronto Island Residents Association (TIRA) was journalist (and later CBC radio personality) Peter Gzowski, who had owned a cottage on the island since 1964. (The residents' cause was also given prominence on the popular CBC-TV drama of the 1980s, *Street Legal*, since the left-leaning lawyer on the show, Leon Robinovitch—played by actor Eric Peterson—lived on Ward's Island.) TIRA launched a series of legal challenges, and the courts granted the residents reprieves, though these stays of execution always only delayed the evictions, never lifted the threat permanently.

When John Sewell became mayor, efforts were underway to convince the province to transfer control of Ward's and Algonquin Islands from Metro back to the city, which held a more favourable view of the residents' rights. Paul Godfrey, who was working to expand the Toronto Island airport, adamantly opposed and fought such a move, among other proposed solutions. The province decided to delay its decision by setting up a one-man commission, headed by lawyer Barry Swadron, to investigate further. On Dominion Day, July 1, 1980, Sewell, accompanied by Jane Jacobs, appeared at a rally on Ward's Island. Speaking in front of a huge banner proclaiming "We Will Not Be Moved," he painted Metro as a "destroyer" of communities and declared that "the Toronto Island community is here to stay." Likewise, Jacobs told the boisterous crowd of two thousand supporters that it was "wicked" to destroy such a "lovable" and "unique" community. Godfrey was definitely the villain of the day, and in a revised verse of "O Canada," the crowd sang: "Oh island homes, on Trawnna's fair island; Save island homes from Godfrey's heartless band." Three weeks later, the Ontario Supreme Court decided that Metro's eviction writs, issued eighteen months earlier, were valid and could be served on the 252 Islands homeowners (of a total population of about 700).

That was not the end of this David and Goliath battle. On July 28, 1980, York County sheriff's officers showed up with eviction notices. The islanders had been on high alert on "bicycle and binocular patrols," as the *Star* reported. A peaceful standoff ensued. "We're 700 people, 200 of them are children, with no place to go and no compensation," said Elizabeth Amer, who was a member of TIRA. "It's a desperate situation." The officer in charge, Acting Sheriff Joseph Bremner, was moved enough by such pleas to give the residents another twenty-four hours. Meanwhile, the islanders' lawyer, Peter Atkinson, made his case for an appeal of the court's decision, which was granted and which delayed the matter yet again.

This scene was soon followed by Barry Swadron's recommendation that the current residents be permitted to remain in their homes for another twenty-five years, until 2005. Premier Davis and his cabinet accepted Swadron's proposal, and on December 9, 1981, the communities on Ward's and Algonquin Islands were saved. To say that Godfrey was angry is an understatement. He vowed to "wage an all-out war to block the legislation," as the *Globe and Mail* reported. The fight continued after both Sewell and Godfrey were out of politics, and was finally resolved in the residents' favour in 1993 with the passage of the Toronto Islands Residential Community Stewardship Act, which enabled the residents of Ward's and Algonquin Islands to obtain ninety-nine-year leases from a land trust.

SEWELL AND GODFREY also clashed over the actions and attitudes of the Metropolitan Toronto Police Force. Though not uncritical, Godfrey generally held the police in high regard and was prepared to give them the benefit of the doubt; Metro's safety and security depended on it. Sewell (who later wrote a book about urban policing in Canada), on the other hand, believed that the force was in need of serious reform.

Among numerous controversial cases that the police handled poorly was the arrest of nurse Susan Nelles, who was charged in March 1981 in the deaths of four babies, among thirty-six who had died at the Hospital for Sick Children in a nine-month period during 1980 and 1981. Following autopsies, it was determined that many of the infants had high levels of digoxin, a cardiac drug, in their systems. Desperate to find someone to blame, the police focused on Nelles, a petite twenty-six-year-old nurse, who remained composed when questioned and asked to speak to a lawyer. The police inexplicably deemed that her calm demeanour and request for counsel were proof of guilt, and Crown lawyers supported this rush to judgment. At the time Nelles was arrested, Attorney General Roy McMurtry was travelling with his family. As he recalled in an interview in April 2007, upon his retirement as Chief Justice of Ontario, he was livid with the police and the prosecutors when he returned and learned what had transpired.

More than a year later, the case fell apart for the simple reason that there was no evidence against Nelles, a conclusion shared by Judge Samuel Grange in his Royal Commission report about the deaths. Nevertheless, police chief Jack Ackroyd refused to state publicly that Nelles was no longer a suspect, even when asked to do so by Nelles's lawyer. And as the Grange inquiry was ending in the fall of 1984, Staff Sergeant Jack Press, who had arrested Nelles, in a classic example of tunnel vision maintained that he still believed she was responsible for the death of at least one of the babies. Nelles sued the police and McMurtry for malicious prosecution and settled with the police for $190,000 and the province for $60,000. Another suspect at the hospital was nurse Phyllis Trayner, yet she was never charged.

Grange's finding that perhaps as many as twenty-three of the babies were murdered left suspicions that someone who worked at the hospital was culpable. More than three decades later, the deaths remain a mystery, though it is probable that no crime was ever committed. According to a 2011 book about the case by retired London (Ontario) doctor Gavin Hamilton, several factors likely contributed to the deaths, most notably Mercaptobenzothiazole or MBT, a chemical compound found in the rubber seals of IV lines and plastic syringes. The digoxin medical authorities believed they had found in the infants' blood was more than likely MBT.

Another flashpoint of the Sewell–Godfrey era was the killing of Albert Johnson, a thirty-five-year-old Jamaican immigrant, who had arrived in Toronto in 1971.

On the night of August 26, 1979, the police received a call about a man who was acting "in an abusive and disorderly manner" in an alley near Ossington Avenue and Bloor Street. When police constables William Inglis and Walter Cargnelli arrived to investigate, among the six officers who responded to the call, they drove up the back lane to a house on Manchester Avenue in a lower-middle-class neighbourhood. There they found Albert Johnson, who lived in the house with his wife, Lemonica, and their four children, talking to a neighbour, Alexander Dataky. Johnson, described as a "simple man," had been in trouble with the law in Jamaica, and he also had a history with the Toronto police; his wife had called the police about his violent behaviour on several occasions. Those incidents convinced the police that Johnson was the troublemaker they were searching for.

According to Dataky, the police broke down the fence gate. Fearing the worst, Johnson ran ahead of them and bolted his back door shut. His wife was standing in the kitchen. The officers kicked open the back door and told Johnson that he was under arrest. Johnson claimed he had done nothing wrong. The police said he had been disturbing the peace. Lemonica told her husband to go with the officers, but he refused. A scuffle broke out beside the stove, and he threw a pot of hot rice and beans at the constables. They, in turn, beat Johnson with their batons. His head started bleeding. Johnson managed to run up the stairs, and his wife followed him to check on their ten-year-old daughter, Michelle.

There are differing accounts of what happened next. Johnson appeared at the top of the stairs and threw a bottle of disinfectant at the officers. He started moving down towards them, and the police shouted to each other that he had an axe in his hand. In fact, it was a lawn edger. Johnson's seven-year-old daughter, Colsie, was watching. The officers ordered Johnson to kneel. When he did, Colsie said, they shot him. He died several hours later at the Toronto Western Hospital. Immediately, police officials dismissed Colsie's eyewitness account. "She's seven years old, not a credible person," said Inspector Robert Stirling. He maintained that Johnson had attacked the officers—Constable Cargnelli was said to have a scrape on his neck—and defended the conduct of the two constables, whose "lives were in danger."

Johnson was the eighth person killed by the police in just over a year. Another questionable shooting involved Andrew "Buddy" Evans, a twenty-four-year-old black man shot at the Flying Disco Tavern on King Street West after a brawl with police. In the melee, Evans, who was tall and strong, had grabbed Constable John Clark's billy club and hit him on the head with it. Dazed, Clark had warned Evans to put the baton down. When Evans refused, Clark fired at Evans, killing him. Following an inquest that lasted more than a year, no charges were laid against Clark, who it was concluded had acted appropriately.

Since Toronto's earliest days, relations between the police and the city's minorities were rarely without tension. Prejudice and discrimination were endemic on the Toronto force as they were on every police force in Canada. This was a reflection of the intolerant attitudes prevalent in Canada even after multiculturalism was made official federal government policy in 1971. It was also a result of the fact that, until recently, members of visible minorities did not seek employment on police forces.

All too representative of police attitudes were two controversial articles in the March 1979 edition of the Metropolitan Toronto Police Association's magazine *News and Views*. In one, Staff Sergeant Tom Moclair, who had been a police officer for more than two decades, wrote about "the homosexual fad," in which he referred to gays as "weirdos," "fruits," and "fags," who "smell like polecats." He concluded, "It is impossible to condone, let alone sympathize with homosexuality." Homosexual acts, he added, "are not voluntary acts. They are sick, volitionally despicable actions. If society is to allow and promote homosexuality, why not condone murder, assault and rape?" In the second article, Ken Peglar, a retired officer, wrote that "nobody expects a black man to think of anything except his colour or a Jew to consider anything but his Jewishness. And you know something, they seldom do." Human rights advocates were highly critical of the police association for publishing these two pieces, as was *Globe and Mail* columnist Dick Beddoes, who called them "a hateful smear of hate." Given that gay rights had yet to be accepted by mainstream Canada, Peglar's article received more attention than Moclair's, but initially police officials defended both men.

In the case of Moclair, deputy police chief Jack Ackroyd (who was promoted to chief some months later) inexplicably stated that there was no evidence Moclair "had exhibited bigotry in his work" and that the officer "had a right to his opinion." The *Toronto Sun* also defended the officers and the police journal's right to freedom of expression. Finally, after more than a week of criticism in the other newspapers and from human rights organizations, police chief Harold Adamson conceded that the opinions in the association journal were not the views of the police force. His apology was strained, however.

The black community had a different take. "Being Black in Toronto," sociologist Frances Henry wrote in her history of the Canadian Caribbean community, "automatically meant having to face racism." Or, put another way by Beverley Folkes, a community legal representative, in a 1989 report: "I am black. I never became aware that I was black until I set foot on the shores of this country." Despite Ontario human rights legislation passed during the seventies, a black person trying to rent an apartment in Toronto faced almost insurmountable obstacles. Landlords routinely told prospective black renters that their buildings had no vacancies, only to rent apartments to white tenants an hour later. The police were accused of using the word "nigger" in their dealings with black citizens and with their own few black colleagues, and there was probably not a black man in Metro Toronto who at one time or another had not been hassled by a police officer. Henry Gomez, otherwise known as King Cosmos, an acclaimed musician, was an immigrant from Trinidad who worked his way through school in the seventies driving a taxi. Gomez liked to dress well and was probably the sharpest cab driver in Toronto in 1975. From the police point of view, however, a black man in fine clothes had to be either a pimp or a drug dealer. One night he was arbitrarily arrested, only to have the charges dropped due to a lack of evidence.

Just standing on a street corner was enough to provoke a confrontation, as Michael Thompson recalls. Thompson, who came to Toronto from Jamaica as a young boy in the early seventies, is today a respected city councillor and vice-chair of the Toronto Police Services Board. As a Scarborough teenager, though, he and his friends, most from relatively well-off families, stayed out of trouble but still attracted the unwanted attention of the police. Two incidents stand out in his memory. Once he was with his friends on Yonge Street, minding his own business, when he was attacked by a plainclothes police officer. "He just picked me," recalls Thompson. "He started swearing at me, F-this and that. I had done nothing." On another occasion, he and his buddies were having a bite at a restaurant on Bloor near Dundas. After they had finished eating, they walked to the front to pay their bill. One of his friends, Clyde Walters, had to use the washroom. "All of a sudden, we heard this great big commotion and we saw Clyde and a policeman wrestling on the floor," he remembers. "We were seventeen, four or five black guys in this whole place. What had happened was that there was a police officer in the restaurant. The waitress had returned to the table, saw Clyde exiting the washroom, and accused him of not paying his bill. She complained to the officer and this led to the fight. More policemen arrived. They arrested Clyde, took him to the station, and beat him up."

Albert Johnson's family was also subjected to racist phone calls and hate mail; one persistent caller told his wife, "We are coming back for the rest of you black bastards." The Ontario Provincial Police were assigned to investigate the Johnson shooting, but that was not good enough for welder Dudley Laws, another Jamaican immigrant. Until his death in 2011, he was an outspoken critic of the Toronto police and in 1988 was one of the founders of the Black Action Defence Committee. In the aftermath of Johnson's death, he and many other members of the approximately 100,000-member black community accused the police force of blatant racism and organized several protest marches.

By early September, in an unusual move, former mayor Philip Givens, the head of the Metro Toronto Police Commission, with the support of Paul Godfrey, asked Gerald Emmett Cardinal Carter, the archbishop of Toronto, to serve as mediator and review the use of firearms by the police. Sewell had not been consulted on the appointment, and while he was surprised by it, he suggested the cardinal would need help. He added in a comment to the press that there was "no magical solution to the racial tension that [had] developed between police and some members of the community." Givens and Godfrey stood up for the police, emphasizing the daily threat of violence they faced. The implication was that by his actions, Johnson was somehow responsible for what happened to him. "Those who insist on violence and confrontation with the police," said Godfrey, "must expect police to react in such a way as to maintain the peace."

A few days later, Sewell and Godfrey became embroiled in yet another public argument after Sewell, in a fiery speech to insurance executives, criticized the Metro Police Commission for being "irresponsible and insensitive to the community it says it is trying to serve and protect." He also declared that Albert Johnson's death was "the result of systematic behaviour by the policing agency, representing either a racist attitude or a shoot-first attitude or both." Those remarks incensed Godfrey. He denounced the mayor, saying "[Sewell] distorts the fact, makes statements of half-truth and no-truth [and] issues charges with no substantiation." A majority of Toronto aldermen agreed, and a week later in a 12–9 vote censured Sewell for his "inflammatory" and "inappropriate" comments. After his anger subsided, however, Godfrey agreed with Sewell that there should be an independent review of the complaints against the police force. Ontario attorney general Roy McMurtry concurred and established an independent civilian review board of police matters, which was rightly interpreted as a vote of non-confidence in the Metro Police Commission.

Cardinal Carter's report, delivered at the end of October 1979, highlighted some serious problems within the police force, though Godfrey and police officials regarded the report favourably. Among other reforms, Carter recommended more foot patrols and an improved procedure for handling complaints against the police, and he urged the chief to prohibit racist and verbal abuse of citizens, which he found to be "prevalent." According to Sewell, the cardinal told the police chief that "his officers should not call black officers 'niggers,' even in jest."

Neither the deaths of Buddy Evans and Albert Johnson, nor the astute recommendations of Cardinal Carter marked the end of the issue. Between 1980 and 2010, twelve more black men of African or Caribbean descent were killed by the police, prompting politicians and community activists to demand further reform and a significant change in attitude among the police. Many more investigations, inquests, and reports took place before any positive change occurred—and it was never smooth.

In 2002, for instance, Devon Murray, a forty-six-year-old printer, was arrested and severely roughed up by Toronto police constable William Walker because he was black. Walker was found guilty of assault, a rare occurrence, but was given a conditional discharge. More than a decade later, in May 2013, the city's police board and service were compelled to "settle" with Clem Marshall, a retired African-Canadian teacher, after another case of racial profiling. In 2009, Marshall was driving his car, a 2009 Nissan Altima, and was pulled over by the police in Parkdale. He was told by one of the officers that "he didn't look like someone who could afford the [car] he was driving." As he handed the officer his driver's licence and registration, he asked why he had been stopped. According to Marshall, the constable shouted at him, "Who do you think you are, fucking Obama?"

AT THE SAME TIME John Sewell was fighting to quash racism in the city, he also made a pioneering declaration of support for the city's gay community. Yet with this issue, too, he confronted strong prejudices. It never has been easy to be an openly gay person in Canada, and that was certainly true in the late seventies and early eighties. If you had told Torontonians in 1979 that same-sex marriage would be legal in Canada within twenty-six years, and that the premier of Ontario in 2013, Kathleen Wynne, would be a gay woman, few would have believed you. Today, a majority of Canadians would regard Staff Sergeant Tom Moclair's depiction of homosexuality as repugnant; thirty years ago, it was widely accepted. As the federal justice minister in 1967, Pierre Trudeau took a step forward by decriminalizing homosexuality, stating that the "state has no place in the bedrooms of the nation," yet that did not translate into public or, in some cases, legal approval. At the time, gays and lesbians were not perceived to be a legitimate "minority group," so overt prejudice and discrimination against them were regarded differently and were fought with less resolve.

In Toronto, where there was a visible and growing gay community by the mid-seventies, several high-profile gay-related cases kept the issue on the front pages of the city's newspapers and on television. The 1977 sexual assault and murder of twelve-year-old Emanuel Jaques by three gay men (a forth participant was acquitted) unfairly tainted all gay men. The trial took place in the spring of 1978, a few months before the Toronto Morality Squad laid charges against Pink Triangle Press, the publishers of the gay magazine *The Body Politic*, for running an article in December 1977 about sexual relations between men and young boys.

Six months after that, the police raided the Barracks bathhouse, a gay steam room on Widmer Street near Spadina Avenue, and arrested men engaged in sexual (and S&M) encounters. Among those charged with keeping a common bawdy house was George Hislop, a leading gay spokesman and president of the Community Homophile Association of Toronto. Hislop had been indirectly linked to the Jaques murder case after one of the perpetrators, Saul Betesh, told him what had happened. He convinced Betesh to turn himself in to the police.

As a man of principle and an advocate of social justice, Mayor Sewell felt compelled to speak out. And he did on January 3, 1979, at a rally held at the University of Toronto to protest the trial of Pink Triangle Press's three owners for publishing the controversial article in *The Body Politic*. The main point of Sewell's speech—vetted by Pink Triangle Press's lawyer, Clayton Ruby, to ensure the mayor was not in contempt of court—was "It's not illegal to be gay." Before a crowd of about six hundred people, Sewell declared that it was time to ensure it was equally "legitimate" to be gay and expressed his sympathy for the "wrenching personal agony over the raid at The Barracks."

Sewell is proud of that speech, rightly pointing out that he was one of the first, if not the first, Canadian politician to stand up for gay rights. But at the time there was some fallout. With the Jaques murder and sordid reports about the S&M paraphernalia found at the Barracks still in the news, many Torontonians were not impressed by Sewell's vocal support. City hall phone operators were kept busy for days responding to more than a thousand calls criticizing the mayor's actions, some in hateful language. The *Globe and Mail*'s editors sardonically awarded Sewell "the ill-timing award of 1979"—and it was only the first week of January. Less tactful was the *Star*, which planned to run a political cartoon depicting Sewell carrying a purse on his way out of his office, and a secretary calling after him, "Mr. Sewell, you forgot your briefcase." Wisely, the paper pulled the cartoon. On the other hand, when someone challenged him about the speech at a labour meeting, the person was booed.

Even with his bluntness and forthright positions on a number of contentious matters, Sewell had a decent chance of re-election going into the November 1980 municipal contest. One widely publicized issue that did not help Sewell's public image was his visit to a live sex show while he was in Amsterdam, representing Toronto at events celebrating the liberation of the Netherlands from Nazi occupation. His defence that "I do the things every normal tourist does" did not sit well with many uptight citizens.

His real problem was that the business community, supporters of both the Liberals and the provincial Progressive Conservatives, and powerful personalities like Metro chair Paul Godfrey, had decided to give their full backing to Alderman Art Eggleton, an accountant by profession and, at thirty-seven years old, already an experienced politician. The chair of Eggleton's campaign, for example, was accountant Bill Saunderson, who was later elected as a PC to the Ontario Legislature and served in Mike Harris's cabinet. Eggleton's campaign manager was Barbara Sullivan, who was later elected as a provincial Liberal. He was feted at a $100-a-plate dinner at the Royal York Hotel hosted by former federal finance minister John Turner, who had returned to a Bay Street law practice, and Alan Eagleson, then head of the National Hockey League Players' Association.

In temperament, Sewell and Eggleton were certainly different. Sewell's "passions persuaded him to go in swinging when a more passive posture would have been more in the public interest," as the *Globe and Mail* put it. That was definitely the case for his relationship with the police force, which he continued to trade barbs with for the duration of his term. During the 1980 election campaign, there were press reports of police association officials collecting money for Eggleton, and of posters put up in precinct locker rooms with the words "flush Sewell down the drain."

But apart from the police issue—which Sewell insists was a key factor in the outcome—and perhaps his position on gay rights, he and Eggleton did not differ all that much in their political philosophy. John Piper, Sewell's campaign manager had the best line about his support for gay rights: "Nineteen-eighty," he said after the election, "was a bit too early in the twentieth century for that issue." Eggleton was merely a more conservative version of Sewell, and that was enough to give him the slight edge in the vote. On November 10, in one of the closest civic elections in Toronto's history, he defeated Sewell by a mere 1,767 votes, 87,919 to 86,152.

John Sewell went on to teach, write a newspaper column and several books on urban issues, and serve on several government commissions. In 1999 he ran as an independent in the provincial election and lost, and in 2006 he tried to regain a seat on city council but lost in that contest too. He remains a committed Torontonian, yet an ardent critic of Toronto as a "megacity." As will be seen in Chapter Twelve, he led another grassroots protest, Citizens for Local Democracy, to oppose amalgamation in the late nineties.

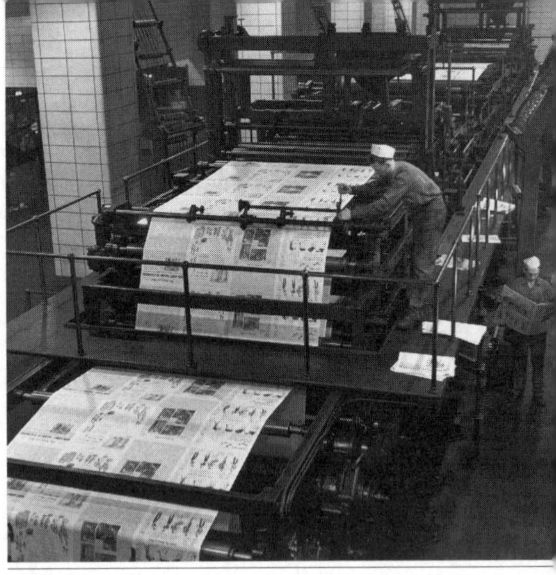

Chapter Eleven

THIS IS WHERE IT'S AT

They're jealous of our success. This is where everything is—the culture, the economy, the people.

—MAYOR MEL LASTMAN, 2002

LONG BEFORE IT WAS available from sea to sea, the *Globe and Mail* styled itself "Canada's National Newspaper." After 1938, thanks to Trans-Canada Airlines, the paper was available for sale across the country, and it began opening bureaus in Canada in the fifties and internationally soon after that. One of editor-in-chief Oakley Dalgleish's more inspired actions was opening a bureau in Peking in 1959, at a time when the American media was not permitted to have a presence in Communist China. He also shrewdly created *Report on Business*, which appeared in 1962, twice a week, before it began running daily five years later. ROB proved popular among the rising business establishment in Toronto and the rest of Canada, and even to subscribers in London, England, and was generally considered as good as or better than the popular weekly *Financial Post*, put out by Maclean Hunter, and its lesser competitor, Southam's *Financial Times*.

The *Globe and Mail*, which was established by business tycoon C. George McCullagh in 1936, has long envisioned itself as Toronto and Canada's newspaper of record. Using the latest satellite technology, the *Globe and Mail* launched its national edition, first to Montreal in 1980 and then in five more major Canadian cities. *Library and Archives Canada / Ronny Jaques*

After Dalgleish died in 1963, managing editor Richard "Dic" Doyle (who was appointed editor-in-chief in 1978), continued to expand the *Globe*'s overseas bureaus. Still, like Toronto itself, the *Globe and Mail* remained "high-minded" and a "bit stuffy," according to its biographer David Hayes. It promoted itself as Canada's *New York Times*, a "paper of record," an elitist image which was dismissed by its Toronto competitors and ignored by readers west of Sault Ste. Marie. Yet, Hayes added, the newspaper's "reputation as a force in Canadian affairs was based on the fact that it was read by agenda-setting policy makers, businesspeople, and academics, [and] its real power was it was used as a primary source by other media outlets, especially the CBC and the national wire service, Canadian Press."

The *Globe*, and, by extension, Toronto, did not gain its true national reach until publisher A. Roy Megarry, with support from new owner Ken Thomson, used the latest satellite technology to launch the *Globe*'s national edition, first to Montreal in 1980 and then in five more major Canadian cities. Besides improving the paper's bottom line, the object was also to live up to the promotion of the *Globe* as the country's "national newspaper." As executive editor Cameron Smith wrote to Megarry about a year before the national edition was a reality: "I can't speak of ad rates and truck routes. I can speak of the soul of a newspaper and the souls of those who write for her. And when I speak of them, I speak of dream and reality intertwined: the dream of a national consciousness, a national mission, sunk deep within the psyches of newsmen." Nonetheless, there was acrimony for several years in the *Globe* newsroom as not every editor or reporter appreciated Megarry's perceived meddling with editorial content or his attempt "to impose an advertiser-driven ethos on the paper," as was pointed out after he left the paper in 1991.

Within eight years, the *Globe*'s national circulation had climbed to 95,000 and then to about 135,000 by 1991. Still, more than half of the approximately 330,000 newspapers it claimed it sold (or gave away at hotels) each day—and its competitors questioned the figures—were purchased by readers who lived in or close to Toronto. By contrast, the *Star*'s daily circulation likely exceeded 400,000. The *Globe and Mail*'s national edition might not have had the overpowering impact Roy Megarry wished for (the year he left the newspaper there was a significant decline in advertising revenue), but it did give the newspaper and Toronto a higher profile across the country.

SEVERAL YEARS BEFORE the *Globe and Mail* tried to dictate national tastes from its home on Front Street West, *Maclean's* magazine had reinvented itself from a tired monthly to a weekly newsmagazine. The chief innovator was Peter C. Newman, "by a wide margin, the most gossiped-about journalist in the country," as Robert Fulford described him—or Canada's most "cussed and discussed" political journalist, as he described himself.

Born in Czechoslovakia, where his father was the wealthy owner of a sugar beet refinery and the family lived well, young Petâ Karel Neumann escaped the Holocaust and immigrated to Canada with his parents in 1940. The Newmans were assimilated Jews, and in Toronto Petâ became Peter Charles Newman. He attended Upper Canada College and embraced everything WASP Toronto had to offer. "I tried desperately to act like a WASP," he recalls in his memoirs, "to think like a WASP, to dress like a WASP. If I had thought I could get away with it, I would have worn a kilt." In time he got a job writing for the *Financial Post*, and then he joined *Maclean's*, becoming its widely read Ottawa columnist.

Newman received more attention when, at the age of thirty-four, he joined forces with Jack McClelland of McClelland & Stewart and published *Renegade in Power*, about John Diefenbaker and his government—his first national bestseller and a book that revolutionized political reporting in the country. A year later he left *Maclean's* and became the Ottawa editor of the *Toronto Star*; by 1969 his column was syndicated in thirty newspapers, including a French translation in Montreal's *La Presse*, reaching an unprecedented two million readers. Hal Dornan, Prime Minister Lester Pearson's assistant, observed in a 1966 confidential memo that his column was "in many ways more important than any combination of commentaries because it is the basis for a large number of editorials, interpretive pieces and even news stories." Newman may not have thought of himself as a representative Torontonian, but his journalistic clout, via the Toronto newspaper with the largest circulation in the country, definitely enhanced the city's media influence.

In 1969 he left his comfort zone and seat of influence in Ottawa and accepted Beland Honderich's offer to become the *Star*'s editor-in-chief. It was a less-than-ideal situation since, as Newman quickly discovered, Honderich really could not share the *Star* with anyone. "As editor-in-chief I was rightly perceived as being responsible for every item and every typo in each of the day's five editions," he remembered. "I was able to confirm my title by glancing at it, on top of the list of editors published daily on the *Star*'s masthead, but I knew that I would always have the second-to-last word. The division of editorial power would haunt my tenure."

While Newman shared Honderich's generally liberal principles, his two-year stint as the newspaper's editor came to an abrupt end after he and Honderich had a disagreement over an innocuous story about Vaughan mayor Garnet Williams. The *Star* was about to erect a state-of-the art $421-million printing plant in Vaughan, north of Toronto, and Honderich wanted to keep Williams happy. The trouble was that Williams was against every issue the *Star* supported, and Newman could not figure out anything positive to write about him. His refusal to abide by Honderich's wishes led to a sharp rift between the two men that could not be healed, and Newman resigned.

One door closed for Newman at the *Star* and another quickly opened back at *Maclean's*. In fact, Lloyd Hodgkinson, the magazine's publisher, had first approached Newman a few months before he left the *Star*. He wanted Newman to become *Maclean's* editor and his wife, the journalist Christina McCall, to become associate editor. The monthly magazine was bleeding money—it lost about $6 million between 1960 and 1970—and Hodgkinson and Newman figured the only way to save it was to recreate it as a Canadian version of *Time* magazine.

The complete overhaul took until 1978, during which time the editorial budget increased from $467,000 to close to $5 million. Newman opened up bureaus across the country and in London, England, and instilled a sense of renewed purpose in the magazine as well as the fear of God into many of his writers. "People who worked for him at *Maclean's*," according to Fulford, "discussed him obsessively, and never (in my experience) with affection. They could rage about him for hours."

Newman did not care. He had to fill forty-five pages a week with original content, and, as he recalled, "the cold-blooded logic of that deadly calculus was that everyone I hired had to produce or leave." He enlisted some of the best writers in the country—Donald Creighton, Bruce Hutchison, Hugh MacLennan, Claude Ryan, Margaret Atwood, Al Purdy, Adrienne Clarkson, Mordecai Richler, among many others—to give the magazine a new and distinctly Canadian feel. His overall plan was helped in no small measure by the federal government's decision in 1974—which he had lobbied hard for—to give tax concessions to businesses buying advertising in Canadian media. That, too, made possible the transformation of *Maclean's* from a monthly to a weekly.

Though *Maclean's* was certainly a Toronto publication, to his credit Newman immediately grasped that, if it was going to succeed, he had to "reflect the mystical nature of the Big Country beyond Toronto's cramped horizons," as he put it in an early memo he wrote for himself. One of the first things he did when he settled into his new office on University and Dundas was to mount a large map of Canada on the wall. He used coloured pins to keep track of all the non-Toronto stories appearing in the magazine. Arguments raged at planning meetings about including Toronto-centric stories and just about every other topic—politics, entertainment, and literature—but Newman persisted.

He was, in the end, only partly successful. Under Newman's firm rule, *Maclean's* did (and still does) "seek talent and sensitivities far beyond Toronto's Family Compact." It also offered its readers, as Newman announced on September 18, 1978, with the magazine's first weekly edition, "an interpretation and a response to world events that is entirely Canadian." Nevertheless, with its Toronto-based editorial staff and collective Toronto consciousness, whether it was held in check or not, *Maclean's* could not completely escape its Hogtown heritage.

NEITHER COULD NEWMAN. As he worked his magic on *Maclean's*, he was also rising each morning at 4:00 AM to write his books. In 1972 he turned away from writing in depth about politics and turned his attention to the businessmen he was now associating with in Toronto. The corporate bosses and bank CEOs were, he wrote later, "secretive, puritanical, uptight, and yet, for all their arrogance, compellingly fascinating." Newman had always been a good listener, all part of his calculating and mischievous strategy to get people to open up to him. And open up they did.

Despite initially being wary of him, everyone from J.A. "Bud" McDougald, who succeeded E.P. Taylor as chairman of Argus Corporation, to Conrad Black, who gained control of Argus following McDougald's death in 1978, spilled their stories, and sometimes their hearts, guts, and tawdry tales to Newman. He became one of them, surreptitiously taking it all in. He accompanied them to their private clubs—the Toronto, Albany, National, and York—and dined with them over two-hour lunches at Winston's Restaurant, where stars like former finance minister John Turner held court at a table perpetually reserved for him. Then Newman did what he had done so well in Ottawa, laying bare the world of politics, except now he exposed the world of the rich and powerful in all its glory in his *Canadian Establishment* books. The volumes were hugely successful, catapulting Newman to the top of the Canadian and Toronto literary scene and making boring business transactions much more fascinating.

Here's Newman in the second volume of his series, *The Acquisitors* (published in 1981), describing Winston's and its graceful owner Giovanni "John" Arena (who had acquired the restaurant in 1966) as only he can: "John Arena's artistry and the roots of his power are demonstrated in the daily dance he performs allocating the tables available on the restaurant's main floor. This is not a matter of filling them. Winston's hasn't had an empty seat in nine years. Each lunch and dinner is staged like a theatrical production (with John Arena in the starring role) to produce the desired dramatic effect... The subtleties of Winston's seating plan have about them the byzantine quality of the pecking order of Louis XIV's court at Versailles." The members of the business establishment in Toronto and other cities claimed that half the material in the books was untrue or exaggerated and cursed the writer—but were equally upset if they were not "Newmanized" and could not find their names in the books' indexes.

Newman's incisive portrait of the establishment caught on with his many readers, not only because he effectively probed the mysteries of corporate power and exposed the underbelly of this modern Family Compact—including the many overlapping links between Canadian business, politics, culture, and high society that up to then everyone except a few academics had ignored—but also because he did so at a time when this wealth and influence were manifesting themselves in Canada as they never had before—especially in Toronto. "The thing is that it used to be hard to get rich in Canada—and harder still to penetrate the preserves of those who had the money," one member of the city's old WASP money class told Christina McCall in 1976 over a roast beef lunch at the York Club (where women were permitted). "In my day you had to conform to a code, but now the country's full of millionaires nobody even knows."

NEWMAN'S VOLUMES also chronicled the gradual demise of WASP domination of Toronto, a process that had started years earlier with Nathan Phillips's election as mayor. By the early eighties, you could be Jewish or Italian, for example, and still be a macher or big shot in Toronto. In Newman's opinion, the city's "WASP hegemony" ended in 1983 with the appointment of Sydney Hermant, and then Eddie Goodman, both Jewish, as successive board chairmen of the Royal Ontario Museum—Toronto's "defining WASP institution." Hermant had built up Imperial Optical, the company he inherited from his father, Percy (who founded it in 1900). He was also one of the few Jews appointed to the board of a Canadian bank in 1960 when he became a director of the Imperial Bank of Canada, a position he held until 1983, by which time the Imperial Bank had merged with the Bank of Commerce to become the Canadian Imperial Bank of Commerce. Eddie Goodman was a Toronto lawyer and key backroom advisor and fundraiser for the Ontario Progressive Conservative Party.

A second transitional moment occurred in the fall of 1994. The Barnes Collection of Impressionist and Post-Impressionist paintings was travelling for the first time, and the Art Gallery of Ontario (AGO) was on its list of stops across North America. To celebrate this historic showing, two high-powered and Jewish Bay Street honchos, Ira Gluskin and Gerry Sheff, who ran a successful wealth management company, Gluskin Sheff & Associates, which was then celebrating its tenth anniversary, hosted one of the great parties in the city's history. They invited "1,700 of their closest friends," as the *Star*'s report of the event put it. The menu was almost sinful: vintage Pol Roger champagne, medallions of veal and racks of lamb, smoked and fresh salmon, and swordfish and halibut steaks. And for dessert, "chocolate-dipped gooseberries and individual dessert plates with five mousses, arranged as an artist's palette with a creme brule in the middle and pencil-thin wafer on the side." Gluskin and Sheff spent an estimated $1.5 million on the soiree and donated another $1 million to the AGO.

Among those privileged to attend was John Macfarlane, then the editor of *Toronto Life*. Not only did he enjoy the champagne and food, but he found the experience enlightening. "I looked around that night," he recalls, "and I realized that this was a changing of the guard. Ira and Gerry were Jews; the WASPs of Toronto, the Eatons and Westons, had never thrown a party for the city like this. If I had been an Eaton or a Weston—and they were there—I would have thought, 'We are no longer running this place anymore.' Other people are running it, Jews, Italians, Poles, and Austrians."

Typical of this new breed, an "ethnic" star of Bay Street, was Andrew Sarlos, a Hungarian immigrant who came to Toronto during the 1956 anti-Soviet revolution. As a student, he had tried to defect to Yugoslavia and was imprisoned for a year. Once he was in Toronto, he became a chartered accountant and briefly worked in Labrador for Bechtel Canada. A self-confessed gambler, he left the safe confines of his administrative jobs and started his own investment company. "If I was in the market only for the money,

I would have quit long ago. I am an advisor but, I must confess, I don't always take my advice. If I had, I'd be much wealthier," he wrote in his autobiography.

Maybe so, but he was a big-time winner. By 1981, the value of funds in his company, HCI Holdings Ltd., was about $700 million, making him one of the most highly regarded wizards at the Toronto Stock Exchange, on Bay Street, and across North America. Each morning, as far away as Zurich, brokers were said to have asked, "What's Andy up to?" Sarlos was a truly decent soul but could go for the jugular. "Good traders," he declared, "rely on what they hear; great traders assimilate the facts, then act on the basis of their gut instincts and sheer nerve. Balls are as important as brains."

When he died suddenly in 1997 at the age of sixty-five from heart failure, his friend Peter Munk, founder of Barrick Gold and another wealthy and influential Hungarian immigrant to the city (he had escaped Nazi-occupied Hungary in 1944 and come to Toronto three years later), said Sarlos "was a giant of a man, a real prince who never said an evil word about anybody, and was more interested in making money for others than for himself."

Moses Znaimer, Zen master, guru, impresario, and "Canadian media visionary" (as his website describes him), took a different path to fame and fortune. He had enormous faith in Toronto's potential to rise above its penchant for provincialism and refused to sacrifice his integrity or creativity. A 1974 newspaper story accurately portrayed him as "a curious blend of ego, chutzpah, [and] inventiveness and... one of TV's rare Original Thinkers." More than three decades later, when he was inducted into the Canadian Broadcast Hall of Fame in 2007, Jay Switzer, head of CHUM Television, who was mentored by Znaimer, said that he had that rare combination among Canadian broadcasters: "creative brilliance and business acumen." In a class by himself, he is still, in his seventies, an entrepreneurial businessman and the founder and head of ZoomerMedia, a company that caters to well-off, aging baby boomers.

Even as a child, Znaimer had a media presence. The cover of *The Standard Review* magazine for June 26, 1948, had a large photograph of two young, smiling, Jewish refugees, who had survived the horrors of the Second World War and landed in Halifax with their families to start a new life. The little girl in the photo was Nasha Rosenberg (now Norma Kirsh) and the boy with the Red Cross sign tied to his coat was six-year-old Moses Znaimer. They had found each other on the voyage over from Europe aboard the SS *Marine Falcon*, a converted U.S. Navy supply ship.

In 1942, Znaimer's parents, Aron and Chaya, had met while fleeing from Nazi-occupied eastern Europe. They made it to Kulyab, Tajikistan, in central Asia, then part of the Soviet Union. Moses was born soon after they got there. After the war ended, the family snuck back to Poland and then to a displaced person's camp in Kassel, southwest of Berlin, in a region of Germany controlled by the Americans. Their only surviving relative lived in Montreal, and he helped them emigrate to Canada. Aron Znaimer worked in a shoe store and Chaya as a waitress. They instilled in Moses and his siblings, Libby, a well-known television personality, and Sam, a Vancouver-based venture capitalist, the desire to achieve.

Znaimer's university education, a mixture of ideas and practicality, paved the way for his career path. He received a BA in philosophy at McGill and a master's degree at Harvard in government. A job in the media suited his personality. In the late sixties he joined the CBC as the popular host of the radio program *Cross Country Checkup* and then co-hosted the television show *Take 30* with future governor general Adrienne Clarkson. A disciple of Marshall McLuhan—in many ways, he was more "McLuhanesque" than McLuhan himself—Znaimer was stifled by CBC's bureaucracy and structure. Ahead of his time, he conceived of television's potential impact and influence on a much broader canvas than almost anyone else of his generation. He later articulated his mantra this way: "It's my view the battle for hearts and minds will be won by those who recognize that television is not a problem to be managed, but an instrument to be played." And he was a virtuoso.

He resigned from the CBC and soon became part of a pioneering consortium, the brainchild of Alberta journalist and television executive Phyllis Switzer (the mother of Jay Switzer), lawyer (and later senator) Jerry Grafstein, and Ed Cowan, the head of public relations firm Carleton, Cowan. In late 1971, the CRTC granted them a licence for a UHF frequency channel, then little used, in Toronto. They raised $2 million and from a studio on Queen Street East launched Citytv, channel 79, on September 28, 1972—opposite the decisive and nail-biting game eight of the Canada–Soviet Summit hockey series (which most of their staff watched). That didn't matter. Citytv was as hip, cool, and popular as Znaimer, its thirty-something program director and creative genius, who told the *Globe and Mail* in November 1974 that "the most significant thing is that my name is not John Bassett, E.P. Taylor or Beland H. Honderich."

From the start, the new station prided itself on providing forty-two hours of original programming each week, at a time when CBC and CTV were running nothing close to that number. Znaimer put the first business show on television, *The Money Game*; gave an unheard-of two and a half hours to local news; and made stars of such TV personalities as Brian Linehan, Dr. Morton Shulman, and Jeanne Beker. Yet what got Znaimer and Citytv the most notoriety was the decision to run adult, albeit artistic, films each Friday night at midnight on *Baby Blue Movies*. Though the station was kept busy dealing with complaints and frequent visits from the morality squad, thousands of uninhibited Torontonians tuned in. (One of the station's earliest hits was the racy BBC series *Casanova*, which featured more "bare bosom and buttock shots" than had ever been seen on Canadian television.) Znaimer made no apologies then or ever. "Toronto is a sophisticated city and we will have sophisticated programs," he had declared in June 1972. He spent the next four decades proving that point and "seeking out the different."

In 1981, CHUM bought Citytv and made Znaimer a vice-president and executive producer of the station's programming. A few years later, CHUM moved its operations to the old Ryerson Press building on Queen Street West, which immediately became what Znaimer called "the temple of television." His imagination took off again; he understood specialty television before most of his industry rivals, and in time he established twenty-two stations, including MuchMusic (with John Martin), Bravo!, Space, FashionTelevision, and BookTelevision, before his initial retirement in 2003. Because he always believed that television had to be a two-way communication between a network and its viewers, he created Speaker's Corner beside the CHUM building, which enabled everyone and anyone to record their feedback or rants, or even sing a song. In the pre-Internet age, before Facebook and YouTube made such commentary the norm, Speaker's Corner was an instant sensation, just the way Moses Znaimer envisioned it.

THERE WAS MONEY to be made in Toronto, and lots of it in land development, construction, the transportation industry, oil, mining, and the burgeoning retail business, as Christina McCall noted in a 1976 *Saturday Night* article. With wealth came prestige and extravagance. Hence, the sumptuous dinners at Winston's and the emergence of Bay and Bloor as a shopping mecca where a Saturday afternoon outing with mandatory stops at Cartier, Birks, and Creeds knew no bounds.

Still, as McCall understood more than most female journalists, in the halls of power on Bay Street, at the staid Albany and York clubs, as well as in newsrooms, Toronto remained largely a man's world. True, the feminist movement was making waves, and more women were beginning to enter traditional male professions like law, politics, and academia. At the University of Toronto, women were finally admitted to Hart House, the university's co-curricular centre, in 1972. And a year later, in another first, the U of T appointed Jill Ker Conway the vice-president of internal affairs, a position she held for two years. (At the same time, male faculty objected mightily to the university funding a new daycare on campus.) Author Margaret Atwood, thirty-three years old, was featured on the cover of *Saturday Night* for the first time in November 1972. She had already published two novels, *The Edible Woman* and *Surfacing*, which had made her one of the most significant and talked-about writers in the country, a voice for women and cultural nationalism. To that end, she was one of the founders of the Writers' Union of Canada in 1973. In typical Canadian fashion, the *Report of the Royal Commission on the Status of Women*, published in December 1970, received all the attention, even if it merely confirmed what everyone already knew. The commissioners found that there were few women in managerial positions and that, despite provincial pay equity laws, a majority of women in the workforce still were paid less than their male counterparts for the exact same jobs. McCall was a sharp critic of the report, arguing that it "was so lacking in passion that it might be a report on freight rates." Several years later she wrote, "In real life, in Canada, the ideal role for women was to be wife and mother with an impeccably run household, its food cellar stocked with preserves, its laundry whiter than the neighbours', and its children better than good. Any woman who didn't fit this circumscribed pattern was an 'old maid.'"

She broke that mould, however. Born in Toronto in 1935 into a middle-class family, McCall was ambitious, bright, and creative, with a style all her own. Upon her death in 2005, her first husband, Peter C. Newman, aptly and lovingly described her as "the quintessential WASP *shiksa* who never misplaced her captivating aura." She attended the University of Toronto in the fifties and, despite its stuffiness, embraced her various studies, especially her classes with the already acclaimed English scholar Northrop Frye. She was initially skeptical of Frye's stellar reputation, but as she later recalled, she quickly discovered after sitting through the first lecture he presented at the start of her third year that he really was "that good."

With the idea of being a writer, McCall took a job at *Maclean's* in 1956 as an editorial secretary—which she soon learned meant fetching coffee and train tickets rather than editing articles—for the low weekly salary of $45. Pierre Berton, the magazine's managing editor, remembered her as a "pudgy jill-of-all-trades," while she remembered Berton as "a managing editor with the ego as big as his libido roar." Unwilling to be relegated to a role as an assistant for male journalists, she persevered and was soon writing articles for *Maclean's* and, later, the *Globe and Mail*, *Saturday Night*, and *Chatelaine*. She also wrote several political bestsellers, including *Grits: An Intimate Portrait of the Liberal Party* (1982), still regarded as one of the most penetrating Canadian political analyses ever published. McCall ultimately became "the star woman journalist of her time," as Eleanor Wachtel of CBC called her, "a gifted dame in a man's world." Respect from Toronto's male-dominated culture often remained elusive, however.

Early in October 1974, McCall and Newman, the influential journalistic couple of the day, were invited to a dinner party at the Forest Hill home of Brigadier Richard S. "Dick" Malone, publisher of the *Globe and Mail* (Malone had been the publisher of the *Winnipeg Free Press* and was an executive of FP Publications, which owned the *Globe* from 1965 to 1980). Newman was then the editor of *Maclean's*, and McCall was a member of his editorial board and contributing insightful political pieces about the first years of the Trudeau era. She was not all that keen on attending the dinner, which she anticipated would be a "bloody bore." The Brigadier was, by all accounts, a knowledgeable newspaper proprietor who lived in the past, revelled in all things British, and enjoyed a good war story. The guest that evening was the seasoned Victoria-based journalist Bruce Hutchison, whom Newman and McCall were acquainted with.

After a dinner of "acceptable" food and "splendid" wine, as McCall later described it, Hutchison inquired of Newman for the inside news and gossip on Trudeau and his government. Malone had stepped out of the dining room momentarily. Newman told Hutchison that he had not been to Ottawa for many months, but that McCall had recently returned and she should be the one to explain the situation. She proceeded to relate the conflict then ongoing between Trudeau and his finance minister, John Turner.

"Just as I got to a particularly affecting piece of news about what Turner's deputy minister thought of [Marc] Lalonde's social welfare ideas, our host came back into the room," she writes. "Hutchison, eyes bright with interest, turned to him and called out, 'Dick, come quick and sit down. Peter is telling me some fascinating stuff about what's going on in Ottawa.' All three men began to immediately discuss sagaciously the implications of what had just been said—without ever acknowledging the fact that I was the one who had said it—while I sat there holding my demitasse so tightly I thought it would shatter in my hands. Nearly an hour later, when we made our own goodbyes—and the publisher and the editor had each pecked me on the cheek and remarked on how lovely I certainly looked—I was still in a state of shock."

There were other female journalistic stars as well. June Callwood, eleven years older than McCall, had begun writing for the *Globe and Mail* in 1942. In a career that spanned more than five decades, she churned out columns, magazine articles (for *Maclean's*, among other publications), and books on every conceivable subject. After she married Trent Frayne, also a *Globe* writer, she was compelled to keep her maiden name because it would have been unacceptable to the newspaper's readers to have a husband and wife on staff at a time when married women were expected to stay home. Nonetheless, she became a staple of the Toronto media and a high-profile social activist.

A different type of female journalist was Diane Francis, who immigrated to Toronto in 1965 with her husband, Frank. A decade later she decided to become a journalist and by 1981 had been hired by the *Toronto Star* as a business writer, the first woman to cover that beat. She was soon wooed away from the *Star* to the new *Sun* by its publisher, a very determined Paul Godfrey, who made her an offer she could not refuse. In addition to writing for the *Sun*, he also arranged for her to write columns for *Maclean's* and the *Financial Post*.

The *Sun* was ahead of its time: Barbara Amiel, another writer with a conservative bent who cut her teeth as a features writer for Newman's *Maclean's* in the seventies, joined the *Sun* as columnist in 1981. Two years later, the British-born Amiel was appointed editor, the first woman to hold such a position in Canada. In 1985 she left the *Sun* and

Toronto, returning to London, where she wrote first for the *Times* and, following her marriage in 1992 to media baron Conrad Black, for the *Daily Telegraph*—acquired by Black in 1985. Meanwhile, Francis, who for a time was writing columns for *Maclean's*, the *Sun*, and the *Financial Post*, was named the *Post*'s editor in 1991.

Even as these talented female journalists, and other women, were breaking through barriers, the only women who truly seemed to count in Toronto in the late seventies and eighties were the wealthy wives of the city's business elite, whose prime objective was to raise hundreds of thousands of dollars for hospitals, schools, and other worthy charities at extravagant balls and lavish fundraisers—and to look fabulous doing so. The more media attention they received—feature stories, magazine covers, mentions of their comings and goings in the society pages—the better. Reflecting the changes in the business community, these women, too, were a new breed. Some were WASP, others were Jewish and "ethnic," a reflection of the expansion of the city's upper-class structure. Rosemary Sexton, the former *Globe and Mail* society columnist, immortalized them as the "glitter girls" in her 1993 book, which chronicles their significant contributions as well as their colourful antics and gossipy sniping. (According to Sexton, most of the women she wrote about still talked to her after the book appeared, but not all.) Operating in an era of excess, when the money amassed on Bay Street was enormous, "the Toronto socialites reached the apex of their power," wrote Sexton. "Their galas were numerous and opulent, their gowns expensive and glamorous, their networks ever expanding, and their ball profits enormous."

Among the group of Forest Hill, Rosedale, and Bridle Path hostesses was the late Patricia Appleton, whose husband, Michael, is managing partner at the law firm Fogler Rubinoff; the late Anna Maria de Souza, who once dated Conrad Black and whose second husband was the investment banker Ivan de Souza; Catherine Nugent, a true Rosedale diva, who is said to have gone through $2 million given to her by her first husband, Crown attorney Stephen Leggett, in two years, and whose second husband is David Nugent, a cosmetics and fashion entrepreneur; Carole Grafstein, whose husband, Jerry, is a lawyer, key Liberal Party organizer, and a senator from 1984 to 2010; and Liz Tory, whose husband, the late John Tory, was the Thomson family lawyer.

One of many nirvana moments they experienced occurred in October 1991 at a gala dinner at the Royal York with Prince Charles and Princess Diana in attendance. Only a select 850 guests were invited to the fundraising dinner and dance ($25,000 per table), hosted by grocery magnates Galen and Hilary Weston (Ontario's lieutenant governor from 1997 to 2002). In her book, Sexton relates various telling arguments between Maria Groussman, wife of Dean Groussman, CEO of Canadian Tire at the time, and the Westons and other socialites. "Do you know to whom you are speaking?" Galen Weston asked Groussman after one heated discussion. The debates over the seating arrangement were epic. "We've paid $25,000 and you're going to put us in the second row!" went one conversation between Groussman and Marlene DelZotto. "You can't put people like the Munks and Conrad Black in the second row. You just can't do that." According to Sexton, the night of the gala Hilary Weston became "irate at [Maria Groussman's] shameless monopolizing of Prince Charles."

When royalty was not visiting, the highlight of the season for these women and their friends was the Brazilian Ball, or, simply, "the Braz," the creation of the Brazilian-born Anna Maria de Souza. In 1966 she organized a small fundraiser in the basement of St. Agnes Church at Dundas and Grace Street. Year after year, the Rio Carnival-like ball, complete with Latin music, scantily clad female samba dancers, male hunks wearing not much more than gold glitter, gallons of expensive liquor, and fine food, grew to legendary proportions. In its day "it was the biggest and glitziest Hogtown event around," media executive Ivan Fecan said in a 2012 interview. "You saw politicians, bankers, [and] captains of industry, cheek-to-cheek with semi-naked Brazilian dancers, all in the name of charity." The hype and success of the ball was another indication Toronto the Good had shed much of its reputation.

Just being named to the organizing committee was considered a great honour. Soon the ball was being held at larger venues, like the Four Seasons Hotel, eventually winding up at the Metro Convention Centre with a guest list of more than a thousand people. Amidst the festivities, the money flowed, with tickets costing $1,200 or $25,000 for a table (rising to $50,000 in 2012). At the 1990 ball, de Souza and her friends managed to raise $720,000 for the Hospital for Sick Children. She outdid herself in 2002 when the ball was held outside Paris at the Château de Versailles. The upper crust of Toronto flew over for the party, which raised an estimated $2 million for the Louis Pasteur Institute, an infectious disease research centre. De Souza died of cancer in 2007, and her husband, Ivan, decided that 2012's ball, number 46, was to be the final one. All told, the ball raised an impressive $60 million for a variety of causes and institutions in Canada and South America.

TORONTO'S FINANCIAL SWAY over the rest of the country, on display at the Brazilian Ball, was boosted by the success of René Lévesque and the separatist Parti Québécois in the Quebec provincial election of November 1976. Lévesque's victory terrified many Anglo Quebeckers, triggering an exodus of people and businesses from which Montreal has never truly recovered. The destination of the majority of these disenchanted English-speaking migrants was Toronto. It was not by coincidence that between 1971 and 1981 Metro Toronto's population surpassed that of Metro Montreal, making the GTA the largest urban centre in Canada, with 2.99 million people in 1981 compared to 2.82 in Montreal. Within twenty years that disparity widened further, with the GTA reaching a population of 4.68 million and Montreal rising to 3.42 million. By 1984 there were an estimated 80,000 former Montrealers in the Toronto area alone, two thousand of whom attended a gala reunion at Roy Thomson Hall in September 1984 to celebrate Toronto's 150th birthday. One of the highlights of that evening for Mayor Art Eggleton was sitting with Montreal mayor Jean Drapeau in the middle of the stage and chatting with the audience.

A series of prominent moves from Montreal to Toronto, some directly related to the PQ victory, enhanced Toronto's business status at the expense of Montreal's. One of the first to leave Quebec was Montreal's pre-eminent law firm Stikeman Elliott, established by Heward Stikeman and Fraser Elliott in 1952. The firm had established a satellite branch in Toronto in 1970, but the seemingly unstable political environment of Quebec led the principals to move the head office to that city. The Royal Bank of Canada made a similar move in 1976, the Bank of Montreal a year later, and Sun Life Assurance a year after that.

By the mid-eighties, the head offices of close to half of Canada's most successful corporations were crammed into a few blocks around Bay and King Streets. Led by the big five banks, with combined assets exceeding $300 billion, Toronto-based companies were generating an estimated $2 billion of wheeling and dealing across the globe every twenty-four hours, five days a week. In 1966, the total amount of cheques cleared in Toronto was $188 billion, compared to $149 billion in Montreal. By 1980, in contrast, the total amount of cheques cleared in the city was $3,079 billion—greater than the combined total of all cheques cleared through Montreal, Vancouver, Winnipeg, Calgary, and other Canadian cities ($2,295 billion). The price of downtown real estate in Toronto skyrocketed to $1,000 a square foot, placing the city in the same league as New York.

Almost overnight, Toronto became the sixth-most-important financial centre in the world. "Until the West gets more population, I don't care how much goddamn oil they discover in Alberta," media magnate John Bassett told Peter C. Newman in 1980. "Toronto and not Calgary is going to be the place where you do the deals—just like it's New York and not Houston where you go for the really big business. It's all a matter of geography. You get out to Western Canada, for Christ's sake... and you're away from the action. This is where it's at."

All good things must end—or at least take a rest. In the case of Toronto's economic primacy, the impact of the recession of the early nineties lingered for a long time. It was "Canada's economic version of a Roman candle firework," as *Globe and Mail* business writer Bruce Little put it in late 1994, "a spectacular 25 percent increase in employment during the 1980s, followed by a fizzling 11 percent slide in the 1990s." Between 1990 and 1992, Toronto lost more than 175,000 jobs. Crime rates increased—in 1991 there were a record eighty-nine homicides in Toronto, most related to an increase in gang violence—as did the number of people who were homeless, which rose from an estimated 3,440 in 1982 to at least three or four times as many by 1994.

The recession led to some high-profile casualties, especially in the financial, manufacturing, and real estate sectors. One of the victims was Sydney Hermant's Paja Group, the parent company of Imperial Optical. Hermant's financing was too closely linked to the volatile real estate market, and he was also caught up in the CIBC's anxiety over its vulnerability in the collapse of the Reichmann empire (Hermant had served as a director of the bank for many years). Hermant, who was about to celebrate his eightieth birthday, was so distressed by these developments that on December 23, 1992, the day his company went into receivership due to an $84-million debt to the bank, he had a heart attack and died.

Another financial fatality was Irving Gerstein and his ever-expanding company, Peoples Jewellers, a family firm established in 1919 by Gerstein's grandfather Frank, a Jewish immigrant from Lithuania and a trained watchmaker. Frank Gerstein opened Peoples' first store on Yonge Street in a small shop above a bank. His grandson, who lived the high life in a Bridle Path mansion, belonged to all the right clubs and boards and got carried away with his own dreams of transforming Peoples into the largest jewellery conglomerate in North America. Using risky and pricey junk bonds (engineered by Michael Milken), Gerstein financed a takeover of the Zale Corporation, a large Texas-based retail jewellery operation, in 1987. He scrambled for a few years to pay $100-million-plus interest payments before Zale's debt troubles brought down Peoples Jewellers in July 1993. The final blow was delivered by Gerstein's elderly uncle, Marvin, who voted against a multi-million-dollar restructuring of the company.

By far, the most disastrous financial collapse in the tight circle of the Toronto establishment involved the Eaton's dynasty. The landmark Eaton Centre on Yonge Street had revamped the city's downtown. Yet by 1999, the venerable 130-year-old company that was so connected to Toronto's history was gone. How did it happen?

One major problem was the unimaginative and weak management of founder Timothy Eaton's great-grandsons: Fredrik, the company president from 1977 to 1988; his brother George, president from 1988 to 1997; and their two brothers, John Craig and Thor. The company also refused to adapt. While Eaton's chief department store competitor, the Bay, started accepting bank credit cards in 1978, Eaton's refused to do so until the early eighties. The company lost good talent through neglect or excessive top-down control. Eaton's expanded when it should not have, had poor inventory control, and, perhaps worst of all, did not heed customers' wishes. "The Eatons walked through their stores with blinders on," retailer Harry Rosen told the *Star* in April 1997. "They didn't want to see those awkward people known as customers."

Fred Eaton became the Christmas Grinch in 1982 when he cancelled the traditional Eaton's Santa Claus Parade, an event the company had sponsored since 1905. At a cost of $250,000 the parade was an expensive promotional and marketing tool, which Eaton claimed the company did not benefit from. Still, it was a significant part of Toronto's heritage and was ultimately rescued by the province and nineteen corporations, which amassed a fund of $1.5 million to sustain it.

Tired of the day-to-day headaches, Fred Eaton, who enjoyed hunting and sailing, resigned as president in 1988 in favour of his younger brother George. A few years later, Brian Mulroney appointed Fred Canada's high commissioner to the United Kingdom, the best patronage posting there is. The company was now in the hands of forty-three-year-old George, whose credentials as a retail merchant were suspect. (George lived in a mansion in Caledon, about seventy kilometres northwest of the city, and built a heliport on top of the south tower of the Eaton's Centre, though he never used it.) According to business journalist and Eaton's historian Rod McQueen, George was responsible for instituting the "most disastrous strategy" in Eaton's history: "everyday value pricing." He did away with the always popular Trans-Canada Sale and opted to go for all-year low pricing, thereby avoiding advertising expenses.

"You can't run Eaton's like a Wal-Mart," one veteran buyer told him. "Oh yes, we can," said George. Except he couldn't and he was forced to backtrack two years later. Annual sales, nonetheless, continued to drop drastically, and in 1995 the family was forced to sell its vast real estate holdings (about $100 million worth) to stay afloat. That was only a stopgap measure. By 1997 Eaton's owed the banks and its suppliers $330 million, which it did not have, and was forced to seek protection under the Companies' Creditors Arrangement Act.

The media was less than sympathetic. One Toronto radio station, CHFI, suggested Eaton's new slogan should be "We want to be your store, and for a small down payment, we can be." And the *Globe and Mail* commented, "At times the four Eaton brothers have seemed to consider retailing a chore that took time away from broadcasting, thoroughbreds, politics, patronage appointments and charity golf tournaments... To inquisitive outsiders, the Eatons have been as warm and communicative as the government of Albania." A $10-million dividend given to family members in November 1996 through their private company, Eaton's of Canada, was returned four months later when news of it became public. The brothers also increased their shares in Baton Broadcasting and made a tidy profit of $173 million.

As the company struggled to survive, George Eaton stepped down as CEO in favour of experienced retail manager George Kosich, who was leaving his position as CEO of the Bay. Kosich was, however, unable to stop the bleeding—in 1997, Eaton's had $1.7 billion in sales, but lost $153 million—and quit after only a year. Brent Ballantyne of Beatrice Foods, who succeeded Kosich, took the company public for the first time. That raised some money but not nearly enough, and in August 1999 Eaton's was forced into bankruptcy. Sears acquired the company's assets for the bargain basement price of $50 million and also obtained control of Toronto's Eaton Centre, among other store properties. The family survived the debacle, and old Toronto customers shared shopping memories, reported with great nostalgia in a slew of melancholy press stories about the loss of yet another Canadian institution. Fifteen years later, Torontonians, even those who are not old enough to have shopped at Eaton's, still lovingly refer to the massive mall that stretches from Dundas to Queen and from Yonge to Bay as the Eaton's Centre.

IT WAS IMPOSSIBLE for Peter C. Newman to chronicle Toronto's establishment without writing about Conrad Black, arguably the most fascinating business personality the city has ever produced. Black was born in Montreal in 1944 but moved with his parents, George Montegu and Jean Elizabeth "Betty" (Riley) Black and his older brother Montegu to Toronto as an infant. His father was head of Canadian Breweries and an associate of E.P. Taylor. Controversy swirled around Conrad even as a young man: in 1959 he was expelled from Upper Canada College for stealing exam papers and selling them. His goal, he recalls, was "to reduce the school's whole academic system, except for the senior matriculation class, to utter chaos."

In 1978, at the age of thirty-three, the young tycoon masterminded the takeover of Argus Corporation in a move that would have impressed his hero, Napoleon Bonaparte, for its audacity and cunning. He moved into the "Greek temple" (as he calls it) of the company's stylish headquarters on quiet Toronto Street, and from this base and the Bridle Path estate he inherited from his parents, there was no stopping his march toward destiny. Within a few years he had sold off most of Argus's assets, created a complex structure of holding companies, such as Hollinger (Argus had an investment in Hollinger Mines), and reinvented himself as a media baron. Black started small, owning the *Sherbooke Record*, a Quebec daily, but in time he gained control of the *Jerusalem Post*, the *Chicago-Sun Times*, and hundreds of other newspapers. His most astute move was acquiring London's *Daily Telegraph*, a newspaper with a circulation of a more than a million subscribers, which was steeped in British history and had great business potential. An original capitalist if there ever was one, he not only did multi-million-dollar deals and eventually was appointed to the British House of Lords as Lord Black of Crossharbour, but also studied and wrote history—including a 1977 biography of Quebec premier Maurice Duplessis and, in later years, similar tomes on Franklin Roosevelt and Richard Nixon. He gave new meaning to the word "erudite."

Newman, who first met Black in 1974, devoted his book *The Establishment Man*, published in 1982, to Black, who had been more than happy to feed Newman information. Thereafter, Newman liked to say that he "invented" Black (and his second wife, journalist Barbara Amiel). Black took great umbrage with this comment, especially after the two men fell out over Newman's critical treatment of Black and Amiel in Newman's 2004 memoir *Here Be Dragons*, for which Black launched one of his many libel lawsuits. In the first volume of his own memoirs (published in 1993), Black conceded that *The Establishment Man* "was more than generous to me," though he added that he was "in general agreement with the many people who said I was an unworthy subject of such an extensive and flattering work." Black's somewhat fond memories of the book do not match the letter he sent Newman following its publication (reproduced in Newman's memoir) in which he had harsh words for the "largely fictitious image" of a "chillingly ruthless and rather conceited person" he accused Newman of creating. As for Newman, he wrote that "interviewing Black on and off for most of three decades, I found that his pomposity grew tiresome." At the same time, he admitted that "Black was too good a story to pass up" and that he had "a sense of destiny about him."

In Canada, Black's company started buying up shares in the 115-year-old Southam newspaper chain in 1992 and within four years had gained control of it. Now Black had a stable of profitable newspapers across the country, with the notable exception of Toronto. He had coveted the *Globe and Mail* but his bid to buy it was beaten by Ken Thomson's. Black's business sense compelled him to establish the *National Post* in 1998—after he had acquired the *Financial Post* from Sun Media in a deal he did with its chairman, Paul Godfrey. If Canadian opinion was set by the CBC, the *Globe and Mail*, *Maclean's*, and, to a lesser extent, the *Toronto Star*, then creating a second national newspaper based in Toronto was a no-brainer from his point of view. Moreover, Black believed, as did many other media critics, that the *Globe*'s status as the country's "national newspaper" was a "scam." He desired a high-quality newspaper with a more conservative voice, unafraid to challenge the powers that be, and which featured daily some of the most talented writers in the country. He found the person to draw it all together in Ken Whyte.

A soft-spoken yet smart journalist who had once worked for Ted Byfield's right-wing *Western Report*, Whyte moved east in the early nineties to become the editor of *Saturday Night* magazine, which Black purchased in 1987. Black's ownership of *Saturday Night* led to a spate of resignations by a host of the magazine's writers—Sandra Gwyn, Ron Graham, and editor Robert Fulford, among others—who could not work for a publication Black owned (though Fulford changed his mind in 1999 when he began writing columns for the *National Post*). In fact, with both the magazine and the *National Post*, Black operated as any wise nineteenth-century proprietor would have, permitting the people he hired to run his enterprises with limited interference from him. (Ironically, in 2001, after Black sold the former Southam newspapers to Izzy Asper and his CanWest Global Corporation, along with a 50 percent interest in the *National Post*, Asper adopted a much more hands-on control of editorial content, and the editors and journalists pined for Black.) Even Peter C. Newman begrudgingly admitted that Black "improved every major paper he bought, and the only one he started, the *National Post*, significantly uplifted the standards of Canadian journalism, particularly under its founding editor, Ken Whyte."

Under Whyte's astute stewardship, the *National Post* was launched in October 1998. With four dailies, Torontonians had not had so many newspapers competing for their attention since John A. Macdonald was prime minister. With such writers as Andrew Coyne, Christie Blatchford, Mark Steyn, David Frum, and Linda McQuaig, the columns and op-ed pages of the *National Post* were an intellectual and always enlightening smorgasbord of ideas. As for the criticism that, under Whyte, the *Post* was staunchly pro-American, Black says this was "simply irritation with Canadian smugness, and with the national media's addiction always to claim superiority to the United States in all intangible and human qualities." The *Post*, he adds, "never advocated absorption into the U.S.; we advocated an overthrow of the Toronto-centric, narcissistic Canadian fantasyland of moral exaltedness, and successful friendly Canadian competition with the U.S."

The only problem was the newspaper cost Black a lot of money, yet it could not attract the requisite advertising. Determined to reduce his company's debt, Black was more than open to Izzy Asper's overtures to pay $3.2 billion for the thirteen former Southam newspapers,136 smaller operations, as well as half the *Post*—until that arrangement proved impossible and Black reluctantly walked away from the *Post* in 2001. The complex deal included non-compete payments that were later to contribute to Black's controversial legal problems in the United States, which led to his forty-two-month incarceration between 2007 and 2012. Fittingly, even while he was in prison, Black continued to write a weekly column for the *Post*, which the financially troubled CanWest Global was finally forced to sell, along with its other newspaper assets, to Paul Godfrey—who had sold the *Financial Post* to Black in 1998—and his Postmedia network. Such is the incestuous nature of the Toronto business world.

THEY MIGHT NOT have liked each other much, but the careers of Conrad Black and Peter C. Newman intersected in another very Toronto way. In 1976, it was Newman (at least according to one version of this story) who introduced Black to Jack McClelland of McClelland & Stewart with a recommendation that M&S publish Black's biography of Duplessis, which it did. M&S had also published Newman's 1963 bestseller on John Diefenbaker, *Renegade in Power*, which had sent his writing career into orbit.

That the lives of both men were affected by Jack McClelland, the "prince" of the Toronto and Canadian publishing industry, is not surprising. No one more epitomized the successes and sheer will to beat the odds of the publishing business than McClelland. "Economically speaking," Roy MacSkimming wrote in *The Perilous Trade*, his aptly titled 2003 book on the Canadian publishing industry, "publishing books in Canada doesn't make a lot of sense. It's a high risk, low-margin business conducted on the fringes of empire." Or, as author Morley Callaghan observed, Canada is "a country that is no publisher's paradise." But Jack persevered, sometimes to the detriment of his health and sanity. About the only subjects that he would rather have discussed than books, he told one writer in 1963, were "beautiful women or sailboats."

In 1946, at the age of twenty-four, he began working for McClelland & Stewart, the publishing house founded in 1919 by his father, John, and his partner George Stewart. The firm's main competitors were a handful of publishing houses headquartered in Toronto—Macmillan of Canada, W.J. Gage, Copp Clark, J.M. Dent & Sons, Oxford University Press, Thomas Nelson & Sons, Clarke, Irwin & Company, Ryerson Press, and the University of Toronto Press—that primarily functioned as distributors of books published in the United States and Britain or that published educational and scholarly books.

There were Canadian authors at the time, such as Morley Callaghan, Hugh MacLennan, Sinclair Ross, Thomas Raddall, Robertson Davies, and Donald Creighton, to note several. But advances were non-existent, there were no literary agents or gala book launches at the Park Plaza Hotel, and the only major book prize was the Governor General's Literary Award. "[I] doubt," John Morgan Gray of Macmillan told a writers' conference in 1955, "that any Canadian publisher derives any important part of his revenue (or any net profit) from Canadian general [trade] publishing; his commercial welfare is therefore not identified with that of any Canadian writers. Similarly, those Canadian writers who derive any important part of their income from their books (apart, of course, from textbooks) do not earn it in Canada and are not dependent on a Canadian publisher."

To Jack McClelland, this business model was unacceptable. After he assumed control of the company in the early fifties, he discovered and nurtured a stable of talented home-grown authors—the long list eventually included Pierre Berton, Farley Mowat, Margaret Laurence, Peter C. Newman, Mordecai Richler, and Margaret Atwood—and emerged as the most significant figure in the establishment of the Canadian book publishing industry. His protégé, publisher and author Anna Porter, fittingly called him the "Prince of Publishers... the most successful, the most colourful, certainly the most persistent and imaginative publisher to have erupted onto the world stage."

McClelland adopted an "author is king" approach and constantly reminded his staff that they could make any mistake at M&S and be given a second chance—other than "rudeness or arrogance in dealing with its authors, no matter who they are." That, he told them in a memo in 1969, "I will not tolerate." And while his authors frequently complained to him that their books were not receiving the attention they deserved, M&S writers loved him. He listened to them and coddled them, and they produced and generally remained loyal to him. "He is a Canadian pioneer," Margaret Laurence declared in 1986. "He risked his life for us Canadian writers." Similarly, Margaret Atwood compared him to "a swashbuckling pirate" who awakened Canadians to a literature they "did not believe they had."

A born troublemaker and raconteur, McClelland, with Pierre Berton, established the celebrated Sordsmen's Club, an excuse for Toronto's male writers, publishers, artists, and other cultural personalities to get together, insult each other in witty speeches, and revel in raucous five-hour lunches at various hotel restaurants (the Franz Josef Room at the Walker House on Front Street was a favourite.) When McKenzie Porter brazenly exposed the debauchery in his *Toronto Telegram* column in 1963, he was ostracized and vilified for years.

With his flowing long hair, which in time turned from light blonde to white, tweed sports coat, and trademark cravat, McClelland "resembled an English aristocrat who just happened to drop into the office for an hour or two," as his biographer James King perfectly described him. Like a character out of the television show *Mad Men*, he also smoked—averaging two packs of Rothmans cigarettes a day—and drank far too much vodka. "Sometimes my day is like the story of the drunk who's charged for setting fire to his hotel bed with a lighted cigarette," he told a journalist in 1978. "He pleads not guilty, 'Oh no, your honour, the bed was on fire when I got into it.'"

Yet behind that contrived image was a marketing genius. More than most of his contemporaries in the business, McClelland innately understood the power of promotion and knew how to create buzz for a book. Posters, ads, author signings (like a "Meet the Authors" dinner at the Royal York in April 1959, with sixty-nine M&S authors in the spotlight), book clubs, and other gimmicks might not have always worked, but for the most part it kept the authors—a tough group to please then and now—more or less content. His zaniest, and, admittedly, not all that effective, stunt was standing on Bloor Street on a bitterly cold day dressed in a Roman toga and gold laurels with author Sylvia Fraser, who was similarly garbed, to promote her 1980 novel *The Emperor's Virgin*. It was fun, though as Fraser recalls, Jack had parked in a no-parking zone, had accumulated several tickets while the two of them were visiting bookstores in the area, and had locked his keys in the car.

Such promotion made sense to McClelland; reviews of his books were another matter. He detested lousy reviews and castigated newspapers and their reviewers (more than once) for their perceived inadequacies. In one case he urged William French, the perceptive *Globe and Mail* book critic, to write about more of them, providing, of course, he did so "favourably."

McClelland's advocacy and promotion of authors and books, and his cocktail parties at the rooftop bar of the Park Plaza Hotel, helped create the myth of the larger-than-life (at least in their own minds) Toronto literati that still dominates the industry. This has led to the wholly specious, as well as absurd, division of Canadian authors into "national" writers who are based in or near Toronto—and, perhaps, Montreal—and "regional" writers who live and work everywhere else in the country. Ironically, McClelland, who spent his entire working life in Toronto, was never truly satisfied with the city and what he perceived to be the publishing industry's inadequacies. "There is little community of interest, no literary core, no literary establishment," he asserted in a speech he gave at the end of October 1969. "Toronto is a cold and dispiriting literary scene in other ways. Few notable authors live here. Indeed, so sparse is the literary population that we are frequently called on to round out the numbers at literary parties by sending staff members... [to] impersonate distinguished authors. As a result Torontonians on occasion find themselves unexpectedly encountering Stephen Leacock, Bliss Carman, Ralph Connor and others who have long gone to a better world... Only in Toronto [could the manager of the Maple Leafs] Punch Imlach become Author of the Week."

But as McClelland's career was winding down, Toronto's paramount position as the publishing and literary centre of the universe was a given. Literary agents, who McClelland did not always appreciate (though he briefly became one himself after he sold M&S), like Bella Pomer, Beverley Slopen, Denise Bukowski, Helen Heller, and Bruce Westwood, who merged several agencies in 1995 to create Westwood Creative Artists in 1995, were all based in the city and gradually became an accepted and necessary aspect of the business, as they were in the United States. Prestigious awards like the Giller Prize, established by Toronto entrepreneur Jack Rabinovitch in 1994 in honour of his late wife Doris Giller, a literary columnist for the *Toronto Star*, though not necessarily given to a Toronto author, have also enhanced the self-importance of Toronto publishing. Canadian fiction has steadily become "more Toronto-centric," according to Douglas Gibson, a seasoned editor and publisher who was associated with Macmillan and M&S during his career. He fought against the notion that an author had to relocate to Toronto in order to achieve critical success, but he has seen it happen. "All my editorial life," he wrote in his 2011 book *Stories about Storytellers*,

"I have fought against the idea that you need to move to Toronto to hit the literary big time, and maybe I was wrong."

Economic realities intervened as well in this dynamic, resulting in further Toronto concentration among publishers and booksellers. For all his love of and devotion to writers and books, McClelland's life story was equally the chronicle of one financial crisis after another. Quite simply, despite a talented staff, led by such luminaries of the business as Anna Porter and Linda McKnight, and a steady stream of bestsellers—Peter C. Newman estimates that the eight books he did with McClelland sold 800,000 copies—M&S was constantly in debt. The company faced severe competition from foreign-owned publishing conglomerates with much deeper pockets, and it competed in a dwindling number of bookstores for shelf space in a market flooded with American and British books. During the seventies, M&S was rescued by the Ontario Development Corporation, an agency of the Ontario government, which provided an interest-free loan of close to $1 million. In 1983, McKnight, who was then president of the company with McClelland as chairman, held a massive fire sale at the Atrium on Bay Street; over a weekend they sold more than 200,000 books for $600,000 or an average of three dollars a book. It was a great ploy, but this hardly made a dent in the company's debt of $5 million.

Eventually McClelland, almost sixty years old, had had enough. In late 1985 he sold the company to businessman Avie Bennett, a member of the M&S board. Fifteen years later, in 2000, Bennett, facing the same dire economic challenges as McClelland, donated 75 percent of the company to the University of Toronto and sold the balance to Random House, itself owned by the mammoth German media company Bertelsmann. More recently, M&S became wholly owned by Random House and now operates as one of its many divisions.

Beyond ever-changing consumer habits and the advent of technological innovations like e-book readers, Canadian publishers felt a tremendous impact from the transformation of the bookselling business. Again, Toronto was ground zero for these critical developments, which started with the whirlwind entrance into the book industry of Lawrence "Larry" Stevenson, the head of a venture capitalist group. As a former captain in the Canadian Airborne Regiment, who obtained a Harvard MBA, Stevenson acted with military precision and possessed the intellectual tools necessary to succeed. In 1994, he and his partners in Chapters, Inc., set out to essentially monopolize the book-retailing business. His model, he said, was Foyles bookstore chain in the United Kingdom.

Chapters soon bought out SmithBooks (W.H. Smith of Canada) and Coles and drove other competitors out of business by its predatory pricing and large box stores—its main Toronto store was on the north side of Bloor Street, midway between Avenue Road and Bay Street—complete with Starbucks Coffee, comfy chairs, and children's play areas. The list of its victims in Toronto alone is a long one: the Book Cellar, the Children's Bookstore, Writers & Company, and ten Lichtman's stores.

One of the few survivors to leave on its own terms was Albert Britnell Book Shop on Yonge Street, south of Bloor. Britnell's had been in operation since Albert Britnell, a staunch temperance advocate, established the business farther south on Yonge in 1893. Albert's son Roy, who died in 1983, had moved the store to its location near the Metro Toronto Library. His family fended off the rise of Chapters and Indigo, but eventually the members of the fourth generation lost their will to fight. They sold the store in 1999 to Books for Business, which continues to use the Britnell name for its online operations. Naturally, the Britnell store, with its fine wood panelling, became a Starbucks.

Meanwhile, Stevenson and Chapters marched on. Through its wholesale distribution arm, Pegasus, which opened in Brampton in 1999, Stevenson demanded discounted terms from publishers, placed larger orders, took forever to pay, and returned thousands of books. (By July 2000, Chapters owed HarperCollins $10 million on books that had been delivered to the company at least eight months earlier.) "Publishers realized," explained Roy MacSkimming, "Stevenson hadn't been buying their books so much as borrowing them, fully returnable, to wall paper his edifice complex." The demise of Stoddart and its subsidiary General Distribution Services in 2002 was particularly telling. The head of the company, Jack Stoddart, whose father, Jack Sr., had started the family firm back in the late fifties, had debts of $45 million by the time of his bankruptcy, in large part caused by Chapters' discounting and return policies.

Besides the Internet giant Amazon, which pioneered the online book business, Chapters' one real competitor was Indigo Books and Music, founded in 1996 by Heather Reisman and backed by her husband, Gerald Schwartz of the Onex Corporation. (Schwartz's total income in 1997 was reportedly $18.7 million, an increase of 124 percent from the previous year.)

There's rich in Toronto and then there's Gerry and Heather. In a 2005 *Toronto Life* magazine profile of the city's premier billionaire power couple, Marci McDonald described their comings and goings like this: "Whether hobnobbing with Michael Douglas and Catherine Zeta-Jones or jetting between their Palm Beach and Beverly Hills homes on a private Gulfstream II, they have cultivated a lifestyle so extravagant that most book buyers could only conceive of it in the pages of an airport potboiler. Their much-ballyhooed birthday gifts to one another outstrip most Indigo staffers' salaries. For Schwartz's 50th, Reisman bought him a red Porsche; for her 40th, he arranged a reunion of the Kingston Trio—or, at least, two-thirds of it. 'The third one was dead,' Schwartz quipped later. 'I couldn't get him to come.'"

Schwartz, born in 1941, is a Winnipeg boy, which likely accounts for his always affable demeanour—except, perhaps, when it comes to writers who ask too many probing questions. Both he and Reisman guard their privacy closely, or as much as possible for a couple who cannot avoid the spotlight. He obtained a law degree from the University of Manitoba and then an MBA from Harvard. His high finance career began in the late seventies and early eighties, when he and his partner, the future media mogul Izzy Asper—whom Schwartz had articled with as a young law student—established the Winnipeg-based merchant bank CanWest Capital Corporation. By then, Schwartz had spent time on Wall Street working for Bear Stearns & Company and learned everything there was to know about becoming a leveraged buyout specialist. Asper and Schwartz parted ways in 1983 after they disagreed about the sale of their biggest asset, the Monarch Life Insurance Company. At the time, Schwartz was in the process of relocating from Winnipeg to Toronto. He soon set up Onex Corporation, an equity firm now worth more than $6 billion, and settled down with his new bride, Heather Reisman.

She was born in Montreal in 1948 and studied to become a social worker. Her father, Mark (or Moe), was a real estate broker and her mother, Rose, owned a stylish clothing boutique, Mary Cullen. She was Reisman's role model on how to make it as a woman in a business world dominated by men. For a time, Heather worked as a consultant for Claude Frenette at his Intergroup office, which is how, according to the various stories told about this, she met Gerry Schwartz, who was in Montreal scouting businesses to acquire. Their first date was in New York, where he took her to see the musical *Annie*. They were married in Toronto on May 15, 1982, with the reception at the posh Four Seasons Hotel. Izzy Asper helped arrange it, complete with a fake newscast from Global Television announcing the nuptials. Settling in Toronto, she and her business partner, South African Peter Cooper, founded their own consulting firm. She then had a stint as president of the Cott Corporation, the soft-drink company owned by Gerry Pencer, who had been one of Schwartz's first investors in Onex.

After leaving Cott in 1995, Resiman decided to enter the book business. The American bookstore chain Borders was intending to create a Canadian subsidiary, Borders Canada, that would have been a direct challenge to Chapters' supremacy, and Reisman was to be its first CEO. In early 1996, however, the federal government—egged on by former Ontario premier David Peterson, a one-time friend of Reisman who had become the chair of Chapters' board—killed that idea when it ruled that such an expansion contravened its foreign ownership regulations for booksellers. Reisman then opted for Plan B. Backed by Schwartz and a handful of other investors, she opened her first Indigo megastore in Burlington in September 1997. Exemplifying the difference between Reisman and her rival, Larry Stevenson, Indigo was more stylish and classier than Chapters. The chain's downtown Toronto store opened some months later in the Manulife Centre, half a block from the Chapters store, setting the stage for a brief war of words.

That fight came to an abrupt end in 2000. Unwilling to be dragged down by Chapters, Reisman and Schwartz engineered a hostile takeover of the company at a cost of $121 million. Chapters' prime Bloor Street store was soon shut down, and Resiman became one of the most important players in the Canadian book industry.

Around the same time, the couple decided they needed a bit more room at home. They lived in a beautiful Rosedale mansion, but starting in early 2000, they began buying up million-dollar-plus houses around them, spending a total of about $8 million on the properties. Then, much to the consternation of their genteel neighbours, they tore down these homes and embarked on a three-year building project to construct a compound, "Castle Onex," complete with a separate guest house, separate men's and women's washrooms, private screening room, and a "massive conservatory-style gym with enough workout stations to accommodate the entire [Toronto] Raptors lineup."

Schwartz does have a sense of humour about it all. At a ritzy Liberal fundraiser in mid-December 2003, held at the mammoth Toronto Convention Centre, Schwartz, a good friend and backer of Liberal leader Paul Martin, hosted the affair. He joked to the four thousand people in attendance that he would have had the event at his home, but "we can only seat 3,000—3,500 max." The dynamic duo are also generous philanthropists and have contributed to such institutions as Mount Sinai Hospital, with a $15-million donation for the Schwartz–Reisman Emergency Centre, and the University of Toronto, where they established the Heather Reisman Chair in Perinatal Nursing Research.

COMPETITION IN TORONTO'S RESTAURANT SCENE was almost as intense as that in the book business, and Joanne Kates was in the best position to observe it all. In 1968 she was home for a visit from Wellesley College, the elite liberal arts university for women in Massachusetts, when her uncle, well-connected lawyer Morris Gross, treated her to lunch at one of the finest and most formal restaurants in Toronto, Three Small Rooms at the Windsor Arms Hotel, hidden away on St. Thomas Street just off Bloor. The hotel and its world-class eatery were owned by the debonair George Minden, Gross's close friend and the son of his late partner, Arthur Minden. There, Kates experienced for the first time hearts and cream. "It was heavy cream, curdled with crème fraîche in a heart-shaped mould with fresh raspberry sauce," she recalls with a smile. "It was as good a dessert as I had ever tasted."

Kates went on to attend a cooking school in France before becoming Toronto's premier restaurant reviewer, first with *Toronto Life* magazine and then with the *Globe and Mail* from 1974 to 2012. In those early days, apart from some acceptable but lowbrow Hungarian, Chinese, and Italian restaurants and Jewish delis, there were few "fancy high-end" dining establishments such as Winston's, "and those were only for the rich," she says. People ate out infrequently, and if husbands occasionally took their wives out for dinner or dancing it was to La Scala on Bay Street or the Pump Room at the classy Lord Simcoe Hotel, a favourite spot for weddings and bar-mitzvah receptions in the sixties. In general, food "was of no interest to Torontonians. When people at parties said: 'What do you do?' and I told them, they always did a quick exit... there were barely enough restaurants of interest to review, and you could count the serious chefs and wait staff on the fingers of one hand, all of whom worked in expensive, fancy, formal places—hardly the normal stomping grounds of somebody (then) my age or income."

The first review she wrote for the *Globe and Mail* was published on April 22, 1974. It was a critique of Noodles on Bloor and Bay, the restaurant that she suggests truly changed Toronto's dining scene. Its astute owner was the same George Minden of Three Small Rooms, who had spent more than $400,000 creating Noodles, which opened in 1973. There were no red-and-white-checkered table cloths, boring spaghetti, or dripping candles in old Chianti bottles that were found in every other Italian restaurant in the city. Instead, Noodles, with its neon lights and custom-designed chairs, bridged the gap between formal and informal dining. Or, as Kates put it in her 1974 review, "Noodles is a classy restaurant that isn't stuffy, a place where you can dine comfortably in jeans or a dinner jacket." Moreover, it was possible to eat a reasonably priced plate of pasta without facing the recriminations from haughty waiters you would have received at Winston's or Three Small Rooms for not ordering a three-course dinner. At Noodles, the pasta was "made from scratch"; according to Kates, you could not have found "a fresher noodle in Canada." It was not only the exceptional food that kept bringing customers back, however. Noodles was as hip a place as there was for middle-class Torontonians of that era, the place to be seen. "It was the great equalizer," Kates says today, "everybody with taste [real or not] and money went there."

Every dog and restaurant has its day, and that certainly applied to the Toronto restaurant scene, then and since. By 1985, Noodles had become somewhat stale, eclipsed by what Kates calls another "game-changer," Franco Prevedello, who opened Pronto in 1981, Centro in 1987, and Splendido four year after that (his most recent establishment is Nota Bene). Then, in a surprising move, Minden sold Noodles to the Windsor Arms Hotel's talented executive chef, Dante Rota, who gave it new life. Rota, who died in Italy in September 2012 at the age of eighty-two, re-established Noodles as the city's supremo Italian bistro. In particular, his devoted customers came from miles around for his gnocchi in gorgonzola sauce.

Under Rota, the Windsor Arms's Three Small Rooms had specialized in what Kates calls "grand excesses." The hotel's chic Courtyard Café and the adjacent oh-so-cool bar Club 22 became the haunt of visiting Hollywood stars shooting movies in the city, as well as of the major players who produced Canadian films (some not all that bad) and laid the groundwork for the city's live musical theatre and glamorous Toronto International Film Festival (TIFF). The café and the piano bar (featuring pianist Paul Drake) were definitely the places to be and be seen. Among the regulars were such movers and shakers as Bob Cooper, Robert Cohen, Jon Slan, Garth Drabinsky, David Pearlmutter, George Mendeluck, Michael McCabe (head of the cash-rich Canadian

Film Development Corporation from 1978 to 1980), and Bill Marshall, the first director of the Festival of Festivals, now TIFF.

Born in Glasgow, Scotland, in 1939, Marshall arrived in Canada at the age of fifteen. He had a knack for communications and marketing and initially used his skills working as David Crombie's assistant. But he was also that rarest of creatures—an ambitious and creative Canadian-based filmmaker. Marshall had two partners: the much beloved lawyer and real estate dealmaker turned movie producer Murray "Dusty" Cohl (he acquired the nickname as a youngster while attending a radical labour Jewish summer camp), who never went anywhere without his trademark black cowboy hat; and film producer Henk Van der Kolk. The trio decided that they needed a venue where they could present their own work and that of the other fledgling Canadian filmmakers (six in total by Marshall's estimation). In the spring of 1976, they travelled to Cannes, schmoozed with anyone who would listen to them, and announced the birth of a film festival in Toronto with the snappy name Festival of Festivals. Each of them later took credit for originating the idea, though when Cohl died in January 2008 from cancer, Marshall said that "the festival was Dusty's gift to the city. There would be no festival without Dusty."

Naturally, there were skeptics. Alderman Art Eggleton, the budget chief, refused a modest funding request of $5,000, though that decision was overturned by city council's executive committee. (Marshall forgave Eggleton for this transgression and helped get him elected mayor in 1980.) As the festival's first executive director, Marshall brazenly announced that such movie stars as Jack Nicholson, Warren Beatty, and Julie Christie would attend. To the major movie studios, however, "Toronto was as notable as Toledo, Ohio," Bryan Johnson noted in the *Globe and Mail*'s history of TIFF, and the Los Angeles heavyweights would not permit their new releases to be premiered in Canada. Hence, Nicholson et al. did not show up in 1976. Yet in time these celebs and nearly every other paparazzi-chased star on the planet would bless the city and TIFF with their glorious presence.

The Festival of Festivals—wisely renamed the Toronto International Film Festival in 1994—screened 127 local and European films over the course of a week in its inaugural year and resonated with the nascent film industry, intellectual and cultural literati, and public. Thereafter, its prominence gradually grew: some of the films that had their world or North American premieres at the festival were *Midnight Express* in 1978; *And Justice for All* in 1979; *Chariots of Fire* in 1982, which went on to win Best Picture at the Academy Awards; *The Big Chill* in 1983; and Quentin Tarantino's *Reservoir Dogs* in 1992. There were the usual glitches—as in 1978, when the festival sold four thousand tickets to a screening of Robert Lantos's feature *In Praise of Older Women* in the 1,600-seat Elgin Theatre; or 1982, when up-and-comer Atom Egoyan, soon to be the toast of the Canadian film business, organized his own screening of his work after the festival ignored him. In 2006, actor Sean Penn caused a scene when he dared smoke a cigarette during a media conference at the Sutton Hotel; he was unaware of Ontario's tough no-smoking laws.

By its thirty-fifth anniversary in 2011, TIFF, now based in the snazzy new Bell Lightbox at the corner of John and King Streets (complete with high-tech studios and three main theatres), had inexplicably become, next to Cannes, the most important film festival in the world. Each year, thousands of movie producers, filmmakers, and celebrities, as well as more than a thousand members of the media from forty-plus countries descended on Toronto to join an estimated 250,000 festival goers and select from more than 300 films (the 2012 catalogue was 456 pages) originating from every corner of the earth. The festival now generates in excess of $135 million.

"The world knows Toronto because of TIFF, not the CN Tower," argued festival pioneer Bill Marshall in a *National Post* opinion piece in May 2012. "Statistics Canada calls us 'an eclipse event,' meaning if you're going to do something bad in Canada, do it during TIFF because we use up all of the country's news allotment worldwide. We are the centre of the media universe for 10 days every September."

ONE OF THE HIGHLY TOUTED FILMS premiered at the 2012 TIFF was Barry Avrich's *Show Stopper: The Theatrical Life of Garth Drabinsky*. The ninety-seven-minute documentary tracked the rise and fall of one of Toronto's great theatre impresarios, the disgraced founder of Cineplex and Livent—"the Ziegfeld of Canada" or "Garth Vader" depending on your perspective—who was incarcerated for seventeen months as part of a five-year sentence for fraud before he was granted day parole in a Toronto halfway house in November 2012 (he was granted full parole on January 20, 2014). Avrich visited Drabinsky while he was still at Beaver Creek, a minimum-security institution near Gravenhurst, Ontario, north of Toronto, though he never asked him to be interviewed for the film. Drabinsky's still-supportive friends and associates were eager to share their generally positive memories of the ambitious and flawed show business executive. Avrich concluded that it was not greed that accounted for Drabinsky's downfall. "If it was greed," he said in a 2012 interview, "it was greed for legitimacy and power."

Other than Ed and David Mirvish, few individuals breathed life into Toronto's popular entertainment industry like Drabinsky. He had a typical Jewish Toronto upbringing, with the notable exception of contracting polio prior to his fourth birthday in 1953. The many operations he endured as a child left him with a noticeable limp. He had an early avid interest in the entertainment industry, and after he graduated with a law degree from the University of Toronto in 1973, he quickly became one of the country's leading entertainment lawyers before he was thirty-five years old.

By all accounts, Drabinsky was a workaholic with unbounded drive and unbridled ambition—and sizable ego to match both. "He must win," one of his former associates told Anne Kingston of *Maclean's* in 2009. "He will not brook interference. He won't tolerate anyone who fails to get it or see it or agree. If they don't, they're not just wrong but ignorant and stupid and dismissed." That approach propelled him to the top of the entertainment business in Toronto and beyond, to New York and Los Angeles, but it proved to be his undoing as well.

Within a few years he began investing in film projects and a movie magazine, which led to his first big venture in 1979. He and Nat Taylor established Cineplex and its then innovative eighteen-screen theatres in a renovated parking garage beneath the Eaton Centre. At the time it was the largest such cinema venue in the world. Cineplex grew and went public in 1982, which enhanced the company's balance sheet but significantly reduced Drabinsky's control and that of his new partner and second-in-command, Myron Gottlieb, an investment broker with a good track record. From the moment the two met in 1978, they became fast friends. When MCA, one of the largest American entertainment conglomerates, which owned close to 50 percent of Cineplex, ousted Drabinsky and Gottlieb from the board in a nasty corporate battle in 1989, the two quickly moved on, establishing Live Entertainment of Canada, Inc., or Livent.

Livent's first big hit was the wildly successful Canadian production of *The Phantom of the Opera*, the mega-musical by Andrew Lloyd Webber, in the magnificently refurbished Pantages Theatre on Yonge Street. "No expense was spared," Drabinsky boasted in September 1989. "The whole idea was to ensure elegance." He was not kidding. It cost $18 million to restore the theatre to its 1920s vaudevillian glory, another $6 million for the show, and millions more for marketing. But despite the usual griping from critics about such popular musicals, *Phantom*, with the unheard-of top ticket price of $85, had advance sales of $24 million, convincing Drabinsky and Gottlieb that they had struck oil. And, indeed, the show had a remarkable ten-year run, cementing Toronto as Canada's Broadway.

There was no stopping the duo or curtailing their P.T. Barnum-like determination. Not only did their productions, like *Kiss of the Spider Woman*, brilliantly succeed in Toronto; they were also able to accomplish what almost every Canadian in the entertainment industry strives for: acceptance and triumphant success on Broadway in New York City. Livent achieved this several times, winning Tony awards and gaining respect from the tough New York theatre crowds.

In 1991, Drabinsky and Gottlieb concluded a sweet deal with North York mayor Mel Lastman. Using both public and private money, Lastman had the $48-million North York Performing Arts Centre (now the Toronto Arts Centre) built for them and gave them an exclusive contract to manage it. There were snickers, as the *Star* noted, about erecting a cultural centre in North York, which many regarded as "a contradiction in terms." Yet Drabinsky was not deterred, proclaiming that North York was "the actual geo-centre of Toronto... We'll be the catalyst for the creation of a whole new entertainment area. All the way up to Highway 7 people are yearning for this."

He soon drew more attention to the project, much of it controversial, with the announcement that the venue's first big production would be the Hal Prince revival of *Show Boat*, which angered members of the city's black community because of the musical's stereotypical and denigrating portrayal of African-Americans. For months, an angry argument raged in Toronto about the appropriateness of running an allegedly racist production; at one point the North York board of education decided not to permit its students to see it, a decision Drabinsky called "patently absurd."

From the moment he decided to stage *Show Boat*, Drabinsky was, in fact, mindful of the issue. In his autobiography he points out that he "consulted widely inside Canada and out with such people as entertainer Harry Belafonte and Washington lawyer and civil-rights advocate Vernon Jordan. Both men encouraged me to use the original lyrics, because it reflected the history and social condition of post-Reconstruction America." He also enlisted Lincoln Alexander, the former lieutenant governor of Ontario, to arrange a meeting with key members of the city's black community to allay their concerns.

Nevertheless, in early October 1993, a protest led by the grassroots group Coalition to Stop Show Boat turned into a rowdy clash with police in front of the theatre. The fact that everyone connected with *Show Boat* was Jewish—Drabinsky, Gottlieb, and Lastman, as well as the show's original creators, Jerome Kern and Oscar Hammerstein II, and Edna Ferber, the author of the 1927 novel the musical was based on—led to accusations and counter-accusations about negative Jewish attitudes towards blacks and vice versa. The story received prominent coverage all over the continent, including in the *New York Times*. Drabinsky dismissed the vocal protest and said that it "would blow over"—which it largely did—though he was angered by what he calls the "scurrilous, hysterical, anti-Semitic commentary in *Share*," the Toronto black community's weekly.

In the end, Toronto audiences were not dissuaded by the storm around the musical. *Show Boat* had a long run at the North York theatre before it opened on Broadway and won the Tony award for Best Revival of a Musical in 1995. Drabinsky soon had his own theatres in New York (the lavishly redone Lyric and Apollo Theatres) and followed up *Show Boat* with a musical version of novelist E.L. Doctorow's *Ragtime* in 1996.

"The theatre is not a business," David Mirvish has said. "It's a disease." To outsiders, Livent seemed to be a smooth and successful operation, but in fact Drabinsky and Gottlieb were managing a massive debt and barely hanging on. As was later determined, they were also fiddling with the books. "Livent itself was an accounting illusion every bit as spellbinding as its big budget special effects," according to Ann Kingston in *Maclean's*. "Numbers were moved like chess pieces: in one example, a net loss before taxes of $41 million was 'adjusted' to a profit of $14 million. Income was boosted, pre-production costs transferred to fixed assets, all to bolster investor confidence and allow the show and the company's bold vision to go on."

Following an investigation of Livent's financial collapse with a $334-million debt in 1998, Drabinsky and Gottlieb were charged in 2002 with defrauding Livent investors out of millions of dollars in an alleged scheme that had carried on for nearly a decade. The two fought the charges and the justice system for six years. Finally, after a two-month trial, on August 5, 2009, Drabinsky was found guilty of fraud and forgery and sentenced to a seven-year jail term. His lawyers appealed, and the Ontario Court of Appeal reduced the jail time by two years. Gottlieb was also convicted of fraud and received a six-year sentence, which was reduced to four. At a parole hearing in the fall of 2012, Drabinsky told the parole board that he wants to again work as a theatre producer as well as teach. "I want to return to my artistic roots and I want to contribute to the cultural landscape of the country," he said. He was more adamant at the hearing that ultimately granted him full parole in January 2014, promising, as the *Star* reported, that "his role in the future will be strictly as a creative consultant" and that he would never be involved again in the financing of any production.

DRABINSKY'S IDEA OF HIGH CULTURE and entertainment was not cheap. The best seats in the house for a Saturday evening performance of *Show Boat* cost $82.50; even the *crème de la crème* gold seats at Maple Leaf Gardens to watch the perennially underperforming Leafs were less by $17.50 in 1993. Economics thus dictated that only a certain class of Torontonian—Rosedale, Forest Hill, the Bridle Path—could afford such expensive social outings. That certainly did not mean there was nothing else to do in the city. On the contrary, starting in the mid-seventies, Toronto bustled with clubs, jazz joints, and small and innovative theatres like Tarragon. You could read about many of these happenings in *NOW*, the free alternative weekly started in 1981 by two idealistic and leftist university graduates, Michael Hollett and Alice Klein. Their objective was to launch a Toronto version of New York City's *Village Voice* and focus on Toronto's grassroots' culture, events, issues, and people that were not covered in the "mainstream media."

Though *NOW* was a small operation in the eighties, from its funky headquarters on the Danforth it published investigative pieces about corruption, militarism, and Canadian foreign policy in Asia and other locales that did not generally make the daily news. Stephen Dale, who wrote freelance articles, recalled that the paper's "mission was to keep powerful people honest and to expose injustices, discrimination, and abuse." One of its columnists in the nineties was former mayor John Sewell, who wrote about municipal affairs from his unique perspective. *NOW* gave space for articles and ads about the city's gay culture, gradually transforming Toronto the Good into one of the gay-friendliest cities in North America, and it was also a big promoter of Toronto's ever-expanding indie music scene. "Its club listings," says John Lorinc, "are to music what the car ads are to the automotive sector." Over the years, as a result of economic constraints—investigative journalism is expensive—and an attempt to attract a wider readership in the face of competition, *NOW* has arguably lost some of its edge.

For Toronto's more socially refined citizens, there were traditional cultural attractions to keep them busy. Popular were performances by the National Ballet of Canada and readings at the International Festival of Authors, which started small in 1980 from its home at Harbourfront and became one of the largest literary festivals in the world. There were concerts by the Canadian Opera Company (COC) and the Toronto Symphony Orchestra (TSO)—which got a new home in 1982, the circular glass-encased $57-million Roy Thomson Hall, designed by Arthur Erickson at the corner of King and Simcoe Streets.

That was the same year the Toronto musical community lost one of its most brilliant artists. In early October, pianist Glenn Gould died of a stroke at the age of fifty. He had grown up in the Beaches area of the city and as a teenager had studied at the Royal Conservatory of Music. From then on, he impressed everyone with his virtuoso performances of Bach, Schoenberg, and others. In March 1955, when he was twenty-two, he received what became a standard rave review of a concert he gave with the TSO. Typical was John Kraglund's assessment in the *Globe and Mail*, in which he compared Gould's artistry to such giants of the music world as Johannes Brahms and Frédéric Chopin. "If Mr. Gould has not already won a local following to compete with the best of today's artists anywhere," Kraglund wrote, "it is because he has not yet turned to the standard popular repertoire."

Gould always followed his own path; in time, his various eccentricities and strange mannerisms—the way he slouched in his chair at the piano and his unremitting humming as he played—attracted as much attention as his musicality. "The nut's a genius," wryly commented George Szell, conductor of the Cleveland Orchestra, after working with Gould in a 1957 concert. In the late fifties and early sixties, Gould performed in the U.S. and Europe, but he grew increasingly disdainful of audience expectations and behaviour and gave his last live performance in 1964. After that he devoted his time to studio recordings and was a staple of CBC radio and television. It is unlikely that Gould would ever have performed in Roy Thomson Hall, but following his death, its officials acquired his Yamaha piano.

Expenditures on high culture frequently take a back seat to financing multi-million-dollar sports and other large public facilities—and it was no different in Toronto. Thus it took three decades of political wrangling and a few false starts before the COC could relocate from its Front Street venue at the old O'Keefe Centre—which became the Hummingbird Centre in 1996 and, since 2007, the Sony Centre for the Performing Arts—to a magnificent new home on University Avenue, the Jack Diamond-designed Four Seasons Centre for the Performing Arts.

Apart from the generous $20-million donation from Isadore "Issy" Sharp of Four Seasons Hotels and Resorts, the one individual who made the Four Seasons Centre a reality was Richard Bradshaw. Born in the British Midlands, Bradshaw, a world-renowned musician and conductor, arrived in Toronto in 1988 after stints in London and San Francisco—he had been conductor of the San Francisco Opera since 1977—as a guest conductor of the COC's production of *Tosca*. A year later he signed on as the company's chief conductor and head of music, and within a decade he had been appointed general director. By all accounts he embraced Toronto but bemoaned the financial problems that had repeatedly wrecked plans for a new theatre. "We are a great and rich country and getting richer," he declared in a speech he gave in 2006, "but we have Third World investment in the arts."

Dedicated, passionate, and unrelenting, he used all means at his disposal to get the new theatre built. In particular, he would not take no for an answer when he approached a potential contributor and then usually asked for more than the person was offering—and got the higher amount. He was "both an artist who could inspire his musicians and an entrepreneur who could see his vision," according to the *Globe and Mail*'s Sandra Martin. To launch the Four Seasons Centre in the fall of 2006, he staged Richard Wagner's *Ring Cycle*. Demand for tickets was intense (at least among a certain clientele). Bradshaw's sudden death from a heart attack in August 2007 was a shock to the company and the city.

LESS HIGHBROW was a night out grooving to the cool sounds of jazz great Moe Koffman at George's Spaghetti House on Dundas Street near Sherbourne—the restaurant was the brainchild of Doug Cole, who died in June 2012 at the age of eighty-seven—or rockin' at the iconic El Mocambo on Spadina, a block from College Street. The El Mocambo was hot, loud, crowded, smoky (before the provincial government killed that), and generally raunchy. Yet being treated to such artists as U2, Stevie Ray Vaughan, Lou Reed, Jimi Hendrix, and Elvis Costello, all of whom played at the club, was an intimate and unforgettable experience.

The club's most memorable moment, or at least the most publicized, was the night in March 1977 that the Rolling Stones performed, billed as "The Cockroaches." That live concert, their first at a club venue in more than a decade, gained even more notoriety due to the presence in the audience of Margaret Trudeau, the twenty-eight-year-old flower-child wife of Prime Minister Pierre Trudeau. The couple had recently separated, yet this had not been made public.

Margaret was already the focus of intense media scrutiny and gossip, and her antics that night triggered an avalanche of unwanted publicity for her and the prime minister. The band's drummer, Charlie Watts, later remarked, "I wouldn't want my wife associating with us." The media later speculated that Margaret, who as far as journalists knew was still the devoted wife of the country's leader, had hooked up with Mick Jagger. But guitarist Ron Wood was the attraction, a fact revealed in his autobiography published thirty years later. "I was the one who invited her to the El Mo concerts," he wrote. "She was my pal and from the moment I met her, we spent as much time together as possible... No one in the band judged me for what I was doing, but they recommended I be cautious. We both knew it was something that couldn't have a future, but we shared something special for that short time."

The El Mocambo closed in 2001 and was reopened ten years later, thanks to the efforts of two local entertainment entrepreneurs, Sam Grosso and Marco Petrucci. They spent an estimated $20,000 restoring the club's trademark palm tree neon sign.

If, as some Canadians outside the GTA suggest, Toronto has always been a great city to laugh about, it has also been a great city to laugh in. Those Kings of Comedy Johnny Wayne and Frank Shuster set the standard and perfected the shticky art of the sketch, soon to be brilliantly emulated by Lorne Michaels, Shuster's son-in-law at the time, on the enduring NBC television show *Saturday Night Live*. "Frank had a huge influence on me," Michaels said in a 2002 interview. "There are very few times when I am thinking some problem through in the studio that something he said doesn't pop up in my mind... How to shoot a sketch. How to keep the reaction close to the joke. How to throw away a laugh." From a Canadian and Toronto perspective, Wayne and Shuster were also unique because they had demurred when their American agent constantly begged them to move south permanently. "They turned down the Canadian Dream—to not be working in Canada," Michaels added, "and there was an entitlement that came with that."

By the early seventies, however, some of their allure was fading, and though it was still funny, their comedy belonged to an earlier age. Second City, born in Chicago in 1959, was equally an inspiration for *SNL* and offered an edgier, more contemporary brand of comedy that appealed to the educated, pot-smoking, sexually liberated sixties generation. This new movement coalesced in Toronto in 1972. According to James Kaplan, writing in the *New Yorker* a decade and a half later, "Toronto in 1972 resembled one of those artistic nexuses that crop up now and then, like Paris in the twenties, Los

Angeles in the thirties, London just before the First World War. Often an influx of expatriates is involved. In 1972, in Toronto, the influx came from Chicago and from elsewhere in Canada."

He points specifically to the production of the rock musical *Godspell*, which debuted at Ed Mirvish's Royal Alexandra Theatre in late May of that year. The show later relocated to the smaller Bayview Playhouse. *Godspell* featured a stellar cast of comedy hall of famers and future SNL and Second City alumni—Gilda Radner (who was visiting from Detroit), Martin Short, Eugene Levy, and Andrea Martin, among them. Victor Garber starred as Jesus, the beginning of his career as an actor, and Paul Shaffer, who wound up as David Letterman's sidekick, was the musical director, having given up on his family's idea that he should go to law school. The generally cynical Toronto media loved the show—a "deluge of dazzlements," the *Globe and Mail* called it—as did the steady stream of theatregoers.

In 1973, Gilda Radner, as well as cast members Derek McGrath, Jayne Eastwood, and Don Scardino, left the show to join the ensemble at the new Second City, which soon moved into its Toronto home at the Old Fire Hall on Lombard Street. Radner went on to even greater fame and fortune as a member of *SNL*'s first cast in 1975, while a host of superb comedy talent—John Candy, Joe Flaherty, Eugene Levy, Andrea Martin, Catherine O'Hara, Rick Moranis, and Dave Thomas—honed their skills at Second City, culminating with the premiere of the hilarious and marvellous television show *SCTV* in 1976.

Around the same time, Mark Breslin, twenty-four in 1976 and a graduate of York University, decided that he wanted to do something beyond becoming a lawyer or accountant. For a brief time he worked at Harbourfront as its director of theatre and music. After he lost his job due to cutbacks, he came up with the novel idea of opening the city's first stand-up comedy cabaret.

Yuk Yuk's, still going strong nearly four decades later, started small. Breslin made a deal with the Church Street Community Centre to lease him the basement room every Wednesday night for a few hours. For the price of two dollars, Torontonians could revel in American-style and usually racy comedy routines. Real and would-be stand-up comedians lined up to show their stuff, and so did the audiences. "Comedy in Toronto is where folk music was at in 1962," Breslin said in an August 1976 interview with the *Globe and Mail*, two months after he had opened. "A market can be created here without limitations. It's an apocalyptic art form; it works best in insecure times, which this is. It can happen." He was right. Within two years, his success allowed him to open his own regular club at a permanent location on Bay Street. The shows were not always sensational, but Yuk Yuk's launched the careers of a slew of comedians, including Howie Mandel, Rick Moranis, Larry Horowitz, Jim Carrey, Norm Macdonald,

Tom Green, Mike MacDonald, Jeremy Hotz, and Russell Peters. The club also made Breslin a key Toronto show business entrepreneur and enabled him to build and expand his comedy empire.

Not in the mood for laughs? You could while away a day at the new Metro Toronto Zoo, which opened in August 1974 on a parcel of land in Scarborough, or at the Royal Ontario Museum. The ROM became embroiled in its own *Show Boat*-type controversy in 1990 when the black community and a handful of academics protested that its "Into the Heart of Africa" exhibit about African life and British imperialism presented a skewed, even racist, portrait of Africans in the nineteenth century. The debate was so heated that several U.S. museums backed out of an agreement to display the ROM exhibit in their own institutions—resulting in a loss to the ROM of at least $100,000—and the exhibit's curator, anthropologist Dr. Jeanne Cannizzo, was compelled to resign her teaching position at the University of Toronto following months of harassment and unfounded accusations that she was a racist. This episode, as well as the one that ensnared Garth Drabinsky and *Show Boat* two years later, was evidence of a power shift among the city's minority groups, who were no longer willing to be passive.

In many ways, the controversy at the ROM, as well as the growth of a dynamic cultural life and entertainment industry—whether highbrow, lowbrow, or somewhere in the middle—was yet another example of Toronto's maturity as a city. Despite grumblings across the country about Toronto's inflated ego, John Bassett was right: the city really was "where it's at."

Chapter Twelve

MULTICULTURALISM, MERGER AND MEL

Toronto is...a city where almost everyone has come from elsewhere—a market, a caravansary—bringing with them their different ways of dying and marrying, their kitchens and songs. A city of forsaken worlds; language a kind of farewell.

—ANNE MICHAELS, *FUGITIVE PIECES*, 1996

The Caribana festival inaugurated in 1967 epitomized Toronto's self-styled development as the "most multicultural city in the world." That designation might be a myth, yet it is hard to dispute the reality of the city's famed cultural diversity. *Archives of Ontario RG 14-151-3-149*

BLAND WAS POWER AT Toronto city hall in the eighties. How else to explain the remarkable success of the city's longest-serving mayor, Arthur "Art" Eggleton, an affable "Clark Kent look-alike" accountant who grew up in Cabbagetown? "You make Joe Clark look charismatic," Eggleton was caustically told by Fraser Kelly of CBC-TV the night before his second victory in November 1982. The mayor merely shrugged. "I'll be back to work tomorrow," he said matter-of-factly. And he was then and in the two subsequent elections. Eggleton retired from municipal politics in 1991 at the close of his fourth term, ending his long career at city hall, which had begun back in 1969 with his election at age twenty-six as the youngest alderman to serve on council. In October 1993 he decided to run federally for the Liberals in the Toronto riding of York Centre and won easily. He served as a cabinet minister in Jean Chrétien's government and was appointed to the Senate by Paul Martin in 2005.

As Toronto's mayor, Eggleton now says, the secret to his success was "to try not to irritate the people and be a good communicator." That strategy worked. "He's dull and boring, but he's the most underestimated politician in Toronto," NDP alderman Richard Gilbert said in an interview in June 1988. "He's a very clever person and has good political sense. He's not overly endowed with principles." Eggleton was an astute people pleaser. He favoured downtown development like the SkyDome, Convention Centre, Harbourfront and Roy Thomson Hall. During his mayoralty, office skyscrapers like Scotia Plaza and BCE Place were erected at a fairly steady pace. When there was a rumour that the new CBC building might be constructed in Scarborough, he called Prime Minister Brian Mulroney and used his influence to ensure that the new headquarters was built on Front Street, where, he says, "it belonged." Accused of being in the pockets of the developers, he countered, "Yes, I'm pro-development. I'm pro good development." Liberal in his views and tied to the Liberal Party, Eggleton had a social conscience and continually promoted more housing for lower-income families (which was, he said in late 1986, the "biggest single challenge facing Toronto," but one not easily resolved). These various attributes made him an unbeatable incumbent.

On November 8, 1982, for example, he defeated his closest opponent, A. Hummer, the alias used by singer and playwright Deanne Taylor—she liked to point out that "city hall was no place for politicians"—by close to 108,000 votes. The city council contest that year was similarly predictable, except for one major upset. In downtown Ward 6, the two incumbents were former mayor John Sewell and Dr. Gordon Chung, who was a business supporter. Sewell easily held on to his seat. But Chung lost his to Jack Layton, an idealistic and popular left-leaning thirty-two-year-old Ryerson political science professor, whom Sewell had recruited. He beat Chung by about 1,600 votes. Thus began Layton's up-and-down political career, which culminated with his election as the leader of the federal NDP in 2003. Eight years later, in the election of May 2, 2011, in which the NDP surprisingly won fifty-nine of seventy-five seats in Quebec, he became the leader of the opposition, three months before his death.

Like Sewell, his mentor, Layton wore blue jeans most days and rode his bike to public engagements. He had stylish long hair accentuated by his trademark moustache and had a knack for attracting a lot more media attention than most of his fellow aldermen. By inclination, he was drawn to the plight of the underdog—workers at the Eaton's Centre who were trying to unionize, AIDS victims, and the homeless. He took on environmental causes and campaigned to end smoking in public places. In his first few years, if Eggleton and a majority of city council were in favour of some deal or policy, the odds were Layton opposed it. He did not realize the image he projected until one night in 1985 when he met one of his brothers at a pub and was introduced to his brother's friend. "Oh, you're Jack Layton," the friend said to him. "I thought your name was

But Jack Layton. You know, you read in the paper, 'The mayor proposes this, but Jack Layton,' or, 'They want to do this, but Jack Layton.'" That criticism cut to the bone. "I was opposing things," he recalled in a June 2011 interview. "I always got the most satisfaction out of life from proposing things." Layton began to reassess his approach.

The rising number of homeless people in Toronto particularly concerned him (so much so that he wrote a book on the subject in 2000), as it did Art Eggleton. The city had had shelters and mission houses to help the destitute since the late nineteenth century, yet the issue was generally off the radar of mainstream Toronto. In those days, you would not have had to step over homeless people sleeping on subway grates in the downtown area because the police would never have permitted it. In 1970, for instance, there was an estimated ten thousand men residing in Toronto's skid row, an area between Yonge and River Streets and Carleton and King Streets. Shelters like Seaton House, which had opened in 1931 to help transients during the Depression, provided temporary haven, though many were crowded and disease ridden. Layton, who spent a night at Seaton House to experience it for himself, called it "a hellish existence." After that, he understood why many homeless men took their chances living on the street or at so-called Tent City, a dilapidated homeless refuge near the Waterfront where about a hundred squatters resided until Home Depot, which had acquired the property, evicted them in 2002.

Under any circumstances, the number of homeless individuals in the city trying to survive on the streets was always, and still is, much greater than the number of beds available in shelters. In one of many reports on homelessness undertaken in Toronto over the decades, the Wellesley Institute noted in 2006 that "more than 30,000 women, men and children crowd into the city's homeless shelters annually. Many thousands more sleep on the streets or join the ranks of the 'hidden homeless'. There are about 70,000 households on Toronto's social housing waiting list. And on the brink of homelessness, are 150,000 households paying more than half their income on shelter."

Toronto's politicians and newspapers finally began to pay attention to what city council later deemed a "disaster" in December 1985, with the death of Drina Joubert, a forty-one-year-old South African immigrant who died from exposure to the cold. Though she had sought treatment and help at a women's shelter, she suffered from alcoholism and mental illness, and during the winter was living in the back of an abandoned pickup truck in an old garage in a laneway near Dundas and Sherbourne Streets, where she was discovered.

The tragedy of Drina Joubert was good copy for a few days and compelled Art Eggleton, who was genuinely appalled by what had happened, together with provincial and federal politicians and a dedicated group of social activists, to take positive steps. "The homeless, the hungry and the poor have been my Number One priority," Eggleton declared. Studies and reports were completed and more public money was made available for social housing through Cityhome, the city's housing company, and other agencies. With financial backing from Ottawa and Queen's Park, thousands of social housing units were built during Eggleton's decade as mayor. In the spring of 1990, Eggleton and other officials were proudly on hand for the ceremony to open StreetCity, a new shelter built inside an abandoned warehouse at Front and Cherry Streets.

The former mayor still points to StreetCity and the social housing units as one of his most important accomplishments, and rightly so. (Jack Layton was more circumspect. "No one can doubt his sincerity about assisting the needy," Layton said in 1989, "but he'll be remembered more for letting the development industry run loose for 10 years... the man whose policies have lowered the quality of life in the city, with oversize buildings bringing more traffic and more pollution.") Yet these projects—including StreetCity's seventy-two beds—only made a tiny dent in a very large problem: a problem that was exacerbated by poverty, mental illness, alcoholism, and the gentrification of downtown property. Moreover, soon after StreetCity began operations, the economy took a turn for the worse and federal and provincial funds dried up. When Mike Harris and the Conservatives took over Queen's Park from Bob Rae and the NDP in June 1995, almost the first item on Harris's agenda was halting Rae's plans for 18,000 social housing units. "Homelessness [is] generally people who have made a decision—and for whatever reason we regret they make it," Harris said in a classic blame-the-victim statement on CBC Radio in April 1996. Such attitudes, what the *Star*'s columnist Joey Slinger called "a stupefyingly silly notion," and the accompanying policy decisions had dire consequences.

A few months earlier, one bitterly cold night in early January, Jack Layton and his wife, Olivia Chow, a Metro councillor, came across two homeless men wrapped in sleeping bags in an alcove on Spadina Avenue. As he usually did, Layton checked on the men, but they did not respond to his questions of concern, so he and Chow moved on. Near Grossman's Tavern there was another homeless man seeking refuge in a bus shelter, though he did not catch their attention. The next morning they heard on a radio news report that this homeless man, Eugene Upper, had died from the freezing weather. Further news stories eventually confirmed that two other homeless people, in other parts of the city, Irwin Anderson and Mirsalah-Aldin Kompani died that night as well.

In the wake of these and other tragedies, yet more inquiries were undertaken, most notably one in 1998 at the behest of Mayor Mel Lastman. As thorough as it was, this action task force, headed by Dr. Anne Golden, president of the United Way, arrived at much the same conclusion as nearly every other study: insurmountable social problems coupled with a lack of affordable housing and inadequate services to monitor mentally ill patients from hospitals and other facilities made the homelessness situation in Toronto difficult to cure. Frustration with the situation exploded on June 16, 2000, when a protest march on Queen's Park, organized by a group of about one thousand anti-poverty activists and homeless people, turned ugly and violent. Dozens of demonstrators were arrested and more than thirty police officers and marchers were injured. The clash solved nothing and led to a backlash against the chief organizer, John Clarke of the Ontario Coalition Against Poverty.

In her *National Post* column a day later, the no-nonsense Christie Blatchford put the riot in perspective: "The comfortable, in the form of the governing Mike Harris Tories, weren't afflicted because the legitimate crisis of the homeless, whose fate this government's cost-cutting has certainly exacerbated though not caused, was lost in the melodrama; the afflicted, which is to say the poor, weren't comforted in the slightest. There are beggars everywhere in this city, you know—a legion of the seriously mentally ill, booze- or drug-addicted, disenfranchised and a large number of street teens—and a good many of them are truly without decent places to live and dependent on shelters. Very few human beings would choose to eke out an existence like this; those who are on the street are either incapable of choice or have run out of choices."

More than a decade later, little has changed and Toronto's homeless population remains a serious concern. At the end of December 2013, during the ice storm that crippled the city, Richard Ian Kenyon, who was discovered dead on Carleton Street, became the 733rd name added to Toronto's Homeless Memorial since 1985. According to Steve Barnes, a policy analyst at the Wellesley Institute, and Beth Wilson, a senior researcher at Social Planning Toronto, provincial and municipal politicians are partly to blame. "Toronto's housing crisis is not inevitable and the negative consequences of homelessness can be avoided if all Torontonians have a decent home," they wrote in a January 2014 *Toronto Star* op-ed article. "But two budget cuts—one municipal and one provincial—are making it harder for many to find and keep a home... It's time for Toronto and Ontario to step up and do the right thing for people in need of housing support."

WHILE HOMELESSNESS REMAINED an intractable problem, the city was beginning to revel in what had previously been viewed as a grave threat, its multiculturalism. Art Eggleton extolled Toronto's celebrated diversity so often that journalists covering city hall would roll their eyes when he began what they referred to cynically as "The Speech." "A lot of people have heard of Toronto but do not know much about it," he said in a *Maclean's* interview in 1988. "There is a strong sense of tradition, of neighbourhood life and family here. It has a reputation as a safe and clean city. People here come from many nations, so it is rich culturally, and diversity is a strength" (like the city's motto, "Diversity Our Strength," says).

Rhetoric aside, Toronto and the surrounding region was indeed shaped by diversity unmatched even by New York City and London. The bastion of all things British for much of its history, Toronto might not be the "most multicultural city in the world," and the mix of people didn't always get along as easily as the city's media and politicians frequently portray it, yet it is hard to dispute the reality of Toronto's famed cultural diversity.

Consider the Caravan festival, for example. This celebration was launched in 1969 by journalist and multicultural promoter Leon Kossar and his wife Zena. For the low price of two dollars, Torontonians of all backgrounds could enjoy the culture and food of many different ethnic groups at dozens of pavilions set up around the city. They could also forget for a moment that the long history of prejudice and discrimination in Toronto and Canada was far more complex than sharing perogies and spring rolls. Still, the crowds flocked to the festival, which encouraged people "to reach out [and] talk to their new neighbours," as former mayor David Crombie remembered.

After a three-and-a-half-decade run, Caravan became less popular and eventually was cancelled in 2004 for lack of interest and funding sponsorship. Torontonians, who could now find ethnic food on most street corners, had grown tired of the event and were weary of having multiculturalism waved in their faces, as Robert Fulford argued. Or put less cynically by Crombie, "what really happened to Caravan was that the city became Caravan. The real sweetness to the story is that. You don't have to organize a 10-day celebration to enjoy cuisine, culture and language differences, you just have to get on the subway."

Crombie was correct about one thing: immigration and multiculturalism were a fact of life in Toronto. By 2001, established ethnic groups like Italians (with a population of 324,090), Jews (179,100), and Germans (57,260) continued to grow and make their presence known in the Toronto Census Metropolitan Area (CMA)—a demographic designation that included Metro Toronto and the counties of Halton, Peel, York, and Durham. When Italy won the World Cup of Soccer in 1982, more than 200,000 deliriously happy Italians paraded on St. Clair Avenue.

Between 1980 and 1996, the population of the CMA increased by approximately 1.25 million, from 2.9 million to 4.2 million. Of that total, an estimated one million or 80 percent were immigrants. Many came from Asia, Africa, the Caribbean, and Central and South America, quite literally changing the face of Toronto. By 1991, 59 percent of people living in the Toronto region were non-British and non-French, representing more than one hundred different ethnic groups. One in four Torontonians was now a member of a visible minority. (The East Indian population in the CMA went from about 255,000 in 1996 to almost 485,000 only five years later.) This was a stunning development for an urban area that in 1961 had a population that was 60 percent of British origin.

To outsiders, it appeared that the city was an ethnic-relations paradise, an aberration in a world where extreme nationalism and racism were still prevalent. In a May 1990 article comparing Toronto with Detroit, *The Economist* concluded that "Toronto has avoided creating the bitter social divide from which Detroit suffers, between an inner-city government and the independent municipalities of its suburbs, between its haves and have-nots, between its 'visible minorities' and its whites." The magazine should have taken a closer look. Because whether most Canadians wanted to accept it or not, the issue was more layered. Toronto and Canada were hardly hate-free zones.

Until the early seventies, a majority of Metro Toronto's Chinese population (about 25,000) still lived in the downtown core, between Bloor and Queen Streets and west of Bathurst. The heart of Chinatown moved west down Dundas to Spadina, replacing Jewish businesses that began moving out as early as the late fifties. Emblematic of this development was the China Court shopping mall on Spadina, south of Dundas, that opened in 1974.

However, almost overnight, wealthy Hong Kong immigrants changed the image of the downtrodden Chinese immigrant. "They are Chinese 'refugees' more likely to come by luxury liner than by boat and Canada has become a haven for them," noted the *Star*'s Tony Wong in July 1988. Flattering news stories abounded about, among others, real estate tycoon Steve Wong; land developers Henry and Daniel Hung, who turned an old roller-skating rink into the Dragon Centre, the first Asian-themed shopping mall in Agincourt in Scarborough; clothing entrepreneur Phoebus Wong, the owner of Artex Sportswear; and venture capitalist Richard Li, youngest son of Hong Kong billionaire Li Ka-shing, who acquired the Harbour Castle Hilton in the mid-eighties.

They and thousands more transformed the so-called 905 suburbs of Markham and Richmond Hill in north Toronto, creating tight-knit and upper-middle-class Chinese enclaves or "ethnoburbs," to use geographer Wei Li's term. In 1995, Markham's population totalled 165,000, of which 45,000 or 27 percent were Chinese Canadian. Following the Hungs' model in Scarborough, Asian malls sprang up at the Toronto Market Village and the nearby Pacific Mall at the corner of Kennedy Road and Steeles Avenue, which according to a Markham website "offer visitors a grand Asian shopping experience."

Chinese immigrants in Markham and across Toronto—in 1991 there were a total of 231,840 Chinese in the Toronto CMA and 391,405 by 2001—reported being content and privileged to live in Ontario. "The more I travel and the more I see of the world, I really feel fortunate to live in Toronto," Andy Ng, a vice-president at Merrill Lynch, said in a 1999 interview from his home in North York. But as in the past, such dramatic ethnic change, even if it involved well-off and educated immigrants, elicited resentment.

In Markham, older white residents were not as enthusiastic about this makeover. Carole Bell, Markham's deputy mayor in the early nineties, became embroiled in controversy in 1995 when she publicly admitted that if she were making the decision then, she would not have moved to the area. "Everything is going Chinese," she said. "This is a racial monopoly... We have citizens demanding we pass by-laws prohibiting signage in a language we can't read... at Chinese malls whose developers are focusing on one group, giving the impression... that non-Chinese basically weren't welcome... The growing concentration of ethnic groups is causing social conflict."

Predictably, her remarks caused a backlash; at one council meeting four hundred Chinese residents demanded that she apologize, as did almost every mayor in the GTA. (To be fair, many Chinese Canadians living in Markham and Richmond also were concerned about the area becoming "an ethnic ghetto" and "alienating residents.") Bell refused to apologize, though she eventually did leave Markham, which became even more diverse and Chinese. In 2001 its population had reached 208,615, of which 62 percent were ethnic minorities and 62,335 or nearly 30 percent were Chinese.

The experience of other Chinese immigrants, who had not grown up enjoying the benefits Hong Kong offered, was more typical. In 1992, Chinese women in Toronto doing piecework toiled long hours sewing skirts for a paltry $1.10 a skirt. In a good year, they might have earned $8,000, well below the poverty line. They did not speak English and rarely ventured beyond the downtown Chinatown. According to a poll conducted by the *Star* and Goldfarb Consultants in 1992, 46 percent felt that Canada was not the land of opportunity they thought it would be, and 63 percent believed that there was "some prejudice" directed towards them.

THOUGH ACTRESS NIA VARDALOS WAS BORN and grew up in Winnipeg, when it came time to shoot her acclaimed 2002 comedy *My Big Fat Greek Wedding*, she knew there was only one location in Canada that had the right "feel" for her movie: in and around "The Danforth." Since the early seventies, when thousands of Greek immigrants made the neighbourhood east of the Don River their own, the avenue has been the bustling hub of Toronto's Greektown—and the place to find the best souvlaki, tzatziki, and baklava west of Athens. On Saturday nights, especially when the weather is decent, the crowds are plentiful, the ouzo flows, the fast-paced bouzouki tunes can be heard for blocks around, and at the mini European-style piazza at the corner of Logan and Danforth, in the shadow of a statue of Alexander the Great, heated conversations about Old World politics—in both Greek and English—continue long into the night. The crowds are even larger each March 25 when they celebrate Greek Independence Day with a colourful parade, as well as in August during the Taste of Danforth street festival, when there is live music and plenty of Greek treats to munch on. It may be classic Canadian multicultural kitsch, but it is hard to argue with the Hellenic atmosphere it generates.

Like the city's Italians, the more than 100,000 Greeks who ventured from their homeland after the Second World War and arrived in Canada were pushed from Europe by a terrible economy and (until 1974) political instability. They were drawn mainly to

Toronto and Montreal via a chain migration. Almost all of them were sponsored by friends and relatives, reinforcing the strong clustering effect around Danforth, especially between Hampton Avenue and Dewhurst Boulevard and as far south as Queen Street East. The completion of the Bloor-Danforth subway extension in 1968 made the location even more attractive for largely unskilled immigrant workers who could not afford a car. In a relatively short period, or so it seemed, The Danforth sprang up, with Greek shops, restaurants, churches, and professional services run by other Greeks for Greeks. By 1971, the Greek population in Metro Toronto (plus the regional municipalities of Durham, Halton, Peel, and York) had reached 51,145, and twenty years later it had increased to 64,015. While in 1991, this represented only 1.66 percent of the population in the CMA, it gave Toronto the largest number of Greek citizens in the Greek diaspora outside of New York and Melbourne.

Higher education and financial success, as well as economic practicality, have gradually reduced the number of Greeks who actually live in or near Greektown. In a typical trend, they moved east to Scarborough or to neighbourhoods up north, where in the 1980s newer homes were more affordable and accessible—since the children of immigrants, unlike their parents, owned and drove cars. As early as 1986, property values around Danforth began shooting up as the neighbourhood attracted affluent yuppies who appreciated its quaintness and had the money to purchase lower-middle-class residences and renovate them. (One Greek restaurant that was opened in 1974 for $80,000 sold twelve years later for $875,000.) "Eighty per cent of our customers used to be Greek," commented Athens-born Jim Karygiannis, who in 1986 was the Danforth Village president (and since 1988 has been an outspoken Toronto Liberal MP). "We've kept them, but now they're only 40 per cent." Nonetheless, due to the strong presence in the area of Greek businesses and community organizations, this internal migration has not diminished the Greek character or flavour of The Danforth.

The experience of Portuguese immigrants was somewhat different. The small number of Portuguese immigrants who arrived in the fifties and sixties settled in and around Kensington Market, in the same homes where Jews and Italians once lived. By 2007, Toronto's Portuguese population reached 96,815, while"Little Portugal" expanded to an area between Bathurst, College, Queen, and the rail yards.

As in Greektown, however, success, assimilation, and a desire to live in a larger house has dissipated the actual number of Portuguese who still reside in the neighbourhood to about 12,075 or 12.4 percent. Many more now live in Brampton, Mississauga, Oakville, and Newmarket, and other suburban locales. The odds of a property in Little Portugal being sold to someone Portuguese are next to nil according to recent research conducted by geographer and community expert Carlos Teixeira. That reality has led to clashes between the older Portuguese residents and the new urban professionals who have moved in—over something as mundane as smoked meat. "Superior Sausage... is a smoke house that has existed at Dundas and Montrose since God gave them the ability to make sausages," one Portuguese homeowner in the area told Teixeira. "Every Wednesday the smokestack spews forth the smoke needed for all the delicacies they produce. Apparently over the last year inspectors at every level have given them a hard time... the [non-Portuguese residents] have decided that the smoke interferes with their enjoyment of Wednesday mornings."

Still, as was the case in Greektown, the absence of Portuguese from the neighbourhood has not diminished its Portuguese identity. A victory by Portugal in a World Cup soccer match will inevitably lead to a boisterous patriotic display on Dundas or College Streets by Portuguese Torontonians who do not live in Little Portugal. To them, however, it will always be, as Teixeira says, "a magnet for Portuguese from across the GTA."

ON APRIL 29, 1992, in a courtroom in Simi Valley, California, sixty-seven kilometres northwest of Los Angeles, three of the four police officers charged in the brutal beating of African-American Rodney King on the side of an LA freeway more than a year earlier were acquitted of all charges. The fourth was also cleared of assault with a deadly weapon, and the jury was deadlocked on whether or not he used excessive force. The jury's verdict triggered large-scale rioting in Los Angeles.

Three days later in Toronto, Constable Robert Rice of the Metro Police Force, who is white, shot and killed Raymond Lawrence, a twenty-two-year-old black Jamaican, who had been living in Toronto for two years on a visitor's permit that had expired. According to the police, Constable Rice and five other plainclothes officers were pursuing Lawrence and two other men in the west end near Wallace and Landsdowne Avenues. They suspected that the men were dealing drugs. Rice cornered Lawrence in a backyard and Lawrence threatened him with a knife. Rice fired a warning shot and ordered Lawrence to stop. When he failed to do so, Rice said he had no choice but to shoot. The police found a small amount of crack cocaine and three wallets containing more than $1,000 in Lawrence's possession. His family and friends, on the other hand, insisted that he was an innocent victim of police abuse.

An independent investigation ultimately confirmed Rice's version of the events. But this much was also true: one more black man, the fourteenth since 1978, and the eighth (none of whom had a gun) in four years, had been killed by a white Toronto police officer. Despite studies, commissions of inquiries, and official promises that the force would adopt a more enlightened and respectful attitude, little seemed to have changed. All too typical was the experience of Toronto-based journalist Cecil Foster, who in 1979, at the age of twenty-five, had emigrated to the city from Barbados. One day in February 1996, by which time he had established himself as a writer for the *Globe and Mail* and a broadcaster for CFRB (where he was, as he says, the only "black talk-show host on any mainstream radio station in the country"), he was driving a nice car when he was randomly pulled over by an angry police officer in what he calls a DWBB violation—"Driving While Being Black." The constable told him he had been speeding; Foster did not think that he was and figured he had been stopped only because the officer believed the car was stolen.

The Caribbean community, a diverse group of immigrants mainly from Jamaica, Trinidad and Tobago, and Haiti, took pride in annual celebrations of its culture like Caribana. Inaugurated in 1967 as a small two-day festival on Centre Island, by the late nineties Caribana attracted up to a million people. To many Torontonians, including many police officers, however, Caribana was merely an illusion. Lurking up north was the true black and Caribbean immigrant story, a harsher narrative of drugs, crime, gangs, and guns, which played out daily in the nasty Jane and Finch corridor, and to the south at Allen Road and Lawrence Avenue in the rough Lawrence Heights housing projects, derisively dubbed "The Jungle" by cab drivers.

Like most stereotypes, this one was not completely untrue—black-related crime, some of it linked to drugs and gangs, was a fact of life in Toronto as it was in New York, Detroit, Los Angeles, and other large urban centres. In February 1989, Staff Inspector Julian Fantino—who later became chief of the Toronto police and commissioner of the Ontario Provincial Police before he was elected to Parliament as a Conservative in 2010—caused an uproar when he released crime statistics which indicated that "while blacks made up 6 per cent of the Jane-Finch population last year, they accounted for 82 per cent of robberies and muggings, 55 per cent of purse-snatchings and 51 per cent of drug offences." A few years later a provocative *Globe and Mail* series on the connection between Jamaican immigrants and crime in Metro Toronto in the summer of 1992 highlighted that "40 per cent of Metro's robberies involve blacks"; one officer maintained that "90 to 95 per cent of it is Jamaican."

Portraying an entire community of more than 130,000 people as a poverty-stricken, crime-infested drug culture raised by single parents was both patently unfair and false. It was no different than treating all Italians as if they belonged to the Mafia, and few people in Toronto would have done that. York University sociologist Frances Henry said it all with the subtitle of her 1994 scholarly study *The Caribbean Diaspora in Toronto: Learning to Live with Racism*.

A week after the Lawrence shooting, black activists decided to organize what was supposed to be a peaceful march to the U.S. consulate on University Avenue to protest alleged police abuse in Toronto and the verdict in the King case. But within a short time the demonstration turned into a riot. Windows in stores on Yonge Street were smashed—by black and white teenagers—and at least thirty people were arrested for disorderly conduct over a six-hour melee.

The riot was yet another cathartic moment for the city, and the analysis and self-reflection continued for months. Toronto was not Los Angeles many commentators argued. "Metropolitan Toronto is not burning," declared Metro chairman Alan Tonks. And he had a point. Asked on a local radio show why he had broken windows, a young unnamed white teen said, "It was just something to do."

Nevertheless, the relationship between the city's black citizens and the police force left much to be desired. While acknowledging racism as a factor, the *Globe and Mail* put the blame for the ongoing tension on "severe social problems"—broken families, higher-than-average drop-out rates from secondary school, and consequently high unemployment rates. Likewise, in her diagnosis of the problem, *Maclean's* writer Barbara Amiel, never one to pull punches, argued that "the real problem America and Canada must face is the growth of an increasingly violent underclass."

Maybe so. Yet, regardless of Amiel's contention that "Canadian society was not racist," these socio-economic problems were also evidence of a hard truth: being black in Toronto meant that you were frequently treated unequally or disrespectfully by the police. "The anger that spilled over into violence in Toronto two nights ago has underscored the urgent need for honesty in agreeing that there is a serious problem between the police and the black community," Clifton Joseph, a black poet and journalist, wrote in an opinion piece for the *Star*. "The regular deadly use of force by the police, the over-representation of blacks in jails, the practice of knee-jerk support by many citizens and officials, and the performance so far of the criminal justice system, including the courts, send out the signals that no matter what the police do, they will be supported." Stephen Lewis, who was appointed by Ontario premier Bob Rae to investigate the riot and its related issues, came to the same conclusion: there was "systematic discrimination" in Toronto and "palpable fear" of the police by many of the city's visible minorities.

THE SITUATION SIMMERED for a while, until a fateful night in early April 1994. No restaurant in Toronto served a more delicious carrot cake topped with rich cream cheese icing than the Just Desserts Café on Davenport Road. The decor was decidedly modern, dominated by large black and white square tiles on the floor, and local art was displayed on the walls. The only negative at Just Desserts was that it was too small, seating fewer than fifty patrons, and the tables were so tightly squeezed together that it wasn't difficult to eavesdrop on the conversation of the people dining next to you. On a typical Saturday night, you usually had to wait in a line that sometimes snaked outside and around the block towards Avenue Road. For the "yuppies" of the Annex, who worked on Bay Street and drove Jaguars, Porsches, and BMWs, as well as for struggling grad students at the nearby University of Toronto, a weekend evening almost always ended with coffee and cake at Just Desserts.

That the café opened in the late seventies in the Annex was not surprising. The surrounding area, with its mix of high-priced, renovated old homes and rustic apartment blocks, had exactly the mixed clientele Just Desserts wanted to attract. An upper-class neighbourhood for decades, the Annex had become a bit rundown in the fifties and early sixties. Then it was reborn and began attracting Toronto's up-and-coming upper and middle classes, especially artists and writers. By the early eighties, these cultural aficionados were snapping up old homes and transforming them into elegant residences and studios. "Late at night, if you listen closely, you may pick up one dominant sound: the clicking of word-processor keys," Robert Fulford quipped about the Annex. "The impression that writers sometimes outnumber houses is not always false."

So Just Desserts thrived. It was the place to relax, hang out, and be seen. On Tuesday April 5, 1994, that was what brought Georgina "Vivi" Leimonis, a vivacious twenty-three-year-old hairdresser, and her friend Tom Drambalas, whom she had known since high school, to the café.

At about eleven o'clock that evening, while Leimonis and Drambalas and other customers were enjoying cake, coffee, and pleasant conversations, four men entered the restaurant. They cased it out and then abruptly left. Minutes later, three of them returned. One man was carrying a sawed-off shotgun. The trio yelled at the staff and patrons to move to the back of the café and hand over their purses, wallets, and jewellery. Two male customers refused to give the men their wallets and a fight broke out. In the ensuing struggle, the robber with the shotgun fired wildly, hitting Leimonis in the chest with more than two hundred pellets. In a panic, the men fled from the restaurant. Leimonis was rushed to the hospital and died a few hours later.

This was arguably the moment Toronto the Good truly lost its innocence. Security cameras had captured part of the robbery in grainy black-and-white video. It was clear that all four men who had first come into the restaurant and the three who had committed the crime were black.

The Just Desserts robbery and murder instantly became national news. Pictures from the video were splashed across newspapers and television. In the Ontario Legislature, politicians bemoaned the horrific murder. Within days, one man, Lawrence Brown, who was later identified as the shooter of Leimonis, had turned himself in, and his three accomplices were soon arrested. All of them were immigrants from Jamaica, who lived in Lawrence Heights.

Brown's story was an ordinary one. He had arrived in Toronto in 1976 at the age of seven with his brother George, who was two years older than him. Their mother,

Josephine Pascoe, had already been in the city for five years. She had found a job at the Prince Hotel, working in the kitchen. She scrimped and saved until she had put away enough to bring her sons to Toronto. Brown was certainly not destined for a life of crime. He attended school and church and became in every way an active and happy Canadian youngster. But when his dreams of becoming rich did not pan out, he became involved with the wrong crowd. Petty theft turned to gangs and drug dealing, which ultimately led him down the path towards that fateful night in April 1994.

Police spoke of the crime as "urban terrorism," and the tragedy led to more virulent denunciations of the city's Caribbean population. *Globe and Mail* columnist Michael Valpy wrote that "the barbarians are inside the gate," suggesting that civilized Toronto, as well as other large Canadian cities, were being invaded by a dangerous and cowardly underclass. The country's immigration rules were called into question, and Torontonians seriously wondered about the safety of their streets.

Three thousand people attended Leimonis's funeral, and a shrine of flowers and letters was left by the café's doorway. One note pleaded for people not to blame the crime on the black community, but it was quickly defaced. "Kill your own," someone wrote across it. "Leave us alone." In a city that prided itself on its acceptance of diversity and lack of prejudice, the killing and the reaction to it were eye-opening.

It took nearly five years of legal wrangling before Lawrence Brown and the other men involved in Vivi Leimonis's murder were brought to court and received their punishment: Brown was given a life sentence with no chance of parole for twenty-five years.

There were a lot more violent and dangerous cities than Toronto in the 1990s and early 2000s. Indeed, in 2012 you had a much greater chance of being killed in Winnipeg or Prince George than near Yonge and Bloor. According to a 2011 survey of crime data from major Canadian cities, Toronto's violent crime severity index of 85.3 ranked far down the list behind Winnipeg at 173.8, Saskatoon at 134.5 and Regina at 123.5. Nonetheless, in the years after the Just Desserts murder, several high-profile gun-related crimes reinforced Toronto's image, as exaggerated as it was, of an urban centre under attack by gangs—especially black gangs.

No tragedy since the death of Vivi Leimonis received more attention than the senseless murder of fifteen-year-old Jane Creba, a student at Riverdale Collegiate Institute, who was an innocent bystander in a gang shooting on Yonge Street near the Eaton's Centre on Boxing Day in 2006. She was white and her assailants were almost all black. By 2010, two young men had been convicted of second-degree murder and two more were found guilty of manslaughter. Race was not an issue in the shooting. The primary victim could easily have been white or brown, male or female, a teen or a senior citizen. "Six others wounded in the incident were indeed of all races, ages, backgrounds," noted the *Star*'s Rosie DiManno. "Yet race—Creba's whiteness, the defendants' blackness, except for one minor-age party to the standoff... has been promoted as the reason police and the Crown attorneys' office were so aggressive with their prosecution, charging just about everyone in sight." Homicide Detective Savas Kyriacou, who was in charge of the lengthy investigation, later said that "Toronto has finally lost its innocence."

That assessment might have been historically inaccurate and even melodramatic. The deaths of Vivi Leimonis and Jane Creba truly did wound the city's collective psyche and raised legitimate questions about housing projects, where gangs and drug crime were cultivated, and allegedly loose immigration policies. But the true victims of gang crime were likely to be gang members themselves or the defenceless residents of Regent Park, Lawrence Heights, and other similar housing complexes—as evidenced by a string of tragic gang-related events that started with a shooting at the Eaton's Centre on June 2, 2012, involving members of a Regent Park gang. Several more serious shootings, including one at a block party on Danzig Street in Scarborough, followed during the summer. (In a bizarre coincidence, Jessica Ghawi, a twenty-four-year-old aspiring journalist working in Denver, was visiting Toronto and witnessed the Eaton's Centre shooting, only to be killed a month later in the shooting at a movie theatre in Aurora, Colorado, on July 20, 2012.)

As for the meaning of it all, Acting Deputy Police Chief Jeff Maguire had what *National Post* columnist Christie Blatchford—who was critical of the hyper-hysterical coverage of the latest Eaton's Centre shooting—said was "the single smartest sentence" she'd heard: "One idiot with a gun doesn't speak to the state of affairs in Toronto."

ART EGGLETON SPENT MANY YEARS attempting to defuse the racial tension provoked by the murder of Vivi Leimonis. He tried as well to repair the relations between the police and many of the city's ethnic communities. By the time he decided to retire in 1991, he had only partly succeeded in this "formidable task," as he described it in a 1989 speech.

His decision to relinquish the mayor's office surprised most people at city hall, including Jack Layton, who could not pass up the opportunity to seek Toronto's highest civic position. During the ensuing mayoralty campaign, he tried hard to reinvent himself by adopting a more professional demeanour. He got a haircut, traded his glasses for contact lenses and started wearing suits instead of jeans. Yet he still came across as too arrogant and as a potential mayor the influential business community could not quite trust.

In the end it became a contest between Layton and the more pro-business law-and-order candidate June Rowlands, a veteran and tough-minded city councillor (as of 1989, Toronto aldermen became known as city councillors), whose recent stint as chair of the Police Commission had given her a high profile. On November 12, 1991, Rowlands, sixty-seven years old, defeated Layton by close to 50,000 votes, becoming Toronto's sixtieth mayor and the first woman to hold that position. It had taken only 157 years.

The loss was a humbling and learning experience for the forty-one-year-old Layton. "I know I came across as too pushy, too ambitious to be mayor, too anxious to stick to the principle rather than say, 'Hey, let's be reasonable'. But people who first think that almost always take a different view of me after we've worked together," he recalled two decades later. He returned to teaching, started an environmental consulting firm, and began laying the groundwork for his eventual success as a federal NDP politician.

"Mayor June" had good intentions. In November 1992 she was forced to double as budget chief when right-wing councillor Tom Jakobek was voted out of that position—councillor Barbara Hall and her five NDP colleagues had accused him of surreptitiously obtaining $100,000 for the Toronto Philharmonic Orchestra from funding allocated to the Toronto Arts Council. Jakobek denied the charges and was indeed vindicated a year later following a lengthy investigation. Truth be told, however, Rowlands was out of her depth.

"June Rowlands wanted to be mayor of Toronto in 1991. At least, she assumed she wanted to be mayor," wrote her former campaign manager John Laschinger in a sharp assessment a year after the election. "She was one of those politicians who seek public office without any clear sense of what they want to do with power once they have it. If Rowlands had a vision for Toronto, she did not share it."

Almost from the start, Rowlands got into trouble. While on holidays, she famously agreed to ban the pop group Barenaked Ladies from performing in Nathan Phillips Square, arguing that the band's name "objectifies women." Six months later, city council, in its wisdom, lifted the ban providing the group and any other organization abided by the Ontario Human Rights Code. Rowlands was criticized for not stopping a council meeting discussing parking regulations when a riot broke out on Yonge Street in May 1992. Mostly, though, she went through the motions of being mayor without accomplishing all that much.

On the eve of a re-election attempt that pitted her against the savvy councillor Barbara Hall, a *Star* editorial summed up Mayor June this way: "It is not that Rowlands is a bad person. She is honest, hard-working, and knowledgeable about city affairs. She would make a good budget chief... But a mayor needs to be more than that; he or she must be a leader. Instead, Rowlands has a habit of disappearing or ducking at times when a mayor's voice is most needed... And on controversial development projects that have come before city council in the past three years, she has chosen to go with the flow rather than take charge and hammer out a compromise." The *Star* supported Hall in the 1994 election and so did a majority of Torontonians. Yet it was not a runaway; Hall received 43.05 percent of the vote to Rowlands's 36.11 percent, which translated into a victory of only 11,296 votes—70,248 to 58,952.

A lawyer by training, Hall had first been elected to city council in 1985. Though she ran for mayor as an independent, she had strong links to the NDP at a time when the public's enthusiasm for the province's NDP government under Premier Bob Rae was waning. Hall's real strength was her successful self-promotion as a "practical progressive" with an intellectual bent who promised to move the city forward. She turned out to be, in the words of Toronto urban affairs writer John Lorinc, "the best mayor Toronto's had since David Crombie."

Besides Hall's win, the other interesting result in 1994, and the one that was to shape the next few years, was the fact that in a non-binding referendum, 58 percent of Toronto voters supported the abolition of the Metro government (since 1988, part of the Metro council had been determined by election). After more than fifty years, Metro had become a dinosaur, outliving its original purpose. The Greater Toronto Area and the outlying region of Halton, Peel, Durham, and York was a hodgepodge of municipal governments with overlapping responsibilities, all trying to govern an ever-expanding geographic area of nearly five million people by 1996. Though police and ambulance services in Metro had been amalgamated years earlier, the same kind of co-ordination was not in place for everything from fire service to a uniform smoking bylaw for restaurants. The property tax system left much to be desired; residents of high-priced homes in Forest Hill and Rosedale paid lower property taxes than homeowners in Scarborough, and the various cities each had their own expensive bureaucracies. And Metro had yet to solve the GTA's unending transportation issues.

"It's interesting to reflect on the fact that when Metro was created in 1953 about half of the land area which is now Metropolitan Toronto was rural, agricultural land," remarked urban planner Ken Greenberg in a *Globe and Mail* discussion of February 1997. "We now have an almost perfect analogy: The urbanized area of Toronto is now perhaps a little less than half of the GTA."

So it was agreed that the Metro system needed fixing. How exactly to do it became the great topic of debate in the mid-nineties. Although most Torontonians like to think of themselves as cosmopolitan, they are as afraid of real change as most Canadians are—especially when that change is rammed down their throats by a provincial government that seems to have no regard for the democratic process. In some quarters, the controversial decision to abolish the Metro government and amalgamate the six lower-tier municipalities into one "megacity" with one large council was like a sequel to the Stop the Spadina Expressway movement, except this time the Ontario premier wore the black hat and did not save the day.

Local history and identity were also under siege as a result of amalgamation. Suddenly, being from North York or Etobicoke took on a whole new meaning, and the demise of municipal governments meant a loss of power for local politicians in the new civic order. "You won't find North York anywhere on the map! North York is gone!" declared the always colourful mayor of North York, Mel Lastman, at one anti-megacity rally. "They're carving us up like a turkey and it isn't even Thanksgiving!"

This made-in-Toronto soap opera started in the spring of 1995. Three months before his crushing defeat by Mike Harris and the Progressive Conservatives in a provincial election, NDP premier Bob Rae established the Greater Toronto Area Task Force led by Dr. Anne Golden, the president of the United Way of Greater Toronto. Golden and the four other commissioners spent months studying this complex issue and received more than three hundred submissions. They delivered their 270-page report to the Harris government in January 1996. Among other recommendations, the task force urged that the Metro government be dissolved and replaced by an appointed GTA regional council that would be responsible for coordinating certain services in the current Metro area and beyond into the outlying regions. Separate municipal governments, like Toronto's city council, would continue with revised powers. The report also suggested revamping the property tax system to make it more equitable.

For the most part, the report received almost universal support from urban planners, and political scientists. Toronto newspapers thought the idea of a GTA council made sense. But the politicians were more skeptical. Metro councillors were not in favour of their own demise, while the four big mayors—Toronto's Barbara Hall, Mel Lastman of North York, Hazel McCallion of Mississauga and Nancy Diamond in Oshawa—who were protective of their own local interests and power, did not believe that Metro or a new regional council was necessary. "Reconstituting a modern city-region on the scale of Greater Toronto requires a degree of political effort that would have daunted the Fathers of Confederation," John Barber, the *Globe and Mail*'s urban columnist, pointed out. "So would-be reformers find themselves cooking eggs above the falls, fatally exposed to the gales of entrenched localisms and special interests."

Most tellingly, Premier Mike Harris and municipal affairs and housing minister Allan Leach, the ultimate decision makers, were less than impressed with the Golden report, especially the idea of establishing a large GTA regional council that would be in direct competition with the provincial jurisdiction. It soon became clear that Harris and Leach favoured one option and one option only: amalgamation, with one megacity council for the entire Metro area. Such a move, Leach said on many occasions, would result in substantial economic savings—predicted to be more than $800 million over three years and then $300 million each year after that—which was in line with the Reganesque "Common Sense Revolution" Harris had promised during the election in order to reduce the size of government and the enormous provincial deficit left to him by the Rae administration.

Reflecting on this decision now, Harris says that, "politically, it would have been easier to keep the municipal governments small, allowing much more [provincial] control. You don't want one big monster. But it was the right thing to do, though I wish it came together a bit better. Golden's plan would have met with more favouritism, but I don't think it was the right way to go." What later cost Harris popular support was the fact that he presented his proposal with an arrogance that further angered his already angry opponents. As a result, the overall "common sense" part of the package got lost.

For more than a year, Golden's report and other possibilities—such as the idea of consolidating only Metro's six municipalities into one urban government, without adding in the outlying regions, which was recommended in a December 1996 report by former mayor David Crombie, who had been asked by the province to study the matter further—were the subject of countless debates and received almost daily media coverage. By a long shot, amalgamation was the least popular option, yet Harris and Leach stubbornly refused to budge. Before the end of 1996, Bill 103, an act to amalgamate Metro Toronto, was introduced in the legislature, and it was given royal assent in April 1997, despite a creative and exhausting ten-day filibuster by the NDP and Liberals. The new city government was to be implemented by January 1, 1998.

By then, Toronto was in the grip of "Mega-Madness," as Joe Chidley of *Maclean's* rightly described it. "To the provincial Conservatives and their supporters, it is a tale of solid municipal policy and sound fiscal management," he explained. "But to many Torontonians, who fear that the province's reforms will destroy their city, it has taken on the proportions of a horror movie—Megacity: The Tory Monster that Ate Toronto." There was lots of shouting, several votes denouncing the plan, and a series of referendums in March 1997 in which an overwhelming number of Torontonians opposed the idea. John Sewell, who was irate at what he perceived as the arrogance and anti-democratic attitude of the government, organized, à la Spadina, a grassroots protest that attracted thousands, and Citizens for Local Democracy was born.

One day, Leach recalls, Sewell showed up at his house unannounced, wanting to talk about the proposal. Leach invited him in and the two men debated amalgamation. "We talked about it," says Leach, "but Sewell got so frustrated that he got up and slammed the door." (Sewell agrees that there was a heated discussion, but he maintains that he did not slam the door as he was leaving.) Harris adds: "I am not a John Sewell fan. Generally, if he was for something, I was opposed to it, and he'd probably say the same." Even the urban prophet Jane Jacobs, about to celebrate her eighty-first birthday, weighed in with her censure of Harris's plan. "Anyone who supposes harmony will prevail and efficiency reign after whole-hog amalgamation has taken leave of common sense," she declared at a provincial hearing. "These six cities really are different, and the differences won't be erased by everybody trying to mind everybody else's business and beat down every local vision different from their own."

Anne Golden, among others, was beside herself. Where did this idea of amalgamation come from, she wondered. "I can't figure it [the amalgamation proposal] out," she said in an interview in mid-January 1997. "It just seemed to emerge as a full-grown idea... What is amazing me is that people have leapt to that conclusion." Of the three hundred submissions her task force received, "only one person advocated amalgamation"—and that one person was Paul Godfrey, the "megacity Machiavelli," as the *Globe and Mail* dubbed him, former Metro chairman, the man who got the SkyDome built, and the head of the *Toronto Sun*. Blaming Godfrey, as his old nemesis John Sewell does, is convenient and may well have played a part in Harris's decision.

The truth of the matter is somewhat less conspiratorial. In late 1996, Harris and Leach did convene what turned into a long meeting at the Albany Club to discuss this issue. Among those invited to attend and consult on the amalgamation question were Paul Godfrey, David Crombie, and MPP David Johnson, chair of the Harris cabinet's management board and the former mayor of East York. "I was asked my opinion," Godfrey recalls, "and I said I thought the city had outgrown the present form of government. There was too much bickering between the local municipalities and Metro. And the only reason to keep the two-tier system of the government was to satisfy the local representatives, mayors and councillors. I thought that an amalgamated city made more sense. Other people spoke and I was quite surprised that so many others in the room repeated the same view." There were no ulterior motives, Leach insists. "We needed to consult and by the end of the meeting it was universally agreed that [amalgamation] was the way to go."

David Crombie also dismisses any notions of a conspiracy. The former mayor was by no means ideologically in sync with Harris, but he concurs that the merger was inevitable. "Amalgamation was always going to be the goal," he says. "It had to be. Metro was a process. It became much more centralizing over the years, taking more and more responsibility. So the precedent was there for one government."

John Sewell took some pleasure in pointing out, in a December 2000 op-ed piece, that amalgamation did not generate the tremendous savings Harris and Leach assured everyone it would. While expenses did decrease in some areas, "surprise, surprise," Sewell wrote, "the net cost of amalgamation over the first two years was $20 million even with the substantial cuts to staff. Amalgamation did not save money—it imposed costs, just as it has done in virtually every other North American urban area that has been amalgamated." Seven years later, on the tenth anniversary of the forced merger, a University of Toronto study came to the same conclusion. By 2007, the civic bureaucracy had swelled—the city employed 4,105 more people (mostly in the TTC) than it did in 1998—and had become even more remote from the citizens it served, just as Jane Jacobs had predicted.

"The current system is not functional," says Anne Golden, who maintains her view that amalgamation was a mistake. "The council is too small to cover the whole economic region. It does not address the region-wide issues of transportation and economic development. But it is too big to provide genuine responsiveness and accountability." As for the question of savings, and irrespective of academic claims to the contrary, she is in agreement with Mike Harris, Allan Leach, David Crombie, and others. "It's impossible to tell if there are savings or not because things got merged and you can't trace it," she says. "The second thing is that in the areas that they said there would be savings, there's no evidence to prove that."

Regardless, there is no turning the clock back. Critics condemned the Harris government's decision to download transit, public housing, and a portion of social services costs to the civic government in exchange for the province taking complete control of education funding. The plan worked fairly well for some municipalities but less so for the city of Toronto. "With its aging subway system and tens of thousands of crumbling public housing units, downloading proved disastrous," according to John Lorinc. The TTC was left hanging and, as Lorinc added, "without adequate provincial funding, the city had no choice but to cut service and stop planning for expansion." The TTC was forced to refurbish older and outdated buses rather than buy new ones. And the city continued to borrow too much money—extra provincial funding in the form of a large no-interest loan that was offered to offset the extra expense was wholly insufficient. Mel Lastman called Premier Mike Harris a "liar" for claiming that amalgamation would be "revenue neutral" and then was compelled to apologize for his intemperate language.

The quest for the megacity mayoral crown in the election of November 1997 pitted Lastman against Barbara Hall. Both had opposed amalgamation, Hall more vehemently than Lastman. At age sixty-four, Lastman was the older of the two and, as mayor of North York since 1972, the more experienced politician—the fifty-year-old Hall had been the City of Toronto's mayor for only three years. Though Hall was a strong contender and had transformed herself into an effective promoter, she could not match Lastman's famous shoot-from-the-hip bluster that he had fashioned in Kensington Market where he grew up and as the multi-millionaire owner of Bad Boy Furniture ("Nobody beats Bad Boy, nooooobody"). As a novice politician in North York in 1969, Lastman ran for the position of controller. After he won the election, he famously asked, "What does a controller do?"

For much of the campaign, Lastman was ahead two-to-one, but a few slip-ups—such as when he claimed that North York had no homeless people on the same day that a homeless woman was discovered dead at a North York gas station a few blocks from Lastman's office—allowed Hall to narrow the gap. "I have no fear of Barbara Hall," Lastman had said just prior to declaring his candidacy. "She's no problem. The only thing I fear is my own mouth." He was right to fear it, and his tendency to speak without thinking was part of the reason the *Globe and Mail*, the *Star*, and the arts community endorsed Hall. The contest was close, with Lastman defeating Hall by 41,396 (mainly suburban) votes—387,848 to 346,452—making "Mayor Mel" of North York, "Megamayor Mel," the first leader of megacity Toronto and its new fifty-seven-member council.

IF CIVIC POLITICS DIVIDED Torontonians in the eighties and nineties, then baseball, especially the back-to-back World Series victories of the Toronto Blue Jays in 1992 and 1993, united them in a triumphant fervour not seen in years. For a few all-too-brief shining moments, everyone in Canada was cheering for Toronto and the Jays.

And thank God for that, because during much of the eighties and nineties, the Leafs were in a big rut. They had lost their two great stars in foolish trades, first Lanny McDonald in 1979, and then Darryl Sittler in early 1982. In 1984–85, the Leafs won only twenty games and were the worst team in the NHL. Following the death of owner Harold Ballard in 1990, the on-ice situation improved, and with such stars as Doug Gilmour and Dave Andreychuk, and Felix Potvin in net, the Leafs became competitive. In the 1993–94 season, they got farther in the post-season than they had in years, only to lose the conference final series to the Vancouver Canucks.

Meanwhile, the Blue Jays were plugging along, making trades, and gradually building a true contender. Things started to turn around for the team under manager Bobby Cox in 1982. Three years later the Jays finished first in the American League East division, but then lost the best-of-seven AL championship series to the Kansas City Royals, four games to three. However, this was a harbinger of future success.

In June 1989, the Jays, who had been using Exhibition Stadium, finally got a proper venue to play in when SkyDome, with its sci-fi retractable roof, opened. Toronto architect Rod Robbie had won the competition to design it in 1985 and promised it could be built for the agreed-upon budget of $225 million. That proved highly optimistic; by the time SkyDome opened, the cost had risen to an astounding $650 million (which included interest charges), much of which had to be covered by Ontario taxpayers.

Robbie envisioned the stadium as a "secular cathedral," but most other professionals were less than impressed. After studying the proposal, Toronto's planning staff deemed SkyDome "too big, too wide, too high and too ugly." Nevertheless, the debt-ridden behemoth (eventually sold by the province to John Labatt, Ltd., in 1994 for the bargain basement price of $151 million) rose up beside the waterfront, and Torontonians grew to love what Robbie called "a pleasure palace for the people." Remembering Robbie, who died in January 2012 at the age of eighty-three, John Bentley Mays, the *Globe and Mail*'s architecture columnist, put the SkyDome—as of 2005 the Rogers Centre—into perspective: "It may be ugly; but it has become our ugly—a living part of the Toronto story, a memory of something Toronto wanted to be, and a dream about the sprawling, hard-driving, hard-playing North American metropolis that, rightly or wrongly, we still want to be."

The opening ceremonies on June 3, 1989, did not quite display the dome's genius, however. With dignitaries and a cast of all-star Canadian talent on hand, SkyDome executives decided in their wisdom that the highlight of the night would be the opening of the roof. Except it was raining, and as the roof magically retracted over twenty-four minutes, thousands of elated Torontonians got soaked. Host Alan Thicke sang a specially composed tune that featured the line "Open up the dome!" but the drenched audience yelled back at him, "Close it! Close it!"

Two days later the Blue Jays played their first game in the SkyDome in front of more than 48,000 fans, the largest crowed to watch a baseball game in the city's history. After great deliberations and intense scrutiny of weather charts, it was decided to keep the roof open. It did not make a difference as the Jays ruined the storybook night by losing to the Milwaukee Brewers 5–3. Fred McGriff hit the team's first home run in the dome.

The most popular moment at SkyDome was undoubtedly during a game on May 15, 1990. It was not the action on the field that pleased the crowd, however, but the action in one of the rooms of the SkyDome Hotel overlooking the field. A couple staying at the hotel believed they could not be seen having sex in front of the window in their room. They were mistaken, as were two other couples over the years.

The march to the World Series began in earnest with the astute promotion of hitting coach Cito Gaston to manager in 1989. He got the support he needed from the team's chief executive, Paul Beeston, and general manager, Pat Gillick. In December 1990, Gillick made a bold move in a monster trade with the San Diego Padres. He swapped popular first baseman Fred McGriff and all-star shortstop Tony Fernández for outfielder Joe Carter and second baseman Roberto Alomar. Both highly talented players would bring tremendous excitement to Toronto, making huge contributions to the team's World Series victories. Alomar, in particular, as sports writer Stephen Brunt put it, was the "finest second baseman of his generation, the best position player in the history of the Toronto Blue Jays, the first player in franchise history selected to wear the team's cap into the Hall of Fame... the first to have his number retired, [and] an athlete who at one time enjoyed the celebrity wattage of a teen idol."

In 1992, the Jays again finished first in the American League East division, helped by the stellar performance of newly acquired pitcher Jack Morris. In the AL championship series their opponents were the Oakland Athletics. Heading into the fourth game in Oakland on October 11, the Jays had played well and were leading two games to one, but the fourth game did not start well. By the third inning the A's had scored five runs and the Jays one. The A's added another run in the sixth. The Jay's amazing comeback started in the eighth inning and culminated in the ninth with Alomar's two-run homer off A's pitcher Dennis Eckersley. This was, Brunt has argued, "the watershed moment in franchise history." The Jays wound up winning the game 7–6 in 11 innings and eventually took the series.

They faced the National League champion Atlanta Braves in the World Series and united Toronto and Canada in common cause by winning in six games. Alomar, Carter, David Cone, Dave Winfield, Pat Borders, and the rest of the superstar team became household names. "Don't feel guilty about cheering for the Blue Jays," wrote Kent Gilchrist of *The Province* in Vancouver, expressing a sentiment that spread far beyond the 401, across the nation. "Give thanks they are a Canadian team, even if there are no Canadians playing for it." Arriving home as world champions on October 26, the Jays were given a short downtown parade as 250,000 delirious fans lined the streets. Another 50,000 or so crammed into SkyDome to cheer the best thing that had happened in the city, sports-wise at least, since the Leafs had won the Stanley Cup way back in 1967. "I'm so proud of you guys, you're the greatest," declared Cito Gaston. "Let's do it again."

He wasn't kidding. There were changes—Dave Winfield and Tom Henke were gone—but the 1993 Blue Jays were an unstoppable team and easily won the East division again. They took the Chicago White Sox in the AL championship, four games to two, and then met the Philadelphia Phillies in the World Series.

On October 23, in game 6, the Jays were leading the series 3 to 2. With the score 6–5 for the Phillies, the Jays had one last chance in the bottom of the ninth. There were two men on base, Rickey Henderson (the former Oakland A's star had signed with the Jays in August) and Paul Molitor, when Joe Carter came up to bat.

With the count 2–2, Carter took a swing and hit the most important and exciting home run in the team's brief history. "I just wanted to make contact," he later said. As he leaped for joy around the bases, the SkyDome erupted, and in living rooms across the country, Canadians who detested Toronto but loved the Jays cheered loudly. Forever after, Canadian baseball fans would remember this moment with great fondness. Only once before had a home run clinched a World Series victory and that was in 1960, when Bill Mazeroski did it for the Pittsburgh Pirates. This was also the first time a team had won consecutive World Series championships since the New York Yankees had done it in 1977 and 1978.

The Blue Jays were the most feted team in the city, but in the years since those glorious celebrations, the team has not performed well enough to play in the post-season playoffs.

The city's National Basketball Association team, the Raptors, played their first games in the shadow of the Blue Jays' second World Series win, and they have also struggled. The team did not make the playoffs until 2000, when its star player, Vince Carter, led the way. They did it again the next two years, though only once, in 2001, did they make it past the first round. The team qualified for the playoffs in 2007 and 2008 with similar results. Since then, despite the presence of Chris Bosh for seven seasons, the Raptors have floundered. They ended the 2012–13 season with thirty-four wins against forty-eight losses, placing the team tenth in the fifteen-team eastern division.

The Leafs have also had a dismal playoff record since 1993. But one of the more significant moments in the franchise's storied history occurred in 1999 when, after sixty-eight years, Maple Leaf Gardens was closed and the Leafs joined the Raptors in the ultra-modern $265-million Air Canada Centre. (As of 1998, both sports franchises were owned by Maple Leaf Sports and Entertainment under the control of Steve Stavro and Larry Tanenbaum.)

Naturally, the end of the Gardens era resulted in an avalanche of sappy media coverage, with reminiscences from just about anyone who had ever attended a game or concert at the arena. Far away in Victoria, Jeff Rud of the *Times Colonist* even tried to make a case that the "schlock sentiment" was legitimate. "More so perhaps than any other building, Maple Leaf Gardens is woven into the cultural fabric of this country," he wrote. Christie Blatchford sensibly dismissed it all. "I come to bury Maple Leaf Gardens, not to praise it," she wrote in her *National Post* column on the Gardens' last day. "Having watched/read/listened to weeks of wretched excess about the Grand Old Lady of Carlton Street, I know I stand pretty much alone here. Is there an aged Gardens' builder or original subscriber still alive who did not come creaking out of the woodwork to pose, with enchanting grandchild, for the cameras, and archly suggest that they ought to be at the final game? ... A visiting player who has not been forced to come up with some cherished reminiscence before being allowed to leave?" And, of course, in that last game the Leafs lost 6–2 to the Chicago Blackhawks.

As disappointing as it often has been to be a Toronto sports fan, the real drama was about to erupt at city hall. Over the course of a decade, a trio of megacity mayors provoked a gamut of emotions—laughter, disbelief, anger, and humiliation—in a struggle of power and wills that was to divide the city like never before.

Chapter Thirteen

MEGACITY MACHINATIONS (OR MADNESS)

Toronto is a place with great aspirations, run by a small-town mentality.

—KELLY MCPARLAND, *NATIONAL POST*, 2012

The construction of Toronto's new city hall, opened in 1965, was enthusiastically promoted by Nathan Phillips, mayor of the city from 1955 to 1962. Despite its controversial modern design, the iconic landmark, distinguished by the twin curving towers of different heights and the circular council chamber, has become one of Toronto's enduring symbols. *City of Toronto Archives, Fonds 200, Series 374, Item 17*

CANADIAN MAYORS come in all shapes and sizes—businessmen, intellectuals, and promoters. Mel Lastman, who was fond of expensive cigars and fine food, and who celebrated his sixty-fifth birthday in March 1998, a few months into his new job as megacity mayor, was of the salesman variety, a generally politically astute raconteur and dealmaker who did everything he could to improve the lives of the citizens he represented—at least by his definition. A pro-development booster, he believed that bigger was always better. He had pushed a massive construction project around Yonge and Sheppard (the work of the late Murray Menkes, an industrious and trend-setting entrepreneur who registered the first condominium in the province in 1969). Lastman also supported sports and cultural projects, and served the citizens of North York well during his twenty-five years in office, transforming the post-war "sleepy suburb" into a much more dynamic city.

But the transition from North York to Toronto city hall was challenging, and it would have been for anyone. Despite the fact that the new megacity council resembled, in jurisdiction at least, the old Metro council, Lastman was still responsible for a civic administration that was essentially being built from the ground up—not to mention, as the *Star*'s Royson James later reflected, a $6-billion budget, which

was more than twenty times greater than the budget he had looked after in North York. And Lastman now had to manage "homeless [people] he said didn't exist, welfare moms, poor people without dentures, Bay Street bigwigs, the TTC, ambulance workers, 6,500 restaurants and bars, almost 50,000 workers, small business and big business, tourism, the police, garbage pickup and the state of cultural institutions" as well. There were bound to be growing pains.

Lastman sometimes spoke without thinking, a dangerous affliction for any politician. Nor did the mayor help his own or Toronto's reputation during the winter of 1999. There is a truism about winter weather in Canada: in January it snows, even in Toronto. On January 14, climatologists warned that Torontonians should brace themselves for a wicked blizzard that was about to descend on the GTA, adding to an already unusual amount of snow that had been dumped on the city. Sure enough by mid-morning the next day, approximately twenty-five centimetres of snow had fallen, made worse by bitterly cold winds. It was the worst winter storm in the city in fifty years.

Even before a snowflake had hit the ground, Lastman conceded that he was "petrified." He was not about to let the city be shut down, so he did what any creative mayor would have (perhaps) done: he called in the army to help clear the snow. The zany plan received the full support of defence minister and former mayor Art Eggleton, and almost immediately more than four hundred soldiers arrived in Toronto with shovels at the ready. Another thousand were on standby. Frequently a one-man show, Lastman acted without consulting his fellow city councillors, who later criticized him for ignoring them. In defending his solo actions, the mayor declared that he did not want to cause a panic and argued that the more people who spoke about the "crisis," the worse the situation would have become.

The storm forced the subway and GO train to suspend service, thousands of flights were cancelled at Pearson Airport, and the city did come to a standstill—as lots of cities in Canada and the United States do in January during a blizzard. The Canadian Forces helped clear the streets and sidewalks and got the city moving again. For their efforts, the soldiers were rewarded with free tickets to a Maple Leafs hockey game.

Needless to say, the rest of the country howled then and later at Toronto's misfortune. "'Troops enter Toronto.' A westerner's fondest dream? The plot line of a forthcoming CBC made-for-television movie?" asked Lorne Gunter in his *Edmonton Journal* column. "No, the headline of a bemused, half-gloating lead story about Toronto's recent snow storms carried in the *Ottawa Citizen* on January 15." Gunter added that it was difficult for the army to clear the streets "because their armoured plows were too wide to navigate the streets without scratching the parked Lexuses and Benz." A witty cartoon by Terry Mosher (Aislin) in the *Montreal Gazette* ridiculed Torontonians with the caption "Item: World Class Wimps in Toronto Call in the Army to Deal with a Bit of Snow," as a man from Toronto's financial sector shouted into his cell phone, "Mayday! Mayday! My Volvo won't start."

When the city was hit again in February 2007, CBC comedian Rick Mercer produced a hilarious *Fifth Estate* parody entitled "Snow in Toronto!" Portraying a frazzled and fearful Torontonian circa 1999, actress Sonja Smits, in tears, cried out, "I remember it just like it was last week. I opened the door and there it was. It was everywhere... I always thought that this was the kind of thing that happened to other people. But when I saw the snow, I started screaming, 'Where is the army? Where is the police? Why me?'"

As was his style, Lastman refused to second-guess his decision. On the tenth anniversary of the '99 storm, the retired former mayor was asked whether he would have done anything different. "Would I do it again?" he said defiantly. "You're darn right I would!"

Lastman's over-the-top reaction to the blizzard may have provided the rest of Canada with some good laughs, but inside the GTA he was still—next to Mississauga's legendary mayor Hazel McCallion, who had been in office since 1978—the most popular civic politician. The economy was in good shape, construction in the city was buzzing again, and property taxes were frozen, as Lastman had promised they would be. He had obtained federal funding for more social housing, part of his campaign on behalf of the homeless, and had also garnered federal and provincial money for a proposed $17-billion waterfront revitalization plan. He had tackled and vastly improved the inadequate system of public health inspections for the city's restaurants. In short, he had given Torontonians solid, if uninspired, leadership. More damaging to his reputation was his public acknowledgment of a fourteen-year affair he had had decades earlier with Grace Louie, a former employee at his Bad Boy store, with whom he fathered two sons.

As vulnerable as he may have been, no credible candidate dared to challenge him in the election of November 2000, and he easily won with an impressive 80 percent of the vote. Running a distant second in the race was the late environmental activist Tooker Gomberg, whose claim to fame was obtaining an endorsement from Jane Jacobs. He received 51,111 votes to Lastman's 483,277. (Enza Anderson, a well-known transvestite model, came in third with 13,595 votes.) Not as favourable for Lastman was the re-election of a cadre of city councillors who were less than enamoured of "His Melness." Led by lawyer David Miller, the group included Michael Walker (who Lastman once said "was a good excuse for birth control"), Howard Moscoe, Joe Mihevc, Anne Johnston, Jack Layton, and several others who made up a sizable minority among the now forty-four councillors.

Gaffe followed gaffe during Lastman's second term. In June 2001 the city was bidding to host the 2008 Summer Olympics (building on its unsuccessful bid for the 1996 games). The committee members were certain that Lastman's acclaimed abilities as a salesman would enhance their bid. About a month before the International Olympic Committee (IOC) was to decide on the host city, Lastman was on his way to Mombasa, Kenya, to convince African IOC delegates that Toronto was the right choice. Then, yet again, he spoke without understanding the ramifications of his words. "What the hell do I want to go to a place like Mombasa," he told a *Star* journalist jokingly. "Snakes just scare the hell out of me. I'm sort of scared about going there, but the wife is really nervous. I just see myself in a pot of boiling water with all these natives dancing around me." His insensitive remarks were widely reported and he was forced to apologize one more time. His comments likely played no role in Toronto losing its bid for the Olympics. A *Star* editorial rightly suggested everyone in the city should get a grip. Lastman was no racist and his silly statement, as the paper suggested, did not "blacken this city's reputation for diversity and multicultural harmony." If anything, it was just one more example of Lastman's unsophisticated style, which made some members of the self-aggrandizing Toronto elite cringe.

Next he shook hands with Hell's Angel bikers who were in Toronto for a convention, only to explain later that he had no idea the motorcycle gang was involved in illicit activities. "[A biker] put out his hand and I shook his hand," he later said. "Please understand, I've never turned my back on anybody who gave me their hand. In retrospect, maybe I did the wrong thing, I don't know."

There was still more. In the spring of 2003, Toronto was one of several cities seriously affected by the deadly severe acute respiratory syndrome, or SARS, pandemic. Of the estimated eight hundred people who died worldwide from the disease, forty-four were from the GTA. As a necessary precaution, medical authorities quarantined several hospitals, and some public events were postponed. For a few weeks the World Health Organization (WHO) recommended that travelling to Toronto was not advisable, a decision that did not sit well with Lastman and other city leaders, who were concerned about the impact of SARS on tourism.

At the end of April, the mayor appeared on CNN to comment on WHO's travel advisory. "I don't know who this group is; I've never heard of them before, I've never seen them before, they've never talked to us," Lastman declared. It was yet another case of Lastman speaking without first doing his homework. Comedian Jon Stewart could not resist poking fun at him. "You know, I was thinking of going to Toronto," he said on his comedy news show, "but I've heard the mayor is kind of a dick. By the way, for more information on Toronto, pick up a copy of the mayor's new city guide, *Toronto: What the Hell?*" Many Torontonians could only sigh and shake their heads with embarrassment.

Some months earlier, Lastman had announced that he would not run in the next election. His decision was based partly on his age and health concerns, but he also had been hurt by allegations about corruption involving the leasing of computers for city hall—charges that later proved to be all too true following an extensive inquiry. Justice Denise E. Bellamy, who wrote the 486-page report released in 2005, uncovered what she called "massive bureaucratic mismanagement that ended up costing the city millions of dollars." Lastman himself was not directly guilty of taking money under the table, as other city officials were, though he was wilfully blind to what had been happening on his watch. He had not set proper ethical standards and ignored the fact that "at every turn in the [contract] drafting process, key participants failed to protect the city's interests."

When he finally relinquished the mayor's chair in the fall of 2003, the full extent of the scandal and his culpability in it had yet to be revealed. Premier Ernie Eves (who had taken over from Mike Harris) praised him as "the little mayor with the big heart"—which is what he was: a politician who truly loved the city, but whose "big" personality and personal flaws and foibles continually got him into trouble. The city desperately required a professional fixer, a twenty-first-century leader with the intellectual bent and integrity to clean up the mess at city hall and make Torontonians proud. In November 2003, voters believed they had found such a talented individual in David Miller.

THE CITY COUNCIL MEETING on May 21, 2002, was unusually boisterous. Accusations flew over Mel Lastman's choice of candidates to serve as various committee chairs. In particular, councillor David Miller was not impressed with the mayor's slate and was not shy about expressing his dissatisfaction. "If you slavishly follow the rules you get rewarded," he stated, "even if that results in screw-ups, even if it results in mismanagement of the city's affairs, even if it results in corruption, you seem to get rewarded."

Throwing around a term like "corruption" is contentious, and within a day Lastman and his allies, who were offended by the accusation, went after Miller. Lastman, who had not yet announced that he was stepping down as mayor, had heard rumours that Miller was vying for his job. "I am not joking about this," Lastman yelled at Miller. "I am asking for a legal opinion, and I will sue you for everything you can possibly lay your hands on." Then, in what must be one of the more ironic declarations ever made at city council, he added, "This is irresponsible. You will never be mayor of this city. This I can tell you right now, because you say stupid and dumb things. You can call a politician stupid and you can call him dumb. But you can't call him a thief and corrupt."

In a sign of things to come, Rob Ford, who had been elected to council in Etobicoke North in the election of 2000—and who was aptly described by John Barber of the *Globe and Mail* as a "loose cannon"—also shouted at Miller for trying to "intimidate" other councillors. Deputy mayor Case Ootes, who ruled that Miller's remarks were "unparliamentary" and "impugned the integrity of council," demanded that Miller withdraw them. He refused. In a subsequent vote on the matter, twenty-seven councillors voted against Ootes's motion (only sixteen voted in favour), which was rightly interpreted as a slap in the face to the mayor. That challenge to Miller's integrity, as he recalls, "launched my [mayoralty] campaign" for the civic election of November 2003.

David Miller was born in San Francisco in 1958. His father, Joe, died when he was an infant, prompting his mother, Joan, who was British, to return with David to England. The two then settled in Toronto in 1967. Education was paramount to Joan and, as Miller recalls, "she worked three jobs to put me through private school." He attended Lakefield College School, near Peterborough, where he played rugby with his fellow student Prince Andrew (at a June 2003 reunion luncheon at Lakefield, Prince Andrew was pleased to wear a "Miller for Mayor" button). Miller went on to do an undergraduate degree at Harvard and a law degree at the University of Toronto. In 1984 he joined the Bay Street corporate law firm Aird & Berlis, which he returned to in 2010 after he left civic politics.

During this period, Miller became active in politics as a member of the NDP. Twice during the 1990s he vied for federal and provincial seats but lost both times. Instead he found his niche in municipal politics. He first ran for a seat on Metro council in 1991, but lost. Three years later he tried again and this time won by 1,100 votes. When Metro was dissolved, he ran in the 1997 election and won a seat on the inaugural megacity council. Appointed to the TTC, he earned a name for himself as a bright and astute left-wing councillor who made informed arguments. "A lot of times during city council debates there is a lot of noise and no one is paying attention," says John Lorinc, one of the best writers on urban politics in the country. "But when Miller stood up to speak, people listened." And a lot of them liked what they heard.

In what was a Toronto first, forty-four individuals ran for mayor in the 2003 election (coming in last, with 110 votes, was thirty-three-year-old Barry Pletch, then the arts editor for the *Etobicoke Guardian*, a community paper). The main contenders who emerged from this unwieldy pack were Miller; Barbara Hall, the former mayor and initial frontrunner, who eventually faded; former Liberal MP John Nunziata, best remembered for his expulsion from the federal Liberal caucus because he opposed the GST; long-time city councillor Tom Jakobek, who was done in because of his links to the computer leasing scandal; and John Tory, a well-connected and polished lawyer, businessman, and Conservative Party political backroom advisor, who represented Toronto's old WASP establishment.

By early November, the election had come down to an ideological and personality battle between Tory and Miller. Both were charismatic and smart candidates. Tory offered a more traditional economic platform that included a much-needed review of program spending, cuts to councillors' budgets, a hiring freeze for the civic bureaucracy, and a sale of "non-core" assets. Miller, with endorsements from Jane Jacobs, Olivia Chow, Margaret Atwood, Michael Ondaatje, and others, promised to clean up the corruption at city hall—he effectively used a broom as a prop to make his point—tackle the city's perpetual transit problems, and, more specifically, stop the federally controlled Toronto Port Authority's proposed $15-million bridge linking the downtown to the city's island airport. Miller was the anti-Lastman, David Crombie-like candidate—an appealing, educated, and articulate left-of-centre spokesman, backed by the unions and intelligentsia, but who was not without support in the suburbs and among the city's diverse ethnic groups. He promised to find new government revenue for the perpetually cash-strapped city, even if that meant raising property taxes.

The 2003 civic election, says Lorinc, "was the first [true] megacity election. That was the moment when Torontonians were able to look at this big city that had been created and had by that time moved beyond the chaos of amalgamation and had asked, 'Who do we want as a leader?'" The answer was David Miller, who squeaked out a victory over Tory by only 36,000 votes (and over Hall by more than 235,000 votes).

"I led an activist government," Miller says today. "I was clear that I was going to be activist." He was true to his word. Almost immediately he convinced council to stop construction of the proposed bridge to the island airport, yet he was unable to stop Robert Deluce's Porter Airlines from taking off in 2006, literally and commercially. Though Miller was by no means the only politician to oppose the expansion of the downtown airport, it became a bit of an obsession for him. "The island is a residential place," he says, defending his position. "It is our Central Park, and you shouldn't have an airport in the middle of a residential area." But as Lorinc wryly remarks, "The person who deserves the most credit for getting Porter Airlines off the ground is David Miller because he gave it more free advertising than Deluce could ever have paid for."

Miller's main objective was, as the *Star*'s Christopher Hume put it, to become "the face of progressive civic politics." To this end, during his seven years in office (the mayor's term of office was extended to four years from three in 2006) he supported a wide range of economic, environmental, and cultural initiatives, including a bid for Expo 2015 (that was awarded to Milan), $70 million of enhancements to Toronto's waterfront, money for bike paths, a mayor's roundtable on arts and culture, improved governance, and his much-debated five-cent fee on plastic bags for retail stores, which was part of a comprehensive environmental strategy. He makes no apologies for any of it.

"My goal," he says, "was to try to turn the city government around. When I first got elected, it was mired in scandal. We achieved open and transparent government. We reformed the government and made it far more efficient. We also adopted a community safety strategy that was not just the absence of crime but the creation of communities where everyone is equally valued."

Yet the civic government structure in which he was forced to operate was flawed. The city never had enough money to fund the transit, improved services, building projects, and social programs Torontonians expected. Miller inherited a deficit of $344 million, and given the lean, cost-cutting times in which he served, the province refused to increase its grant. So he did what had to be done: he pushed council to increase property and business taxes, though only modestly. He had more success working with federal and provincial authorities when it came to obtaining funding for public housing and the TTC. That led to the construction of the controversial St. Clair Avenue right-of way project, which speeded up streetcar service but also added to the traffic congestion at the western end of the street. More notable was Toronto Transit City, a fifteen-year plan he unveiled with TTC chair Adam Giambrone in the spring of 2007. The light rail (or LRT) network it proposed is desperately needed to improve the city's terribly inadequate public transportation system, but as evidenced by the bitter debate over building new subways or less-expensive LRT during Rob Ford's first term, it remains to be seen whether Transit City will survive to be Miller's greatest legacy.

In his second election campaign in November 2006, Miller's chief opponent was city councillor Jane Pitfield, who tried to beat him by portraying him as an irresponsible spender. Though she had an impressive team of Liberal and Progressive Conservative Party strategists running her campaign and was touted by the media as a strong candidate, Miller, who said he was going to raise taxes and create new ones, received nearly 60 percent of the vote. With that mandate, he embarked on his second term with two of his less-popular decisions: the detested sixty-dollar vehicle-registration tax (scrapped as soon as Rob Ford became mayor in 2010) and a slightly more tolerable, and enduring, 1.5 percent land-transfer tax, which in 2013 brought in more than $340 million.

His most difficult challenge was the protracted municipal workers' strike during the summer of 2009, and the manner in which he handled it lost him the support of many Torontonians. Miller had had a good relationship with the Canadian Union of Public Employees (CUPE), but that did not stop two locals representing about 30,000 civic workers from walking off the job on June 22 to protest negotiations over a new contract—job security and the banking of sick days were the main sticking points. Garbage pickup stopped, city daycares were closed, and the ferry service was halted. Mounds of garbage became the strike's most visible and aggravating symbol.

Miller was ideologically opposed to privatizing garbage collection and resisted the idea whenever it was up for discussion. But that meant the city was hostage to the unions, and as piles of smelly garbage accumulated throughout Toronto in the hot weather, Miller became as much a target of public hostility as the CUPE leaders who had called the strike. (The only ones delighted with the strike were Toronto's army of scavenger raccoons, which feasted on the debris.)

The labour action lasted thirty-nine days, with both sides declaring victory at the end. Miller believed that the negotiated pay increases, plus the agreement to phase-out banking of unused sick days, which had been in place for fifty years, demonstrated his tough resolve. But many councillors and observers argued that the city had "caved in" to union demands and were adamant that the mayor was arrogant and wrong to declare that he had bested the union. "The people of Toronto are not happy," councillor Michael Thompson declared in a comment that was typical of the anti-Miller faction. "They have been left holding the bag literally and figuratively as a result of a bungled process led by the mayor."

Miller dismisses such carping. "The strike was very difficult," he recalls, "and CUPE was incredibly misguided to go on strike. But the criticism of the settlement was unfair. We went public with our offer and the union accepted virtually exactly what we offered. Some of the media portrayed that as caving in. I find that just incomprehensible."

Less than two months later, Miller surprised the city with the announcement that he would not be seeking a third term. The media generally interpreted this as a reflection of his unpopularity and his fear that he would lose in 2010. An Ipsos Reid poll conducted at the end of the strike found that close to 80 percent of the respondents wanted Miller to step down. He maintained then and now that his decision to leave civic politics was a personal one and nothing to do with perceptions about who won the strike or any other policy decision, for which he has absolutely no regrets. The truth was that he had a young family and the job consumed him. On a typical day he was up at five-thirty in the morning for a run before sitting down for radio interviews at seven. He might deliver a breakfast speech, followed by morning briefings at city hall. Next were executive committee or city council sessions, and telephone calls to other Canadian mayors to co-ordinate strategies for dealing with federal and provincial authorities. There was usually another speech at lunch and more briefings in the afternoon. His evenings were generally taken up with five to seven different events. "In the early years," he remembers, "after all of that I'd stop at McDonald's for two quarter-pounders with cheese and was home around eleven. I did this day after day." After gaining some weight, he stopped the late night visits to McDonald's at his family's behest. But by the fall of 2009, he realized that another four-year term would mean his two teenage children would go through their high school years without their father around. And that, he decided, was too much of a personal sacrifice.

For the next year, the ups and downs of his civic career were endlessly debated in op-ed pieces and letters to the editor. Much of the commentary was critical, even hostile. "I would honestly like to know what David Miller has done that has been positive for the City of Toronto?" asked *Star* reader Trevor Jones of North York, who then proceeded to list every negative aspect of the mayor's two terms he could come up with. In the *National Post*, columnist Kelly McParland derided Miller for his "imperviousness to reality." The mayor's achievements, he argued, "have come at the price of ever-more-precarious financial machinations. The budget has grown from \$6.7-billion to \$8.7-billion, accompanied by annual crises, shortfalls and pleas to Queen's Park to save the city yet again. Contingency reserves have been pilfered, fees and surcharges ratcheted up, a convoluted new trash collection system instituted, accompanied by monster bins and garbage control technicians skilled at discovering arcane reasons why this week's trash doesn't qualify for their attention." Meanwhile, McParland's fellow columnist Robert Fulford publicly flagellated himself for voting for Miller—but only once. "How can I explain myself?" he wondered. "I knew people who knew him and said he was a good man. He seemed plausible when you met him and if you could bring yourself to endure the boredom of a Miller speech he made, well, a sort of sense. Perhaps, in some colonized corner of my brain, I also thought: How stupid can a Harvard man be? (Now I know.)"

A *Globe and Mail* editorial was slightly kinder, noting that "David Miller's announcement that he would not run for a third term as Toronto's mayor marks the beginning of the end of an ambitious mayoralty that never quite found its footing. Mr. Miller had some undoubted successes... but his attempt to govern as a centrist was fraught. He could not rein in expenditures or union influence, making him unable to meet the high expectations most Torontonians had for him."

Shown the *Globe* article three years later, Miller angrily dismisses it as being out of hand. "You are running one of North America's major cities, of course you are going to run into obstacles," he says. Judging David Miller will take more time—and given the fiasco of the Ford years that followed, he now seems a much more attractive politician, despite any of his perceived flaws. "History will show," says John Lorinc, bucking the anti-Miller trend, "that many of the things he promoted were the right things to do—sustainability and transit development. He made city government more accountable and made Toronto a more independent city."

MILLER HAD ONE LAST MAJOR HEADACHE to deal with before he returned to the quiet confines of his law practice—and for this one he was more or less an innocent bystander. At the end of June 2010, it was Canada's turn to host the G-20 summit, the annual gathering of heads of government from around the world. These meetings rarely accomplish much beyond the symbolic. The security costs are enormous, and the presence of so many leaders attracts mass protests, some led by misguided students and adults dressed in black who have used the summit as an excuse for senseless violence and destructive vandalism.

Rather than convening the meeting in a remote location, as originally planned, Prime Minister Stephen Harper opted to hold it at the Metro Convention Centre in downtown Toronto. When the city was first notified that it was hosting the summit, Miller had been led to believe it would be held at Exhibition Place, a locale that was containable. He later expressed anger at not being properly consulted, and being informed after the fact, about the decision to move the summit downtown. Indeed, holding such a high-profile meeting at the convention centre proved to be a nightmare for the police. It ended up costing Canadians an estimated $858 million, a good portion of which was spent on security that turned downtown Toronto into a restricted armed encampment. As many as 20,000 police officers and soldiers guarded the area, which was protected by a three-metre-high security fence snaking 3.5 kilometres around Toronto's core. The only thing missing was the electric current running through it.

The protests started more than a week before the summit began and became more rowdy and out of control as world leaders arrived in the city. Legitimate grievances about globalization or environmental concerns were quickly hijacked by so-called black bloc members, young thugs who attacked downtown businesses, smashing windows, setting fires to cars, and wreaking as much havoc as they could get away with. The cost later paid by the federal government to cover damage to property and lost revenue was approximately $1.5 million—which included a bill for $5,886 from the Zanzibar strip club on Yonge Street.

Led by Toronto police chief Bill Blair, the police made two tactical errors that came back to bite them. First, they claimed incorrectly that they had been given near martial-law power to arrest and detain people coming near the security fence. No such power existed. Second, when they found themselves unable to control the situation or stop the black bloc, they began using tear gas, pepper spray, and rubber bullets to disperse the crowds, roughed up anyone who got in their way, and detained and arrested hundreds of people, guilty or not.

In one notable case, a group of police officers badly beat up twenty-seven-year-old Adam Nobody, who was merely a spectator of a demonstration at Queen's Park. Once they arrested him, they asked him his name. When he told them, they thought he was being a "smartass." He was then kicked in the face several times, an act captured on a widely viewed YouTube video. Blair initially argued the video had been doctored, but he was finally compelled to admit it was an accurate portrayal of what had transpired. Three years later, one constable, Babak Andalib-Goortani, was charged and found guilty of assaulting Nobody with his baton.

One of the most needless and foolish moments, at least from a public relations perspective, came on June 28. Believing that they had trapped some black bloc demonstrators, the police "kettled" or enclosed hundreds of protestors for several hours at the corner of Queen Street and Spadina Avenue in the middle of a rainstorm. "It's unfortunate some innocent people had to stand in the rain," Chief Blair later said. "We had to stand in the rain with them."

Despite differences over budgets and union issues, David Miller's relations with the police had been fairly good, and as the summit unfolded, he wholeheartedly backed them. "We were met this weekend with a number of people—certainly several hundred—who wished to use the opportunity available to them during a peaceful democratic protest to commit violent acts," he said. Officers showed "admirable professionalism" and did an "extraordinary job in almost impossible circumstances."

Many commentators later agreed with that analysis of the police actions, though with reservations. "In letting his police force run wild during last summer's G-20 summit, Bill Blair wasn't being sinister," suggested *Globe and Mail* writer Adam Radwanski. "He was just in over his head... His inability to keep some of his officers under control—leading to violent treatment of peaceful protesters, along with people who happened to be in the wrong place at the wrong time—thus begins to look a little more like incompetence than anything calculated."

Nearly two years later, however, a report by the Office of the Independent Police Review Director (OIPRD), a provincial agency, was scathing in its assessment of the Toronto police actions during the summit. "Some police officers ignored basic rights citizens have under the Charter and overstepped their authority when they stopped and searched people arbitrarily and without legal justification," concluded Gerry McNeilly, head of the OIPRD. "Numerous police officers used excessive force when arresting individuals and seemed to send a message that violence would be met with violence."

Somewhat reluctantly, Chief Blair proceeded with charges against more than a dozen of his officers for alleged misconduct.

One civic politician who had no doubts that Blair and the police acted appropriately during the G-20 riots was Etobicoke councillor and 2010 mayoralty candidate Rob Ford, who declared that he would have ordered the police to arrest anyone suspected of violence or vandalism. "Either you support the police or you don't support the police here," he said at a forum with other candidates. "This is black or white. I support the police." Three long years later, the Ford–Blair relationship was less black or white following sensational revelations about Mayor Ford smoking crack cocaine.

IN THE ANNALS OF TORONTO CIVIC POLITICS, there had never been anything quite like the manic circus surrounding Rob Ford, which virtually brought city hall to a standstill. The seemingly endless melodrama started in mid-May 2013 when the American website *Gawker* and the *Toronto Star* broke a story alleging the existence of a video showing the mayor smoking crack cocaine. Six months later, after Ford's vehement denials that he had ever done such a thing, the police confirmed the video existed. This was followed by Ford's confession that he had indeed smoked crack cocaine while he was in "a drunken stupor" (which made the *Toronto Sun* dub him a "global stupor-star"). The police alleged the mayor had partied with known criminals; the mayor conceded that he had occasionally driven his car while drunk. Following weeks of non-stop media coverage, a majority of city councillors voted to strip the mayor of much of his power. Throughout this poor excuse for a sordid reality TV show, Ford, backed by his brother and lone ally, councillor Doug Ford, steadfastly refused to resign. Each day in November 2013 brought yet another heartfelt apology from the mayor, blaming the "tremendous, tremendous stress" he was under, which he admitted was "largely of my own making," but always framed in a narcissistic construct that portrayed him as a champion of the people and the only bulwark against taxpayer abuse.

According to section 134 of the City of Toronto Act, 2006, among the duties of the mayor are "to provide leadership to council; act as the representative of the City both within and outside the City, and promote the City locally, nationally and internationally; and participate in and foster activities that enhance the economic, social and environmental well-being of the City and its residents." Ford refused to acknowledge that his personal actions made carrying out these duties impossible—and that the worldwide attention, and ridicule, he was receiving, especially from American late-night TV talk shows, was hardly promoting the city in the way the act had in mind. The most honest moment in this whole sorry affair was the Ford brothers' interview with Matt Lauer, host of NBC's *The Today Show*. "You have brought disgrace to this office and you know that's true," Lauer said. The mayor merely gave one of his patented responses that he was "embarrassed" and that he had made "mistakes." He also achieved something unprecedented in the city's journalistic history: all four Toronto newspapers were unanimous that Rob Ford must resign as mayor.

None of this made an iota of difference to thousands of Ford supporters and apologists, who accused the media of "bullying" the mayor and who insisted that they would vote for him in 2014 (according to Forum Research polls, support for Ford has remained fairly constant at 44 percent from 2011 until February 2014). This despite the fact that Ford's policies had not saved the city's taxpayers $1 billion, as he and his brother repeatedly claimed, using a series of contrived math calculations. "There's nothing wrong with Ford Nation," the *National Post*'s Kelly McParland insisted. "They're honest people who thought they had a champion. He let them down. It happens."

TO UNDERSTAND HOW it happened, you have to separate the Ford saga into two parts, before and after the release of the crack video. Ford the city councillor was a meat-and-potatoes politician who offered disgruntled Torontonians a return to common sense and parsimony in civic affairs. In the October 2010 municipal election, he emerged as the unlikely successor to David Miller.

Then, he was merely uncouth, blunt, and sometimes just plain silly. Built like the ex-football lineman (who has seen better days) that he once was, Ford was regarded as an opinionated neo-Conservative, but one who could also bring an end to the alleged tax-and-spend policies of the Miller years. Or, as one *National Post* pro-Ford reader suggested: "We don't want to be a 'world-class' city. We want a city that is safe for our wives and children, one where we can get to work easily and inexpensively. We don't like opera or classical music and can't afford to attend a $100 performance. We want low taxes so that we can continue to live in our bungalows and to have efficient household services like clean water and trash pick-up. We want to send our children to good local public schools...Mr. Ford represents this for us. He does stupid things from time to time, but our family and friends forgive us our sins."

Those Torontonians who shook their heads in disbelief that someone like Ford, with all his many personal failings, could become mayor were simply not paying attention to the mood of the city in the fall of 2010, or were lulled into a false sense of security. "Tell me something: What did you expect?" asked the *Globe and Mail*'s Marcus Gee in a March 2012 column entitled "An open letter to those who elected Rob Ford." Gee's frustration was palpable. "Mr. Ford had been on city council for 10 years when he ran for mayor," he wrote. "Thanks to his antics, he was in the news quite a bit. Unless you were living under a rock, you had to have a pretty good idea what he was about."

The official and sanitized version of the Ford story goes something like this: Rob Ford, the youngest child in a family of four, grew up in an upper-middle-class home.

By the time he was born in 1969, his father, Doug Ford Sr. (who passed away from cancer in 2006), had established—with his partner and neighbour Ted Herriott—a highly successful business, DECO Labels and Tags. In 2012, the company, now run by Ford's older brother, city councillor Doug Ford, had sales exceeding $100 million, making Rob Ford's claim that he was an "ordinary guy" defending the city from the "rich, elitist people" slightly preposterous. (By the *Globe and Mail*'s estimation, the Ford family had property in the GTA, Muskoka, and Florida worth more than $10 million.)

The brothers naturally looked up to their father as a role model. Not only did he show them how to persevere and build a profitable enterprise, he also was the first Ford to enter politics, winning a seat as a Progressive Conservative in the 1995 provincial election that made Mike Harris the premier of Ontario by a landslide. (According to *Toronto Star* reporter Robyn Doolittle, Doug Ford Jr.'s experience working on Doug Holyday's winning mayoral campaign in Etobicoke in 1994 was even more of an inspiration for Rob Ford's political ambitions.)

As a high school student at Scarlett Heights, Rob became a decent football player, at the centre position. He attended Carleton University in Ottawa, though he was never a starter for the Ravens, the university team, and left without graduating. He later took some continuing courses at York University and began working for the family business.

The less palatable and darker version of the family's history was chronicled in a feature article in the *Globe and Mail* on May 25, 2013. Following an eighteen-month investigation, reporters Greg McArthur and Shannon Kari, basing their case largely on anonymous sources, portrayed brother Doug Ford as Etobicoke's prime hashish supplier in the early eighties, from about the time he was fifteen until he was twenty-two years old. There were also tales of the drug-related involvement of siblings Randy, who was once arrested for his part in a plot to kidnap a drug buyer who owed Randy and his friends money, and Kathy, who was allegedly connected to dealers, gun violence, and members of the Canadian Ku Klux Klan. Naturally, Doug Ford, who the paper pointed out had never been "criminally charged for illegal drug possession or trafficking," repudiated the story, calling it "disgusting" and "a personal shot at our family." Ford complained to the Ontario Press Council about the story, but following hearings in early September 2013, the council ruled a month later that the *Globe and Mail*'s coverage was "reasonably reliable and the reporters were sufficiently diligent in their efforts to verify their conclusions."

At age twenty-eight, Rob Ford ran in the first megacity council election but came in fourth out of six candidates running for two seats in Ward 3. Three years later he beat incumbent Elizabeth Brown in Ward 2, Etobicoke North, by 1,628 votes. He won by much more substantial margins in 2003 and 2006, by which time he had established his reputation as a councillor who paid attention to the bottom line—he famously only spent $2 of his $53,000 councillor's budget—but who also attracted headlines for the wrong reasons. In March 2008, police were summoned to his house to resolve a domestic dispute. His wife, Renata, complained about an assault and a death threat, though the charges were dropped because her story of what had happened changed.

From almost the first day of his career as a politician, Ford, like Mel Lastman, spoke whatever was on his mind, showing himself to be something of a redneck and a buffoon. He could be counted on to vote against almost anything David Miller proposed, and he racked up a long list of questionable, even outrageous, comments: he labelled councillor Giorgio Mammoliti, "a scammer"; demanded that Toronto be declared a "refugee-free zone" to halt the immigration of undesirable newcomers; suggested that a bylaw protecting Toronto's trees was an example of "communism"; called councillor Gloria Lindsay Luby a "waste of skin"; told cyclists that "it's their own fault" if they are involved in traffic accidents or killed; was kicked out of a Maple Leafs game at the Air Canada Centre for being drunk and abusive; and in 2008, in a throwback to the 1950s, stated that "Oriental people work like dogs... They're slowly taking over." Nevertheless, his constituents in Etobicoke loved him and loved the fact that he always personally returned their phone calls.

When Miller announced in September 2009 that he was not running in the next election, there was much speculation in the media about his possible successors. Prominently mentioned were John Tory, who had lost to Miller in 2003; Adam Giambrone, head of the TTC; George Smitherman, a Liberal MPP, minister of health, and deputy premier to Dalton McGuinty; Joe Pantalone, Miller's deputy mayor; and Rocco Rossi, a Liberal Party strategist. There was also Sarah Thomson, a self-styled "social entrepreneur" and transit advocate. At the bottom of the list was councillor Rob Ford, considered to be a long shot at best.

By the spring of 2010, the election shaped up as a contest between Smitherman, who was also the first openly gay MPP, Pantalone, Rossi, and Ford, who at the end of March announced his candidacy to a room full of loyal and exuberant supporters—soon to be anointed members of the "Ford Nation." Conventional wisdom was that Smitherman would coast to victory. But within a month of Ford's entry into the race, Smitherman and his supporters, as well as the unabashedly pro-Smitherman *Toronto Star*, started to become nervous. Each day it seemed that Ford was gaining in popularity. "I don't believe city council would follow Rob Ford," councillor Kyle Rae told the *Star*. "He's not informed, he doesn't read the agenda, [and] doesn't read reports." Rae's opinion proved to be all too prophetic.

In a smart campaign managed by Nick Kouvalis, a PC Party operative, Ford tapped into the anti-Miller backlash that had been simmering in the city. Whether they lived downtown or in the suburbs, a lot of Torontonians detested Miller's new taxes and what they perceived as excessive and wasteful spending. If Miller was the anti-Lastman, then Ford was the anti-Miller. Nearly everything Miller was proud of—from the LRT plan to the five-cent plastic bag tax, as well as such necessary levies as the sixty-dollar vehicle registration tax—Ford vowed to eliminate. "What are we, the ministry of transport?" he asked sarcastically about the vehicle registration tax. He was proudly pro-subway and pro-car, and declared that roads were primarily meant for automobiles, not bicycles. Most decisively of all, he promised to "stop the gravy train" at city hall.

Smitherman, meanwhile, ran a lousy campaign. He never articulated precisely why he wanted to be the mayor and was the victim of anti-homosexuality attack ads in several ethnic communities. Despite several high-profile endorsements, he faded quickly and never recovered. Even when Ford put his foot in his mouth, as he did when he suggested Toronto's population growth should be curbed, or when he agreed with Wendell Brereton, a black fundamentalist Christian pastor (and one-time mayoral candidate), that same-sex marriage could "dismantle the very ethical fibers of what a healthy democratic civilization is," his momentum could not be halted. By mid-September, about a month before the vote, Ford was more than twenty points ahead of Smitherman in the polls, 45.8 percent to 21.3.

The few voices who spoke against Ford were ignored. "Can anything stop Rob Ford?" Marcus Gee of the *Globe and Mail* wondered in exasperation. How could people vote for a candidate, Gee asked, who "has promised both to cut taxes and to build new costly subway lines, a howling contradiction from a guy who claims he wants to run Toronto like an efficient private business." Over at the *Star*, an editorial strongly endorsed Smitherman and deemed Ford "not the sort of person who should be representing the city as its chief magistrate."

Ford later stopped speaking to the *Star* and subsequently boycotted the paper after it published a story about an alleged confrontation between Ford and one of his players in Ford's role as a high school football coach. Ford insisted that the *Star* apologize for the football story of July 2010, which he vehemently denied, and the newspaper absolutely refused to do so. "We won't apologize for the story, ever," says the *Star*'s city columnist Royson James. Relations between Ford and the newspaper deteriorated, of course, after the *Star* broke the story of the contentious crack video in May 2013. (When Ford referred to journalists hounding him about the video as "maggots," you can figure that he had in mind James and his *Star* colleagues.)

On October 25, 2010, 47.1 percent of the 813,984 Torontonians who voted, the vast majority of whom lived in the suburbs, chose Rob Ford. It took all of eight minutes after the polls closed for Ford to be declared the victor and the new mayor of Toronto. The win was not "the largest mandate in Canada's history," as Ford later claimed in an interview with the CBC's Peter Mansbridge, but it was decisive. At his victory celebration at the Congress Centre, with "Eye of the Tiger," the theme song from *Rocky III* playing in the background, Ford announced that "Toronto is now open for business, ladies and gentlemen!"

In the months ahead, as Ford showed many times that he was not quite up to the task of being mayor, there was much hand-wringing and head-scratching at this outcome, but the explanation was simple. A lot of Torontonians were angry; their paycheques weren't going as far and they did not much like the inefficiencies and bureaucracy at city hall. "People were nervous," recalls John Lorinc. "This was an election at an angry time. There was a lot of economic uncertainty. And when people are nervous, they don't always make the best choices."

A few weeks before the election, Sarah Fulford, the editor of *Toronto Life*, conceded that she was not voting for Ford but definitely understood why so many people were. "In 2008, I bought a house in a neighbourhood not far from downtown," she explained. "The land transfer tax cost me thousands of dollars, and I didn't like it much. The following summer, I was disposing of my own garbage, my community pool was closed, and my subway ride on the Yonge line was so packed that my commute became an exercise in ritual humiliation. After the strike, the union pretty much got what it wanted, and, a few months later, the price of a single subway ride went up to $3. This is why I understand the appeal of Rob Ford. The citizens of Toronto are angry. They're paying more and getting less... Ford, on the other hand, is now resonating with voters who crave a leader with nerve."

IT WAS OBVIOUS that things were about to become really interesting at city hall when *Hockey Night in Canada* commentator Don Cherry, dressed in one of his trademark "hot-pink floral" jackets, showed up to swear Rob Ford in as mayor and remarked about "all the pinkos out there that ride bicycles." As Marci McDonald later observed, "Not only did Cherry's tirade crystallize much of the inchoate fear and frustration that had helped bring Ford to power, it also set the tone for the new administration, designating anyone who wasn't onside as the enemy."

As soon as Ford moved into his new digs and ended Miller's open-door policy, he and his brother Doug got to work dismantling as much of the Miller legacy as was possible. The vehicle registration tax was gone. The LRT and Transit City were also, at least initially, gone in favour of more and more subways. He awarded garbage contracts to private companies, reduced councillors' and the mayor's office budgets, and rewarded his followers at city council with plum committee appointments. Joe Mihevc, an NDP councillor and a strong social rights advocate with a PhD in theology, who had been chair of the board of health from 2000 to 2003, was told by Ford that he was "going to be on the pencil-sharpening committee." (That was an exaggeration: Mihevc, who remained a strong critic of Ford, was later appointed vice-chair of the board of health and was elected chair in February 2013.)

After the first seven months, the Ford parade of controversy began and only got worse. Starting in the summer of 2011, a long list of tactical missteps, poor decisions, and foolish pronouncements dogged him and brother Doug: Doug's rants about closing libraries and his ignorance about writer Margaret Atwood; Doug's ill-conceived development scheme (complete with Ferris wheel) for the Port Lands waterfront area, which was rejected by council and just about every other interested party; and Rob's loss of several key council votes. The most notable was the rejection of his January 2012 budget. At stake were millions in spending cuts and his all-or-nothing subway (or, at least, underground LRT) transportation scheme, which pitted him against TTC chairman Karen Stintz, who proposed a different plan. This was followed in February and March 2012 with anti-Ford and pro-LRT council votes for Eglinton Avenue, Finch Avenue West, and Sheppard Avenue East.

Added to this were imprudent decisions and sheer acts of folly: for two years he absolutely refused to attend the annual gay pride week celebrations, finally showing up in June 2013 for a flag-raising ceremony; he fired the TTC general manager because he did not agree with his advice; he called the police when comedian Mary Walsh showed up at his house as her *This Hour Has 22 Minutes* alter ego Marg Delahunty, Warrior Princess, to have some harmless fun and interview him; he used his power to have city staff clean up the street in front of his family business; he left an important council meeting to coach his high school football team (the Toronto Catholic District School Board fired him in May 2013 during the crack video hoopla, though its officials never said that was the reason); he chased and confronted a *Toronto Star* reporter who was hanging around his home; and he got caught reading while driving his car in slow traffic on the Gardiner Expressway. "Yeah, probably, I'm busy," he responded when asked about the driving infraction.

And then there were months of needless debate and court proceedings to determine whether the mayor should be removed from office for violating conflict of interest rules (he voted on an issue in which he had a personal interest); whether or not he should repay the $3,150 in donations to his Rob Ford Football Foundation that he had solicited from lobbyists in his position as a city councillor. The entire affair, from the lower court's decision that he was guilty to the appeal court's ruling that he was (more or less) not, displayed both his lack of judgment and the pettiness of his frustrated opponents.

After Ford was cleared of conflict of interest charges in January 2013, *National Post* columnist Kelly McParland wrote. "He's not subtle. He's often not very diplomatic. He tends to treat opposing views dismissively. He provokes opponents when it might be better politics to accommodate... He's anything but a downtown sophisticate. He drives a big fat Cadillac Escalade... He dislikes streetcars... preferring subways. He's too often in the news for the wrong reasons, and has a tendency to act without completely thinking through the situation. He is, in short, human. Very human." He was also elected "with 47 percent of the vote, more than ten percentage points ahead of his nearest challenger... to get the city's budget under control."

Fair enough. But when you cut to the bare bones of this first phase of the unstoppable hullabaloo engulfing Rob Ford and his friends, it is hard not to come to one inescapable conclusion: despite Ford's partial success at keeping taxes nearly at bay, dealing with the unions (though as one journalist noted in May 2013, the lack of labour unrest was due to the fact that "he hasn't asked much of the union"), and curbing much of the questionable spending at city hall, he lacked the skill set and temperament to run the sixth-largest government in Canada. "The legitimate criticism of Ford," Toronto radio broadcaster and commentator John Moore noted at the end of January 2013, "is that he barely has a presence at city hall and doesn't seem to have a plan or agenda. He has few formal appointments a day and seems to spend the rest of his time making site inspections of public housing or personally answering calls from citizens about downed trees and broken sewer grates." He even made Mel Lastman look a lot better, an opinion shared by Lastman himself. "I'm not a genius, obviously," said the former mayor in October 2012, "but he makes me look like one."

In the first months of 2013, Ford received a slap on the wrist for overspending on his 2010 election campaign and for "improperly" borrowing money from his family's company. Then, at a dinner in March 2013, an inebriated Ford was accused by former mayoral candidate Sarah Thomson of grabbing her buttocks. Ford denied the allegation, suggesting Thomson was not "playing with a full deck."

It was all downhill after that. Ford's May denial—"I do not use crack cocaine, nor am I an addict of crack cocaine"—proved to be a bald-faced lie. When he finally admitted to smoking crack in November, Kelly McParland revised his earlier assessment of the mayor. "Mr. Ford needs to get help," he wrote on November 5, 2013. "Pledging to be a better mayor and more admirable human being down the road isn't enough. It's a sad tale, but the city can't cease to operate while an elected leader struggles with personal demons."

Torontonians have long loved to read and hear about themselves and their city in U.S. newspapers and on television news shows, but not this way. From CNN to late-night talk shows, Americans could not get enough of Rob Ford, whether he was having a few too many beers at the Taste of Danforth festival in August 2013 (which led to another round of hyperventilating in the Toronto media about the mayor's disgraceful behaviour) or denying to journalists that he had told a former female staffer "I want to eat your pussy" because, he said, "I'm happily married, I have more than enough to eat at home" (which likely ranks as the most vulgar public declaration in all of Canadian political history). Many, but certainly not all, the citizens of Toronto were utterly humiliated. "We didn't have to become the fourth-largest metropolis in North America, or promote our diverse makeup and lack of crime to make international headlines," opined *Maclean's* Toronto-based columnist Emma Teitel. "All we had to do was elect Rob Ford mayor, and wait... Toronto has morphed into a desperate reality-television show character... the city that delights in all and any outsider attention." Even Ford's beloved Toronto Argonauts asked him not to wear an Argos jersey or show up at the 2013 Grey Cup. He ignored both requests and caused a scene at the Rogers Centre during the CFL championship game.

On November 14, a majority of city councillors literally turned their backs to Ford as he spoke. The next day they stripped him of his mayoral power to appoint and dismiss committee chairs or the deputy mayor and to govern the city in a state of emergency. A few days later they also cut his office budget (giving the money to the office of the deputy mayor) and took away further powers to run council meetings.

In spite of this, Ford filed his nomination papers for the October 2014 civic election on January 2, 2014, insisting he would be mayor for another term. "I've got the strongest track record," he declared. "I've been the best mayor that this city's ever had. My record speaks for itself."

His critics disagreed. They argued that Ford, no matter what happened in the 2014 election, would be remembered as "the worst mayor in the modern history of cities and the most anti-urban mayor ever to preside over a large global city," as Richard Florida of the University of Toronto's Rotman School of Management portrayed him. Ironically, as Myer Siemiatycki, a professor of urban politics at Ryerson University pointed out, "Rob Ford's greatest achievement to date has been to reinvigorate a more robust civic democracy." But this fiasco showed, too, that democracy is not perfect and can backfire when a mayor acts in a reprehensible manner and there is no democratic method to remove him from office unless he is convicted of a crime and sent to jail.

In any event, in a city where a controversial figure like Rob Ford is mayor and, a few subway stops away at Queen's Park, Kathleen Wynne (as of May 2014) is the first female premier of Ontario and the first openly gay premier in Canada, there's always hope that anything and everything is possible.

TIGER CITY, ALPHA CITY

If you stay in Toronto, the longing remains deep in the soul, and since it can't be satisfied you can't be wearied, and your mind and your imagination, should become like a caged tiger. O Toronto! O my tiger city!

—MORLEY CALLAGHAN, 1951

If any street has defined Toronto in the public imagination and throughout the city's history it has been Yonge Street. It was nothing but a treacherous muddy wagon path when it started being used in the 1790s as a north-south route, yet the area from around Bloor Street south to the waterfront ultimately evolved into the heart of the city's cultural, entertainment and social centre. *Felix Lam photo*

BRIAN BURKE, the gruff and embattled former president and general manager of the Toronto Maple Leafs, did not suffer fools gladly. During his stint as the Leafs' boss from late 2008 to early 2013, he had no patience for the city's intrusive sports journalists who dared to question him about his strategy to improve the city's hapless NHL team. In 2004 he famously dismissed most sports scribes as "scumbags and maggots" and "idiots." Asked in a February 2012 interview on TSN radio why Toronto sports fans did not like the Leafs' coach Ron Wilson (who was fired a month later), he retorted, "The reason the fans don't like our coach is because the media doesn't like our coach."

Apart from the seemingly irrelevant fact that in three and a half seasons the Leafs under Wilson had only managed to win 130 of 310 games (with 45 ties), Burke did have a point about the power of the Toronto media. Such was the downside of running the most valuable franchise in the NHL (and the only team valued at $1 billion as of 2013) in Canada's "alpha city"—as John Lorinc has appropriately labelled Toronto. In happier days, when Burke was asked about the prospects of running the club, he had replied, "If you're Catholic, this is The Vatican." Yet the price he had to pay for this papal-like responsibility and distinction in a city with four daily newspapers, a dozen television stations, and countless bloggers, twitterers, and amateur know-it-alls was a media scrutiny comparable to that which exists in Ottawa and Washington, D.C., for politicians.

Only in Toronto would there be a dissection of Leafs forward and star Phil Kessel's shooting position choices or a serious Lincolnesque deliberation on whether or not the Leafs' Mikhail Grabovski actually bit the arm of Montreal Canadiens forward Max Pacioretty during an altercation in a game in early February 2013. Leafs fans are indeed a tough group to placate and always have been. "I've only been in Toronto for three months and I hate playing at [Maple Leaf] Gardens, to tell you the truth," said defenceman Dave Shand in a January 1981 interview, three months after he had been traded to the Leafs from the then Atlanta Flames. "We got up two goals against Hartford (in last week's 7–2 loss) and you could have heard a pin drop. It's the weirdest place I've ever played hockey. It's almost as though they're waiting for you to make a mistake and then they're happy."

THE LEAFS AND OTHER LOCAL SPORTS TEAMS have never been the only subject of this hyper-analysis, of course, either now or in the past. It is endemic to Toronto, where anything and everything—from developing the waterfront (a perpetual civic work-in-progress) to building new bike lanes or installing a "scramble" crosswalk at Yonge and Dundas, to bemoaning the lack of residential parking—generates endless amounts of print and electronic commentary, introspection, back-and-forth discussion, and angst. In short, Toronto is one self-absorbed fishbowl. Moreover, since these obsessive debates have to do with Toronto, imagined and real, many of them take on a monumental importance; they are often regarded as of the utmost national significance by the city's political, media, academic, and cultural elites, which for the life of them cannot understand why the rest of the country does not want to hear their endless griping and problems.

Consider two fairly recent and classically Toronto-centric examples of this compulsive navel-gazing—or, from a Toronto perspective, lively public discourse. In 2007, the opening of architect Daniel Libeskind's admittedly unique $250-million "Crystal" expansion (officially the Michael Lee-Chin Crystal, after its major donor) to the Royal Ontario Museum sent the city—or the self-styled cultural arbiters of good taste, at any rate—into a tailspin. For weeks the question "Do you like the new ROM addition?" was the most common conversation starter in the GTA, all very annoying to the ROM's CEO William Thorsell, who had conceived the project.

The answers were mixed. In the minority corner was the *Star*'s Christopher Hume, who took a wait-and-see approach, arguing that many famous architectural icons, from the Parthenon to the Eiffel Tower, were hated at first. Leading the majority was the

Globe's Lisa Rochon, declaring that "Daniel Libeskind's brutal vision of emptiness works for Berlin, but not for Toronto. It's hard, aggressive and in your face. It cantilevers dangerously over the street, shifting the ground from under our feet. Mostly, though, the new ROM rages at the world. This rage I cannot pretend to understand."

The always insightful and entertaining Robert Fulford had the best observation, not about Libeskind's architecture, but about the pompous and pretentious "Torontoish" ceremony that opened it. "Imagine, then, this spectacle: Like Big Brother in George Orwell's *1984*, the face of William Thorsell, director of the ROM, suddenly loomed several stories high over Bloor Street, projected onto the museum's new cladding," he wrote in his *National Post* column a few days after the festivities. "It was realistic enough to be terrifying. And it spoke! It said, of course, that this was a great moment, but the disembodied god-like presence left us trembling... Most of the evening was dead ordinary, but the Big Brother imagery at least delivered an element of primitive horror. And its spiritual implications fit the evening's theme."

Two years later, another insult: the *Washington Post*'s noted art and architecture critic Philip Kennicott awarded the Crystal addition the prize for "The Ugliest Building of the Decade." "Sure, there were a lot of Wal-Marts thrown up in the Aughts," he wrote, "but Daniel Libeskind's addition to the Royal Ontario Museum in Toronto surpasses the ugliness of bland functional buildings by being both ugly and useless. His aluminum-and-glass-clad crystalline forms grow out of the building's original 1914 structure, and from the street it's dramatic. But go inside and you need a map to move around its irrational and baffling dead spaces." It was one thing for Toronto to be dissed by Canadian critics, quite another to take it on the chin in a major American newspaper. The ego-bruising pronouncement was duly reported as national news and received the requisite defensive Toronto reaction.

Another, though much different, kind of navel-gazing involving Toronto's landscape was the short-lived, highly emotional casino debate of 2012–13. It began with an announcement in October 2012 that a casino would be built in the downtown area as part of a massive renovation of the Metro Toronto Convention Centre. The initial proposal from Oxford Properties was for two seventy-storey towers, a combination of offices and residences. A slew of Las Vegas entrepreneurs wielding a great deal of cash, including Sheldon Adelson, billionaire CEO of the Las Vegas Sands Corporation, also expressed an interest in turning part of Front Street into a mini Las Vegas-style Strip, complete with a hotel, offices, residences, and lots of space for blackjack and craps.

The ever-enthusiastic Paul Godfrey, in his capacity as chairman of the Ontario Lottery and Gaming Corporation (OLG), declared the concept to be a "once-in-a-generation" opportunity and was adamant that it should be located downtown rather than in the suburbs. Mayor Rob Ford, too, was an avid supporter, as were members of the carpenters union. David Whitaker, president and CEO of Toronto Tourism, thought it was a great idea for attracting much bigger conventions.

But a casino, so symbolic of greed, sin, and corruption, was bound to be controversial and indeed caused an intense bout of conniption, at a level not seen in Toronto for quite some time. The usual suspects weighed in. Left-leaning councillor Adam Vaughan warned of a "parking calamity" on Front Street. "It's insane," he said. "It's just the wrong project in the wrong part of the city. None of it is real. It's a fantasy proposal designed to snare a casino." A trio of former mayors, David Crombie, John Sewell, and Art Eggleton, issued a public letter declaring that a casino was absolutely the wrong type of establishment for the downtown and would only increase crime and parking problems. "It is not in our city's best interest to establish commercial casino operations in Toronto," they wrote. (From a historical perspective, the sight of Crombie and Sewell taking on Paul Godfrey once again brought warm feelings of nostalgia to long-time Torontonians.)

Likewise, urban planners and designers A.J. Diamond and Ken Greenberg, and Rob Simpson, former CEO of the Ontario Problem Gambling Research Centre, denounced the concept and dismissed any notions of its job creation and revenue-generating benefits. "For a city, particularly one with a strong, healthy and diverse local economy like Toronto," they argued, "to squander valuable lands based on faulty premises would be an egregious mistake." Rosie DiManno of the *Star* noted that she had "zero moral qualms about gambling," but locating a casino complex in an already cluttered downtown location—with more ongoing construction projects than anywhere else in North America—did not make a lot of sense in her view. Put it in "Scarberia" she suggested.

And writing on the *Huffington Post Canada* website, the U of T's Richard Florida proclaimed that "casino building is city-ruining of the highest order." Toronto did not need a casino, he added in an interview with the *Globe and Mail*. "They smack of desperation. Casinos aren't for cities on their way up. They're for cities out of options." Maybe so, but that did not explain how in 2012 a city like Melbourne, Australia, could be rated the most livable city in the world by *The Economist* for a second year in a row (Toronto was in fourth place after Vienna and Vancouver) while running a casino in the heart of its downtown. (According to John Masanauskas, the urban affairs writer for the *Melbourne Herald Sun*, the city "experienced isolated incidents involving drunkenness and other anti-social behaviour by people leaving the complex, but generally it is a family-friendly environment with an array of restaurants, cafes, shops and cinemas in the immediate vicinity.")

In mid-May 2013, when it became clear that the Ontario Liberal government did not share the same vision for the casino as Paul Godfrey, he was coerced into resigning his position as chairman of the OLG. More hand-wringing and heated and passionate arguments continued until the end of May, when city council voted 38 to 6 against the downtown casino proposal. It was another slap in the face to Ford, who had championed the idea.

THE CRITICAL REACTION to the casino was indicative of the pessimistic cloud that had been hovering over the city, making locals feel that Toronto was on the verge of a collapse akin to the fall of Rome. "Toronto is a mess," John Macfarlane, editor and co-publisher of *Walrus* magazine, recently concluded. "The city finds itself in this fix due to a litany of bad decisions by politicians, planners, and voters." And the gloomy Richard Florida added, "The same forces of globalization that have powered Toronto's rise are also behind the class divide that increasingly defines this city. Maps developed by my colleagues at the Martin Prosperity Institute [at the University of Toronto] show that Toronto's professional, knowledge and creative workers tend to live in the core and radiate out along transit lines. Lower-income and low-skill service workers get pushed farther afield. Traditional mixed-income neighbourhoods, once the norm, have become narrow buffer zones between a wealthy downtown and impoverished inner suburbs."

Thus, as of 2013 there was a lengthy list of unresolved headaches: the Gardiner Expressway was falling apart; traffic congestion was a major headache; commuting from the suburbs downtown or vice versa (the latest trend) could take up to eighty minutes each way. Newly anointed Ontario premier Kathleen Wynne introduced a plan for a massive infusion of tax money and fees to improve transportation in the Greater Toronto and Hamilton Areas. Meanwhile, Toronto city politics, which experienced a year of hell in 2013, was dysfunctional, partisan, and petty—and in light of the maelstrom (more like a political polar vortex) surrounding Rob Ford, that is putting it mildly. More importantly, the city did not have enough money to improve its infrastructure. And there are likely far too many high-priced condominiums being built from the waterfront to Richmond Hill. In late 2012, Tridel, the largest builders of condos in the GTA was offering a three-bedroom 1,305-square-foot condo at the bottom of York Street for $920,000, with a possession date in 2017. With small semi-detached houses in middle-class neighbourhoods selling for more than $500,000, owning a house in Toronto had become difficult, if not impossible, for anyone but the well-off. This is why nearly half of Torontonians, especially so-called echo boomers, the adult children of the baby boomers, are renters.

Finally, let's also be honest about the Leafs. The team had a good season in 2012–13 (yet missed the playoffs the year after). But it will take a while to get over the heartbreaking loss in game seven of the first-round playoff series with Boston. The Leafs had a 4–1 lead with less than six minutes to play in the third period and then fell apart. The chances of the Leafs winning a Stanley Cup any time before the city's two-hundredth anniversary in 2034 seem slim. Regardless, that will hardly stop the ever-loyal members of Leafs Nation from paying absurdly high ticket prices and filling the ACC for every home game.

On a more positive note, the Toronto media took some solace in summer of 2012 from an Angus Reid poll which showed that 70 percent of the respondents in the U.K. and U.S. felt that Toronto was indeed "a world-class city."

TORONTO'S ARROGANCE AND SWAGGER are arguably part of its charm, and have been since that day in 1793 when John Graves Simcoe set eyes on the harbour and envisioned a great city. Over the course of the nearly four hundred years presented in this biography, Toronto was transformed from an aboriginal outpost to a sleepy provincial town in the nineteenth century, to a homogenous WASP enclave "dominated by the Orange Order, and greatly derided by the rest of Canada for its smugness, its snobbery, and its sterility," as scholar Northrop Frye remembered it in the late twenties. As it grew into the country's pre-eminent financial and cultural urban centre, it eventually shed its sterility, but kept the smugness and snobbery.

After the Second World War, another great tidal wave of immigrants from every corner of the earth joined Toronto's Jews, Italians, and the small Chinese community, descending on the city. These exotic newcomers upset the relatively neat Anglo hierarchy—from the point of view of the Brits and Scots, the city's most aggravating blight for decades were the Irish Catholics, who did not know their proper place—and literally changed the face of the city forever. By 2006, about half of Toronto's population, 1.23 million people, had been born outside of Canada.

Too much, perhaps, has been made of Toronto's celebrated diversity; prejudice and discrimination remain alive and well in the city, as they do in the rest of tolerant, multicultural Canada. Notwithstanding the generally upbeat message found in the annual reports of the Ontario Human Rights Commission over the last decade, as well as in numerous anti-racism education initiatives, conferences, and events, hate crimes, anti-Semitism, racial discrimination, and racial profiling still occur in Toronto. The racism is much subtler than it was in the forties and fifties, but from time to time incidents occur. They likely always will.

Yet some perspective is also required. Considering the current insurmountable problems caused in the world by religious, national, and ethnic differences, Toronto's example of accommodation and the relatively peaceful co-existence of people who elsewhere might be at each other's throats bodes well for the city's reputation and greatness. Toronto's motto, "Diversity Our Strength," is not merely a catchphrase, but truly does resonate across the GTA in a positive way. At the same time, there has been a shift in ethnic identity for such long-established groups as Jews and Italians. In 2013, both the

Canadian Jewish News and the *Corriere Canadese* ran into severe economic problems and were forced to suspend operations. Though the *CJN* bounced back with a smaller staff, it is undeniable that the sizable Jewish and Italian communities of Toronto are now more mainstream and assimilated, and in the Internet age the importance of an ethnic press has declined.

Like any large North American metropolitan area, Toronto has crime, much of it ugly, brutish, senseless, and, in the past few years, gang related. The city's police are also far from perfect. On the night of July 27, 2013, while travelling on a streetcar on Dundas Street West, Sammy Yatim, by all accounts a pleasant eighteen-year-old Syrian immigrant, threatened other passengers with a knife. The reason for his actions remains unclear, though eyewitnesses said he was agitated. Frightened, the other passengers exited the car, while the driver stayed put. Soon the police arrived and a brief standoff ensued—all captured on cellphone video by witnesses. A group of armed officers surrounded the streetcar where Yatim was brandishing his knife. Instead of waiting it out, however, Constable James Forcillo suddenly fired nine times at Yatim, who fell to the floor of the car. Another officer then tasered him. The video of the incident went viral on the Internet. Police officials were at a loss to explain why Yatim was shot. Within a month, in a rare occurrence, Forcillo was charged with second-degree murder, a charge supported by a majority of Torontonians.

This became a national news story, in part, because such an incident is so rare; unlike many similar U.S. cities, Toronto remains, a safe place to live—a teeming collection of unique and vibrant neighbourhoods with a tremendous assortment of superb ethnic restaurants and a range of high- and lowbrow cultural pursuits and entertainment. Despite suggestions to the contrary, Dundas Square will never be mistaken for New York City's Times Square, but that's okay. It is precisely the fact Toronto has been (and remains) kinder and gentler and decidedly is not New York that has sustained and nurtured its growth. This was the reason that Jane Jacobs once hailed Toronto as the healthiest city in North America.

"THIS CITY IS WHAT IT IS because our citizens are what they are," Plato once said about Athens. That dictum certainly applies to Toronto. The city has never lacked inspirational and innovative leaders who make a difference in the lives of the people they touch and are the reason Toronto truly is a "world-class city."

Think, for example, of the impressive work of Karl Subban, the tough and dedicated principal of Brookview Middle School in the troubled Jane Street and Finch Avenue neighbourhood, who has brought a new sense of purpose and order to his young students. Success is possible even when you grow up around Jane and Finch. From those mean streets came Anthony Bennett, who, thanks to the tutelage of his diligent and caring mother Edith, was chosen as the number one pick in the 2013 National Basketball Association draft.

There is Yacov Fruchter, a thirty-two-year-old transplant from Montreal and a spiritual leader, who has, with a lot of help from his wife, Ryla Braemer (one of many former Winnipeggers living in Toronto), Bram Belzberg, and Richard Meloff, made the Annex Shul popular among young Jews seeking to reconnect with synagogue and their religion. And there is Kevin Lee, one of the brains behind the Scadding Court Community Centre at Dundas and Bathurst, who manages programs aimed at at-risk children, immigrants, people living with disabilities, and seniors. A few years ago, Lee and his team, with assistance from Adam Vaughan, purchased shipping containers that were turned into food-vending stalls as part of Market 707.

At city hall, councillors Kristyn Wong-Tam and Karen Stintz (a 2014 candidate for mayor) have both shown a lot of political courage, standing up for what they believe in despite criticism. And Ken Greenberg, the inheritor of Jane Jacobs's mantle, is a truly original urban thinker who spends his days contemplating and writing about the "big picture" and Toronto's future potential and development. Cameron Bailey, TIFF's creative artistic director, has found new ways to grow the festival, while the Hudson Bay Company's former president (and current vice-chairman) Bonnie Brooks, with her distinctive voice and charm, breathed new life into the department store chain. (In January 2014, in what was billed as "the biggest expansion of the Eaton Centre since it was built," HBC sold its flagship store on Queen Street West, and the adjoining Simpson's Tower, to Cadillac Fairview, the mall owners, for $650 million. HBC is opening Canada's first Saks Fifth Avenue store in the new south end of the centre and leasing a smaller space for a new Bay store.) And Ratna Omidvar, president of the Maytree Foundation, has doggedly worked on behalf of immigrants and has stopped at nothing to transform Toronto into the tolerant, diverse city it claims to be.

Or what about the trio of women appointed to the Order of Ontario in early 2013: Phyllis Creighton, described as "a passionate advocate for mental and reproductive health care, social justice, peace and the environment"; Deepa Mehta, internationally acclaimed film director and human rights advocate; and physician Gail Robinson, co-founder of the country's first rape crisis centre? Each of these individuals is a star in her respective fields, and each has enhanced the lives of the citizens of Toronto.

THEN THERE IS DAVID MIRVISH, my vote for inspirational Torontonian of the past half century. Mirvish comes by his love for Toronto naturally. As the only child of "Honest Ed" Mirvish, he grew up with a sense of purpose instilled in him at a young age. Soft-spoken and dignified, he exudes a passion for Toronto that has motivated him as the city's most important theatre impresario, art promoter, businessman, and, most recently, land developer. Nearly seventy years old, he could be taking it easy. Instead, he continues to search for imaginative ways to move forward personally, professionally, and as a Torontonian committed to the city. In October 2012, around the time the debate over the casino proposal started raging, he and well-known architect Frank Gehry sent shock waves through the city by announcing what may turn out to be the most momentous development in Toronto in the last five decades.

As originally conceived, their bold plan was to tear down Mirvish's Princess of Wales Theatre on King Street West and redevelop the area with three towers as high as eighty-five storeys, complete with 2,600 private condos, retail space, and, the main attraction, a 60,000-square-foot public art museum, three times larger than the Art Gallery of Ontario, complete with adjacent classrooms and exhibition space for OCAD University. But as Mirvish insisted in January 2013, "I am not building condominiums. I am building three sculptures for people to live in." The impetus, he said, was to create a "destination" that would permit the largest display of twentieth-century contemporary art in the country, while his broader objective in this massive undertaking was to "engage" the public in a way that transformed the King and John Street cultural corridor even more profoundly than his father had done. "Can we create something that nowhere else can be compared to?" he asks.

The reaction to the announcement was exactly what Mirvish and Gehry anticipated. As Ken Greenberg stated, "Change at this scale and rate can be terrifying." Media and architectural commentators were not sure what to think of Mirvish's plan to demolish the historic Princess of Wales Theatre, yet most decided that the term "visionary" was an apt way to describe him. "Like it or not," added Greenberg, "Toronto is becoming a different city. It's now clear that it's transitioning to a city with a vastly different level of intensity. There's an echo of Manhattan in the mid-20th century, when wave after wave of building radically altered the form of New York and produced the kind of hyper-dense, hyper-animated environment that makes that city unique."

In December 2013, Toronto city planners expressed serious reservations about the size and scope of the project. Not wanting to become embroiled in a long-drawn-out confrontation with civic bureaucracy, Mirvish and Gehry unveiled a slightly scaled-back version of the development in May 2014. The new design will maintain the Princess of Wales Theatre and incorporate two condominium towers, rather than three. While one of the towers is to be ninety-two storeys, six higher than the tallest (or tallest tower) originally proposed, the general consensus among city planners and local architects was positive.

IT IS FOUR O'CLOCK on a cold and wet day in late January 2013 and I'm having a coffee at Hannah's Kitchen on Yonge Street, south of Eglinton, not far from where

Montgomery's Tavern stood, the headquarters for William Lyon Mackenzie and his rebels in 1837. Sitting opposite me is one of Mackenzie's illustrious successors as mayor, the fifty-sixth mayor of Toronto, David Crombie, who three and a half decades after leaving office is still regarded by most Torontonians with unbounded affection and respect. A few months shy of his seventy-seventh birthday, he tells me that he is not quite as active as he was as a civic and federal politician in the seventies and eighties—though the day before our meeting the letter he wrote with John Sewell and Art Eggleton that was critical of the casino proposal had been issued, and one day after the meeting he was named a member of the transition team for the new Ontario premier, Kathleen Wynne. In any event, he is "chronically cheerful," as he describes himself, and is as optimistic about Toronto as he ever was.

He claims that if he were younger, he would want to be mayor again, pointing out that the amalgamated city council is really not that different from the old Metro council in structure and responsibility. He also agrees that Toronto's most serious problem is transportation. "We once had the best subway system," he says, "but the province pulled away financially. Then people who had been through the wars of the sixties and seventies truly believed we were the 'city that worked.' There was this idea that God did it all and you did not need to do anything else." If he were in charge, he says he would raise taxes and negotiate with the province for proper funding. "There are too many cars on the road and the public transportation is inadequate," he adds. "I've seen huge crowds three and four deep waiting in the morning to get on jammed streetcars and buses. We are brutalizing people and one day they are going to erupt."

Finally, I ask him if Toronto is a "world-class city" and he laughs loudly. "It never has been," he says, with a glint in his eye. "It can't be New York or Montreal or any other city. We want to be the best we can be. No one else is getting up in the morning and saying, 'How can we make a better Toronto?' It is only us. That's all we need. It sounds corny. We have people from all over the world. They have seen great cities. They just want to have a place where they can raise their kids, make a living, get ahead, and enjoy life. It is not any more complicated than that."

True enough. In the larger perspective, however, Toronto in the last sixty years has been transformed from a rather pedestrian provincial town to a significant economic urban player. Few cities have experienced such sustained growth. That in itself puts tremendous pressure on people and institutions. The various political, social, and economic issues that have nearly torn Toronto apart in recent years are a by-product of that process. If the past is any indication, this clash of visions about Toronto's future will endure for a while yet, but they could produce something wonderful.

SELECTED BIBLIOGRAPHY

Ackroyd, Peter. *London: The Biography*. London: Random House, 2009.

Anisef, Paul, and Michael Lanphier, eds. *The World in a City*. Toronto: University of Toronto Press, 2003.

Armstrong, Christopher, and H.V. Nelles. *The Revenge of the Methodist Bicycle Company: Sunday Streetcars and Municipal Reform in Toronto, 1888–1897*. Toronto: Peter Martin Associates, 1977.

Armstrong, Frederick H. *Toronto: The Place of Meeting*. Toronto: Windsor Publications and the Ontario Historical Society, 1983.

———. "William Lyon Mackenzie, First Mayor of Toronto: A Study of a Critic in Power." *Canadian Historical Review* 48, 4 (December 1967): 309–31.

Armstrong, Jackson W., ed. *Seven Eggs Today: The Diaries of Mary Armstrong 1859 and 1869*. Waterloo, ON: Wilfrid Laurier University Press, 2004.

Arthur, Eric. *Toronto: No Mean City*. Toronto: University of Toronto Press, 1986.

Bain, David. "John Howard's High Park." *Ontario History* 101, 1 (Spring 2009): 1–24.

Baskerville, Peter A. "Entrepreneurship and the Family Compact." *Urban History Review* 9, 3 (February 1981): 15–34.

Battan, Jack. *The Annex: The Story of a Toronto Neighbourhood*. Toronto: Boston Mills Press, 2004.

———. *Honest Ed's Story*. Toronto: Doubleday Canada, 1972.

Beddoes, Dick. *Pal Hal: An Uninhibited No-Holds Barred Account of the Life and Times of Harold Ballard*. Toronto: Macmillan of Canada, 1989.

Berton, Pierre. *Flames across the Border 1813–1814*. Toronto: McClelland & Stewart, 1981.

———. *The Great Depression, 1929–1939*. Toronto: McClelland & Stewart, 1990.

———. *My Times: Living with History, 1947–1995*. Toronto: McClelland & Stewart, 1995.

———. *The New City: A Prejudiced View of Toronto*. Toronto: Macmillan of Canada, 1961.

———. *1967: The Last Good Year*. Toronto: Doubleday Canada, 1997.

Betcherman, Lita-Rose. *The Little Band: The Clashes between the Communists and the Political and Legal Establishment in Canada, 1928–1932*. Ottawa: Deneau, 1982.

Black, Conrad. *A Life in Progress*. Toronto: Key Porter, 1993.

———. *A Matter of Principle*. Toronto: McClelland & Stewart, 2011.

Bliss, Michael. *A Canadian Millionaire: The Life and Times of Sir Joseph Flavelle, Bart. 1858–1939*. Toronto: Macmillan of Canada, 1978.

———. *Northern Enterprise: Five Centuries of Canadian Business*. Toronto: McClelland & Stewart, 1987.

Boles, Derek. *Toronto's Railway Heritage*. Charleston, SC: Arcadia, 2009.

Burrill, William. *Hemingway: The Toronto Years*. Toronto: Doubleday Canada, 1994.

Cameron, Elspeth, and Janice Dickin, eds. *Great Dames.* Toronto: University of Toronto Press, 1997.

Campbell, Lara. *Respectable Citizens: Gender, Family and Unemployment in Ontario's Great Depression.* Toronto: University of Toronto Press, 2009.

Caplan, Kimmy. "There Is No Interest in Precious Stones in a Vegetable Market: The Life and Sermons of Rabbi Jacob Gordon of Toronto." *Jewish History* 23 (2009): 149–67.

Careless, J.M.S. *Brown of the Globe.* Vol. 1, *The Voice of Upper Canada 1818–1859.* Toronto: Dundurn, 1989.

———. *Brown of the Globe.* Vol. 2, *Statesman of Confederation 1860-1880.* Toronto: Dundurn, 1989.

———. *Toronto to 1918: An Illustrated History.* Toronto: Lorimer, 1984.

———. *The Union of the Canadas: The Growth of Canadian Institutions 1841–1857.* Toronto: McClelland & Stewart, 1967.

Chan, Arlene. *The Chinese in Toronto from 1878.* Toronto: Dundurn, 2011.

Chimbos, Peter D. *The Canadian Odyssey: The Greek Experience in Canada.* Toronto: McClelland & Stewart, 1980.

Clark, C.S. *Of Toronto the Good: The Queen City of Canada as It Is.* Montreal: The Toronto Publishing Company, 1898.

Clarke, Brian P. *Piety and Nationalism: Lay Voluntary Associations and the Creation of an Irish-Catholic Community in Toronto, 1850–1895.* Montreal and Kingston: McGill-Queen's University Press, 1993.

———. "Religious Riot as Pastime: Orange Young Britons, Parades and Public Life in Victorian Toronto." In *The Orange Order in Canada,* edited by David A. Wilson, 109–27. Dublin: Four Courts Press, 2007.

Colantonio, Frank. *From the Ground Up: An Italian Immigrant's Story.* Toronto: Between the Lines, 1997.

Colton, Timothy J. *Big Daddy: Frederick G. Gardiner and the Building of Metropolitan Toronto.* Toronto: University of Toronto Press, 1980.

Cottrell, Michael. "St. Patrick's Day Parades in Nineteenth-Century Toronto: A Study of Immigrant Adjustment and Elite Control." *Histoire sociale/Social History* 25, 49 (May 1992): 57–73.

Coyne, James H., ed. *The Talbot Papers.* Ottawa: Transactions of the Royal Society of Canada, 1909.

Craig, Gerald M. *Upper Canada.* Toronto: McClelland & Stewart, 1963.

Croucher, Sheila L. "Constructing the Image of Ethnic Harmony in Toronto, Canada: The Politics of Problem Definition and Nondefinition." *Urban Affairs Review* 32 (January 1997): 319–47.

Cumbo, Enrico T. Carlson. "'As the Twig's Bent, the Tree's Inclined': Growing Up Italian in Toronto." PhD dissertation, University of Toronto, 1996.

Dawson, Hilary J. "From Immigrant to Establishment: A Black Family's Journey." *Ontario History* 99, 1 (Spring 2007): 31–43.

De Klerck, Denis, and Corrado Paina, eds. *College Street: Little Italy.* Toronto: Mansfield Press, 2006.

Dendy, William. *Lost Toronto.* Toronto: Oxford University Press, 1978.

Desfor, Gene, and Jennifer Laidly, eds. *Reshaping Toronto's Waterfront.* Toronto: University of Toronto Press, 2011.

Doolittle, Robyn. *Crazy Town: The Rob Ford Story.* Toronto: Viking, 2014.

Doyle, Richard J. *Hurly-Burly: A Time at the Globe.* Toronto: Macmillan of Canada, 1990.

Drabinsky, Garth. *Closer to the Sun.* Toronto: McClelland & Stewart, 1995.

Driedger, Sharon Doyle. *An Irish Heart: How a Small Immigrant Community Shaped Canada.* Toronto: HarperCollins, 2010.

Duffy, Dennis. "Furnishing the Pictures: Arthur S. Goss, Michael Ondaatje and the Imag(in)ing of Toronto." *Journal of Canadian Studies* 36, 2 (Summer 2001): 106–29.

Earl, David W., ed. *The Family Compact: Aristocracy or Oligarchy?* Toronto: Copp Clark, 1967.

Errington, Jane. *The Lion, the Eagle, and Upper Canada: A Developing Colonial Ideology.* Montreal and Kingston: McGill-Queen's University Press, 1987.

Fairley, Margaret, ed. *The Selected Writings of William Lyon Mackenzie, 1824–1837.* Toronto: Oxford University Press, 1960.

Filey, Mike. *Toronto Sketches.* Toronto: Dundurn, 1992.

———. *More Toronto Sketches.* Toronto: Dundurn, 1993.

———. *Toronto Sketches 3.* Toronto: Dundurn, 1994.

———. *Toronto Sketches 4.* Toronto: Dundurn, 1995.

———. *Toronto Sketches 5.* Toronto: Dundurn, 1997.

———. *Toronto Sketches 10.* Toronto: Dundurn, 2010.

Finkelstein, Bernie. *True North: A Life in the Music Business.* Toronto: McClelland & Stewart, 2012.

Firth, Edith. *The Town of York, 1793–1815: A Collection of Documents of Early Toronto.* Toronto: Champlain Society, 1962.

———. *The Town of York, 1815–1834: A Further Collection of Documents of Early Toronto.* Toronto: Champlain Society, 1966.

Fitzgerald, James. *What Disturbs Our Blood.* Toronto: Random House, 2010.

Flaherty, David H., ed. *Essays in the History of Canadian Law.* Vol. 2. Toronto: University of Toronto Press, 1983.

Fleming, R.B. *The Railway King of Canada: Sir William Mackenzie 1849–1923.* Vancouver: UBC Press, 1991.

Foster, Cecil. *A Place Called Heaven: The Meaning of Being Black in Canada.* Toronto: HarperCollins, 1996.

Fowler, Marian. *The Embroidered Ten: Five Gentlewomen in Early Canada.* Toronto: Anansi, 1982.

Fox, William S., ed. *Letters of William Davies, Toronto 1854–1861.* Toronto: University of Toronto Press, 1945.

Frager, Ruth. A. "Class, Ethnicity, and Gender in the Eaton Strikes of 1912 and 1934." In *Gender Conflicts: New Essays in Women's History,* edited by Franca Iacovetta and Mariana Valverde, 189–228. Toronto: University of Toronto Press, 1992.

———. *Sweatshop Strife: Class, Ethnicity and Gender in the Jewish Labour Movement of Toronto 1900–1939.* Toronto: University of Toronto Press, 1992.

Fraser, Graham. *Fighting Back: Urban Renewal in Trefann Court.* Toronto: Hakkert, 1972.

Friedland, Martin L. *The University of Toronto: A History.* Toronto: University of Toronto Press, 2002.

Frost, Karolyn Smardz. *I've Got a Home in Glory Land: A Lost Tale of the Underground Railroad.* Toronto: Thomas Allen, 2007.

Fryer, Mary Beacock. *Elizabeth Postuma Simcoe 1762–1850: A Biography.* Toronto: Dundurn, 1989.

Fryer, Mary Beacock, and Christopher Dracott. *John Graves Simcoe, 1752–1806: A Biography.* Toronto: Dundurn, 1998.

Fulford, Robert. *Accidental City: The Transformation of Toronto.* Toronto: Macfarlane Walter & Ross, 1995.

———. *Best Seat in the House: Memoirs of a Lucky Man.* Toronto: Collins Publishers, 1988.

Garner, Hugh. *Cabbagetown.* Toronto: The Ryerson Press, 1950.

Gelman, Susan. "Anatomy of a Failed Strike: The T. Eaton Co. Lockout of Cloakmakers, 1912." *Canadian Jewish Historical Society Journal* 9, 2 (Fall 1985): 93–119.

Gibson, Douglas. *Stories about Storytellers.* Toronto: ECW Press, 2011.

Gibson, Sally. *More Than an Island: A History of the Toronto Island.* Toronto: Irwin Publishing, 1984.

Glazebrook, G.P. de T. *The Story of Toronto.* Toronto: University of Toronto Press, 1971.

Goheen, Peter G. *Victorian Toronto, 1850–1900: Pattern and Process of Growth.* Chicago: University of Chicago Press, 1970.

Graham, Roger. *Old Man Ontario: Leslie M. Frost.* Toronto: University of Toronto Press, 1990.

Granatstein, J.L., and Desmond Morton. *A Nation Forged in Fire: Canadians and the Second World War 1939–1945.* Toronto: Lester & Orpen Dennys, 1989.

Gray, Charlotte. *The Massey Murder: A Maid, Her Master and the Trial That Shocked a Country.* Toronto: HarperCollins, 2013.

———. *Mrs. King: The Life and Times of Isabel Mackenzie King.* Toronto: Viking, 1997.

Greer, Allan. "1837–38: Rebellions Reconsidered." *Canadian Historical Review* 76, 1 (March 1995): 1–18.

Guillet, Edwin C. *Early Life in Upper Canada.* Toronto: The Ontario Publishing Company, 1933.

———. *The Great Migration.* Toronto: University of Toronto Press, 1963 (originally published 1937).

———. *The Life and Times of the Patriots.* Toronto: University of Toronto Press, 1968 (originally published 1938).

Hale, Katherine. *Toronto: Romance of a Great City.* Toronto: Cassell & Company, 1956.

Harney, Robert F., ed. *Gathering Place: Peoples and Neighbourhoods of Toronto, 1834–1945.* Toronto: Multicultural History Society of Ontario, 1985.

Harney, Robert F., and Harold Troper. *Immigrants: A Portrait of the Urban Experience, 1890–1930.* Toronto: Van Nostrand Reinhold, 1975.

Harris, Amy Lavender. *Imagining Toronto.* Toronto: Mansfield Press, 2010.

Harris, Marjorie. *Toronto: The City of Neighbourhoods.* Toronto: Key Porter, 1984.

Harris, Richard. *Creeping Conformity: How Canada Became Suburban, 1900–1960.* Toronto: University of Toronto Press, 2004.

———. *Unplanned Suburbs: Toronto's American Tragedy, 1900 to 1950.* Baltimore: Johns Hopkins University Press, 1996.

Hayes, David. *Power and Influence: The Globe and Mail and the News Revolution.* Toronto: Key Porter, 1992.

Hayes, Derek. *Historical Atlas of Toronto.* Vancouver: Douglas & McIntyre, 2009.

Henderson, Stuart. *Making the Scene: Yorkville and Hip Toronto in the 1960s.* Toronto: University of Toronto Press, 2011.

Henry, Frances. *The Caribbean Diaspora in Toronto: Learning to Live with Racism.* Toronto: University of Toronto Press, 1994.

Hewitt, W.A. *Down the Stretch: Recollections of a Pioneer Sportsman and Journalist.* Toronto: Ryerson, 1958.

Hiebert, Daniel J. "Jewish Immigrants and the Garment Industry of Toronto, 1901–1931: A Study of Ethnic and Class Relations." *Annals of the Association of American Geographers* 83, 2 (June 1993): 243–71.

Hoffman, Frances, and Ryan Taylor. *Across the Waters: Ontario Immigrants' Experiences 1820–1850.* Milton, ON: Global Heritage Press, 1999.

———. *Much To Be Done: Private Life in Ontario from Victorian Diaries.* Toronto: Natural Heritage Books, 2007.

Horn, Michiel, ed. *The Dirty Thirties: Canadians in the Great Depression.* Toronto: Copp Clark, 1972.

Hounsom, Eric W. *Toronto in 1810.* Toronto: Ryerson, 1970.

How, Douglas. *Canada's Mystery Man of Finance.* Hantsport, NS: Lancelot Press, 1986.

Hubbard, Stephen L. *The Story of William Peyton Hubbard: Black Leader and Municipal Reformer.* Toronto: Dundurn, 1987.

Humphrey, C.W. "The Capture of York." *Ontario History* 51, 1 (March 1960): 1–21.

Iacovetta, Franca. *Such Hardworking People: Italian Immigrants in Postwar Toronto.* Montreal and Kingston: McGill-Queen's University Press, 1992.

James, Cathy. "Reforming Reform: Toronto's Settlement House Movement, 1900–20." *Canadian Historical Review* 82, 1 (March 2001): 1–20.

Kaplan, Harold. *Urban Political Systems: A Functional Analysis of Metro Toronto.* New York: Columbia University Press, 1967.

Kealey, Gregory S. *Toronto Workers Respond to Industrial Capitalism 1867–1892.* Toronto: University of Toronto Press, 1980.

Keane, David, and Colin Read. *Old Ontario: Essays in Honour of J.M.S. Careless.* Toronto: Dundurn, 1990.

Kennedy, Betty. *Hurricane Hazel.* Toronto: Macmillan of Canada, 1979.

Kilbourn, William, *The Firebrand: William Lyon Mackenzie and the Rebellion in Upper Canada.* Toronto: Clarke, Irwin, 1956.

———, ed. *The Toronto Book.* Toronto: Macmillan of Canada, 1976.

———, ed. *Toronto Remembered: A Celebration of the City.* Toronto: Stoddart, 1984.

King, James. *Jack: A Life with Writers; The Story of Jack McClelland.* Toronto: Knopf, 1999.

Layton, Jack. *Homelessness: How to End the National Crisis.* Toronto: Penguin Canada, 2008.

Lemon, James. *Toronto Since 1918: An Illustrated History.* Toronto: Lorimer, 1985.

LeSueur, William Dawson. *William Lyon Mackenzie: A Reinterpretation.* Toronto: Macmillan of Canada, 1979.

Levine, Allan. *The Devil in Babylon: Fear of Progress and the Birth of Modern Life.* Toronto: McClelland & Stewart, 2005.

———. *King: William Lyon Mackenzie King: A Life Guided by the Hand of Destiny.* Vancouver: Douglas & McIntyre, 2011.

———. *Scrum Wars: The Prime Ministers and the Media.* Toronto: Dundurn, 1993.

———, ed. *Your Worship: The Lives of Eight of Canada's Most Unforgettable Mayors.* Toronto: Lorimer, 1989.

Levitt, Cyril, and William Shaffir. *The Riot at Christie Pits.* Toronto: Lester & Orpen Dennys, 1987.

Levy, Edward J. *Rapid Transit in Toronto: A Century of Plans, Progress, Politics and Paralysis.* Toronto: Neptis Foundation, 1913.

Luftspring, Sammy. *Call Me Sammy.* Scarborough, ON: Prentice-Hall of Canada, 1975.

MacSkimming, Roy. *The Perilous Trade: Publishing Canada's Writers.* Toronto: McClelland & Stewart, 2003.

Mandres, Marinel. "The Dynamics of Ethnic Residential Patterns in the Toronto Census Metropolitan Area." PhD dissertation, Wilfrid Laurier University, 1998.

Mann, W.E. *The Underside of Toronto.* Toronto: McClelland & Stewart, 1970.

Marshall, William. *Film Festival Confidential.* Toronto: McArthur & Company, 2005.

Marquis, Greg. "The Police as a Social Service in Early Twentieth-Century Toronto." *Histoire sociale/ Social History* 25, 50 (November 1992): 335–358.

Martyn, Lucy Booth. *The Face of Early Toronto: An Archival Record 1797–1936.* Sutton West, ON: Paget, 1982.

———. *Toronto: 100 Years of Grandeur.* Toronto: Pagurian, 1978.

Masters, D.C. *The Rise of Toronto 1850–1890.* Toronto: University of Toronto Press, 1947.

Maynard, Steven. "'Horrible Temptations': Sex, Men and Working-Class Male Youth in Urban Ontario, 1890–1935." *Canadian Historical Review* 78, 2 (June 1997): 191–235.

McAree, J.V. *Cabbagetown Store.* Toronto: Ryerson, 1953.

———. "The Jews in Canada." *Maclean's* 24, 1 (May 1912): 17–27.

———. "The Jews in Canadian Business." *Maclean's* 24, 3 (August 1912): 55–59.

McCall, Christina. *My Life as a Dame: The Personal and Political Writings of Christina McCall.* Edited by Stephen Clarkson. Toronto: House of Anansi Press, 2008.

McCalla, Douglas. "The Commercial Politics of the Toronto Board of Trade, 1850–1860." *Canadian Historical Review* 50, 1 (March 1969): 51–67.

McDougall, A.K. *John P. Robarts: His Life and Government.* Toronto: University of Toronto Press, 1986.

McGowan, Mark G. *The Waning of the Green: Catholics, the Irish, and Identity in Toronto, 1887–1922.* Montreal and Kingston: McGill-Queen's University Press, 1999.

McKillop, Brian. *Pierre Berton: A Biography.* Toronto: Random House of Canada, 2011.

McParland, Kelly. *The Lives of Conn Smythe.* Toronto: McClelland & Stewart, 2011.

McQueen, Rod. *The Eatons: The Rise and Fall of Canada's Royal Family.* Toronto: Stoddart, 1998.

Menkis, Richard, and Norman Ravvin, eds. *The Canadian Jewish Studies Reader.* Calgary: Red Deer Press, 2004.

Mickleburgh, Rod, with Rudyard Griffiths. *Rare Courage: Veterans of the Second World War Remember.* Toronto: McClelland & Stewart, 2005.

Miller, Ian Hugh Maclean. *Our Glory and Our Grief: Torontonians and the Great War.* Toronto: University of Toronto Press, 2002.

Moore, Christopher. *The Loyalists.* Toronto: Macmillan of Canada, 1984.

Morton, Desmond. *Mayor Howland: The Citizens' Candidate.* Toronto: Hakkert, 1973.

Myers, Jay. *The Great Canadian Road: A History of Yonge Street.* Toronto: Red Rock, 1977.

Nash, Catherine Jean. "Contesting Identity: Politics of Gays and Lesbians in Toronto in the 1970s." *Gender, Place and Culture* 12, 1 (March 2005): 113–35.

Nash, Knowlton. *The Microphone Wars: A History of Triumph and Betrayal at the CBC.* Toronto: McClelland & Stewart, 1994.

Nathanson, Deena. "A Social Profile of Peddlers in the Jewish Community of Toronto, 1891–1930." *Canadian Jewish Studies* 1 (1993): 27–40.

Nelles, H.V. *The Politics of Development: Forests, Mines and Hydro-Electric Power in Ontario, 1849–1941.* Toronto: Macmillan of Canada, 1974.

Newman, Peter C. *The Canadian Establishment.* Vol. 1. Toronto: McClelland & Stewart, 1975.

———. *The Canadian Establishment.* Vol. 2, *The Acquisitors.* Toronto: McClelland & Stewart, 1981.

———. *The Canadian Establishment.* Vol. 3, *Titans: How the New Canadian Establishment Seized Power.* Toronto: Viking, 1998.

———. *The Canadian Revolution: From Deference to Defiance.* Toronto: Viking, 1995.

———. *Here Be Dragons: Telling Tales of People, Passion and Power.* Toronto: McClelland & Stewart, 2004.

Nolan, Michael. *CTV: The Network That Means Business.* Edmonton: University of Alberta Press, 2001.

Osbaldeston, Mark. *Unbuilt Toronto: A History of the City That Might Have Been.* Toronto: Dundurn, 2008.

———. *Unbuilt Toronto 2: More of the City That Might Have Been.* Toronto: Dundurn, 2011.

Panofsky, Ruth. *The Literary Legacy of the Macmillan Company of Canada: Mapping Books and Mapping Culture.* Toronto: University of Toronto Press, 2012.

Paris, Erna. *Jews: An Account of Their Experience in Canada.* Toronto: Macmillan of Canada, 1980.

Patterson, Marian A. "The Cholera Epidemic of 1832 in York, Upper Canada." *Bulletin of the Medical Library Association* 46, 2 (April 1958): 165–84.

Pearson, W.H. *Recollections and Records of Toronto of Old.* Toronto: William Briggs, 1914.

Phillips, Nathan. *Mayor of All the People.* Toronto: McClelland & Stewart, 1967.

Piva, Michael J. *The Condition of the Working Class in Toronto 1900–1921.* Ottawa: University of Ottawa Press, 1979.

Prince, Bryan. "The Case of Isaac Brown: Fugitive Slave." *Ontario History* 99, 1 (Spring 2007): 18–30.

Raible, Chris. *Muddy York Mud: Scandal and Scurrility in Upper Canada.* Creemore, ON: Curiosity House, 1992.

Rasporich, Anthony W., ed. *William Lyon Mackenzie.* Toronto: Holt, Rinehart and Winston of Canada, 1972.

Read, Colin, and Ronald J. Stagg, eds. *The Rebellion of 1837 in Upper Canada.* Toronto: The Champlain Society / Ottawa: Carleton University Press, 1985.

Riddell, William Renwick. *The Life of John Graves Simcoe.* Toronto: McClelland & Stewart, 1926.

Ridout, Thomas. *Ten Years of Upper Canada in Peace and War, 1805–1815.* Edited by Matilda Edgar. Toronto: William Briggs, 1890.

Robertson, Heather. *Driving Force: The McLaughlin Family and the Age of the Car.* Toronto: McClelland & Stewart, 1995.

Robertson, John Ross. *The Diary of Mrs. John Graves Simcoe.* Toronto: William Briggs, 1911.

———. *Old Toronto.* Edited by E.C. Kyte. Toronto: Macmillan of Canada, 1954.

Robinson, Danielle. "Modernism at a Crossroad: The Spadina Expressway Controversy in Toronto, Ontario ca. 1960–1971." *Canadian Historical Review* 92, 2 (June 2011): 295–322.

Robinson, Percy. *Toronto during the French Regime.* Toronto: University of Toronto Press, 1965 (originally published 1933).

Rogers, Edward S., and Donald B. Smith, eds. *Aboriginal Ontario: Historical Perspectives on the First Nations.* Toronto: Dundurn, 1994.

Rose, Albert. *Governing Metropolitan Toronto: A Social and Political Analysis.* Berkeley: University of California Press, 1972.

———. *Regent Park: A Study in Slum Clearance.* Toronto: University of Toronto Press, 1958.

Rosenfeld, Max, and Earle Beatie. *A Blot on the Face of the City.* Toronto: Toronto Telegram, 1955.

Russell, Victor L., ed. *Forging a Consensus: Historical Essays on Toronto.* Toronto: University of Toronto Press, 1984.

Rust-D'Eye, George H. *Cabbagetown Remembered.* Erin, ON: Boston Mills Press, 1984.

Rutherford, Paul. *When Television Was Young: Prime Time Canada, 1952–1967.* Toronto: University of Toronto Press, 1982.

Saddlemyer, Ann, ed. *Early Stages: Theatre in Ontario, 1800–1914.* Toronto: University of Toronto Press, 1990.

Santink, Joy L. *Timothy Eaton and the Rise of his Department Store.* Toronto: University of Toronto Press, 1990.

Saunders, Leslie H. *An Orangeman in Public Life.* Toronto: Britannia Printers, 1981.

Saywell, John T. *"Just Call Me Mitch": The Life of Mitchell F. Hepburn.* Toronto: University of Toronto Press, 1991.

———. *Someone to Teach Them: York University and the Great University Explosion, 1960–1973.* Toronto: University of Toronto Press, 2008.

Scadding, Henry. *Toronto of Old.* Abridged and edited by F.H. Armstrong. Toronto: Oxford University Press, 1966 (first published in 1873).

Scadding, Henry, and J.C. Dent. *Toronto Past and Present: Historical and Descriptive.* Toronto: Hunter, Rose and Company, 1884.

Schmalz, Peter S. *The Ojibwa of Southern Ontario.* Toronto: University of Toronto Press, 1991.

Sewell, John. *The Shape of the City: Toronto Struggles with Modern Planning.* Toronto: University of Toronto Press, 1993.

———. *The Shape of the Suburbs: Understanding Toronto's Sprawl.* Toronto: University of Toronto Press, 2009.

———. *Up against City Hall.* Toronto: James Lewis & Samuel, 1972.

———. *Urban Policing in Canada.* Toronto: Lorimer, 1985.

Sexton, Rosemary. *Glitter Girls: Charity and Vanity Chronicles of an Era of Excess.* Toronto: Macmillan Canada, 1993.

Shadd, Adrienne, Afua Cooper, and Karolyn Smardz Frost. *The Underground Railway: Next Stop Toronto!* Toronto: Natural Heritage Books, 2002.

Shapiro, Shmuel Mayer. *The Rise of the Toronto Jewish Community.* Toronto: Now & Then Books, 2010.

Sharp, Rosalie, Irving Abella, and Edwin Goodman, eds. *Growing up Jewish: Canadians Tell Their Own Stories.* Toronto: McClelland & Stewart, 1997.

Sharp, Rosalie Wise. *Rifke: An Improbable Life.* Toronto: ECW Press, 2007.

Siggins, Maggie. *Bassett: John Bassett's Forty Years in Politics, Publishing, Business and Sports.* Toronto: Lorimer, 1979.

Smith, Denis. *Rogue Tory: The Life and Legend of John G. Diefenbaker.* Toronto: Macfarlane Walter & Ross, 1995.

Smith, Mary Larratt, ed. *Young Mr. Smith in Upper Canada.* Toronto: University of Toronto Press, 1980.

Sonmor, Jean. *The Little Paper That Grew: Inside the Toronto Sun Publishing Corporation.* Toronto: Toronto Sun, 1993.

Speisman, Stephen. *The Jews of Toronto: A History to 1937.* Toronto: McClelland & Stewart, 1979.

———. "Munificent Parsons and Municipal Parsimony: Voluntary vs. Public Poor Relief in Nineteenth Century Toronto." *Ontario History* 45, 1 (March 1973): 33–49.

Sprigley, Katrina. *Breadwinning Daughters: Young Women in a Depression-Era City, 1929–1939.* Toronto: University of Toronto Press, 2010.

Strange, Carolyn. *Toronto's Girl Problem: The Perils and Pleasures of the City, 1880–1930.* Toronto: University of Toronto Press, 1995.

Taylor, Alan. *The Civil War of 1812.* New York: Knopf, 2010.

Thompson, Richard H. *Toronto's Chinatown: The Changing Social Organization of an Ethnic Community.* New York: AMS Press, 1989.

Torcyzyner, James L., Shari L. Brotman, and Jay Brodbar. *Rapid Growth and Transformation: Demographic Challenges Facing the Jewish Community of Greater Toronto.* Toronto: Jewish Federation of Greater Toronto, 1995.

Tulchinsky, Gerald. *Branching Out: The Transformation of the Canadian Jewish Community.* Toronto: Stoddart, 1998.

———. *Joe Salsberg: A Life of Commitment.* Toronto: University of Toronto Press, 2013.

———. *Taking Root: The Origins of the Canadian Jewish Community.* Toronto: Stoddart, 1992.

Valverde, Marianne. *The Age of Light, Soap, and Water: Moral Reform in English Canada, 1885–1925.* Toronto: McClelland & Stewart, 1991.

Van Hasselt, Caroline. *High Wire Act: Ted Rogers and the Empire That Debt Built.* Mississauga, ON: Wiley, 2007.

Van Steen, Marcus. *Governor Simcoe and His Lady.* Toronto: Hodder and Stoughton, 1968.

Vipond, Mary. "A Canadian Hero of the 1920s: Dr. Frederick G. Banting." *Canadian Historical Review* 63, 4 (December 1982): 461–85.

Walden, Keith. *Becoming Modern in Toronto: The Industrial Exhibition and the Shaping of a Late Victorian Culture.* Toronto: University of Toronto Press, 1997.

———. "Toronto Society's Response to Celebrity Performers, 1887–1914." *Canadian Historical Review* 89, 3 (September 2008): 373–97.

Walker, Frank N. *Sketches of Old Toronto.* Toronto: Longmans Canada, 1965.

Weintraub, William. *City Unique: Montreal Days and Nights in the 1940s and '50s.* Toronto: McClelland & Stewart, 1996.

West, Bruce. *Toronto.* Toronto: Doubleday Canada, 1979.

White, Randall. *Too Good To Be True: Toronto in the 1920s.* Toronto: Dundurn, 1993.

Williams, Lorraine O'Donnell. *Memories of the Beach: Reflections on a Toronto Childhood.* Toronto: Dundurn, 2010.

Williamson, Ronald F., ed. *Toronto: A Short Illustrated History of Its First 12,000 Years.* Toronto: Lorimer, 2008.

Wilson, David. A., ed. *The Orange Order in Canada.* Dublin: Four Courts Press, 2007.

Wilton, Carol. *Popular Politics and Popular Culture in Upper Canada 1800–1850.* Montreal and Kingston: McGill-Queen's University Press, 2000.

Winks, Robin W. *The Blacks in Canada: A History.* Montreal and Kingston: McGill-Queen's University Press, 1997.

———. "Negro School Segregation in Ontario and Nova Scotia." *Canadian Historical Review* 50, 2 (June 1969): 164–91.

Wright, Barry. "Sedition in Upper Canada: Contested Legality," *Labour/Le Travail* 29 (Spring 1992), 7–57.

Zucchi, John E. *Italians in Toronto: Development of a National Identity, 1875–1935.* Montreal and Kingston: McGill-Queen's University Press, 1988.

NOTES

ABBREVIATIONS

CHR *Canadian Historical Review*

DCB *Dictionary of Canadian Biography*

GL *Globe* (1844–1936)

GM *Globe and Mail* (1936–present)

ME *Mail and Empire* (1895–1936)

NP *National Post*

OH *Ontario History*

SN *Saturday Night*

TE *Empire* (1887–1895)

TL *Toronto Life*

TM *Toronto Daily Mail* (1872–1895)

TN *News* (1881–1919)

TO *Torontoist*

TS *Toronto Star*

The *Star* has had three names: *Evening Star* (1892–1899); *Toronto Daily Star* (1900–1971); and *Toronto Star* (1971–present). For convenience sake, the newspaper is generally noted as the *Toronto Star* throughout the book.

TT *Toronto Telegram* (1876–1971)

TW *The World* (Toronto) (1880–1920)

INTRODUCTION: YONGE AND BLOOR

PAGE

1 **"If you're born in a city":** TS, August 5, 1995.

2 **According to the Toronto Board of Trade's:** Toronto Board of Trade, *Toronto as a Global City: Scorecard on Prosperity* (Toronto: Toronto Board of Trade 2012), 51 (www.tfsa.ca/storage/reports/Toronto_Global_City_Scorecard2012.pdf).

And in one of the few: Toronto Region Board of Trade, "A Green Light to Moving the Toronto Region: Paying for Public Transportation Expansion," discussion paper, March 2013, 5-6 (http://letsbreakthegridlock.com/wp-content/uploads/2013/03/discussion_paper_march15.pdf).

To the English poet: Rupert Brooke, *Letters from America* (New York: 1913), 83–84.

The consequence is: "Worst Traffic List Puts Vancouver, Montreal before Toronto," CBC News, October 12, 2012.

3 **This and other travels:** John Barber, "A Street of Many Cultures," *Maclean's*, October 13, 1986, 20–21.

4 **Home to some:** Derek Flack, "The Top 20 Novels Set in Toronto," Blog TO, August 25, 2011 (www.blogto.com/books_lit/2011/08/the_top_20_novels_set_in_toronto/).

Michael Ondaatje's *In the Skin*: Amy Lavender Harris, *Imagining Toronto* (Toronto: Mansfield Press, 2010), 13–32.

Great cities: Peter Ackroyd, *London: The Biography.* (London: Random House, 2009), 1–2 (see also the publisher's catalogue description of the book, http://www.randomhouse.com/acmart/catalog/display.pperl?isbn=9780385497718&view=print).

Revelling in his: Author's interview with Mike Harris, January 29, 2013.

The GTA has: Richard Florida, "What Toronto Needs Now," TL, November 2012, 80–82; Statistics Canada, "Canada at a Glance 2012: Population" (www.statcan.gc.ca/pub/12-581-x/2012000/pop-eng.htm).

5 **"What Toronto chose":** Peter C. Newman, *The Canadian Revolution: From Deference to Defiance* (Toronto: Viking, 1995), 108.

Part of the issue: Author's interview with Peter Mansbridge, October 22, 2012.

From his office at the *Walrus*: Author's interview with John Macfarlane, October 24, 2012.

By 2006, approximately half: "Toronto's Racial Diversity," City of Toronto website (www.toronto.ca/toronto_facts/diversity.htm).

6 **The city was:** Harris, *Imagining Toronto*, 17.

That turned out: Michael J. Doucet, "The Anatomy of an Urban Legend: Toronto's Multicultural Reputation, 2001," at the Ceris–Ontario Metropolis Centre website (http://ceris.metropolis.net/Virtual%20Library/other/doucet3.html).

"There is a school of thought": GM, June 30, 2003.

7 **According to WealthInsight:** TS, May 9, 2013.

Of the fifty: "50 Most Influential 2012: A ranking of Toronto's Top Tycoons, Backroom Operators and Supersize Egos," TL, December 2012, 44–50, 54, 56, 58, 60, 62 (www.torontolife.com/informer/features/2012/12/03/50-most-influential-2012/).

"For cities to have": *Financial Times*, March 27, 2012.

"Christ, I hate to leave": Hemingway to Isabel Simmons, June 24, 1923, in Ernest Hemingway, *Ernest Hemingway, Selected Letters, 1917–1961*, ed. Carlos Baker (New York: Scribner, 1981), 84.

"Once it was fashionable": Margaret Atwood, *Cat's Eye* (Toronto: McClelland & Stewart, 1988), 13–14.

"Clearly, if Confederation": Eric Nicol and Peter Whalley, *100 Years of What?* (Toronto: Ryerson, 1966), cited in *Ottawa Citizen*, June 25, 2007.

8 **The first shot:** See Lister Sinclair, "We All Hate Toronto," in *A Play on Words and Other Radio Plays* (Toronto: J.M. Dent, 1948), 255–78; Kevin Plummer, "The City That Nobody Loves," TO, November 21, 2009 (http://torontoist.com/2009/11/historicist_the_city_that_nobody_loves/); *Calgary Herald*, June 16, 2006; NP, April 2, 2007.

The mockingly outrageous: Arrogant Worms, "The Toronto Song" (www.lyricsmode.com/lyrics/t/three_dead_trolls_in_a_baggie/the_toronto_sucks.html); TS, March 9, 2002.

A harsher and more: Bert Archer, "Making a Toronto of the Imagination," in *UTOpia: Towards a New Toronto*, ed. Jason McBride and Alana Wilcox (Toronto: Coach House, 2005), 220.

"Toronto is recognized": NP, October 6, 2012.

Or, as the Toronto-born: GM, January 19, 2014.

CHAPTER ONE: THE CARRYING PLACE

9 **"My people have survived":** Chief Bryan LaForme, "A Layered City: 200 Years of the Mississaugas and Toronto," William Kilbourn Memorial Lecture, 2012 (www.youtube.com/watch?v=9fhxiepJNzk).

The name was likely: "The Real Story of How Toronto Got Its Name," Natural Resources Canada (http://www.nrcan.gc.ca/earth-sciences/geography/place-names/education-resources/9226?destination=node/5697); Derek Hayes, *Historical Atlas of Toronto* (Vancouver: Douglas & McIntyre, 2009), 15.

He was among: David Hackett Fischer, *Champlain's Dream* (Toronto: Knopf Canada, 2009), 239.

10 **After many months:** "Etienne Brule," DCB (www.biographi.ca/en/bio/brule_etienne_1E.html).

"It is clear": Father François Du Creux, *The History of Canada or New France*, vol. 1, trans. with an introduction by Percy J. Robinson, ed. with notes by James B. Conacher (Toronto: Champlain Society, 1951–1952), 182.

"Brûlé was unfortunately": Cited in "Etienne Brule," DCB.

Or, like other young: Ibid.

In September 1615: Ibid.; Fischer, *Champlain's Dream*, 328.

As historian Percy Robinson: Percy Robinson, *Toronto during the French Regime* (1933; Toronto: University of Toronto Press, 1965), 2.

Some historians now: "Did Étienne Brûlé Visit Toronto in 1615?" *Arts and Culture. Museums: Virtual Exhibits—The History of Toronto: An 11,000-Year Journey—Natives and Newcomers, 1600–1793*, on the City of Toronto website (www.toronto.ca/culture/history/history-natives-newcomers.htm).

11 **In his memoir:** Alexander Henry, *Travels and Adventures in Canada and the Indian Territories between the Years 1761 and 1776* (New York: I. Riley, 1809), 180 (www.biographi.ca/009004-119.01-e.php?BioId=37033).

Though he did enlist: "Etienne Brule," DCB.

Either way, in the years: Fischer, *Champlain's Dream*, 500.

In 1628, on: Ibid., 500–501; "Etienne Brule," DCB.

Thousands of years: Ronald F. Williamson, ed., *Toronto: A Short Illustrated History of its First 12,000 Years* (Toronto: Lorimer, 2008), 26.

Though these hunting: Edward S. Rogers and Donald B. Smith, eds. *Aboriginal Ontario: Historical Perspectives on the First Nations* (Toronto: Dundurn, 1994), 26–32, 35–36, 44.

12 **Over the years:** Ibid., 27, 39.

More recently, entire Huron: Ibid, 38–39; "The Alexandra Site," Toronto Historical Plaques website (www.torontohistory.org/Pages_ABC/Alexandra_Site.html); GL, May 24, 1881; Williamson, *A Short Illustrated History*, 42.

By the time Jacques Cartier: Rogers and Smith, *Aboriginal Ontario*, 41–42; Williamson, *A Short Illustrated History*, 38–52.

In time, however: "Disease and Dislocation among the First Nations in the 17th Century," *Arts and Culture. Museums: Virtual Exhibits—The History of Toronto: An 11,000-Year Journey—Natives and Newcomers, 1600–1793*, on the City of Toronto website (www.toronto.ca/culture/history/history-natives-newcomers.htm).

This high death rate: Rogers and Smith, *Aboriginal Ontario*, 51–52.

Steckley recalls: Steckley to author, October 15, 2012.

But another soon: See "West Don Lands" on the Waterfront Toronto website (www.waterfrontoronto.ca/explore_projects2/west_don_lands).

It had easy access: Eric Arthur, *Toronto: No Mean City* (Toronto: University of Toronto Press, 1986), 5.

13 **"The site was a natural":** Williamson, *A Short Illustrated History*, 50.

Teiaiagon does not: Arthur, *No Mean City*, 6.

Some of La Salle's: Ibid., 50; Robinson, *Toronto during the French Regime*, 26–33.
In 1701, the Seneca: Peter S. Schmalz, *The Ojibwa of Southern Ontario* (Toronto: University of Toronto Press, 1991), 21.

In 1720, under the direction: Robinson, *Toronto during the French Regime*, 77–78.

Unhappy with this: Ibid;, 61–84; Williamson, *A Short Illustrated History*, 55–56; Bruce West, *Toronto* (Toronto: Doubleday Canada, 1979), 7; Arthur, *No Mean City*, 7.

14 **The small post:** Pierre Robinau de Portneuf," DCB (www.biographi.ca/en/bio/robinau_de_portneuf_pierre_3E.html).

Not wanting to lose: Robinson, *Toronto during the French Regime*, 97, 101–3; "Pierre Robinau de Portneuf," DCB.

Fort Rouillé, named: "Pierre Robinau de Portneuf," DCB; Arthur, *No Mean City*, 7; "Zacharie Robutel del la Noue," DCB (www.biographi.ca/en/bio/robutel_de_la_noue_zacharie_2E.html); Robinson, *Toronto during the French Regime*, 122.

The trade with: La Jonquière to Rouille, October 6, 1751, cited in Robinson, *Toronto during the French Regime*, 113–14, 127.

When the British arrived: Henry Scadding, *Toronto of Old* (Toronto: Oxford University Press, 1966), 22; Robinson, *Toronto during the French Regime*, 139.

15 **Born in Massachusetts:** "Robert Rodgers," DCB (www.biographi.ca/en/bio/rogers_robert_4E.html).

"The soil here": *Journals of Major Robert Rogers*, (London: J. Millan, 1765), 149 (www.archive.org/stream/journelsofmajorr00709 2mbp#page/n1/mode/2up).

Baby was born: "Jacques Dupéront Baby," DCB (www.biographi.ca/en/bio/baby_jacques_4E.html)

At some point: Ibid.

16 **By then, his eldest son:** Ibid.; Arthur, *No Mean City*, 8.

In 1770, the elder Rousseau: "John Baptist Rousseaux St. John," DCB (www.biographi.ca/en/bio/rousseaux_st_john_john_baptist_5E.html).

He set out with: Robinson, *Toronto during the French Regime*, 210.

General Thomas Gage: Ibid., 147; Peter C. Mancall, *Deadly Medicine: Indians and Alcohol in Early America* (Ithaca, NY: Cornell University Press, 1997), 162–63.

Jean-Baptiste had learned: "John Baptist Rousseaux St. John," DCB.

17 **Though he built:** Ibid.; Arthur, *No Mean City*, 8; Robinson, *Toronto during the French Regime*, 209.

In his role: Rogers and Smith, *Aboriginal Ontario*, 106.

Since 1763, the British: Christopher Moore, *The Loyalists* (Toronto: Macmillan of Canada, 1984), 137.

On September 23, 1787: Percy J. Robinson, "The Chevalier De Rocheblave and the Toronto Purchase," *Transactions of the Royal Society of Canada*, 3rd series, 31, sec. 2, (1937), 138–46; TS, June 10, 2006; "Distribution of Arms, Ammunition and tobacco made by Sir John Johnson at the Head of the Bay of Quinté on the 23rd September 1787, at which time they made a formal Cession of Lands on the north side of Lake Ontario to the Crown," in Library and Archives Canada, RG 10, vol. 15, 195. Victoria Jane Freeman, "'Toronto Has No History!' Indigeneity, Settler Colonialism and Historical Memory in Canada's Largest City" (PhD dissertation, University of Toronto, 2010), 56–75.

Once land surveyors: Arthur, *No Mean City*, 10; TS, June 8, 2010.

CHAPTER TWO: BRITISH MUDDY YORK

19 **"Toronto was born":** William Kilbourn, ed. *Toronto Remembered: A Celebration of the City* (Toronto: Stoddart, 1984), 12–14.

When he first: John Ross Robertson, *Old Toronto* (Toronto: Macmillan of Canada, 1954), 32.

John Graves Simcoe: Mary Beacock Fryer and Christopher Dracott, *John Graves Simcoe, 1752–1806: A Biography* (Toronto: Dundurn, 1998), 12–13; "John Graves Simcoe," DCB (www.biographi.ca/en/bio/simcoe_john_graves_5E.html).

20 **Plundering and abusing:** Fryer and Dracott, *Simcoe*, 37–38, 75.

This assault was: Robin Winks, *The Blacks in Canada: A History* (Montreal and Kingston: McGill-Queen's University Press, 1997), 31.

Another British commander: Ibid., 79; Mary Beacock Fryer, *Elizabeth Postuma Simcoe 1762–1850: A Biography* (Toronto: Dundurn, 1989), 25.

21 **He was a natural:** Alan Taylor, *The Civil War of 1812* (New York: Knopf, 2010), 15.

22 **Simcoe was certain:** Gerald M. Craig, *Upper Canada* (Toronto: McClelland & Stewart, 1963), 20–21.

The new colony: Simcoe to Sir Joseph Banks, January 8, 1791, in *The Correspondence of Lieut. John Graves Simcoe*, ed. Brigadier E.A. Cruikshank, vol.1 (Toronto: Ontario Historical Society, 1923),18; Jane Errington, *The Lion, the Eagle, and Upper Canada: A Developing Colonial Ideology* (Montreal and Kingston: McGill-Queen's University Press, 1987), 13.

There, Elizabeth indulged: Fryer and Dracott, *Simcoe*, 170–71; Mary Quayle Innis, ed., *Mrs. Simcoe's Diary* (Toronto: Dundurn, 2007), 125–26.

The name "Fort York": Carl Benn, *Historic Fort York*, 1793–1993 (Toronto: Dundurn, 1993), 13.

Unhappy with the choice: Innis, *Mrs. Simcoe's Diary*, 24.

23 **Simcoe's vision angered:** Moore, *The Loyalists*, 181.

Moreover, Kingston was: Edith Firth, *The Town of York, 1793–1815: A Collection of Documents of Early Toronto* (Toronto: Champlain Society, 1962), xxxvi, xxxvii–xxxviii, 21–22, 47–48, 85–86.

He told Major General Alured Clarke: Cited in West, *Toronto*, 23.

"We embarked on board the 'Mississauga'": John Ross Robertson, *The Diary of Mrs. John Graves Simcoe* (Toronto: William Briggs, 1911), 179.

"I still distinctly": Robertson, *Old Toronto*, 508.

24 **As she reasoned:** Innis, *Mrs. Simcoe's Diary*, 153; Marian Fowler, *The Embroidered Ten: Five Gentlewomen in Early Canada* (Toronto: Anansi, 1982), 21.

In good spirit: Fowler, *The Embroidered Ten*, 21; Duke de la Rochefoucauld, *Travels through the United States of North America: The Country of the Iroquois, and Upper Canada in the Years 1795, 1796, and 1797* (London: R. Phillips, 1799), 241–42 (http://archive.org/details/travelsthroughunoolaro).

To remind her: Innis, *Mrs. Simcoe's Diary*, 85.

"The Governor and Mrs. Simcoe": Cited in West, *Toronto*, 27.

In 1794, a brutal: Firth, *The Town of York*, 219.

In the spring of 1794: Arthur, *No Mean City*, 20.

On one occasion: Innis, *Mrs. Simcoe's Diary*, 25.

25 **"His favourite topics":** Mary Delany, Lady Llanover, ed., *The Autobiography and Correspondence of Mary Granville, Mrs. Delany*, vol. 2 (London: Richard Bentley, 1862), 409; Fowler, *The Embroidered Ten*, 37.

"He thinks every": *Correspondence of Simcoe*, vol. 3 (Toronto: Ontario Historical Society, 1925), 109.

Minor transgressions: West, *Toronto*, 33.

Nonetheless, Simcoe had: J.M.S. Careless, *Toronto to 1918: An Illustrated History* (Toronto: Lorimer, 1984), 21.

Mann came up: Arthur, *No Mean City*, 11.

He devised a: Ibid., 16; Firth, *The Town of York*, xxxii.

26 **Both surveyors lacked imagination:** Arthur, *No Mean City*, 16–17.

"A more imaginative city": Robert Fulford, *Accidental City: The Transformation of Toronto* (Toronto: Macfarlane Walter & Ross, 1995), 42.

In an early example: Firth, *The Town of York*, xxxvii–xxxviii, 17.

Another path: Robertson, *Old Toronto*, 35; Eric W. Hounsom, *Toronto in 1810* (Toronto: Ryerson, 1970), 25.

27 **Embroiled in a:** L.F. Gates, "Roads, Rivals, and Rebellion: The Unknown Story of Asa Danforth, Jr.," OH 76 (1984): 233–54; see also "Asa Danforth," DCB (www.biographi.ca/en/bio/danforth_asa_6E.html).

The American attack: "John Graves Simcoe," DCB (www.biographi.ca/en/bio/simcoe_john_graves_5E.html); Craig, *Upper Canada*, 31.

Hence, it was: Firth, *The Town of York*, lxv.

Born in Ireland: "Peter Russell," DCB (www.biographi.ca/en/bio/russell_peter_5E.html).

28 **In the mid-1760s:** Ibid.

During Russell's tenure: G.P. de T Glazebrook, *The Story of Toronto* (Toronto: University of Toronto Press, 1971), 18–19.

29 **At different times:** Firth, *The Town of York*, liv–lv; "Russell," DCB.

There is no denying: "Russell," DCB; Craig, *Upper Canada*, 48–49.

Designed by William Berczy: Hounsom, *Toronto in 1810*, 64–65; Arthur, *No Mean City*, 24–25.

"You would be": Russell to Osgoode, September 13, 1798, in Firth, *The Town of York*, 226.

At best, Russell: Firth, *The Town of York*, xxviii, lxxviii; Winks, *The Blacks in Canada*, 49–50.

Russell was a fair: Winks, *The Blacks in Canada*, 51.

In a February 1806: *Upper Canada Gazette*, February 18, 22, 1806; West, *Toronto*, 41.

30 **Similar advertisements:** Robertson, *Old Toronto*, 210; West, *Toronto*, 41.

"For God's sake": Cited in Glazebrook, *The Story of Toronto*, 38. See also Firth, *The Town of York*, 229–30, 136–37.

John White: Craig, *Upper Canada*, 56–57.

Rank, privileges, government positions: Firth, *The Town of York*, lxxxix; Glazebrook, *The Story of Toronto*, 16–17.

The men enjoyed: Firth, *The Town of York*, lxxxii; Glazebrook, *The Story of Toronto*, 39; Hounsom, *Toronto in 1810*, 121–27.

To mark the occasion: Firth, *The Town of York*, 225.

Public drunkenness: "Minutes of the General Quarter Sessions of the Peace, Home District, July 14, 1802," in Firth, *The Town of York*, 100–101.

31 **It was enough to:** Abel Stevens, *Life and Times of Nathan Bangs* (New York: Carlton & Porter, 1863), 361 (http://archive.org/details/lifeandtimesnatoostevgoog).

York attracted: Firth, *The Town of York*, xlvii, 94–95; West, *Toronto*, 43.

The market's pillory: Firth, *The Town of York*, 249; Robertson, *Old Toronto*, 210.

The first man hanged: *Upper Canada Gazette*, January 25, 1800; Firth, *The Town of York*, 96; Katie Rook, "At the Heart of the City, a Site with a Gruesome Past," GM, June 15, 2005, A15.

In contrast, four years: "Wabakinine," DCB (www.biographi.ca/en/bio/wabakinine_4E.html).

And in truth: Firth, *The Town of York*, xlviii, 84–85.

"York never was": Stuart to Mountain, September 14, 1801, in ibid., 118.

32 **A popular joke:** West, *Toronto*, 115.

Mary (Gapper) O'Brien: Glazebrook, *The Story of Toronto*, 52. See also Audrey Saunders Miller, ed., *The Journals of Mary O'Brien*, 1828–1838 (Toronto: Macmillan of Canada, 1968).

In 1816, a stagecoach: Robertson, *Old Toronto*, 292.

By 1800, York magistrates: Ibid., 225; Firth, *The Town of York*, xlix.

It was, therefore: *Upper Canada Gazette*, December 18, 1802; Firth, *The Town of York*, 101.

In an 1802 ordinance: "Minutes of the General Quarter Sessions of the Peace, Home District, July 14, 1802," in Firth, *The Town of York*, 100–101.

As late as the 1830s: Glazebrook, *The Story of Toronto*, 68.

33 **Neither John White:** On the White–Small feud see "John White," DCB (www.biographi.ca/en/bio/white_john_1800_4E.html), and "John Small," DCB (www.biographi.ca/en/bio/small_john_6E.html).

That evening: White to Peter Russell, January 2, 1800, cited in "Law Society's First Treasurer Killed in Duel—Jan. 1800," Law Society of Upper Canada newsletter, January 2003 (www.lsuc.on.ca/with.aspx?id=365).

He shot White: "Russell's Report to Serjeant [sic] Shepherd, Lincoln's Inn," in Firth, *The Town of York*, 231.

Mrs. Small's reputation: Firth, *The Town of York*, lxxx; Mrs. W.D. Powell to George Murray, New York, January 24, 1808, in ibid., 271–72.

Later, the Smalls' son: "James Edward Small," DCB (www.biographi.ca/en/bio/small_james_edward_9E.html); "Samuel Peters Jarvis," DCB (www.biographi.ca/en/bio/jarvis_samuel_peters_8E.html); Chris Raible, *Muddy York Mud: Scandal and Scurrility in Upper Canada* (Creemore, ON: Curiosity House, 1992), 71–74.

34 **Allan ventured to:** "William Allan," DCB (www.biographi.ca/en/bio/allan_william_8E.html); Glazebrook, *The Story of Toronto*, 18.

More colourful was: "Laurent Quetton St. George," DCB (www.biographi.ca/en/bio/quetton_st_george_laurent_6E.html); Glazebrook, *The Story of Toronto*, 31.

35 **He also built:** Arthur, *No Mean City*, 34, 39.

In 1808, U.S. authorities: "Laurent Quetton St. George," DCB.

Half of York: Firth, *The Town of York*, lvi–lvii, 126; 134; James Powell, "British Colonies in North America: The Early Years (pre-1841)," in "A History of the Canadian Dollar," on the Bank of Canada website (www.bankofcanada.ca/publications-research/books-and-monographs/history-canadian-dollar/).

In the fall: "Laurent Quetton St. George," DCB; "William Dummer Powell," DCB (www.biographi.ca/en/bio/powell_william_dummer_6E.html).

Dr. William Baldwin: "William Warren Baldwin," DCB (www.biographi.ca/en/bio/baldwin_william_warren_7E.html).

36 **His most lasting:** "Spadina," on the City of Toronto website (www1.toronto.ca/wps/portal/contentonly?vgnextoid=919d2271635af310VgnVCM10000071d60f89RCRD)

Baldwin would have: Firth, *The Town of York*, lxxxi; "William Warren Baldwin," DCB.

He merely saw: "William Warren Baldwin," DCB.

Opposing moderates: Pierre Berton, *Flames across the Border*, 1813–1814 (Toronto: McClelland & Stewart, 1981), 39.

37 **He condemned the United States:** John Strachan, "A Sermon Preached at York before the Legislative Council and House of Assembly, August 2, 1812" (York, Upper Canada, 1812), 20 (https://archive.org/stream/cihm_41179#page/n5/mode/2up).

Ironically for someone: "John Strachan," DCB (www.biographi.ca/en/bio/strachan_john_9E.html).

By 1803, he had: Ibid.

That explains the: William Kilbourn, "John Toronto: Variations on Strachan," in *The Toronto Book*, ed. William Kilbourn (Toronto: Macmillan of Canada, 1976), 115.

38 **Before his untimely:** "Sir Isaac Brock," DCB (www.biographi.ca/en/bio/brock_isaac_5E.html).

On the morning: Firth, *The Town of York*, xc; Alan Taylor, *The Civil War of 1812* (New York: Knopf, 2010), 214; Richard Gerrard, historian, War of 1812 Bicentennial, Museum Services Toronto, to author May 6, 2013. See also Robert Malcomson, *Capital in Flames: The American Attack on York, 1813* (Montreal: Robin Brass Studio, 2008).

39 **Dr. William Beaumont:** Cited in West, *Toronto*, 86.

Nevertheless, during the: Firth, *The Town of York*, xci; C.W. Humphries, "The Capture of York," OH 51, 1 (March 1960): 1–21.

Isaac Wilson: Wilson to Jonathan Wilson, December 5, 1813, cited in Firth, *The Town of York*, 293.

On the other hand: Penelope Beikie to John Macdonnell, May 5, 1813, cited in Firth, *The Town of York*, 299–300.

"Those who abandoned": John Beikie to Miles Macdonnell, March 19, 1814, cited in ibid., 322–23; Taylor, *The Civil War of 1812*, 215.

The worst event: Taylor, *The Civil War of 1812*, 217.

40 **Then in 1934:** "The Mace," website of the Speaker of the Legislative Assembly of Ontario (http://speaker.ontla.on.ca/en/at-the-assembly/the-mace/).

Still, compared to other atrocities: Glazebrook, *The Story of Toronto*, 49; Taylor, *The Civil War of 1812*, 210–13; George S. Burkhardt, *Confederate Rage, Yankee Wrath: No Quarter in the Civil War* (Carbondale: Southern Illinois University Press, 2007).

Nearly three months: Glazebrook, *The Story of Toronto*, 50; Taylor, *The Civil War of 1812*, 305–7; Mary Beacock Fryer and William A. Smy, *Rolls of the Provincial (Loyalist) Corps, Canadian Command American Revolutionary Period* (Toronto: Dundurn, 1981), 45.

Strachan again negotiated: "John Strachan," DCB.

Not everything about: Careless, *Toronto to 1918*, 33.

As John Beverley Robinson: *Christian Guardian*, April 9, 1834.

CHAPTER THREE: THE REBELLION

41 **"Toronto is like a":** Anna B. Jameson, *Winter Studies and Summer Rambles in Canada*, vol. 1 (London: Saunders and Otley, 1838), 98.

"The people of": Cited in Paul Romney, "A Struggle for Authority," in *Forging a Consensus: Historical Essays on Toronto*, ed. Victor L. Russell (Toronto: University of Toronto Press, 1984), 14.

York was indeed: *York Patriot*, December 7, 1832.

42 **The influential and fashionable:** "Christopher Widmer," DCB (www.biographi.ca/en/bio/widmer_christopher_8E.html); Edith Firth, *The Town of York, 1815–1834: A Further Collection of Documents of Early Toronto* (Toronto: Champlain Society, 1966), lii.

For the next six: Arthur, *No Mean City*, 62.

Yet enough residents: Firth, *Town of York, 1815–1834*, xvii, 2.

Getting to and from: Ibid., 66; *Upper Canada Gazette*, June 13, 1808; Jay Myers, *The Great Canadian Road: A History of Yonge Street* (Toronto: Red Rock, 1977), 67–70.

43 **Besides drinking:** Firth, *Town of York, 1815–1834*, lxxxiv–lxxxv; Arthur, *No Mean City*, 73.

Completed in 1817: *Lucy Booth Martyn, The Face of Early Toronto: An Archival Record 1797–1936* (Sutton West, ON: Paget, 1982), 69; Robertson, *Old Toronto*, 38.

Similarly, Captain George Taylor: "The Denisons" on the Kensington Market Historical Society website (www.kmhs.ca/george-taylor-denison-i/)

But he was not: "William Botsford Jarvis," DCB (www.biographi.ca/en/bio/jarvis_william_botsford_9E.html).

44 **"The Town of York":** Firth, *Town of York, 1815–1834*, 322–23.

In the 1835 edition: George Henry, *The Emigrant Guide, or Canada As It Is* (Quebec: William Gray & Company, 1835), 101–5 (www.archive.org/stream/cihm_35678#page/n5/mode/2up).

"York looked pretty": E.S. Dunlop, ed., *Our Forest Home: Being Extracts from the Correspondence of the Late Frances Stewart* (Montreal: Gazette Printing and Publishing, 1902), 14–15.

In 1818, a young: Firth, *Town of York, 1815–1834*, lxvi.

Public lashings: Ibid., lxvii; Robertson, *Old Toronto*, 165.

This multitude comprised: J.M. Bumsted, *History of the Canadian Peoples* (Toronto: Oxford University Press, 2003), 131–38; Edwin C. Guillet, *The Great Migration* (Toronto: University of Toronto Press, 1963), 2–3.

45 **Poverty, slums, crime:** Rabbi Jonathan Sacks, "Reversing the Decay of London Undone," *Wall Street Journal*, August 20, 2011.

A well-known joke: Guillet, *The Great Migration*, 15, 3.

"I really do bless": James Dobbie to his father, April 24, 1826, in *Third Report from the Select Committee on Emigration from the United Kingdom* (London: House of Commons, 1827), 166.

At the same time: Firth, *Town of York*, 1815–1834, lxxxiv.

Thereafter, to hide: William Kilbourn, *The Firebrand: William Lyon Mackenzie and the Rebellion in Upper Canada* (Toronto: Clarke, Irwin, 1956), 11.

46 **Upper Canadians were:** Romney, "A Struggle for Authority," 16.

The legacy of: See Allan Levine, *King: William Lyon Mackenzie King; A Life Guided by the Hand of Destiny* (Vancouver: Douglas & McIntyre, 2011), 39–40.

As he later recalled: Charles Lindsey, *The Life and Times of William Lyon Mackenzie* (Toronto: P.R. Randall, 1862), 40.

Idealistic and slightly naïve: *Colonial Advocate*, June 5, 1828; Craig, *Upper Canada*, 211.

47 **Progressive for his:** Margaret Fairley, ed., *The Selected Writings of William Lyon Mackenzie, 1824–1837* (Toronto: Oxford University Press, 1960), 54–55, 63, 173, 220, 363.

In a May 1912: Firth, *Town of York, 1815–1834*, xvi; TS, June 7, 1912.

That was certainly: Lindsey, *The Life and Times of William Lyon Mackenzie*, 5.

As historians Frederick Armstrong: "William Lyon Mackenzie," DCB (www.biographi.ca/en/bio/mackenzie_william_lyon_9E.html).

The first time: Cited in John Sewell, *Mackenzie: A Political Biography* (Toronto: Lorimer, 2002), 68.

48 **By 1833 he had:** William Lyon Mackenzie, *Sketches of Canada and the United States* (London: Effingham Wilson, 1833), 361, 408–9. See also *Colonial Advocate*, June 10, 1824, in Fairley, *Selected Writings*, 264–66; David W. Earl, ed., *The Family Compact: Aristocracy or Oligarchy?* (Toronto: Copp Clark, 1967), 12–14; and Anthony W. Rasporich, ed., *William Lyon Mackenzie* (Toronto: Holt, Rinehart and Winston of Canada, 1972), 54.

Theirs was a noble: Craig, *Upper Canada*, 109–10, 165–66.

The Compact leaders: Ibid., 109.

They sought to: Colin Read and Ronald J. Stagg, eds., *The Rebellion of 1837 in Upper Canada* (Toronto: The Champlain Society / Ottawa: Carleton University Press, 1985), xxii; Craig, *Upper Canada*, 189.

49 **The Reform movement:** In 1838, Anna Jameson, a writer and the wife of Robert Jameson, attorney general of Upper Canada, used the term "Reformers" to describe Toronto politicians in her book about Canada. See Jameson, *Winter Studies and Summer Rambles in Canada*, vol. 1, 147. Thanks to Prof. Ron Stagg for pointing this out to me.

Principled and sensitive: "Robert Baldwin," DCB (www.biographi.ca/en/bio/baldwin_robert_8E.html).

"I am left": Cited in John Ralston Saul, *Extraordinary Canadians: Louis Hippolyte Lafontaine and Robert Baldwin* (Toronto: Penguin Canada, 2010), 49.

A month after Baldwin: Michael Cross, *A Biography of Robert Baldwin: The Morning-Star of Memory* (Toronto: Oxford University Press, 2012), 365–66.

"The Game is": Robert Stanton to John Macaulay, June 2, 1826, in Firth, *Town of York, 1815–1834*, 96.

His insulting references: *Colonial Advocate*, May 18, 1826; Craig, *Upper Canada*, 113.

Led by the hot-headed: "William Lyon Mackenzie," DCB; Craig, *Upper Canada*, 114; Firth, *Town of York, 1815–1834*, 96–97; Raible, *Muddy York Mud*, 3–5, 79–80.

50 **Mackenzie's political career:** "William Lyon Mackenzie," DCB.

Twenty of the 178: Marian A. Patterson, "The Cholera Epidemic of 1832 in York, Upper Canada," *Bulletin of the Medical Library Association* 46, 2 (April 1958): 169.

As more and more: Ibid., 170.

Medical understanding about: Ibid., 173–75.

51 **In truth, they were:** Angus MacMurchy and T.A. Reed, *Our Royal Town of York. Historical and Romantic Associations of Down-Town Toronto, and the Site of the Royal York Hotel* (Toronto: 1929), 206.

Victims could have: Patterson, "The Cholera Epidemic of 1832," 179–80; Careless, *Toronto to 1918*, 51.

By the time: Careless, *Toronto to 1918*, 53.

Officials had opted: Ibid., 54.

Though William Lyon Mackenzie: *Colonial Advocate*, March 6, 1834, in Fairley, *Selected Writings*, 338–39.

Then, in a contest: "John Rolph," DCB (www.biographi.ca/en/bio/rolph_john_9E.html); Frederick H. Armstrong, "William Lyon Mackenzie, First Mayor of Toronto: A Study of a Critic in Power," *Canadian Historical Review* 48, 4 (December 1967): 313–15.

52 **Though he designed:** Armstrong, "William Lyon Mackenzie," 316–17.

During one heated: Mark Maloney, "Toronto's Mayors: Scoundrels, Rogues and Socialists," TS, January 2, 2010.

When Gurnett refused: Armstrong, "William Lyon Mackenzie," 325–27.

As mayor, Mackenzie: Romney, "A Struggle for Authority," 24.

In one notable case: Henry Scadding and J.C. Dent, *Toronto Past and Present: Historical and Descriptive* (Toronto: Hunter, Rose and Company, 1884), 162; "Court House Square," Toronto Historical Plaques website (www.torontohistory.org/Pages_ABC/Court_House_Square.html); Romney, "A Struggle for Authority," 24–25.

Among the victims: "Francis Collins," DCB (www.biographi.ca/en/bio/collins_francis_6E.html).

53 **Mackenzie quickly tired:** Armstrong, "William Lyon Mackenzie," 320–21.

In 1833, the two men: "William Lyon Mackenzie," DCB; *Colonial Advocate*, June 12, 1834, in Fairley, *Selected Writings*, 339–41; Craig, *Upper Canada*, 215–16.

Mackenzie, whom he: Sir Francis Bond Head, *A Narrative* (London: John Murray, 1839), 3.

Never discreet: David Mills, *The Idea of Loyalty in Upper Canada 1784–1850* (Montreal and Kingston: McGill-Queen's University Press, 1988), 80; Carol Wilton, *Popular Politics and Popular Culture in Upper Canada 1800–1850* (Montreal and Kingston: McGill-Queen's University Press, 2000), 179.

Mackenzie, who had: William Lyon Mackenzie to John Neilson, December 28, 1835, in Fairley, *Selected Writings*, 345; "William Lyon Mackenzie," DCB.

54 **Meanwhile, throughout the summer:** "William Lyon Mackenzie," DCB.

By the fall: Wilton, *Popular Politics,* 187; Craig, *Upper Canada*, 246; Read and Stagg, *The Rebellion of 1837*, xxiv.

In a more decisive: "William Lyon Mackenzie," DCB.

Mackenzie sat in a wagon: Mary Larratt Smith, ed., *Young Mr. Smith in Upper Canada* (Toronto: University of Toronto Press, 1980), 12.

55 **As it turned out:** Read and Stagg, *The Rebellion of 1837*, xliii.

Powell, who did: Ibid., xliii. Thanks to Prof. Ron Stagg for providing me with the correct chronology of these events.

About the same time: Robert M. Stamp, "Chapter 5: Tories and Reformers," in *Early Days in Richmond Hill: A History of the Community to 1930* (Richmond Hill, ON: Richmond Hill Public Library Board, 1991), electronic edition (http://edrh.rhpl.richmondhill.on.ca/default.asp?ID=s5.6).

As the trio tried: "Capt. Hugh Stewart's Account of Colonel Moodie's Death," in Read and Stagg, *The Rebellion of 1837*, 144–47.

56 **Perhaps because Mackenzie:** "William Lyon Mackenzie," DCB; "Statement of James Latimer, December 21, 1837," in Read and Stagg, *The Rebellion of 1837*, 158.

Robert Horne, an official: "Robert Charles Horne," DCB (www.biographi.ca/en/bio/horne_robert_charles_7E.html).

Next, he moved on: Read and Stagg, *The Rebellion of 1837*, xlviii.

That evening, Mackenzie: Ibid., xlv, li; Samuel Thompson, *Reminiscences of a Canadian Pioneer for the Last Fifty Years: An Autobiography* (Toronto: Hunter, Rose and Company, 1884), 119–20 (www.gutenberg.ca/ebooks/thompsons-reminiscences/thompsons-reminiscences-00-h.html).

Early in the morning: Read and Stagg, *The Rebellion of 1837*, liii.

A brief battle: Ibid., liv; "John Montgomery," DCB (www.biographi.ca/en/bio/montgomery_john_1879_10E.html).

57 **Back in Toronto:** Read and Stagg, *The Rebellion of 1837*, liii.

"I hope you have": "Chief Justice's Address to Samuel Lount and Peter Matthews," *Christian Guardian*, April 4, 1838, in ibid., 381–82.

Mrs. Lount even: Read and Stagg, *The Rebellion of 1837*, xc.

As he was led: Toronto Historical Plaques, "Samuel Lount and Peter Matthews," Toronto Historical Plaques website (www.torontohistory.org/Pages_STU/Samuel_Lount_and_Peter_Matthews.html).

58 **And the worst:** Craig, *Upper Canada*, 255.

In his report: *Report Of Lord Durham On the Affairs of British North America* (1839), Claude Bélanger's Quebec History website (http://faculty.marianopolis.edu/c.Belanger/quebechistory/docs/durham/1.htm). See also "John George Lambton," DCB (www.biographi.ca/en/bio/lambton_john_george_7E.html).

However, they did follow: "Act of Union," and "Province of Canada" in Gerald Hallowell, ed., *The Oxford Companion to Canadian History* (Don Mills, ON: Oxford University Press, 2004), 22, 511.

CHAPTER FOUR: A CITY OF ORANGE AND GREEN

59 **"He hated the neighbourhood":** Hugh Garner, *Cabbagetown* (Toronto: Ryerson, 1950), 106.

"There never was": William Clyde Wilkins, ed., *Charles Dickens in America* (London: Chapman and Hall, 1911), 79.

Apart from desiring: Matthew Pearl, "Dickens V. America," *More Intelligent Life*, n.d. (http://moreintelligentlife.com/story/dickens-vs-america).

60 **"Every attention that":** *Toronto Patriot*, May 6, 1842.

During their brief: West, *Toronto*, 142.

One of the invitees: Smith, *Young Mr. Smith in Upper Canada*, 14–15, 18–46, 51–57, 77; Stamp, "Chapter 6: 'Stagecoach Lines and Railways,'" in *Early Days in Richmond Hill* (http://edrh.rhpl.richmondhill.on.ca/default.asp?ID=s6.3).

As for the admired author: Charles Dickens, *American Notes* (London: Chapman Hall, 1913), 167; Myers, *The Great Canadian Road*, 97; William Kilbourn,"Toronto on the Eve of Confederation," in Kilbourn, *The Toronto Book*, 42.

61 **A week later:** Dickens to John Forster, May 12, 1842, in Charles Dickens, *The Letters of Charles Dickens: 1842–1843*, vol. 3, ed. Madeline House and Graham Storey (London: Oxford University Press, 1974), 235–36; see also Bill Taylor, "When Dickens Visited Toronto," TS, December 20, 2007.

Waiting for them: Peter Vronsky, "Toronto Police in 1834–1860: Formidable Engines Of Oppression," at the History of Policing in Toronto website (www.russianbooks.org/crime/cph3.htm); "John Munro," DCB (www.biographi.ca/en/bio/monro_george_10E.html).

62 **Near St. James Cathedral:** "John Munro," DCB; "John Henry Dunn," DCB (www.biographi.ca/en/bio/dunn_john_henry_8E.html).

There were reported: Nicholas Rogers, "Serving Toronto the Good: The Development of the City Police Force 1834–84," in Russell, *Forging a Consensus*, 118.

The dozen or so: *Examiner* (Toronto), March 24, 1841, November 11, 1841; Rogers, "Serving Toronto the Good," 118.

"It is a matter": Dickens, *American Notes*, 167.

63 **They did not mince:** "Report of the Commissioners Appointed to Investigate Proceedings at Toronto, Connected with the Election for That City, Laid before the House by Message from His Excellency the Governor General, dated Kingston, 3rd August, 1841," in Appendix to the *First Volume of the Journals of the Legislative Assembly of the Province of Canada, Session 1841* (Kingston: George Desbarats and Thomas Carey, 1842), S1-6 (http://eco.canadiana.ca/view/oocihm.9_00955_1/351?r=0&s=1); Gregory S. Kealey, "Orangemen and the Corporation: The Politics of Class during the Union of the Canadas," in Russell, *Forging a Consensus*, 51.

In the hallways: Christopher Armstrong and H.V. Nelles, *The Revenge of the Methodist Bicycle Company: Sunday Streetcars and Municipal Reform in Toronto, 1888–1897* (Toronto: Peter Martin Associates, 1977), 13.

By the early 1860s: Kealey, "Orangemen and the Corporation," 43.

Tightly knit: Ibid., 42; see also Table 2, "Mayors of Toronto" 47.

64 **For much of this:** "Sir Adam Wilson," DCB (www.biographi.ca/en/bio/wilson_adam_12E.html); Rogers, "Serving Toronto the Good," 119.

Its loyal members: Kealey, "Orangemen and the Corporation," 46, 49.

Davis was not: Ibid., 48–49, 51; GL, December 9, 1845.

The newspaper cheered: Kealey, "Orangemen and the Corporation," 51.

Orange Order members: Smith, *Young Mr. Smith in Upper Canada*, 69.

65 **The Order was at the centre:** Kealey, "Orangemen and the Corporation," 43–45.

Yet the only other: Rogers, "Serving Toronto the Good," 119.

Predictably, when news: *Examiner*, November 8, 1843; J.M.S. Careless, *The Union of the Canadas: The Growth of Canadian Institutions 1841–1857* (Toronto: McClelland & Stewart, 1967), 82.

The Orange mob was: Kealey, "Orangemen and the Corporation," 56.

66 **The government's decision:** Ibid., 23, 56; Robertson, *Old Toronto*, 133–35.

Indeed, it was a bloody fight: "Michael Murphy," DCB (www.biographi.ca/en/bio/murphy_michael_9E.html); Brian P. Clarke, *Piety and Nationalism: Lay Voluntary Associations and the Creation of an Irish-Catholic Community in Toronto, 1850–1895* (Montreal and Kingston: McGill-Queen's University Press, 1993), 158–62; Michael Cottrell, "St. Patrick's Day Parades in Nineteenth-Century Toronto: A Study of Immigrant Adjustment and Elite Control," *Histoire sociale/Social History* 25, 49 (May 1992): 64–65.

In the earliest days: Clarke, *Piety and Nationalism*, 162.

The widely accepted: Ibid., 160; *Toronto Leade*r, May 11, 12, 17, 1858; GL, April 9, 1858.

In the summer of 1855: The story of the circus riot can be found in the GL, July 16, 17, 19, 24, 1855; Kealey, "Orangemen and the Corporation," 68–69.

67 **Asked later to:** GL, July 3, 19, 24, 27, 1855; Kealey, "Orangemen and the Corporation," 69–73.

Sensible Tories: Rogers, "Serving Toronto the Good," 117, 122–23.

In one of their first: Ibid., 123–26.

68 **After problems in Kingston:** John Martineau, *The Life of Henry Pelham, Fifth Duke of Newcastle 1811–1864* (London: John Murray, 1908), 297.

Early in the evening: GL, September 8, 1860; Martineau, *Life of Henry Pelham*, 297.

69 **This angered the crowd:** Rogers, "Serving Toronto the Good," 130; D.C. Masters, *The Rise of Toronto 1850–1890* (Toronto: University of Toronto Press, 1947), 85–86.

The city did not have: Masters, *The Rise of Toronto*, 13.

"It seems like magic": GL, February 5, 1853; Careless, *Toronto to 1918*, 76.

"There is a Yankee": Charles McKay, *Life and Liberty in America, or Sketches of a Tour of the United States and Canada in 1857–58* (New York: Harper and Brothers, 1859), 374.

Late on the night: Frederick H. Armstrong, *Toronto: The Place of Meeting* (Toronto: Windsor Publications and the Ontario Historical Society, 1983), 91–92; Marla Friebe, *A History of the Toronto Fire Services 1874–2002* (Toronto: City of Toronto, 2003).

70 **Of note, too:** C.K. Clarke, *A History of the Toronto General Hospital* (Toronto: William Briggs, 1923), 63–68; Careless, *Toronto to 1918*, 86–89.

Until it was demolished: Charlotte Gray, *Mrs. King: The Life and Times of Isabel Mackenzie King* (Toronto: Viking, 1997), 204; Allan Levine, *Scrum Wars: The Prime Ministers and the Media* (Toronto: Dundurn, 1993), 8.

"Let us in the West": GL, March 19, 1850; Masters, *The Rise of Toronto*, 16.

In mid-October 1851: Derek Boles, *Toronto's Railway Heritage* (Charleston, SC: Arcadia, 2009), 7.

In time, the Northern: Armstrong, *Toronto: The Place of Meeting*, 92–93; Careless, *Toronto to 1918*, 77–78; Masters, *The Rise of Toronto*, 16–17; Hayes, *Historical Atlas of Toronto*, 46–57.

71 **The fact that the GTR:** Douglas McCalla, "The Commercial Politics of the Toronto Board of Trade, 1850–1860," *Canadian Historical Review* 50, 1 (March 1969): 56.

Indeed, as Toronto railway historian: Boles, *Toronto's Railway Heritage*, 8.

Frederick Capreol, the entrepreneur: "Frederick Chase Capreol," DCB (www.biographi.ca/en/bio/capreol_frederick_chase_11E.html).

Caught up in: "John George Bowes," DCB (www.biographi.ca/en/bio/bowes_john_george_9E.html); "Sir Francis Hincks," DCB (www.biographi.ca/en/bio/hincks_francis_11E.html).

72 **It was no coincidence:** Careless, *Toronto to 1918*, 81; McCalla, "The Commercial Politics of the Toronto Board of Trade," 51.

By 1861, the Toronto Street Railway: Myers, *The Great Canadian Road*, 98; West, *Toronto*, 129–30.

Typical of the new: "William Gooderham," DCB (www.biographi.ca/en/bio/gooderham_william_1790_1881_11E.html); see also Sally Gibson, *Toronto's Distillery District: History by the Lake* (Toronto: Distillery Historic District, 2008).

In later years: "Gooderham Flatiron Building 1892," on the Ontario Heritage Trust website (www.heritagetrust.on.ca/Conservation/Conservation-easements/Visit-our-easement-properties/Gooderham-Building-(Toronto),-1891-92.aspx).

73 **Tragic victims of:** *Cork Examiner*, October 6, 1847, cited in Paul Bew, *Ireland the Politics of Enmity, 1789–2006* (New York: Oxford University Press, 2007), 197.

Of the million who: Sharon Doyle Driedger, *An Irish Heart: How a Small Immigrant Community Shaped Canada* (Toronto: HarperCollins, 2010), 18–19; France Hoffman and Ryan Taylor, *Across the Waters: Ontario Immigrants' Experiences 1820–1850* (Milton, ON: Global Heritage Press, 1999), 130–34.

In the summer of 1847: Robert Whyte, *The Journey of an Irish Coffin Ship* (1848; Cork, Ireland: Mercier Press, 1994), 96–97.

One of the early victims: "Michael Power," DCB (www.biographi.ca/en/bio/power_michael_7E.html)

An asylum had: "Report of the Managing Committee of the Widows and Orphans' Asylum, for the Care and Maintenance of the Destitute Widows and Orphans of the Emigrants of 1847" (Toronto: Rowsell & Thompson, 1848); "Immigrants to Canada: Widows and Orphans of 1847," at Marjorie P. Kohli's website (http://jubilation.uwaterloo.ca/~marj/genealogy/papers/children1847.html).

Anglican bishop John Strachan: Glazebrook, *The Story of Toronto*, 87; Susan E. Houston, "Victorian Origins of Juvenile Delinquency: A Canadian Experience," *History of Education Quarterly* 12 (1972): 255–56.

By 1851, one in four: Clarke, *Piety and Nationalism*, 16, 44; *Canadian Freeman*, January 5, 1865; *Irish Canadian*, March 9, 1864, September 13, 1869.

74 **At best, many were:** Murray W. Nicolson, "Peasants in an Urban Society: Irish Catholics in Victorian Toronto," in *Gathering Place: Peoples and Neighbourhoods of Toronto, 1834–1945*, ed. Robert F. Harney (Toronto: Multicultural History Society of Ontario, 1985), 60; *Irish Canadian*, September 29, 1869.

The prejudice and discrimination: Clarke, *Piety and Nationalism*, 44.

Brown was hard: J.M.S. Careless, *Brown of the Globe: The Voice of Upper Canada 1818–1859*, vol. 1 (Toronto: Dundurn, 1989), 99.

Brown was a staunch: Ibid., 123.

75 **It was later said:** Levine, *Scrum Wars*, 7.

"Rome has but": GL, August 7, 1857. See also John Higham, *Strangers in the Land: Patterns of American Nativism 1860–1925* (New York: Atheneum, 1978), 5–6.

The *Toronto Mirror*: *Toronto Mirror*, April 25, 1851; Daniel Connor, "The Irish-Canadian: Image and Self-Image 1847–1870" (master's thesis, University of British Columbia, 1976), 67–68.

His intolerance: See Christopher Moore, *1867: How the Fathers Made a Deal* (Toronto: McClelland & Stewart, 1997), 10–12.

Almost as soon: GL, April 21, 1847; Connor, "The Irish-Canadian," 52, 80.

In a February 1856: GL, February 18, 1856.

76 **For many years:** GL, July 2, 14, 1857, December 10, 1857; Barrie Dyster, "Captain Bob and the Noble Ward," in Russell, *Forging a Consensus*, 103.

Some, like John McGee: Clarke, *Piety and Nationalism*, 19–21; "Sir Frank Smith," DCB (www.biographi.ca/en/bio/smith_frank_13E.html).

There was no Irish ghetto: Clarke, *Piety and Nationalism*, 23.

"Surrounded by a": Cited in GL, November 18, 1846; Connor, "The Irish-Canadian," 20.

A feeling of isolation: Connor, "The Irish-Canadian," 20–21.

77 **Similarly, Irish Catholics and Protestants:** J.M.S. Careless, "The Emergence of Cabbagetown in Victorian Toronto," in Harney, *Gathering Place*, 25; Clarke, *Piety and Nationalism*, 23; Nicolson, "Peasants in an Urban Society," 52–3.

Every stereotype about: GL, November 25, 1859; Connor, "The Irish-Canadian," 74.

"Irish beggars are": GL, February 11, 1858; Mark G. McGowan, *The Waning of the Green: Catholics, the Irish, and Identity in Toronto, 1887–1922* (Montreal and Kingston: McGill-Queen's University Press, 1999), 17.

A few years later: GL, September 15, 1864, February 14, 1866; Clarke, *Piety and Nationalism*, 25.

Protestant sensibilities were: Clarke, *Piety and Nationalism*, 129–31; Nicolson, "Peasants in an Urban Society," 58.

78 **The Toronto press:** GL, July 6, 11, 1850; Masters, *The Rise of Toronto*, 83–84.

Newspapers recorded the: GL, November 21, 25, 1856, May 26, 1860.

At the end of May 1860: GL, May 26, 1860.

"Yesterday Patrick O'Brien": GL, December 28, 1865.

Such lurid accounts: Clarke, *Piety and Nationalism*, 28.

Of the nearly five thousand: Scadding and Dent, *Toronto Past and Present*, 213; Masters, *The Rise of Toronto*, 78–79.

79 **Based on arrest:** Clarke, *Piety and Nationalism*, 26–27; Connor, "The Irish-Canadian," 72, 153.

More serious was: GL, July 15, 18, 1857; Clarke, *Piety and Nationalism*, 158–59.

In 1864, the sad: Paul Robert Magocsi, ed., *Encyclopedia of Canada's Peoples* (Toronto: University of Toronto Press, 1999), 744; Nicolson, "Peasants in an Urban Society," 58.

80 **Though it attracted:** Adrienne Shadd, Afua Cooper, and Karolyn Smardz Frost, *The Underground Railway: Next Stop Toronto!* (Toronto: Natural Heritage Books, 2002), 15.

In 1985, the ruins: Karolyn Smardz Frost, *I've Got a Home in Glory Land: A Lost Tale of the Underground Railroad* (Toronto: Thomas Allen, 2007), xi.

Fearing that Lucie: Ibid., 12–47, 171–74, 176–81.

Ultimately, Chief Justice: Ibid., 209–31.

Some years later: Shadd et al., *The Underground Railway*, 55–56; John Boyko, *Blood and Daring: How Canada Fought the American Civil War and Forged a Nation*, (Toronto: Knopf Canada, 2013), 15–59.

81 **In that case:** "John Anderson," DCB (www.biographi.ca/en/bio/anderson_john_1831_62_9E.html).

After living in Amherstburg: Frost, *I've Got a Home in Glory Land*, 256.

All three became: Dan Hill, "The Blacks in Toronto," in Harney, *Gathering Place*, 79; Rochelle Williams, "First Baptist Church: A Journey in Courage," First Baptist Church of Toronto website (http://fbctoronto.ca/index.php?option=com_content&view=article&id=50&Itemid=55).

Thornton's first job: Frost, *I've Got a Home in Glory Land*, 262–63; Shadd et al., *The Underground Railway*, 5–6.

By the 1840s: Frost, *I've Got a Home in Glory Land*, 268–69.

Thornton and Lucie: Ibid., 269–70, 349.

82 **Alfred Lafferty was born:** Hilary J. Dawson, "From Immigrant to Establishment: A Black Family's Journey," OH 99, 1 (Spring 2007): 31; *Toronto Leader*, January 5, 1863; Robin W. Winks, "Negro School Segregation in Ontario and Nova Scotia," *Canadian Historical Review* 50, 2 (June 1969): 178.

His father, Wilson: "Wilson Ruffin Abbott," DCB (www.biographi.ca/en/bio/abbott_wilson_ruffin_10E.html).

Anderson was one: "Anderson Ruffin Abbott," DCB (www.biographi.ca/en/bio/abbott_anderson_ruffin_14E.html).

83 **In particular, they objected:** "Petition from People of Colour residing in the City of Toronto," October 1841, in City of Toronto Archives, Series 1081, File 57 (www.toronto.ca/archives/petitiontranscription.htm); Hill, "The Blacks in Toronto," 86; Winks, *The Blacks in Canada*, 149–50; Dawson, "From Immigrant to Establishment," 34–35.

They also spearheaded: Winks, *The Blacks in Canada*, 254; Dawson, "From Immigrant to Establishment," 36.

Toronto civic officials: Winks, *The Blacks in Canada*, 149–50, 228, 248. See also Levine, King, 286–87.

Lord Elgin, who: Ged Martin, "British Officials and Their Attitude Towards the Negro," OH 66, 1 (March 1974): 86.

"We fear that": Hill, "The Blacks in Toronto," 87, 98.

Abolitionists and black journalists: Henry Highland Garnet, *The Past and the Present Condition and the Destiny of the Colored Race* (Tory, New York, 1848), 27; Dawson, "From Immigrant to Establishment," 35.

Likewise, it manifested: See Boyko, *Blood and Daring*, 164, 189, 228, 285–86.

84 **The *Globe* publisher:** Dyster, "Captain Bob and the Noble Ward," 109; Hill, "The Blacks in Toronto," 98.

The *Globe* regularly: See, for example, GL, September 19, 1850; March 1, 1851; April 1, 1851; January 3, 1863; Careless, *Brown of the Globe*, vol. 1, 103; Fred Landon, "The Anti-Slavery Society of Canada," *The Journal of Negro History* 4, 1 (January 1919): 33–40, 36–39.

One of the society's: GL, April 3, 1851. See also April 1, 8, 10, 1851.

The ringing of the bells: C.C. Taylor, *Toronto "Called Back": From 1888 to 1847 and the Queen's Jubilee* (Toronto: William Briggs, 1888), 177; West, *Toronto*, 131; Richard Gwyn, *John A.: The Man Who Made Us; The Life and Times of John A. Macdonald*, vol. 1 (Toronto: Random House, 2007), 436.

85 **Yet it could be argued:** Monck to Brown, November 13, 1868, cited in Careless, *Brown of the Globe*, vol. 2, 253; Levine, *Scrum Wars*, 8.

During the preceding: Careless, *Toronto to 1918*, 102–4; Careless, *Brown of the Globe*, vol. 1, 311–22; Moore, *1867: How the Fathers Made a Deal*, 27–29.

But in 1864: Moore, *1867: How the Fathers Made a Deal*, 28.

Brown had stayed: Careless, *Brown of the Globe*, vol. 2, 251–52; GL, July 1, 1867.

From a purely Toronto: Careless, *Toronto to 1918*, 104.

CHAPTER FIVE: HOGTOWN THE GOOD

86 **"Down to the docks":** Hugh Hood, *The Swing in the Garden* (Ottawa: Oberon, 1975), 175.

William Davies was: "William Davies," DCB (www.biographi.ca/en/bio/davies_william_15E.html); D.R. McDonald, "The Stockyard Story," on the Old Time Trains website (www.trainweb.org/oldtimetrains/stockyards/stock.htm).

The secret to his: "William Davies," DCB.

87 **With Flavelle at:** Ibid.; Michael Bliss, *A Canadian Millionaire: The Life and Times of Sir Joseph Flavelle, Bart. 1858–1939* (Toronto: Macmillan of Canada, 1978), 52.

For them and other: See Marguerite Van Die, *Religion, Family, and Community in Victorian Canada: The Colbys of Carrollcroft* (Montreal and Kingston: McGill-Queen's University Press, 2006), 15; Ramsay Cook, *The Regenerators: Social Criticism in Late Victorian English Canada* (Toronto: University of Toronto Press, 1985), 33–37; "William Davies," DCB; "Sir Joseph Wesley Flavelle," DCB (www.biographi.ca/en/bio/flavelle_joseph_wesley_16E.html).

Part of that growth: Careless, *Toronto to 1918*, 124; "History of Danforth," on the Danforth website (www.thedanforth.ca/index.php/history-of-the-danforth).

Howard was born: David Bain, "John Howard's High Park," OH 101, 1 (Spring 2009), 2; "John George Howard," DCB (www.biographi.ca/en/bio/howard_john_george_11E.html).

88 **At the time Howard:** "Colborne Lodge," *Arts and Culture. Museums: Explore Toronto's Historic Sites*, on the City of Toronto website (www.toronto.ca/); "John George Howard," DCB.

Still, it took: Bain, "John Howard's High Park," 15–17.

Inexplicably, he shot a round: GL, July 25, October 13, November 1, 4, 1882; David Wencer, "Historicist: John Howard's Enduring Monument," TO, December 7, 2013 (http://torontoist.com/2013/12/historicist-john-howards-enduring-monument/).

It was also: Armstrong and Nelles, *The Revenge of the Methodist Bicycle Company*, 4; Peter G. Goheen, *Victorian Toronto, 1850–1900: Pattern and Process of Growth* (Chicago: University of Chicago, 1970), 220.

"If the sons and": *Toronto Illustrated* (Toronto: Toronto Consolidated Illustrating Company, 1893), 34.

89 **"Altogether, Sunday in":** W.T. Crosweller, *Our Visit to Toronto, the Niagara Falls and the United States of America* (London: 1898), 69–70. See also Armstrong and Nelles, *The Revenge of the Methodist Bicycle Company*, 6.

However, an altercation: Martin A. Galvin, "The Jubilee Riots in Toronto, 1875," *CCHA Report*, 26 (1959): 93–97.

Orange groups like: GL, September 30, 1875; Brian Clarke, "Religious Riot as Pastime: Orange Young Britons, Parades and Public Life in Victorian Toronto," in *The Orange Order in Canada*, ed. David A. Wilson (Dublin: Four Courts Press, 2007), 117, 123–24.

At a well-attended: Galvin, "The Jubilee Riots in Toronto, 1875," 98.

The defiant young men: Clarke, "Religious Riot as Pastime," 125.

90 **The battle raged from:** Galvin, "The Jubilee Riots in Toronto, 1875," 100–101.

In the aftermath: TM, October 4, 1875; GL, October 5, 1875; Galvin, "The Jubilee Riots in Toronto, 1875," 101–4.

Surprisingly, considering the number: Timothy Edgar Strauch, "Walking for God and Raising Hell: The Jubilee Riots, the Orange Order and the Preservation of Protestantism in Toronto, 1875" (master's thesis, Queen's University, 1999), 54–64, 72–82.

Three years later: TM, February 23, 1878, March 30, 1878; GL, March 27, 1878; Clarke, "Religious Riot as Pastime," 118–19.

Yet the actions: See Clarke, "Religious Riot as Pastime," 120–27; James T. Watt, "Anti-Catholic Nativism in Canada: The Protestant Association," *Canadian Historical Review* 48, 1 (March 1967), 45–58; "Christopher William Bunting," DCB (www.biographi.ca/en/bio/bunting_christopher_william_12E.html).

91 **In 1871, the city:** Goheen, *Victorian Toronto*, 66.

"The industrial and social": G. Mercer Adam, *Toronto Old and New* (Toronto: Mail Printing Company, 1891), 42.

Within the city's: Gregory S. Kealey, *Toronto Workers Respond to Industrial Capitalism 1867–1892* (Toronto: University of Toronto Press, 1980), 20; Armstrong and Nelles, *The Revenge of the Methodist Bicycle Company*, 3.

William McMaster's career: "William McMaster," DCB (www.biographi.ca/en/bio/mcmaster_william_11E.html).

Among McMaster's contemporaries: Careless, *Toronto to 1918*, 117; "George Albertus Cox," DCB (www.biographi.ca/en/bio/cox_george_albertus_14E.html); "James Austin," DCB (www.biographi.ca/en/bio/austin_james_12E.html); "Sir Edmund Boyd Osler," DCB (www.biographi.ca/en/bio/osler_edmund_boyd_15E.html).

92 **Before Eaton and Simpson:** Careless, *Toronto to 1918*, 115; "Thomas Thompson," DCB (www.biographi.ca/en/bio/thompson_thomas_9E.html).

One of Timothy Eaton's: Cited in Masters, *The Rise of Toronto*, 104.

"We are made": Cited in Joy L. Santink, *Timothy Eaton and the Rise of his Department Store* (Toronto: University of Toronto Press, 1990), 8.

Guided by the motto: W.A. Hewitt, *Down the Stretch: Recollections of a Pioneer Sportsman and Journalist* (Toronto: Ryerson, 1958), 36; Santink, *Timothy Eaton*, 122.

He and his brother: Santink, *Timothy Eaton*, 37–38; "Timothy Eaton," DCB (www.biographi.ca/en/bio/eaton_timothy_13E.html).

Initially Eaton ran: Santink, *Timothy Eaton*, 120.

93 **As his biographer:** "Timothy Eaton," DCB; Santink, *Timothy Eaton*, 30–31, 63–64.

Annual sales increased: Santink, *Timothy Eaton*, 155.

At a huge New Year's: *Golden Jubilee 1869–1919: A Book to Commemorate the Fiftieth Anniversary of the T. Eaton Company. Ltd.* (Toronto: T. Eaton Company, 1919), 222; Ruth A. Frager, "Class, Ethnicity, and Gender in the Eaton Strikes of 1912 and 1934," in *Gender Conflicts: New Essays in Women's History*, ed. Franca Iacovetta and Mariana Valverde (Toronto: University of Toronto Press, 1992), 189.

Eaton sensibly reduced: Santink, *Timothy Eaton*, 85–7; 112–14.

94 **His story is:** "Robert Simpson," DCB (www.biographi.ca/en/bio/simpson_robert_12E.html).

However, he was: "Our History: Acquisitions: Retail: The Robert Simpson Company Limited," HBC Heritage website (http://www.hbcheritage.ca/hbcheritage/history/acquisitions/retail/simpsons.asp).

He was crippled: "Robert Simpson," DCB.

Another businessman who: "Hart Almerrin Massey," DCB (www.biographi.ca/en/bio/massey_hart_almerrin_12E.html).

Vincent Massey, who in: Ibid.

95 **Like a shepherd:** Ibid.; Kealey, *Toronto Workers Respond to Industrial Capitalism*, 196–97.

At every step: Allan Levine, *The Devil in Babylon: Fear of Progress and the Birth of Modern Life* (Toronto: McClelland & Stewart, 2005), 162; Kealey, *Toronto Workers Respond to Industrial Capitalism*, 44–45.

In assessing the: GL, January 26, 1871; Masters, *The Rise of Toronto*, 107; Careless, *Brown of the Globe*, vol. 2, 290.

A year later: Careless, *Brown of the Globe*, vol. 2, 290–91; Richard Gwyn, *Nation Maker: Sir John A. Macdonald; His Life, Our Times*, vol. 2 (Toronto: Random House, 2011), 195.

He dismissed out of hand: GL, March 23, 1872; Kealey, *Toronto Workers Respond to Industrial Capitalism*, 133.

96 **A pro-strike rally:** *Toronto Leade*r, April 4, 1872; Careless, *Brown of the Globe,* vol. 2, 294; Gwyn, *Nation Maker*, 195.

As a final resort: Kealey, *Toronto Workers Respond to Industrial Capitalism*, 133–34, 217; Careless, *Brown of the Globe*, vol. 2, 295.

For years, Macdonald: Levine, *Scrum Wars*, 11–14; "John Ross Robertson," DCB (www.biographi.ca/en/bio/robertson_john_ross_14E.html).

97 **Riel had imprisoned:** "John Ross Robertson," DCB.

He also had a reputation: Stephen J. Harper, *A Great Game: The Forgotten Leafs and the Rise of Professional Hockey* (Toronto: Simon & Schuster, 2013), 23–32; Scott Young, *100 Years of Dropping the Puck: A History of the OHA* (Toronto: McClelland & Stewart, 1989), 46.

In early 1872: Levine, *Scrum Wars*, 15–17.

One afternoon in: *Toronto World*, June 26, 1891; GM, February 15, 1955; Armstrong and Nelles, *The Revenge of the Methodist Bicycle Company*, 69.

"The first number": Cited in Gwyn, *Nation Maker*, 193.

98 **About the printers':** Macdonald to Patteson, March 30, 1872, in the Provincial Archives of Ontario, Thomas Patteson Papers, F-1191.

Patteson lasted: Levine, *Scrum Wars*, 18–24.

On March 25, 1880: Careless, *Brown of the Globe*, vol. 2, 366–72.

The Knights supported: Kealey, *Toronto Workers Respond to Industrial Capitalism*, 186–87, 196–97; Careless, *Toronto to 1918*, 130; "Daniel John O'Donoghue," DCB (www.biographi.ca/en/bio/o_donoghue_daniel_john_13E.html).

99 **The Knights were outraged:** "Hart Almerrin Massey," DCB.

Support for the: Kealey, *Toronto Workers Respond to Industrial Capitalism*, 198–99.

Under the terms: Armstrong and Nelles, *The Revenge of the Methodist Bicycle Company*, 28–9.

An astute entrepreneur: Ibid., 29–30; "Sir Frank Smith," DCB (www.biographi.ca/en/bio/smith_frank_13E.html).

TRC workers soon: TM, May 10, 1886; Armstrong and Nelles, *The Revenge of the Methodist Bicycle Company*, 31; "Sir Frank Smith," DCB; Desmond Morton, *Mayor Howland: The Citizens' Candidate* (Toronto: Hakkert, 1973), 53; Kealey, *Toronto Workers Respond to Industrial Capitalism*, 200; TN, March 10, 1886.

100 **Within a few:** TN, March 11, 1886; Kealey, *Toronto Workers Respond to Industrial Capitalism*, 202.

"You have by your": TN, March 11, 1886; Morton, *Mayor Howland*, 48.

Nevertheless, as the: TN, March 13, 1886; Morton, *Mayor Howland*, 48–49; Kealey, *Toronto Workers Respond to Industrial Capitalism*, 203–4.

It had been established: Armstrong and Nelles, *The Revenge of the Methodist Bicycle Company*, 10; "Edmund Ernest Sheppard," DCB (www.biographi.ca/en/bio/sheppard_edmund_ernest_15E.html); Keith Walden, "Toronto Society's Response to Celebrity Performers, 1887–1914," *Canadian Historical Review* 89, 3 (September 2008), 373.

The *News* thought: TN, May 12, 1886; Kealey, *Toronto Workers Respond to Industrial Capitalism*, 204–6.

101 **This started with:** Walden, "Toronto Society's Response to Celebrity Performers," 373–76.

At Hanlan's Point: Keith Walden, *Becoming Modern in Toronto: The Industrial Exhibition and the Shaping of a Late Victorian Culture* (Toronto: University of Toronto Press, 1997), 255–56.

Each September starting: Ibid., 36–39, 91, 136–37.

102 **This was despite:** TM, October 13, 1879; Gerald Lenton-Young, "Variety Theatre," in *Early Stages: Theatre in Ontario, 1800–1914*, ed. Ann Saddlemyer (Toronto: University of Toronto Press, 1990), 188–89.

And, foreshadowing the: "Social and Personal," SN, April 19, 1890, 2; Walden, "Toronto Society's Response to Celebrity Performers," 382.

Whatever the activity: TM, March 6, 1884.

As Wilfrid Laurier: Cited in Gray, *Mrs. King*, 184.

Born in 1843: GM, October 2, 1944; *The Newmarket Era and Express*, January 13, 1944.

His uncle William Cawthra: Ron Haggart, "The Merchant Princes," in Kilbourn, *The Toronto Book*, 128–29; "William Cawthra," DCB (www.biographi.ca/en/bio/cawthra_william_10E.html).

103 **They had six:** "Cawthra Mulock," DCB (www.biographi.ca/en/bio/mulock_cawthra_14E.html); TS, February 18, 1963; Haggart, "The Merchant Princes," 128–29; "Royal Alexandra Theatre," on Canada's Historic Places website (www.historicplaces.ca/en/rep-reg/place-lieu.aspx?id=1137&pid=0).

He also oversaw: Martin L. Friedland, *The University of Toronto: A History* (Toronto: University of Toronto Press, 2002), 100.

When Emily Stowe: Ibid., 85.

And when students: Levine, *King*, 37–39.

The *Globe*'s social: GL, June 22, 1899.

104 **John King was:** Levine, *King*, 30–33

"Arthur and Ethel": Library and Archives Canada, William Lyon Mackenzie King Diaries, R10383-0-6-E, June 21, 1899 (hereafter King Diary).

Among other literary: "Goldwin Smith," DCB (www.biographi.ca/en/bio/smith_goldwin_13E.html); "John Ross Robertson," DCB.

In Smith's view: Gerald Tulchinsky, *Taking Root: The Origins of the Canadian Jewish Community* (Toronto: Stoddart, 1992), 231–34; Allan Levine, *Coming of Age: A History of the Jewish People of Manitoba* (Winnipeg: Jewish Heritage Centre of Western Canada and Heartland Publications, 2009), 55–56.

105 **In 1946, when:** King Diary, February 20, 1946. On King's attitudes to Jews and other ethnic groups, see Levine, *King*, 286–92.

He touched a: "Goldwin Smith," DCB.

She sported: TW, August 31, 1882; TT, September 2, 1882; Walden, *Becoming Modern in Toronto*, 80.

One story claimed: Walden, *Becoming Modern in Toronto*, 81–4; TW, September 2, 3, 1882.

Her secret was: TT, September 12, 18, 1882; GL, September 8, 1882; Walden, *Becoming Modern in Toronto*, 84.

106 **Charlatan or not:** Walden, *Becoming Modern in Toronto*, 84.

On Christmas Eve: Glazebrook, *The Story of Toronto*, 145.

Civic leaders, physicians, journalists: Levine, *The Devil in Babylon*, 13–14.

"Underneath the seemingly": Cited in Marianne Valverde, *The Age of Light, Soap, and Water: Moral Reform in English Canada, 1885–1925* (Toronto: McClelland & Stewart, 1991), 132.

According to Reverend: S.W. Dean, "The Church and the Slum," *Social Service Council of Canada Congress* (Ottawa, 1914), 127; Valverde, *The Age of Light, Soap, and Water*, 133.

107 **The Methodist Fred Victor:** Glazebrook, *The Story of Toronto,* 147; "Hart Almerrin Massey," DCB. See also Cary Fagan, *The Fred Victor Mission Story: From Charity to Social Justice* (Winfield, BC: Wood Lake Books, 1993).

There was, too, the Haven: John R. Graham, "William Lyon Mackenzie King, Elizabeth Harvie, and Edna: A Prostitute Rescuing Initiative in Late Victorian Toronto," *The Canadian Journal of Human Sexuality* 8, 1 (Spring 1999): 48–49.

By the 1890s: Ibid., 48; Levine, *King,* 39.

Despite the best: King Diary, October 2, 5, 11, 19, 20, 1894; November 22, 1894; December 12, 16, 31, 1894; January 15, 1895; February 3, 10, 1895; Graham, "William Lyon Mackenzie King," 50–51; Levine, *King,* 43.

108 **"Houses of ill fame":** C.S. Clark, *Of Toronto the Good: The Queen City of Canada as It Is* (Montreal: The Toronto Publishing Company, 1898), 106.

By Clark's: Ibid., 131–332, 86–87.

Then again: TE, September 5, 1891; Walden, *Becoming Modern in Toronto,* 50–51.

According to Detective: TS, Feburary 24, 1912.

At McQuarry's Saloon: TM, October 1, 1879, September 25, 1897; Walden, *Becoming Modern in Toronto,* 250.

At midnight, York Street: TM, October 1, 1879; GL, December 5, 1887; TT, September 18, 1885; Clark, *Of Toronto the Good,* 143–46; Charles Pelham Mulvany, *Toronto Past and Present: A Handbook of the City* (Toronto: W.E. Caiger, 1884), 44.

For the truly adventurous: TE, June 20, 1892.

Clark determined that: Clark, *Of Toronto the Good,* 88–89.

109 **A *Globe* feature:** GL, December 5, 1887.

In 1861, the American: Michael Foster and Barbara Foster, *A Dangerous Woman: The Life, Loves, and Scandals of Adah Isaacs Menken, 1835–1868, America's Original Superstar* (Guilford, CT: Globe Pequot, 2011), xvi; xii; Lenton-Young, "Variety Theatre," 194.

Somewhat more crude: Lenton-Young, "Variety Theatre," 194. See also Kurt Ganzl, *Lydia Thompson: Queen of Burlesque* (New York: Routledge, 2002); Scott Dagostino, "Teasing and Pleasing: Toronto's Not-So-Secret World of Burlesque," *Winterplay* (2011), 19–23 (http://pinkplaymags.com/archive-2011-winterplay.html).

110 **"Picture after picture":** TE, September 17, 1894; Walden, *Becoming Modern in Toronto,* 276–77.

As early as 1871: *Annual Report of Chief Constable* (Toronto, 1887), 13; Carolyn Strange, *Toronto's Girl Problem: The Perils and Pleasures of the City, 1880–1930* (Toronto: University of Toronto Press, 1995), 56.

Young woman "adrift": Strange, *Toronto's Girl Problem,* 22.

In the first week: GL, July 10, 1888; Strange, *Toronto's Girl Problem,* 53.

111 **That same year:** Strange, *Toronto's Girl Problem,* 70.

This was a tragic: Ibid., 62; W.T Stead, "The Maiden Tribute of Modern Babylon," *Pall Mall Gazette,* July 6, 1885, section 15 (www.attackingthedevil.co.uk/pmg/tribute/mt1.php#15).

About the same time: Strange, *Toronto's Girl Problem,* 63.

Seeking refuge for: Ibid., 66–67.

112 **Twenty years later:** Lucy W. Brooking, "Canada's War on the White Slave Trade" (London, 1911), in *The Proper Sphere: Women's Place in Canadian Society*, ed. Ramsay Cook and Wendy Mitchinson (Toronto: Oxford University Press, 1976), 242–49.

From 1880 to 1930: Carolyn Strange, "Wounded Womanhood and Dead Men: Chivalry and the Trials of Clara Ford and Carrie Davies," in Iacovetta and Valverde, *Gender Conflicts*, 177.

The sensational trial: Ibid., 159–64, 170–79. See also Charlotte Gray, *The Massey Murder: A Maid, Her Master and the Trial That Shocked a Country* (Toronto: HarperCollins, 2013).

The son of: "William Holmes Howland," DCB (www.biographi.ca/en/bio/howland_william_holmes_12E.html); Morton, *Mayor Howland*, 15–17.

At the time of: GL, December 14, 1893.

The great Satan: "William Holmes Howland," DCB.

113 **In some quarters:** Morton, *Mayor Howland*, 17.

Throughout the brief: GL, December 2, 23, 1885; Morton, *Mayor Howland*, 20, 24.

On election day: Morton, *Mayor Howland*, 63–64, 68.

He supported the: Ibid., 36; Arthur, *No Mean City*, 201.

The new Romanesque: Careless, *Toronto to 1918*, 136; "Old City Hall," www.toronto.ca/old_cityhall/; Marilyn M. Litvak, *Edward James Lennox: "Builder of Toronto"* (Toronto: Dundurn, 1996), 19–32.

Howland also wanted: GL, October 7, 1886; Morton, *Mayor Howland*, 57, 39–42, 72, 83.

He could claim: TT, February 15, 1887; GL, January 3, 1888; Morton, *Mayor Howland*, 59–61, 67, 71–74, 103.

114 **Howland had more:** GL, May 16, 1886; Greg Marquis, "The Police as a Social Service in Early Twentieth-Century Toronto," *Histoire sociale/Social History*, 25, 50 (November 1992): 335–58.

"The difficulty with": GL, December 1, 1887; David Archibald, "The Suppression of Vice," *Canadian Municipal Journal* (1906): 539.

He planned for alderman: TN, December 31, 1888; Morton, *Mayor Howland*, 95–96, 102; "Report of the Select Committee to Investigate and Report Upon Alleged Combinations in Manufactures, Trade and Insurance," May 16, 1888, in *Journals of the House of Commons*, 1888, appendix 3; House of Commons, *Debates*, February 28, 1888, 28, May 18, 1888, 1544–45.

"The citizens of": TM, January 7, 1888; Armstrong and Nelles, *The Revenge of the Methodist Bicycle Company*, 16.

He was an active: Armstrong and Nelles, *The Revenge of the Methodist Bicycle Company*, 17–19.

115 **He also brought:** Ibid., 18.

For a brief time: TW, May 28, 1889; *Labor Advocate*, June 5, 1891; Armstrong and Nelles, *The Revenge of the Methodist Bicycle Company*, 32–33.

Never a poor: TM, June 24, 1891; TW, April 28, 1891; Armstrong and Nelles, *The Revenge of the Methodist Bicycle Company*, 33–34.

116 **To manage it:** Herbert H. Harwood and Robert S. Korach, *The Lake Shore Electric Railway Story* (Bloomington: Indiana University Press, 2000), 5–6.

"Oiled and smoothed": TW, July 20, 21, August 29, 1891; TM, July 21, 1891; Armstrong and Nelles, *The Revenge of the Methodist Bicycle Company*, 43; R.B. Fleming, *The Railway King of Canada: Sir William Mackenzie 1849–1923* (Vancouver: UBC Press, 1991), 34.

An 1894 investigation: "In the Matter of the Investigation before his Honour Judge McDougall, Pursuant to Resolutions of City Council, dated 8th October 1894 and 13th November 1894," City of Toronto Archives, City Clerk's Department Papers, Evidence, vol. 2, Testimony of William Hall, 651; and Evidence, vol. 3, Testimony of William Laidlaw, 882; Armstrong and Nelles, *The Revenge of the Methodist Bicycle Company*, 43.

Mayor Clarke cuttingly: TW, July 16, 1891.

By the end of August: "Agreement between the Corporation of the City of Toronto and George W. Kiely, William McKenzie, Henry A. Everett and C.C. Woodworth, for Transfer of Toronto Street Railway (1891)" (http://archive.org/details/cihm_28929).

"The stolidity, stupidity": *Labor Advocate*, September 4, 1891; Armstrong and Nelles, *The Revenge of the Methodist Bicycle Company*, 48.

"Oh bliss!": Cited in Frances Hoffman, *Much To Be Done: Private Life in Ontario from Victorian Diaries* (Toronto: Natural Heritage Books, 2007), 21.

In the middle of the afternoon: TE, September 3, 5, 1892; Walden, *Becoming Modern in Toronto*, 3; R.B. Fleming, "The Trolley Takes Command, 1892–1984," *Urban History Review* 19, 3 (February 1991): 220.

Though 1890s Toronto: TM, July 17, 1893; Armstrong and Nelles, *The Revenge of the Methodist Bicycle Company*, 114.

117 **"The character of":** TM, August 7, 1893.

In fact, the yes side: TW, December 21, 1891; TM, January 1, 1892; Armstrong and Nelles, *The Revenge of the Methodist Bicycle Company*, 57–58.

In the end it probably: Armstrong and Nelles, *The Revenge of the Methodist Bicycle Company*, 167, 198, ; TW, May 24, June 12, 1897; Fleming, *The Railway King of Canada*, 82–83.

An especially astute: Lorraine O'Donnell Williams, *Memories of the Beach: Reflections on a Toronto Childhood* (Toronto: Dundurn, 2010), 13–14. See also Agatha Barc, "Nostalgia Tripping: Scarboro Beach Park," Blog TO, May 21, 2011 (www.blogto.com/city/2011/05/nostalgia_tripping_scarboro_beach_park/).

118 **In June 1897:** Fleming, *The Railway King of Canada*, 83.

Like other major: Arthur M. Schlesinger, *The Rise of the City 1878–1898* (New York: Macmillan, 1933), 80, 133; Levine, *The Devil in Babylon*, 11. On the history of telephones in Toronto, see Mike Filey, *Toronto Sketches 9: "The Way We Were"; Columns from the Toronto Sunday Sun* (Toronto: Dundurn, 2006), 44–46.

Toronto may not: Upton Sinclair, *The Jungle* (Memphis, TN: Peachtree Publishers, 1988), 28–40; Levine, *The Devil in Babylon*, 12.

CHAPTER SIX: THE WARD

119 **"In a part":** Lawren Harris, "A Note of Colour," in Gregory Betts, ed., *Lawren Harris in the Ward: His Urban Poetry and Paintings* (Holstein, ON: Exile Editions, 2007), 5.

Jews were wrongly: Zvi Gitelman, *A Century of Ambivalence: The Jews of Russia and the Soviet Union 1881 to the Present* (New York: Schocken, 1988), 2–5; Stephen M. Berk, *Year of Crisis, Year of Hope: Russian Jewry and the Pogroms of 1881–1882* (Westport, CT: Greenwood Press, 1985), 4, 35–8; I. Michael Aronson, *Troubled Waters: Origins of the 1881 Anti-Jewish Pogroms in Russia* (Pittsburgh: University of Pittsburgh Press, 1990), 108–24; Allan Levine, *Scattered among the Peoples: The Jewish Diaspora in Twelve Portraits* (New York: Overlook Press, 2003), 219–26.

120 **About 100,000 made:** Gerald Tulchinsky, *Branching Out: The Transformation of the Canadian Jewish Community* (Toronto: Stoddart, 1998), 357–58.

By the time Sarah: Gerald Tulchinsky, *Joe Salsberg: A Life of Commitment* (Toronto: University of Toronto Press, 2013), 11; "J.B. Remembered: The Life and Career of J.B. Salsberg," at the Ontario Jewish Archives website (www.ontariojewisharchives.org/images/Salsberg_exhibit.pdf).

Located close to: Robert Harney and Harold Troper, *Immigrants: A Portrait of the Urban Experience, 1890–1930* (Toronto: Van Nostrand Reinhold, 1975), 23; John E. Zucchi, *Italians in Toronto: Development of a National Identity, 1875–1935* (Montreal and Kingston: McGill-Queen's University Press, 1988), 38–39; David Skene-Melvin, *Bloody York* (Toronto: Dundurn, 2013), 12–13.

The local school board: Ruth A. Frager, *Sweatshop Strife: Class, Ethnicity and Gender in the Jewish Labour Movement of Toronto 1900–1939* (Toronto: University of Toronto Press, 1992), 35–36.

121 **Much to the chagrin:** "J.B. Remembered," OJA website; Erna Paris, *Jews: An Account of Their Experience in Canada* (Toronto: Macmillan of Canada, 1980), 124–25.

Born in the town: "Francesco Glionna," DCB (www.biographi.ca/en/bio/glionna_francesco_14E.html).

The "push" factors: Zucchi, *Italians in Toronto*, 13–14.

The Old World: Ibid., 61–62.

122 **Though hardly appreciated:** Ibid., 27–31, 36; "Francesco Glionna," DCB.

The corner of Chestnut: Zucchi, *Italians in Toronto*, 54; "Francesco Glionna," DCB.

Still, Toronto's population: Ian Hugh Maclean Miller, *Our Glory and Our Grief: Torontonians and the Great War* (Toronto: University of Toronto Press, 2002), 8.

123 **Alice Randle, who:** Alice Randle, "Suburban Settlement," SN, January 3, 1914, 9. See also GL, November 9, 1907; Richard Harris, *Unplanned Suburbs: Toronto's American Tragedy, 1900 to 1950* (Baltimore: Johns Hopkins University Press, 1996), 1.

The newspaper, along: GL, January 27, 1908; Harris, *Unplanned Suburbs*, 29.

This was the result: Kilbourn, *Toronto Remembered*, 206.

It was also because: ME, July 6, 1911.

The slums of the Ward: Ramsay Wright, "The Civic Cancer," *The Presbyterian*, August 3, 1911, 108.

Here is the festering: Cited in J.S. Woodsworth, *My Neighbour* (1911; Toronto: University of Toronto Press, 1972), 217.

"What a story": King Diary, September 18, 1897.

124 **"Foreign trash":** Levine, *The Devil in Babylon*, 33–34; Valverde, *The Age of Light, Soap, and Water*, 53; House of Commons, *Debates*, January 23, 1914, 140.

In a November 1909: Augustus Bridle, "The Drama of the Ward," *Canadian Magazine* 34, 1 (November 1909): 3–10.

It was also not a: Strange, *Toronto's Girl Problem*, 128.

Leading the charge: Valverde, *The Age of Light, Soap, and Water*, 54–55.

"We may not want": Cited in "John George Shearer," DCB (www.biographi.ca/en/bio/shearer_john_george_15E.html).

With little evidence: GL, November 12, 1910.

"We do not have": Rev. John G. Shearer, "The Redemption of the City," *Address to the Pre-Assembly Congress of the Presbyterian Church of Canada*, 1911, 171–73.

125 **"The danger that lurks":** Mary Joplin Clarke, "Life in the Ward," *Saint Hilda's Chronicle* 7, 20 (1915): 6–9, cited in Cathy James, "Reforming Reform: Toronto's Settlement House Movement, 1900–20," *Canadian Historical Review* 82, 1 (March 2001): 11.

This meant teaching: Valverde, *The Age of Light, Soap, and Water*, 19; Harney and Troper, *Immigrants*, 110; Levine, *The Devil in Babylon*, 40.

Operating after 1892: W.F. Wiggins, "Making Men out of Street Arabs", SN, December 1, 1906, cited at Best of Bill Gladstone.ca website (www.billgladstone.ca/?p=7340).

By the time he accepted: Kevin Plummer, "Historicist: Guarding a City's Health," TO, August 16, 2008 (http://torontoist.com/2008/08/historicist_guarding_a_citys_health/).

Between 1900 and 1911: Michael J. Piva, *The Condition of the Working Class in Toronto 1900–1921* (Ottawa: University of Ottawa Press, 1979), 114.

For years, untreated sewage: Ibid., 118, 128–29.

126 **During the first years:** Charles J. Hastings, "Report of the Medical Health Officer Dealing with the Recent Investigation of Slum Conditions in Toronto," (Toronto: City of Toronto, Department of Health, 1911), 31.

"Thousands [of immigrants] are": Charles J. Hastings, "Medical Inspection of Public Schools," *Canadian Journal of Medicine and Surgery* 21 (1907): 73.

Many white middle-class: *Canadian Jewish Times* (Montreal), March 28, 1913, 1.

By the First World War: John E. Zucchi, *A History of Ethnic Enclaves in Canada* (Ottawa: Canadian Historical Association, 2007), 7; Robert Harney, "The Commerce of Migration," *Canadian Ethnic Studies* 9, 1 (1977): 42–53.

Italian immigrants: Zucchi, *Italians in Toronto*, 84–85, 91.

127 **"Twenty-five years ago":** J.V. McAree, "The Jews in Canada," *Maclean's* 24, 1 (May 1912): 18.

One exception was: TS, February 29, 1912. The newspaper articles referenced in this chapter about the Jewish immigrants of the Ward are mainly derived from journalist Bill Gladstone's superb research and website www.billgladstone.ca.

In Toronto and across: Stephen Speisman, *The Jews of Toronto: A History to 1937* (Toronto: McClelland & Stewart, 1979), 118–21; *Canadian Jewish News*, June 7, 1957.

At the University of Toronto: Friedland, *The University of Toronto*, 324.

Gentile mothers invoked: Cited in William Kurelek and Abraham J. Arnold, *Jewish Life in Canada* (Edmonton: Hurtig, 1976), 52.

Regarded as unwanted: Speisman, *The Jews of Toronto*, 120.

Jewish schoolchildren: Ibid., 121; TS, July 22, 1913; Deena Nathanson, "A Social Profile of Peddlers in the Jewish Community of Toronto, 1891–1930," *Canadian Jewish Studies* 1 (1993): 31.

128 **Hardly a day:** TS, October 28, 1910; GL, September 1, 1914, July 21, 1919.

By 1914 there: Speisman, *The Jews of Toronto*, 101.

A private clinic: "Memoirs of Dorothy Goldstick Dworkin," *The Jewish Standard*, August 15, 1960; Rosalie Sharp, Irving Abella, and Edwin Goodman, eds., *Growing Up Jewish: Canadians Tell Their Own Stories* (Toronto: McClelland & Stewart, 1997), 56; Michael Brown, "Ida Siegel 1885–1982," in *Jewish Women: A Comprehensive Historical Encyclopedia* at the Jewish Women's Archives website (http://jwa.org/encyclopedia/article/siegel-ida); "The Hospital That Philanthropy Built," at the Mount Sinai Hospital Foundation website (http://www.mshfoundation.ca/page.aspx?pid=303).

129 **At a store at:** Shmuel Mayer Shapiro, *The Rise of the Toronto Jewish Community* (Toronto: Now & Then Books, 2010), 23–25.

Here you could attend: Michael Rom, "Cultural and Institutional Life in the Toronto Jewish Community between the Wars," *Student Journal of Canadian Jewish Studies* 2, 1 (Spring 2008): 7–8 (http://web2.concordia.ca/canadianjewishjournal/pdf/MRFinal.pdf); Adam Fuerstenberg, "Yudica: Poet of Spadina's Sweatshops," *Canadian Woman Studies* 16, 4 (Fall 1996): 107–11.

"Thinly fragile is": Cited in Tulchinsky, *Branching Out*, 94.

That evening: Ben Lappin, "May Day in Toronto: Yesteryear and Now," *Commentary* 19, 5 (1955): 477.

More entertaining: Speisman, *The Jews of Toronto*, 238; Sheldon Kirshner, "A Walk through Jewish Toronto of Decades Past," *Canadian Jewish News*, August 28, 2003, B6–8.

130 **His parents made:** Sammy Luftspring, *Call Me Sammy* (Scarborough, ON: Prentice-Hall of Canada, 1975), 7–8.

He learned to: "The History of the Y.M.H.A.," at the Ontario Jewish Archives website (www.ontariojewisharchives.org/exhibits/ymha/index.html).

"For us Jews": Luftspring, *Call Me Sammy*, 20.

Before or after: Lara Rabinovitch, "Of Cabbage Borscht and Kreplach at United Bakers," *Edible Toronto* (Spring 2009), 48–50 (www.edibletoronto.com).

All these events: Rom, "Cultural and Institutional Life in the Toronto Jewish Community between the Wars," 8; Frager, *Sweatshop Strife*, 37.

The *Globe* was: GL, March 21, 1922; Speisman, *The Jews of Toronto*, 320–21.

"An influx of Jews": TT, September 22, 1924; Speisman, *The Jews of Toronto*, 321.

131 **"The foreign quarter":** *Methodist Missionary Outlook*, December 1910; Robert Grunier, "The Hebrew-Christian Mission in Toronto," *Canadian Ethnic Studies* 9, 1 (1977): 18–28.

In 1912, Rohold: Rev. S.B. Rohold, *Presbyterian Church in Canada, Missions to the Jews: Historical Sketch; The Story of Our Church's Interest in Israel* (Toronto: Christian Synagogue, 1918), 16 (https://archive.org/details/cihm_87572); Speisman, *The Jews of Toronto*, 132–35.

The mayor told: Speisman, *The Jews of Toronto*, 125.

By 1931, more: Daniel Hiebert, "Jewish Immigrants and the Garment Industry of Toronto, 1901–1931: A Study of Ethnic and Class Relations," *Annals of the Association of American Geographers* 83, 2 (June 1993): 252; Frager, *Sweatshop Strife*, 16–17.

"At a machine": J.V. McAree, "The Jews in Canadian Business," *Maclean's* 24, 3 (August 1912): 58.

One of the more: Hiebert, "Jewish Immigrants and the Garment Industry of Toronto," 261; Sharp et al., *Growing up Jewish*, 130.

132 **So-called speed-ups:** Susan Gelman, "Anatomy of a Failed Strike: The T. Eaton Co. Lockout of Cloakmakers, 1912," *Canadian Jewish Historical Society Journal* 9, 2 (Fall 1985): 97; Kevin Plummer, "Sewing the Seeds of Discontent," TO, January 15, 2011 (http://torontoist.com/2011/01/historicist_sewing_the_seeds_of_discontent/).

There was a room: Cited in Frager, *Sweatshop Strife*, 19.

Jews were on: Ibid., 39.

The local Cloakmakers' Union: Shapiro, *The Rise of the Toronto Jewish Community*, 116–17.

Joe Salsberg told: Frager, *Sweatshop Strife*, 23.

John Craig Eaton: Ruth A. Frager, "Sewing Solidarity: The Eaton's Strike of 1912," in *A Nation of Immigrants: Women, Workers, and Communities in Canadian History, 1840s–1960s*, ed. Franca Iacovetta, Paula Draper and Robert Ventresca (Toronto: University of Toronto Press, 1998), 316.

133 **The men refused:** Frager, "Class, Ethnicity, and Gender in the Eaton Strikes," 193.

The Jewish community: Ibid., 195; Gelman, "Anatomy of a Failed Strike," 103.

A main problem: *Lance*, March 9, 1912, cited in Gelman, "Anatomy of a Failed Strike," 105.

Many of them were: Frager, "Class, Ethnicity, and Gender in the Eaton Strikes," 196; Gelman, "Anatomy of a Failed Strike," 106.

134 **"Let them swarm":** SN, September 8, 1906, 1; Kathy Paupst, "A Note on Anti-Chinese Sentiment in Toronto before the First World War," *Canadian Ethnic Studies* 9, 1 (1977): 57.

The *Globe* was: GL, October 11, 1907.

Sam Ching operated: Arlene Chan, *The Chinese in Toronto from 1878* (Toronto: Dundurn, 2011), 41.

The city's first Chinese: Dora Nipp, "The Chinese in Toronto," in Harney, *Gathering Place*, 162.

In a December 1896 story: TS, December 17, 1896.

The following year: Ibid., November 6, 1897; Chan, *The Chinese in Toronto from 1878*, 42.

135 **A decade later:** Myer Siemiatycki, Tim Rees, Roxana Ng, and Khan Rahi, "Integrating Community Diversity in Toronto: On Whose Terms?" CERIS Working Paper No. 14 (March 2001), 24 (www.ceris.metropolis.net/wp-content/uploads/pdf/research_publication/working_papers/wp14.pdf).

Feeding the hysteria: GM, June 11, 1994; James W. St. G. Walker, *"Race," Rights and the Law in the Supreme Court of Canada: Historical Case Studies* (Waterloo, ON: Wilfrid Laurier University Press, 1997), 67.

"The bland smiling": *Jack Canuck*, September 14, 16, 30, 1911; Paupst, "A Note on Anti-Chinese Sentiment in Toronto before the First World War," 58; Strange, *Toronto's Girl Problem*, 155; Margaret Bell, "Toronto's Melting Pot," *Canadian Magazine*, July 1913, 238.

In one case in 1913: Chan, *The Chinese in Toronto from 1878*, 81; Clayton James Mosher, *Discrimination and Denial: Systemic Racism in Ontario's Legal and Criminal Justice Systems, 1892–1961* (Toronto: University of Toronto Press, 1998), 77.

For a long time: Chan, *The Chinese in Toronto from 1878*, 163.

Supervised by thirty-four-year-old: TS, September 14, 2012; Mark Osbaldeston, *Unbuilt Toronto 2: More of the City That Might Have Been* (Toronto: Dundurn, 2011), 36.

136 **Amazingly no one:** "The Great Fire of 1904," City of Toronto Archives website (www.toronto.ca/archives/fire1.htm).

In late 1900: Sally Gibson, "An Illustrated History of the King Edward Hotel," at the King Edward website (www.kingedward.ca/flash/assets/pdfs/king_edward_an_illustrated_history.pdf), 2–15; Walden, *Becoming Modern in Toronto*, 329–31.

The *Star* proclaimed: TS, March 14, 1903; Gibson, "An Illustrated History of the King Edward Hotel," 11–12.

A week later: GL, March 25, 1903; Gibson, "An Illustrated History of the King Edward Hotel," 15–18.

137 **Cox, who moved:** "George Albertus Cox," DCB.

Flavelle, who lived by: Michael Bliss, *Northern Enterprise: Five Centuries of Canadian Business* (Toronto: McClelland & Stewart, 1987), 346–47.

In the spring: GL, April 13, 1904; Bliss, *A Canadian Millionaire*, 163.

"With few exceptions": SN, May 21, 1904; Bliss, *A Canadian Millionaire*, 163.

138 **Working with Flavelle:** Friedland, *The University of Toronto*, 202–3.

From that point: Ibid., 203–5, 213.

One of the early: Ibid., 244.

Right from the start: Ibid., 244–48; Lovat Dickson, *The Museum Makers: The Story of the Royal Ontario Museum* (Toronto: Royal Ontario Museum, 1986), 38.

Edmund Walker and Goldwin Smith: "Sir Byron Edmund Walker," DCB (www.biographi.ca/en/bio/walker_byron_edmund_15E.html); "Goldwin Smith," DCB; "History of the Grange," at the Art Gallery of Ontario website (http://www.ago.net/history-of-the-grange); GM, June 29, 1966.

139 **A major expansion:** Fulford, *Accidental City*, 153–54.

Pellatt was born: Bliss, *Northern Enterprise*, 278.

During the 1890s: Ibid., 317; TS, May 17, 2011; H.V. Nelles, *The Politics of Development: Forests, Mines and Hydro-Electric Power in Ontario, 1849–1941* (Toronto: Macmillan of Canada, 1974), 231.

A fair chunk: Bliss, *Northern Enterprise*, 333.

The scheme might: "Sir Adam Beck," DCB (www.biographi.ca/en/bio/beck_adam_15E.html).

He had enlisted: Bill Freeman, *Casa Loma: Toronto's Fairy-Tale Castle and Its Owner, Sir Henry Pellatt* (Toronto: Lorimer, 1999), 36–50.

140 **Pellatt owned a:** Ibid., 54–62.

He took a big: Bliss, *Northern Enterprise*, 381.

There was no heat: Ibid., 347, 381.

An expensive mahogany: Heather Robertson, *Driving Force: The McLaughlin Family and the Age of the Car* (Toronto: McClelland & Stewart, 1995), 194.

For a while it appeared: Bliss, *Northern Enterprise*, 409; "History of Casa Loma," at the Casa Loma website (www.casaloma.org/about.history.gk).

Few events prompted: Ian Hugh Maclean Miller, *Our Glory and Our Grief: Torontonians and the Great War* (Toronto: University of Toronto Press, 2002), 16, 25–27.

141 **And seventy thousand men:** William Burrill, *Hemingway: The Toronto Years* (Toronto: Doubleday Canada, 1994), 54.

On its wall of honour: West, *Toronto*, 173.

At the University of Toronto: Friedland, *The University of Toronto*, 253–55.

Future Canadian prime minister: Lester Pearson, *Mike: The Memoirs of the Right Honourable Lester B. Pearson*, vol. 1 (Toronto: University of Toronto Press, 1972), 17.

Among the many wounded: Friedland, *The University of Toronto*, 258.

"I cannot see": Cited in ibid., 261.

142 **Church took the war:** Burrill, *Hemingway*, 54; West, *Toronto*, 177.

Nevertheless, from Hemingway's: Burrill, *Hemingway*, 258, 259.

Toronto Jews held: GL, March 8, 1915.

When a rumour: TT, April 13, 1917; Miller, *Our Glory and Our Grief*, 64–65.

At a large public: GL, June 2, 4, 1917; Miller, *Our Glory and Our Grief*, 137.

In the "bedlam": TS, June 4, 1917.

143 **The highlight:** TS, August 3, 1917.

What triggered an: TN, June 19, 1918; TS, June 21, 1919; Kevin Plummer, "Historicist: Rough-and-Tumble Politics of Sam McBride," TO, March 27, 2010, (http://torontoist.com/2010/03/historicist_rough-and-tumble_politics_of_sam_mcbride/).

The suave Tommy Church: TS, July 9, 10, 1918; Miller, *Our Glory and Our Grief*, 176–77.

144 **Still, as historian Thomas Gallant:** "The 1919 Anti-Greek Riots in Toronto," a video on the Violent August website (http://violentaugust.com).

The trouble began: TS, August 3, 1918; January 3, 1919; GL, August 3, 1918; Miller, *Our Glory and Our Grief*, 178–80.

An official inquiry: TS, October 3, 1918; Miller, *Our Glory and Our Grief*, 181.

At the end of the month: TW, September 19, 1918; Janice P. Dickin McGinnis, "The Impact of the Epidemic Influenza: Canada, 1918–1919," *Canadian Historical Association Papers* 12, 1 (1977): 120–40.

On September 29: TS, September 30, October 1, 1918; Miller, *Our Glory and Our Grief*, 186.

145 **The epidemic was:** Miller, *Our Glory and Our Grief*, 185–88.

CHAPTER SEVEN: TORONTO THE DULL

146 **"It must be good":** Leopold Infeld, *Quest: An Autobiography* (1941; Providence, RI: American Mathematical Society, 1980), 324.

As he was figuring: Burrill, *Hemingway*, 9–37.

For years, every morning: Hewitt, *Down the Stretch*, 32.

147 **Whether it was raising:** Paul Rutherford, *The Making of the Canadian Media* (Toronto: McGraw-Hill Ryerson, 1978), 56–57; Mary Vipond, "A Canadian Hero of the 1920s: Dr. Frederick G. Banting," *Canadian Historical Review* 63, 4 (December 1982): 471; Trista Vincent, "Manufacturing Consent," *Ryerson Review of Journalism*, March 1999 (http://rrj.ca/m3946/).

The *Star* in those: Morley Callaghan, *That Summer in Paris* (1963; Holstein, ON: Exile Editions, 2006), 8.

At the rate of half-a-cent a word: Ernest Hemingway, "Canuck Whiskey Pouring into the U.S.," *Star Weekly*, June 5, 1920 (http://ehto.thestar.com/marks/canuck-whiskey-pouring-into-us); Randall White, *Too Good to be True: Toronto in the 1920s* (Toronto: Dundurn, 1993), 28–31.

"It is necessary to go": Cited in Michael Marrus, *Mr. Sam: The Life and Times of Samuel Bronfman* (Toronto: Penguin Canada, 1991), 70; White, *Too Good to be True*, 31.

Toronto, where the law: White, *Too Good to be True*, 162; Kilbourn, *Toronto Remembered*, 222.

148 **Hemingway's appointment:** Burrill, *Hemingway*, 99–100.

According to William Burrill: Ibid., 1.

Hindmarsh, enamoured: Ibid., 157–60; Charles A. Fenton, *The Apprenticeship of Ernest Hemingway: The Early Years* (London: Octagon Books, 1975), 272.

Morley Callghan, who: Callaghan, *That Summer in Paris*, 12–14, 29–30.

That Hindmarsh and Hemingway: Burrill, *Hemingway*, 192–94.

Hemingway had been: Ibid., 194–96.

149 **He formally submitted:** Ibid., 222–28.

Anarchist Emma Goldman: TS, December 7, 1927.

In early December 1919: Chris Bateman, "Ambrose Small, Toronto's Most Sensational Mystery," Blog TO, February 4, 2012 (www.blogto.com/city/2012/02/ambrose_small_torontos_most_sensational_mystery/); "Ambrose Small and Toronto's 'Crime of the Century,'" Toronto Then and Now, December 1, 2010 (http://torontothenandnow.blogspot.ca/2010/12/14-ambrose-small-and-torontos-crime-of.html).

Theresa Small waited: Bateman, "Ambrose Small."

No matter how: Ibid.

150 **The shindig in:** White, *Too Good to be True*, 62; C.M. Johnson, E.C. Drury: *Agrarian Idealist* (Toronto: University of Toronto Press, 1986), 198.

For sheer enjoyment: GL, June 29, 1922; Mike Filey, *I Remember Sunnyside: The Rise and Fall of a Magical Era* (Toronto: Dundurn, 1996), 51.

Sunnyside was often: Filey, *I Remember Sunnyside*, 53; White, *Too Good to be True*, 52; West, *Toronto*, 189.

Special events on: James Lemon, *Toronto Since 1918: An Illustrated History* (Toronto: Lorimer, 1985), 26; Filey, *I Remember Sunnyside*, 94–95.

More risqué was: Lemon, *Toronto Since 1918*, 26; West, *Toronto*, 210; Barc, "Nostalgia Tripping,"; "A Century of Midway Madness," The Grid, May 16, 2012 (www.thegridto.com/city/places/a-century-of-midway-madness/).

151 **The city was home:** Lemon, *Toronto Since 1918*, 37, 64.

While proud of this: Burrill, *Hemingway*, 41.

The words "bathroom": Pierre Berton, *The Great Depression, 1929–1939* (Toronto: McClelland & Stewart, 1990), 368; Kilbourn, *Toronto Remembered*, 146.

Before sentencing Sterry: GL, March 16, 1927.

152 **It required no less:** Andrew Lefebvre, "Prohibition and the Smuggling of Intoxicating Liquors between the Two Saults," *The Northern Mariner/Le marin du nord* 11, 3 (July 2001): 33–40; Gerald A. Hallowell, *Prohibition in Ontario 1919–1923* (Toronto: Ontario Historical Society, 1972), ix, 7, 8.

Ferguson's intention: Cited in Robert Bostelaar, *Guardians of Peace: A History of the Sault Ste. Marie Police Force, Ontario, Canada* (Sault Ste. Marie, ON: Board of Commissioners of Police, 1987), 44.

Before you could guzzle: Control Mandate, "Punched Drunk: Alcohol, Surveillance and the LCBO, 1927–1975" (http://puncheddrunk.ca/control-mandate.html); White, *Too Good to be True*, 126.

A notable exception: TS, March 10, 2007.

153 **McBride, who had been:** West, *Toronto*, 196.

His gruff, no-nonsense style: White, *Too Good to be True*, 194; Plummer, "Historicist: Rough-and-Tumble Politics of Sam McBride."

One fight McBride: GL, March 27, May 5, 1926; Kilbourn, *Toronto Remembered*, 297.

Its chief owner: TN, December 15, 1906; Bliss, *A Canadian Millionaire*, 171.

There were never enough: Lemon, *Toronto Since 1918*, 42–43; Harris, *Unplanned Suburbs*, 38.

During the next few years: Lemon, *Toronto Since 1918*, 43, 77.

154 **In 1916 there were 10,000:** Ibid., 44–45, 50; White, *Too Good to be True*, 117.

With no lanes: Robertson, *Driving Force*, 160–61.

Owning a house: Harris, *Unplanned Suburbs*, 50–51, 135. See also Henrik Reitsma, "North York: The Development of a Suburb" (master's thesis, University of Toronto, 1962); Esther Heyes, *Etobicoke: From Furrow to Borough* (Etobicoke, ON: Borough of Etobicoke Civil Centre, 1974).

By 1921, after: Lemon, *Toronto Since 1918*, 33; Harris, *Unplanned Suburbs*, 58–59, 69, 86.

But, it was in the town: Lemon, *Toronto Since 1918*, 77; Mike Filey, *Toronto Sketches* (Toronto: Dundurn, 1992), 88–89.

155 **No one seemed:** Berton, *The Great Depression*, 29–30.

On Front Street: White, *Too Good to be True*, 198–200, 203–4.

Farther south on Avenue: Mike Filey, *Toronto Sketches 3* (Toronto: Dundurn, 1994), 117–19.

156 **Some months earlier:** Knowlton Nash, *The Microphone Wars: A History of Triumph and Betrayal at the CBC* (Toronto: McClelland & Stewart, 1994), 29–31.

In fact, the radio: Levine, *The Devil in Babylon*, 247–48.

As a young boy: Ian A. Anthony, "Rogers' Recollections: A Chronicle of Excellence and Achievement," IEEE Canada website (www.ieee.ca/millennium/alternating_current/ac_recollections.html); TS, September 25, 1925.

Building on that success: Caroline Van Hasselt, *High Wire Act: Ted Rogers and the Empire That Debt Built* (Mississauga, ON: Wiley, 2007), 11–12.

They quickly became: Ibid., 3–4.

157 **The game went:** Nash, *The Microphone Wars*, 31–33; Kelly McParland, *The Lives of Conn Smythe* (Toronto: McClelland & Stewart, 2011), 134–36.

"Toronto is going": TS, March 24, 1928; Lita-Rose Betcherman, *The Little Band: The Clashes between the Communists and the Political and Legal Establishment in Canada, 1928–1932* (Ottawa: Deneau, 1982), 1.

John Gray, a University of Toronto: Kilbourn, *Toronto Remembered*, 146.

With the full support: Betcherman, *The Little Band*, 19–21; Lemon, *Toronto Since 1918*, 53.

In early 1929: TS, January 23, 1929; GL, February 18, 1929; Betcherman, *The Little Band*, 24.

158 **Chief Draper later:** Michiel Horn, "Keeping Canada 'Canadian': Anti-Communism and Canadianism in Toronto 1928–29," *Canada* 3, 1 (1975): 36.

Debate about the: GL, January 24, 1929; Berton, *The Great Depression*, 42; Lemon, *Toronto Since 1918*, 53; Betcherman, *The Little Band*, 28.

Refusing to be intimidated: GL, August 2, 1929; Betcherman, *The Little Band*, 59–61.

On this night: John Morgan Gray, *Fun Tomorrow: Learning to be a Publisher and Much More* (Toronto: Macmillan of Canada, 1978), 179–81; Berton, *The Great Depression*, 20–21; Betcherman, *The Little Band*, 62–65; TS, August 15, 1929.

159 **"Police Rout Communists":** GL, August 14, 15, 1929.

"The story of what happened": TS, August 15, 1929.

If anything, the police repression: Betcherman, *The Little Band*, 64–85; Berton, *The Great Depression*, 23, 69, 95.

Years later they would: Jamie Bradburn, "A Crash Course on Toronto's Black Tuesday," TO, August 12, 2011 (http://torontoist.com/2011/08/crashing_in_on_black_tuesday/).

On October 4, a wave: Berton, *The Great Depression*, 32–34.

160 **At the TSE:** Ibid., 34.

Brokers did not jump: GL, March 15, 1930; Berton, *The Great Depression*, 37.

By May 1932: White, *Too Good to be True*, 216.

"Stock Lists Holding": TS, October 30, 1929; GL, October 30, 1929; White, *Too Good to be True*, 214–15.

Asked by the press: GL, October 30, 1929; Levine, *King*, 191–92.

In late 1934: Lemon, *Toronto Since 1918*, 59; Lara Campbell, *Respectable Citizens: Gender, Family and Unemployment in Ontario's Great Depression* (Toronto: University of Toronto Press, 2009), 3.

161 **Hugh Garner depicted:** Hugh Garner, *Cabbagetown* (Toronto: McGraw-Hill Ryerson, 1968), 70–71.

Only the truly wealthy: Campbell, *Respectable Citizens*, 4.

Asking prices: West, *Toronto*, 203.

In violation of local bylaws: Lemon, *Toronto Since 1918*, 65; George H. Rust-D'Eye, *Cabbagetown Remembered* (Erin, ON: Boston Mills Press, 1984), 39.

In August 1934: H.A. Bruce to R.B. Bennett, August 10, 1934, in *The Dirty Thirties: Canadians in the Great Depression*, ed. Michiel Horn (Toronto: Copp Clark, 1972), 194–98.

Half the houses: Rust-D'Eye, *Cabbagetown Remembered*, 35.

Worse was the "hobo jungle": "Don Valley Brickworks, Don Valley Historical Mapping Project,"http://maps.library.utoronto.ca/dvhmp/don-valley-brickworks.html.

At the luncheon: Lemon, *Toronto Since 1918*, 59, 68.

162 **Construction jobs dried:** Ibid., 60; Marcus Klee, "Between the Scylla and Charybdis of Anarchy and Despotism: The State, Capital, and the Working Class in the Great Depression, Toronto, 1929–1940" (PhD dissertation, Queen's University, 1998), 238; Campbell, *Respectable Citizens*, 76.

The owner of a restaurant: Berton, *The Great Depression*, 242.

Several nasty clashes: TT, June 5, 1933; TS, July 27, 1933; Cyril Levitt and William Shaffir, *The Riot at Christie Pits* (Toronto: Lester & Orpen Dennys, 1987), 26–27.

Businessman and boxing promoter: Sharp et al., *Growing up Jewish*, 120–21.

Similarly, restaurateur Lou Bregman's: Ibid., 151–55.

On average, piece workers: *The Royal Commission on Price Spreads* (Ottawa, 1935) in Horn, *The Dirty Thirties*, 122–23.

As one young woman: Ibid., 122; Frager, *Sweatshop Strife*, 22.

163 **Upset by what they:** Tulchinsky, *Branching Out*, 110–12; Frager, *Sweatshop Strife*, 142–44; Berton, *The Great Depression*, 291–92.

The company used strikebreakers: Frager, "Class, Ethnicity, and Gender in the Eaton Strikes of 1912 and 1934," 204; Plummer, "Sewing the Seeds of Discontent"; TS, January 22, 1935; Berton, *The Great Depression*, 292.

So hostile were the Poslunses: Danielle Gehl, "Bricks and Slingshots," *The Peak*, 51, 6 (May 2012): http://guelphpeak.org/volume51issue1/garmentworkers; Gerald Tulchinksy, *Canada's Jews: A People's Journey* (Toronto: University of Toronto Press, 2008), 259; TS, August 22, 24, 1934.

"People believe he": King Diary, October 6, 1937.

Hepburn was indeed: Levine, *King*, 277; John T. Saywell, *"Just Call Me Mitch": The Life of Mitchell F. Hepburn* (Toronto: University of Toronto Press, 1991), 192, 287.

164 **In the spring of 1937:** Levine, *King*, 277; Laurel Sefton MacDowell, "Oshawa Strike," in *The Oxford Companion to Canadian History*, ed. Gerald A. Hallowell (Don Mills, ON: Oxford University Press, 2004), 467.

After sixteen days: MacDowell, "Oshawa Strike," 467.

As a politician: TS, September 26, 1938.

He was no communist: Cited in Gerald Caplan, *The Dilemma of Canadian Socialism: The CCF in Ontario* (Toronto: McClelland & Stewart, 1973), 71.

165 **Almost immediately:** Lemon, *Toronto Since 1918*, 74.

"To him and to his": TS, September 26, 1938.

When the young new: Speisman, *The Jews of Toronto*, 217.

Even at the more traditional: Ibid., 225–30.

The community's institutions: Ibid., 309–10; Gil Zohar, "Notes on the Early History of Mount Sinai Hospital," Heritage Toronto website, October 28, 1991 (www.gilzohar.ca/articles/canada/c1991-1.html).

Among the throng in 1930: Rosemary Bergeron, "Wayne and Shuster at the National Archives of Canada: The Frank Shuster Fonds," *The Archivist*, 119 (www.collectionscanada.gc.ca/publications/archivist-magazine/015002-2132-e.html).

166 **Harbord had "one other":** Eddie Goodman, *Life of the Party* (Toronto: Key Porter, 1988), 12; Jim Coyle, "The Heroes of Harbord," TS, April 27, 2012. On April 27, 2012, Heritage Toronto unveiled a legacy plaque commemorating the late Frank Shuster and Johnny Wayne during the 120th anniversary celebrations of Harbord Collegiate.

"As Tommy's defeat": TS, July 29, 1930.

Mackenzie King considered: King Diary, July 2, 1940.

It was the virulent anti-Semitism: Levine, *King*, 288–89; Tulchinsky, *Branching Out*, 173–75, 185–88; Irving Abella and Harold Troper, *None Is Too Many: Canada and the Jews of Europe, 1933–1948* (Toronto: Lester and Orpen Dennys, 1982).

"Is it restricted": B.G. Kayfetz, "Only Yesterday" (paper presented to the Toronto Jewish Historical Society, May 1972), cited in Levitt and Shaffir, *The Riot at Christie Pits*, 34.

Signs proclaiming: Irving Abella, "Anti-Semitism," *Canadian Encyclopedia* (www.thecanadianencyclopedia.com/articles/antisemitism); Levitt and Shaffir, *The Riot at Christie Pits*, 35–36; Speisman, *The Jews of Toronto*, 332; "Toronto's First Synagogues: Beach Hebrew Institute," Ontario Jewish Archives website (www.ontariojewisharchives.org/exhibits/TorontoSynagogues/synogogues/Beach/history.html).

167 **Mayor William Stewart:** TS, June 16, 1932, February 24, 1933; *Canadian Jewish News*, December 23, 2004, 12.

On more than one occasion: Enrico T. Carlson Cumbo, "'As the Twig's Bent, the Tree's Inclined': Growing Up Italian in Toronto" (PhD dissertation, University of Toronto, 1996), 130.

When the St. Andrews Golf Club: Tulchinsky, *Branching Out*, 194; TS, January 30, 2010.

Several Toronto newspapers: GL, November 8, 1923; Speisman, *The Jews of Toronto*, 319–20.

During the summer months: Levitt and Shaffir, *The Riot at Christie Pits*, 81–82.

168 **In 1933, these unwanted:** Ibid., 78–79; Speisman, *The Jews of Toronto*, 332–33.

The police: Speisman, *The Jews of Toronto*, 333; Levitt and Shaffir, *The Riot at Christie Pits*, 38–39, 82–85.

Soon after, Mayor Stewart: Speisman, *The Jews of Toronto*, 333.

The simmering animosity: TS, August 15, 1933; Levitt and Shaffir, *The Riot at Christie Pits*, 152–53, 199.

St. Peter's Church and Harbord: Levitt and Shaffir, *The Riot at Christie Pits*, 155–73.

169 **The Christie Pits riot:** TS, August 17, 1933; TT, August 17, 18, 1933; ME, August 17, 1933; GL, August 18, 1933; Levitt and Shaffir, *The Riot at Christie Pits*, 166–75.

The Jewish community's: *Der Yiddisher Zhurnal*, August 22, 1933; Levitt and Shaffir, *The Riot at Christie Pits*, 174.

Most recently, on the eightieth: GM, August 10, 2013; NP, August 10, 2013.

"No, we have no job": Donna Hill, ed. *A Black Man's Toronto 1914–1980: The Reminiscences of Harry Gairey* (Toronto: Multicultural History Society of Ontario, 1981), 7–9, 14, 22, 28.

One day in late: Ibid., 26–27; TS, February 16, 2009.

170 **Herb Carnegie, who:** Cecil Harris, *Breaking the Ice: The Black Experience in Professional Hockey* (London, ON: Insomniac, 2003), 47.

One day the Maple: Signa Butler, "Hockey Pioneer Herb Carnegie Dead at 92," CBC Sports, March 10, 2012 (www.cbc.ca/sports/hockey/nhl/story/2012/03/10/sp-carnegie-herb-obit.html); Harris, *Breaking the Ice*, 47–49.

It is true that: McParland, *The Lives of Conn Smythe*, 42.

Carnegie later played: Harris, *Breaking the Ice*, 44–45.

171 **In 1939, Velma Demerson:** Joan Sangster, "Incarcerating 'Bad Girls': The Regulation of Sexuality through the Female Refuges Act in Ontario, 1920–1945," *Journal of the History of Sexuality* 7, 2 (1996): 239–75.

As she recalls: Velma Demerson, *Incorrigible* (Waterloo, ON: Wilfrid Laurier University Press, 2004), 163. See also Scott Piatkowski, "An Honest Woman," *This Magazine*, July–August 2005 (www.thismagazine.ca/issues/2005/07/honestwoman.php).

Three months after: Demerson, *Incorrigible*, 158; Piatkoswki, "An Honest Woman"; Ruth Brown, "A Woman Called Incorrigible: Velma Demerson," Section 15.ca website, March 21, 2005 (http://section15.ca/features/people/2005/03/21/velma_demerson/).

Thanks to generous grants: Friedland, *The University of Toronto*, 325–26.

More impressive was: Ibid., 329; GL, May 4, 1933.

172 **The legendary hockey:** McParland, *The Lives of Conn Smythe*, 229–30; Conn Smythe and Scott Young, *Conn Smythe: If You Can't Beat 'em in the Alley* (Toronto: McClelland & Stewart, 1981), 176.

In 1926 he was hired: McParland, *The Lives of Conn Smythe*, 40.

Above all, he approached: Ibid.

The deal that saw: Ibid., 78.

173 **"I'm not interested":** Trent Frayne, "Ice Man," *Colliers*, January 24, 1948, 244.

To achieve profitability: McParland, *The Lives of Conn Smythe*, 83–84, 107.

Smythe realized that: Ibid., 107.

174 **The plan began:** Ibid., 111–27; Michael McKinley, *Hockey: A People's History* (Toronto: McClelland & Stewart, 2006), 113–14.

The Gardens had it: McParland, *The Lives of Conn Smythe*, 111–31; GL, November 13, 1931.

With an improved product: McParland, *The Lives of Conn Smythe*, 142.

Thirty-one years old: GM, April 1, 1998.

175 **He looked, as a:** R.E. Knowles, "Presidents and Publishers," SN, November 14, 1936, 5.

Legend has it: Pierre Berton, "The Amazing Career of George McCullagh, *Maclean's*, January 15, 1949, 42: Levine, *Scrum Wars*, 175–76.

"In the Canadian scene": Berton, "The Amazing Career of George McCullagh," 43.

The younger Jaffray: Ibid., 42; Levine, *Scrum Wars*, 143.

Jaffray also deliberately: Levine, *King*, 137–38.

176 **For years, Jaffray:** Levine, *Scrum Wars*, 144.

Not finished yet: Douglas How, *Canada's Mystery Man of Finance* (Hantsport, NS: Lancelot Press, 1986), 12, 104–6.

When Mackenzie King: King Diary, November 19, 1936.

"I have no politics": Cited in David Hayes, *Power and Influence: The Globe and Mail and the News Revolution* (Toronto: Key Porter, 1992), 53; GM, November 22, 1936.

What drove McCullagh: Levine, *Scrum Wars*, 177.

The two men shared: Saywell, *"Just Call Me Mitch,"* 280–83, 319–20; Hayes, *Power and Influence*, 54; Levine, *Scrum Wars*, 177–78.

177 **In a series of:** GM, February 24, July 13, 1939; Richard J. Doyle, *Hurly-Burly: A Time at the Globe* (Toronto: Macmillan of Canada, 1990), 27–28; Saywell, *"Just Call Me Mitch,"* 414–15.

The League became: GM, July 13, 1939, August 6, 1952; Levine, *Scrum Wars*, 178; Hayes, *Power and Influence*, 55–56.

In the forties: Herbert Whittaker and Arnold Edinborough, *Winston's: The Life and Times of a Great Restaurant* (Toronto: Stoddart, 1988), 8, 85.

Winston's, named in: Ibid., 8–9, 15–16; GM, February 4, 1974, December 13, 1988; Peter C. Newman, *The Acquisitors*, vol. 2 of *The Canadian Establishment* (Toronto: McClelland & Stewart, 1981), 281; Jamie Bradburn, "Historicist: Winston's—Where Celebrities Meet to Eat," TO, August 6, 2011 (http://torontoist.com/2011/08/historicist_winstonswhere_celebrities_meet_to_eat/).

An October 1946: GM, October 22, 1946; Bradburn, "Historicist: Winston's."

Celebrities dining at: GM, March 30, 1945, May 21, 1947, December 13, 1988; Whittaker and Edinborough, *Winston's*, 21–25, 32–35. On Harold Shaw, see TS, November 20, 1975.

178 **The Bercellers prided:** Whittaker and Edinborough, *Winston's*, 56–62.

They presented about: Ibid., 21, 27–28; GM, February 4, 1974; Bradburn, "Historicist: Winston's."

The keys, which suggested: Whittaker and Edinborough, *Winston's*, 21; Newman, *The Acquisitors*, 281.

In December 1949, actress: Whittaker and Edinborough, *Winston's*, 18–19; GM, February 4, 1974.; Bradburn, "Historicist: Winston's."

That was his style: Whittaker and Edinborough, *Winston's*, 36–43.

During the forties and fifties: Ibid., 105–6.

CHAPTER EIGHT: SUBWAYS, SUBURBIA, AND PAESANI

179 **"Toronto is the greatest":** Lister Sinclair, "We All Hate Toronto" (1948), cited in Kevin Plummer, "The City That Nobody Loves," TO, November 21, 2009 (http://torontoist.com/2009/11/historicist_the_city_that_nobody_loves/).

On the evening of September 3: TS, September 5, 11, 13, 1939; GM, September 4, 5, 8, 1939.

Instead, the *Athenia*: "Athenia Statistics," in Francis M. Carroll, *Athenia Torpedoed: The U-boat Attack That Ignited the Battle of the Atlantic* (Annapolis, MD: Naval Institute Press, 2012), 159.

180 **The city's economy:** Lemon, *Toronto Since 1918*, 84; James Dow, *The Arrow* (Toronto: Lorimer, 1997), vi–viii.

In October 1942: Saywell, *"Just Call Me Mitch,"* 490–506.

181 **Still, Toronto voters were not:** GM, June 8, 1948; Saywell, *"Just Call Me Mitch,"* 507–11.

To ensure that: Nathan Phillips, *Mayor of All the People* (Toronto: McClelland & Stewart, 1967), 65.

At a conference: Friedland, *The University of Toronto*, 348–49.

In the first month: Ibid., 339.

He also encouraged: McParland, *The Lives of Conn Smythe*, 178–85.

182 **During his recovery:** GM, September 19, 1944; TT, September 19, 1944; McParland, *The Lives of Conn Smythe*, 204–8; Levine, *King*, 348–57.

The Gardens was: McParland, *The Lives of Conn Smythe*, 248.

Ben Dunkelman, the son of: Ben Dunkelman, *Dual Allegiance* (Toronto: Macmillan of Canada, 1976), 7–8, 11–12.

In the fall of 1939: Ibid., 55–56.

In another example: Rod Mickleburgh with Rudyard Griffiths, *Rare Courage: Veterans of the Second World War Remember* (Toronto: McClelland & Stewart, 2005), 31–34; TS, February 21, 1959.

183 **By early 1943:** Tulchinsky, *Branching Out*, 212.

For him, as for: GM, July 10, 1954; Eleanor Drake, *Call Me True: A Biography of True Davidson* (Toronto: Natural Heritage/Natural History, 1997), 83.

"Toronto's City Council": GM, March 24, 1943; Phillips, *Mayor of All the People*, 159.

Dr. Peter Bryce: Cited in Pierre Berton, *Worth Repeating: A Literary Resurrection 1948–1994* (Toronto: Doubleday, 1998), 246.

For historian and alderman: Kilbourn, *Toronto Remembered*, 132–33.

184 **After Norway was invaded:** Sally Gibson, *More Than an Island: A History of the Toronto Island* (Toronto: Irwin Publishing, 1984), 204–5; Filey, *Toronto Sketches*, 9; Donald Jones, "Unravelling Little Norway's Big Secrets," TS, May 10, 1986, A3; Susan Reid, "King Returns to Wartime 'Little Norway,'" TS, November 20, 1987, A6.

About the only: John Sewell, *Up against City Hall* (Toronto: James Lewis & Samuel, 1972), 6.

In 1947, when journalist: Pierre Berton, *My Times: Living with History*, 1947–1995 (Toronto: McClelland & Stewart, 1995), 6.

185 **The city was too hot:** Ibid., 6–7.

He and his family: Ibid., 50–59; Pierre Berton website (www.pierreberton.com/author.htm).

At the time, he recalled: TS, October 5, 2002.

A classic example of: Friedland, *The University of Toronto*, 383–84.

Publication of the term's: Ibid., 384; GM, March 7, 13, 14, 17, 1952.

They were not banned: Friedland, *The University of Toronto*, 325.

186 **After graduating with:** Mary Jane Mossman, "'Contextualizing' Bertha Wilson: Wilson as a Woman in Law in Mid-20th Century Canada," *Supreme Court Law Review* (2008), 41 S.C.L.R. (2d), 20–22; GM, August 9, 2012.

In November 1971: Mossman, "'Contextualizing' Bertha Wilson," 21–22.

When evangelist: TS, June 17, 1946; GM, June 17, 1946; Kilbourn, *Toronto Remembered*, 133; Kevin Kee, "Bobby-Sox to Bach: Charles Templeton and the Commodification of Popular Protestantism in Post-World War II Canada," *Journal of the Canadian Historical Association* 15, 1 (2004): 240.

The backlash against: GM, June 8, 1948; Olenka Melynk, *No Bankers in Heaven: Remembering the CCF* (Toronto: McGraw-Hill Ryerson, 1989), 177–78; Jamie Bradburn, "Vintage Toronto Ads: Booted by a Billboard," TO, October 7, 2008 (http://torontoist.com/2008/10/vintage_toronto_ads_booted_by_a_bil/).

The irony was: Berton, *My Times*, 8.

187 **In 1950, he was:** Roger Graham, *Old Man Ontario: Leslie M. Frost* (Toronto: University of Toronto Press, 1990), 252–53.

"Some proprietors": Cited in Ibid., 253.

Worse, the seemingly endless: Ibid. 253–54.

From his first election: TS, June 14, 1974, June 30, 1995.

Built "like a fire hydrant": GM, November 20, 1999; Ron Haggart, "Situation Comedy in City Hall," in Kilbourn, *The Toronto Book*, 255–56; John Robert Colombo, *Quotations from Chairman Lamport* (Vancouver: Pulp, 1990).

188 **He also became embroiled:** GM, December 9, 10, 11, 30, 1954.

Thirty years later: GM, August 7, 1987.

It was, recalled William Kilbourn: William Kilbourn, "Moreness Versus Chicken Talk: Lamport and McLuhan at City Hall," in Kilbourn, *The Toronto Book*, 266–67.

In that last: GM, December 7, 1949.

Of the 170,000: GM, January 3, 1950.

189 **Much to the chagrin:** GM, December 6, 1961.

The most popular event: GM, May 31, 1961; Filey, *Toronto Sketches*, 38–39; Kevin Plummer, "Historicist: Cup Cake Cassidy and the Burlesque Boom," TO, August 1, 2009 (http://torontoist.com/2009/08/historicist_cup_cake_cassidy_and_the_burlesque_boo/); Robert Fulford, "Crisis at the Victory Burlesk," in *The Underside of Toronto*, ed. W.E. Mann (Toronto: McClelland & Stewart, 1970), 255–58.

According to local legend: Lisa Beaton, "Bad Boys, Booze and Bylines: The Rise and Demise of the Toronto Press Club," *Ryerson Review of Journalism*, March 2003 (www.rrj.ca/m3777/).

190 **He and his key staff:** Ken Carriere, "An Officer and a Journalist," *Ryerson Review of Journalism*, Spring 1996 (www.rrj.ca/m3694/).

He considered that paper: Levine, *Scrum Wars*, 194; Maggie Siggins, *Bassett: John Bassett's Forty Years in Politics, Publishing, Business and Sports* (Toronto: Lorimer, 1979), 60.

In fact, it was the *Star*: Berton, *My Times*, 27; Doyle, *Hurly-Burly*, 86–87; GM, January 5, 1973.

During the 1949: Levine, *Scrum Wars*, 194; Peter Dempson, *Assignment Ottawa: Seventeen Years in the Press Gallery* (Toronto: General Publishing, 1968), 60; Sidney Katz, "How Toronto's Evening Papers Slanted the Election News," *Maclean's*, August 15, 1949, 54.

191 **The most outrageous:** TS, June 25, 28, 1949; Levine, *Scrum Wars*, 195; Ross Harkness, *J.E. Atkinson of the Star* (Toronto: University of Toronto Press, 1963), 365.

"Liberals Paying Off *Star*": Katz, "How Toronto's Evening Papers Slanted the Election News," 54; Harkness, *J.E. Atkinson of the Star*, 366.

When the election: GM, June 28, 1949; TS, June 28, 1949.

The two newspapers: TS, September 3, 4, 8, 1954; Betty Kennedy, *Hurricane Hazel* (Toronto: Macmillan of Canada, 1979), 14–15.

192 **The worst moment:** TS, September 10, 1954; Kennedy, *Hurricane Hazel*, 16.

Doug MacFarlane, now: Carriere, "An Officer and a Journalist."

When the harsh: TS, October 15, 1954; Kennedy, *Hurricane Hazel*, 36–38.

Just after eleven o'clock: Kennedy, *Hurricane Hazel*, 45, 107–22, 148.

193 **On Island Road:** TS, October 16, 1994; Mike Davis, "Hurricane Hazel (The Weird, Ravaging, Black-Hearted Hag): An Extreme Weather Event Reshapes Toronto's Green Infrastructure," June 11, 1999, on Orange Crush website (www3.sympatico.ca/orangecrush/hazel.html).

For days after: Carriere, "An Officer and a Journalist."

It also reaffirmed: Fulford, *Accidental City*, 36.

"Where is the Old": Pierre Berton, *The New City: A Prejudiced View of Toronto* (Toronto: Macmillan of Canada, 1961), 26.

Whether these old-stock: Lemon, *Toronto Since 1918*, 113–14.

The Soviet invasion: TS, January 13, 2010.

194 **As a young war:** Author's interview with Peter C. Newman, June 25, 2012.

By 1958, Paul and Ralph Reichmann: Anthony Bianco, *The Reichmanns: Family, Faith, Fortune, and the Empire of Olympia and York* (Toronto: Random House of Canada, 1997), 231–40.

The majority settled: Franca Iacovetta, *Such Hardworking People: Italian Immigrants in Postwar Toronto* (Montreal and Kingston: McGill-Queen's University Press, 1992), 567, 204–5, 210; Lemon, *Toronto Since 1918*, 197.

Another result was: Denis De Klerck and Corrado Paina, eds., *College Street: Little Italy* (Toronto: Mansfield Press, 2006), 93.

In 1951, more than: Iacovetta, *Such Hardworking People*, Table 11.

Inevitably, many of them: "Tridel History," at the corporate website (www.tridel.com/about-tridel/our-history); GM, February 22, 2005, November 11, 2008.

195 **A skilled plasterer:** GM, December 7, 2005.

Then, with his partners: GM, September 29, 1989; TS, December 10, 2005; *Canadian Business*, December 5, 2005, 30–72.

He was "the Bull": GM, September 29, 1989.

In the early seventies: *Report of the Royal Commission on Certain Sectors of the Building Industry*, vol. 1 (Toronto: Queen's Printer, 1974), 113; *Vancouver Sun*, June 30, 1989.

As was his style: GM, September 29, 1989, December 7, 2005.

196 **He boarded with:** "The Life History of Fortunato Rao: From Calabria to Canadian Labour Leader," Multicultural History Society of Ontario website (www.mhso.ca/ggp/Ethnic_groups/Italian/Lucky_Rao/Rao.html); Nicholas Harney and Frank Sturino, eds., *The Lucky Immigrant: The Public Life of Fortunato Rao* (Toronto: Multicultural History Society of Ontario, 2002).

The plight of the: TS, June 26–28, 1961; De Klerck and Paina, *College Street*, 90–91; Iacovetta, *Such Hardworking People*, 121–22.

"Like many families": TS, June 26, 1961.

As well-intentioned: Iacovetta, *Such Hardworking People*, 122.

A few astute: Peter C. Newman, "Are the New Canadians Hurting Canada?" *Maclean's*, July 18, 1959, 19, 55–57; Hugh Garner, "An Old Canadian Assesses the New Canadians' Case against Us," *Maclean's*, July 18, 1959, 19, 58; Iacovetta, *Such Hardworking People*, 122.

When immigrants rode: Iacovetta, *Such Hardworking People*, 107–9.

Italians were stereotyped: Robert Allen, "Portrait of Little Italy," *Maclean's*, March 21, 1964, 43–46.

Another new arrival: Frank Colantonio, *From the Ground Up: An Italian Immigrant's Story (*Toronto: Between the Lines, 1997), 2–34. On wages in Canada see Abdul Rashid, "Seven Decades of Wage Changes," *Perspectives on Labour and Income* 5, 2 (Summer 1993): Table 1 (www.statcan.gc.ca/studies-etudes/75-001/archive/e-pdf/57-eng.pdf).

197 **His main task:** Colantonio, *From the Ground Up*, 63–65.

Frank and Nella: Ibid., 89.

Despite rescue: Iacovetta, *Such Hardworking People*, 53.

Subsequent investigations revealed: TT, March 18, 25, 1960; Iacovetta, *Such Hardworking People*, 162–63.

"For years they've been": Cited in Laurel Sefton MacDowell and Ian Radforth, eds., *Canadian Working-Class History: Selected Readings* (Toronto: Canadian Scholars' Press, 2006), 365–66.

In March 2010: Colantonio, *From the Ground Up*, 94–97; Jamie Bradburn, "Historicist: Disaster at Hogg's Hollow," TO, March 20, 2010 (http://torontoist.com/2010/03/historicst_disaster_at_hoggs_hollow/).

198 **Born in the Ward:** TS, March 20, 2002.

When Pierre Berton: Berton, *The New City*, 39.

A year earlier: TS, March 20, 30, 1960.

"I know more": TT, March 30, 1960; Iacovetta, *Such Hardworking People*, 171–73.

His death in: TS, March 20, 2002.

On March 30, 1954: TS, March 30, 1954; James Bow, "A History of the Original Yonge Subway," Transit Toronto website (http://transit.toronto.on.ca/subway/5102.shtml).

199 **After a few false starts:** Mike Filey, *The TTC Story: The First Seventy-Five Years* (Toronto: Dundurn, 1997), 70–71.

A year later: GM, April 14, 1947; Lemon, *Toronto Since 1918*, 81.

The first ground: Stan Fischler, *Subways of the World* (Osceola, WI: MBI Publishing, 2000), 46; TS, September 8, 1949.

It would take two: Bow, "A History of the Original Yonge Subway."

200 **Critics of Regent Park:** TS, April 2, 2010, June 9, 2012; NP, June 16, 2012.

Even before its: Albert Rose, *Regent Park: A Study in Slum Clearance* (Toronto: University of Toronto Press, 1958), 65.

The idea for Regent Park: John Sewell, *The Shape of the City: Toronto Struggles with Modern Planning* (Toronto: University of Toronto Press, 1993), 55–56; Carolyn Whitzman, *Suburb, Slum, Urban Village: Transformations in Toronto's Parkdale Neighbourhood, 1875–2002* (Vancouver: UBC Press, 2009), 143; City of Toronto Planning Board, *Master Plan for the City of Toronto and Environs* (Toronto: City of Toronto Planning Board, 1943).

Little had changed: Max Rosenfeld and Earle Beattie, *A Blot on the Face of the City* (Toronto: Toronto Telegram, 1955), 3.

Leaving no stone: Ibid., 3–22.

Led by such: Rose, *Regent Park*, 47–53; Sewell, *The Shape of the City*, 70–71.

201 **The development, managed:** Ibid., 72–73.

With adequate green space: Ibid., 150–58; TS, November 19, 1959; GM, November 21, 1960.

"It's like a palace": TS, March 30, 1949.

The Citizens' Housing: Rose, *Regent Park*, 49, 54.

The housing project: Ibid., 157–67, 220–21.

Toronto Community Housing: "Regent Park Revitalization" Toronto Community Housing website (http://www.torontohousing.ca/investing_buildings/regent_park).

202 **"We don't feel safe":** TS, June 16, 2012; Global News, June 5, 2012.

As the population: "Table 1: Population Growth in Toronto and Region, 1911–1981," in Lemon, *Toronto Since 1918*, 194.

Commuting to and from: Lemon, *Toronto Since 1918*, 134; Timothy J. Colton, *Big Daddy: Frederick G. Gardiner and the Building of Metropolitan Toronto* (Toronto: University of Toronto Press, 1980), 169.

He was "big Eddie": Bliss, *Northern Enterprise*, 468; Peter C. Newman, *Here Be Dragons: Telling Tales of People, Passion and Power* (Toronto: McClelland & Stewart, 2004), 117.

His sizable stable: Bliss, *Northern Enterprise*, 466–68; Peter C. Newman, *The Canadian Establishment*, vol. 1 (Toronto: McClelland & Stewart, 1975), 31–36. See also Richard Rohmer, *E.P. Taylor: The Biography of Edward Plunket Taylor* (Toronto: McClelland & Stewart, 1978).

Taylor's "methods were rough": Bliss, *Northern Enterprise*, 441.

By 1958, when: Libbie Park and Frank Park, *Anatomy of Big Business* (Toronto: James Lewis & Samuel, 1973), 63.

203 **In the late forties:** GM, October 4, 1958, July 1, 1976; NP, April 18, 2001; Newman, *The Canadian Establishment*, 22, 184; Conrad Black, *A Matter of Principle* (Toronto: McClelland & Stewart, 2011), 239.

In 1952, he bought: Sewell, *The Shape of the City*, 81–82.

Influenced by American: Ibid., 80–93.

In short, as the: *Architectural Forum*, June 1954, 148; Sewell, *The Shape of the City*, 93.

Taylor's one stipulation: Rohmer, *E.P. Taylor*, 209.

As Don Mills took: Sewell, *The Shape of the City*, 95–96.

Without access to: Ibid., 177.

204 **Indeed, the story of Metro:** Colton, *Big Daddy*, 83.

Gardiner, as his biographer: Ibid., viii, 149.

So Premier Frost: Ibid., 66–71.

Toronto city council: TS, February 2, 26, 1953.

He had Irish: Colton, *Big Daddy*, 72–73.

"I knew I was": Cited in ibid., 79–80.

Gardiner was regularly: TS, January 5, 1959.

In one of Duncan: TS, December 7, 1958.

205 **"When he really":** Cited in Colton, *Big Daddy*, 105.

Gardiner's objectionable: Robert Fulford, *Best Seat in the House: Memoirs of a Lucky Man* (Toronto: Collins Publishers, 1988), 63.

"If the Americans": TT, June 6, 1958; TS, October 4, 1958; Colton, *Big Daddy*, 141–42.

He made things: Colton, *Big Daddy*, 82.

They considered it: Ibid., 21.

Both schools were: Conrad Black, *A Life in Progress* (Toronto: Key Porter, 1993), 12–19.

206 **Forest Hill culture:** John R. Seeley, R. Alexander Sim, and Elizabeth W. Loosley, *Crestwood Heights* (Toronto: University of Toronto Press, 1956).

The chief author: GM, January 26, 2008; Paul Roberts Bentley, "Martyr for Mental Health: John R. Seeley and the Forest Hill Village Project, 1948–1956" (PhD dissertation, Ontario Institute for Studies in Education, University of Toronto, 2013), 2–3, 96–98 (https://tspace.library.utoronto.ca/bitstream/1807/43489/1/Bentley_Paul_201311_EdD_thesis.pdf).

"Children Spoiled": TS, May 2, 1956; Marsh Jeanneret, *God and Mammon: Universities as Publishers* (Toronto: Macmillan of Canada, 1989), 111.

One reason the Jews: Richard Harris, *Creeping Conformity: How Canada Became Suburban, 1900–1960* (Toronto: University of Toronto Press, 2004), 89–90.

In 1951, 40 percent: Etan Diamond, "Sanctifying Suburban Space," in *The Canadian Jewish Studies Reader*, ed. Richard Menkis and Norman Ravvin (Calgary: Red Deer Press, 2004), 190–93, 196; Colton, *Big Daddy*, 43.

207 **"Our lives in the Forties":** Erna Paris, "Ghetto of the Mind: Forest Hill in the Fifties," *Toronto Live*, November 1972, cited in Kilbourn, *The Toronto Book*, 101–2, 104.

To Toronto Jews: Cited in Diamond, "Sanctifying Suburban Space," 186–87.

The city was: Newman, *Here Be Dragons*, 82.

In 1946, a Gallup poll: Nancy Tienhaara, *Canadian Views on Immigration and Population* (Ottawa: Manpower and Immigration, 1974), 59; Tulchinsky, *Branching Out*, 264.

The Toronto General Hospital: Friedland, *The University of Toronto*, 352.

Much to his dismay: Berton, *My Times*, 23–25.

Jazz drummer Archie Alleyne: TS, February 6, 2012.

A feature story: TS, February 21, 1959.

208 **When the bill abolishing:** McGibbon to Frost, February 17, 1950, and Frost to McGibbon, February 21, 1950, cited in Graham, *Old Man Ontario*, 262–65.

Despite efforts by: Tulchinsky, *Branching Out*, 277.

Frederick Gardiner, for instance: Colton, *Big Daddy*, 44.

As John Seeley: Seeley et al., *Crestwood Heights*, 307–8; Tulchinsky, *Branching Out*, 277–78.

209 **Phillips felt that:** Phillips, *Mayor of All the People*, 90–91.

During the campaign: Ibid., 98–99.

Equally as important: Ibid., 96–97; Siggins, *Bassett*, 124.

The *Globe and Mail* supported: GM, December 3, 4, 6, 15, 17, 24, 1954; Phillips, *Mayor of All the People*, 98.

The night before: Phillips, *Mayor of All the People*, 100–101.

Bitter about the: Leslie Howard Saunders, *An Orangeman in Public Life: The Memoirs of Leslie Howard Saunders* (Pickering, ON: Britannia Printers, 1980), 128.

210 **"Every person should":** TS, December 7, 1954.

Two decades later: TS, January 8, 1976.

In its assessment: Cited in Phillips, *Mayor of All the People*, 104.

And a year later: TS, December 6, 1955.

Though Nathan Phillips: Fulford, *Best Seat in the House*, 64.

He loved the attention: TS, January 8, 1976.

His suggestion that: Kilbourn, *Toronto Remembered*, 295.

211 **Phillips wanted to:** Phillips, *Mayor of All the People*, 105–15; Heritage Toronto website (www.heritagetoronto.org/).

Early in 1964: TS, February 27, 1964; Sam Kashner and Nancy Schoenberger, *Furious Love: Elizabeth Taylor, Richard Burton, and the Marriage of the Century* (New York: HarperCollins, 2010), 92–96.

In December 1955: TS, December 6, 1955, December 4, 1956; Phillips, *Mayor of All the People*, 115–16, 140–41; Mark Osbaldeston, *Unbuilt Toronto: A History of the City That Might Have Been* (Toronto: Dundurn, 2008), 84–90.

The 1956 election: TS, October 6, 1971.

The redevelopment necessitated by: Chan, *The Chinese in Toronto from 1878*, 105.

The businesses that: Ibid., 107–8, 110–11.

212 **Had Nathan Phillips:** Sewell, *The Shape of the City*, 139–40.

According to Rod McQueen: Rod McQueen, *The Eatons: The Rise and Fall of Canada's Royal Family* (Toronto: Stoddart, 1998), 164. See also TS, June 5, 1967; Osbaldeston, *Unbuilt Toronto*, 32–38; Siggins, *Bassett*, 172.

Plans for the new: Phillips, *Mayor of All the People*, 115–16.

Architectural students at: Osbaldeston, *Unbuilt Toronto*, 91.

Whether the criticisms: Ibid.

213 **Sadly, Revell died:** Ibid., 92–98; "Toronto City Hall: A Brief History," City of Toronto website (www.toronto.ca/city_hall_tour/history.htm).

The exception again: City of Toronto, "News Release Issued by the City of Toronto to Mark the 20th Anniversary of Toronto City Hall," September 9, 1985 (www.toronto.ca/city_hall_tour/city_hall_turns_twenty_page1.htm).

The large square: Fulford, *Accidental City*, 3.

By the time: Phillips, *Mayor of All the People*, 142–49; TS, January 9, 1976.

To complement his: TS, April 3, 2013; Kevin Plummer, "Historicist: Henry Moore's Big Bronze Whatchamacallit," TO, July 17, 2010 (http://torontoist.com/2010/07/historicist_henry_moores_big_bronze_whatchamacallit/).

Philip Givens, who: Plummer, "Historicist: Henry Moore's Big Bronze Whatchamacallit."

He negotiated with: Ibid.

The price for: GM, April 9, May 21, 1966; TS, April 3, 2013.

Several city councillors: GM, March 10, 17, 31,1966.

Determined, Givens raised: GM, April 1, May 21, 1966.

That was still: GM, June 23, 1966; Plummer, "Historicist: Henry Moore's Big Bronze Whatchamacallit."

In the end: GM, June 30, 1966; Plummer, "Historicist: Henry Moore's Big Bronze Whatchamacallit."

214 **"Posterity will remember":** GM, October 28, 1966.

For a while: GM, October 26, 1966.

Many voters believed: GM, March 19, 1966; Plummer, "Historicist: Henry Moore's Big Bronze Whatchamacallit."

The Archer might: John Warkentin, *Creating Memory: A Guide to Outdoor Sculpture in Toronto* (Toronto: Becker Associates and the City Institute at York University, 2010), 7; GM, November 25, December 6, 1966.

CHAPTER NINE: THE FASTEST-GROWING CITY IN NORTH AMERICA

215 **It was only below:** Phyllis Brett Young, *The Torontonians* (1960; Montreal and Kingston: McGill-Queen's University Press, 2007), 148.

If you were a "somebody": TS, September 9, 1963; GM, September 10, 1963; Jack Battan, *Honest Ed's Story* (Toronto: Doubleday Canada, 1972), 158–59.

216 **Capped off by:** TS, July 12, 2007; GM, July 12, 2007.

It also later connected: Martin Knelman, "Giving Was Ed's Business," TS, July 12, 2007; author's interview with David Mirvish, January 28, 2013.

His *bris* or ritual: TS, July 12, 2007.

217 **David soon opened:** GM, July 12, 2007.

"We were broke": TS, February 18, 1963.

"Never give credit": TS, July 12, 2007.

He found a job: Battan, *Honest Ed's Story*, 56–59.

At the Sport Bar: Ibid., 61–62.

Among Italian women: Iacovetta, *Such Hardworking People*, 77.

Mirvish struck gold: David Olive, "Ed Mirvish Put Show in Retail Business," TS, July 12, 2007, B1.

The Toronto police: GM, July 12, 2007.

218 **Yet another clever:** Author's interview with David Mirvish.

In July 2013: TS, July 16, October 27, 2013

Mirvish paid $215,000: TS, July 12, 2007; Battan, *Honest Ed's Story*, 151–57.

219 **The Queen was impressed:** GM, July 12, 2007.

"What would the": Richard Ouzonian, "Mirvish Set the Scene for Success," TS, July 12, 2007, E1.

"Behind everything he": Trent Frayne, "Conn Smythe: That Man in the Greens," *Maclean's*, January 15, 1952, 18; McParland, *The Lives of Conn Smythe*, 267.

220 **The change required:** McParland, *The Lives of Conn Smythe*, 298–99.

Not only did: Ibid. 288–89, 303–4.

"He was forty": Punch Imlach with Scott Young, *Hockey Is a Battle: Punch Imlach's Own Story* (Toronto: Macmillan of Canada, 1969), ix.

Stafford united with: Thomas Stafford Smythe with Kevin Shea, *Centre Ice: The Smythe Family, the Gardens and the Toronto Maple Leafs Hockey Club* (Bolton, ON: Fenn Publishing, 2000), 43–44.

The elder Smythe: Ibid., 45; McParland, *The Lives of Conn Smythe*, 318.

According to Stafford's son: Smythe with Shea, *Centre Ice*, 45.

221 **The Fab Four:** TS, September 8, 1964.

Within three years: Smythe with Shea, *Centre Ice*, 47.

Baun refused to quit: TS, April 24, 26, 1964.

Imlach was accused: TS, May 3, 1967.

He later claimed: Imlach with Young, *Hockey Is a Battle*, 114–16.

Imlach, with lots: "The Big M: The Life and Times of Frank Mahovlich," CBC *Life and Times* (www.cbc.ca/lifeandtimes/mahovlich.html).

It happened a: TS, November 3, 1967, April 6, 2012.

222 **The team's two:** TS, May 3, 1967.

The year after that: Smythe with Shea, *Centre Ice*, 107–8; Siggins, *Bassett*, 100–101.

A few weeks later: Smythe with Shea, *Centre Ice*, 109, 114–15; Siggins, *Bassett*, 101.

The ordeal of: Smythe with Shea, *Centre Ice*, 115–16; TS, October 13, 1971.

223 **True to form:** TS, April 12, 1990.

Owing to what: Smythe with Shea, *Centre Ice*, 105–6.

For the next two decades: TS, April 12, 1990. Ballard's interview with Barbara Frum and Dick Beddoes on the CBC radio program *As It Happens* in March 1979 is available online at CBC Digital Archives (www.cbc.ca/archives/categories/arts-entertainment/media/barbara-frum-pioneering-broadcaster/frum-firm-as-canadas-favourite-broad-caster.html).

"In one of the greatest": TS, March 5, 1979.

In the fifties: Newman, *Here Be Dragons*, 85.

In 1960, Diefenbaker: Siggins, *Bassett*, 130; Dempson, *Assignment Ottawa*, 118.

224 **Ironically, it was:** Levine, *Scrum Wars*, 201.

During the 1957 general: Ibid., 185.

His opponent John Diefenbaker: Paul Rutherford, *When Television Was Young: Prime Time Canada, 1952–1967* (Toronto: University of Toronto Press, 1982), 170–71.

Newspaper editors: GM, September 5, 1952; Hayes, *Power and Influence*, 39.

"Undoubtedly television": GM, September 10, 1952.

The editors merely: Rutherford, *When Television Was Young*, 49.

One Sunday in May 1958: "Kings of Comedy: 50th Anniversary of Wayne and Shuster," *The National Magazine*, CBC-TV, October 4, 1996.

One of the best lines: Wayne and Shuster, "Rinse the Blood Off My Toga," transcription at the Informal Music website, Later Latin Society homepage (www.informalmusic.com/latinsoc/rinse.html); *Montreal Gazette*, July 2, 1988; GM, August 11, 2009.

225 **When Frank reviewed:** Marc Glassman, "Wayne and Shuster: Duo Were Canada's Comedy Ambassadors," *Playback*, May 26, 2008.

In March 1963: Rutherford, *When Television Was Young*, 214.

"You know, there's more: "Kings of Comedy: 50th Anniversary of Wayne and Shuster."

More than once: Siggins, *Bassett*, 200–201.

226 **"Toronto was the":** Cited in Michael Nolan, *CTV: The Network That Means Business* (Edmonton: University of Alberta Press, 2001), 88.

During the decade: Fulford, *Best Seat in the House*, 120–21.

Around the *Star*: Newman, *Here Be Dragons*, 270.

Peter C. Newman: Ibid., 45.

On Saturdays in 1970: Ibid., 266–76; Siggins, *Bassett*, 160, 173.

The newsroom, recalled: Cited in Michael Thomas, "Good Stuff, Kid," *Ryerson Review of Journalism*, Summer 2013 (www.rrj.ca/m27726/).

Bassett decided to: Siggins, *Bassett*, 164–65.

227 **Continuing labour troubles:** Ibid., 176–77; Carriere, "An Officer and a Journalist."

Bassett's son John: Siggins, *Bassett*, 173–74, 180–82.

"We are told": Cited in Jean Sonmor, *The Little Paper That Grew: Inside The Toronto Sun Publishing Corporation* (Toronto: Toronto Sun, 1993), 26.

The Guild wanted: GM, September 20, 1971; Sonmor, *The Little Paper That Grew*, 26.

As for the *Tely*'s employees: *Toronto Sun*, November 1, 1996.

228 **"I went to Haight-Ashbury":** The Beatles, *The Beatles Anthology* (San Francisco: Chronicle Books, 2000), 259.

***Globe and Mail* writer Michael Valpy:** Stuart Henderson, *Making the Scene: Yorkville and Hip Toronto in the 1960s* (Toronto: University of Toronto Press, 2011), 236.

229 **In an investigation:** "Yorkville: Hippie Haven," CBC *Newsmagazine*, September 4, 1967, online at CBC Digital Archives (www.cbc.ca/archives/categories/society/youth/hippie-society-the-youth-rebellion/yorkville-hippie-haven.html); Henderson, *Making the Scene*, 172–73.

The story of Yorkville: Bernie Finkelstein, *True North: A Life in the Music Business* (Toronto: McClelland & Stewart, 2012), 42.

Yorkville, a less-than-desirable: TS, June 10, 1965; Henderson, *Making the Scene*, 39–42, 118.

There is no disputing: Nicholas Jennings, *Before the Gold Rush: Flashbacks to the Dawn of the Canadian Sound* (Toronto: Viking, 1997), 21; Finkelstein, *True North*, 42; Nicholas Jennings, "The Riverboat Coffeehouse," NicholasJennings.com, (www.nicholasjennings.com/magazine-articles/the-riverboat-coffehouse).

"The heavy concentration": Colleen Riley Roberts, *The Life and Times of a Single Woman* (Bloomington, IN: Authorhouse, 2005), 82–83.

Berton was castigated: "Pierre Berton's Page: It's Time We Stopped Hoaxing the Kids about Sex," *Maclean's*, May 18, 1963, 66; Berton, *My Times*, 240–48; Brian McKillop, *Pierre Berton: A Biography* (Toronto: Random House of Canada, 2011), 395–97.

230 **So it was hardly surprising:** Pierre Berton, *1967: The Last Good Year* (Toronto: Doubleday Canada, 1997), 173; "Streetsyle: 27 Looks at the Ladies who Lunch in Yorkville," TL, June 8, 2012 (www.torontolife.com/daily/style/toronto-street-style/2012/06/08/toronto-street-style-yorkville-ladies-who-lunch/).

Yorkville had lost: GM, August 4, 5, 1961; Henderson, *Making the Scene*, 54–55.

A few months later: TS, May 1962; Henderson, *Making the Scene*, 55.

On the night: GM, April 10, 1965.

"This is what I remember": Dave Bidini, *On a Cold Road: Tales of Adventure in Canadian Rock* (Toronto: McClelland & Stewart, 1998), 260; Gillian Mitchell, *The North American Folk Music Revival: Nation and Identity in the United States and Canada, 1945–1980* (Surrey, UK: Ashgate, 2007), 125; Jake Schabas, "Throwback Thursday: Yorkville and the Death of Toronto's First Scene," *Spacing Toronto*, June 25, 2009 (http://spacingtoronto.ca/2009/06/25/throwback-thursday-yorkville-and-the-death-of-torontos-first-scene/).

As the drug culture: TS, July 2, 1965; GM, December 16, 1965.

A fistfight between: GM, May 30, 1966; Henderson, *Making the Scene*, 138–41.

231 **A year later:** TS, April 5, May 31, 1967; GM, November 4, 1967.

In mid-August 1967: TS, June 3, 2007; June Callwood, "Digger House," in Mann, *The Underside of Toronto*, 126–27; Henderson, *Making the Scene*, 151.

At a memorable meeting: GM, August 18, 1967.

Three days later: GM, August 21, 1967; Callwood, "Digger House," 123–28.

"We failed in Yorkville": GM, November 4, 1967.

232 **The hippies soon:** Henderson, *Making the Scene*, 213.

"Yorkville today is": TS, June 3, 2007.

E.P. Taylor's Don Mills: Lemon, *Toronto Since 1918*, 136; Edmund Faltermayer, "Toronto, the New Great City," *Fortune Magazine*, September 1974, 137.

Shopping plazas with separate: Sewell, *The Shape of the City*, 112–14.

Yorkdale's genesis began: Kevin Plummer, "Historicist: Yorkdale Mall and the Aesthetics of Commerce," TO, February 25, 2012 (http://torontoist.com/2012/02/historicist-instant-downtown-uptown); Lemon, *Toronto Since 1918*, 136.

233 **The proposed Spadina Expressway:** Plummer, "Historicist: Yorkdale Mall and the Aesthetics of Commerce"; Colton, *Big Daddy*, 141.

The development was: William Zeckendorf with Edward McCreary, *The Autobiography of William Zeckendorf* (New York: Holt, Rinehart and Winston, 1970), 194; James Lorimer, *The Developers* (Toronto: Lorimer, 1978), 35–36.

Trizec, minus Zeckendorf: "Trizec Corporation History," at the corporate website (www.fundinguniverse.com/company-histories/trizec-corporation-ltd-history/); Jay P. Pederson, *International Directory of Company Histories*, vol. 97 (Farmington Hills, MI: Gale, 2008), 10.

The $40-million: TS, February 27, 1964; TT, February 27, 1964; GM, February 27, 1964.

"It's Instant Downtown": Cited in Plummer, "Historicist: Yorkdale Mall and the Aesthetics of Commerce."

234 **The most sensible:** Alison Hymas, "Yorkdale's Interiors: Comments," *Journal of the Royal Architectural Institute of Canada* 42 (June 1965): 51; Plummer, "Historicist: Yorkdale Mall and the Aesthetics of Commerce."

In April 2013: "Yorkdale Shopping Centre Announces $331 Million Expansion," Yorkdale news release, April 8, 2013 (http://yorkdale.com/wp-content/uploads/2013/04/Yorkdale-Expansion-Announcement_REVISED.pdf).

Completed in 1967: Bliss, *Northern Enterprise*, 491; Sewell, *The Shape of the City*, 119.

Indeed, Toronto's skyline: Richard J. Needham, *Boom Town Metro* (Toronto: *Toronto Daily Star*, 1978), 2.

Finally, the Bank of Montreal: Bianco, *The Reichmanns*, 342–55.

235 **At Toronto city hall:** Ibid., 346; TS, February 9, 1971.

Ironically, Fred Eaton: McQueen, *The Eatons*, 194.

The company needed: TS, February 6, April 10, May 19, 1971; McQueen, *The Eatons*, 193–94.

There was much: TS, February 6, 1977; GM, February 11, 1977.

Upstanding Torontonians: Mike Doherty, "Soundscape," NP, March 19, 2011.

236 **In the midst of the clubs:** GM, September 27, 2012.

Still, Yonge had become: GM, July 5, 1975; TS, February 7, 9, 1977; Christina McCall, *My Life as a Dame: The Personal and Political Writings of Christina McCall*, ed. Stephen Clarkson (Toronto: House of Anansi Press, 2008), 120–28.

Full nudity was: NP, March 19, 2011.

The Zanzibar's motto: Edward Brown, "Meanwhile Up on the Zanzibar's Roof," TO, November 24, 2010 (http://torontoist.com/2010/11/zanzibar_women_roof_photos/).

Even Union Station: Pierre Berton, "A Feeling, an Echo: The Life of Union Station," in Kilbourn, *The Toronto Book*, 228.

In December 1968: Osbaldeston, *Unbuilt Toronto*, 45–48.

Predictably, city council: Sewell, *Up against City Hall*, 99–102; Osbaldeston, *Unbuilt Toronto*, 48–50.

237 **"The decision to terminate":** Cited in Graham, *Old Man Ontario*, 357. See also Denis Smith, *Rogue Tory: The Life and Legend of John G. Diefenbaker* (Toronto: Macfarlane Walter & Ross, 1995), 308–9, 319–23.

The day after: TS, February 21, 1959; GM, February 21, 23, 25, 1959; TT, February 21, 1959; Smith, *Rogue Tory*, 320, 636 n.158.

The perception that Diefenbaker: Smith, *Rogue Tory*, 323–25.

More than two thousand: *Montreal Gazette*, February 25, 1959; GM, February 25, 1959; Michael Bliss, "Shutting Down the Avro Myth," *Report on Business Magazine* 5, 8 (February 1989): 29, 31.

238 **But the myth:** Bliss, *Northern Enterprise*, 476–77.

The trio hatched: Newman, *Here Be Dragons*, 261–63.

CHAPTER TEN: JANE'S DISCIPLES

239 **Before the real city:** Michael Ondaatje, *In the Skin of a Lion* (Toronto: McClelland & Stewart, 1987), 29.

"If you are going to make": Cited in Sewell, *Up against City Hall*, 25.

240 **Going against the:** *New York Times*, November 5, 1961.

"Like a construction gang": *New York Times*, April 25, 2006.

"It was as if": Cited in Fulford, *Accidental City*, 76.

A bit of a loner: Sewell, *Up against City Hall*, 67; Graham Fraser, *Fighting Back: Urban Renewal in Trefann Court* (Toronto: Hakkert, 1972), 7; Kilbourn, *Toronto Remembered*, 104–5; Victor L. Russell, "David Crombie: Remaking Toronto," in *Your Worship: The Lives of Eight of Canada's Most Unforgettable Mayors*, ed. Allan Levine (Toronto: Lorimer, 1989), 104–5.

241 **"Our houses are old":** Cited in Fraser, *Fighting Back*, 70.

It was later: Ibid., 77.

The *Star*'s columnist: TS, March 6, 9, 1965.

Unwilling to back: Sewell, *Up against City Hall*, 15–16.

John Sewell became involved: Ibid., 17–18.

242 **He and his fellow:** Ibid., 27, 30.

It was audacious: Albert Rose, *Governing Metropolitan Toronto: A Social and Political Analysis* (Berkeley: University of California Press, 1972), 139.

243 **Construction of the:** Danielle Robinson, "Modernism at a Crossroad: The Spadina Expressway Controversy in Toronto, Ontario ca. 1960–1971," *Canadian Historical Review* 92, 2 (June 2011): 303; "Allen (Spadina) Expressway," Get Toronto Moving Transportation Committee (www.gettorontomoving.ca/Allen_Expressway.html).

In his last: Colton, *Big Daddy*, 145, 172; TS, November 1, 1961, December 13, 1961; GM, December 13, 1961.

To mark Canada's: "History of Rathnelly," Toronto Neighbourhood Guide website (www.torontoneighbourhoods.net/neighbourhoods/midtown/rathnelly/history); NP, July 7, 2012.

244 **Its leading proponents:** Robinson, "Modernism at a Crossroad," 306–7; GM, March 14, 1970.

Well-connected and creative: City of Toronto Archives, Colin Vaughan fonds, series 427, file 6, "Stop Spadina Committee, 1970"; Robinson, "Modernism at a Crossroad," 308.

Better still, Jacobs: GM, October 16, 1970; GM, February 5, 1969.

The well-organized: TS, January 23, 1970.

Urban intellectuals and activists: TS, February 21, 1970; Robinson, "Modernism at a Crossroad," 311.

"The crux of the": GM, February 17, 1970.

At the *Star*: Newman, *Here Be Dragons*, 272.

245 **Still, Ontario premier John:** GM, March 11, 1970.

They hired John: Rose, *Governing Metropolitan Toronto*, 138–39; TS, February 17, 1971.

An affable "Red Tory": Carolyn Hughes Tuohy, "Red Tory Redux," NP, April 4, 2011.

He wasted little: Author's interview with Bill Davis, September 17, 2012; NP, April 4, 2011.

"If we are": GM, June 4, 1971.

McMurtry, an old friend: Roy McMurtry to the author, May 22, 2013; Adam Vaughan, "City Father: Adam Vaughan on Colin Vaughan," TL, March 2000, 82.

246 **Reaction across the city:** TS, June 4, 1971.

Members of the Stop: Ibid.; Vaughan, "City Father," 82.

Dennis Lee wrote: Dennis Lee, "The Day We Stopped Spadina," in *The City: Attacking Modern Myths*, ed. Alan T.R. Powell (Toronto: McClelland & Stewart, 1972), 114.

The Frederick Gardiner era: Colton, *Big Daddy*, 180.

After a few more: "Allen (Spadina) Expressway," Get Toronto Moving Transportation Committee.

"Not that I'm": "Editor's Letter: The Real Spadina Expressway Legacy," TL, September 2011, 18.

247 **He paid attention:** Robinson, "Modernism at a Crossroad," 320. See also Gerald Killan and George Warecki, "The Algonquin Wildlands League and the Emergence of Environmental Politics in Ontario, 1965–1974,"*Environmental History Review* 16, 4 (Winter 1992): 1–27.

There were scandals: John Wilson, "Ontario Political Culture at the End of the Century" in *Revolution at Queen's Park: Essays on Governing Ontario*, ed. Sidney Noel (Toronto: Lorimer, 1997), 60–64.

Crombie was indeed: Russell, "David Crombie: Remaking Toronto," 107–9; Sewell, *The Shape of the City*, 182; Fulford, *Accidental City*, 65.

"For years": Fulford, *Accidental City*, 64.

Crombie had learned: Russell, "David Crombie: Remaking Toronto," 108.

It was idealistic: GM, November 9, 18, 1972; Russell, "David Crombie: Remaking Toronto," 110.

248 **"We knew in the late 60s":** Tomasz Bugajsk, "David Crombie on Toronto's Mayoral Race," Blog TO, July 9, 2010 (www.blogto.com/city/2010/07/david_crombie_on_torontos_mayoral_race/).

As the new mayor: Graham Fraser, "Toronto's Quiet Revolutionary," *Montreal Gazette*, February 17, 1979.

For the next six: Russell, "David Crombie: Remaking Toronto," 101.

It was not by: Anthony Astrachan, "A City That Works," *Harper's*, December 1974, 14–19.

Like a well-prepared: Russell, "David Crombie: Remaking Toronto," 120–23.

His motto, which: Ibid., 121; author's interview with David Crombie, January 29, 2013.

Nevertheless, developers were: Sewell, *The Shape of the City*, 183; Bianco, *The Reichmanns*, 346; Faltermayer, "Toronto, the New Great City," 137.

Four decades later: Author's interview with David Crombie.

249 **It took vision:** Fulford, *Accidental City*, 84; author's interview with John Sewell, September 13, 2012.

It required two years: J. David Hulchanski, "Planning New Urban Neighbourhoods: Lessons from Toronto's St. Lawrence Neighbourhood," University of British Columbia Planning Papers, no. 28, September 1990.

No one could: Russell, "David Crombie: Remaking Toronto," 115–20; Toronto Community Housing website (www.torontohousing.ca).

"He grabbed many": Author's interview with John Sewell.

Crombie has fond: Author's interview with David Crombie.

250 **Yet he did not see:** Author's interview with John Sewell. In early 2013, after two *Globe and Mail* articles portrayed Sewell as a "famously radical former mayor" and "arguably Toronto's most leftist mayor," he fired off a letter to the editor listing his many achievements. "The support of the electorate [in the 1978 and 1980 municipal elections] speaks well for my ability as mayor to serve the public in a balanced way," he wrote. GM, January 28, February 2, February 6, 2013.

He insists that: Author's interview with John Sewell.

"The first walk": Ibid.

On election day: GM, November 14, 1978.

Indeed, Sewell was: Graham Fraser, "Toronto's Quiet Revolutionary," *Montreal Gazette*, February 17, 1979.

251 **"I don't know":** Author's interview with Paul Godfrey, October 22, 2012.

Working closely with Labatt: TS, October 8, 1985, June 28, 2008; NP, December 1, 2008; "Postmedia Network Canada Corp. Completes Acquisition of Canwest Publishing Print and Online Assets," Postmedia news release, July 13, 2010 (www.postmedia.com/2010/07/13/postmedia-network-canada-corp-completes-acquisition-of-canwest-publishing-print-and-online-assets/).

Thirty years later: TS, June 28, 2008.

"As we came on": Author's interview with Paul Godfrey.

"I think we can": GM, November 14, 1978.

According to Jean Sonmor: Sonmor, *The Little Paper That Grew*, 114.

252 **Godfrey could and:** GM, January 9, 1979; Fraser, "Toronto's Quiet Revolutionary."

For decades the: GM, October 5, 1937; Sally Gibson, "Sense of Place—Defence of Place: A Case Study of the Toronto Island" (PhD dissertation, University of Toronto, 1981), 137–38.

Questions about the: Gibson, *More Than an Island*, 240–41.

At public meetings: Ibid. 275–76.

One of those: R.B. Fleming, *Peter Gzowski: A Biography* (Toronto: Dundurn, 2010), 134.

253 **On Dominion Day:** GM, July 2, 1980; Gibson, *More Than an Island*, 289–90.

Three weeks later: GM, July 2, 1980.

The islanders had been: TS, July 29, 1980; GM, July 29, 1980.

To say that Godfrey: GM, December 10, 1981.

The fight continued: See "Toronto Islands Residential Community Trust," at the Toronto Island Community website (http://torontoisland.org/Trust).

254 **Among numerous controversial:** Justice Samuel G.M. Grange, *Report of the Royal Commission of Inquiry into Certain Deaths at the Hospital for Sick Children and Related Matters* (Toronto: Ontario Ministry of the Attorney General, 1984), 49–152 (http://archive.org/stream/reportofsickkids00onta#page/n3/mode/2up).

Following autopsies: Gavin Hamilton, *The Nurses Are Innocent: The Digoxin Poisoning Fallacy* (Toronto: Dundurn, 2011), 17–18. While Dr. Hamilton's theory has not been officially confirmed, it is widely accepted by medical authorities. See I. Ralph Edwards, "Lethal, Odd and 'New' in Pharmacovigilance," *Upsala Reports* (World Health Organization) 61 (April 2013): 10; author's interview with Dr. Gavin Hamilton, February 7, 2014.

At the time: GM, April 4, 2007.

More than a year: Grange, *Report of the Royal Commission of Inquiry into Certain Deaths at the Hospital for Sick Children*, 213.

Nevertheless, police chief: GM, April 20, 1983.

And as the Grange inquiry: GM, September 6, 1984.

More than three decades: Hamilton, *The Nurses Are Innocent*, 71–84, 172–84; Peter Bowal and Kelsey Horvat, "What Happened to the Prosecution of Susan Nelles," *LawNow*, September/October 2011, 55–60 (www.lawnow.org/d/sites/default/files/LN361FamousCases.pdf); Brian Bethune, "The Baby Killer at Toronto's Sick Kids Was Rubber," *Maclean's*, December 22, 2011 (www2.macleans.ca/tag/susan-nelles/).

255 **On the night of:** Catherine Jean Nash, "Contesting Identity: Politics of Gays and Lesbians in Toronto in the 1970s," *Gender, Place and Culture* 12, 1 (March 2005): 126.

There they found: GM, August 27, 28, 1979.

There are differing accounts: GM, August 27, 28, 29, 1979.

Another questionable shooting: GM, August 10, 1978, October 4, 5, 1979.

256 **This was a reflection:** John Sewell, *Urban Policing in Canada* (Toronto: Lorimer, 1985), 114–15. See also Clayton James Mosher, *Discrimination and Denial: Systemic Racism in Ontario's Legal and Criminal Justice Systems, 1892–1961* (Toronto: University of Toronto Press, 1998); Charles C. Smith, *Crisis, Conflict and Accountability: The Impact and Implications of Police Racial Profiling* (Toronto: African Canadian Coalition on Racial Profiling, March 2004), 1–3.

All too representative: GM, March 21, 1979.

In the case of: *Montreal Gazette*, March 22, 28, 1979; GM, March 21, 1979; Nash, "Contesting Identity: Politics of Gays and Lesbians in Toronto in the 1970s," 113.

The *Toronto Sun*: *Toronto Sun*, March 29, 1979; Nash, "Contesting Identity: Politics of Gays and Lesbians in Toronto in the 1970s," 123.

"Being Black in": Frances Henry, *The Caribbean Diaspora in Toronto: Learning to Live with Racism* (Toronto: University of Toronto Press, 1994), 258.

Or, put another way: Sheila L. Croucher, "Constructing the Image of Ethnic Harmony in Toronto, Canada: The Politics of Problem Definition and Nondefinition," *Urban Affairs Review* 32 (January 1997): 327–28.

Despite Ontario human: Martin O'Malley, "Blacks in Toronto," in Mann, *The Underside of Toronto*, 131–33.

The police were accused: GM, September 11, 1979; Sewell, *Urban Policing in Canada*, 115; Henry, *The Caribbean Diaspora in Toronto*, 188–91; author's interview with Henry Gomez, October 24, 2012.

257 **Two incidents stand:** Author's interview with Michael Thompson, October 24, 2012.

Albert Johnson's family: GM, September 17, 1979.

In the aftermath: "A Short History of Community Organizing against Police Brutality in Toronto: The History of B.A.D.C. and Beyond," *BasicsNews.ca*, March 21, 2008 (http://basicsnews.ca/2008/03/a-short-history-of-community-organizing-against-police-brutality-in-toronto-the-history-of-b-a-d-c-and-beyond/); GM, October 15, 1979.

By early September: GM, September 7, 1979.

258 **A few days later:** GM, September 11, 18, 1979.

After his anger: GM, September 12, 17, 1979; TS, September 18, 1979; Nash, "Contesting Identity: Politics of Gays and Lesbians in Toronto in the 1970s," 126–27.

Cardinal Carter's report: TS, October 30, 1979; GM, October 30, 31, 1979; "Report to the Civic Authorities of Metropolitan Toronto and its Citizens, Cardinal G. Emmett Carter, for the Municipality of Metropolitan Toronto" (Toronto, 1979); Toronto Police Service, *Policing a World Within a City: The Race Relations Initiatives of the Toronto Police Service*, January 2003, at the Toronto Police website (www.torontopolice.on.ca/publications/files/reports/2003.02.13-policingaworldwithinacity.pdf).

According to Sewell: Sewell, *Urban Policing in Canada*, 115; author's interview with John Sewell.

Between 1980 and: See Gabriella Pedicelli, *When Police Kill: Police Use of Force in Montreal and Toronto* (Montreal: Véhicule Press, 1998), 64; Smith, *Crisis, Conflict and Accountability*, 4–5; TS, October 26, 2002; "Factsheet on Police Containment of and Violence in the African Community" compiled by Dr. Ajamu Nangwaya, Toronto Media Co-Op website, February 7, 2011 (http://toronto.mediacoop.ca/blog/ajamu-nangwaya/6183).

In 2002: TS, October 19, 2004, January 18, 2005, October 18, 2006.

More than a decade: TS, May 14, 2013.

259 **As the federal justice:** John English, *Citizen of the World: The Life of Pierre Elliott Trudeau*, vol. 1, *1919–1968* (Toronto: Random House, 2009), 447.

At the time, gays: As late as 1964, journalist Sidney Katz, writing in *Maclean's* in an article entitled "The Homosexual Next Door," observed that "the homosexual is rarely the weird sex monster so often depicted in psychiatric case histories, police records and lurid fiction... The vast majority are industrious, law-abiding citizens with regular jobs—some of them positions of great responsibility... The average homosexual is a much maligned individual, unfairly discriminated against by our laws and society." Cited in Scott Steele and Mary Nemeth, "Coming Out: The State Is out of the Bedroom, But after 25 Years, Old Attitudes Still Linger," *Maclean's*, May 16, 1994, 40–43.

The trial took: GM, January 4, 1979; Nash, "Contesting Identity: Politics of Gays and Lesbians in Toronto in the 1970s," 113–14.

Six months after: GM, December 11, 1978, January 4, 1979; Nash, "Contesting Identity: Politics of Gays and Lesbians in Toronto in the 1970s," 113–14.

Among those charged: TS, December 20, 2005.

260 **The main point:** GM, January 4, 1979.

The *Globe and Mail*'s editors: GM, January 5, 1979.

Less tactful was: Fraser, "Toronto's Quiet Revolutionary"; author's interview with John Sewell.

One widely publicized: GM, May 12, 24, 1980.

His real problem: TS, May 2, 1991; author's interview with Art Eggleton, October 22, 2012; author's interview with Paul Godfrey.

Sewell's "passions persuaded": GM, September 18, 1979.

261 **During the 1980:** Sewell, *Urban Policing in Canada*, 198; author's interview with John Sewell.

John Piper, Sewell's campaign: GM, November 11, 1980.

CHAPTER ELEVEN: THIS IS WHERE IT'S AT

262 **They're jealous of:** TS, March 9, 2002.

One of editor-in-chief: Hayes, *Power and Influence*, 49, 67–69.

Still, like Toronto: Ibid., 107–8.

263 **As executive editor:** Cited in ibid., 157.

Nonetheless, there was acrimony: Ibid., 171–257; *Wall Street Journal*, August 10, 1989; CanWest News, December 16, 1991; *Financial Post*, December 19, 1991.

Within eight years: Hayes, *Power and Influence*, 219; Doyle, *Hurly-Burly*, 415–19; TS, April 25, 1991; *Ottawa Citizen*, January 25, 1992.

The chief innovator: Fulford, *Best Seat in the House*, 148; "Peter C. Newman," in Writers' Trust of Canada, *A Writer's Life: The Margaret Laurence Lectures* (Toronto: Random House of Canada, 2011), 403.

"I tried desperately": Newman, *Here Be Dragons*, 82.

264 **A year later:** Levine, *Scrum Wars*, 256–57.

Hal Dornan: Cited in ibid., 257.

"As editor-in-chief": Newman, *Here Be Dragons*, 268.

The trouble was: Ibid., 269–70, 275–76; author's interview with Peter C. Newman.

The monthly magazine: Author's interview with Peter C. Newman; Newman, *Here Be Dragons*, 353–55.

265 **"People who worked":** Fulford, *Best Seat in the House*, 150.

He had to fill: Newman, *Here Be Dragons*, 378.

His overall plan: Suzy Aston and Sue Ferguson, "*Maclean's*: The First 100 Years," on the *Maclean's* website (www2.macleans.ca/about-macleans/macleans-the-first-100-years/).

Though *Maclean's* was: Newman, *Here Be Dragons*, 361.

He was, in the: Ibid., 375–76; Aston and Ferguson, "*Maclean's*: The First 100 Years."

The corporate bosses: Newman, *Here Be Dragons*, 461; Val Ross, "With Strategy, Style and a Sweeping Sense of History," GM, October 12, 1991.

266 **He accompanied them:** Newman, *The Acquisitors*, 270–71; author's interview with Peter C. Newman.

Here's Newman: Newman, *The Acquisitors*, 259.

"The thing is that": McCall, *My Life as a Dame*, 139.

267 **In Newman's opinion:** Newman, *Here Be Dragons*, 86; Peter C. Newman, *The Canadian Revolution: From Deference to Defiance* (Toronto: Viking, 1995), 112.

They invited: TS, September 17, 1994; Peter C. Newman, *Titans: How the New Canadian Establishment Seized Power*, vol. 3 of *The Canadian Establishment* (Toronto: Viking, 1998), 121.

"I looked around": Author's interview with John Macfarlane. Still, this perception requires qualification. In a study conducted by Wallace Clement, a sociologist at Carleton University, in the mid-eighties, of 2,377 people in power in Canada, he found that the majority were still Anglos—cited in TS, November 3, 1985.

"If I was in": Andrew Sarlos, *Fireworks: The Investment of a Lifetime* (Toronto: Key Porter, 1993), 211.

268 **Each morning:** Newman, *The Acquisitors*, 161.

"Good traders": Cited in Peter C. Newman, "The Life and Death of Bay Street's Guru," *Maclean's*, May 12, 1997, 50.

When he died: Ibid.

A 1974 newspaper: GM, November 9, 1974.

More than three decades: Cited in Etan Vlessing, "Moses Znaimer—Television: TV Guru Revolutionized Small Screen," *Playback: Canada's Broadcast and Production Journal*, June 25, 2007, 36.

269 **In the late sixties:** GM, November 9, 1974; TS, July 26, 2009.

He later articulated: Vlessing, "Moses Znaimer," 36.

They raised $2 million: NP, September 22, 2012; "Genesis, Genius and Tumult at Citytv Recalled 40 Years On," *Broadcaster Magazine*, October 1, 2012.

Citytv was as: GM, November 9, 1974.

Znaimer made no apologies: GM, June 15, 1972.

270 **He spent the next:** Newman, *Titans*, 303.

A few years later: Vlessing, "Moses Znaimer," 36.

There was money: McCall, *My Life as a Dame*, 139.

At the University of Toronto: Jill Ker Conway, *True North: A Memoir* (New York: Knopf, 1994), 111–25.

At the same time: Friedland, *The University of Toronto*, 534–35, 540.

271 **McCall was a sharp critic:** McCall, *My Life as a Dame*, 162–66.

Several years later: GM, October 13, 1975.

Upon her death: Peter C. Newman, *Heroes: Canadian Champions, Dark Horses and Icons* (Toronto: HarperCollins, 2010), 72.

She attended the: McCall, *My Life as a Dame*, 21.

Pierre Berton, the magazine's: Berton, *My Times*, 47; McCall, *My Life as a Dame*, 43.

McCall ultimately became: McCall, *My Life as a Dame*, 1.

272 **After a dinner:** The story of the dinner is from Christina McCall, "Women and Political Power: What's Holding Us Back?" *Chatelaine*, December 1982, cited in McCall, *My Life as a Dame*, 182–84.

After she married: GM, April 16, 2007.

She was soon wooed: Sonmor, *The Little Paper That Grew*, 279–81; Diane Francis to author, February 11, 2014.

273 **Operating in an:** Rosemary Sexton, *Glitter Girls: Charity and Vanity Chronicles of an Era of Excess* (Toronto: Macmillan Canada, 1993), 1.

Among the group: See ibid., and Rosemary Sexton, "Tarnished crown?" *Maclean's*, June 16, 2005, 46–48.

In her book: Sexton, *Glitter Girls*, 66–73.

274 **In its day:** GM, September 8, 2012.

At the 1990 ball: Leah McLaren, "A Look Back at the Brazilian Ball, the Annual Black-Tie Extravaganza That Taught Toronto to Party," TL, August 14, 2012 (www.torontolife.com/daily/hype/print-edition/2012/08/14/the-last-hurrah-the-brazilian-ball/2/); Sexton, *Glitter Girls*, 26–40.

De Sousza died: TS, September 15, 2012.

275 **By 1984, there:** GM, September 25, 1984.

One of the first: Richard W. Pound, *Stikeman Elliott: The First Fifty Years* (Montreal and Kingston: McGill-Queen's University Press, 2002), 81.

By the mid-eighties: Lemon, *Toronto Since 1918*, 198.

"Until the West gets": Cited in Newman, *The Acquisitors*, 154.

It was "Canada's economic": GM, November 14, 1994.

Crime rates increased: TS, September 5, 2010; Nick Falvo, "Homelessness, Program Responses, and an Assessment of Toronto's Streets to Homes Program," *Canadian Policy Research Networks Research Report*, February 2009, 9–19 (www.cprn.org/documents/50981_EN.pdf).

276 **One of the victims:** GM, December 29, 1992; Newman, *The Canadian Revolution*, 112–14.

Using risky and pricey: GM, June 21, 1991, July 30, 1993; *Financial Post*, July 30, 1993; *Edmonton Journal*, July 31, 1993; "Divided Dynasties," *Maclean's*, September 6, 1993, 38–39; Newman, *The Canadian Revolution*, 114–16

While Eaton's chief: McQueen, *The Eatons*, 205.

The company lost: Ibid., 207, 211–13.

"The Eatons walked": TS, April 28, 1997.

277 **At a cost of:** GM, August 10, October 9, November 15, 1982; McQueen, *The Eatons*, 215–16.

The company was now: McQueen, *The Eatons*, 226.

According to business journalist: Ibid., 228.

"You can't run Eaton's": Cited in ibid., 228–29.

"We want to be your store": Cited in ibid., 256.

And the *Globe and Mail*: GM, March 1, 1997.

A $10-million dividend: Newman, *Titans*, 76.

278 **Controversy swirled around:** Black, *A Life in Progress*, 13–15.

He moved into: Black, *A Life in Progress*, 334–50.

279 **Thereafter, Newman liked:** Newman, *Here Be Dragons*, 418; Conrad Black, *A Matter of Principle* (Toronto: McClelland & Stewart, 2011), 315.

In the first volume: Black, *A Life in Progress*, 295.

Black's somewhat fond memories: Newman, *Here Be Dragons*, 417.

As for Newman: Ibid., 409–11.

Moreover, Black believed: Black, *A Matter of Principle*, 32–34.

Black's ownership: Black, *A Life in Progress*, 386.

280 **Ironically, in 2001:** Peter C. Newman, *Izzy: The Passionate Life and Turbulent Times of Izzy Asper, Canada's Media Mogul* (Toronto: HarperCollins, 2008), 291–321; author's interview with Christie Blatchford, July 19, 2012.

Even Peter C. Newman: Newman, *Here Be Dragons*, 415.

As for the criticism: Black, *A Matter of Principle*, 36.

In 1976, it was: Newman, *Here Be Dragons*, 411.

281 **"Economically speaking":** Roy MacSkimming, *The Perilous Trade: Publishing Canada's Writers* (Toronto: McClelland & Stewart, 2003), 1.

Or, as author Morley Callaghan: Cited in Bruce Whiteman, *Lasting Impressions: A Short History of English Publishing in Quebec* (Montreal: Véhicule Press, 1994), 65.

About the only subjects: Cited in McKillop, *Pierre Berton: A Biography*, 441.

"[I] doubt": John M. Gray, "Book Publishing," in *Writing in Canada: Proceedings of the Canadian Writers' Conference, Queen's University*, ed. George Whalley, July 28–31, 1955 (Toronto: Macmillan, 1956), 58.

His protégé, publisher: Cited in MacSkimming, *The Perilous Trade*, 118.

282 **McClelland adopted an:** James King, *Jack: A Life with Writers; The Story of Jack McClelland* (Toronto: Knopf, 1999), 173–74.

"He is a Canadian pioneer": Sam Solecki, ed., *Imagining Canadian Literature: The Selected Letters of Jack McClelland* (Toronto: Key Porter, 2002), 289.

Similarly, Margaret Atwood: Cited in King, *Jack: A Life with Writers*, 381.

When McKenzie Porter: McKillop, *Pierre Berton: A Biography*, 442–43.

With his flowing long: King, *Jack: A Life with Writers*, 72.

"Sometimes my day": Tim Heald, "A Day in the Life of Jack McClelland," *Weekend Magazine*, April 8, 1978, 12.

His zaniest: TS, September 21, 1996; King, *Jack: A Life with Writers*, 344–45.

283 **In one case:** Elspeth Cameron, "Adventures in the Book Trade," SN, November 1983, 37.

"There is little community": Speech on publishing, October 30, 1969, cited in King, *Jack: A Life with Writers*, 174–75.

"All my editorial life": Douglas Gibson, *Stories about Storytellers* (Toronto: ECW Press, 2011), 152; author's interview with Douglas Gibson, June 28, 2012.

284 **It was a great ploy:** TS, April 19, 1983; King, *Jack: A Life with Writers*, 363–64.

Eventually, McClelland: TS, December 31, 1985.

In 1994, he and: Newman, *Titans*, 311.

Chapters soon bought: MacSkimming, *The Perilous Trade*, 360–61; "Lichtman's Files for Bankruptcy Protection," CBC News, March 7, 2000 (www.cbc.ca/news/business/story/2000/03/07/lichtman000307.html).

285 **His family fended off:** John Lorinc, "Britnell IV: Century-Old Bookselling Institution Revived by a New Generation," *Quill & Quire*, June 1993, 1, 8; TS, January 29, 1999; GM, January 29, 1999.

"Publishers realized": MacSkimming, *The Perilous Trade*, 363–64.

The head of the company: Ibid., 377–83.

Schwartz's total income: Newman, *Titans*, 219.

In a 2005 *Toronto Life* magazine: Marci McDonald, "The Heather and Gerry Show," TL, June 2005, 56.

286 **Both he and Reisman:** When Marci McDonald was researching her feature article on Schwartz and Reisman for *Toronto Life* in 2005, she notes that she received this two-page missive from Schwartz: "You and the writer are hereby put on notice," it said, "that all records, notes and source documentation used in the course of preparing the proposed article must be maintained for litigation should this become necessary," ibid., 57.

By then, Schwartz had: Newman, *Izzy*, 85–109.

For a time, Heather: Newman, *Heroes*, 286–87; McDonald, "The Heather and Gerry Show," 59.

They were married: Newman, *Izzy*, 98–100.

Settling in Toronto: Michael Brown, "Heather Resiman," in *Jewish Women: A Comprehensive Historical Encyclopedia* at the Jewish Women's Archives website (http://jwa.org/encyclopedia/article/reisman-heather); McDonald, "The Heather and Gerry Show," 62.

After leaving Cott: GM, February 9, 1996, September 4, 1997.

287 **Unwilling to be:** McDonald, "The Heather and Gerry Show," 62–63.

They lived in a: TS, April 8, 2000; NP, May 21, 2001; McDonald, "The Heather and Gerry Show," 57.

At a ritzy Liberal: TS, December 10, 12, 2003; McDonald, "The Heather and Gerry Show," 57.

The dynamic duo: TS, August 28, 1999.

"It was heavy cream": Author's interview with Joanne Kates, October 23, 2012.

In those early days: Ibid.; Jamie Bradburn, "Historicist: Lord Simcoe's Folly," TO, August 20, 2011 (http://torontoist.com/2011/08/historicist_lord_simcoes_folly/).

288 **In general, food:** Author's interview with Joanne Kates; GM, May 26, 2012.

Or, as Kates put: GM, April 22, 1974.

Rota, who died: GM, October 12, 2012.

289 **Among the regulars:** Newman, *Here Be Dragons*, 348–51.

Marshall had two: GM, January 12, 2008; TS, January 12, 2008; Jules Ross, "Bill Marshall Interview," WILDSound website (www.wildsound-filmmaking-feedback-events.com/bill_marshall_interview.html); William Marshall, *Film Festival Confidential* (Toronto: McArthur & Company, 2005), 1.

Marshall forgave Eggleton: Marshall, *Film Festival Confidential*, 13.

As the festival's first: GM, September 6, 2000.

To the major movie: Bryan Johnson, ed., *TIFF: A Reel History, 1976–2012* (Toronto: *Globe and Mail*, 2012), 8; Marshall, *Film Festival Confidential*, 14.

290 **There were the usual:** GM, September 6, 2000.

In 2006, actor: TS, August 24, 2011.

The festival now: Ibid.

"The world knows": NP, May 31, 2012.

One of the highly touted: GM, January 6, September 18, October 24, 2012; NP, September 18, 2012.

The ninety-seven-minute: TS, February 20, 2013, January 20, 2014; NP, January 20, 2014.

Avrich concluded that: GM, September 13, 2012.

He had a typical: Garth Drabinsky, *Closer to the Sun* (Toronto: McClelland & Stewart, 1995), 13–15, 42.

291 **By all accounts:** Newman, *Titans*, 350–51; Anne Kingston, "The Illusionist," *Maclean's*, April 13, 2009, 30–33.

"He must win": Kingston, "The Illusionist," 31.

Within a few years: Drabinsky, *Closer to the Sun*, 141–49.

From the moment: Ibid., 111–12.

"No expense was": TS, September 3, 1989.

He was not: GM, September 21, 1989.

292 **There were snickers:** TS, October 2, 1993.

For months: Ibid., July 6, 1994.

From the moment: Drabinsky, *Closer to the Sun*, 474–75; TS, October 6, 1993.

The fact that everyone: *New York Times*, May 1, 1993; John Bemrose, "Roll On, Big River: Show Boat," *Maclean's*, November 1, 1993, 71–72; Drabinsky, *Closer to the Sun*, 475–87; *Ottawa Citizen*, March 26, 1995.

293 **"The theatre is not":** GM, May 17, 2012. Entrepreneur Aubrey Dan learned this lesson the hard way as well. In 2007 he launched his live theatre company, Dancap Productions, in Toronto with a $50-million investment; five years later he suspended operations after losing

about $40 million, despite the popularity of the musical *Jersey Boys*, his most profitable show. See GM, May 17, 2012.

"Livent itself was an": Kingston, "The Illusionist," 32.

Finally, after a two-month: NP, October 15, 2011.

At a parole hearing: GM, October 24, 2012.

He was more: TS, January 20, 2014.

You could read: "About *NOW*," *Now* website (www.nowtoronto.com/about/about.cfm); Kara Aaserud, "That Was Then, This Is *NOW*," *Ryerson Review of Journalism*, June 2003 (www.rrj.ca/m3804/); Rachel Horner, "Alice Klein," *On the Danforth*, July 19, 2009 (http://onthedanforth.ca/2009/07/19/alice-klein/).

294 **Stephen Dale, who wrote:** Aaserud, "That Was Then, This Is *NOW*."

"Its club listings": John Lorinc to author, May 23, 2013.

That was the same: GM, October 5, 1982.

He had grown up: Ibid.; Kevin Bazzana, *Glenn Gould: The Performer in the Work; A Study in Performance Practice* (Oxford: Clarendon Press, 1997), 1–5.

Typical was John Kraglund's: GM, March 31, 1955. See also Kraglund's review of another Gould concert with the TSO, GM, December 7, 1960.

Gould always followed: Glenn Gould and Jonathan Cott, *Conversations with Glenn Gould* (Chicago: University of Chicago Press, 2005), 11.

"The nut's a": Cited in ibid., 11, 132.

295 **Gould performed in the:** GM, October 5, 1982.

It is unlikely: GM, August 23, 1983.

"We are a great": "Richard Bradshaw of Canadian Opera Company Dies at 63," CBC, August 16, 2007 (www.cbc.ca/news/arts/music/story/2007/08/16/richard-bradshaw-obit.html?ref=rss).

Dedicated, passionate, and unrelenting: GM, August 18, 2007; NP, August 25, 2007.

The El Mocambo was hot: CBC News, November 5, 2001; GM, June 15, 2012.

296 **The band's drummer:** Heath McCoy, "Sympathy for the Devils: The Greatest Rolling Stones Scandals," *Calgary Herald*, October 26, 2005.

"I was the one": Ron Wood, *Ronnie* (London: Macmillan, 2007), 144.

The El Mocambo closed: TS, July 23, 2012.

"Frank had a huge influence": Cited in Brian D. Johnson, "A Comic 'Gold Standard,'" *Maclean's*, January 28, 2002, 52.

"There are very few": Cited in TS, June 20, 1999.

"They turned down": Johnson, "A Comic 'Gold Standard,'" 52.

297 **According to James Kaplan:** James Kaplan, "Paul Shaffer," *New Yorker*, January 16, 1989, 36.

***Godspell* featured a:** "Toronto's Legendary Production of *Godspell*," http://godspell.ca/stories.htm; David Kamp, "The Cat's Meow," *Vanity Fair*, January 2013, 107.

The generally cynical: GM, June 2, 1972; TS, June 2, 1972; *Toronto Sun*, June 2, 1972.

After he lost: Sheldon Kirshner, "Mark Breslin Brings Edge to Canada's Comedy Scene," *Canadian Jewish News*, March 1, 2012, 45.

"Comedy in Toronto": GM, August 28, 1976.

298 **Within two years:** Kirshner, "Mark Breslin Brings Edge to Canada's Comedy Scene," 45.

The ROM became: TS, July 13, 1990.

The debate was so: GM, October 17, 1990.

CHAPTER TWELVE: MULTICULTURALISM, MERGER AND MEL

299 **Toronto is:** Anne Michaels, *Fugitive Pieces* (Toronto: McClelland & Stewart, 1996), 89.

Bland was power: TS, June 19, 1988, November 10, 1989.

"You make Joe Clark": GM, November 9, 1982; TS, November 10, 1982.

300 **As Toronto's mayor:** Author's interview with Art Eggleton, October 22, 2012.

"He's dull and boring": TS, June 19, 1988.

Accused of being: TS, October 13, 1991; author's interview with Art Eggleton.

Liberal in his: TS, December 31, 1986.

On November 8, 1982: GM, November 9, 1982.

By inclination: GM, August 22, 2011.

"Oh, you're Jack": John Geddes, "The Making of Jack Layton," *Maclean's*, June 27, 2011, 24.

301 **In 1970, for:** Keith Whitney, "Skid Row," in Mann, *The Underside of Toronto*, 66.

Layton, who spent: Jack Layton, *Homelessness: How to End the National Crisis* (Toronto: Penguin Canada, 2008), 67, 167–68.

In one of many: "The Blueprint to End Homelessness in Toronto," Wellesley Institute, 2006, 2 (http://tdrc.net/uploads/file/blueprint_short_(final_02).pdf).

Toronto's politicians and newspapers: "Inquest into the Death of Drina Joubert: Verdict of Coroner's Jury," February 25, 1986, Canadian Urban Policy Archive at the Centre for Urban and Community Studies website (www.urbancentre.utoronto.ca/pdfs/policyarchives/1986DrinaJoubert.pdf); TS, January 10, 1999.

"The homeless, the hungry": TS, November 19, 1989.

302 **The former mayor:** Author's interview with Art Eggleton; TS, December 31, 1986.

"No one can doubt": TS, November 10, 1989.

When Mike Harris and: TS, January 10, 1999; Layton, *Homelessness*, 13.

"Homelessness [is] generally": TS, April 2, 4, 1996.

A few months earlier: Layton, *Homelessness*, 19–35.

As thorough as: Mayor's Homelessness Action Task Force, *Taking Responsibility for Homelessness* (Toronto: City of Toronto, 1999), available at the Human Services and Justice Coordinating Committee website (http://www.hsjcc.on.ca) in the Social Determinants of Health folder under the Education & Resources tab.

303 **Dozens of demonstrators:** TS, June 19, 2000; NP, June 17, 2000; GM, June 17, 2000.

In her *National Post* column: NP, June 17, 2000.

More than a decade: Steve Barnes and Beth Wilson, "Time for City and Province to Tackle Urgent Homelessness Crisis," TS, January 21, 2014; TS, December 31, 2013.

Art Eggleton extolled: TS, November 13, 1985.

"A lot of people have": Carl Mollins, "A City That Works," *Maclean's*, June 20, 1988, 37.

The bastion of all: Doucet, "The Anatomy of an Urban Legend" (http://ceris.metropolis.net/Virtual%20Library/other/doucet3.html); Croucher, "Constructing the Image of Ethnic Harmony in Toronto," 320; Harris, *Imagining Toronto*, 190; TS, December 5, 2007.

304 **Still, the crowds:** TS, April 4, 2009.

Torontonians, who could: NP, June 25, 2005; TS, April 4, 2009.

By 2001, established: Michael Ornstein, *Ethno-Racial Groups in Toronto, 1971–2001: A Demographic and Socio-Economic Profile* (Toronto: Institute for Social Research, York University, 2006), Table 1.1, 99 (www.isr.yorku.ca/download/Ornstein--Ethno-Racial_Groups_in_Toronto_1971-2001.pdf); Charles Shahar and Tina Rosenbaum, "2001 Census Analysis Series: The Jewish Community of Toronto," UJA of Greater Toronto, 2003, 4.

When Italy won: Michael Buzzelli, "From Little Britain to Little Italy: An Urban Ethnic Landscape Study in Toronto," *Journal of Historical Geography* 27, 4 (2001): 574.

Between 1980 and 1996: Paul Anisef and Michael Lanphier, eds, *The World in a City* (Toronto: University of Toronto Press, 2003), 195; Michael Ornstein, *Ethno-Racial Groups in Toronto, 1971–2001*, Appendix: Table 1.1.

By 1991, 59 percent: TS, February 23, 1991.

In a May 1990: "Toronto and Detroit: Canadians Do It Better," *The Economist*, May 19, 1990, 18.

305 **Until the early seventies:** Chan, *The Chinese in Toronto from 1878*, 131–34.

"They are Chinese": TS, July 10, 1988.

Flattering news stories: TS, January 30, February 8, April 27, 1987, November 25, 1996, January 14, 2005; Chan, *The Chinese in Toronto from 1878*, 154.

They and thousands: Chan, *The Chinese in Toronto from 1878*, 127, 156; TS, July 3, 2005; "Pacific Mall and Market Village in Markham," GuidingStar.ca (www.guidingstar.ca/Pacific_Mall_&_Market_Village_in_Markham.htm).

"The more I travel": TS, May 10, 1999.

"Everything is going Chinese": Matt Lee, "Ethnic Relations II: Carole Bell and Markham's Racial Tensions," *Green Beam City* (cached on April 20, 2011, at http://www.zoominfo.com/CachedPage/?archive_id=0&page_id=-270979619&page_url=//green.hyperdot.net/culture/ethnic-relations/&page_last_updated=2011-04-20T21:41:05&firstName=Carole&lastName=Bell); TS, August 24, 1995; Chan, *The Chinese in Toronto from 1878*, 162.

306 **Predictably, her remarks:** TS, July 4, 1995, July 3, 2005.

According to a poll: TS, July 12, 1992.

They were drawn: Peter Chimbos, "Greeks," in *Encyclopedia of Canada's Peoples*, ed. Paul Robert Magocsi (Toronto: University of Toronto Press, 1999), 617–19; Peter D. Chimbos "The Greeks in Canada: An Historical and Sociological Perspective," in *The Greek Diaspora in the Twentieth Century*, ed. Richard Clogg (New York: St. Martin's, 1999), 91–92.

307 **In a relatively short:** Marinel Mandres, "The Dynamics of Ethnic Residential Patterns in the Toronto Census Metropolitan Area" (PhD dissertation, Wilfrid Laurier University, 1998), 151–53.

While in 1991: Ornstein, "Ethno-Racial Groups in Toronto, 1971–2001," Appendix: Table 1.2.

"Eighty per cent": TS, June 16, 1986.

The small number: Anisef and Lanphier, *The World in a City,* 148–49.

As in Greektown: Ibid., 149; Carolos Teixeira, "Toronto's Little Portugal: A Neighbourhood in Transition," Research Bulletin #35, Centre for Urban and Community Studies (March 2007), 1–7 (www.urbancentre.utoronto.ca/pdfs/researchbulletins/CUCSRB35Teixeira.pdf); Carlos Teixeira, "The Portuguese in Toronto: A Community on the Move," *Portuguese Studies Review* 4 (1995): 57–75; Carlos Teixeira and R.A. Murdie, "The Role of Ethnic Real Estate Agents in the Residential Relocation Process: A Case Study of the Portuguese Homebuyers in Suburban Toronto," *Urban Geography* 18 (1997): 497–520.

The odds of a property: Teixeira, "Toronto's Little Portugal," 4.

308 **"Superior Sausage":** Ibid., 7.

A victory by Portugal: Ibid.

Three days later: Paul Kaihla and Ross Laver, "Black and Angry," *Maclean's,* May 18, 1992, 24–29; TS, May 19, 1992.

According to the police: TS, May 19, 1992. See also TS, May 5, 8, 17, 1992; GM, May 5, 1992.

An independent investigation: Croucher, "Constructing the Image of Ethnic Harmony in Toronto," 327.

All too typical: Cecil Foster, *A Place Called Heaven: The Meaning of Being Black in Canada* (Toronto: HarperCollins, 1996), 4–5.

309 **Inaugurated in 1967:** Henry, *The Caribbean Diaspora in Toronto,* 178; Foster, *A Place Called Heaven,* 248–60.

Like most stereotypes: TS, Feburary 19, 1989; GM, July 10, 1992, August 13, 2005; Henry, *The Caribbean Diaspora in Toronto,* 191–200.

In February 1989: TS, February 19, 1989.

A few years later: GM, July 7, 13, 1992.

But within a: GM, May 5, 1992; TS, May 5, 6, 1992.

310 **"Metropolitan Toronto is not":** *Edmonton Journal,* May 6, 1992.

While acknowledging: GM, May 7, 1992.

Likewise, in her diagnosis: Barbara Amiel, "Racism: An Excuse for Riots and Theft," *Maclean's,* May 18, 1992, 15.

Yet, regardless of: Ibid.; TS, May 7, 1992.

"The anger that": TS, May 7, 1992.

Stephen Lewis, who: Stephen Lewis, "Advisory Report on Race Relations in Toronto," June 9, 1992, 2–3 (http://www.ontla.on.ca/library/repository/mon/13000/134250.pdf); Croucher, "Constructing the Image of Ethnic Harmony in Toronto," 328.

311 **"Late at night":** Robert Fulford, "2001 real estate guide," TL, February 2001, insert.

The Just Desserts robbery: TS, April 9, 1994.

He had arrived: GM, December 7, 1999.

312 **Police spoke:** Ibid.

***Globe and Mail* columnist:** GM, April 7, 1994; John Miller, "How Canada's Daily Newspapers Shut Out Minorities," *Media Magazine*, July 1994, 30–32.

One note pleaded: John Miller, "Covering Diversity," Diversity Watch, Ryerson University School of Journalism (www.diversitywatch.ryerson.ca/course/).

Indeed, in 2012: See, for example, "Canada's Most Dangerous Cities," *Maclean's*, December 7, 2012 (www2.macleans.ca/2012/12/07/canadas-most-dangerous-cities/); *Winnipeg Free Press*, July 25, 2012.

No tragedy since: TS, November 21, 2008, December 30, 2009, April 3, 2010.

"Six others wounded": TS, April 2, 2010.

313 **Homicide Detective:** *Montreal Gazette*, January 3, 2006.

Several more serious: NP, June 16, July 17, 2012; GM, July 18, 23, 2012; CTV News, July 20, 2012. See also Amy Marie Siciliano, "Policing Poverty, Race, Space and the Fear of Crime after the Year of the Gun (2005) in Suburban Toronto" (PhD dissertation, University of Toronto, 2010).

As for the meaning: NP, June 4, 2012.

By the time: TS, February 9, 1989.

Yet he still: GM, August 22, 2011.

314 **"I know I came":** NP, May 28, 2011.

In November 1992: TS, November 12, 1992, November 3, 1993; "The Lie: Betty Disero's Accusations against Tom Jakobek Cost Him His Job as Budget Chief and Turned City Council into a Snake Pit," TL, January 1994, 40–47.

"June Rowlands wanted": John Laschinger and Geoffrey Stevens, *Leaders and Lesser Mortals: Backroom Politics in Canada* (Toronto: Key Porter, 1992), 180–85.

While on holidays: TS, January 8, 1992, November 29, 1992; GM, June 1, 1992.

On the eve of: TS, November 12, 1994.

315 **Hall's real strength:** TS, November 15, 1994.

She turned out: John Lorinc, "The Battle to Be Megamayor," TL, October 1997, 84.

Though police and: Joe Chidley, "The Fight for Toronto," *Maclean's*, March 17, 1997, 46–50.

The property tax: TS, January 17, 1996; January 19, 1997.

"It's interesting to": GM, February 15, 1997.

316 **"You won't find":** Chidley, "The Fight for Toronto," 48.

They delivered their: Dr. Anne Golden (Chair), Jack Diamond, Thomas W. McCormack, Professor J. Robert S. Prichard, Dr. Joseph Y.K. Wong, "Report of the GTA Task Force, January 1996" (Toronto: Publications Ontario, 1996), 13-14 (www.scribd.com/doc/99998119/English); John Sewell, *The Shape of the Suburbs: Understanding Toronto's Sprawl* (Toronto: University of Toronto Press, 2009), 194; GM, January 15, 1996; TS, January 17, 1996.

For the most part: One exception was Andrew Sancton, an urban government expert at the University of Western Ontario in London, who was critical of a "powerful Greater Toronto Authority." See GM, February 15, 1997.

"Reconstituting a modern": GM, January 15, 1996.

Most tellingly: TS, November 1, 1996.

Such a move: TS, October 24, 1996, November 1, 1996.

317 **Reflecting on this:** Author's interview with Mike Harris.

What later cost: Author's interview with John Matheson, January 28, 2013.

By then, Toronto: Chidley, "The Fight for Toronto," 46.

There was lots: GM, February 27, 1997.

One day, Leach: Author's interview with Allan Leach, February 1, 2013; author's interview with Mike Harris. John Sewell to author, February 14, 2014.

"Anyone who supposes": GM, February 4, 1997.

318 **Where did this idea:** GM, January 14, 1997.

Of the three hundred submissions: GM, November 11, 1996, January 14, 1997; TS, February 27, 1996; Sewell, *The Shape of the Suburbs*, 198.

In late 1996: Author's interviews with Paul Godfrey, Mike Harris, and Allan Leach.

David Crombie also: Author's interview with David Crombie.

While expenses did: *Montreal Gazette*, December 2, 2000.

Seven years later: NP, December 29, 2007; GM, January 19, 2008. A 2013 study by Professors Enid Slack and Richard Bird of the Munk School of Global Affairs at the University of Toronto came to a slightly more positive conclusion on the benefits of amalgamation. See Enid Slack and Richard Bird, *Merging Municipalities: Is Bigger Better?* IMFG Papers on Municipal Finance and Governance 14 (Toronto: Munk School of Global Affairs, University of Toronto, 2013).

319 **"The current system":** Author's interview with Anne Golden, January 25, 2013.

"With its aging subway": John Lorinc, "How Toronto Lost Its Groove: And Why the Rest of Canada Should Resist the Temptation to Cheer," *Walrus*, November 2011 (http://thewalrus.ca/how-toronto-lost-its-groove/?ref=2011.11-society-how-toronto-lost-its-groove&page=).

Mel Lastman called: GM, January 6, 1998.

The quest for: Lorinc, "The Battle to Be Megamayor," 84–90.

As a novice: TS, November 11, 2000.

For much of: GM, November 7, 8, 1997.

320 **"I have no fear":** Cited in GM, November 4, 1997.

He was right: GM, November 7, 1997; TS, November 8, 1997; *Financial Post*, November 15, 1997.

Robbie envisioned the: GM, January 7, 2012.

After studying the: TS, December 17, 1985.

Nevertheless, the debt-ridden: Canadian Press, November 29, 2004 (www.tsn.ca/story/print/?id=106352); GM, January 6, 2012.

Remembering Robbie: GM, January 6, 2012.

321 **The most popular moment:** TS, May 17, 1990, May 13, 1996.

Alomar, in particular: GM, July 23, 2011.

322 **This was, Brunt has argued:** Ibid.

"Don't feel guilty": *The Province* (Vancouver), October 13, 1992.

"I'm so proud of you": TS, October 27, 1992.

"I just wanted to": TS, April 10, 2007; GM, October 23, 2012.

323 **Naturally, the end:** NP, February 13, 15, 1999; *Calgary Herald*, February 13, 1999; *Edmonton Journal*, February 14, 1999.

"More so perhaps": *Times Colonist* (Victoria), February 11, 1999.

"I come to bury": NP, February 13, 1999.

CHAPTER THIRTEEN: MEGACITY MACHINATIONS (OR MADNESS)

324 **Toronto is a place:** NP, October 2, 2012.

He had pushed: GM, May 24, 2013.

Despite the fact: TS, January 11, 2003.

325 **Even before a:** *Vancouver Sun*, January 15, 1999; *Ottawa Citizen*, January 18, 1999; NP, January 19, 1999.

Frequently a one-man: TS, January 17, 1999.

326 **"Troops enter Toronto":** *Ottawa Citizen*, January 15, 1999; *Edmonton Journal*, January 24, 1999.

A witty cartoon: *Montreal Gazette*, January 15, 1999; TS, January 16, 1999.

When the city: *Rick Mercer Special Report*, CBC-TV, February 21, 2007.

"Would I do it": TS, January 12, 2009.

He had obtained: TS, February 22, 2000, November 14, 2000; January 11, 2003.

More damaging to: *Vancouver Sun*, December 1, 2000.

327 **As vulnerable as:** NP, November 14, 15, 2000.

Gaffe followed gaffe: See TS, June 21, 22, 2001.

Next he shook: TS, January 15, 2002.

328 **At the end of April:** NP, April 25, 2003; GM, April 26, 2003.

His decision was: Denise E. Bellamy, *Toronto Computer Leasing Inquiry/Toronto External Contracts Inquiry*. vol. 4, *Executive Summary* (Toronto: City of Toronto, 2005), 42, 61; TS, September 13, December 27, 2005; author's interview with John Lorinc, January 28, 2013.

Premier Ernie Eves: TS, October 23, 2003.

"If you slavishly": GM, May 23, 2002.

329 **"I am not joking":** Ibid.

In a sign: Ibid.

Deputy mayor Case Ootes: TS, May 23, 2002.

That challenge to: Author's interview with David Miller, October 23, 2012.

He attended Lakefield: Ibid.; TS, June 16, 2003.

"A lot of times": Author's interview with John Lorinc.

330 **The main contenders:** John Lorinc, "The Right Stuff," TL, April 2003, 61–69.

By early November: NP, November 7, 2003.

"I led an activist": Author's interview with David Miller.

331 **But as Lorinc:** Author's interview with John Lorinc.

Miller's main objective: TS, October 2, 2009.

"My goal": Author's interview with David Miller.

More notable was: TS, March 17, 2007.

With that mandate: TS, August 29, 2013.

332 **Miller believed that:** TS, August 1, 2009.

"The strike was": Author's interview with David Miller.

An Ipsos Reid poll: NP, September 26, 2009; TS, September 26, 27, 2009.

333 **"In the early years":** Author's interview with David Miller.

"I would honestly": TS, September 28, 2009.

In the *National Post*: NP, September 26, 2009.

"How can I explain": NP, October 9, 2010.

A *Globe and Mail* editorial: GM, September 26, 2009.

"You are running": Author's interview with David Miller.

334 **"History will show":** Author's interview with John Lorinc. See also the more positive assessments of Carol Goar, TS, October 15, 2010, and economist Hugh Mackenzie, TS, October 24, 2010.

When the city: TS, June 30, 2010.

The protests started: TS, June 28, 29, 2010; CBC News, October 30, 2012.

335 **In one notable case:** GM, November 30, 2010; NP, January 20, 2012, September 12, 2013.

Three years later: TS, December 9, 2013.

One of the most needless: TS, June 29, 2010.

Despite differences over: *Telegraph-Journal* (Saint John, NB), June 29, 2010.

Many commentators later: GM, December 10, 2010.

Nearly two years: *Ottawa Citizen*, May 17, 2012; NP, May 19, 2012.

336 **"Either you support":** TS, July 21, 2010.

Three long years: GM, November 1, 2013; NP, November 1, 2013.

The seemingly endless: Robyn Doolittle, *Crazy Town: The Rob Ford Story* (Toronto: Viking, 2014), 5, 222–23, 230.

Six months later, after Ford's: NP, May 18, 2013; TS, May 26, 2013; GM, May 28, October 16, 2013; Nicholas Kohler, "The Political Genius of Rob Ford," *Maclean's*, October 18, 2010, 24–28.

This was followed by: *Toronto Sun*, November 6, 2013.

Each day in: GM, November 4, 2013; NP, November 14, 2013; Charlie Gillis, "Rob Ford's Wild Ride," *Maclean's*, November 18, 2013, 25–29.

According to section 134: *City of Toronto Act* 2006, c. 11, Sched. A, s. 134.

The most honest: NP, November 19, 2013.

337 **He also achieved:** NP, TS, *Toronto Sun*, October 31, 2013; GM, November 5, 2013.

None of this: NP, November 22, 2013, and "Letters to Editor," November 23, 2013; Doolittle, *Crazy Town*, 305–6. On Forum Research polls, see *Toronto Sun*, January 23, 2014, CP24, and February 10, 2014.

This despite the fact: John Moore, "Rob Ford Never Was 'Rob Ford,'" NP, November 5, 2013; TS, November 25, 26, 2013.

"There's nothing wrong with": NP, November 18, 2013.

Built like the ex-football: Doolittle, *Crazy Town*, 65–73.

Or, as one *National Post*: "Letters to Editor: Voice from Ford Nation," NP, May 30, 2013, A13.

"Tell me something": GM, March 23, 2012.

The official and: Doolittle, *Crazy Town*, 24–28.

338 **By the *Globe and Mail*'s estimation:** GM, November 23, 2013.

According to *Toronto Star* reporter: Doolittle, *Crazy Town*, 38–40.

The less palatable: GM, May 25, October 16, 2013; Ontario Press Council, "In the Matter Regarding: Complaint from Ms. Connie Harrison regarding an article published by The *Globe and Mail*, dated May 25, 2013 entitled Globe Investigation: The Ford family's history with drug dealing," October 16, 2013 (www.theglobeandmail.com/news/toronto/article14882983.ece/BINARY/OPC+decision+Harrison+vs+Globe+Oct++2013+.pdf).

Three years later: Marci McDonald, "The Incredible Shrinking Mayor," TL, May 2012, 43–44.

339 **In March 2008:** TS, March 27, 2008; GM, March 28, 2008.

He could be counted: TS, April 1, 2010; *Toronto Sun*, August 18, 2010.

When Miller announced: See GM, September 25, 2009.

"I don't believe": TS, April 24, 2010.

340 **Nearly everything Miller:** Kohler, "The Political Genius of Rob Ford," 26.

Even when Ford: "Rob Ford Endorses, Is Endorsed by Pride-Dissing, Anti-Gay-Marriage Pastor. Hilarity Ensues," TL, August 5, 2010; GM, August 24, 2010.

"Can anything stop": GM, August 24, 2010.

Over at the *Star*: TS, July 15, October 17, 2010.

Ford later stopped: TS, December 2, 2011; Royson James to author, February 7, 2013.

The win was not: "Rob Ford Interview with Peter Mansbridge: 7 Key Points," CBC, November 19, 2013.

At his victory celebration: GM, October 26, 2010.

341 **"People were nervous":** Author's interview with John Lorinc.

"In 2008, I bought": Sarah Fulford, "Rob Ford's Powers of Persuasion," TL, October 2010, 15.

It was obvious: Steve Kupferman, "Don Cherry's Speech to Council, Transcribed," TO, December 7, 2010 (http://torontoist.com/2010/12/don_cherrys_speech_to_council_transcribed/).

As Marci McDonald: McDonald, "The Incredible Shrinking Mayor," 46.

Joe Mihevc, an NDP: Ibid.; "Councillor Joe Mihevc," City of Toronto website (www1.toronto.ca/wps/portal/contentonly?vgnextoid=ae893293dc3ef310VgnVCM10000071d60f89RCRD).

342 **Starting in the summer:** See TS, May 3, August 16, 30, October 25, 2012; NP, May 9, November 3, December 29, 2012.

After Ford was cleared: NP, January 26, 2013.

343 **But when you cut:** GM, May 30, 2013.

The legitimate criticism: NP, January 29, 2013.

"I'm not a genius": *Toronto Sun*, October 11, 2012.

In the first months: NP, February 27, 2013.

Then, at a dinner: NP, March 10, 11, 2013.

"Mr. Ford needs to: NP, November 5, 2013.

From CNN to: NP, August 13, 2013, November 14, 2013.

344 **"We didn't have to":** Emma Teitel, "The Biggest Loser," *Maclean's*, June 3, 2013, 30.

Even Ford's beloved: GM, November 14, 2013.

On November 14: GM, November 15, 2013.

The next day: Ibid.; NP, November 18, 2013.

"I've got the": TS, January 2, 2014.

They argued that: GM, November 30, 2012.

Ironically: Cited in McDonald, "The Incredible Shrinking Mayor," 50.

CONCLUSION: TIGER CITY, ALPHA CITY

345 **If you stay:** Morley Callaghan, "Why Toronto?" in *Our Sense of Identity: A Book of Canadian Essays*, ed. Malcolm Ross (Toronto: Ryerson, 1954), 120–23.

During his stint: See TSM, "Whom Are the Toronto Sports Media Dirtbags?" Toronto Sports Media, February 23, 2012 (http://torontosportsmedia.com/sports-and-toronto/whom-are-the-toronto-sports-media-dirtbags/12962).

Such was the: Lorinc, "How Toronto Lost Its Groove"; author's interview with John Lorinc.

In happier days: CBC News, November 29, 2008.

346 **Only in Toronto:** Gus Katsaros, "Tracking Phil Kessel's Shots on Goal," TheLeafsNation.com, January 29, 2013 (http://theleafsnation.com/2013/1/29/tracking-phil-kessel-shots-on-goal).

"I've only been": GM, January 1, 1981.

For weeks: NP, June 1, 2007.

In the minority: TS, May 27, June 23, 2007; NP, May 11, 2007; GM, June 2, 3, 2007.

347 **"Imagine, then, this":** NP, June 9, 2007.

"Sure, there were a": *Washington Post*, December 27, 2009; CBC News, December 29, 2007; City News, December 28, 2009; Global News, December 29, 2007; David Fleischer, "Anything But Crystal Clear," TO, December 31, 2009 (http://torontoist.com/2009/12/anything_but_crystal_clear/?galleryoPic=1).

The ever-enthusiastic: NP, September 22, 2012.

348 **Left-leaning councillor:** TS, October 27, 2012; GM, October 26, 2012.

A trio of former: TS, January 29, 2013.

"For a city": *Daily Commercial News and Construction Record*, December 6, 2012, 1–2.

Rosie DiManno: TS, October 15, 2012.

And writing on the: Huffington Post Canada, April 17, 2013. See also Florida's op-ed piece in the GM, April 11, 2013.

According to John Masanauskas: John Masanauskas to author, April 26, 2013.

In mid-May: NP, May 17, 2013.

349 **"Toronto is a mess":** John Macfarlane, "Editor's Note: The Fix Isn't In," *Walrus*, November 2011 (http://walrusmagazine.com/article.php?ref=2011.11-editors-note). See also Ken Greenberg, "Extreme Makeover: Toronto's Density Challenges," GM, October 2, 2012; Richard Florida, "What Toronto Needs Now," TL, November 2012, 80–82, 84–85.

"The same forces of globalization": Florida, "What Toronto Needs Now," 82.

And there are likely far: GM, December 26, 2012.

This is why: NP, January 22, 2013.

350 **On a more positive note:** TS, July 16, 2012; NP, July 18, 2012.

Over the course: Northrop Frye, *Divisions on a Ground: Essays on Canadian Culture* (Toronto: Anansi, 1982), 68.

By 2006, about half of: "Toronto's Racial Diversity," City of Toronto website (www.toronto.ca/toronto_facts/diversity.htm).

In 2013, both the: NP, May 7, 2013.

351 **On the night of:** See GM, July 30, 31, 2013; NP, August 19, 24, 2013; TS, August 24, 2013.

This was the: GM, November 1, 1969.

Think, for example: See NP, January 19, 2009, April 16, December 10, 2011; TS, August 12, 2011.

352 **In January 2014:** TS, January 27, 2014.

353 **Their bold plan:** TS, October 2, 2012; NP, October 2, 2012; author's interview with David Mirvish. The project's website is http://mirvishandgehrytoronto.com/

As Ken Greenberg stated: GM, October 2, 2012.

In December 2013: NP, May 27, 2014; GM, May 27, 2014.

A few months shy: Author's interview with David Crombie.

354 **Few cities have experienced:** Thanks to John Lorinc for his insight on the city's history and development. Lorinc to author, May 21, 2013.

INDEX

Page numbers in **bold** refer to illustrations.